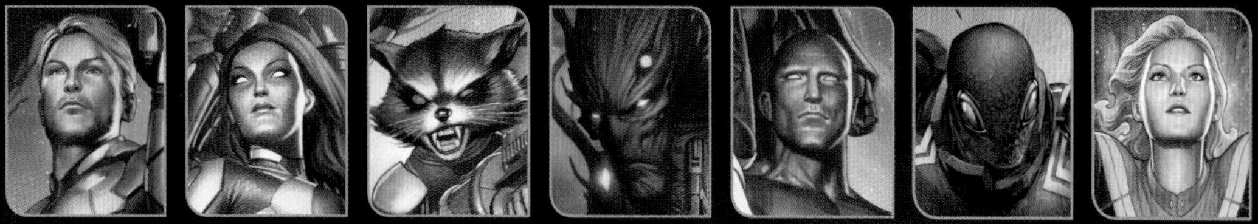

STAR-LORD GAMORA ROCKET RACCOON GROOT DRAX VENOM CAPTAIN MARVEL

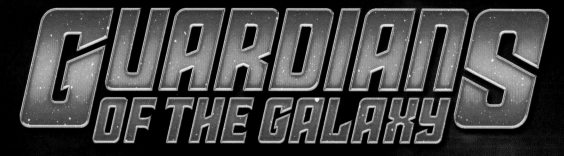

GUARDIANS OF THE GALAXY

WRITER: **BRIAN MICHAEL BENDIS**

ISSUES #18-20

PENCILERS: **ED MCGUINNESS** WITH **VALERIO SCHITI** (#20)
INKERS: **MARK FARMER** (#18-19), **MARK MORALES** (#19), **JOHN LIVESAY** (#19), **ED MCGUINNESS** (#19) & **VALERIO SCHITI** (#20)
COLOR ARTISTS: **JUSTIN PONSOR** (#18) & **JASON KEITH** (#19-20)
COVER ART: **ED MCGUINNESS**, **MARK FARMER** & **JUSTIN PONSOR**

ISSUES #21-27

ARTISTS: **VALERIO SCHITI** WITH **DAVID LOPEZ** (#22)
COLOR ARTIST: **JASON KEITH**
COVER ART: **VALERIO SCHITI** & **JUSTIN PONSOR** (#21), **VALERIO SCHITI** & **JASON KEITH** (#22, #24-27) AND **CHRISTIAN WARD** (#23)

ANNUAL #1

ARTIST: **FRANK CHO**
COLOR ARTIST: **JASON KEITH**
LETTERER: **VC's CLAYTON COWLES**
COVER ART: **FRANK CHO** & **JASON KEITH**

LETTERER: **VC's CORY PETIT**
ASSISTANT EDITOR: **XANDER JAROWEY**
EDITOR: **MIKE MARTS**

COLLECTION EDITOR: **JENNIFER GRÜNWALD** ASSOCIATE EDITOR: **SARAH BRUNSTAD**
ASSOCIATE MANAGING EDITOR: **ALEX STARBUCK** EDITOR, SPECIAL PROJECTS: **MARK D. BEAZLEY**
VP, PRODUCTION & SPECIAL PROJECTS: **JEFF YOUNGQUIST** SVP PRINT, SALES & MARKETING: **DAVID GABRIEL**
BOOK DESIGNER: **ADAM DEL RE**

EDITOR IN CHIEF: **AXEL ALONSO** CHIEF CREATIVE OFFICER: **JOE QUESADA**
PUBLISHER: **DAN BUCKLEY** EXECUTIVE PRODUCER: **ALAN FINE**

GUARDIANS OF THE GALAXY VOL. 3. Contains material originally published in magazine form as GUARDIANS OF THE GALAXY #18-27 and ANNUAL #1. First printing 2016. ISBN# 978-1-302-90008-3. Published by MARVEL WORLDWIDE, INC., a subsidiary of MARVEL ENTERTAINMENT, LLC. OFFICE OF PUBLICATION: 135 West 50th Street, New York, NY 10020. **Printed in China.** ALAN FINE, President, Marvel Entertainment; DAN BUCKLEY, President, TV, Publishing & Brand Management; JOE QUESADA, Chief Creative Officer; TOM BREVOORT, SVP of Publishing; DAVID BOGART, SVP of Business Affairs & Operations, Publishing & Partnership; C.B. CEBULSKI, VP of Brand Management & Development, Asia; DAVID GABRIEL, SVP of Sales & Marketing, Publishing; JEFF YOUNGQUIST, VP of Production & Special Projects; DAN CARR, Executive Director of Publishing Technology; ALEX MORALES, Director of Publishing Operations; SUSAN CRESPI, Production Manager; STAN LEE, Chairman Emeritus. For information regarding advertising in Marvel Comics or on Marvel.com, please contact Vit DeBellis, Integrated Sales Manager, at vdebellis@marvel.com. For Marvel subscription inquiries, please call 888-511-5480. **Manufactured between 5/6/2016 and 7/18/2016 by R.R. DONNELLEY ASIA PRINTING SOLUTIONS, CHINA.**

10 9 8 7 6 5 4 3 2 1

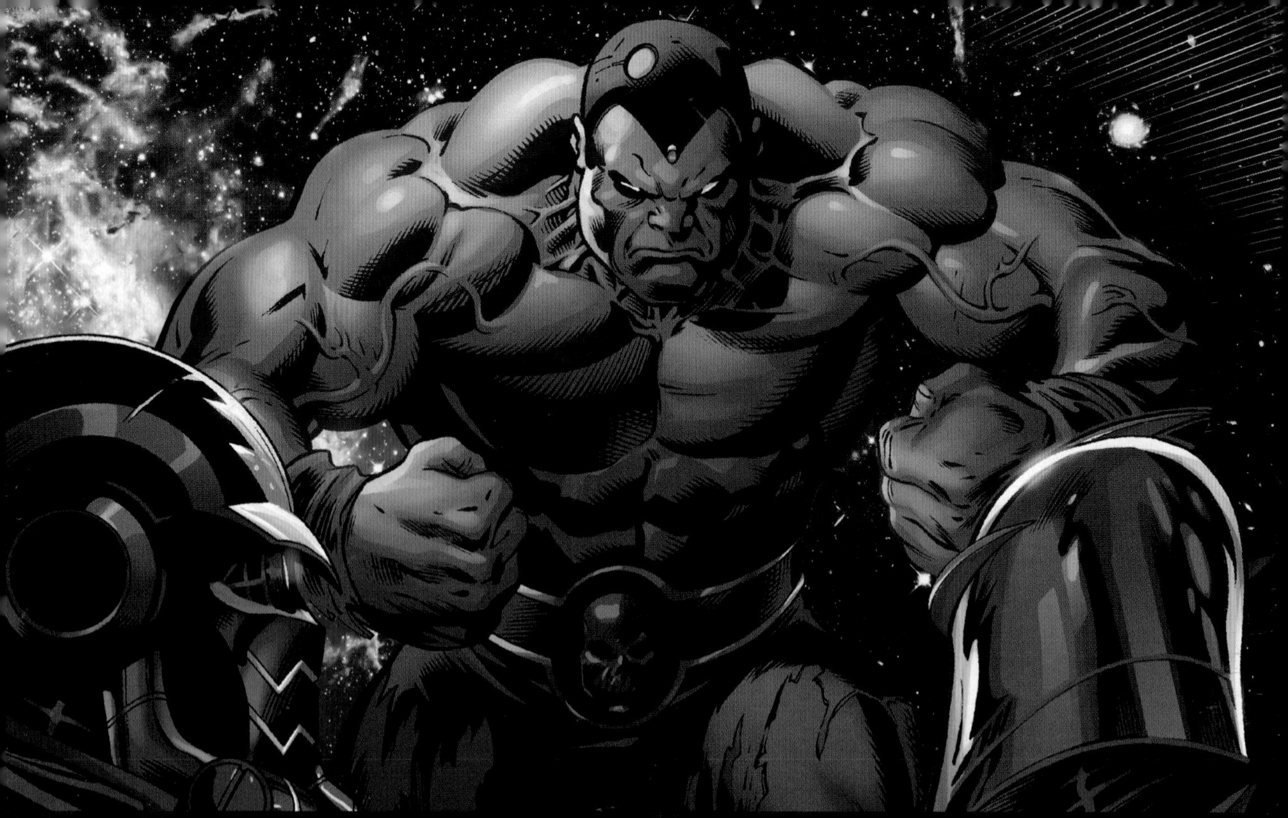

PREVIOUSLY...

DURING A CONFLICT WITH THANOS, PETER QUILL AND RICHARD RIDER, A.K.A. NOVA, AIMED TO STOP THE MAD TITAN ONCE AND FOR ALL BY TRAPPING HIM, ALONG WITH THEMSELVES, IN A PARASITIC PARALLEL DIMENSION KNOWN AS THE CANCERVERSE. A SUICIDE MISSION BY ALL ACCOUNTS, BUT WORTH IT TO SAVE THE GALAXY FROM THANOS. WITH THE COLLAPSE OF THE FAULT THAT CONNECTED THE CANCERVERSE, PETER AND NOVA WERE BELIEVED TRAPPED FOREVER.

AFTER MOURNING THEIR DEATHS, THE REMAINING GUARDIANS WERE RELIEVED TO DISCOVER THAT PETER — ALONG WITH THE FORMERLY DECEASED DRAX — WAS SOMEHOW ALIVE, BUT RELIEF TURNED TO HORROR WHEN THEY REALIZED THANOS HAD SURVIVED THE CANCERVERSE AS WELL. HOW THEY SURVIVED REMAINED A MYSTERY...UNTIL NOW.

MEANWHILE, PETER QUILL MAY HAVE FINALLY SETTLED DOWN FOR A RELATIONSHIP WITH THE X-MEN'S KITTY PRYDE — IF YOU CAN CALL HOLOGRAM CALLS FROM STAR SYSTEMS AWAY "DATING." AND FLASH THOMPSON, A.K.A. VENOM, HAS BEEN PLACED WITH THE GUARDIANS OF THE GALAXY AS THE AVENGERS' EARTH REPRESENTATIVE. HOWEVER, AFTER BEING KIDNAPPED AND SEPARATED FROM THE GROUP, VENOM MAY NOT BE KEEN ON INTERSTELLAR ADVENTURES. SPACE HAS DONE STRANGE THINGS TO HIS SYMBIOTE, AND AS EACH DAY PASSES IT GROWS STRONGER AND MORE DIFFICULT TO CONTROL.

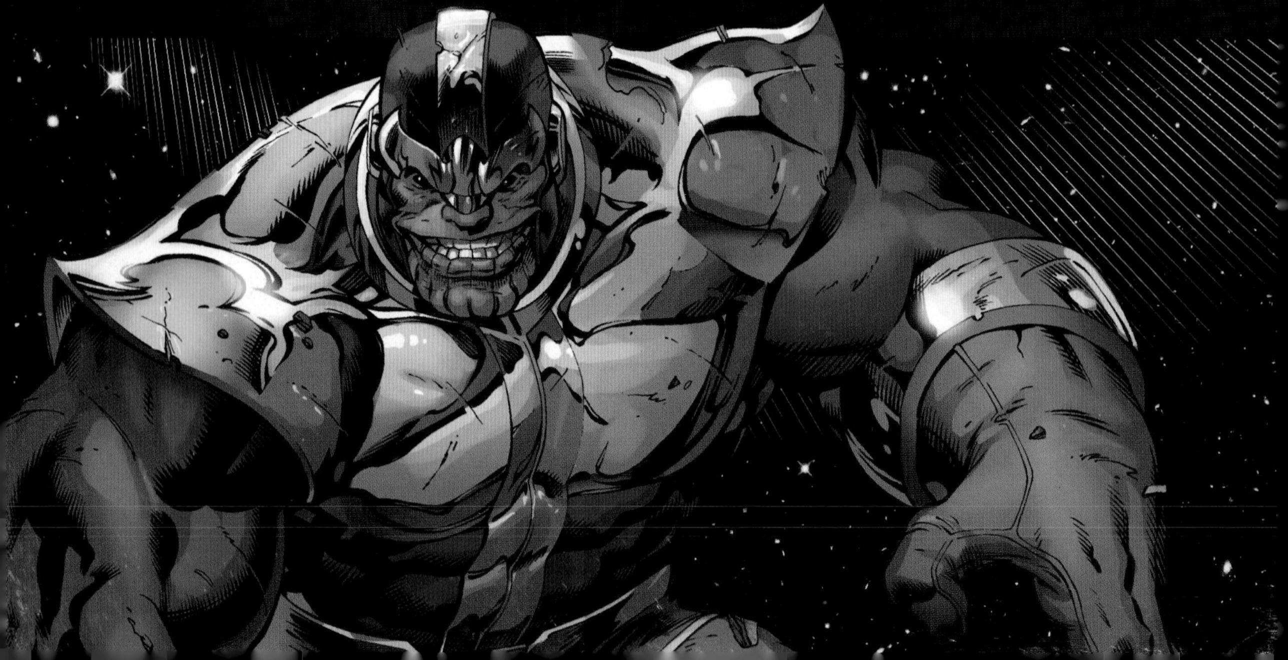

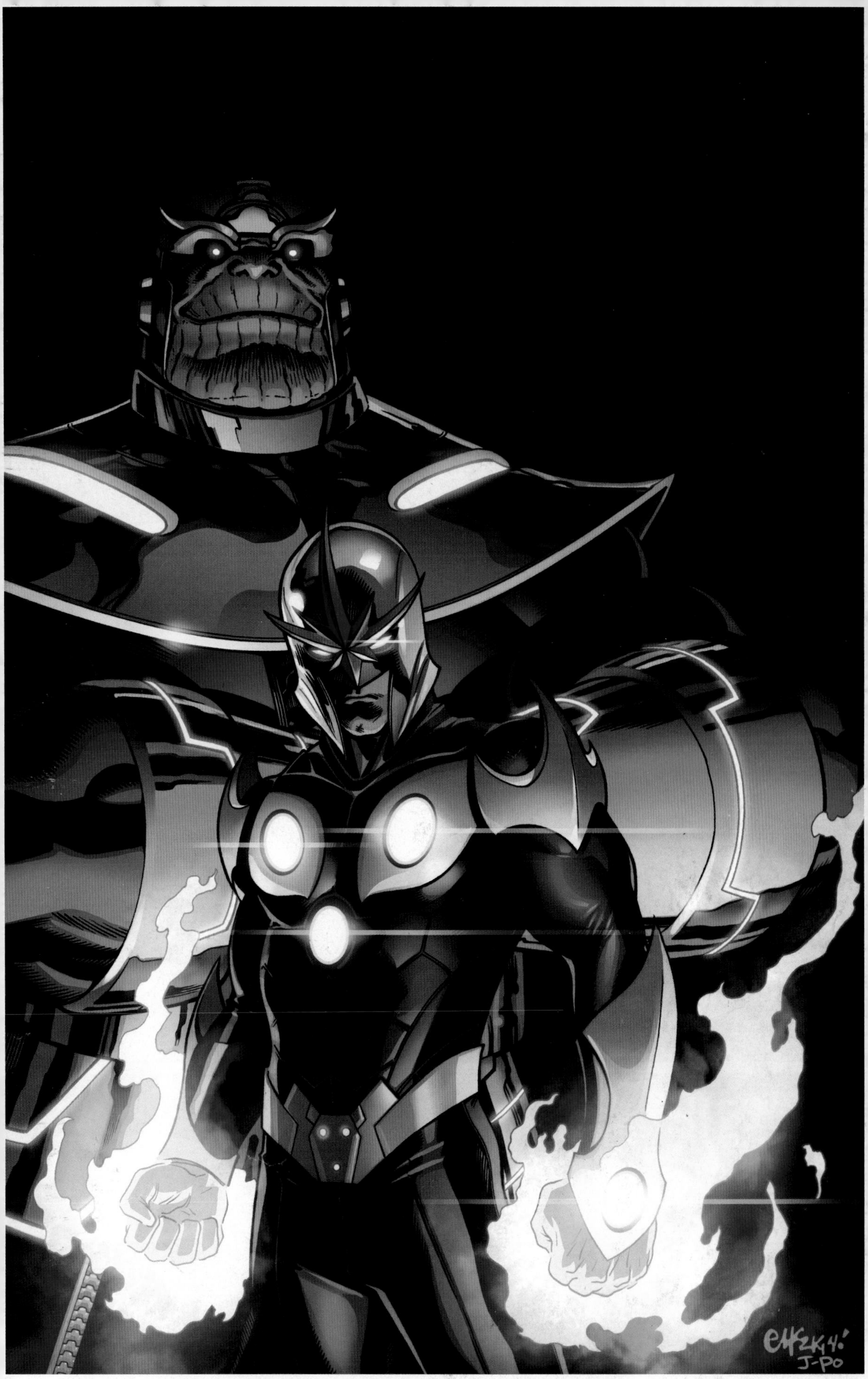

18

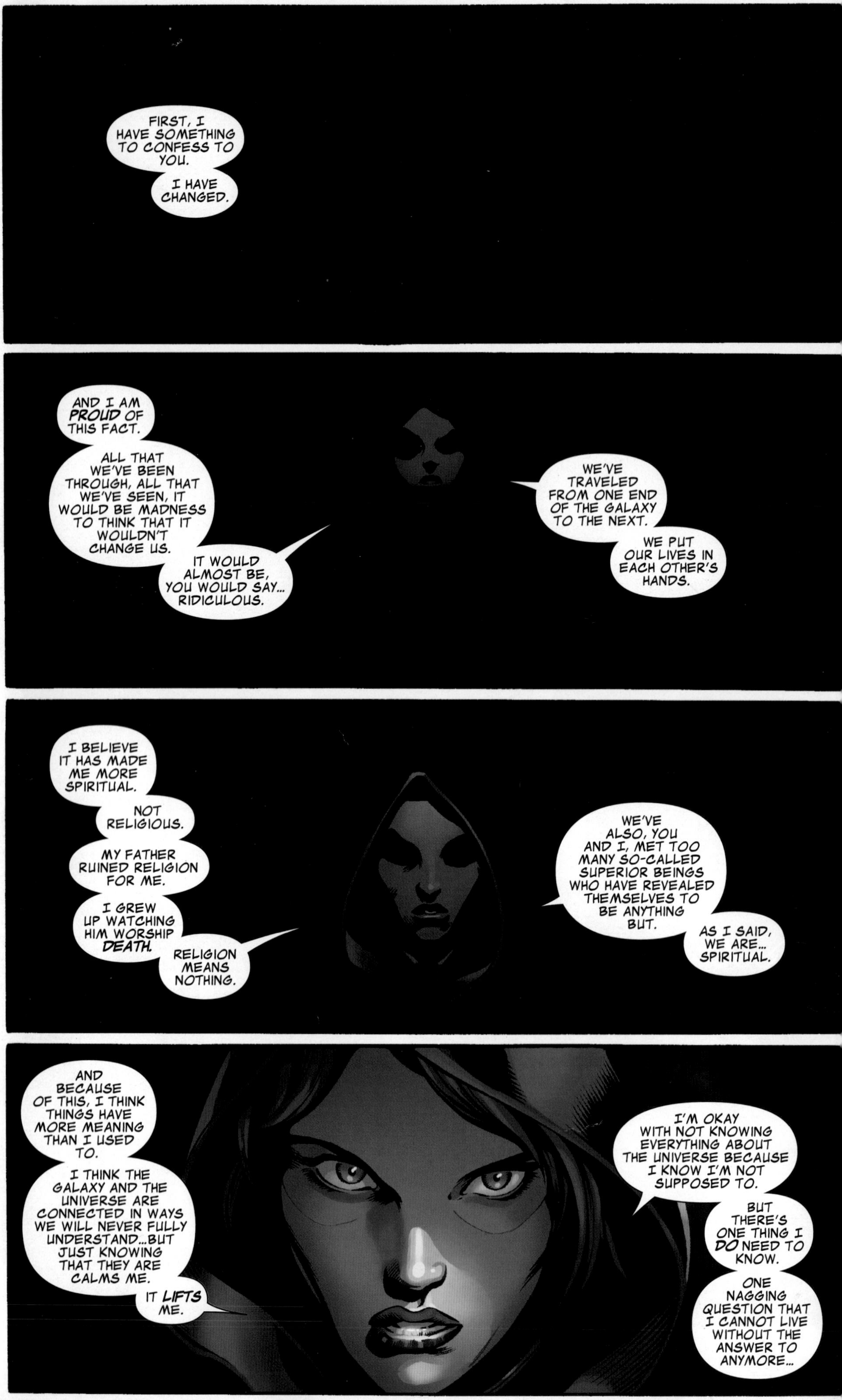
FIRST, I HAVE SOMETHING TO CONFESS TO YOU.
I HAVE CHANGED.
AND I AM PROUD OF THIS FACT.
ALL THAT WE'VE BEEN THROUGH, ALL THAT WE'VE SEEN, IT WOULD BE MADNESS TO THINK THAT IT WOULDN'T CHANGE US.
IT WOULD ALMOST BE, YOU WOULD SAY... RIDICULOUS.
WE'VE TRAVELED FROM ONE END OF THE GALAXY TO THE NEXT.
WE PUT OUR LIVES IN EACH OTHER'S HANDS.
I BELIEVE IT HAS MADE ME MORE SPIRITUAL.
NOT RELIGIOUS.
MY FATHER RUINED RELIGION FOR ME.
I GREW UP WATCHING HIM WORSHIP DEATH.
RELIGION MEANS NOTHING.
WE'VE ALSO, YOU AND I, MET TOO MANY SO-CALLED SUPERIOR BEINGS WHO HAVE REVEALED THEMSELVES TO BE ANYTHING BUT.
AS I SAID, WE ARE... SPIRITUAL.
AND BECAUSE OF THIS, I THINK THINGS HAVE MORE MEANING THAN I USED TO.
I THINK THE GALAXY AND THE UNIVERSE ARE CONNECTED IN WAYS WE WILL NEVER FULLY UNDERSTAND...BUT JUST KNOWING THAT THEY ARE CALMS ME.
IT LIFTS ME.
I'M OKAY WITH NOT KNOWING EVERYTHING ABOUT THE UNIVERSE BECAUSE I KNOW I'M NOT SUPPOSED TO.
BUT THERE'S ONE THING I DO NEED TO KNOW.
ONE NAGGING QUESTION THAT I CANNOT LIVE WITHOUT THE ANSWER TO ANYMORE...

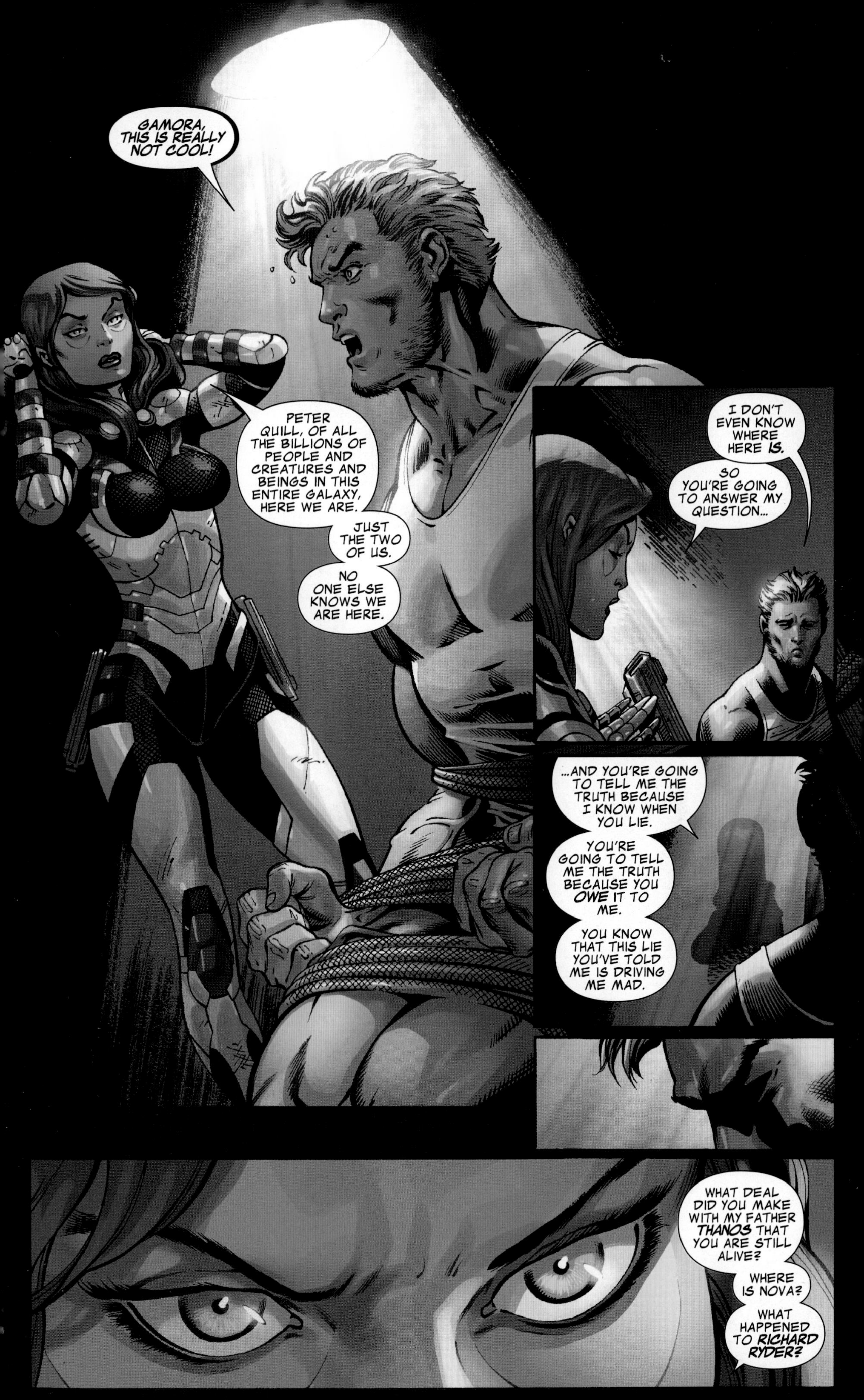
GAMORA, THIS IS REALLY NOT COOL!
PETER QUILL, OF ALL THE BILLIONS OF PEOPLE AND CREATURES AND BEINGS IN THIS ENTIRE GALAXY, HERE WE ARE.
JUST THE TWO OF US.
NO ONE ELSE KNOWS WE ARE HERE.
I DON'T EVEN KNOW WHERE HERE IS.
SO YOU'RE GOING TO ANSWER MY QUESTION...
...AND YOU'RE GOING TO TELL ME THE TRUTH BECAUSE I KNOW WHEN YOU LIE.
YOU'RE GOING TO TELL ME THE TRUTH BECAUSE YOU OWE IT TO ME.
YOU KNOW THAT THIS LIE YOU'VE TOLD ME IS DRIVING ME MAD.
WHAT DEAL DID YOU MAKE WITH MY FATHER THANOS THAT YOU ARE STILL ALIVE?
WHERE IS NOVA?
WHAT HAPPENED TO RICHARD RYDER?

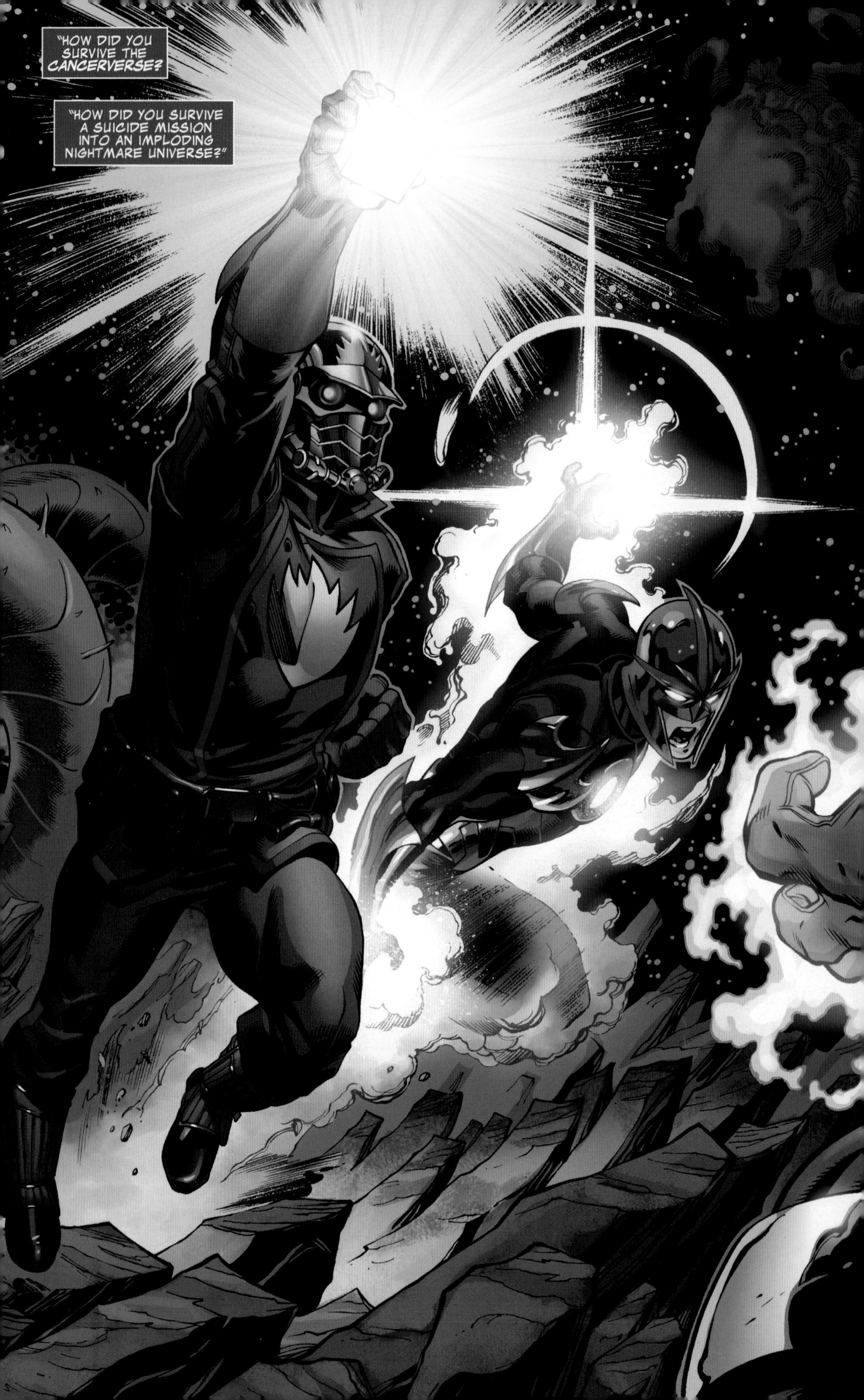
"HOW DID YOU SURVIVE THE CANCERVERSE?
"HOW DID YOU SURVIVE A SUICIDE MISSION INTO AN IMPLODING NIGHTMARE UNIVERSE?"

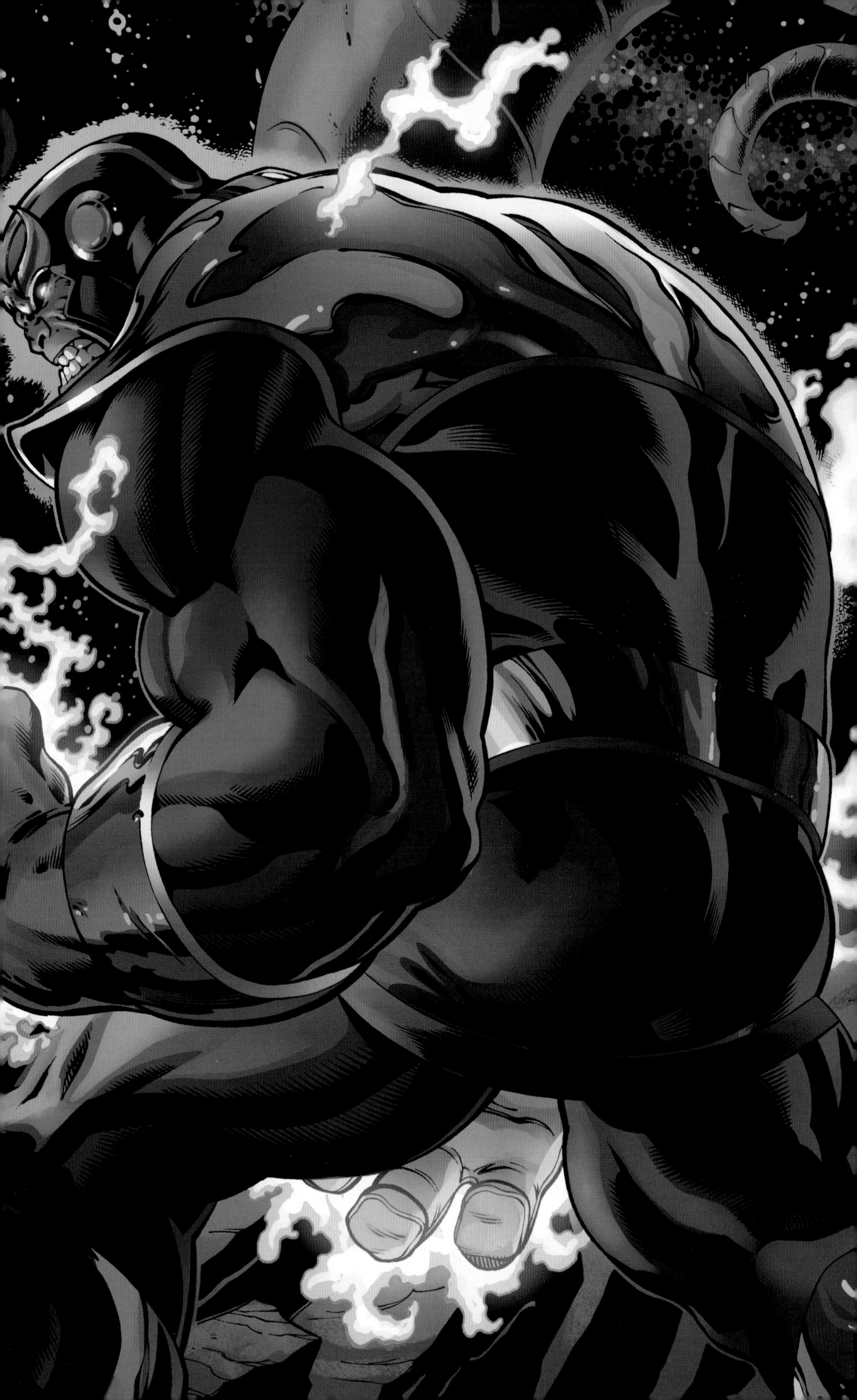

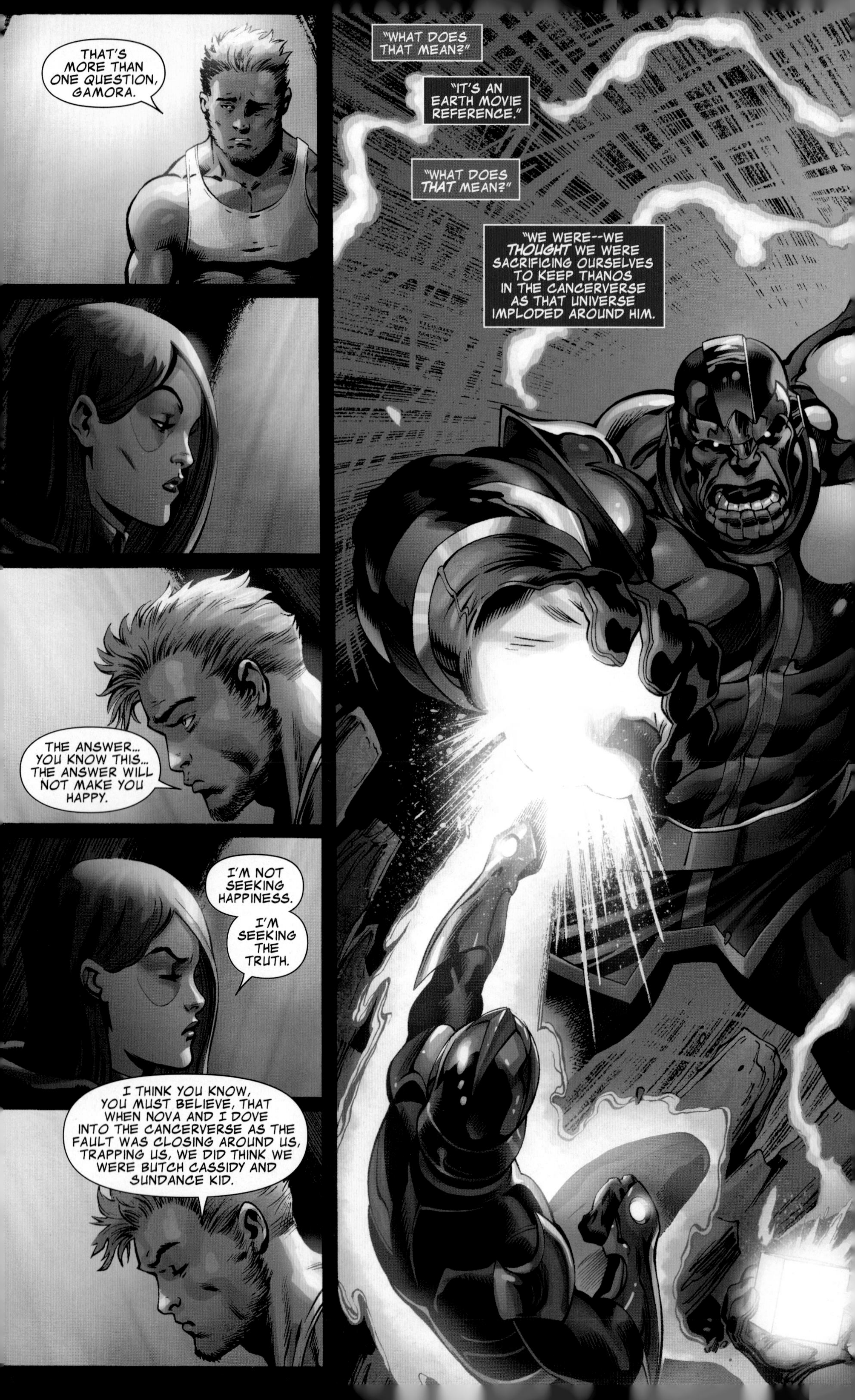
THAT'S MORE THAN ONE QUESTION, GAMORA.
THE ANSWER... YOU KNOW THIS... THE ANSWER WILL NOT MAKE YOU HAPPY.
I'M NOT SEEKING HAPPINESS.
I'M SEEKING THE TRUTH.
I THINK YOU KNOW, YOU MUST BELIEVE, THAT WHEN NOVA AND I DOVE INTO THE CANCERVERSE AS THE FAULT WAS CLOSING AROUND US, TRAPPING US, WE DID THINK WE WERE BUTCH CASSIDY AND SUNDANCE KID.
"WHAT DOES THAT MEAN?"
"IT'S AN EARTH MOVIE REFERENCE."
"WHAT DOES THAT MEAN?"
"WE WERE--WE THOUGHT WE WERE SACRIFICING OURSELVES TO KEEP THANOS IN THE CANCERVERSE AS THAT UNIVERSE IMPLODED AROUND HIM.

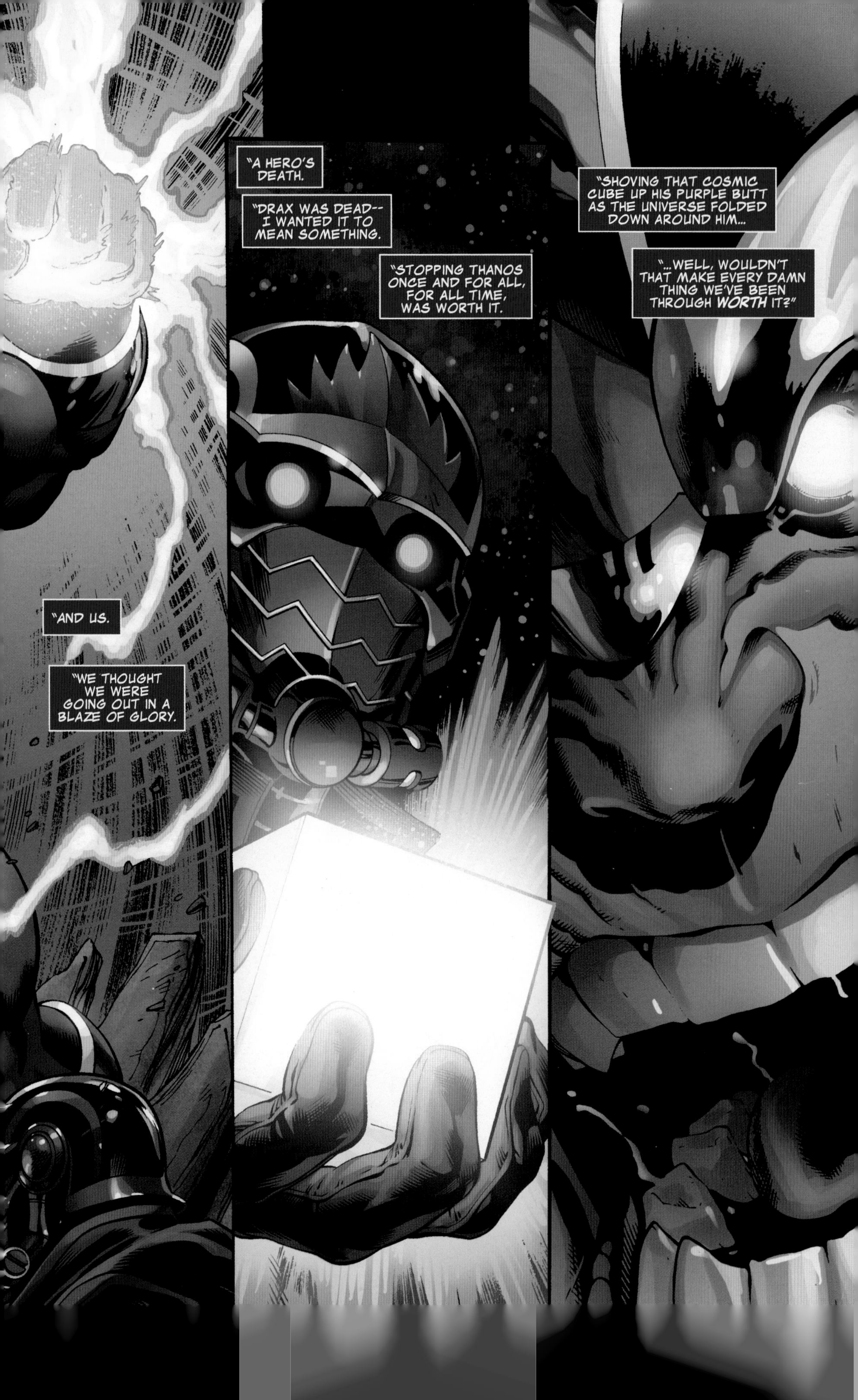
"AND US.
"WE THOUGHT WE WERE GOING OUT IN A BLAZE OF GLORY.
"A HERO'S DEATH.
"DRAX WAS DEAD-- I WANTED IT TO MEAN SOMETHING.
"STOPPING THANOS ONCE AND FOR ALL, FOR ALL TIME, WAS WORTH IT.
"SHOVING THAT COSMIC CUBE UP HIS PURPLE BUTT AS THE UNIVERSE FOLDED DOWN AROUND HIM...
"...WELL, WOULDN'T THAT MAKE EVERY DAMN THING WE'VE BEEN THROUGH *WORTH* IT?"

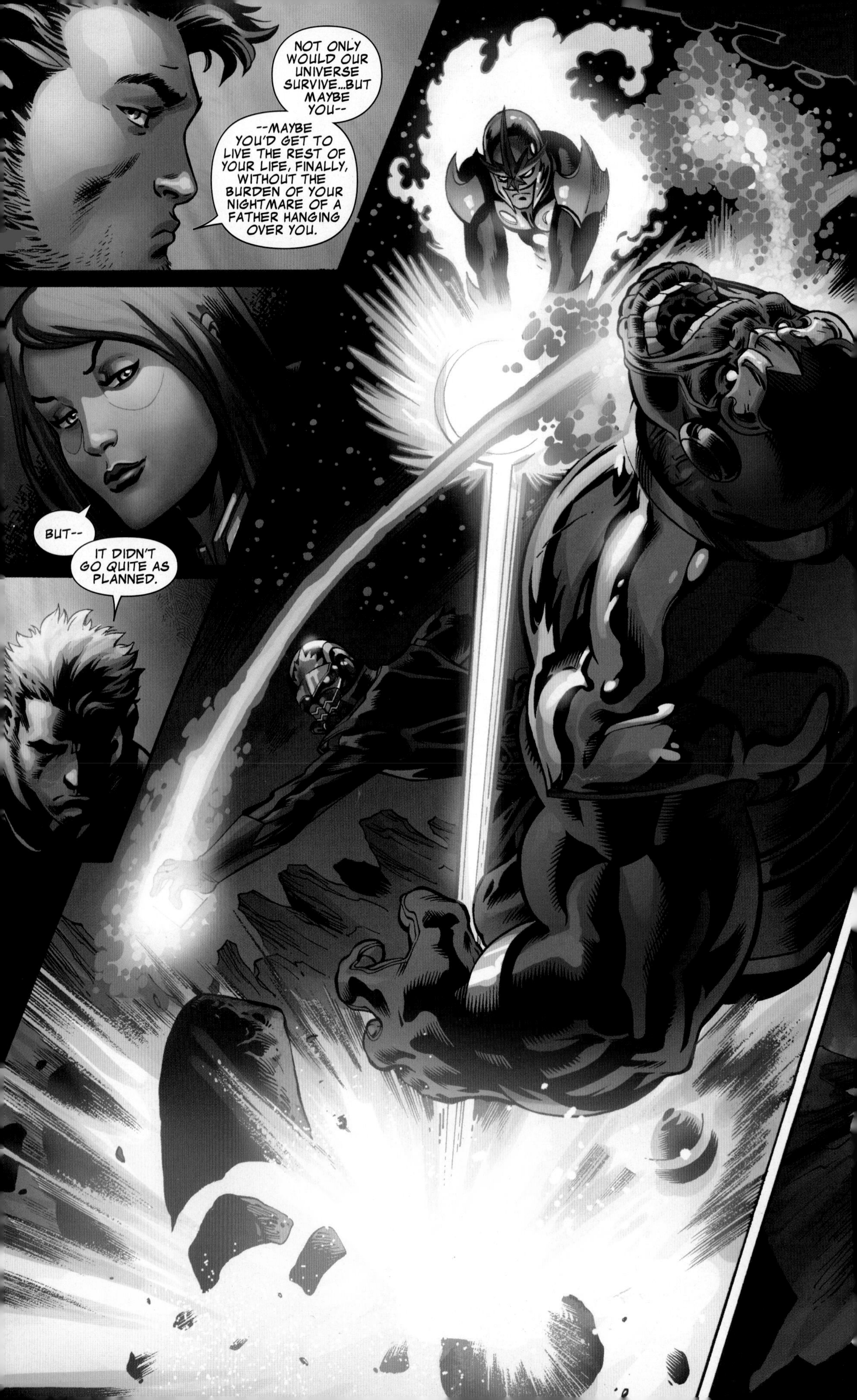
NOT ONLY WOULD OUR UNIVERSE SURVIVE...BUT MAYBE YOU--
--MAYBE YOU'D GET TO LIVE THE REST OF YOUR LIFE, FINALLY, WITHOUT THE BURDEN OF YOUR NIGHTMARE OF A FATHER HANGING OVER YOU.
BUT--
IT DIDN'T GO QUITE AS PLANNED.

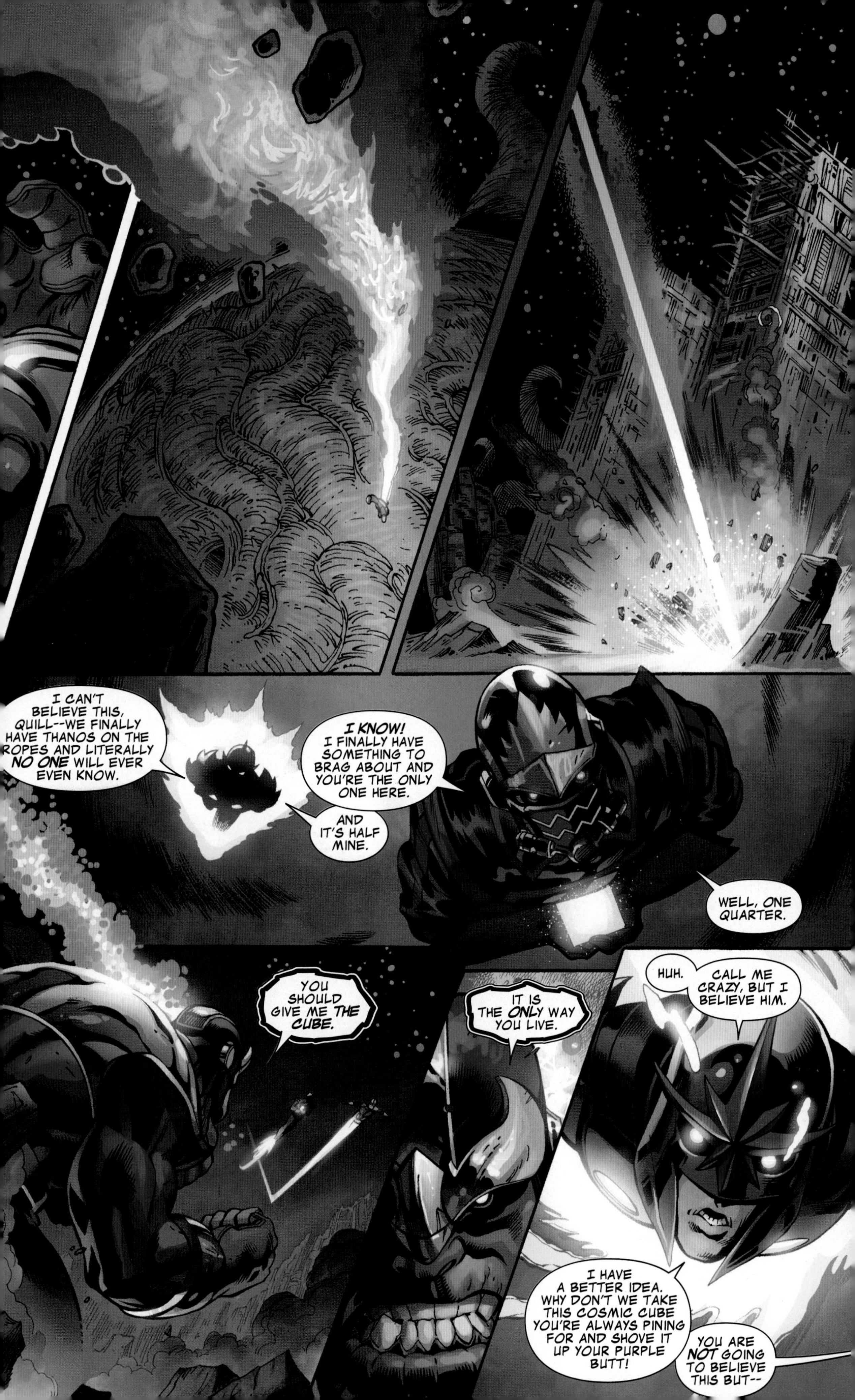
I CAN'T BELIEVE THIS, QUILL--WE FINALLY HAVE THANOS ON THE ROPES AND LITERALLY NO ONE WILL EVER EVEN KNOW.
I KNOW! I FINALLY HAVE SOMETHING TO BRAG ABOUT AND YOU'RE THE ONLY ONE HERE.
AND IT'S HALF MINE.
WELL, ONE QUARTER.
YOU SHOULD GIVE ME THE CUBE.
IT IS THE ONLY WAY YOU LIVE.
HUH.
CALL ME CRAZY, BUT I BELIEVE HIM.
I HAVE A BETTER IDEA. WHY DON'T WE TAKE THIS COSMIC CUBE YOU'RE ALWAYS PINING FOR AND SHOVE IT UP YOUR PURPLE BUTT!
YOU ARE NOT GOING TO BELIEVE THIS BUT--

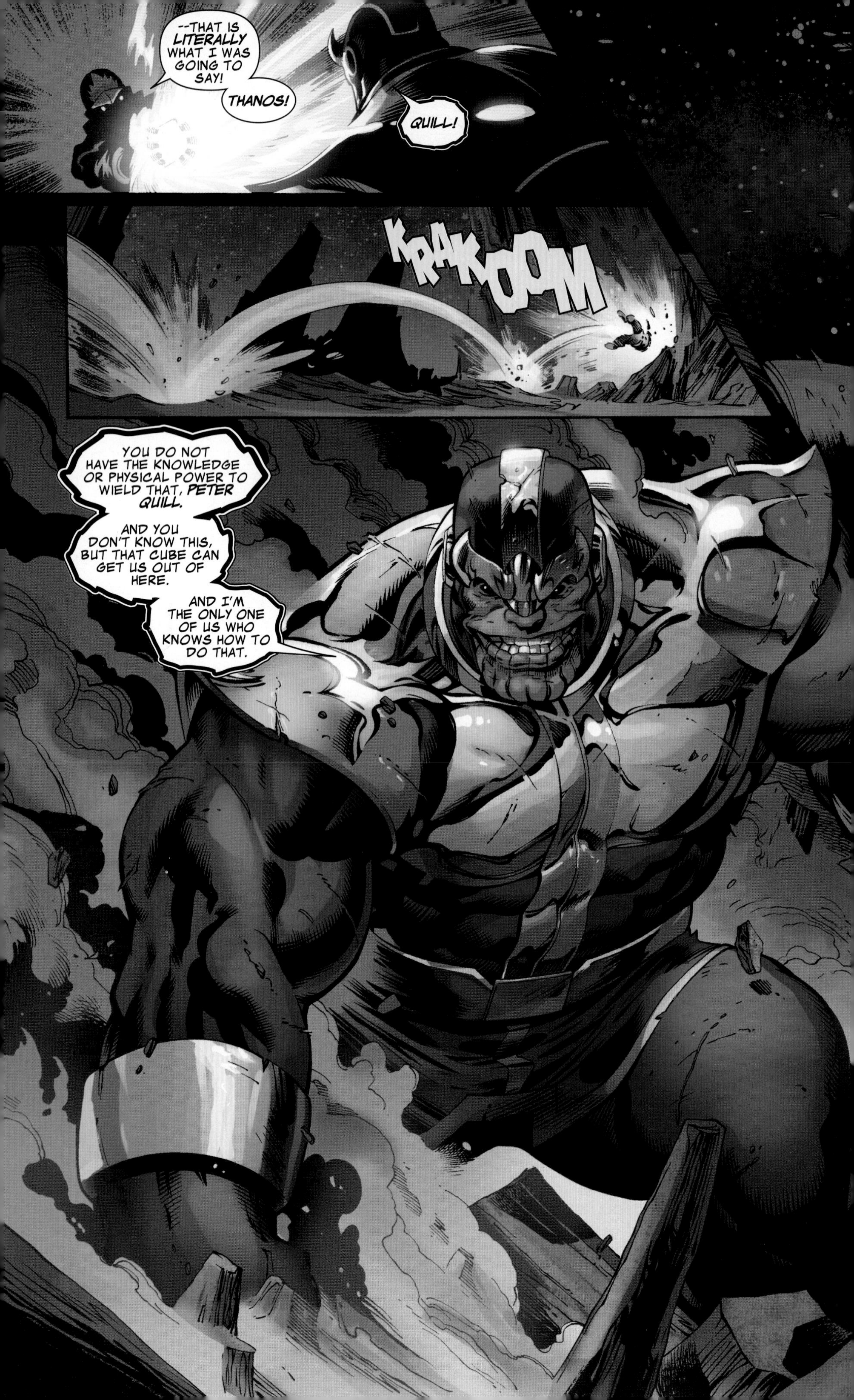
--THAT IS LITERALLY WHAT I WAS GOING TO SAY!
THANOS!
QUILL!
KRAKOOM
YOU DO NOT HAVE THE KNOWLEDGE OR PHYSICAL POWER TO WIELD THAT, PETER QUILL.
AND YOU DON'T KNOW THIS, BUT THAT CUBE CAN GET US OUT OF HERE.
AND I'M THE ONLY ONE OF US WHO KNOWS HOW TO DO THAT.

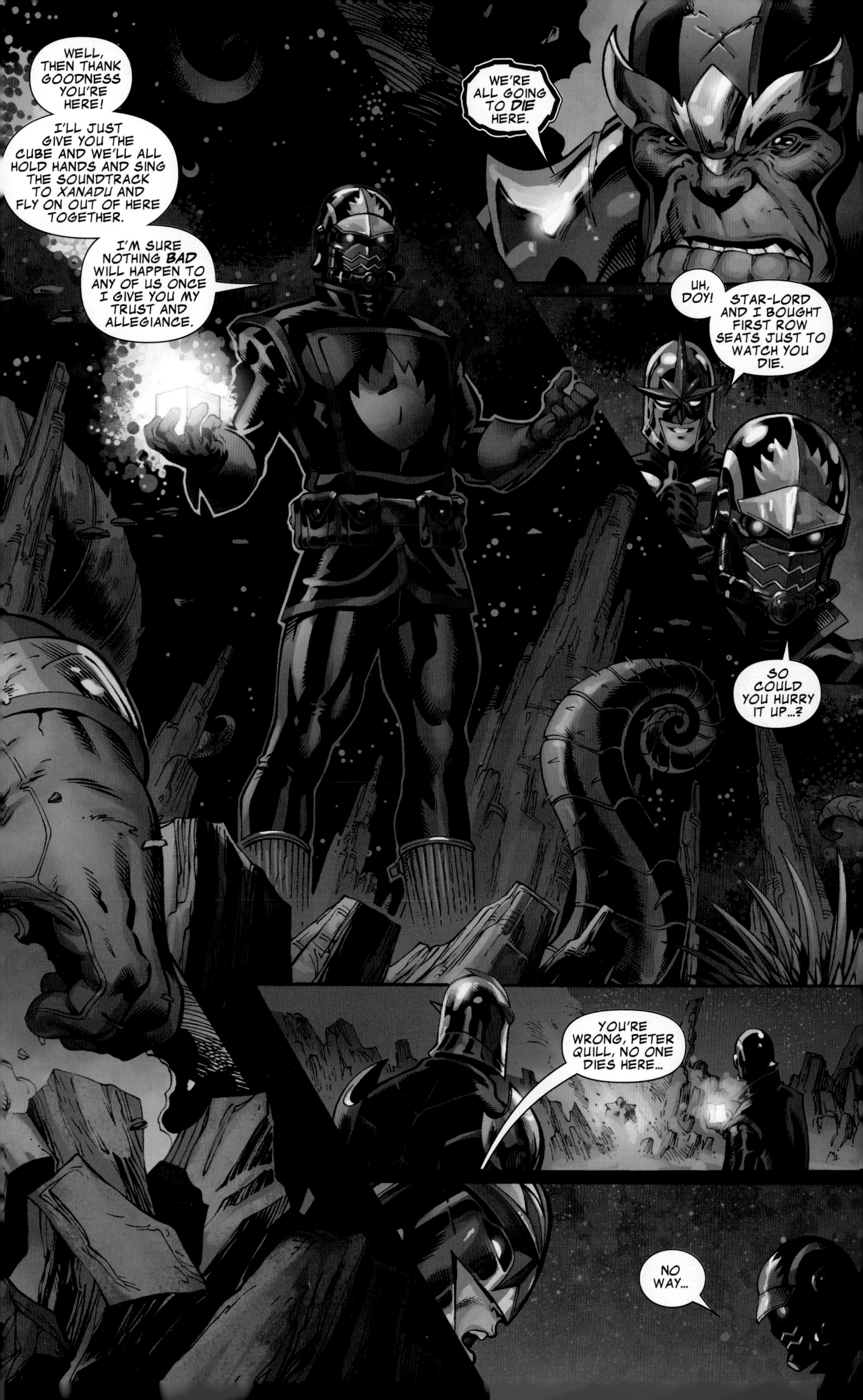
WELL, THEN THANK GOODNESS YOU'RE HERE!
I'LL JUST GIVE YOU THE CUBE AND WE'LL ALL HOLD HANDS AND SING THE SOUNDTRACK TO XANADU AND FLY ON OUT OF HERE TOGETHER.
I'M SURE NOTHING BAD WILL HAPPEN TO ANY OF US ONCE I GIVE YOU MY TRUST AND ALLEGIANCE.
WE'RE ALL GOING TO DIE HERE.
UH, DOY!
STAR-LORD AND I BOUGHT FIRST ROW SEATS JUST TO WATCH YOU DIE.
SO COULD YOU HURRY IT UP...?
YOU'RE WRONG, PETER QUILL, NO ONE DIES HERE...
NO WAY...

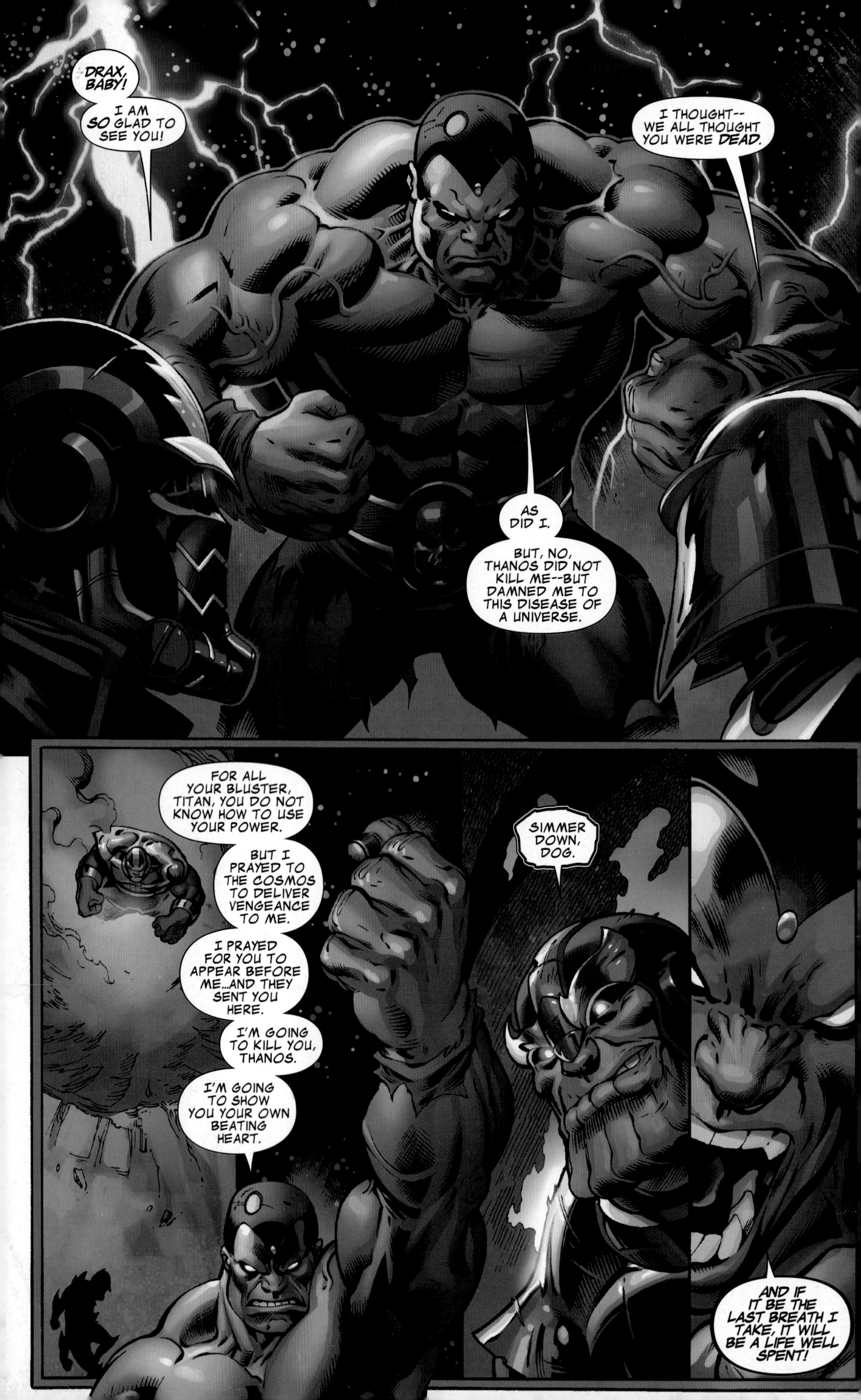
DRAX, BABY!
I AM SO GLAD TO SEE YOU!
I THOUGHT-- WE ALL THOUGHT YOU WERE DEAD.
AS DID I.
BUT, NO, THANOS DID NOT KILL ME--BUT DAMNED ME TO THIS DISEASE OF A UNIVERSE.
FOR ALL YOUR BLUSTER, TITAN, YOU DO NOT KNOW HOW TO USE YOUR POWER.
BUT I PRAYED TO THE COSMOS TO DELIVER VENGEANCE TO ME.
I PRAYED FOR YOU TO APPEAR BEFORE ME...AND THEY SENT YOU HERE.
I'M GOING TO KILL YOU, THANOS.
I'M GOING TO SHOW YOU YOUR OWN BEATING HEART.
SIMMER DOWN, DOG.
AND IF IT BE THE LAST BREATH I TAKE, IT WILL BE A LIFE WELL SPENT!

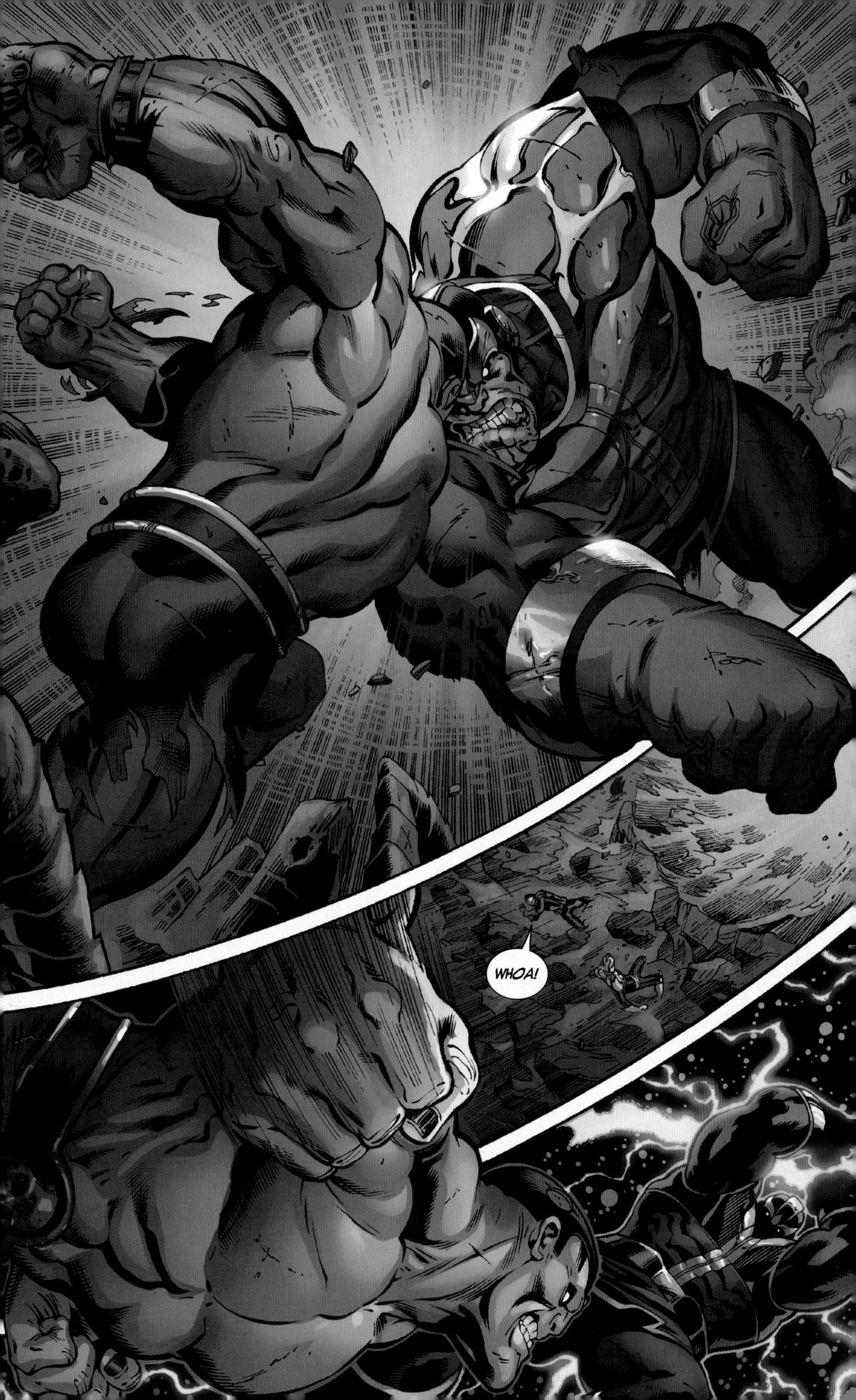
WHOA!

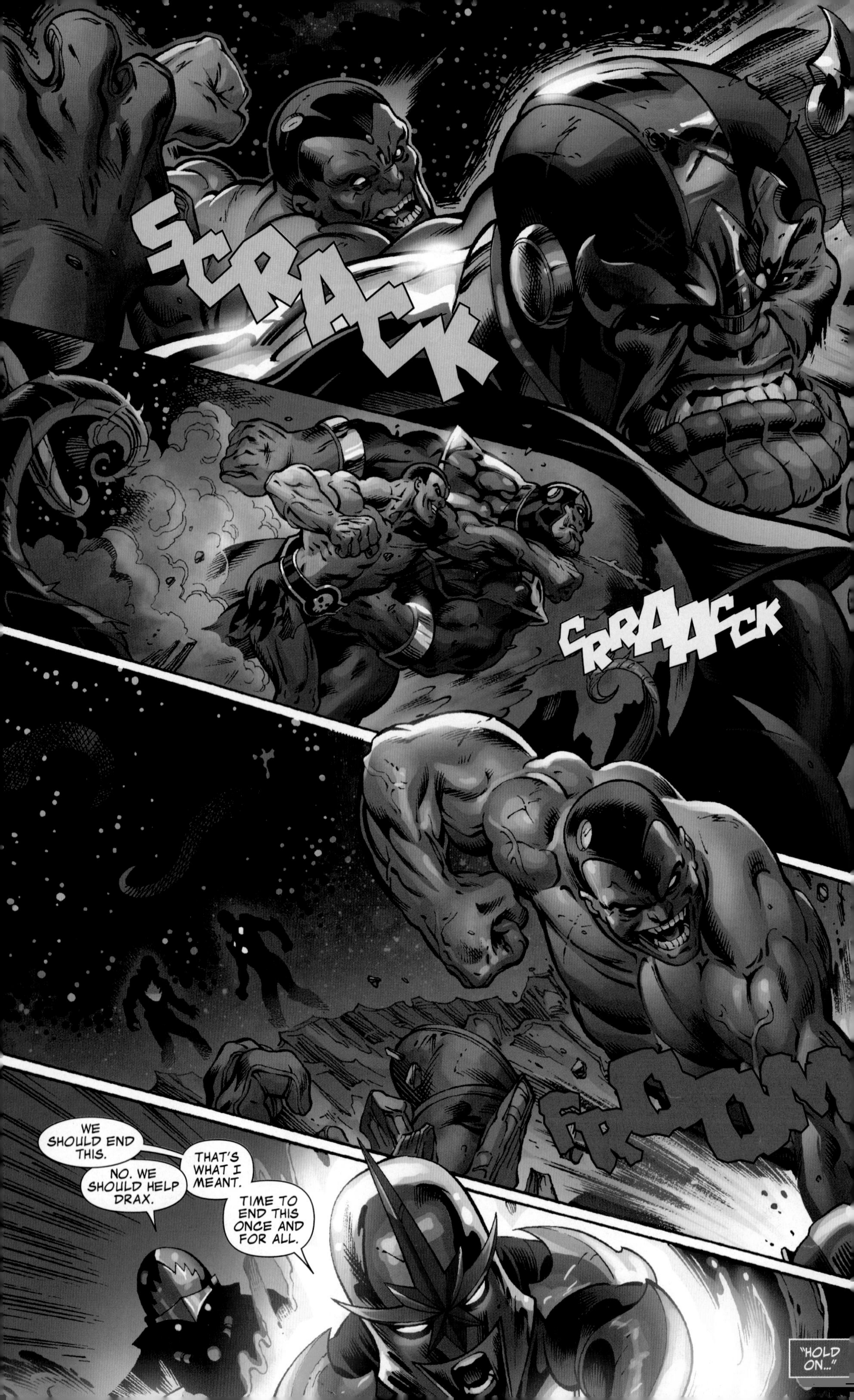
SCRACK
CRRAACCK
WE SHOULD END THIS.
NO. WE SHOULD HELP DRAX.
THAT'S WHAT I MEANT.
TIME TO END THIS ONCE AND FOR ALL.
"HOLD ON..."

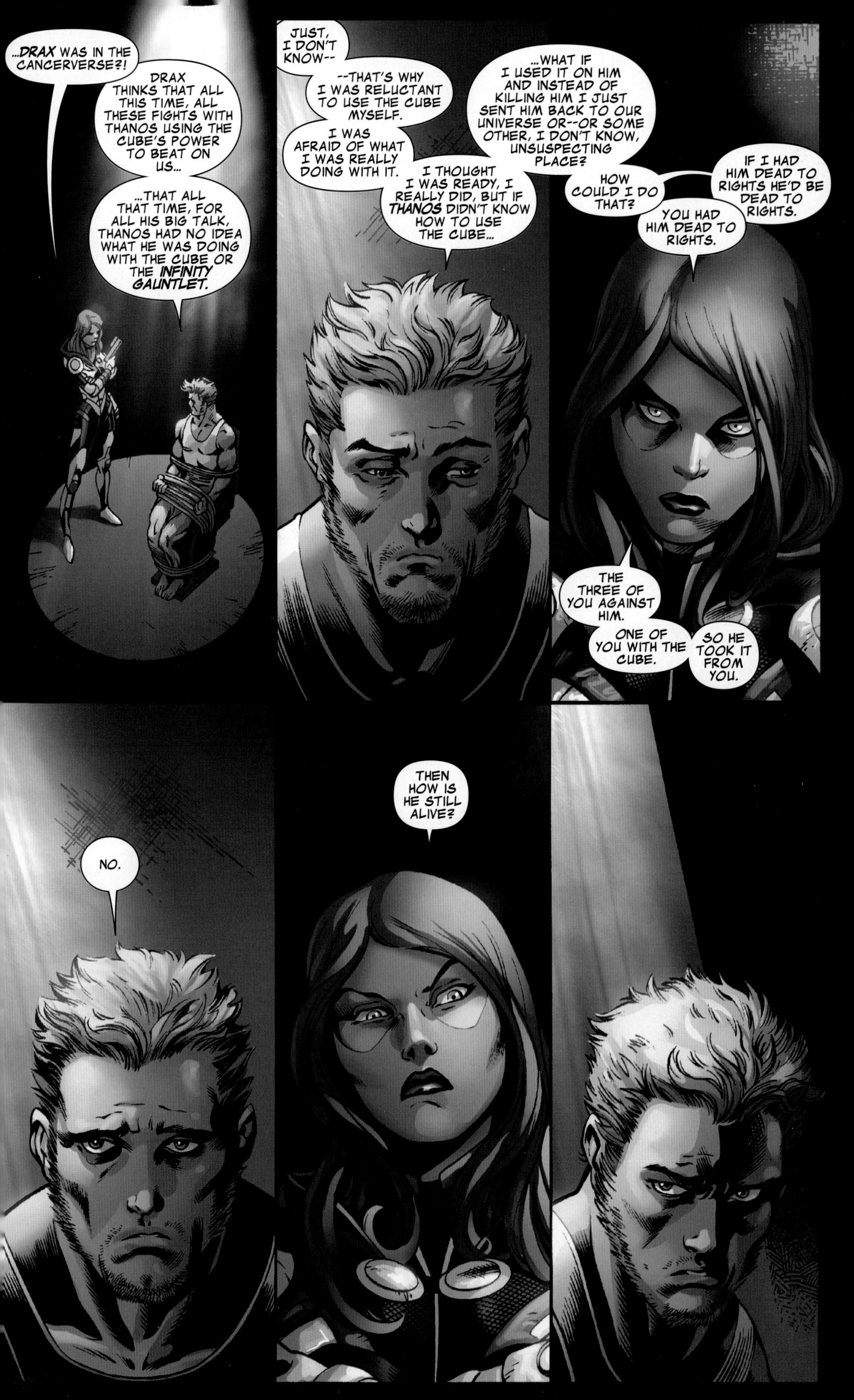
...DRAX WAS IN THE CANCERVERSE?!
DRAX THINKS THAT ALL THIS TIME, ALL THESE FIGHTS WITH THANOS USING THE CUBE'S POWER TO BEAT ON US...
...THAT ALL THAT TIME, FOR ALL HIS BIG TALK, THANOS HAD NO IDEA WHAT HE WAS DOING WITH THE CUBE OR THE INFINITY GAUNTLET.
JUST, I DON'T KNOW--
--THAT'S WHY I WAS RELUCTANT TO USE THE CUBE MYSELF.
I WAS AFRAID OF WHAT I WAS REALLY DOING WITH IT.
I THOUGHT I WAS READY, I REALLY DID, BUT IF THANOS DIDN'T KNOW HOW TO USE THE CUBE...
...WHAT IF I USED IT ON HIM AND INSTEAD OF KILLING HIM I JUST SENT HIM BACK TO OUR UNIVERSE OR--OR SOME OTHER, I DON'T KNOW, UNSUSPECTING PLACE?
HOW COULD I DO THAT?
IF I HAD HIM DEAD TO RIGHTS HE'D BE DEAD TO RIGHTS.
YOU HAD HIM DEAD TO RIGHTS.
THE THREE OF YOU AGAINST HIM.
ONE OF YOU WITH THE CUBE.
SO HE TOOK IT FROM YOU.
NO.
THEN HOW IS HE STILL ALIVE?

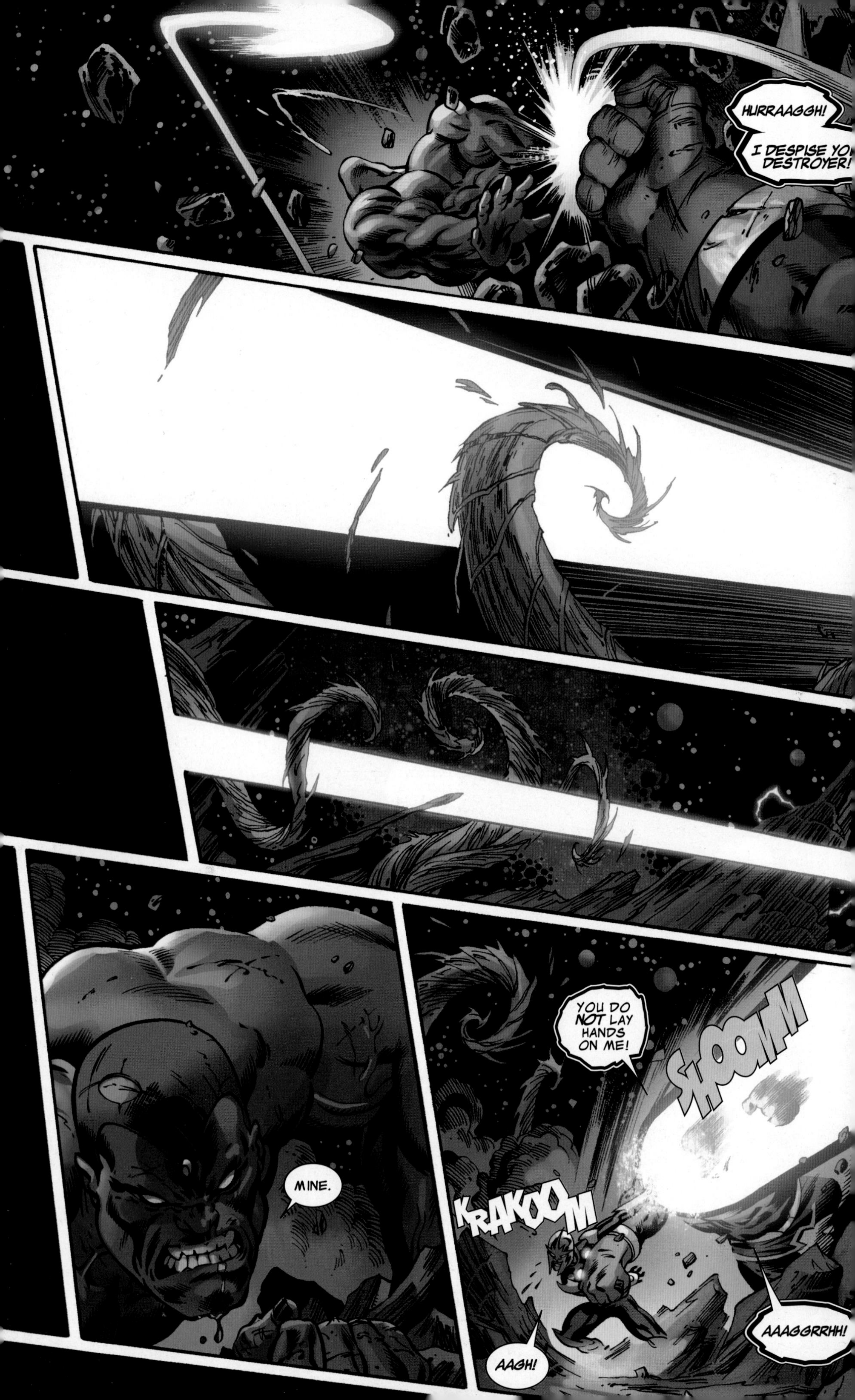
HURRAAGGH!
I DESPISE YO
DESTROYER!
MINE.
YOU DO NOT LAY HANDS ON ME!
SHOOMM
KRAKOOM
AAGH!
AAAGGRRHH!

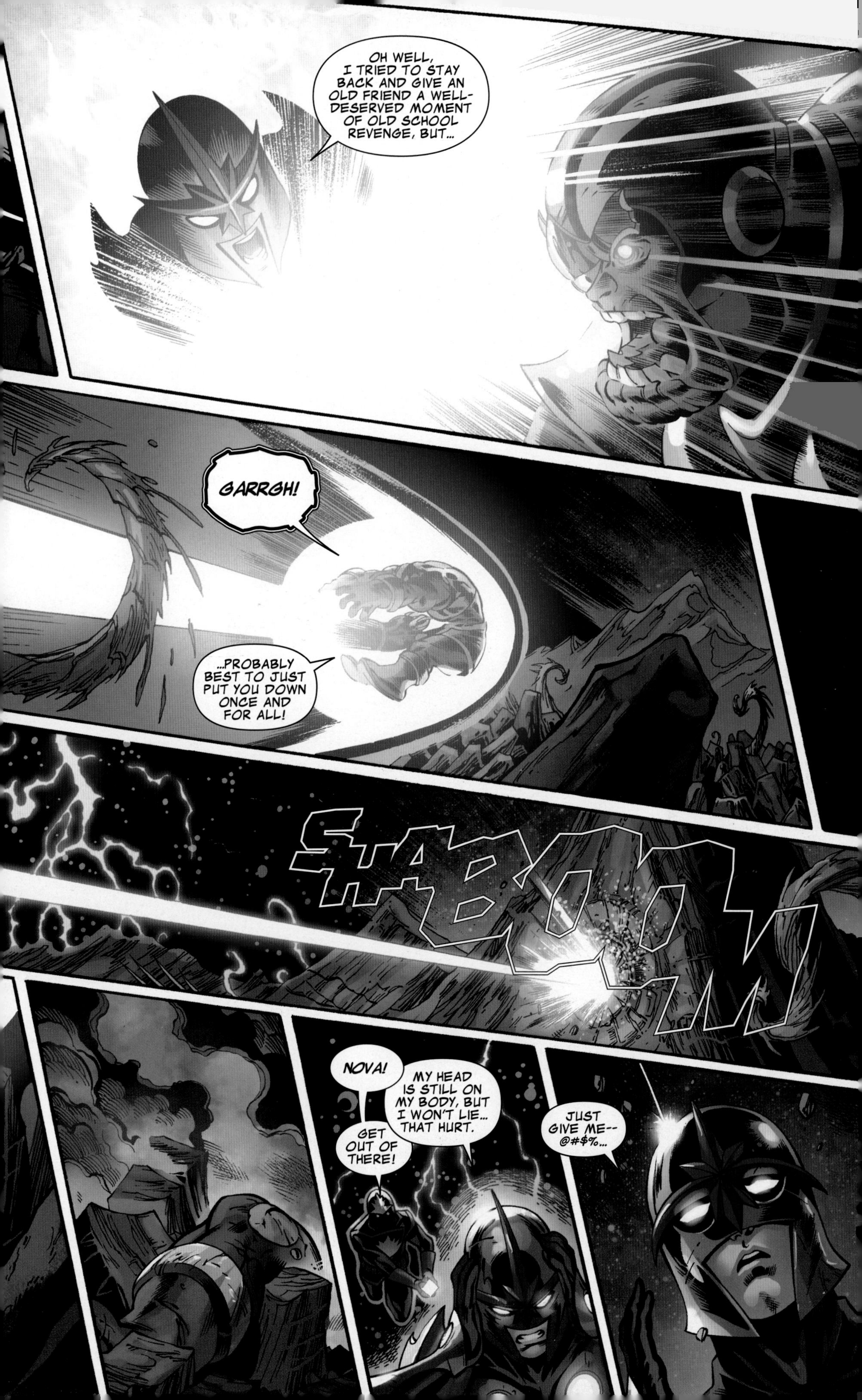
OH WELL, I TRIED TO STAY BACK AND GIVE AN OLD FRIEND A WELL-DESERVED MOMENT OF OLD SCHOOL REVENGE, BUT...
GARRGH!
...PROBABLY BEST TO JUST PUT YOU DOWN ONCE AND FOR ALL!
SHABOOM
NOVA!
GET OUT OF THERE!
MY HEAD IS STILL ON MY BODY, BUT I WON'T LIE... THAT HURT.
JUST GIVE ME-- @#$%...

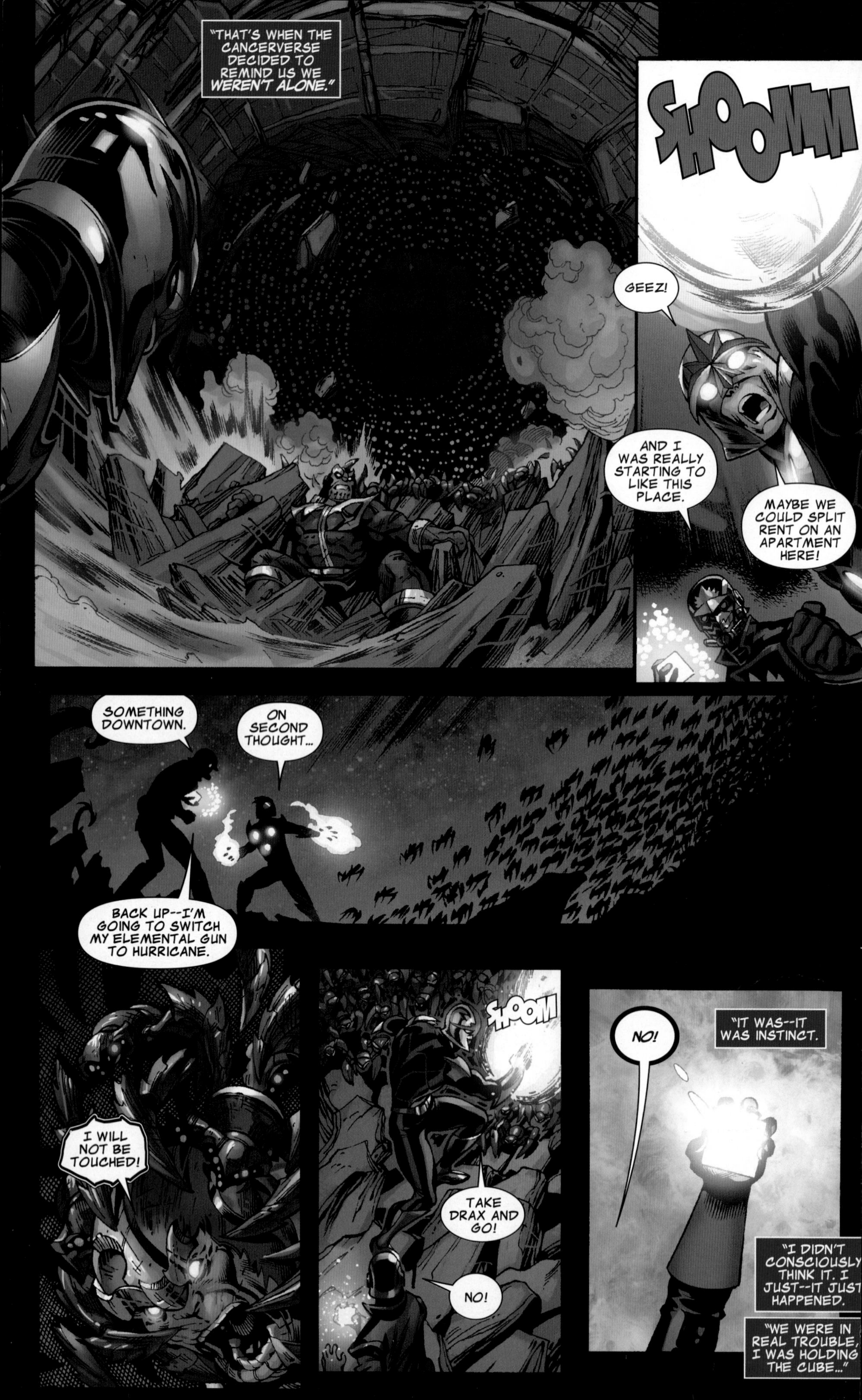
"THAT'S WHEN THE CANCERVERSE DECIDED TO REMIND US WE WEREN'T ALONE."
SHOOMM
GEEZ!
AND I WAS REALLY STARTING TO LIKE THIS PLACE.
MAYBE WE COULD SPLIT RENT ON AN APARTMENT HERE!
SOMETHING DOWNTOWN.
ON SECOND THOUGHT...
BACK UP--I'M GOING TO SWITCH MY ELEMENTAL GUN TO HURRICANE.
I WILL NOT BE TOUCHED!
SHOOM
TAKE DRAX AND GO!
NO!
NO!
"IT WAS--IT WAS INSTINCT.
"I DIDN'T CONSCIOUSLY THINK IT. I JUST--IT JUST HAPPENED.
"WE WERE IN REAL TROUBLE, I WAS HOLDING THE CUBE..."

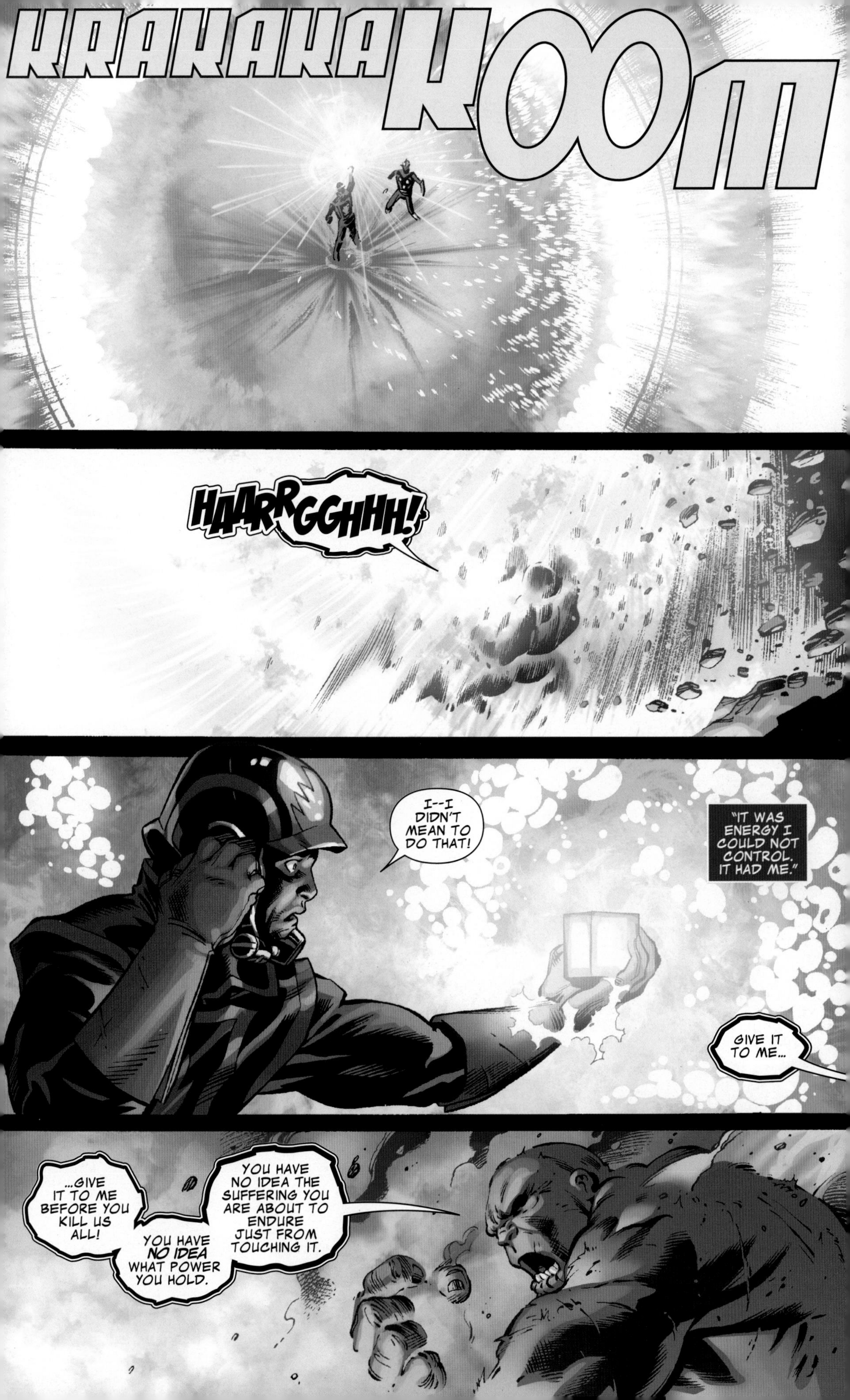
KRAKAKAKOOM
HAARRGGHHH!
I--I DIDN'T MEAN TO DO THAT!
"IT WAS ENERGY I COULD NOT CONTROL. IT HAD ME."
GIVE IT TO ME...
...GIVE IT TO ME BEFORE YOU KILL US ALL!
YOU HAVE NO IDEA WHAT POWER YOU HOLD.
YOU HAVE NO IDEA THE SUFFERING YOU ARE ABOUT TO ENDURE JUST FROM TOUCHING IT.

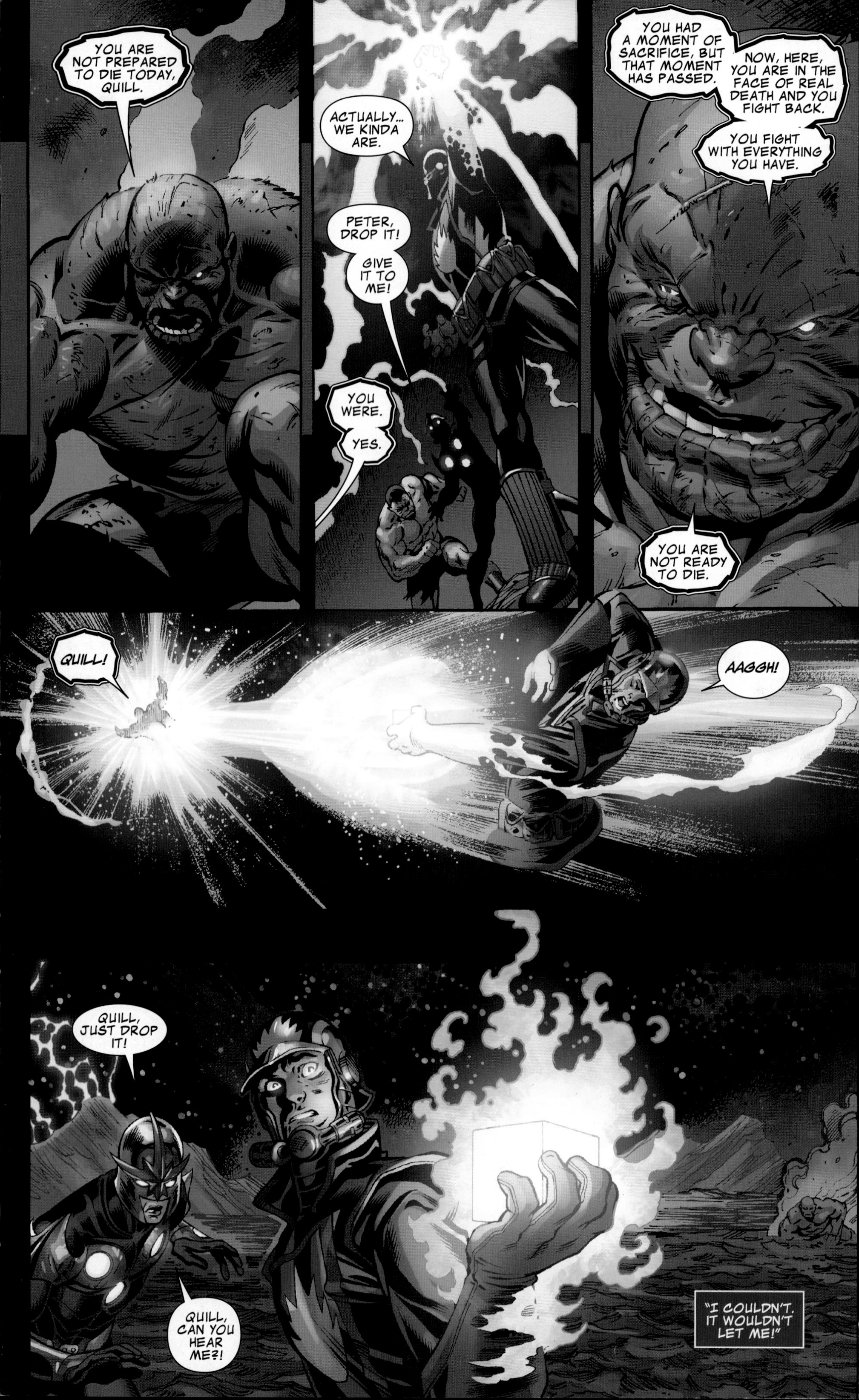
YOU ARE NOT PREPARED TO DIE TODAY, QUILL.
ACTUALLY... WE KINDA ARE.
PETER, DROP IT!
GIVE IT TO ME!
YOU WERE.
YES.
YOU HAD A MOMENT OF SACRIFICE, BUT THAT MOMENT HAS PASSED.
NOW, HERE, YOU ARE IN THE FACE OF REAL DEATH AND YOU FIGHT BACK.
YOU FIGHT WITH EVERYTHING YOU HAVE.
YOU ARE NOT READY TO DIE.
QUILL!
AAGGH!
QUILL, JUST DROP IT!
QUILL, CAN YOU HEAR ME?!
"I COULDN'T. IT WOULDN'T LET ME!"

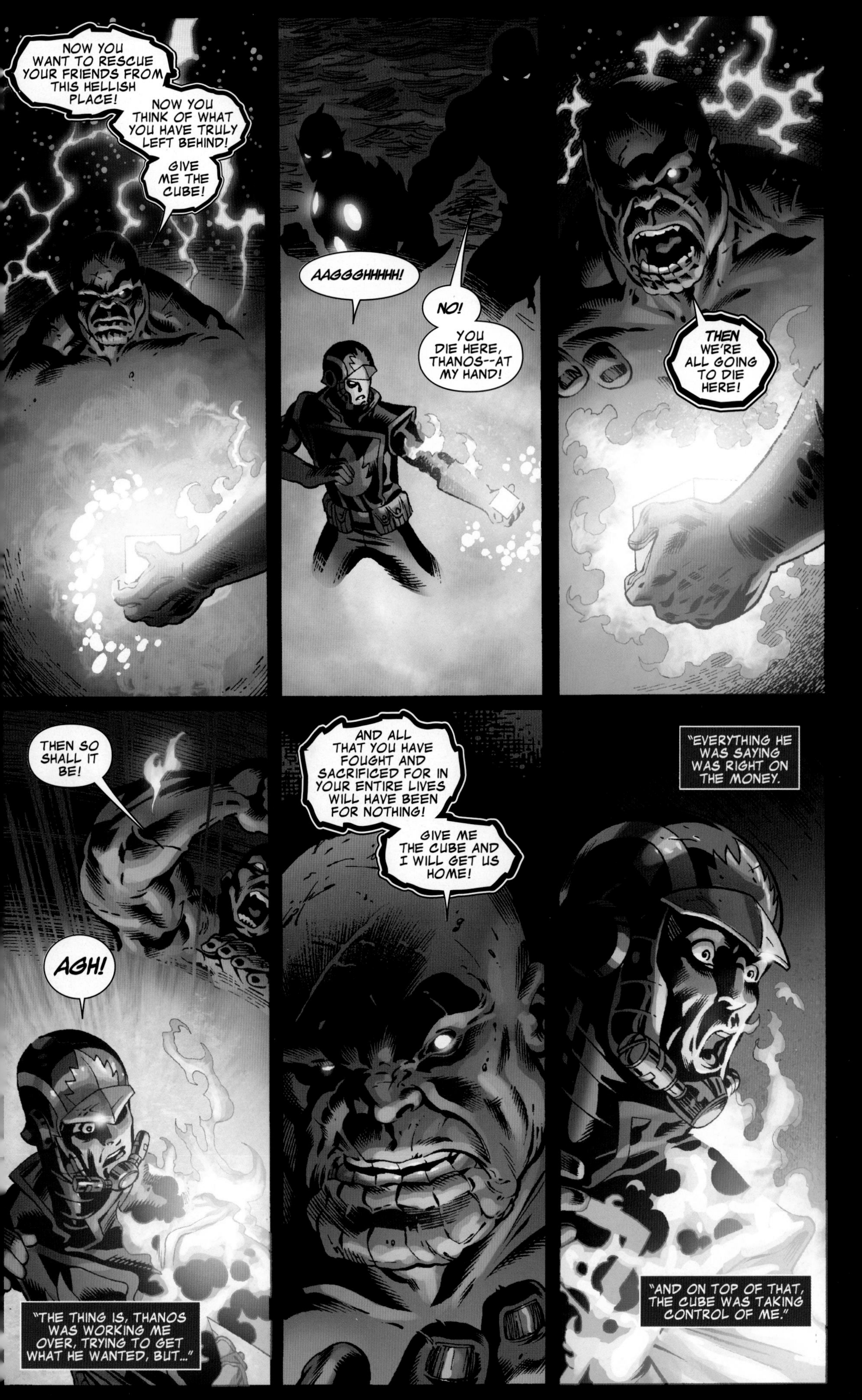
NOW YOU WANT TO RESCUE YOUR FRIENDS FROM THIS HELLISH PLACE!
NOW YOU THINK OF WHAT YOU HAVE TRULY LEFT BEHIND!
GIVE ME THE CUBE!
AAGGGHHHHH!
NO!
YOU DIE HERE, THANOS--AT MY HAND!
THEN WE'RE ALL GOING TO DIE HERE!
THEN SO SHALL IT BE!
AGH!
"THE THING IS, THANOS WAS WORKING ME OVER, TRYING TO GET WHAT HE WANTED, BUT..."
AND ALL THAT YOU HAVE FOUGHT AND SACRIFICED FOR IN YOUR ENTIRE LIVES WILL HAVE BEEN FOR NOTHING!
GIVE ME THE CUBE AND I WILL GET US HOME!
"EVERYTHING HE WAS SAYING WAS RIGHT ON THE MONEY.
"AND ON TOP OF THAT, THE CUBE WAS TAKING CONTROL OF ME."

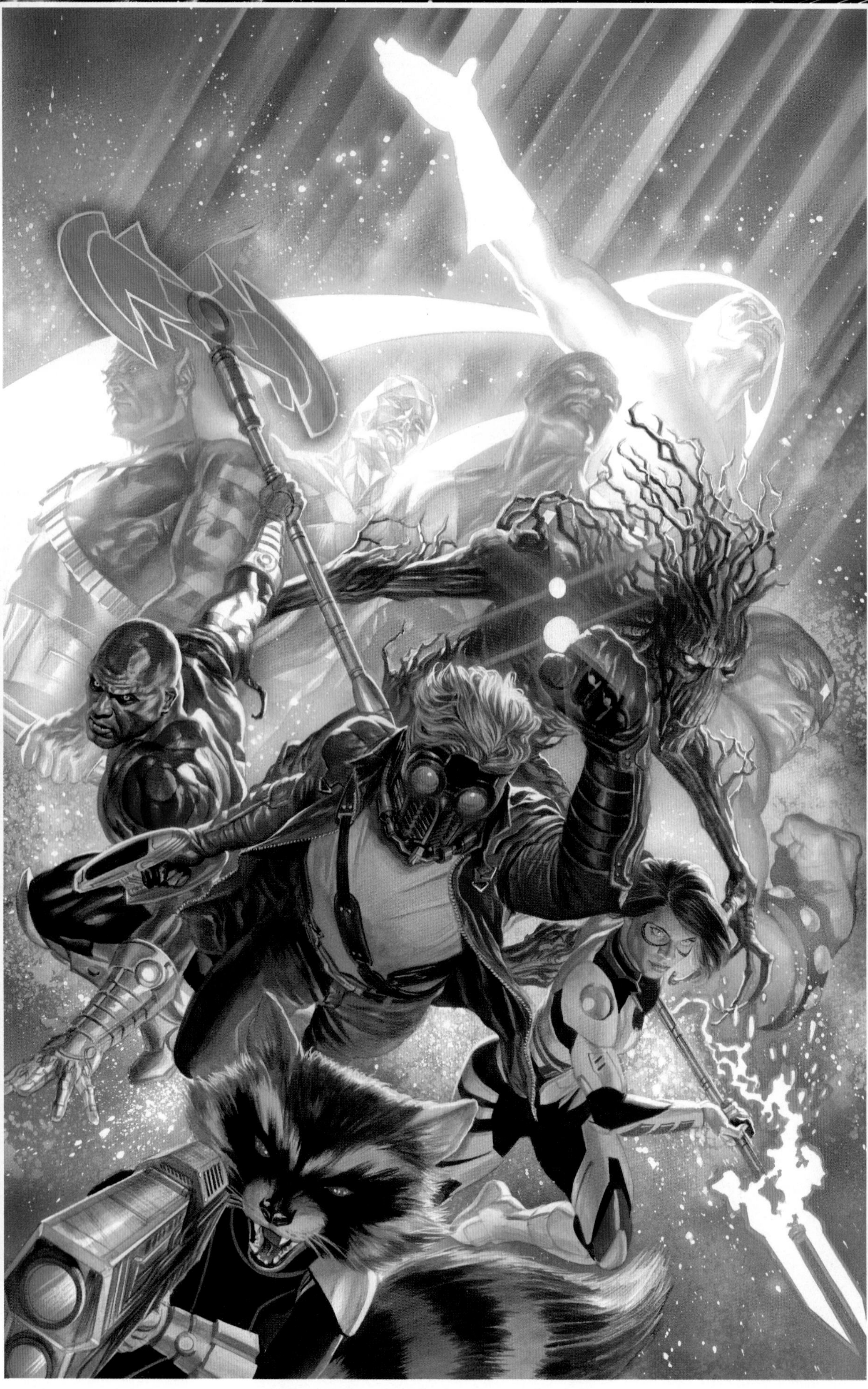

#*18* 75TH ANNIVERSARY VARIANT BY ALEX ROSS

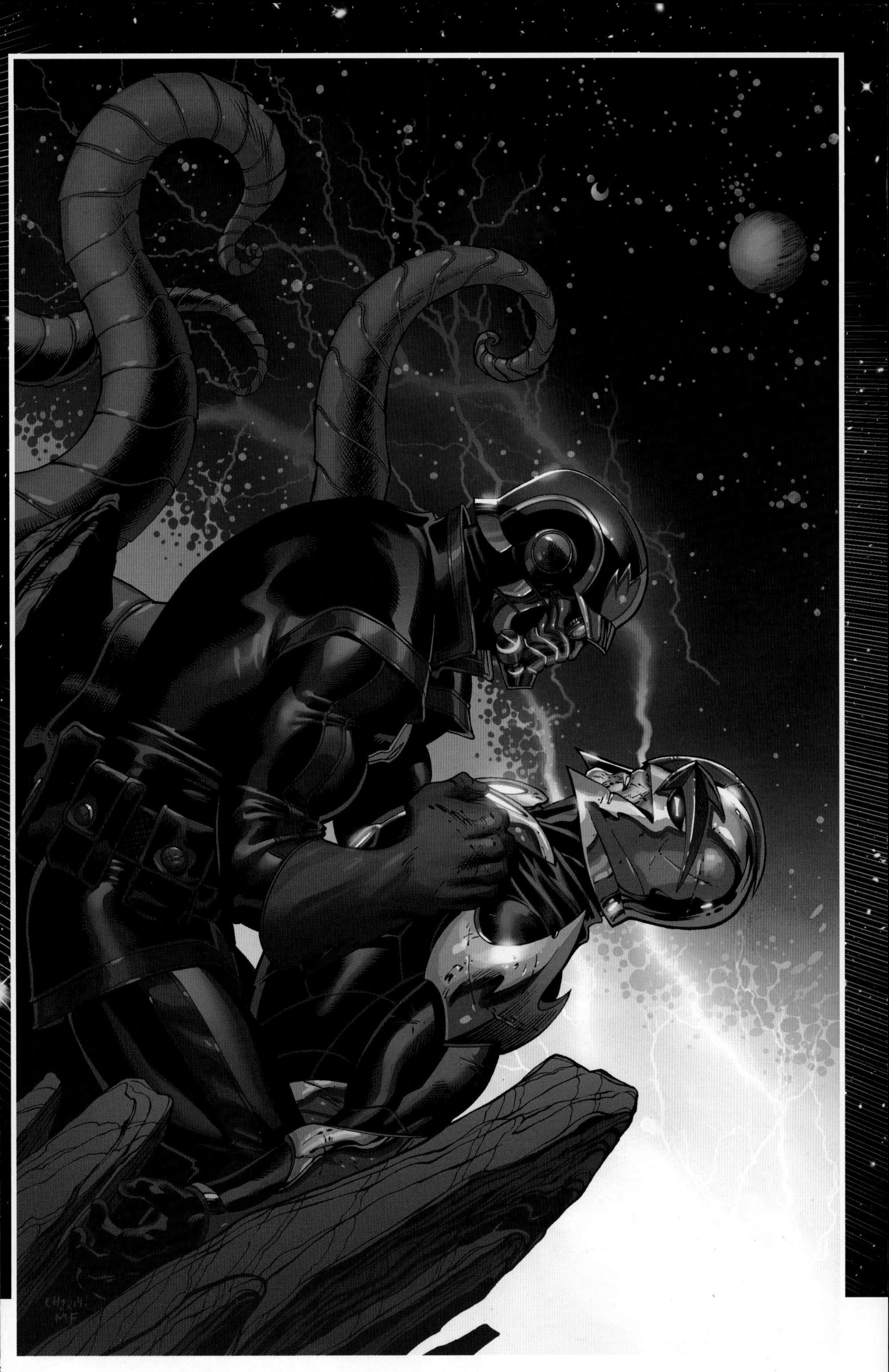

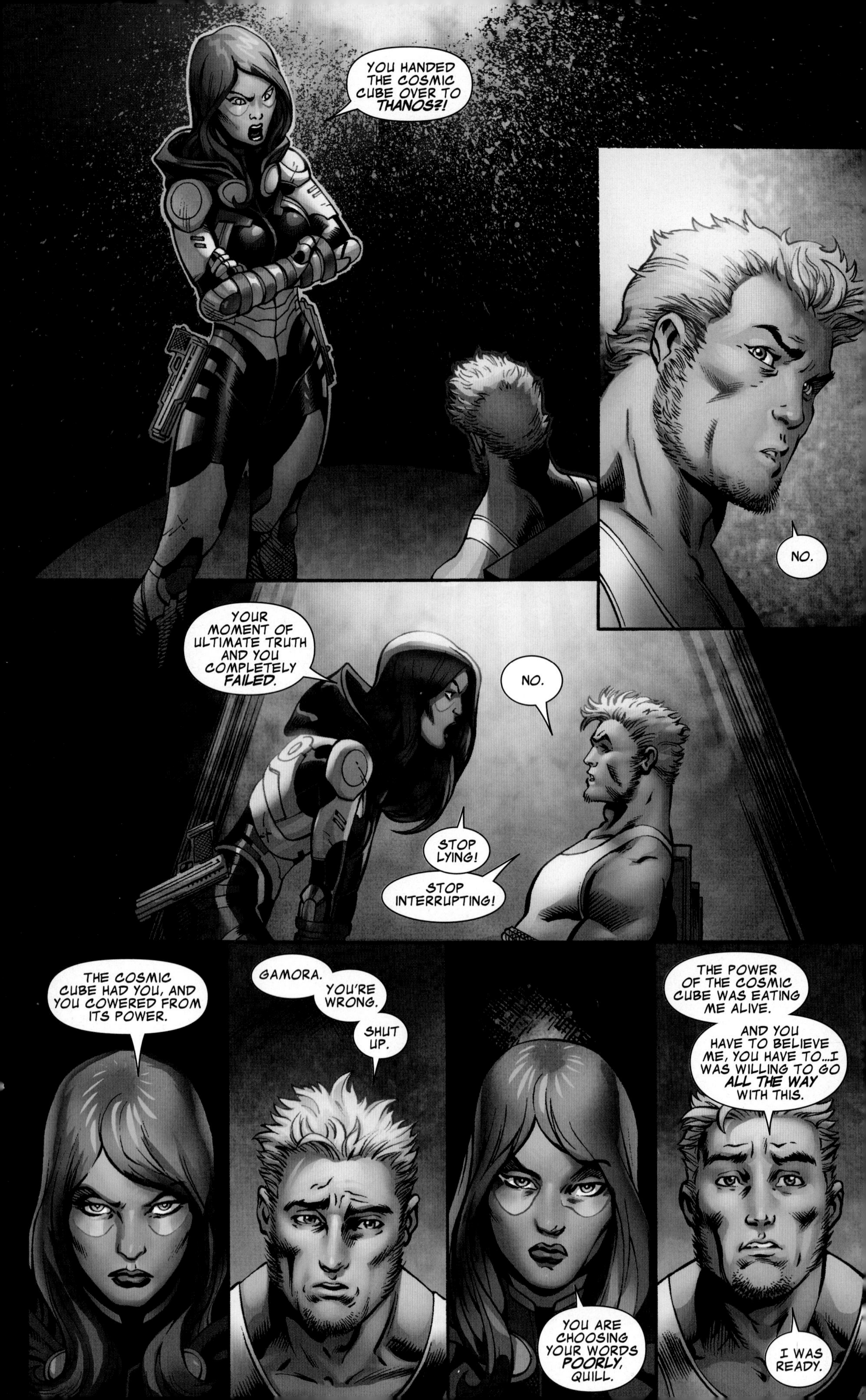
YOU HANDED THE COSMIC CUBE OVER TO *THANOS?!*
NO.
YOUR MOMENT OF ULTIMATE TRUTH AND YOU COMPLETELY *FAILED*.
NO.
STOP LYING!
STOP INTERRUPTING!
THE COSMIC CUBE HAD YOU, AND YOU COWERED FROM ITS POWER.
GAMORA.
YOU'RE WRONG.
SHUT UP.
YOU ARE CHOOSING YOUR WORDS *POORLY*, QUILL.
THE POWER OF THE COSMIC CUBE WAS EATING ME ALIVE.
AND YOU HAVE TO BELIEVE ME, YOU HAVE TO...I WAS WILLING TO GO *ALL THE WAY* WITH THIS.
I WAS READY.

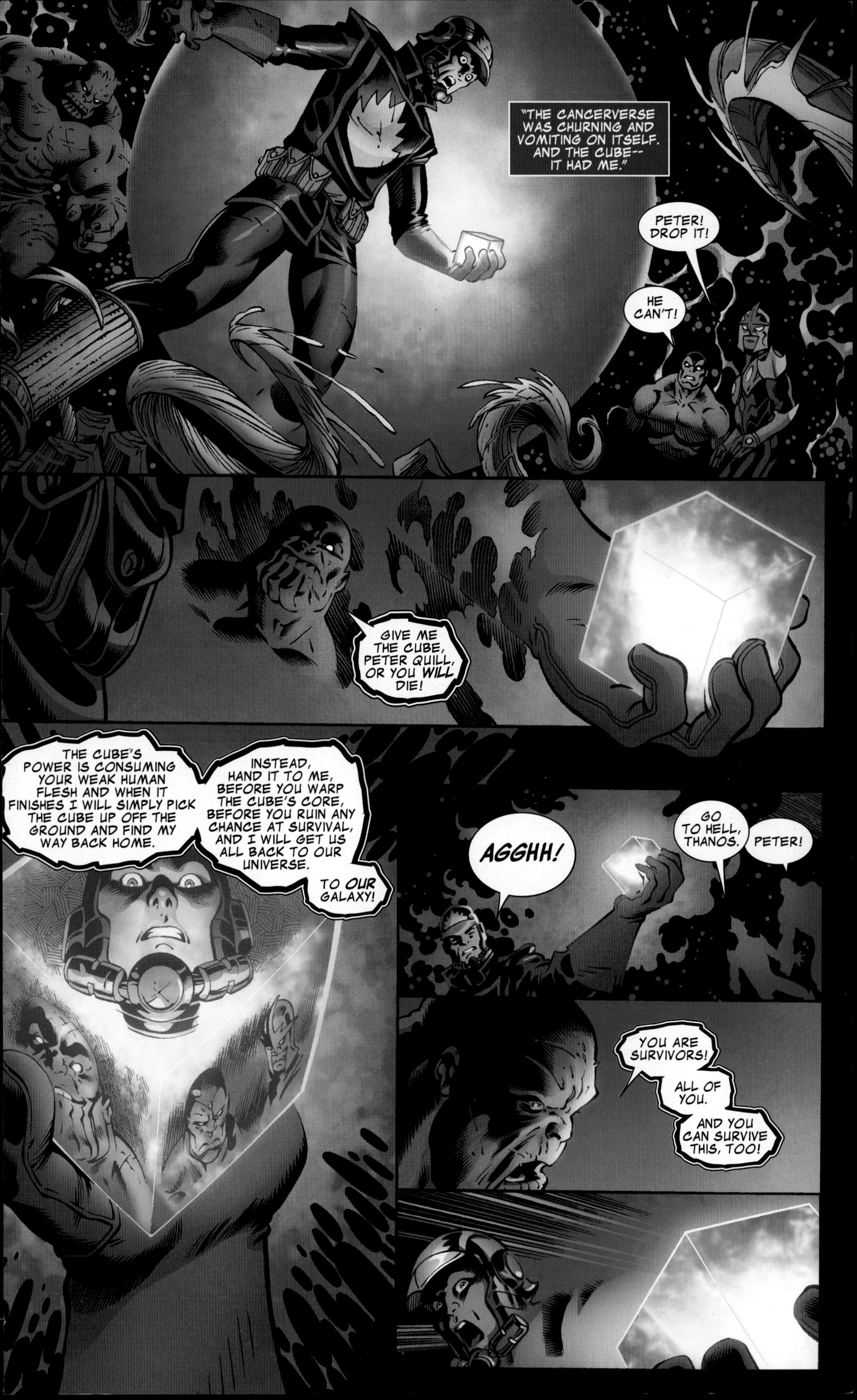
"THE CANCERVERSE WAS CHURNING AND VOMITING ON ITSELF. AND THE CUBE-- IT HAD ME."
PETER! DROP IT!
HE CAN'T!
GIVE ME THE CUBE, PETER QUILL, OR YOU WILL DIE!
THE CUBE'S POWER IS CONSUMING YOUR WEAK HUMAN FLESH AND WHEN IT FINISHES I WILL SIMPLY PICK THE CUBE UP OFF THE GROUND AND FIND MY WAY BACK HOME.
INSTEAD, HAND IT TO ME, BEFORE YOU WARP THE CUBE'S CORE, BEFORE YOU RUIN ANY CHANCE AT SURVIVAL, AND I WILL GET US ALL BACK TO OUR UNIVERSE.
TO OUR GALAXY!
AGGHH!
GO TO HELL, THANOS.
PETER!
YOU ARE SURVIVORS!
ALL OF YOU.
AND YOU CAN SURVIVE THIS, TOO!

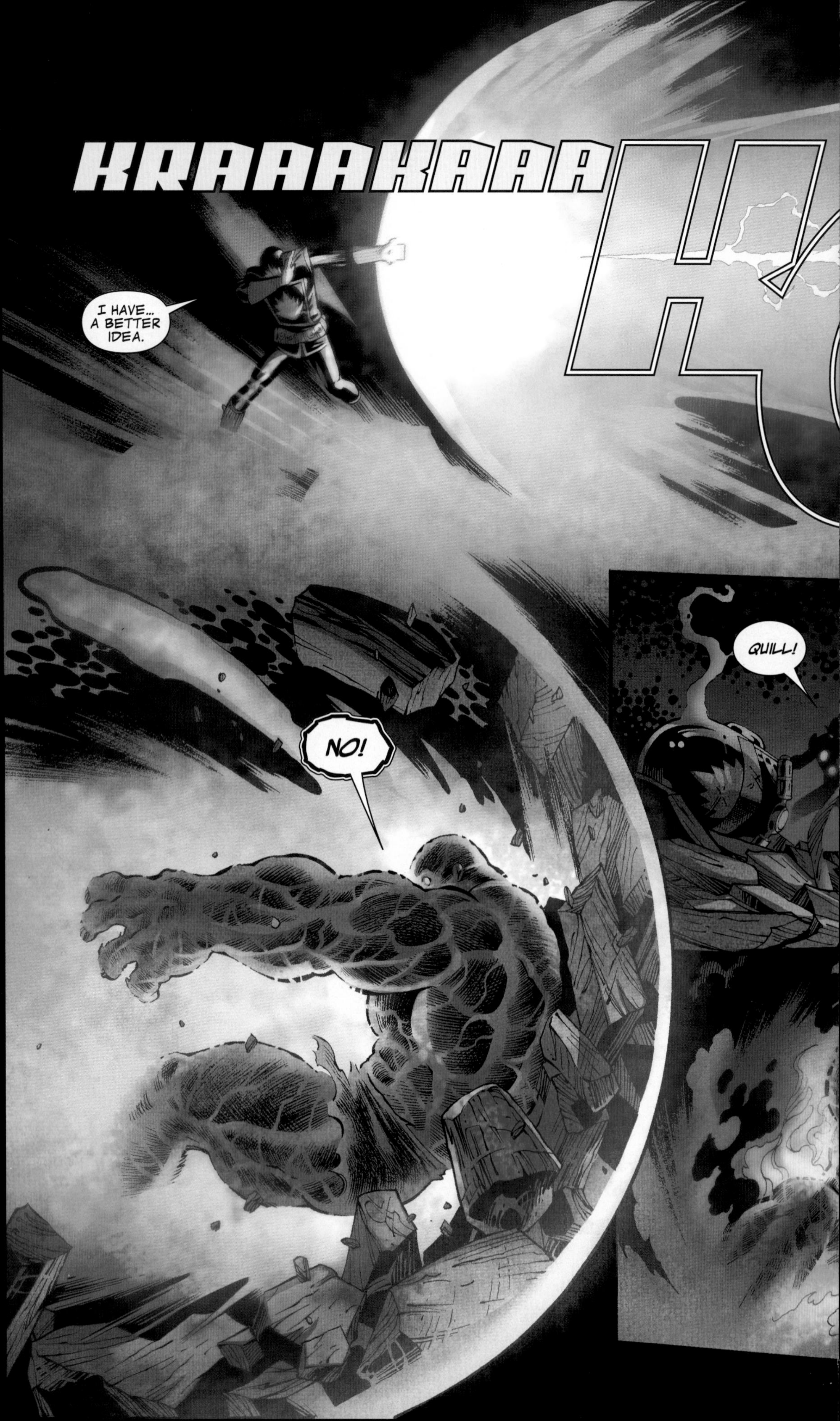
KRAAAKAAA
I HAVE... A BETTER IDEA.
NO!
QUILL!

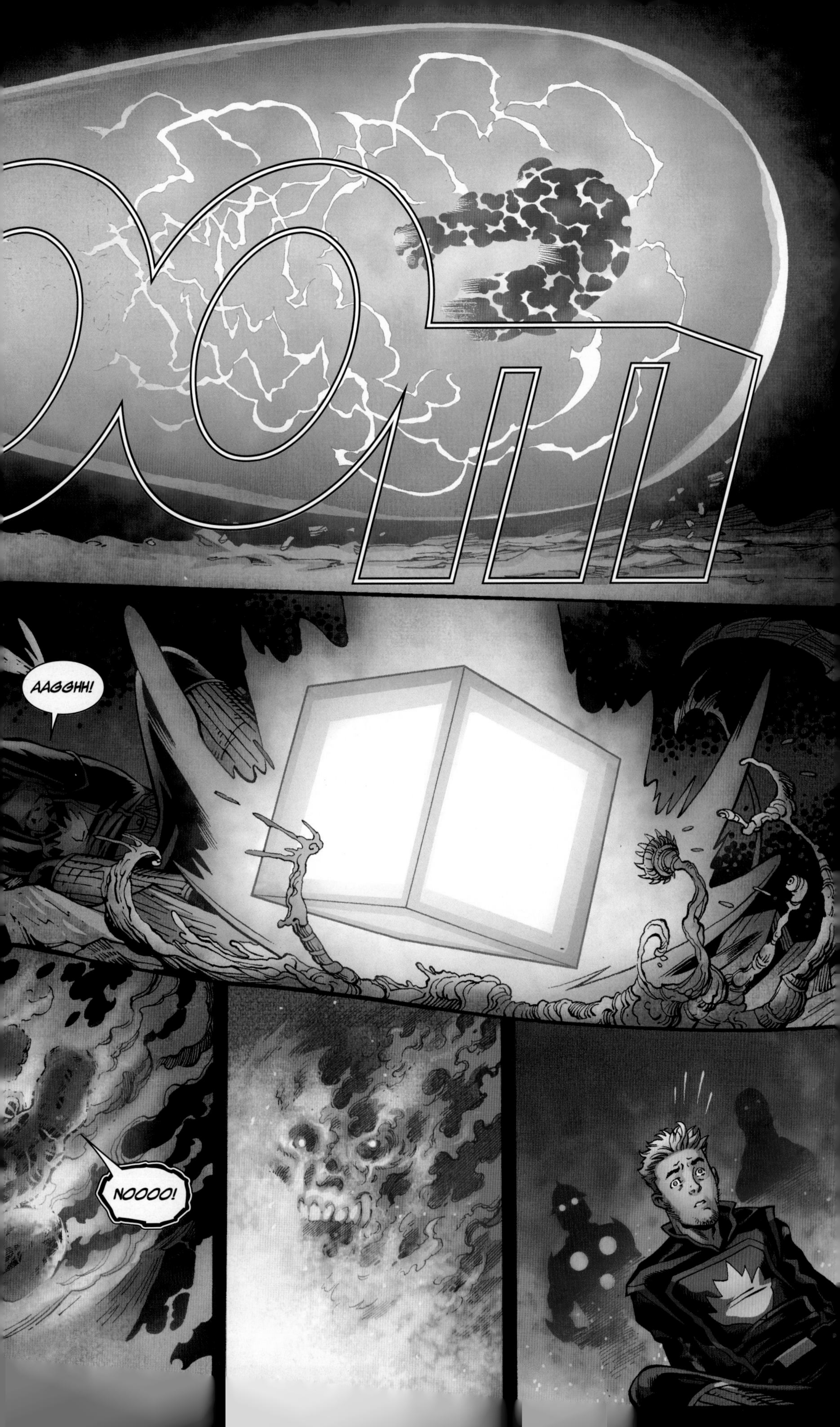
DOOM
AAGGHH!
NOOOO!
! ! !

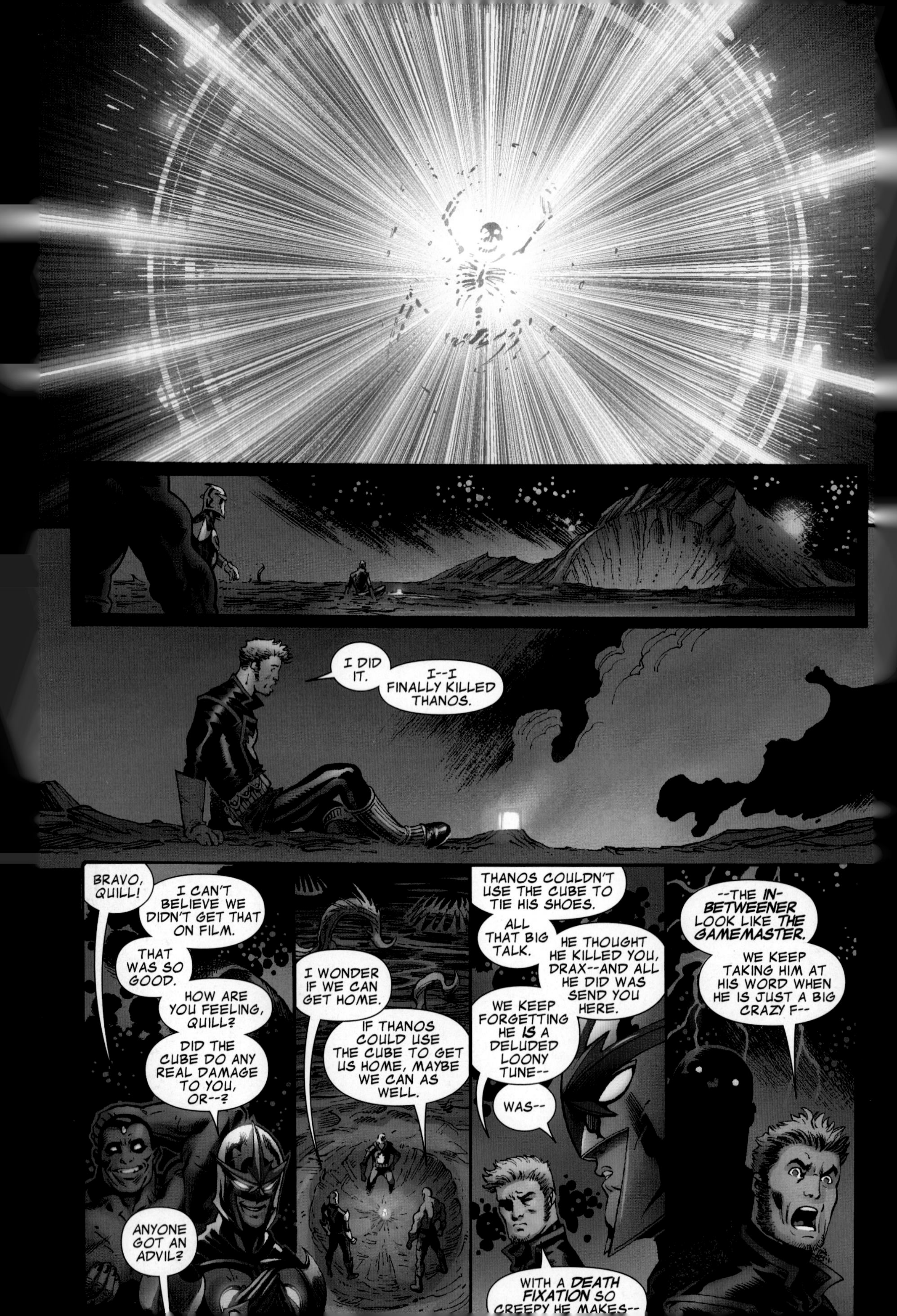

I DID IT.
I--I FINALLY KILLED THANOS.
BRAVO, QUILL!
I CAN'T BELIEVE WE DIDN'T GET THAT ON FILM.
THAT WAS SO GOOD.
HOW ARE YOU FEELING, QUILL?
DID THE CUBE DO ANY REAL DAMAGE TO YOU, OR--?
ANYONE GOT AN ADVIL?
I WONDER IF WE CAN GET HOME.
IF THANOS COULD USE THE CUBE TO GET US HOME, MAYBE WE CAN AS WELL.
THANOS COULDN'T USE THE CUBE TO TIE HIS SHOES.
ALL THAT BIG TALK.
HE THOUGHT HE KILLED YOU, DRAX--AND ALL HE DID WAS SEND YOU HERE.
WE KEEP FORGETTING HE IS A DELUDED LOONY TUNE--
WAS--
WITH A DEATH FIXATION SO CREEPY HE MAKES--
--THE IN-BETWEENER LOOK LIKE THE GAMEMASTER.
WE KEEP TAKING HIM AT HIS WORD WHEN HE IS JUST A BIG CRAZY F--

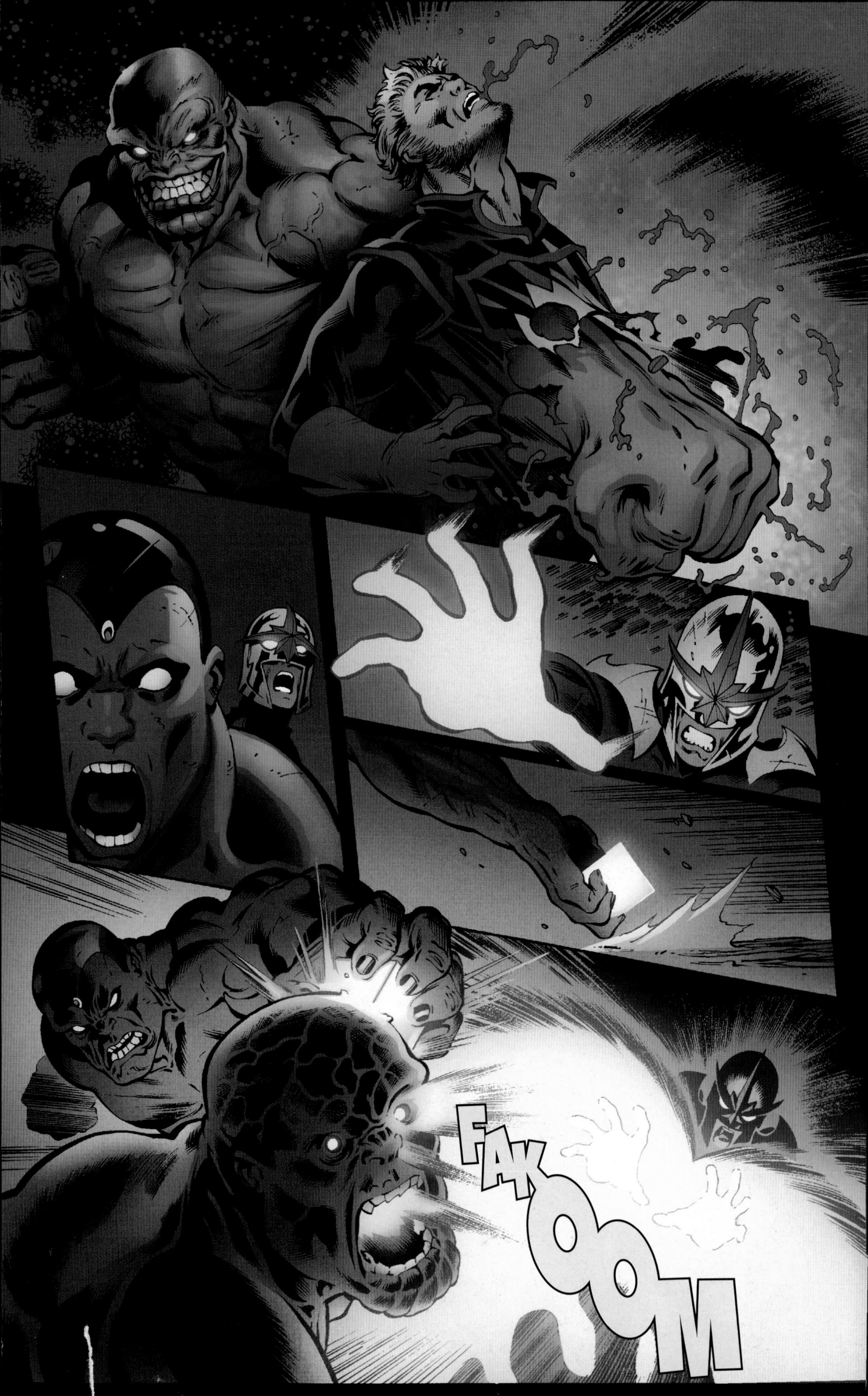
FAKOOOM

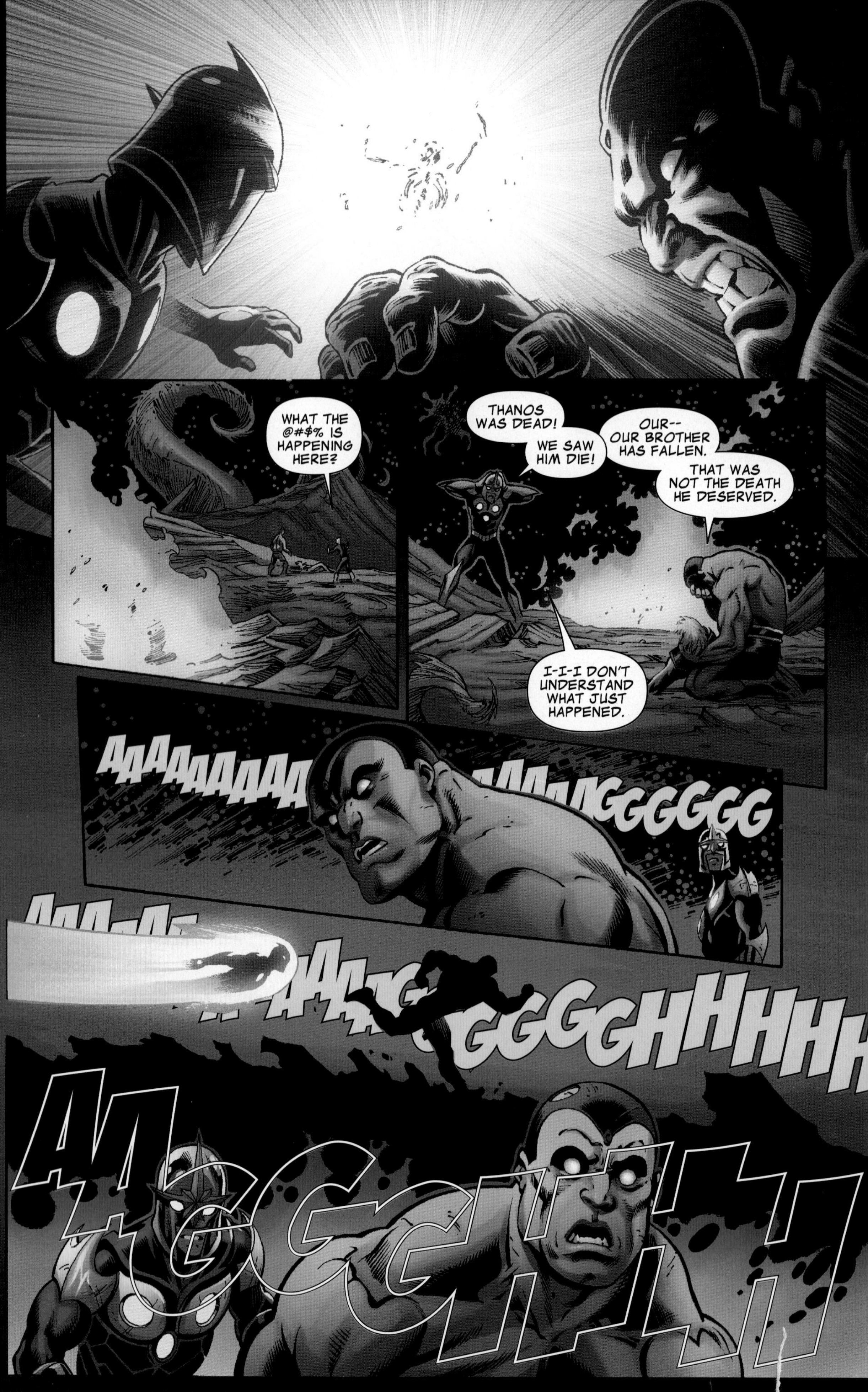
WHAT THE @#$% IS HAPPENING HERE?
THANOS WAS DEAD!
WE SAW HIM DIE!
OUR-- OUR BROTHER HAS FALLEN.
THAT WAS NOT THE DEATH HE DESERVED.
I-I-I DON'T UNDERSTAND WHAT JUST HAPPENED.
AAAAAAAAAAAAAAAGGGGGG
GGGGHHHHH
AAGGHHHH

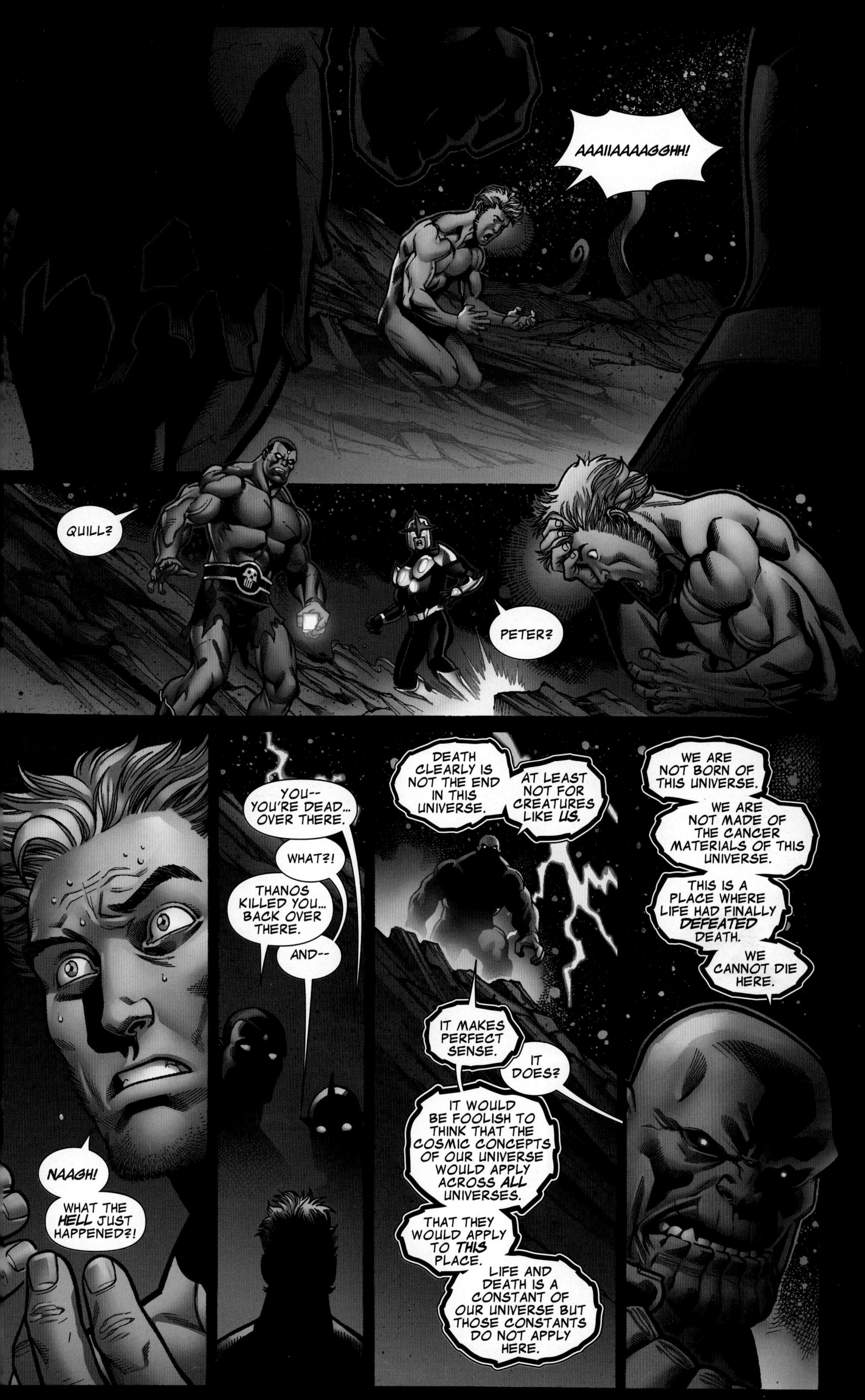
AAAIIAAAAGGHH!
QUILL?
PETER?
YOU-- YOU'RE DEAD... OVER THERE.
WHAT?!
THANOS KILLED YOU... BACK OVER THERE.
AND--
NAAGH!
WHAT THE HELL JUST HAPPENED?!
DEATH CLEARLY IS NOT THE END IN THIS UNIVERSE.
AT LEAST NOT FOR CREATURES LIKE US.
IT MAKES PERFECT SENSE.
IT DOES?
IT WOULD BE FOOLISH TO THINK THAT THE COSMIC CONCEPTS OF OUR UNIVERSE WOULD APPLY ACROSS ALL UNIVERSES.
THAT THEY WOULD APPLY TO THIS PLACE.
LIFE AND DEATH IS A CONSTANT OF OUR UNIVERSE BUT THOSE CONSTANTS DO NOT APPLY HERE.
WE ARE NOT BORN OF THIS UNIVERSE.
WE ARE NOT MADE OF THE CANCER MATERIALS OF THIS UNIVERSE.
THIS IS A PLACE WHERE LIFE HAD FINALLY DEFEATED DEATH.
WE CANNOT DIE HERE.

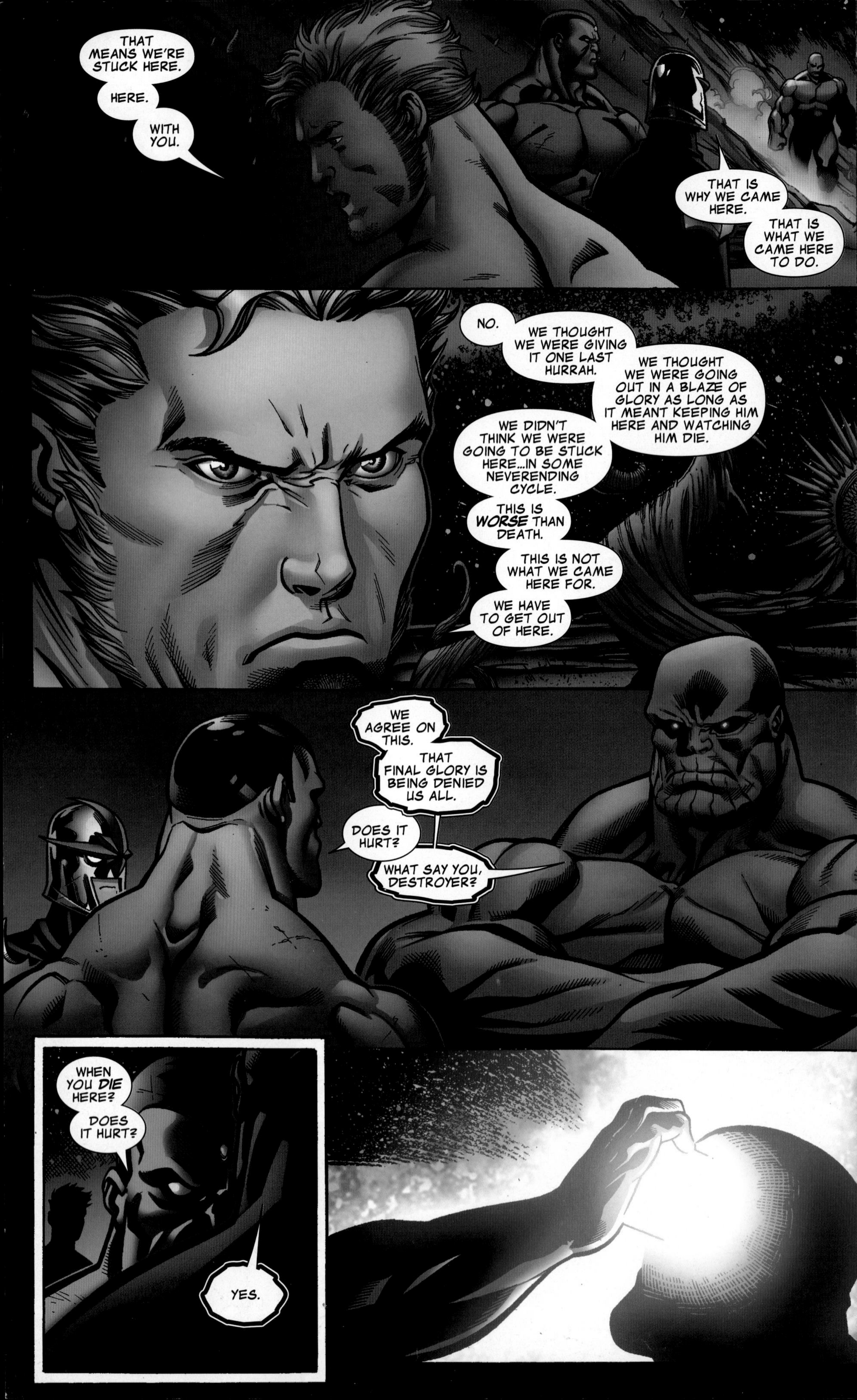
THAT MEANS WE'RE STUCK HERE.
HERE.
WITH YOU.
THAT IS WHY WE CAME HERE.
THAT IS WHAT WE CAME HERE TO DO.
NO.
WE THOUGHT WE WERE GIVING IT ONE LAST HURRAH.
WE THOUGHT WE WERE GOING OUT IN A BLAZE OF GLORY AS LONG AS IT MEANT KEEPING HIM HERE AND WATCHING HIM DIE.
WE DIDN'T THINK WE WERE GOING TO BE STUCK HERE...IN SOME NEVERENDING CYCLE.
THIS IS WORSE THAN DEATH.
THIS IS NOT WHAT WE CAME HERE FOR.
WE HAVE TO GET OUT OF HERE.
WE AGREE ON THIS.
THAT FINAL GLORY IS BEING DENIED US ALL.
WHAT SAY YOU, DESTROYER?
DOES IT HURT?
WHEN YOU DIE HERE?
DOES IT HURT?
YES.

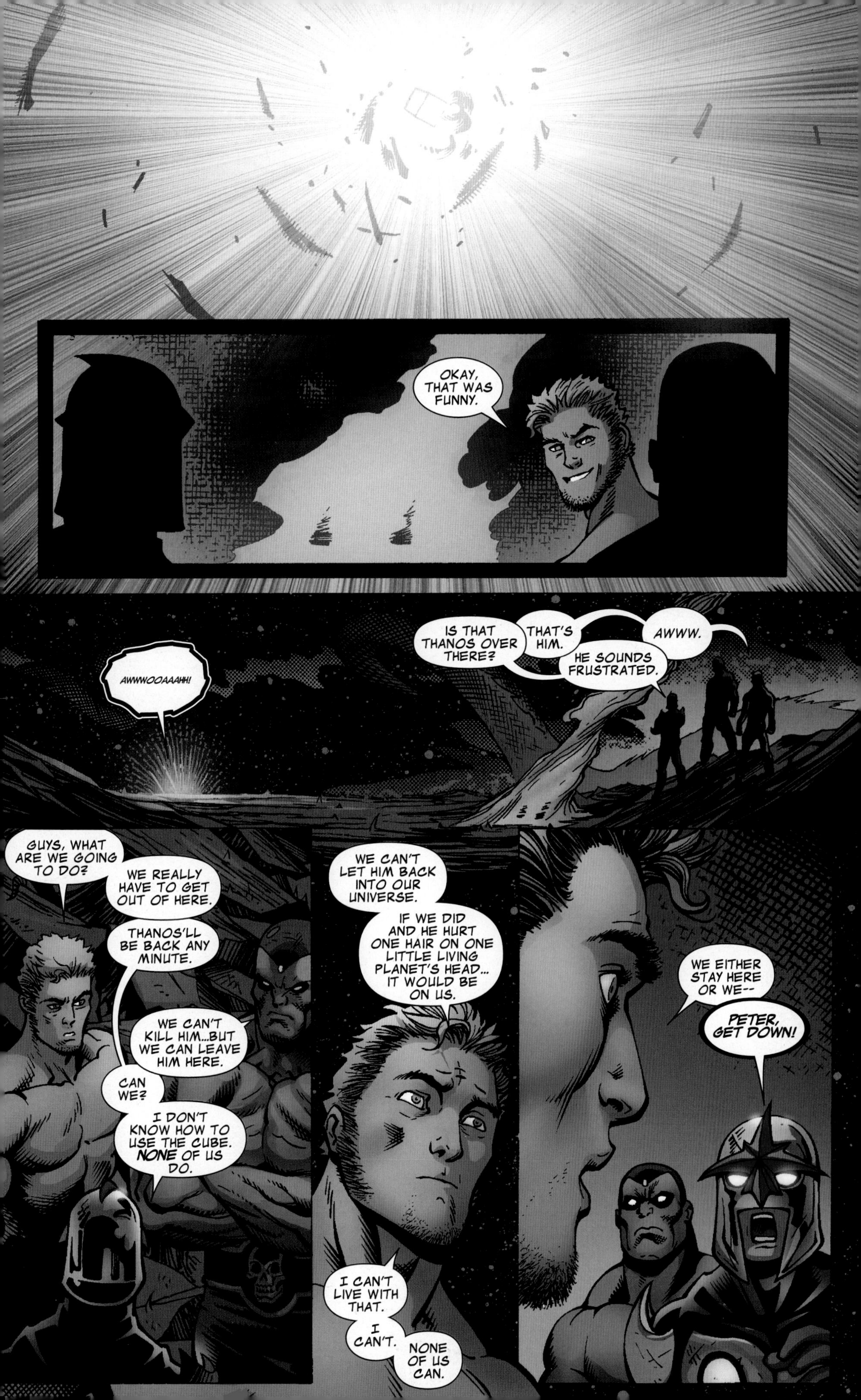
OKAY, THAT WAS FUNNY.
AWWWOOAAAHH!
IS THAT THANOS OVER THERE?
THAT'S HIM.
AWWW.
HE SOUNDS FRUSTRATED.
GUYS, WHAT ARE WE GOING TO DO?
WE REALLY HAVE TO GET OUT OF HERE.
THANOS'LL BE BACK ANY MINUTE.
WE CAN'T KILL HIM...BUT WE CAN LEAVE HIM HERE.
CAN WE?
I DON'T KNOW HOW TO USE THE CUBE. NONE OF US DO.
WE CAN'T LET HIM BACK INTO OUR UNIVERSE.
IF WE DID AND HE HURT ONE HAIR ON ONE LITTLE LIVING PLANET'S HEAD... IT WOULD BE ON US.
I CAN'T LIVE WITH THAT.
I CAN'T.
NONE OF US CAN.
WE EITHER STAY HERE OR WE--
PETER, GET DOWN!

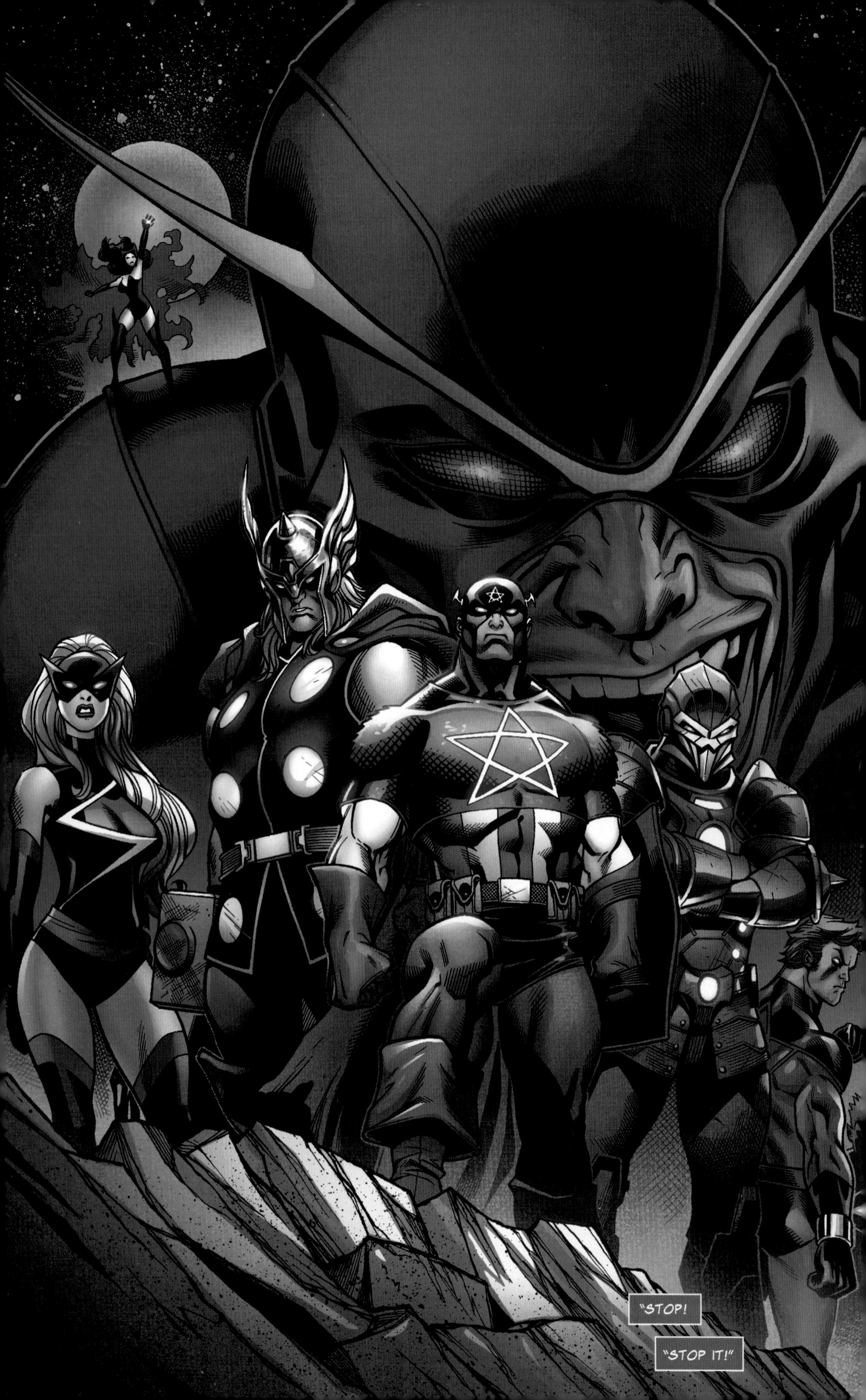
"STOP!
"STOP IT!"

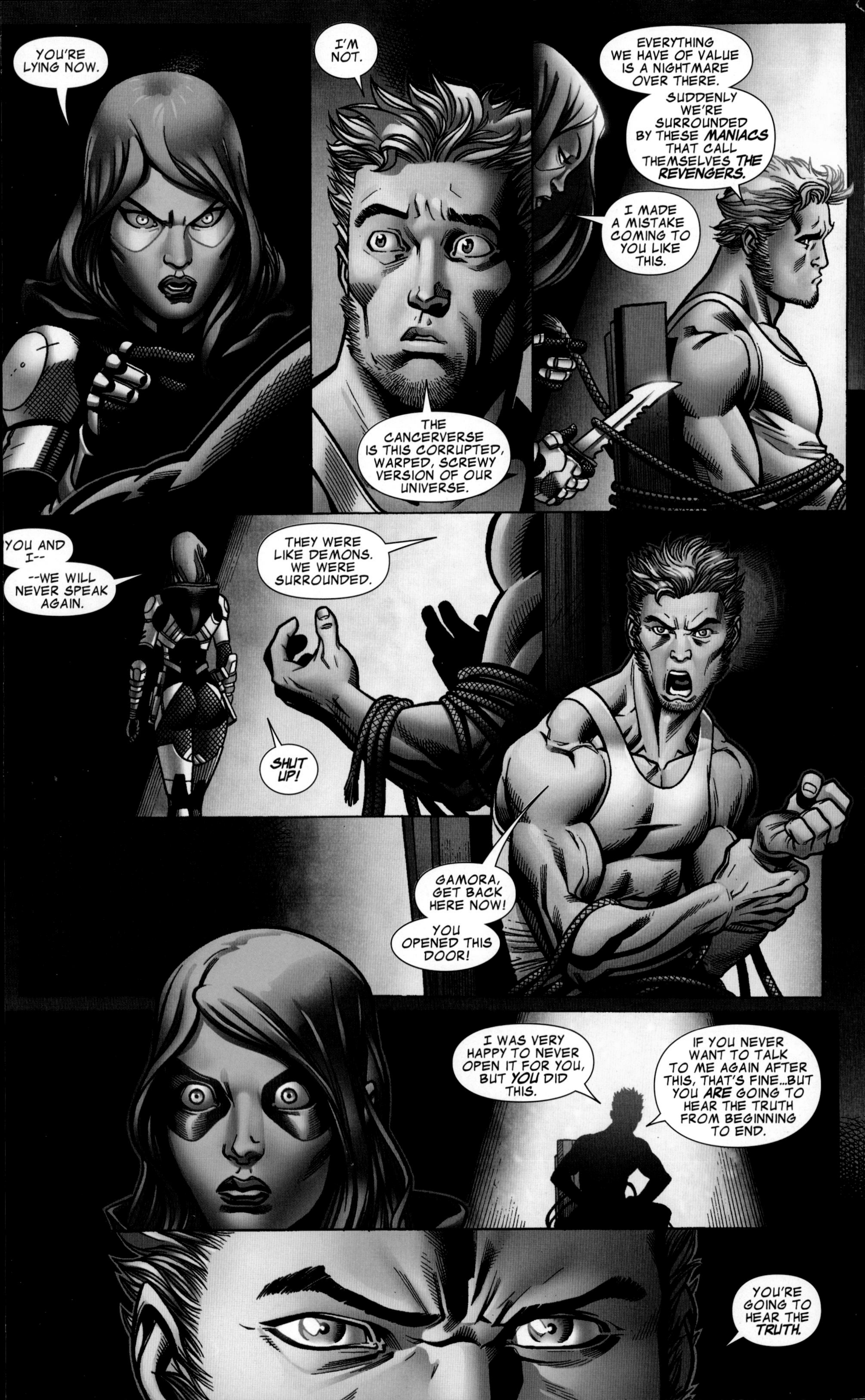
YOU'RE LYING NOW.
I'M NOT.
THE CANCERVERSE IS THIS CORRUPTED, WARPED, SCREWY VERSION OF OUR UNIVERSE.
EVERYTHING WE HAVE OF VALUE IS A NIGHTMARE OVER THERE.
SUDDENLY WE'RE SURROUNDED BY THESE MANIACS THAT CALL THEMSELVES THE REVENGERS.
I MADE A MISTAKE COMING TO YOU LIKE THIS.
THEY WERE LIKE DEMONS. WE WERE SURROUNDED.
YOU AND I--
--WE WILL NEVER SPEAK AGAIN.
SHUT UP!
GAMORA, GET BACK HERE NOW!
YOU OPENED THIS DOOR!
I WAS VERY HAPPY TO NEVER OPEN IT FOR YOU, BUT YOU DID THIS.
IF YOU NEVER WANT TO TALK TO ME AGAIN AFTER THIS, THAT'S FINE...BUT YOU ARE GOING TO HEAR THE TRUTH FROM BEGINNING TO END.
YOU'RE GOING TO HEAR THE TRUTH.

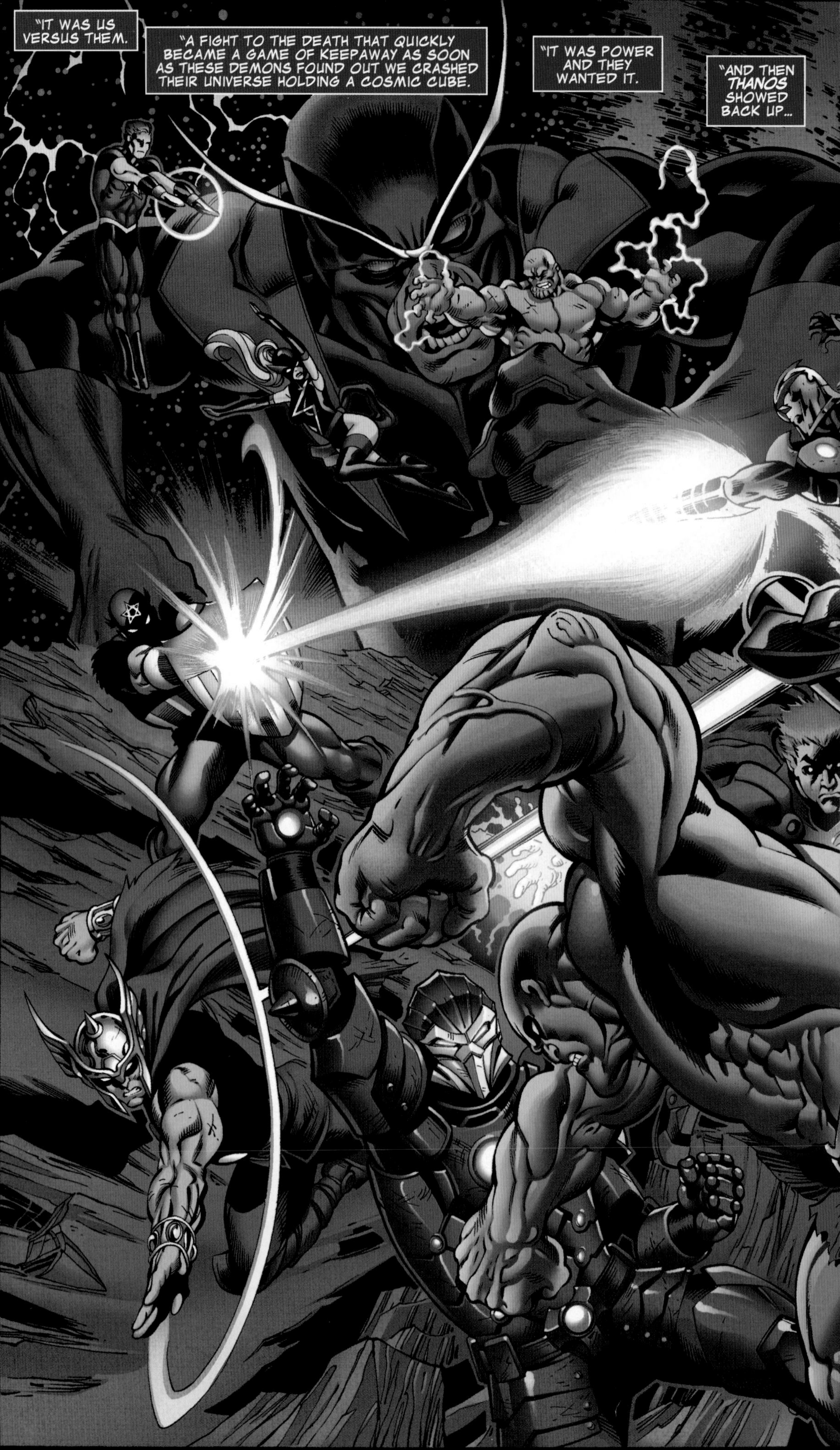
"IT WAS US VERSUS THEM.
"A FIGHT TO THE DEATH THAT QUICKLY BECAME A GAME OF KEEPAWAY AS SOON AS THESE DEMONS FOUND OUT WE CRASHED THEIR UNIVERSE HOLDING A COSMIC CUBE.
"IT WAS POWER AND THEY WANTED IT.
"AND THEN *THANOS* SHOWED BACK UP...

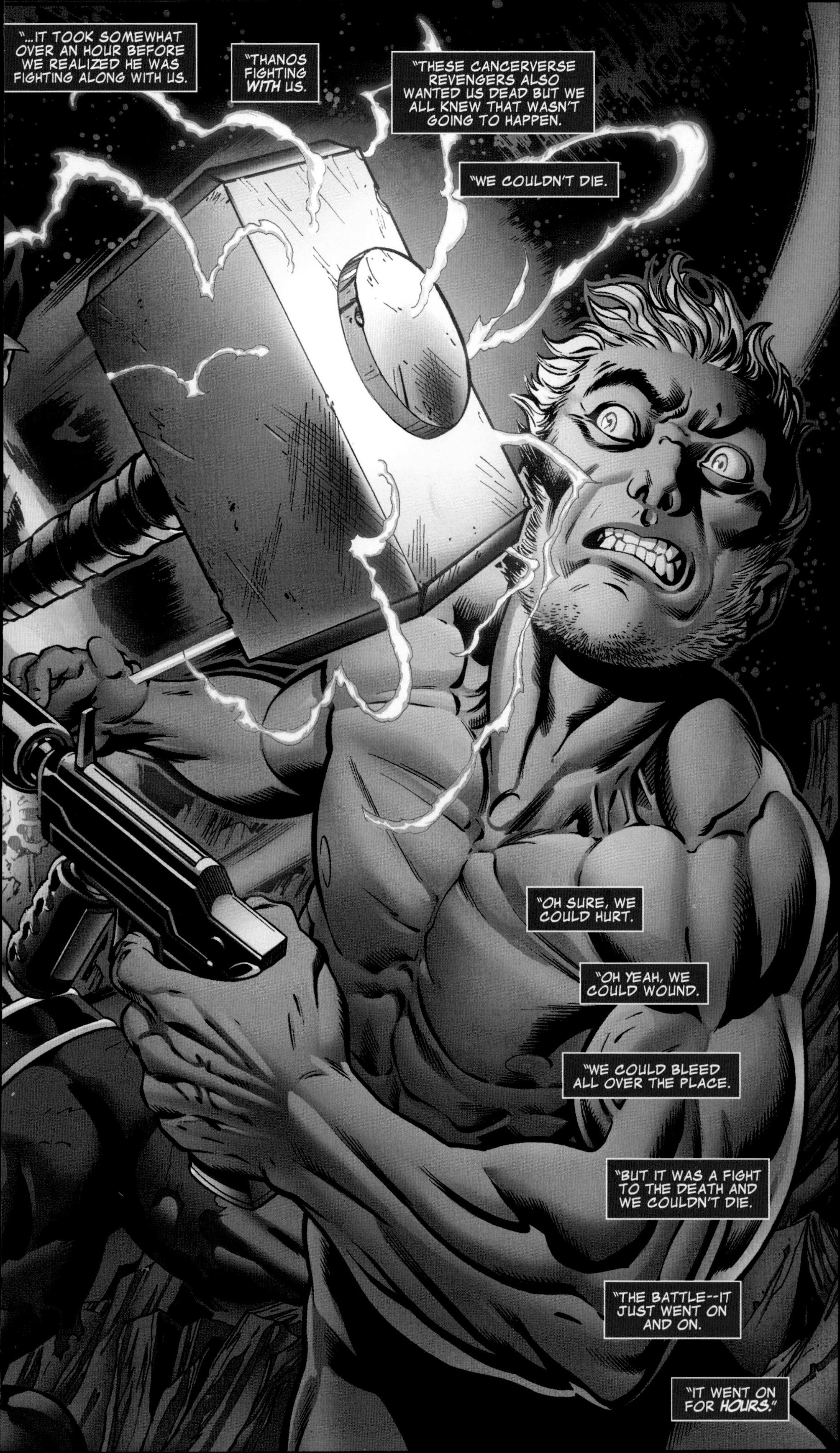
"...IT TOOK SOMEWHAT OVER AN HOUR BEFORE WE REALIZED HE WAS FIGHTING ALONG WITH US.
"THANOS FIGHTING WITH US.
"THESE CANCERVERSE REVENGERS ALSO WANTED US DEAD BUT WE ALL KNEW THAT WASN'T GOING TO HAPPEN.
"WE COULDN'T DIE.
"OH SURE, WE COULD HURT.
"OH YEAH, WE COULD WOUND.
"WE COULD BLEED ALL OVER THE PLACE.
"BUT IT WAS A FIGHT TO THE DEATH AND WE COULDN'T DIE.
"THE BATTLE--IT JUST WENT ON AND ON.
"IT WENT ON FOR HOURS."

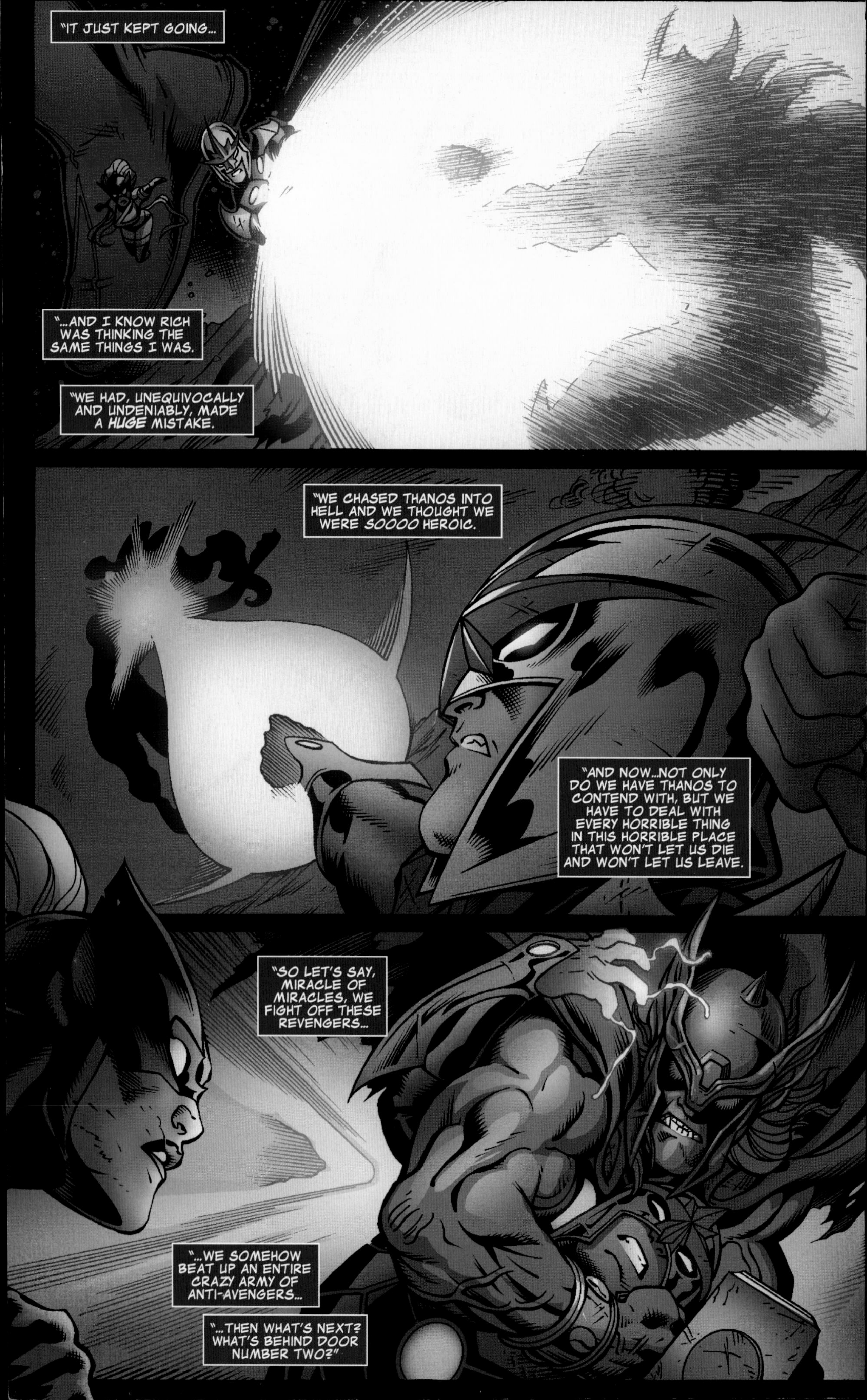
"IT JUST KEPT GOING...
"...AND I KNOW RICH WAS THINKING THE SAME THINGS I WAS.
"WE HAD, UNEQUIVOCALLY AND UNDENIABLY, MADE A *HUGE* MISTAKE.
"WE CHASED THANOS INTO HELL AND WE THOUGHT WE WERE *SOOOO* HEROIC.
"AND NOW...NOT ONLY DO WE HAVE THANOS TO CONTEND WITH, BUT WE HAVE TO DEAL WITH EVERY HORRIBLE THING IN THIS HORRIBLE PLACE THAT WON'T LET US DIE AND WON'T LET US LEAVE.
"SO LET'S SAY, MIRACLE OF MIRACLES, WE FIGHT OFF THESE REVENGERS...
"...WE SOMEHOW BEAT UP AN ENTIRE CRAZY ARMY OF ANTI-AVENGERS...
"...THEN WHAT'S NEXT? WHAT'S BEHIND DOOR NUMBER TWO?"

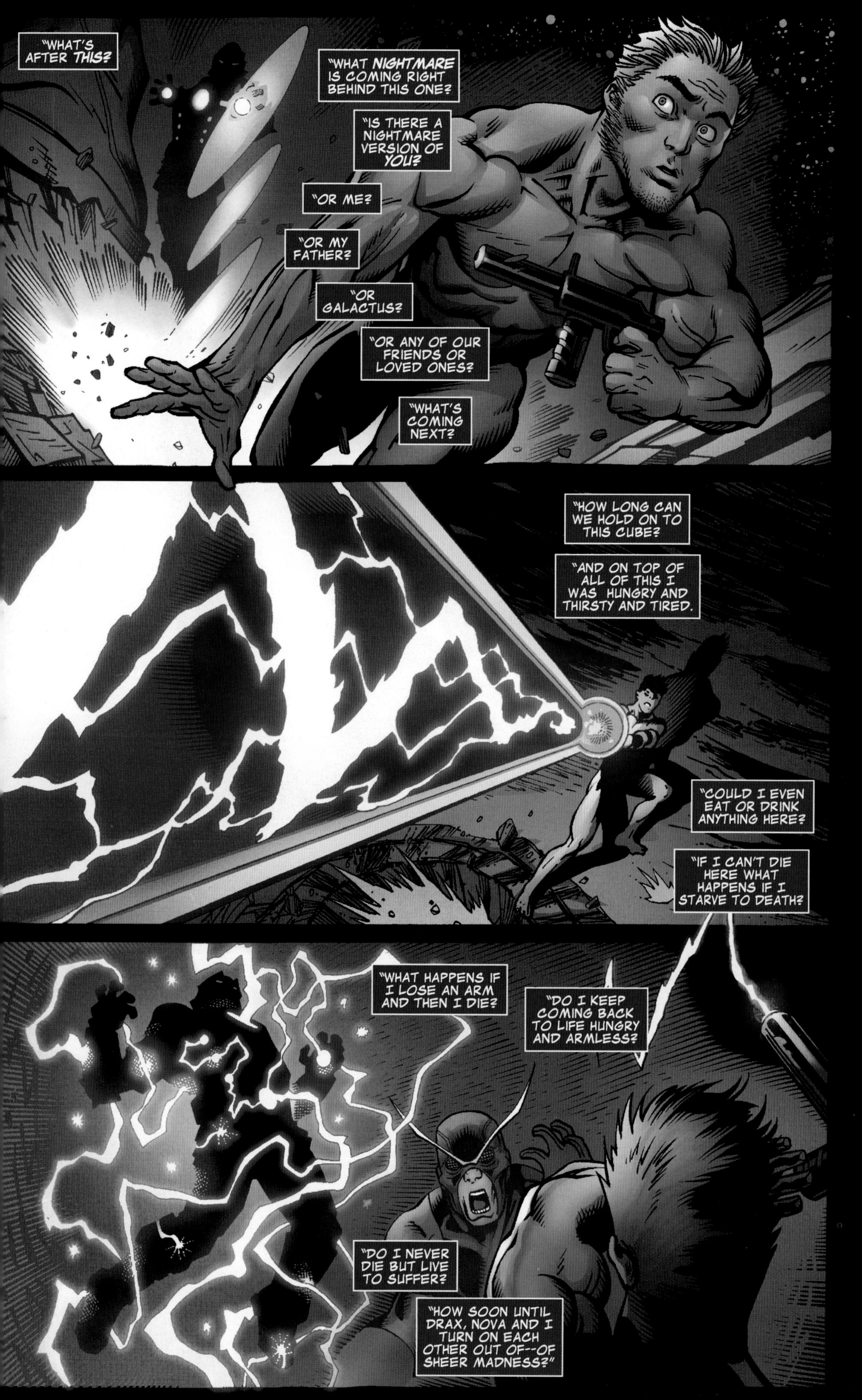
"WHAT'S AFTER THIS?
"WHAT NIGHTMARE IS COMING RIGHT BEHIND THIS ONE?
"IS THERE A NIGHTMARE VERSION OF YOU?
"OR ME?
"OR MY FATHER?
"OR GALACTUS?
"OR ANY OF OUR FRIENDS OR LOVED ONES?
"WHAT'S COMING NEXT?
"HOW LONG CAN WE HOLD ON TO THIS CUBE?
"AND ON TOP OF ALL OF THIS I WAS HUNGRY AND THIRSTY AND TIRED.
"COULD I EVEN EAT OR DRINK ANYTHING HERE?
"IF I CAN'T DIE HERE WHAT HAPPENS IF I STARVE TO DEATH?
"WHAT HAPPENS IF I LOSE AN ARM AND THEN I DIE?
"DO I KEEP COMING BACK TO LIFE HUNGRY AND ARMLESS?
"DO I NEVER DIE BUT LIVE TO SUFFER?
"HOW SOON UNTIL DRAX, NOVA AND I TURN ON EACH OTHER OUT OF--OF SHEER MADNESS?"

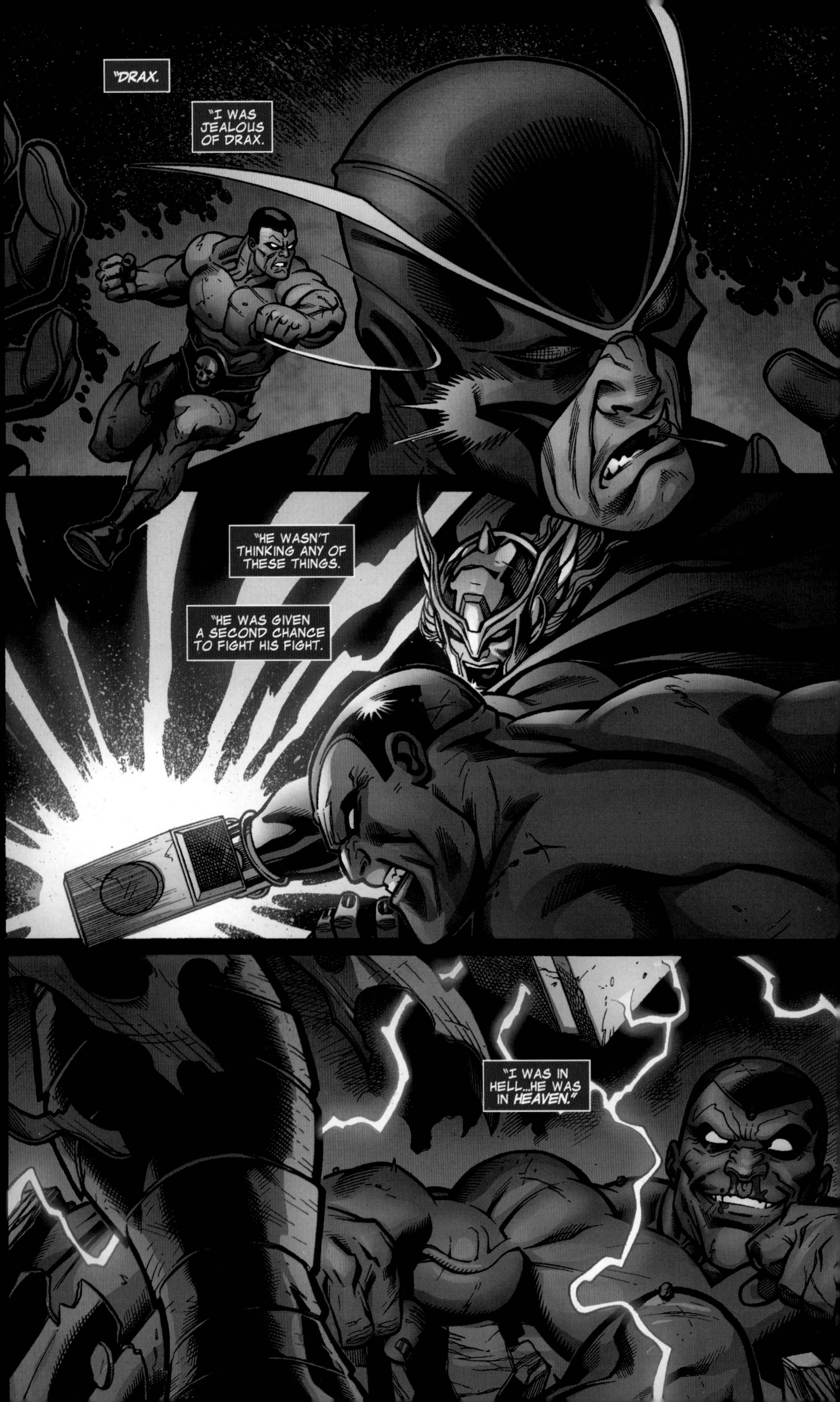
"DRAX.
"I WAS JEALOUS OF DRAX.
"HE WASN'T THINKING ANY OF THESE THINGS.
"HE WAS GIVEN A SECOND CHANCE TO FIGHT HIS FIGHT.
"I WAS IN HELL...HE WAS IN *HEAVEN*."

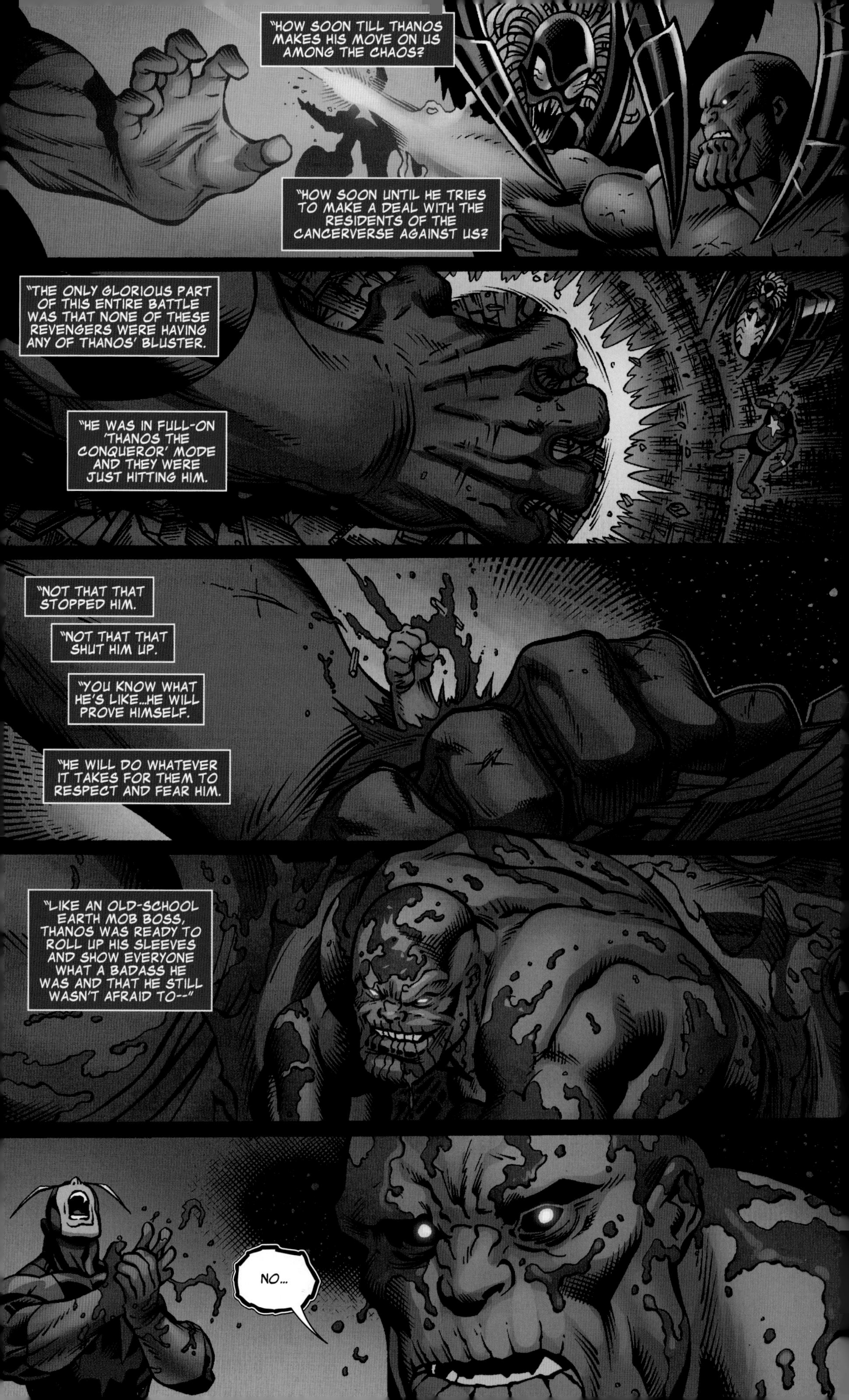
"HOW SOON TILL THANOS MAKES HIS MOVE ON US AMONG THE CHAOS?
"HOW SOON UNTIL HE TRIES TO MAKE A DEAL WITH THE RESIDENTS OF THE CANCERVERSE AGAINST US?
"THE ONLY GLORIOUS PART OF THIS ENTIRE BATTLE WAS THAT NONE OF THESE REVENGERS WERE HAVING ANY OF THANOS' BLUSTER.
"HE WAS IN FULL-ON 'THANOS THE CONQUEROR' MODE AND THEY WERE JUST HITTING HIM.
"NOT THAT THAT STOPPED HIM.
"NOT THAT THAT SHUT HIM UP.
"YOU KNOW WHAT HE'S LIKE...HE WILL PROVE HIMSELF.
"HE WILL DO WHATEVER IT TAKES FOR THEM TO RESPECT AND FEAR HIM.
"LIKE AN OLD-SCHOOL EARTH MOB BOSS, THANOS WAS READY TO ROLL UP HIS SLEEVES AND SHOW EVERYONE WHAT A BADASS HE WAS AND THAT HE STILL WASN'T AFRAID TO--"
NO...

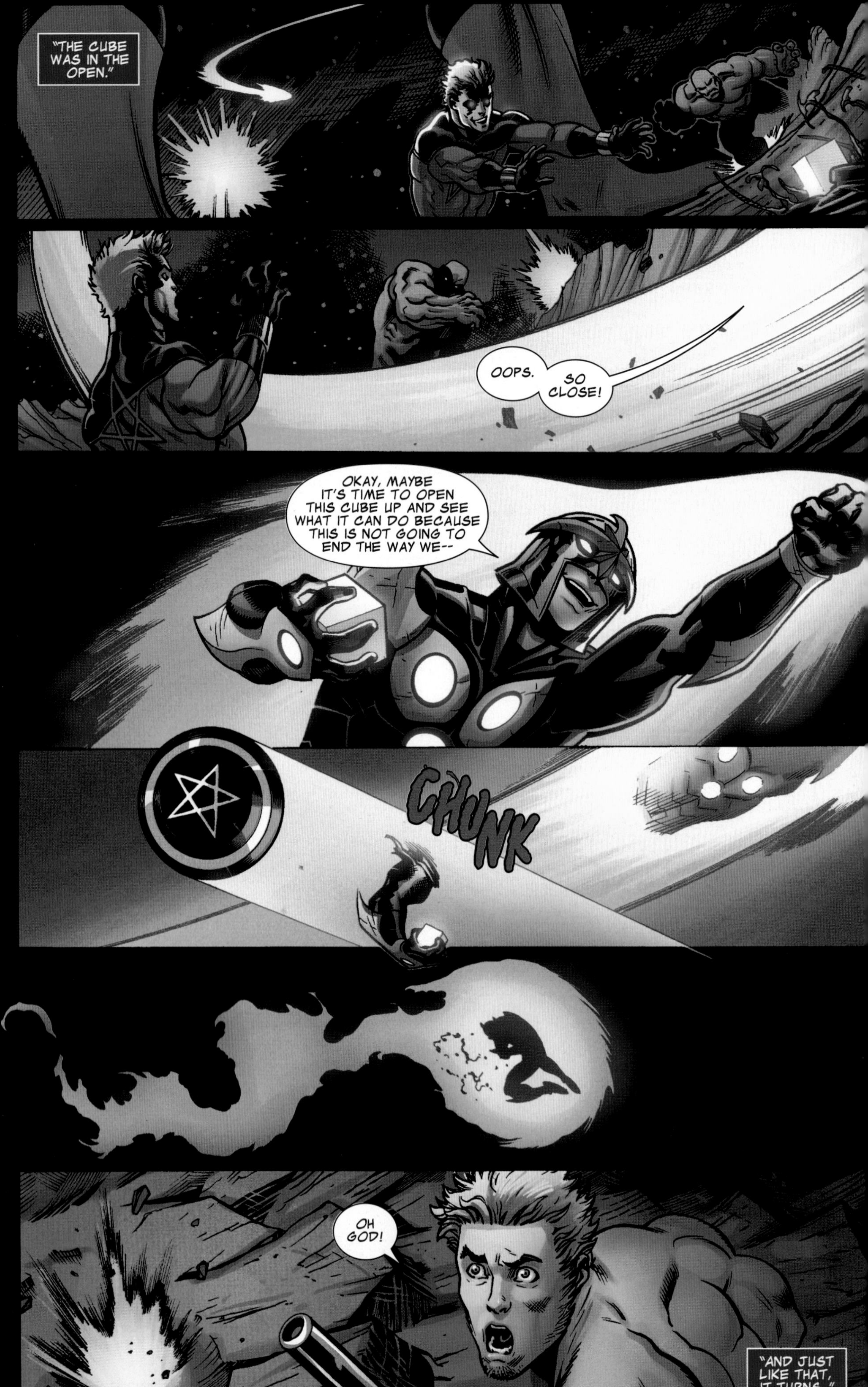

"THE CUBE WAS IN THE OPEN."
OOPS.
SO CLOSE!
OKAY, MAYBE IT'S TIME TO OPEN THIS CUBE UP AND SEE WHAT IT CAN DO BECAUSE THIS IS NOT GOING TO END THE WAY WE--
CHUNK
OH GOD!
"AND JUST LIKE THAT, IT TURNS..."

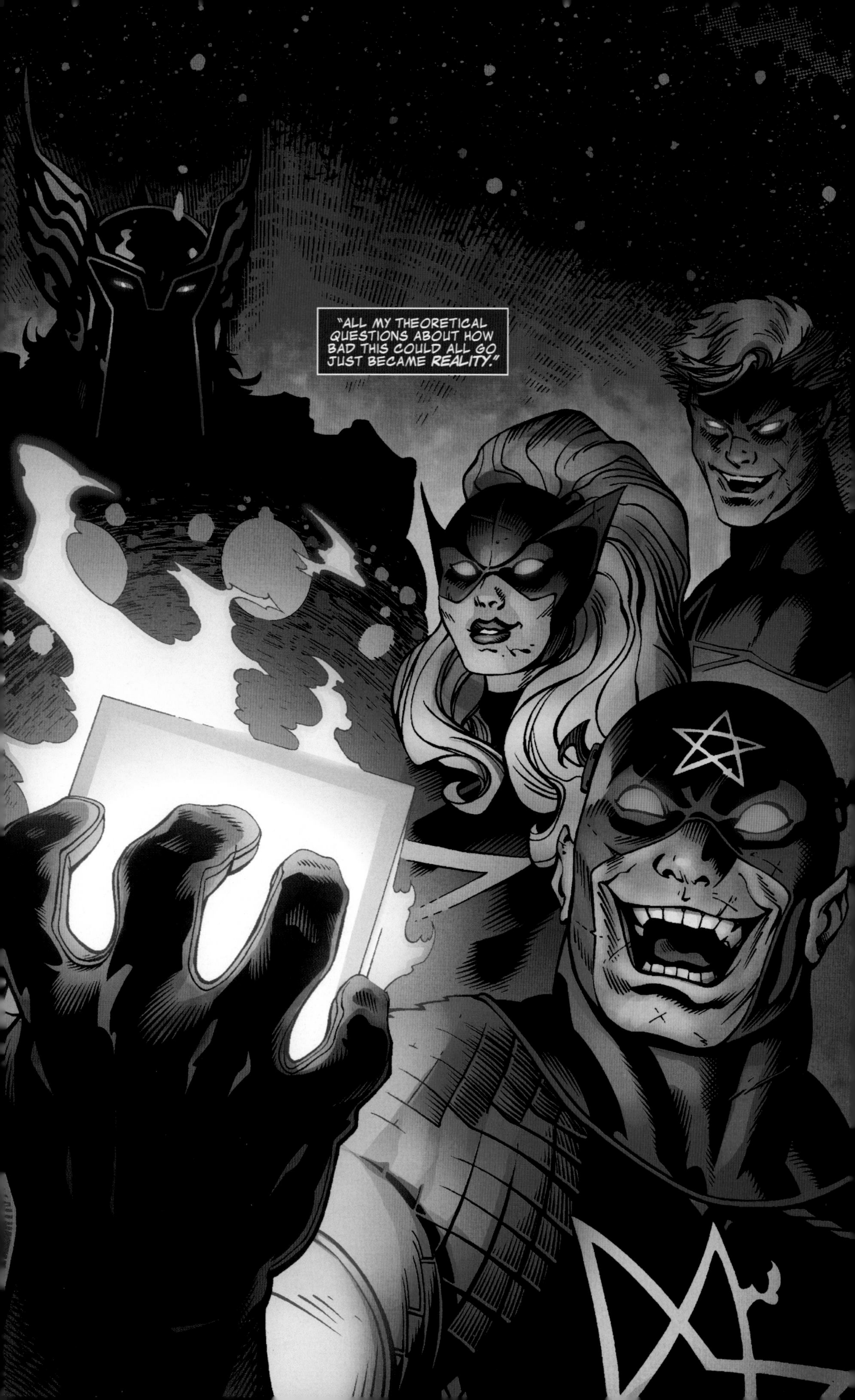
"ALL MY THEORETICAL QUESTIONS ABOUT HOW BAD THIS COULD ALL GO JUST BECAME *REALITY.*"

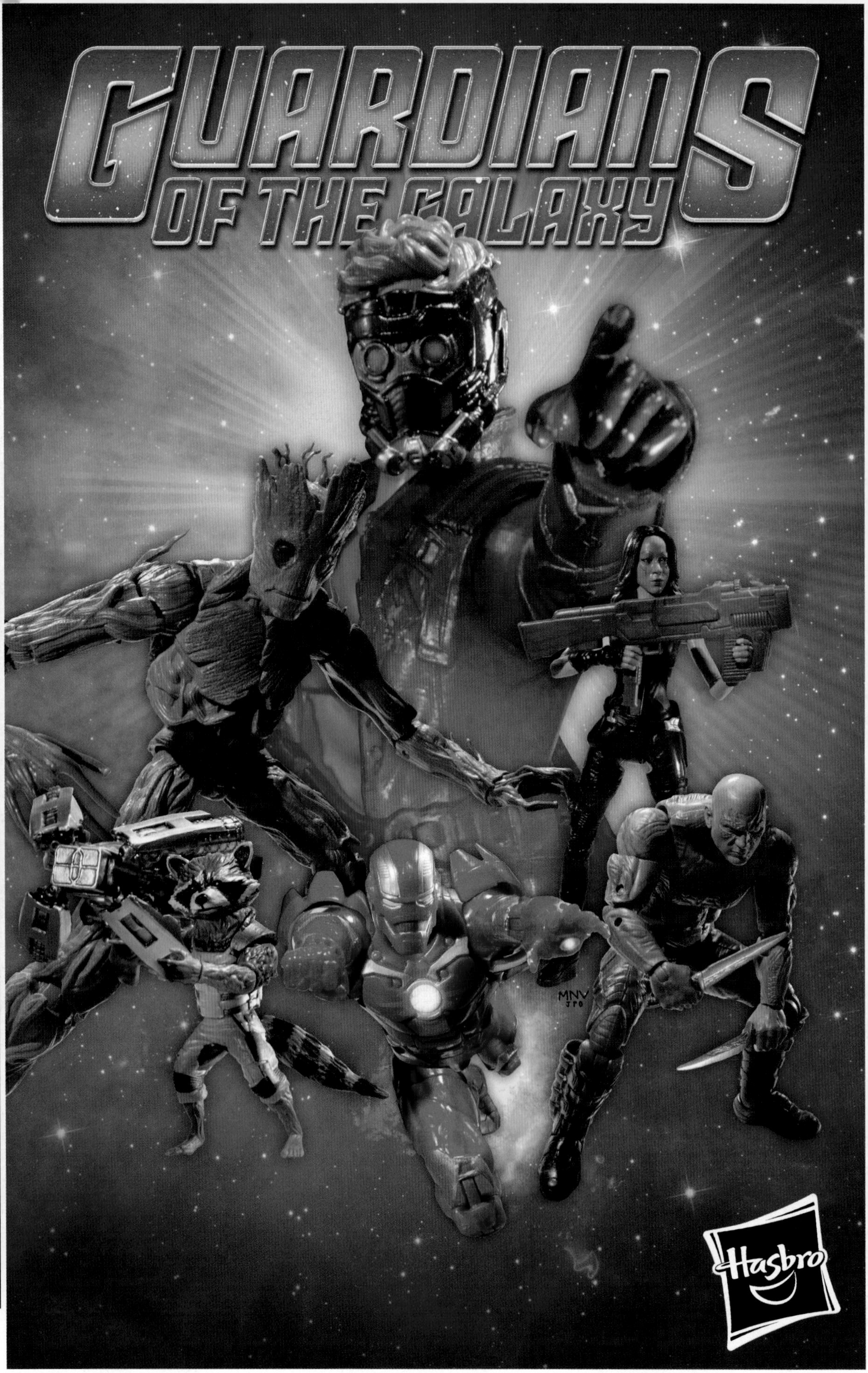
GUARDIANS
OF THE GALAXY
MNV
Hasbro

#20 HASBRO VARIANT

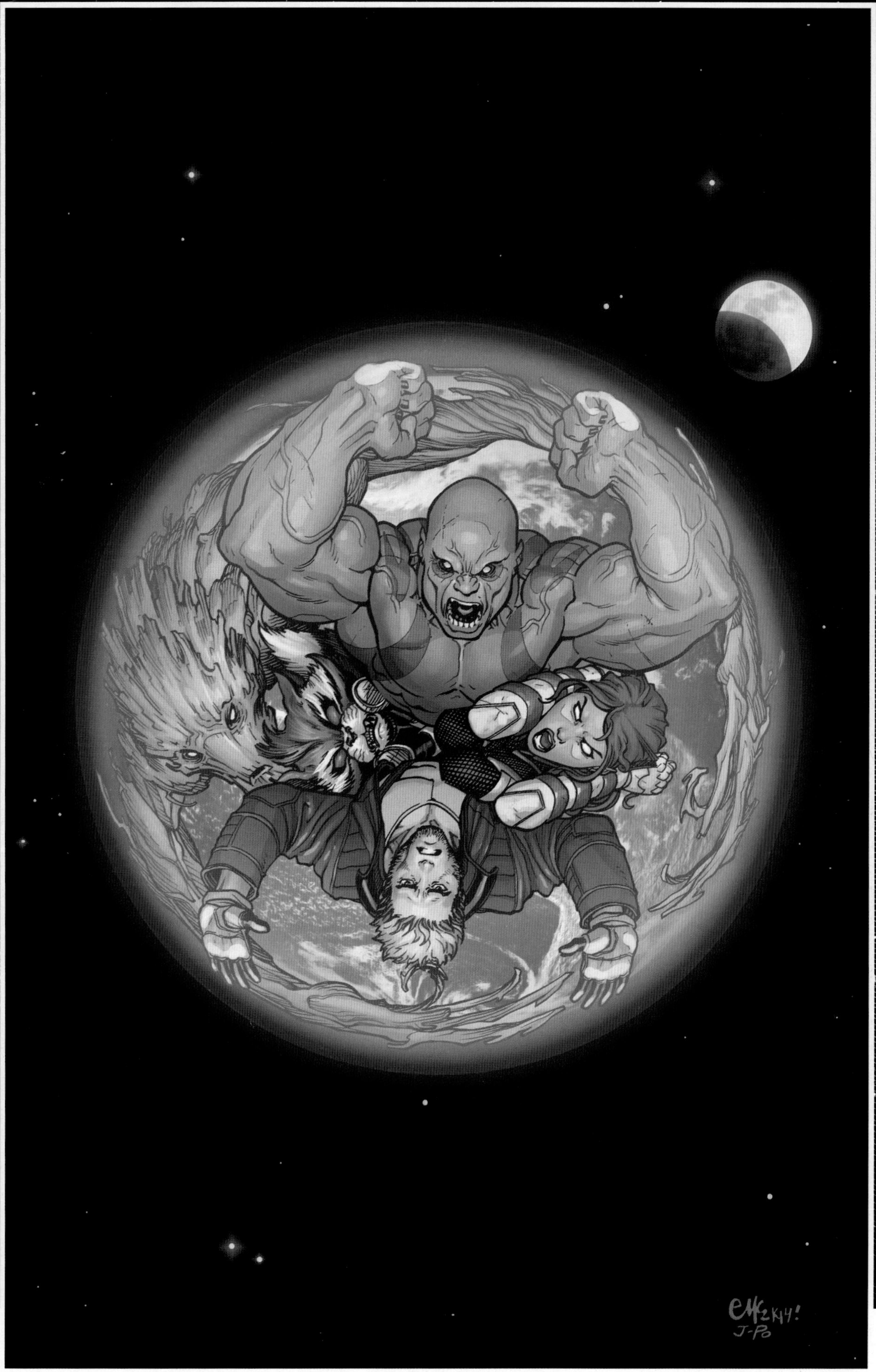

eMc 2K14!
J-Po

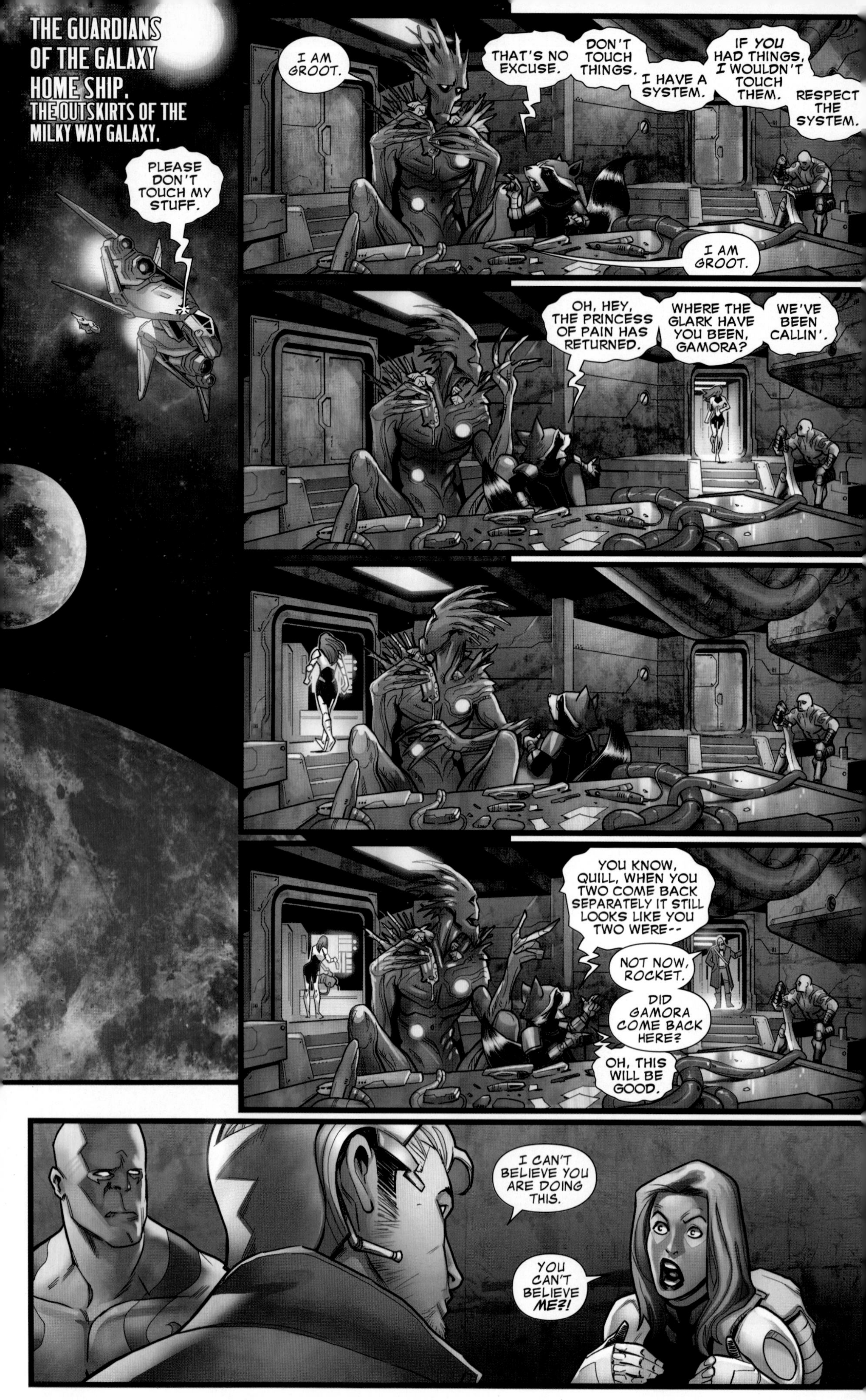
THE GUARDIANS OF THE GALAXY HOME SHIP.
THE OUTSKIRTS OF THE MILKY WAY GALAXY.
PLEASE DON'T TOUCH MY STUFF.
I AM GROOT.
THAT'S NO EXCUSE.
DON'T TOUCH THINGS.
I HAVE A SYSTEM.
IF YOU HAD THINGS, I WOULDN'T TOUCH THEM.
RESPECT THE SYSTEM.
I AM GROOT.
OH, HEY, THE PRINCESS OF PAIN HAS RETURNED.
WHERE THE GLARK HAVE YOU BEEN, GAMORA?
WE'VE BEEN CALLIN'.
YOU KNOW, QUILL, WHEN YOU TWO COME BACK SEPARATELY IT STILL LOOKS LIKE YOU TWO WERE--
NOT NOW, ROCKET.
DID GAMORA COME BACK HERE?
OH, THIS WILL BE GOOD.
I CAN'T BELIEVE YOU ARE DOING THIS.
YOU CAN'T BELIEVE *ME*?!

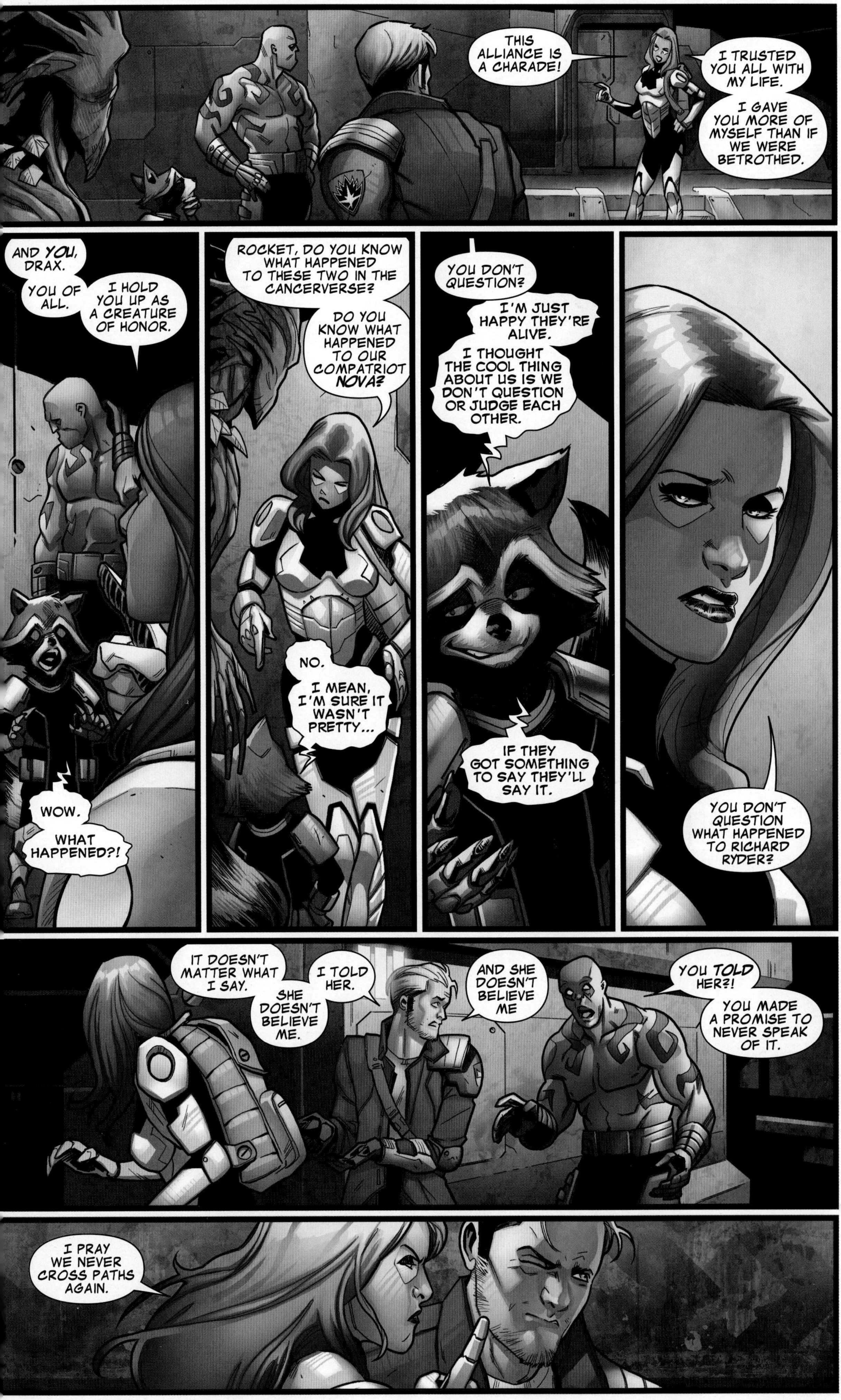

THIS ALLIANCE IS A CHARADE!
I TRUSTED YOU ALL WITH MY LIFE.
I GAVE YOU MORE OF MYSELF THAN IF WE WERE BETROTHED.
AND YOU, DRAX.
YOU OF ALL.
I HOLD YOU UP AS A CREATURE OF HONOR.
WOW.
WHAT HAPPENED?!
ROCKET, DO YOU KNOW WHAT HAPPENED TO THESE TWO IN THE CANCERVERSE?
DO YOU KNOW WHAT HAPPENED TO OUR COMPATRIOT NOVA?
NO.
I MEAN, I'M SURE IT WASN'T PRETTY...
YOU DON'T QUESTION?
I'M JUST HAPPY THEY'RE ALIVE.
I THOUGHT THE COOL THING ABOUT US IS WE DON'T QUESTION OR JUDGE EACH OTHER.
IF THEY GOT SOMETHING TO SAY THEY'LL SAY IT.
YOU DON'T QUESTION WHAT HAPPENED TO RICHARD RYDER?
IT DOESN'T MATTER WHAT I SAY.
SHE DOESN'T BELIEVE ME.
I TOLD HER.
AND SHE DOESN'T BELIEVE ME
YOU TOLD HER?!
YOU MADE A PROMISE TO NEVER SPEAK OF IT.
I PRAY WE NEVER CROSS PATHS AGAIN.

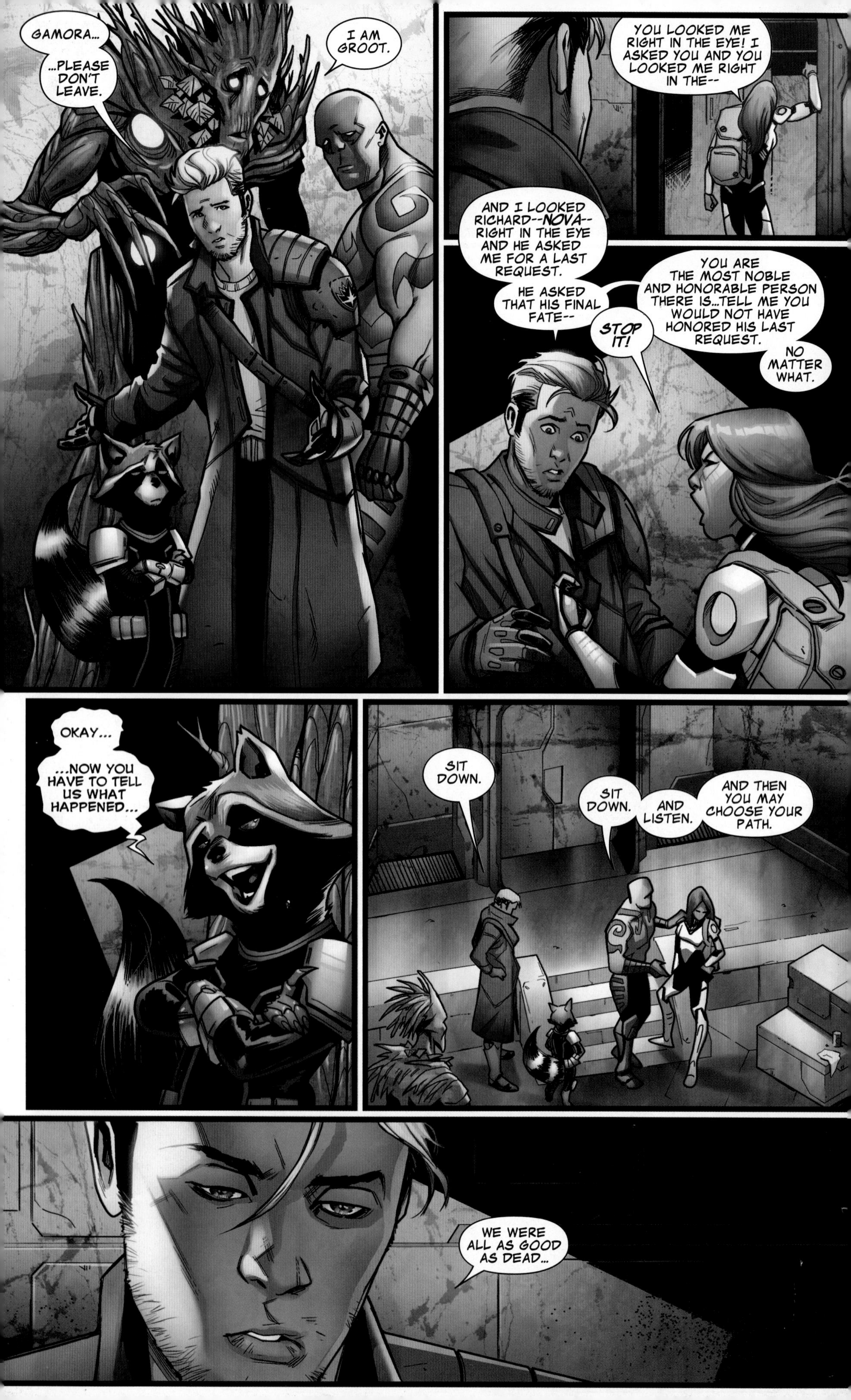
GAMORA...
...PLEASE DON'T LEAVE.
I AM GROOT.
YOU LOOKED ME RIGHT IN THE EYE! I ASKED YOU AND YOU LOOKED ME RIGHT IN THE--
AND I LOOKED RICHARD--NOVA--RIGHT IN THE EYE AND HE ASKED ME FOR A LAST REQUEST.
HE ASKED THAT HIS FINAL FATE--
STOP IT!
YOU ARE THE MOST NOBLE AND HONORABLE PERSON THERE IS...TELL ME YOU WOULD NOT HAVE HONORED HIS LAST REQUEST.
NO MATTER WHAT.
OKAY...
...NOW YOU HAVE TO TELL US WHAT HAPPENED...
SIT DOWN.
SIT DOWN.
AND LISTEN.
AND THEN YOU MAY CHOOSE YOUR PATH.
WE WERE ALL AS GOOD AS DEAD...

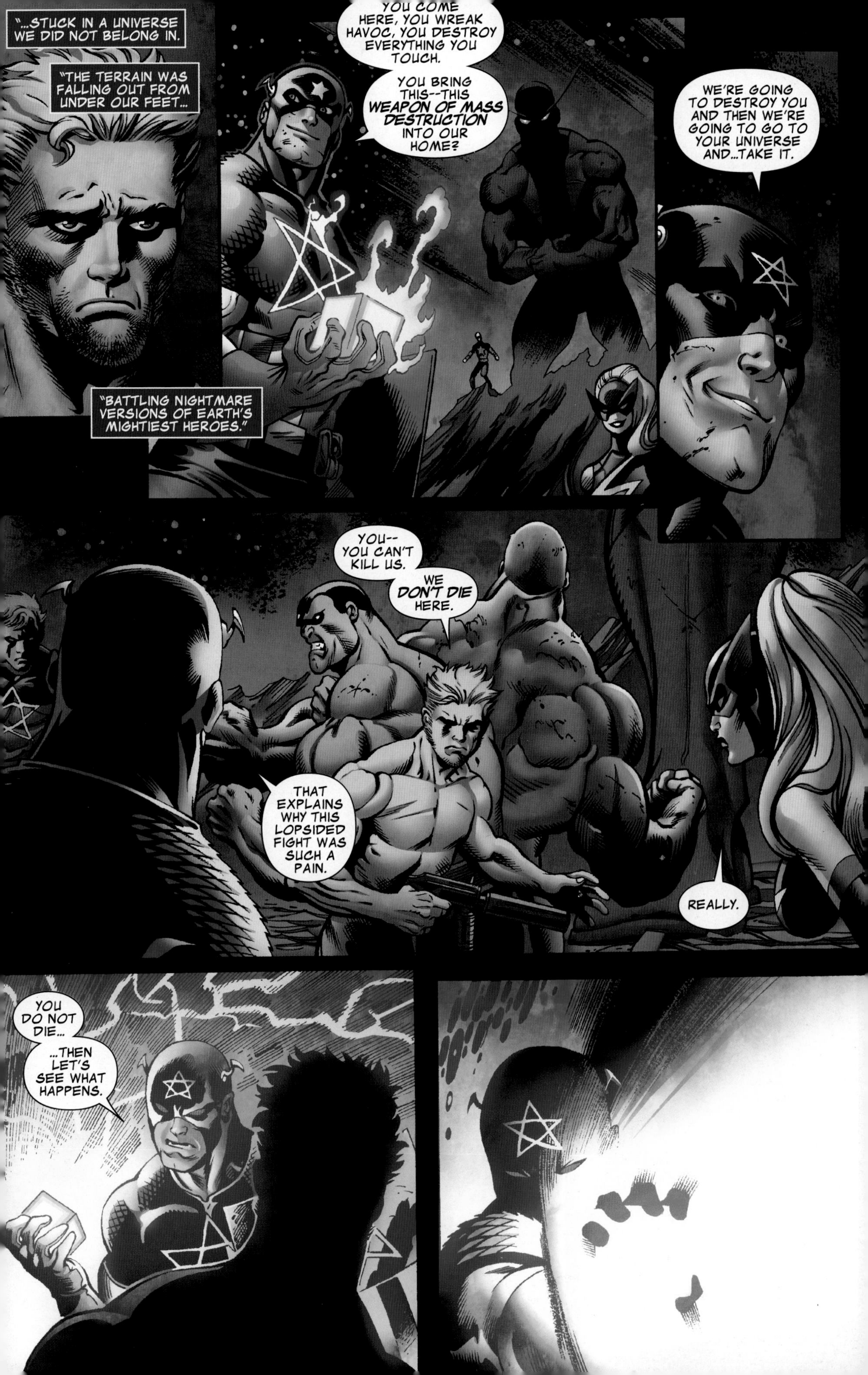
"...STUCK IN A UNIVERSE WE DID NOT BELONG IN.
"THE TERRAIN WAS FALLING OUT FROM UNDER OUR FEET...
YOU COME HERE, YOU WREAK HAVOC, YOU DESTROY EVERYTHING YOU TOUCH.
YOU BRING THIS--THIS WEAPON OF MASS DESTRUCTION INTO OUR HOME?
WE'RE GOING TO DESTROY YOU AND THEN WE'RE GOING TO GO TO YOUR UNIVERSE AND...TAKE IT.
"BATTLING NIGHTMARE VERSIONS OF EARTH'S MIGHTIEST HEROES."
YOU--YOU CAN'T KILL US.
WE DON'T DIE HERE.
THAT EXPLAINS WHY THIS LOPSIDED FIGHT WAS SUCH A PAIN.
REALLY.
YOU DO NOT DIE...
...THEN LET'S SEE WHAT HAPPENS.

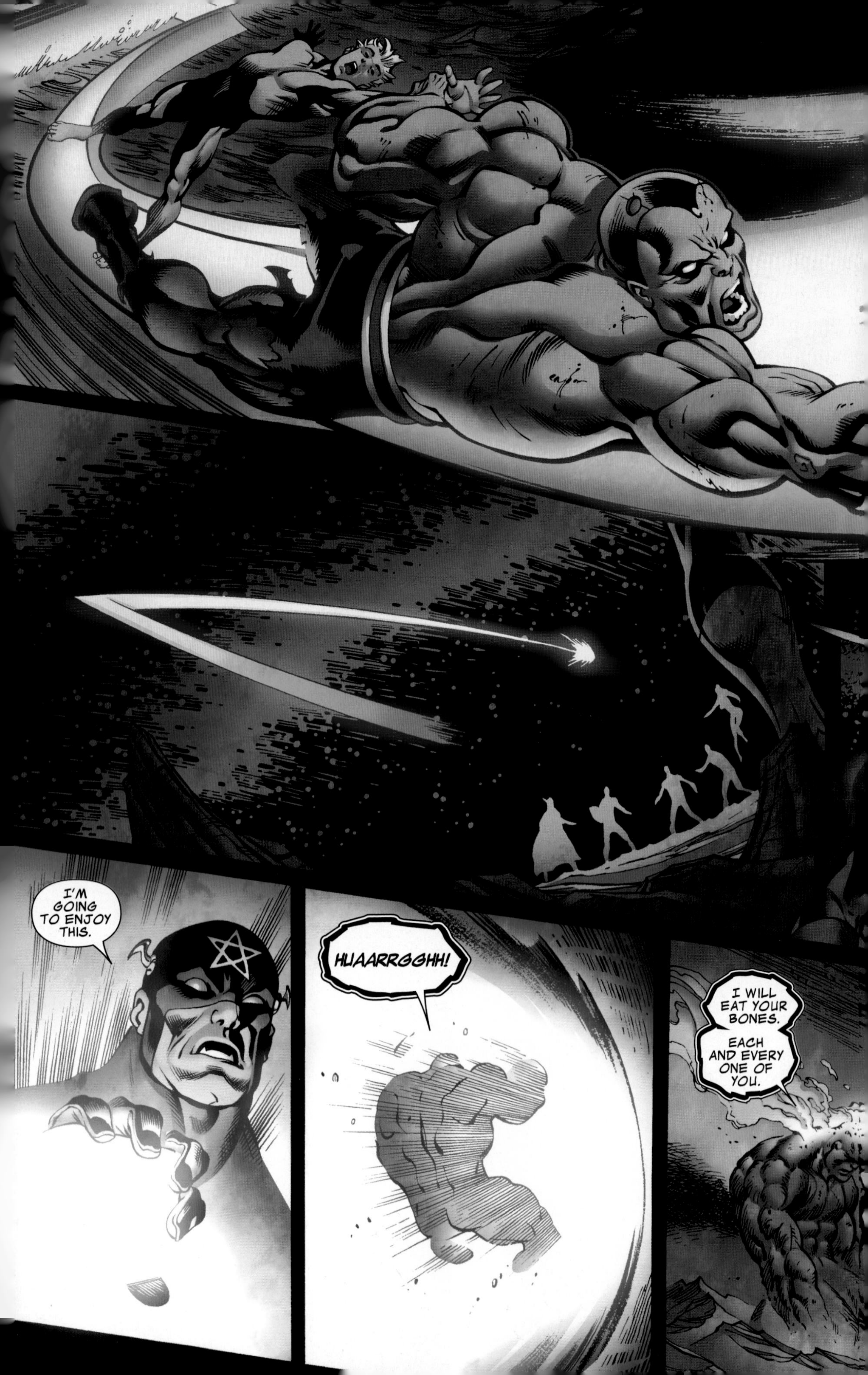
I'M GOING TO ENJOY THIS.
HUAARRGGHH!
I WILL EAT YOUR BONES.
EACH AND EVERY ONE OF YOU.

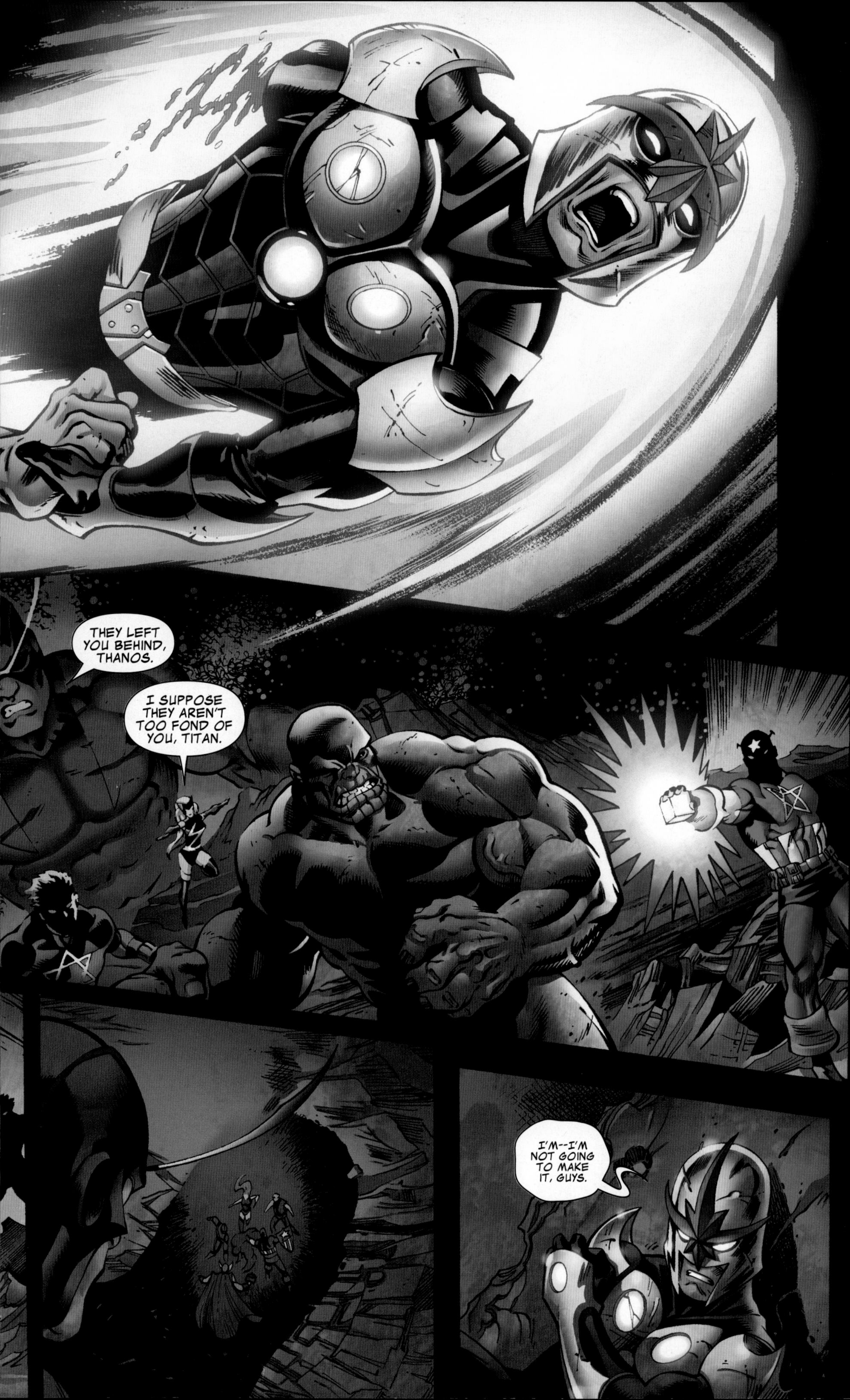
THEY LEFT YOU BEHIND, THANOS.
I SUPPOSE THEY AREN'T TOO FOND OF YOU, TITAN.
I'M--I'M NOT GOING TO MAKE IT, GUYS.

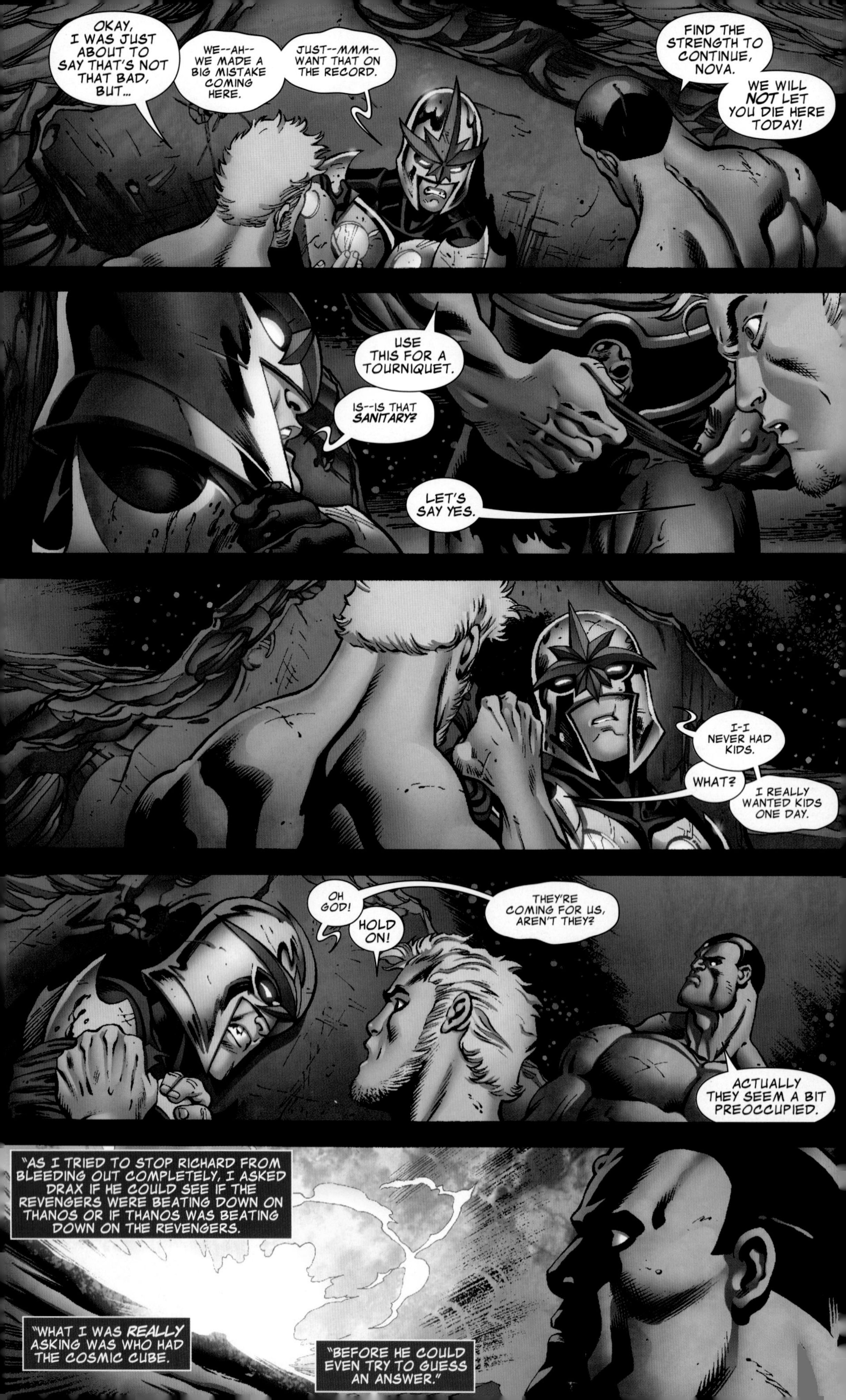
OKAY, I WAS JUST ABOUT TO SAY THAT'S NOT THAT BAD, BUT...
WE--AH-- WE MADE A BIG MISTAKE COMING HERE.
JUST--MMM-- WANT THAT ON THE RECORD.
FIND THE STRENGTH TO CONTINUE, NOVA.
WE WILL NOT LET YOU DIE HERE TODAY!
USE THIS FOR A TOURNIQUET.
IS--IS THAT SANITARY?
LET'S SAY YES.
I-I NEVER HAD KIDS.
WHAT?
I REALLY WANTED KIDS ONE DAY.
OH GOD!
HOLD ON!
THEY'RE COMING FOR US, AREN'T THEY?
ACTUALLY THEY SEEM A BIT PREOCCUPIED.
"AS I TRIED TO STOP RICHARD FROM BLEEDING OUT COMPLETELY, I ASKED DRAX IF HE COULD SEE IF THE REVENGERS WERE BEATING DOWN ON THANOS OR IF THANOS WAS BEATING DOWN ON THE REVENGERS.
"WHAT I WAS REALLY ASKING WAS WHO HAD THE COSMIC CUBE.
"BEFORE HE COULD EVEN TRY TO GUESS AN ANSWER."

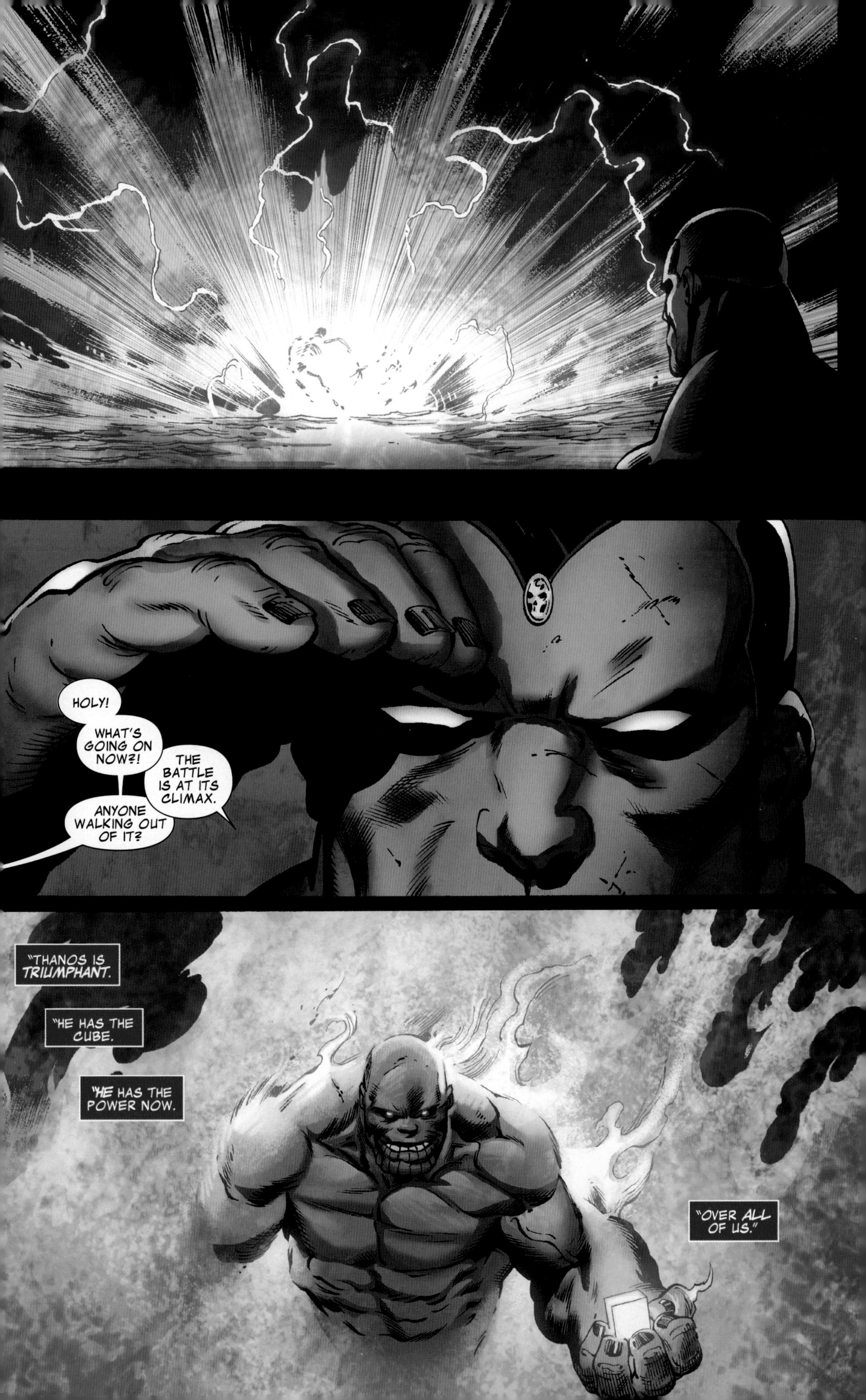
HOLY!
WHAT'S GOING ON NOW?!
ANYONE WALKING OUT OF IT?
THE BATTLE IS AT ITS CLIMAX.
"THANOS IS TRIUMPHANT.
"HE HAS THE CUBE.
"HE HAS THE POWER NOW.
"OVER ALL OF US."

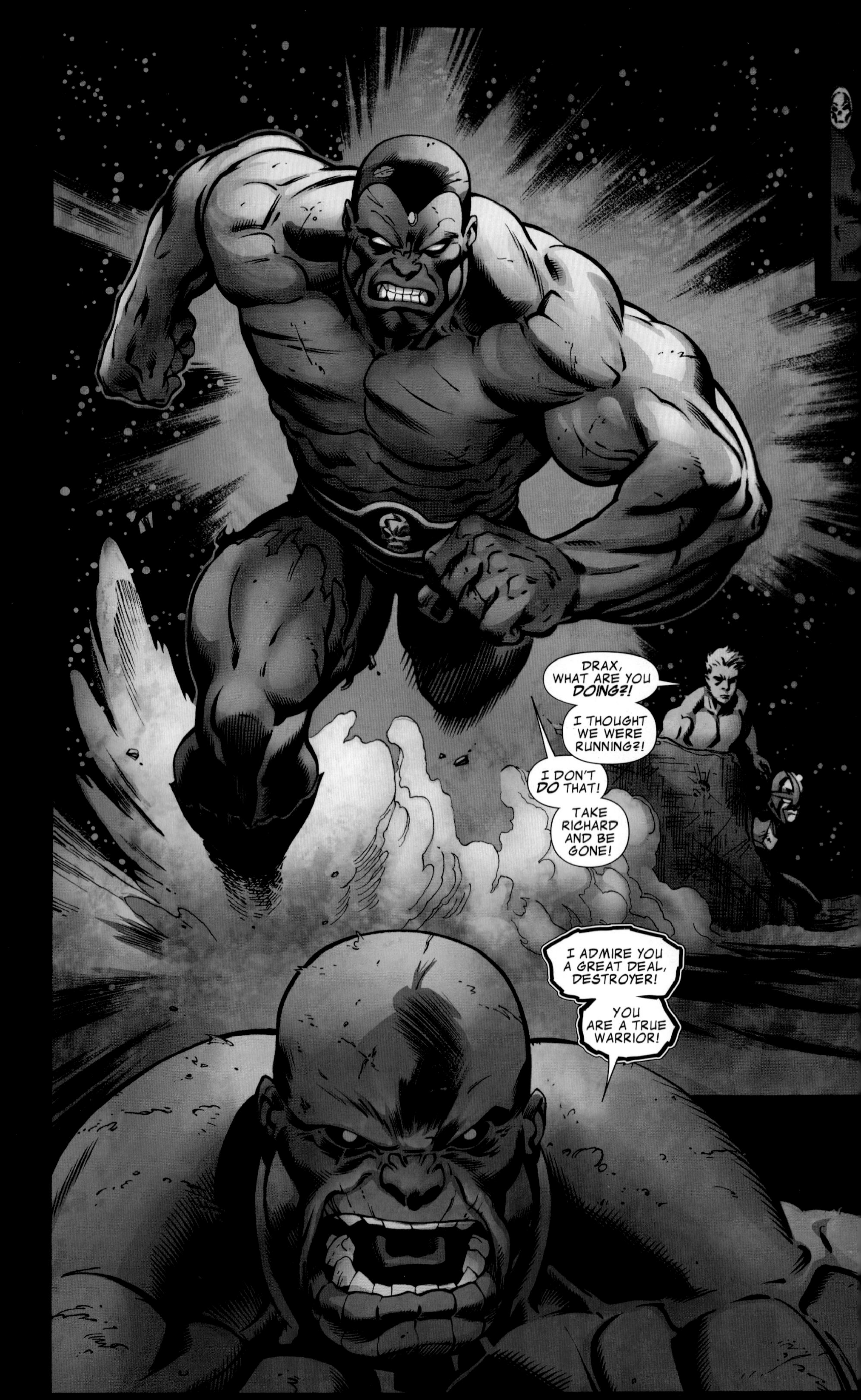
DRAX, WHAT ARE YOU DOING?!
I THOUGHT WE WERE RUNNING?!
I DON'T DO THAT!
TAKE RICHARD AND BE GONE!
I ADMIRE YOU A GREAT DEAL, DESTROYER!
YOU ARE A TRUE WARRIOR!

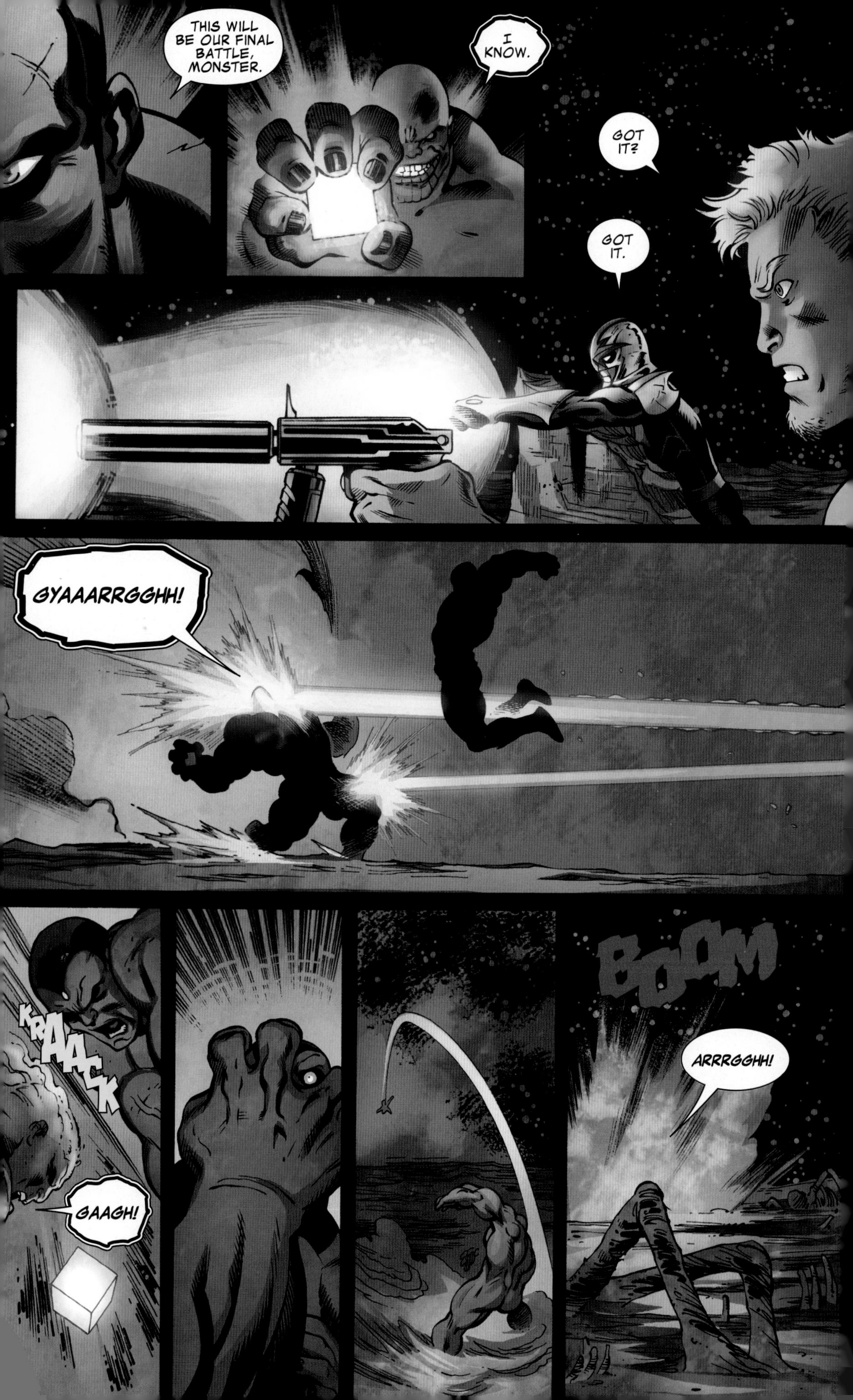
THIS WILL BE OUR FINAL BATTLE, MONSTER.
I KNOW.
GOT IT?
GOT IT.
GYAAARRGGHH!
KRAAACK
GAAGH!
BOOM
ARRRGGHH!

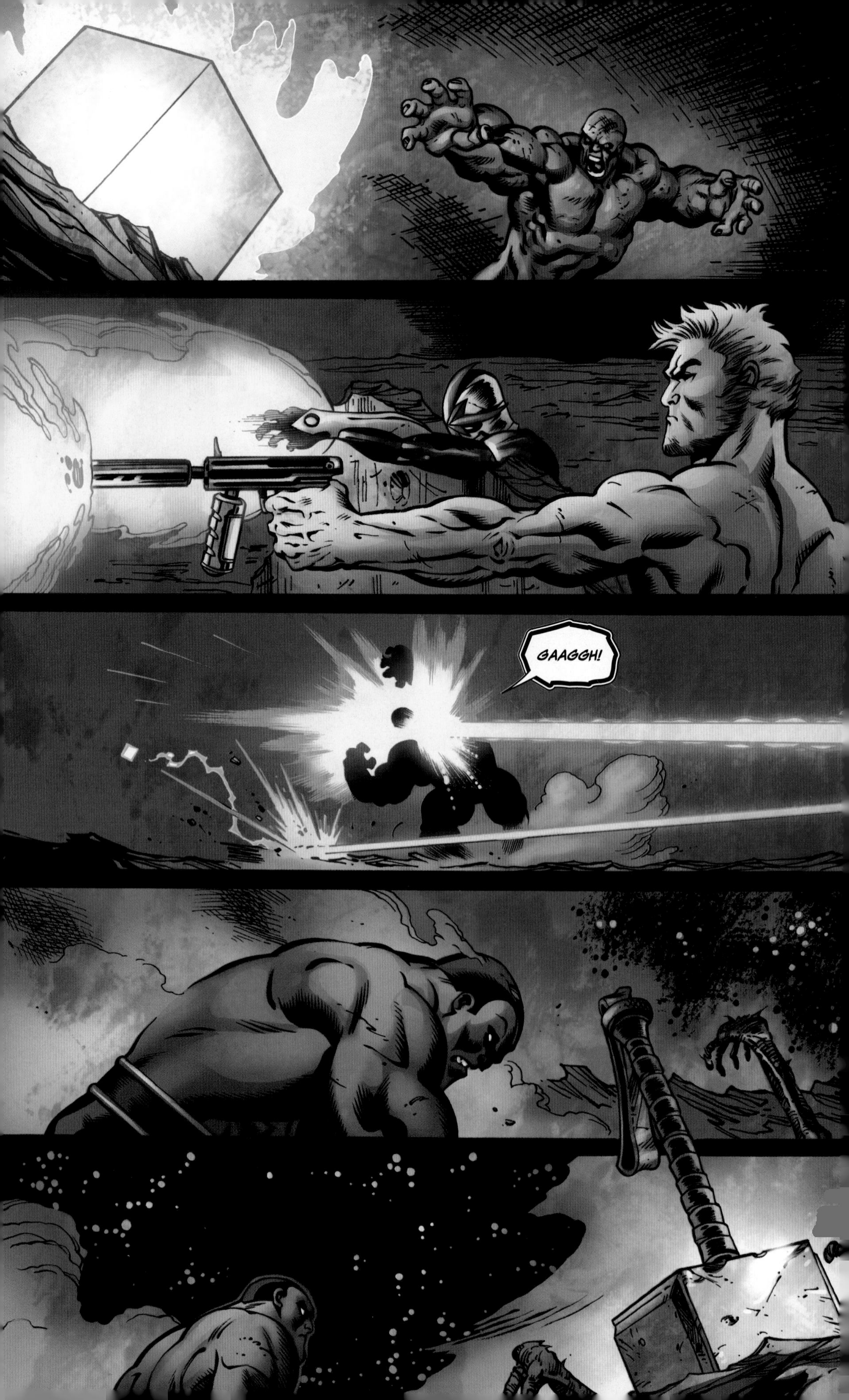
GAAGGH!

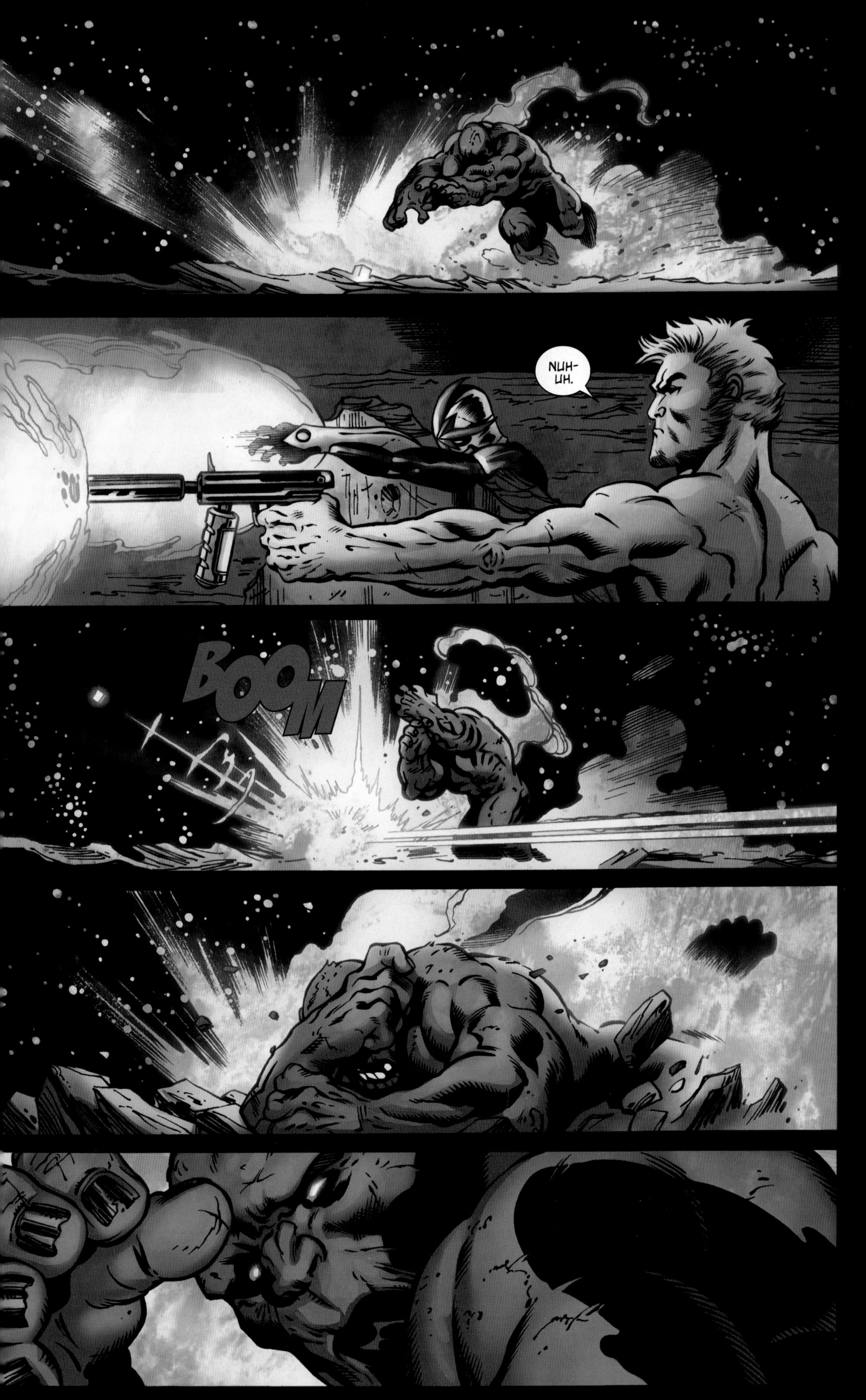
NUH-UH.
BOOM

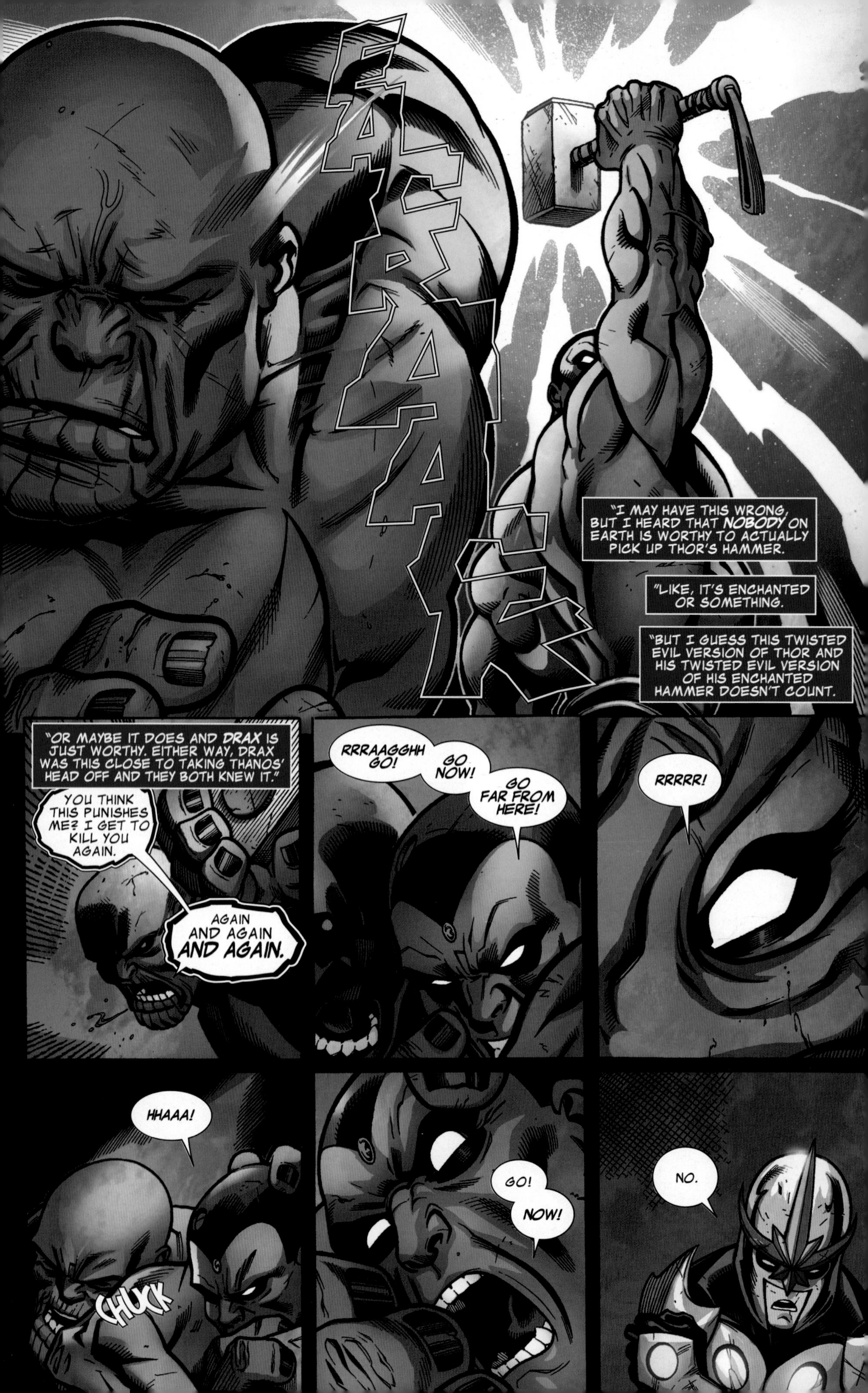
"I MAY HAVE THIS WRONG, BUT I HEARD THAT NOBODY ON EARTH IS WORTHY TO ACTUALLY PICK UP THOR'S HAMMER.
"LIKE, IT'S ENCHANTED OR SOMETHING.
"BUT I GUESS THIS TWISTED EVIL VERSION OF THOR AND HIS TWISTED EVIL VERSION OF HIS ENCHANTED HAMMER DOESN'T COUNT.
"OR MAYBE IT DOES AND DRAX IS JUST WORTHY. EITHER WAY, DRAX WAS THIS CLOSE TO TAKING THANOS' HEAD OFF AND THEY BOTH KNEW IT."
YOU THINK THIS PUNISHES ME? I GET TO KILL YOU AGAIN.
AGAIN AND AGAIN AND AGAIN.
RRRAAGGHH GO!
GO NOW!
GO FAR FROM HERE!
RRRRR!
HHAAA!
CHUCK
GO!
NOW!
NO.

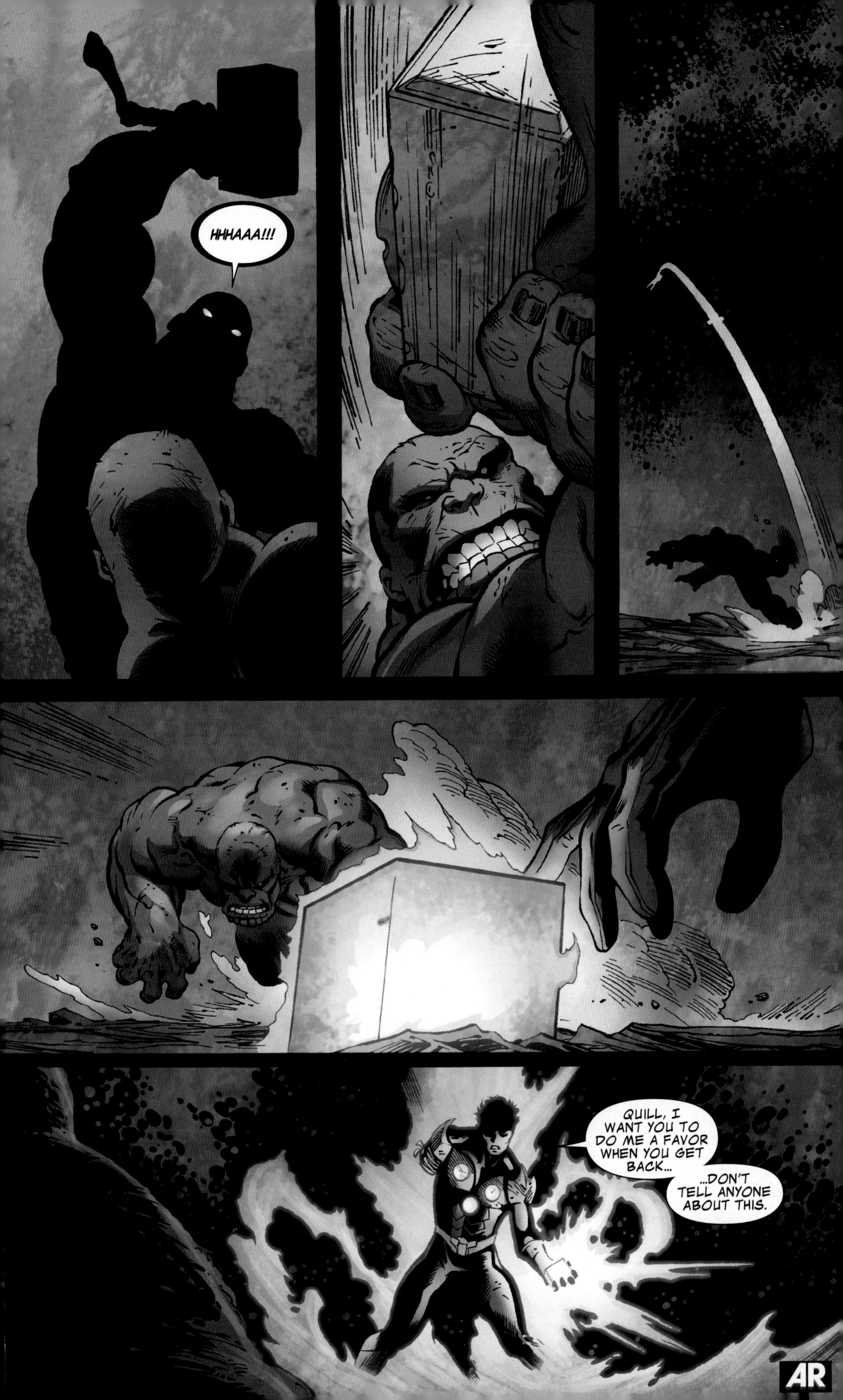
HHHAAA!!!
QUILL, I WANT YOU TO DO ME A FAVOR WHEN YOU GET BACK...
...DON'T TELL ANYONE ABOUT THIS.
AR

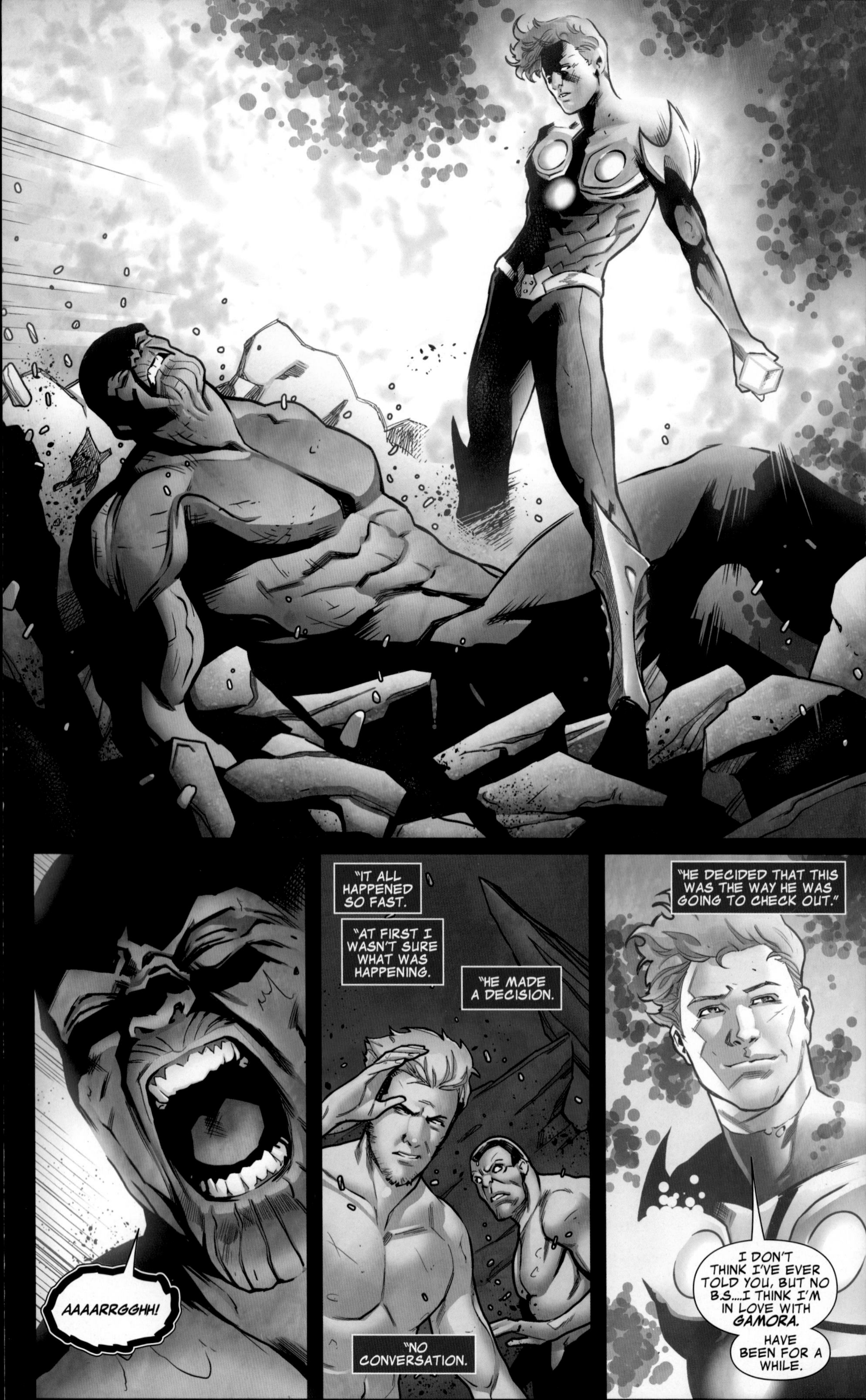
AAAARRGGHH!
"IT ALL HAPPENED SO FAST.
"AT FIRST I WASN'T SURE WHAT WAS HAPPENING.
"HE MADE A DECISION.
"NO CONVERSATION.
"HE DECIDED THAT THIS WAS THE WAY HE WAS GOING TO CHECK OUT."
I DON'T THINK I'VE EVER TOLD YOU, BUT NO B.S....I THINK I'M IN LOVE WITH GAMORA.
HAVE BEEN FOR A WHILE.

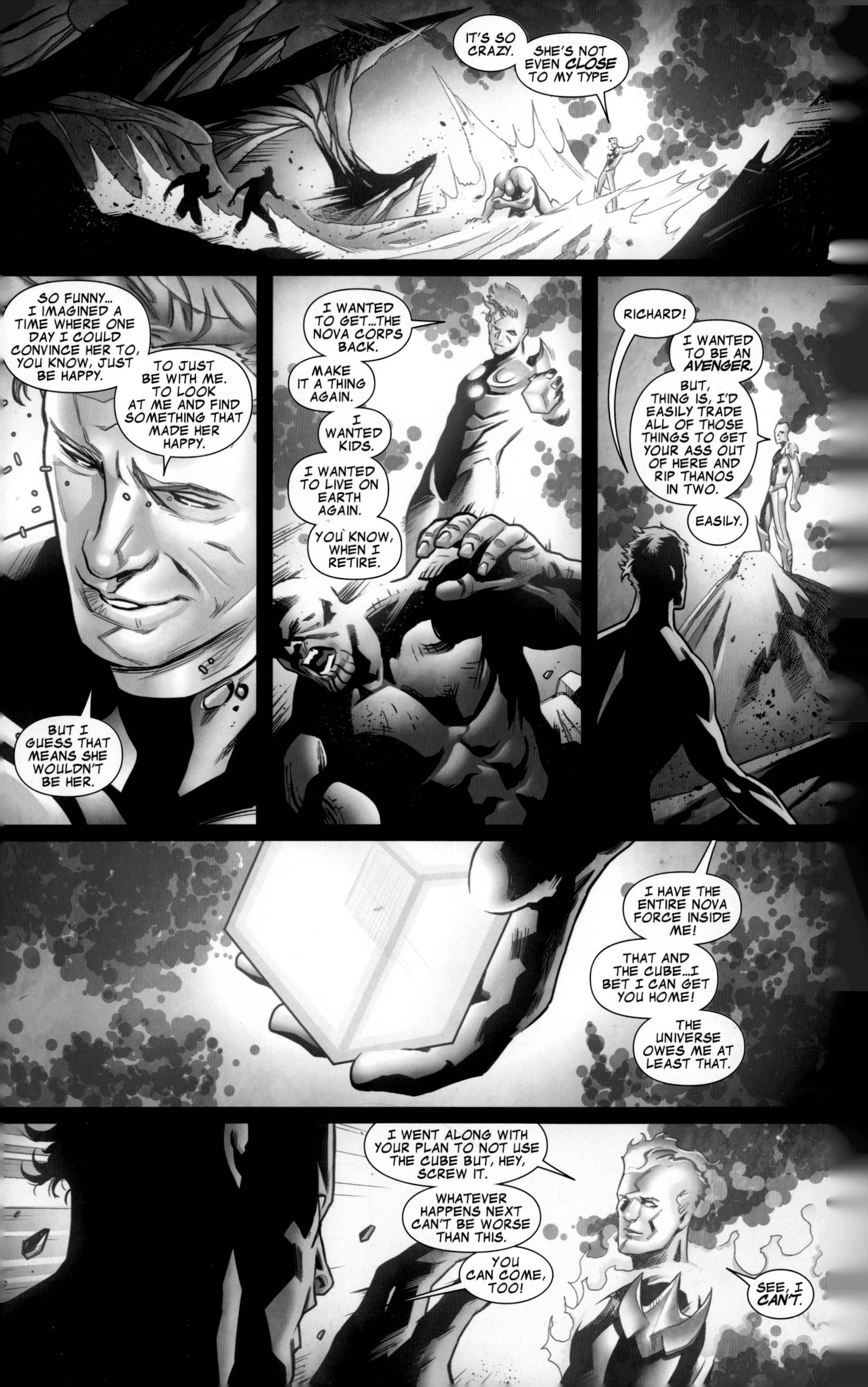
IT'S SO CRAZY.
SHE'S NOT EVEN CLOSE TO MY TYPE.
SO FUNNY... I IMAGINED A TIME WHERE ONE DAY I COULD CONVINCE HER TO, YOU KNOW, JUST BE HAPPY.
TO JUST BE WITH ME. TO LOOK AT ME AND FIND SOMETHING THAT MADE HER HAPPY.
BUT I GUESS THAT MEANS SHE WOULDN'T BE HER.
I WANTED TO GET...THE NOVA CORPS BACK.
MAKE IT A THING AGAIN.
I WANTED KIDS.
I WANTED TO LIVE ON EARTH AGAIN.
YOU KNOW, WHEN I RETIRE.
RICHARD!
I WANTED TO BE AN AVENGER.
BUT, THING IS, I'D EASILY TRADE ALL OF THOSE THINGS TO GET YOUR ASS OUT OF HERE AND RIP THANOS IN TWO.
EASILY.
I HAVE THE ENTIRE NOVA FORCE INSIDE ME!
THAT AND THE CUBE...I BET I CAN GET YOU HOME!
THE UNIVERSE OWES ME AT LEAST THAT.
I WENT ALONG WITH YOUR PLAN TO NOT USE THE CUBE BUT, HEY, SCREW IT.
WHATEVER HAPPENS NEXT CAN'T BE WORSE THAN THIS.
YOU CAN COME, TOO!
SEE, I CAN'T.

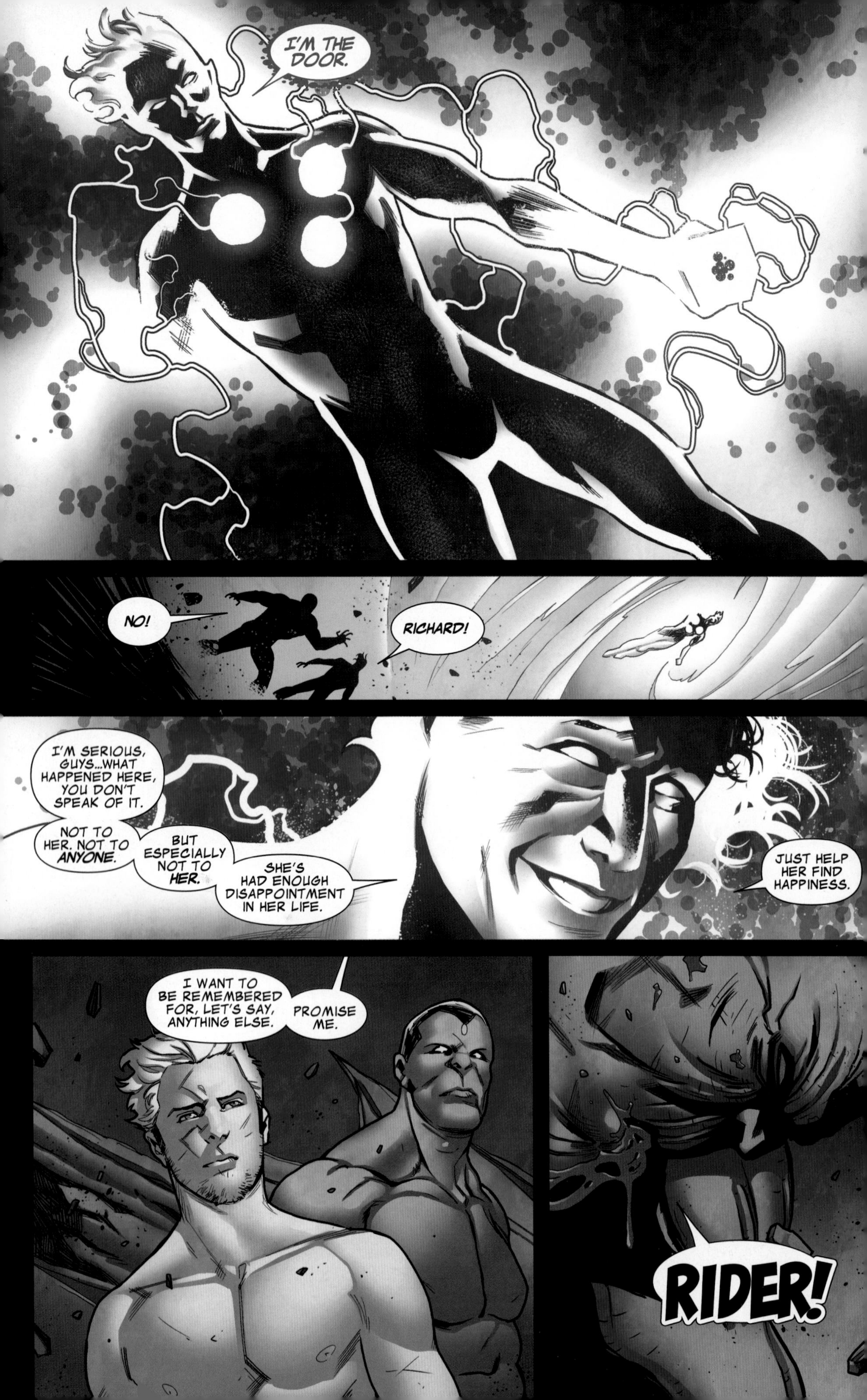
I'M THE DOOR.
NO!
RICHARD!
I'M SERIOUS, GUYS...WHAT HAPPENED HERE, YOU DON'T SPEAK OF IT.
NOT TO HER. NOT TO ANYONE.
BUT ESPECIALLY NOT TO HER.
SHE'S HAD ENOUGH DISAPPOINTMENT IN HER LIFE.
JUST HELP HER FIND HAPPINESS.
I WANT TO BE REMEMBERED FOR, LET'S SAY, ANYTHING ELSE.
PROMISE ME.
RIDER!

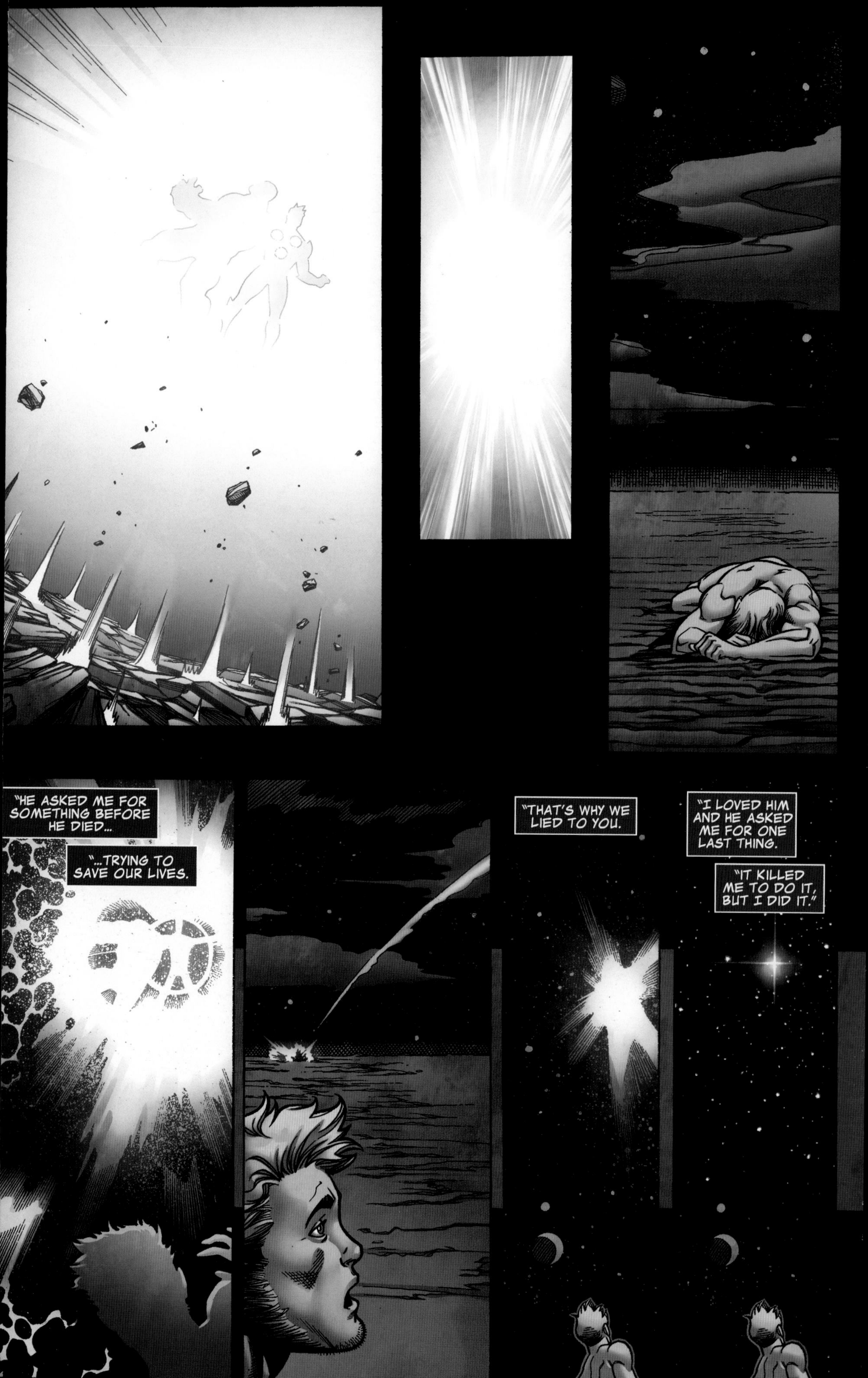
"HE ASKED ME FOR SOMETHING BEFORE HE DIED...
"...TRYING TO SAVE OUR LIVES.
"THAT'S WHY WE LIED TO YOU.
"I LOVED HIM AND HE ASKED ME FOR ONE LAST THING.
"IT KILLED ME TO DO IT, BUT I DID IT."

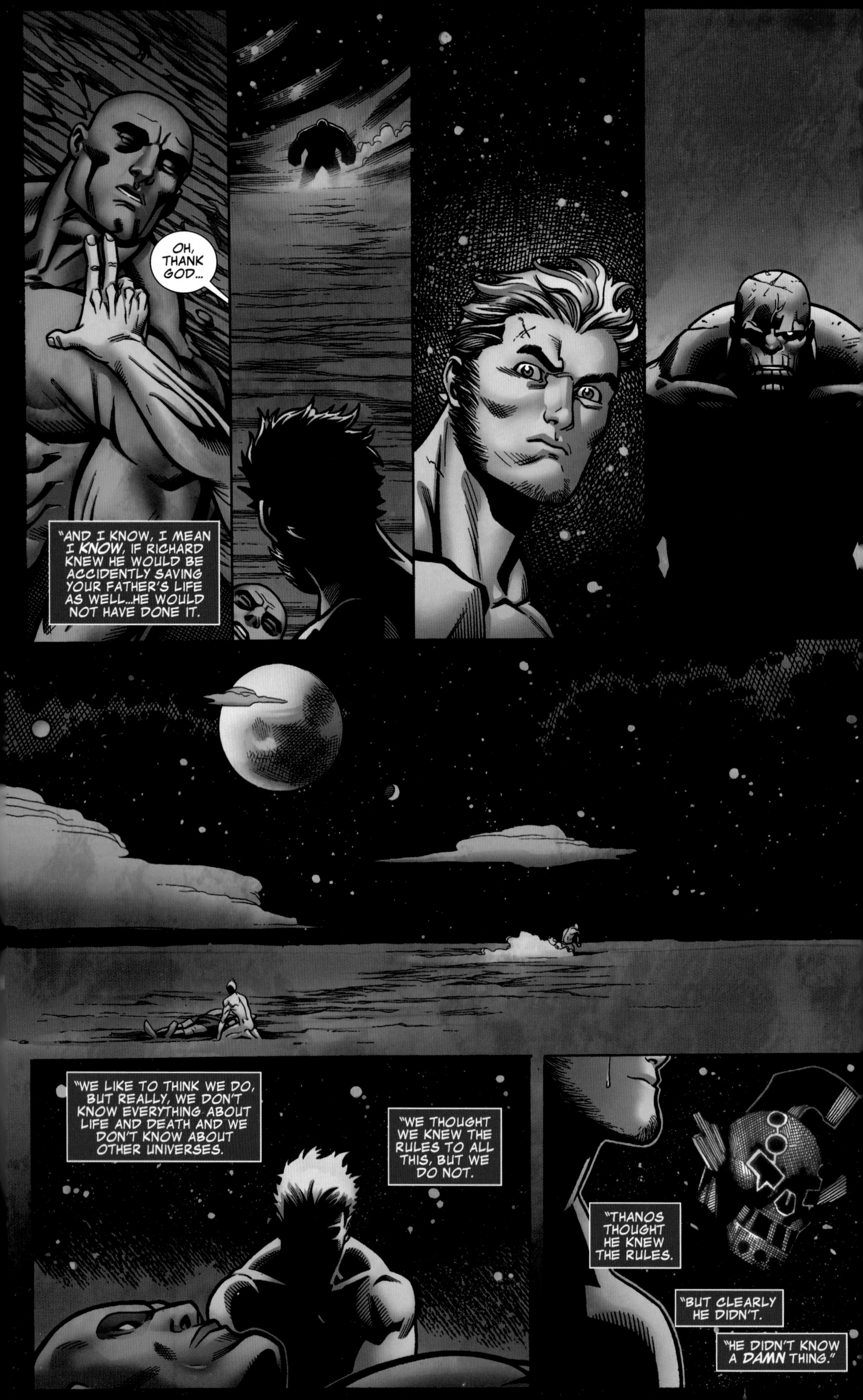
OH, THANK GOD...
"AND I KNOW, I MEAN I KNOW, IF RICHARD KNEW HE WOULD BE ACCIDENTLY SAVING YOUR FATHER'S LIFE AS WELL...HE WOULD NOT HAVE DONE IT.
"WE LIKE TO THINK WE DO, BUT REALLY, WE DON'T KNOW EVERYTHING ABOUT LIFE AND DEATH AND WE DON'T KNOW ABOUT OTHER UNIVERSES.
"WE THOUGHT WE KNEW THE RULES TO ALL THIS, BUT WE DO NOT.
"THANOS THOUGHT HE KNEW THE RULES.
"BUT CLEARLY HE DIDN'T.
"HE DIDN'T KNOW A DAMN THING."

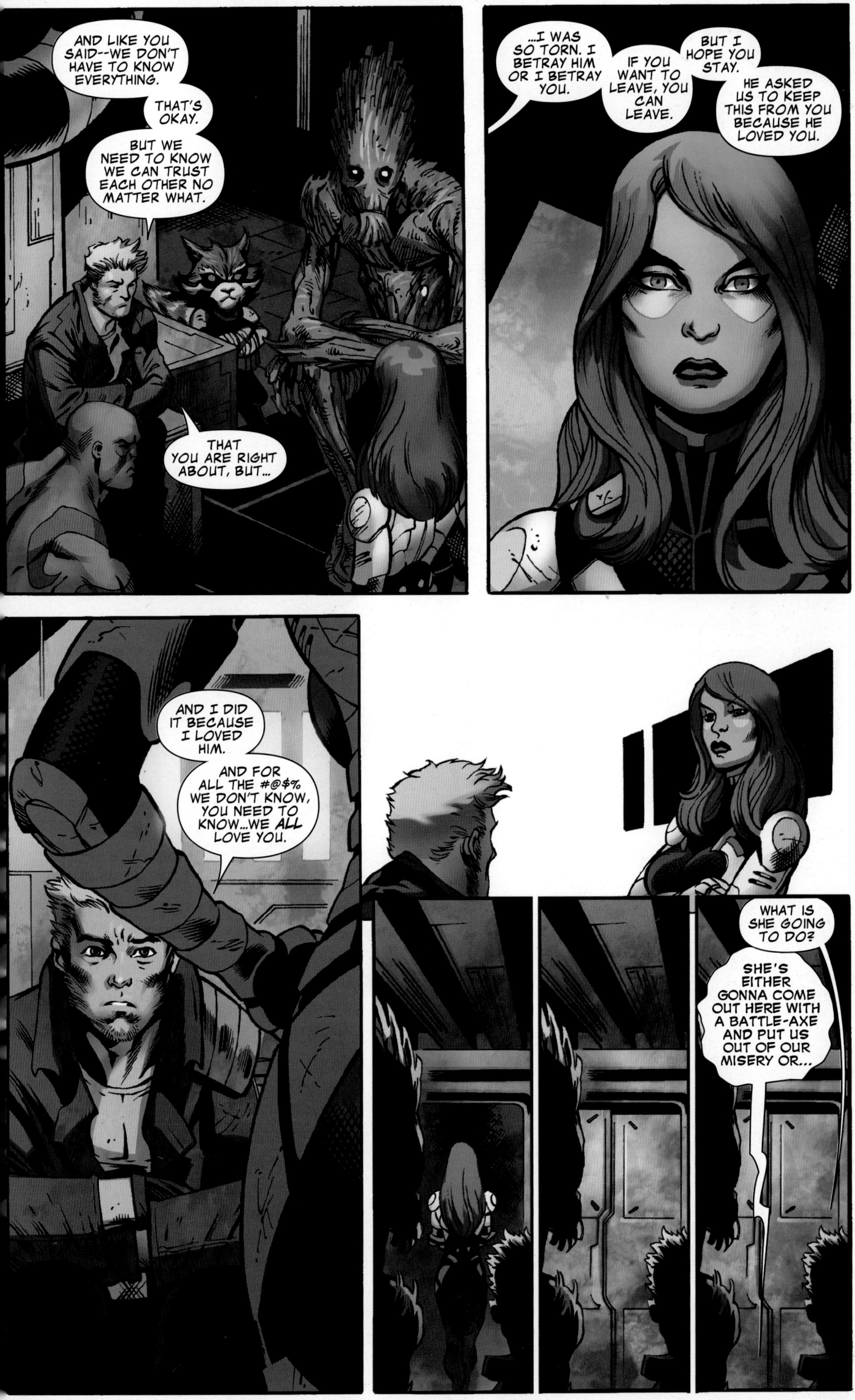
AND LIKE YOU SAID--WE DON'T HAVE TO KNOW EVERYTHING.
THAT'S OKAY.
BUT WE NEED TO KNOW WE CAN TRUST EACH OTHER NO MATTER WHAT.
THAT YOU ARE RIGHT ABOUT, BUT...
...I WAS SO TORN. I BETRAY HIM OR I BETRAY YOU.
IF YOU WANT TO LEAVE, YOU CAN LEAVE.
BUT I HOPE YOU STAY.
HE ASKED US TO KEEP THIS FROM YOU BECAUSE HE LOVED YOU.
AND I DID IT BECAUSE I LOVED HIM.
AND FOR ALL THE #@$% WE DON'T KNOW, YOU NEED TO KNOW...WE ALL LOVE YOU.
WHAT IS SHE GOING TO DO?
SHE'S EITHER GONNA COME OUT HERE WITH A BATTLE-AXE AND PUT US OUT OF OUR MISERY OR...

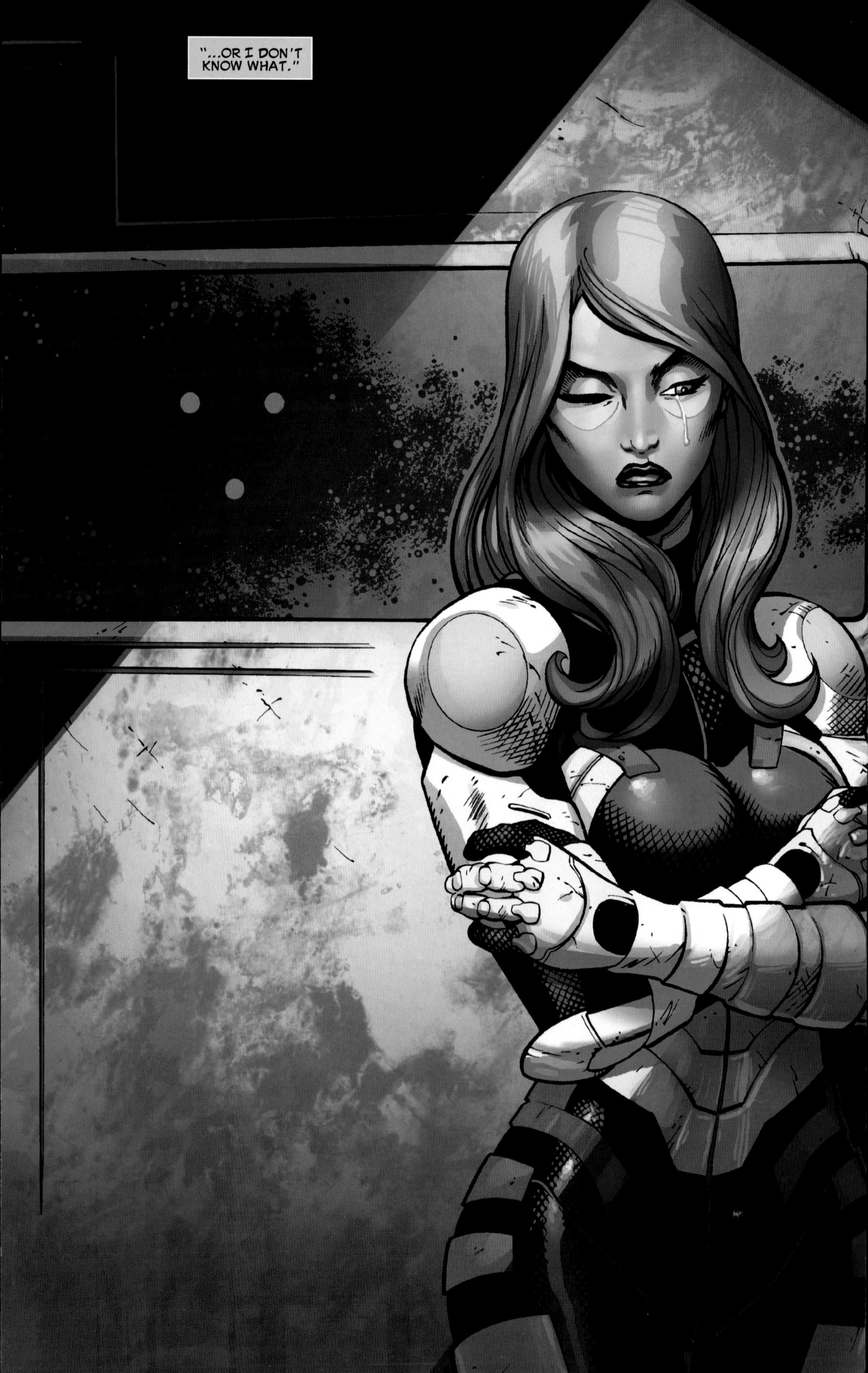
"...OR I DON'T KNOW WHAT."

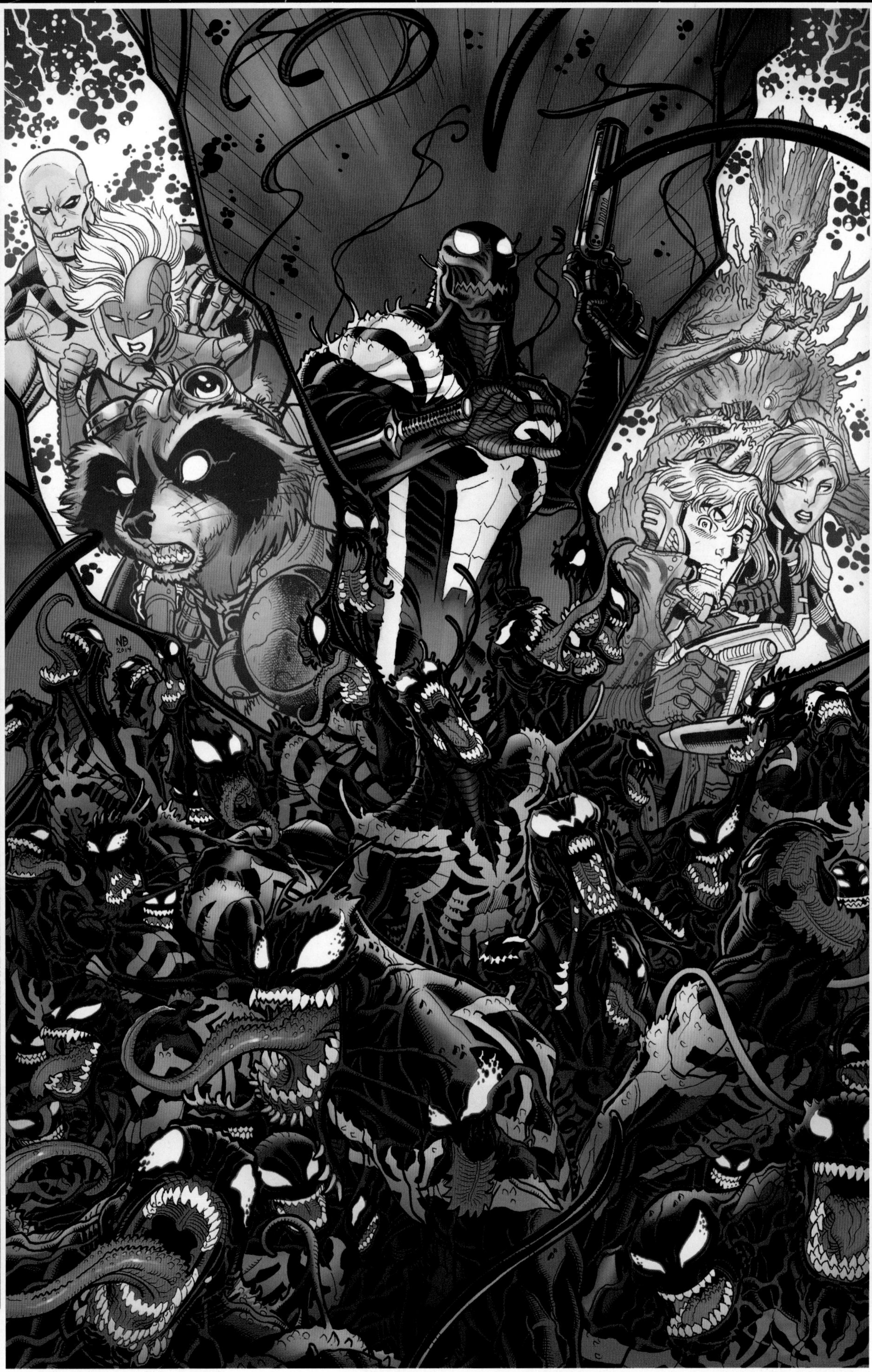

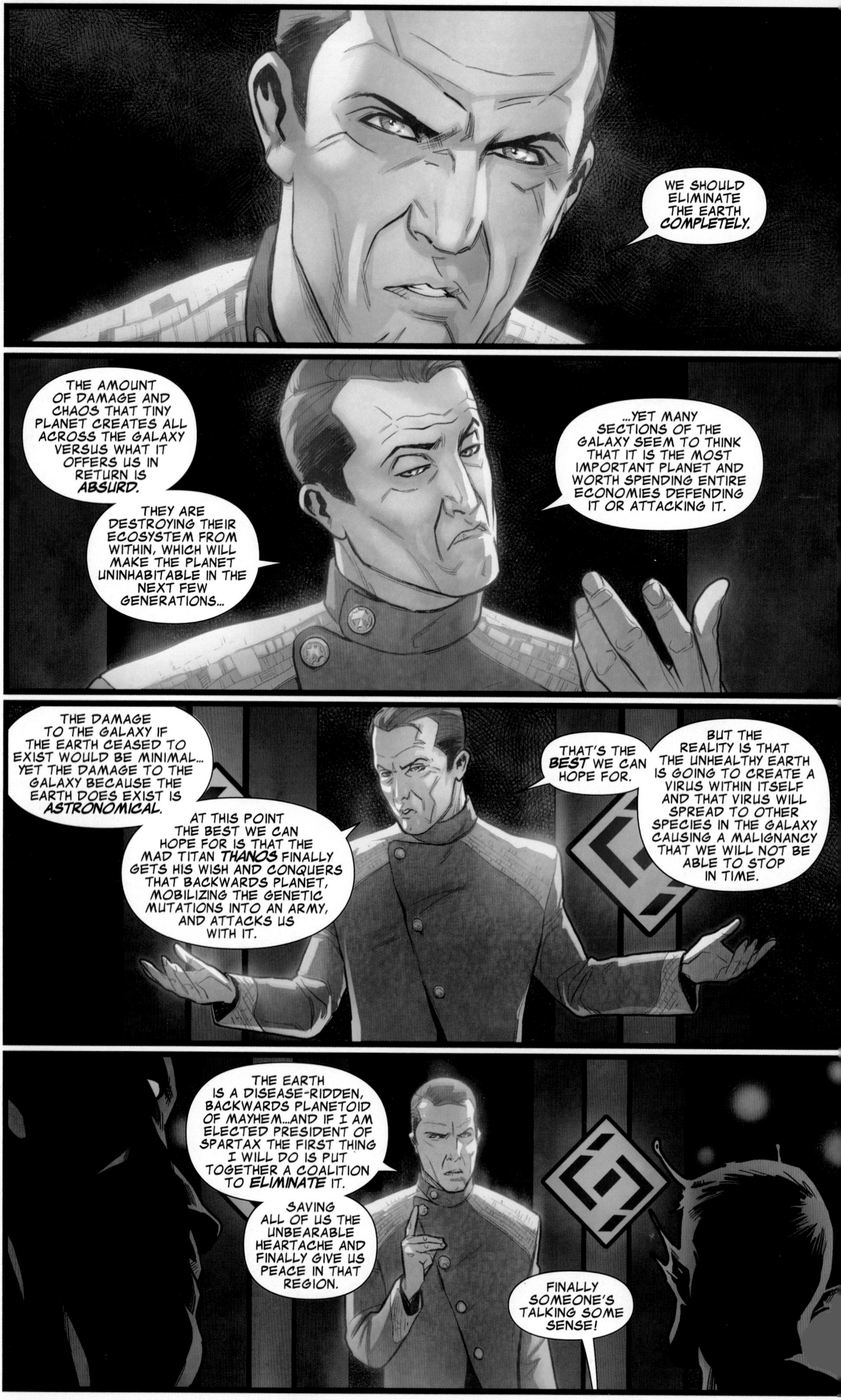
WE SHOULD ELIMINATE THE EARTH COMPLETELY.
THE AMOUNT OF DAMAGE AND CHAOS THAT TINY PLANET CREATES ALL ACROSS THE GALAXY VERSUS WHAT IT OFFERS US IN RETURN IS ABSURD.
THEY ARE DESTROYING THEIR ECOSYSTEM FROM WITHIN, WHICH WILL MAKE THE PLANET UNINHABITABLE IN THE NEXT FEW GENERATIONS...
...YET MANY SECTIONS OF THE GALAXY SEEM TO THINK THAT IT IS THE MOST IMPORTANT PLANET AND WORTH SPENDING ENTIRE ECONOMIES DEFENDING IT OR ATTACKING IT.
THE DAMAGE TO THE GALAXY IF THE EARTH CEASED TO EXIST WOULD BE MINIMAL... YET THE DAMAGE TO THE GALAXY BECAUSE THE EARTH DOES EXIST IS ASTRONOMICAL.
AT THIS POINT THE BEST WE CAN HOPE FOR IS THAT THE MAD TITAN THANOS FINALLY GETS HIS WISH AND CONQUERS THAT BACKWARDS PLANET, MOBILIZING THE GENETIC MUTATIONS INTO AN ARMY, AND ATTACKS US WITH IT.
THAT'S THE BEST WE CAN HOPE FOR.
BUT THE REALITY IS THAT THE UNHEALTHY EARTH IS GOING TO CREATE A VIRUS WITHIN ITSELF AND THAT VIRUS WILL SPREAD TO OTHER SPECIES IN THE GALAXY CAUSING A MALIGNANCY THAT WE WILL NOT BE ABLE TO STOP IN TIME.
THE EARTH IS A DISEASE-RIDDEN, BACKWARDS PLANETOID OF MAYHEM...AND IF I AM ELECTED PRESIDENT OF SPARTAX THE FIRST THING I WILL DO IS PUT TOGETHER A COALITION TO ELIMINATE IT.
SAVING ALL OF US THE UNBEARABLE HEARTACHE AND FINALLY GIVE US PEACE IN THAT REGION.
FINALLY SOMEONE'S TALKING SOME SENSE!

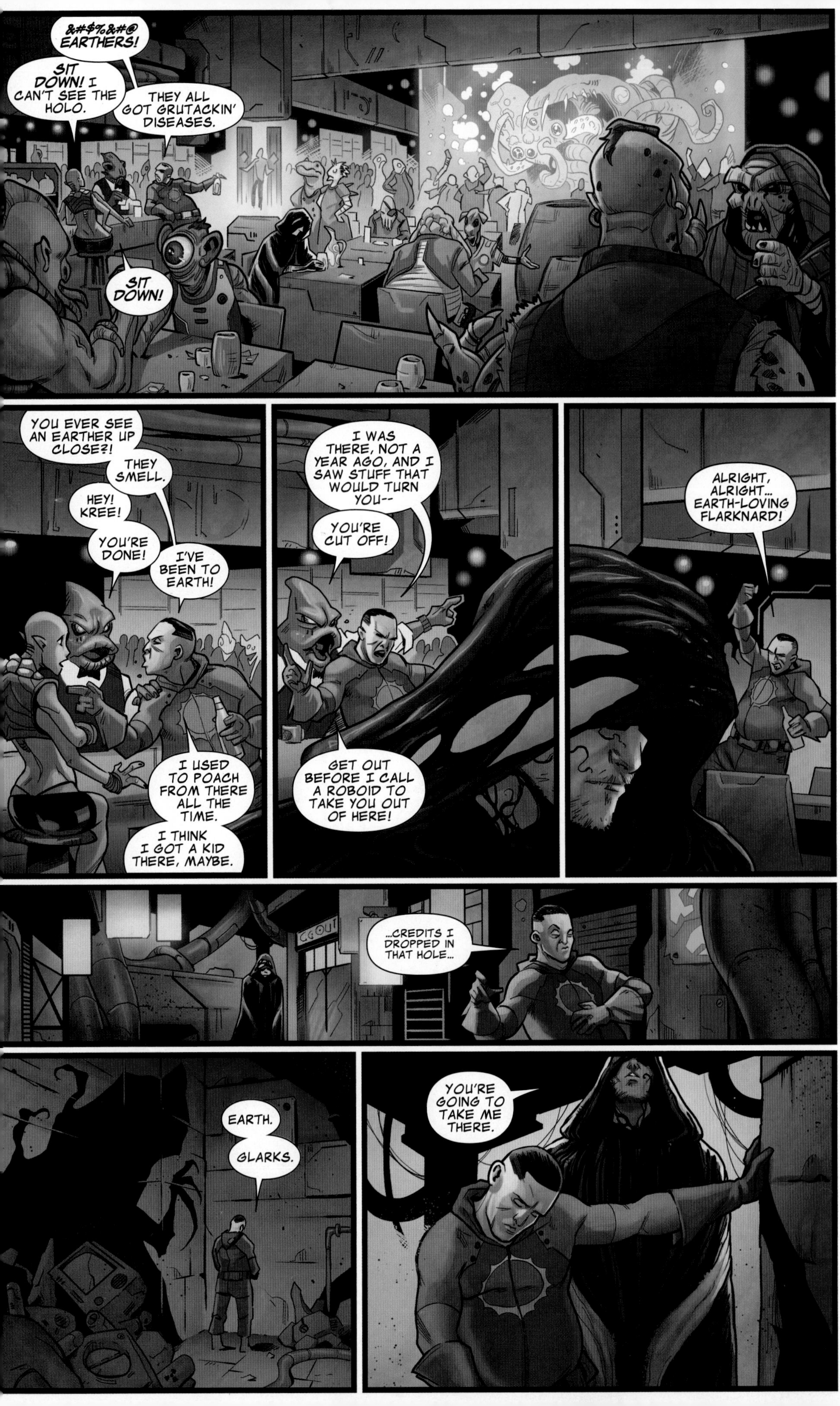
&#$%&#@ EARTHERS!
SIT DOWN! I CAN'T SEE THE HOLO.
THEY ALL GOT GRUTACKIN' DISEASES.
SIT DOWN!
YOU EVER SEE AN EARTHER UP CLOSE?!
THEY SMELL.
HEY! KREE!
YOU'RE DONE!
I'VE BEEN TO EARTH!
I USED TO POACH FROM THERE ALL THE TIME.
I THINK I GOT A KID THERE, MAYBE.
I WAS THERE, NOT A YEAR AGO, AND I SAW STUFF THAT WOULD TURN YOU--
YOU'RE CUT OFF!
GET OUT BEFORE I CALL A ROBOID TO TAKE YOU OUT OF HERE!
ALRIGHT, ALRIGHT... EARTH-LOVING FLARKNARD!
...CREDITS I DROPPED IN THAT HOLE...
EARTH.
GLARKS.
YOU'RE GOING TO TAKE ME THERE.

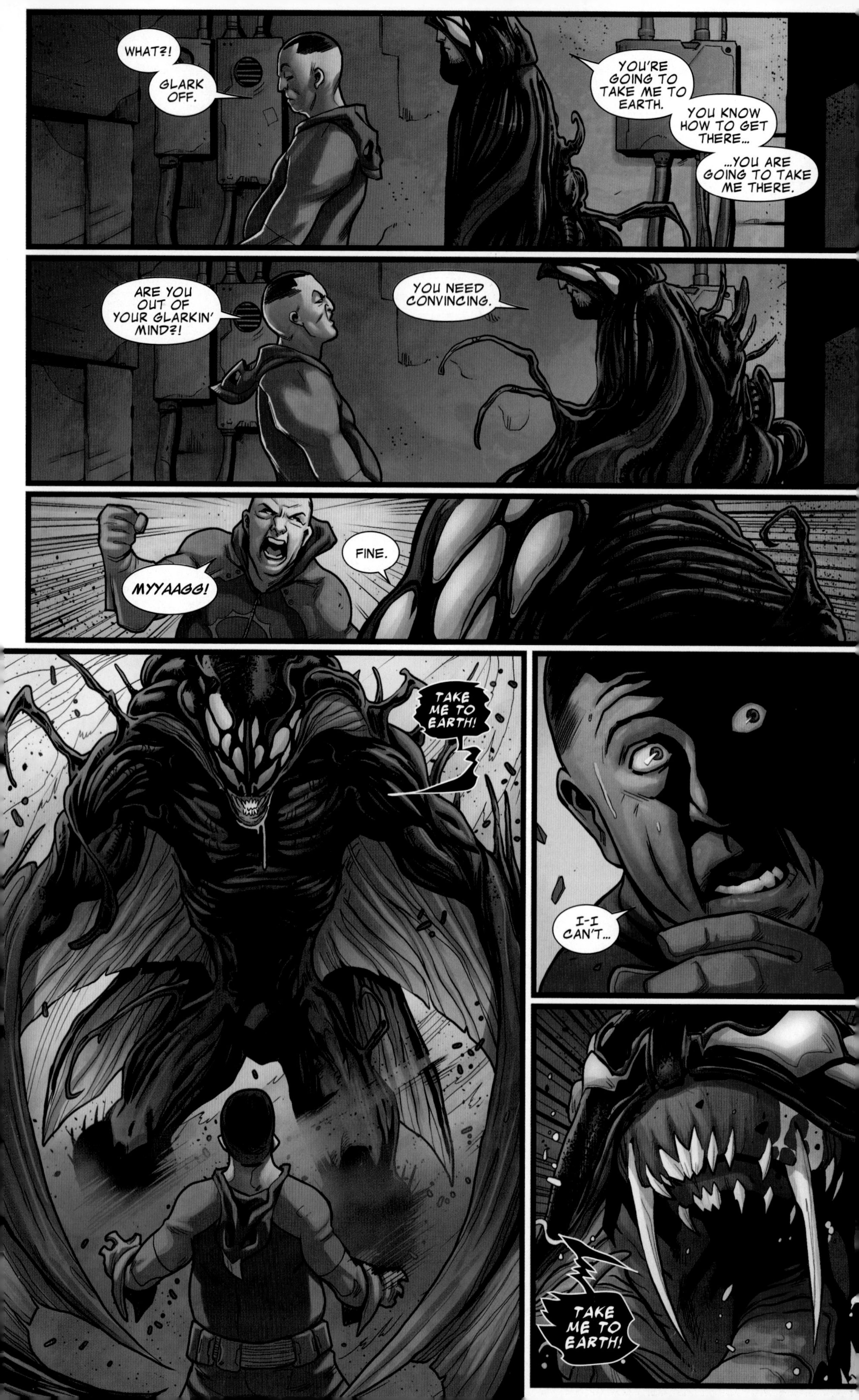
WHAT?!
GLARK OFF.
YOU'RE GOING TO TAKE ME TO EARTH.
YOU KNOW HOW TO GET THERE...
...YOU ARE GOING TO TAKE ME THERE.
ARE YOU OUT OF YOUR GLARKIN' MIND?!
YOU NEED CONVINCING.
MYYAAGG!
FINE.
TAKE ME TO EARTH!
I-I CAN'T...
TAKE ME TO EARTH!

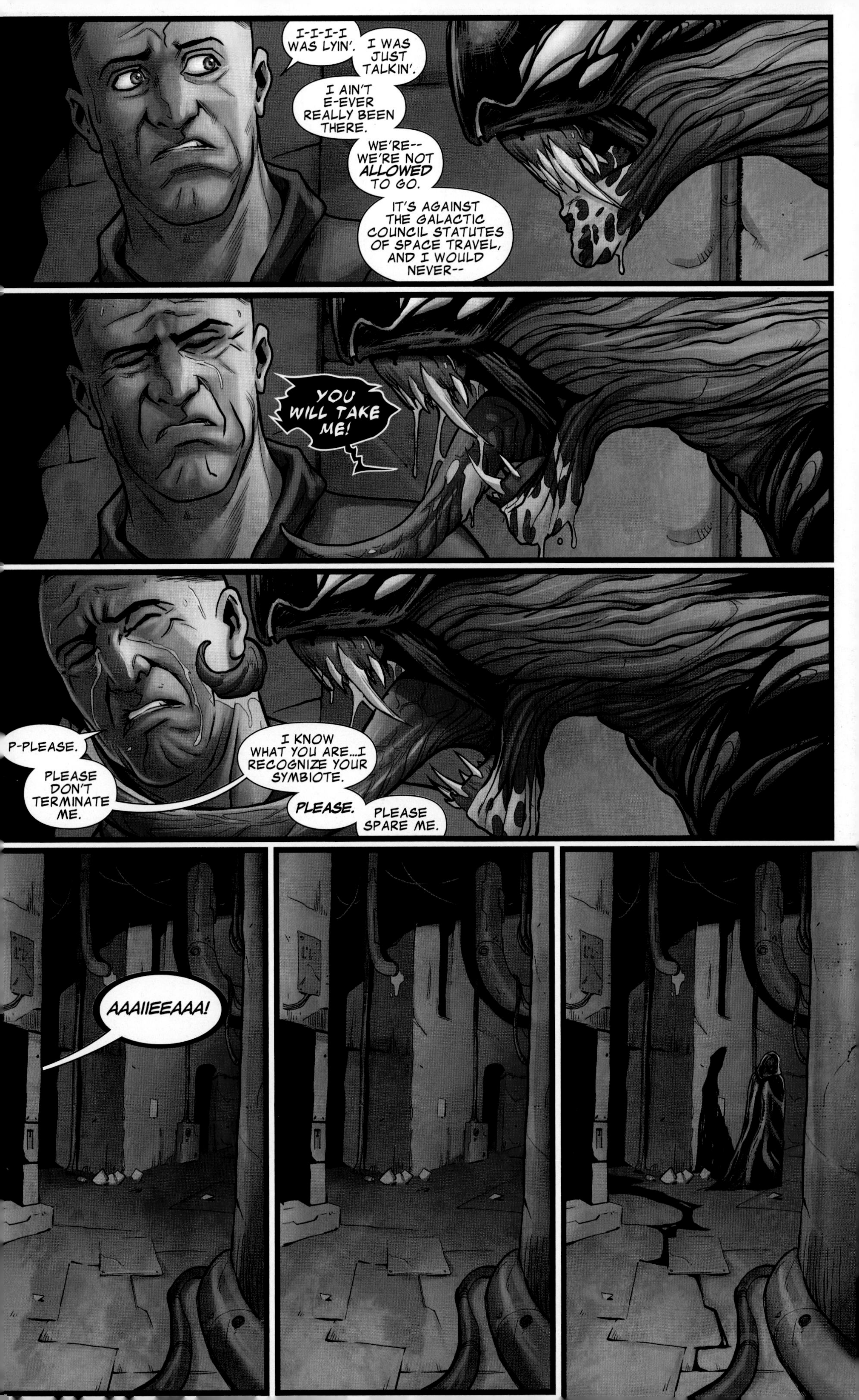
I-I-I-I WAS LYIN'.
I WAS JUST TALKIN'.
I AIN'T E-EVER REALLY BEEN THERE.
WE'RE-- WE'RE NOT **ALLOWED** TO GO.
IT'S AGAINST THE GALACTIC COUNCIL STATUTES OF SPACE TRAVEL, AND I WOULD NEVER--
YOU WILL TAKE ME!
P-PLEASE.
PLEASE DON'T TERMINATE ME.
I KNOW WHAT YOU ARE...I RECOGNIZE YOUR SYMBIOTE.
PLEASE.
PLEASE SPARE ME.
AAAIIEEAAA!

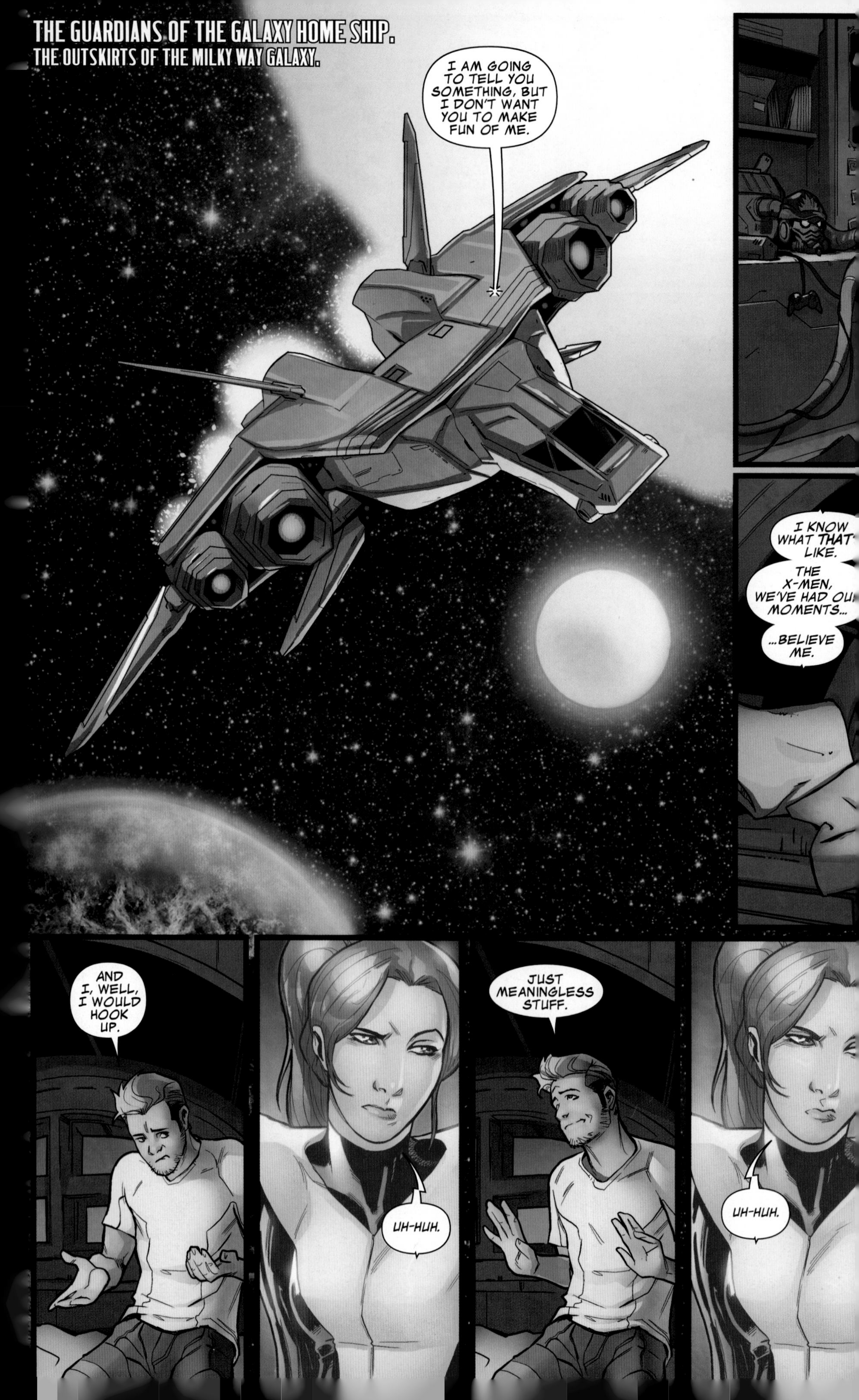
THE GUARDIANS OF THE GALAXY HOME SHIP.
THE OUTSKIRTS OF THE MILKY WAY GALAXY.
I AM GOING TO TELL YOU SOMETHING, BUT I DON'T WANT YOU TO MAKE FUN OF ME.
I KNOW WHAT THAT LIKE.
THE X-MEN, WE'VE HAD OU MOMENTS...
...BELIEVE ME.
AND I, WELL, I WOULD HOOK UP.
UH-HUH.
JUST MEANINGLESS STUFF.
UH-HUH.

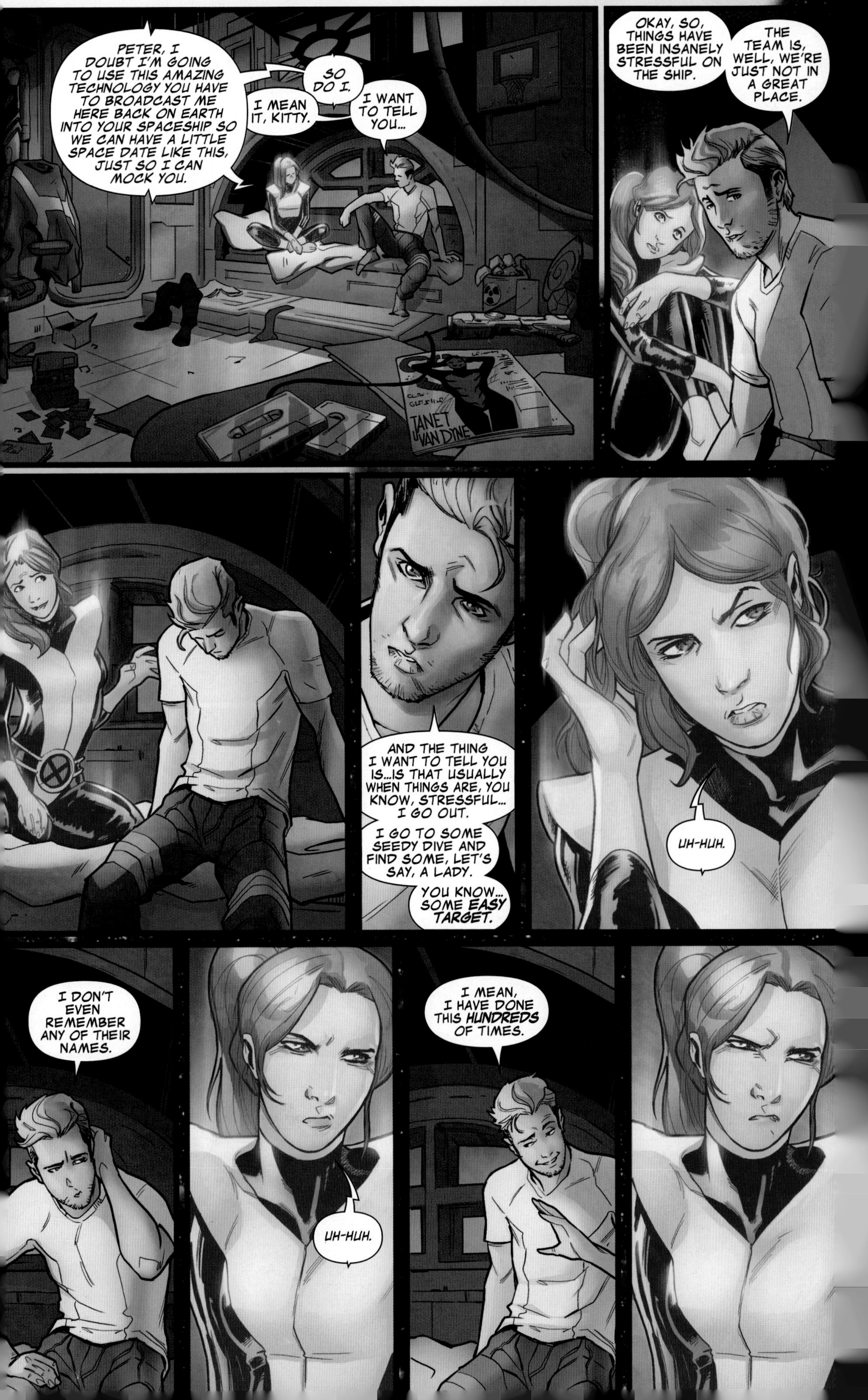
PETER, I DOUBT I'M GOING TO USE THIS AMAZING TECHNOLOGY YOU HAVE TO BROADCAST ME HERE BACK ON EARTH INTO YOUR SPACESHIP SO WE CAN HAVE A LITTLE SPACE DATE LIKE THIS, JUST SO I CAN MOCK YOU.
SO DO I.
I MEAN IT, KITTY.
I WANT TO TELL YOU...
JANET VAN DYNE
OKAY, SO, THINGS HAVE BEEN INSANELY STRESSFUL ON THE SHIP.
THE TEAM IS, WELL, WE'RE JUST NOT IN A GREAT PLACE.
AND THE THING I WANT TO TELL YOU IS...IS THAT USUALLY WHEN THINGS ARE, YOU KNOW, STRESSFUL... I GO OUT.
I GO TO SOME SEEDY DIVE AND FIND SOME, LET'S SAY, A LADY.
YOU KNOW... SOME EASY TARGET.
UH-HUH.
I DON'T EVEN REMEMBER ANY OF THEIR NAMES.
UH-HUH.
I MEAN, I HAVE DONE THIS HUNDREDS OF TIMES.

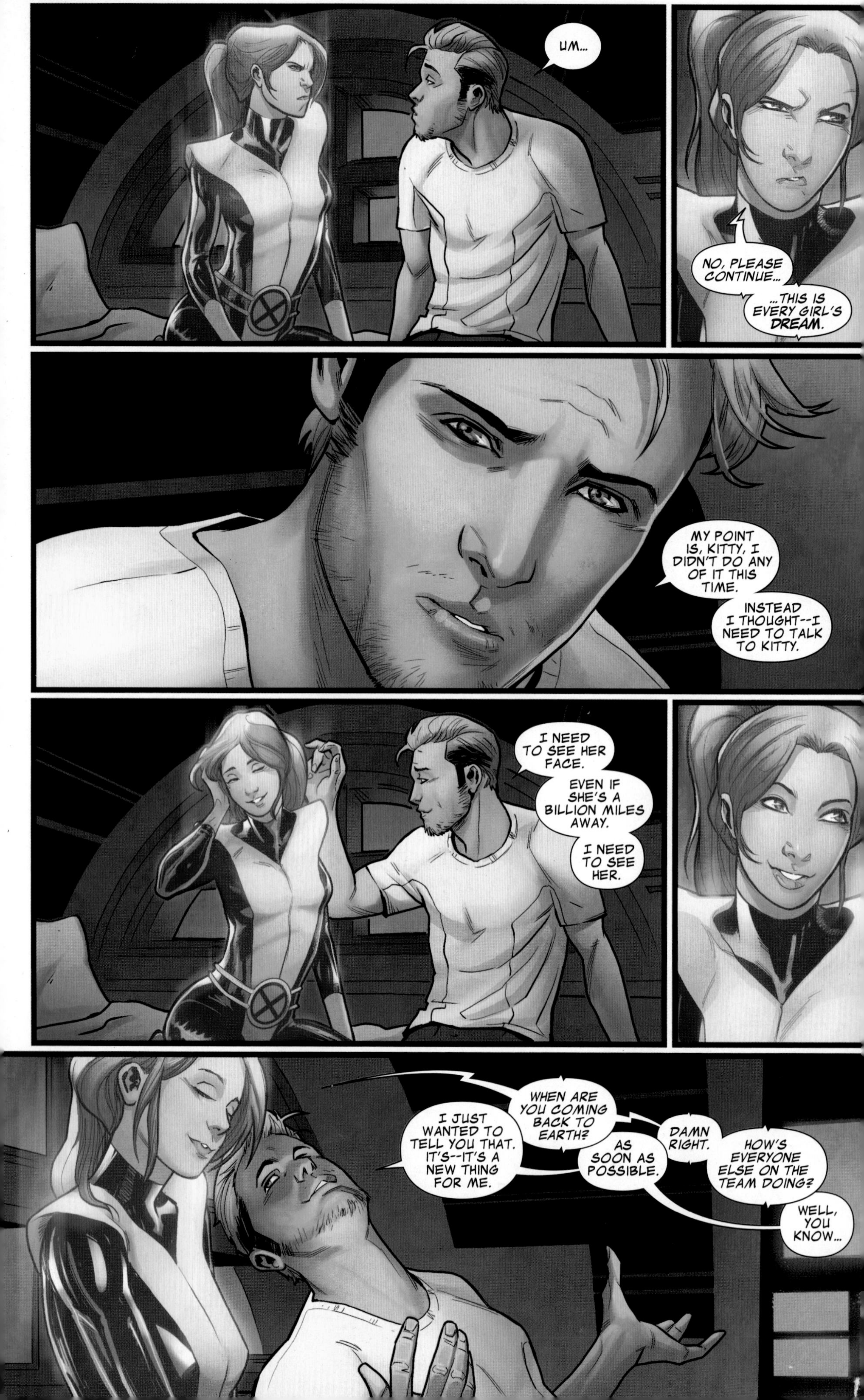
UM...
NO, PLEASE CONTINUE...
...THIS IS EVERY GIRL'S DREAM.
MY POINT IS, KITTY, I DIDN'T DO ANY OF IT THIS TIME.
INSTEAD I THOUGHT--I NEED TO TALK TO KITTY.
I NEED TO SEE HER FACE.
EVEN IF SHE'S A BILLION MILES AWAY.
I NEED TO SEE HER.
I JUST WANTED TO TELL YOU THAT. IT'S--IT'S A NEW THING FOR ME.
WHEN ARE YOU COMING BACK TO EARTH?
AS SOON AS POSSIBLE.
DAMN RIGHT.
HOW'S EVERYONE ELSE ON THE TEAM DOING?
WELL, YOU KNOW...

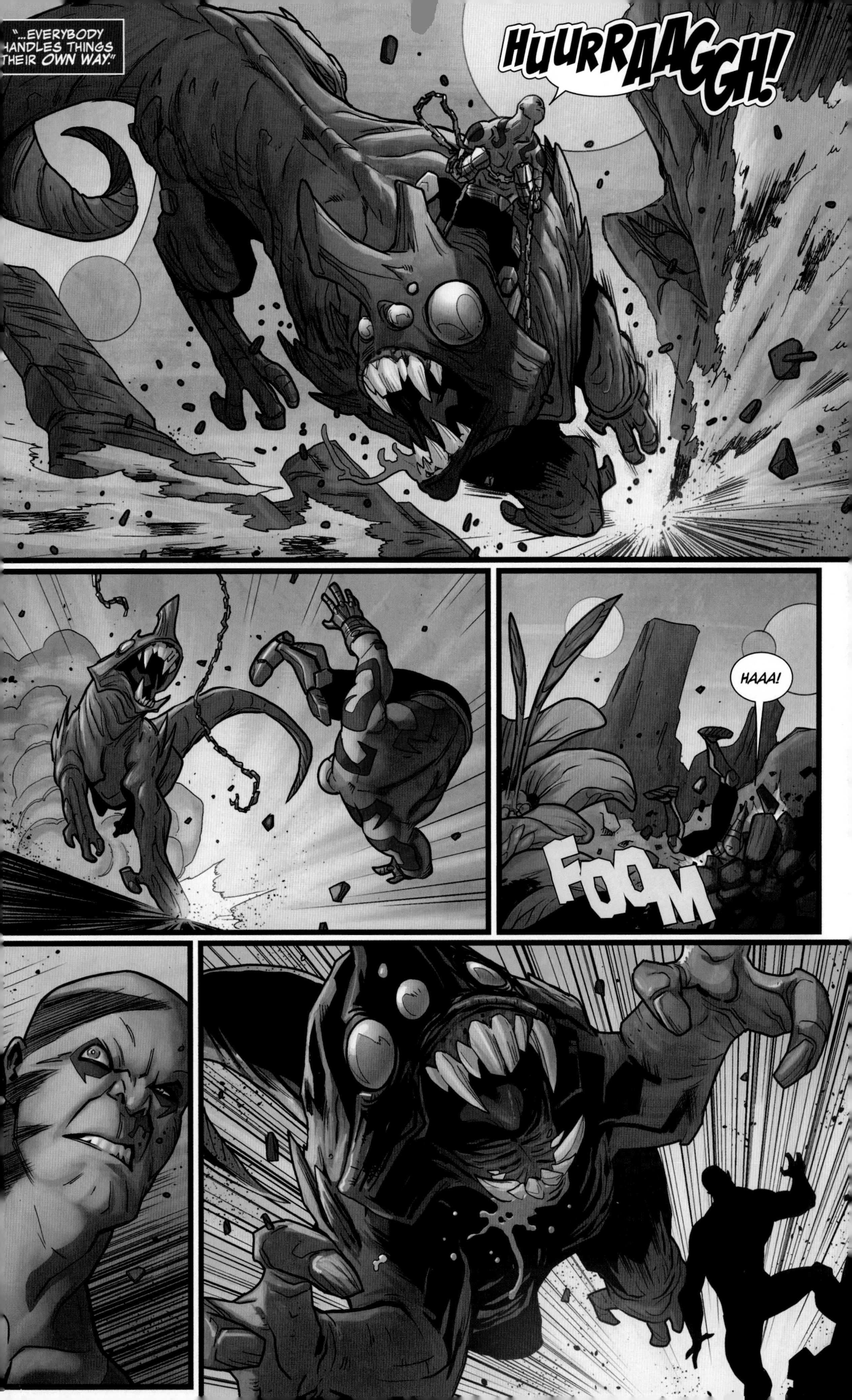
"...EVERYBODY HANDLES THINGS THEIR OWN WAY."
HUURRAAGGH!
HAAA!
FOOM

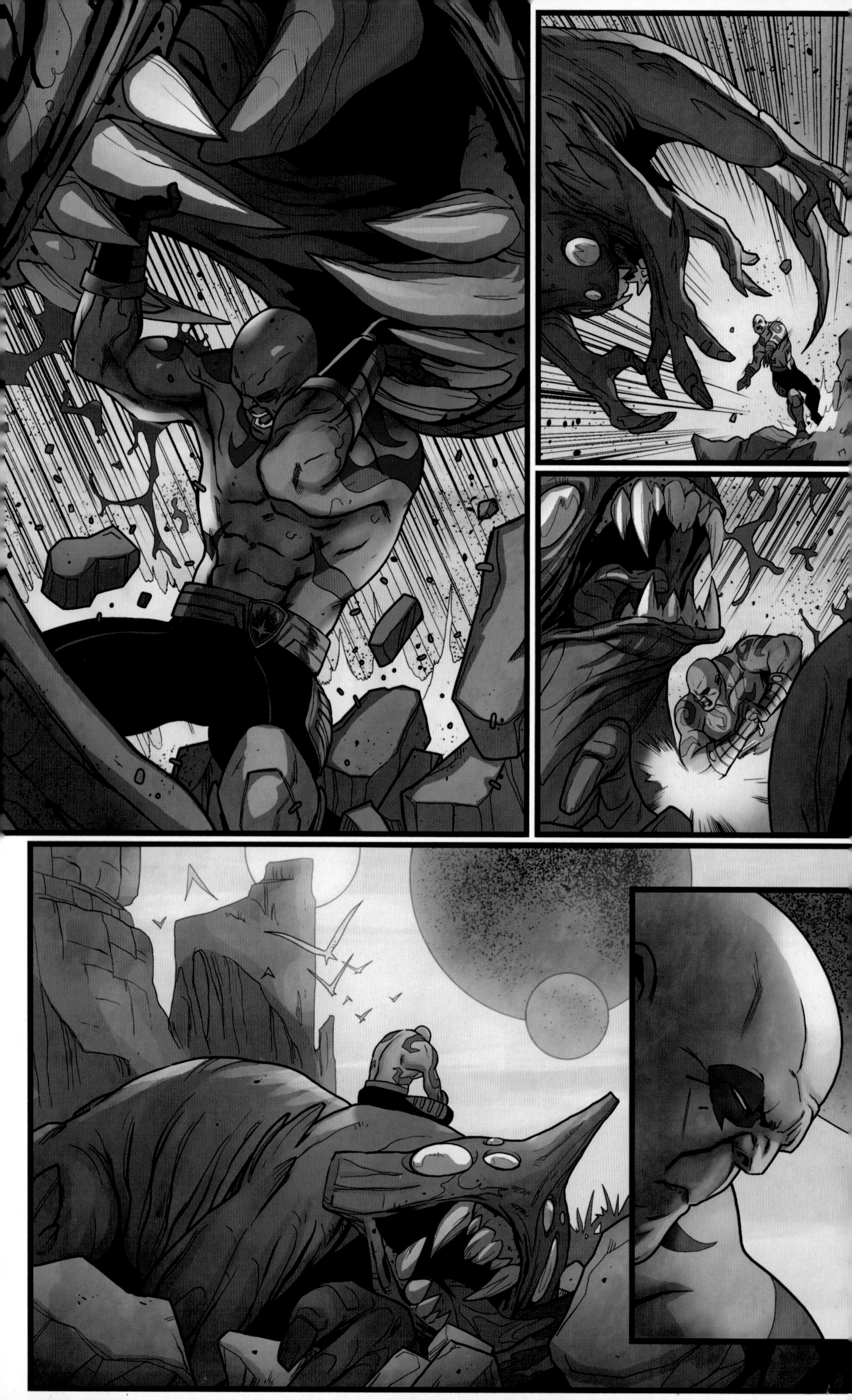

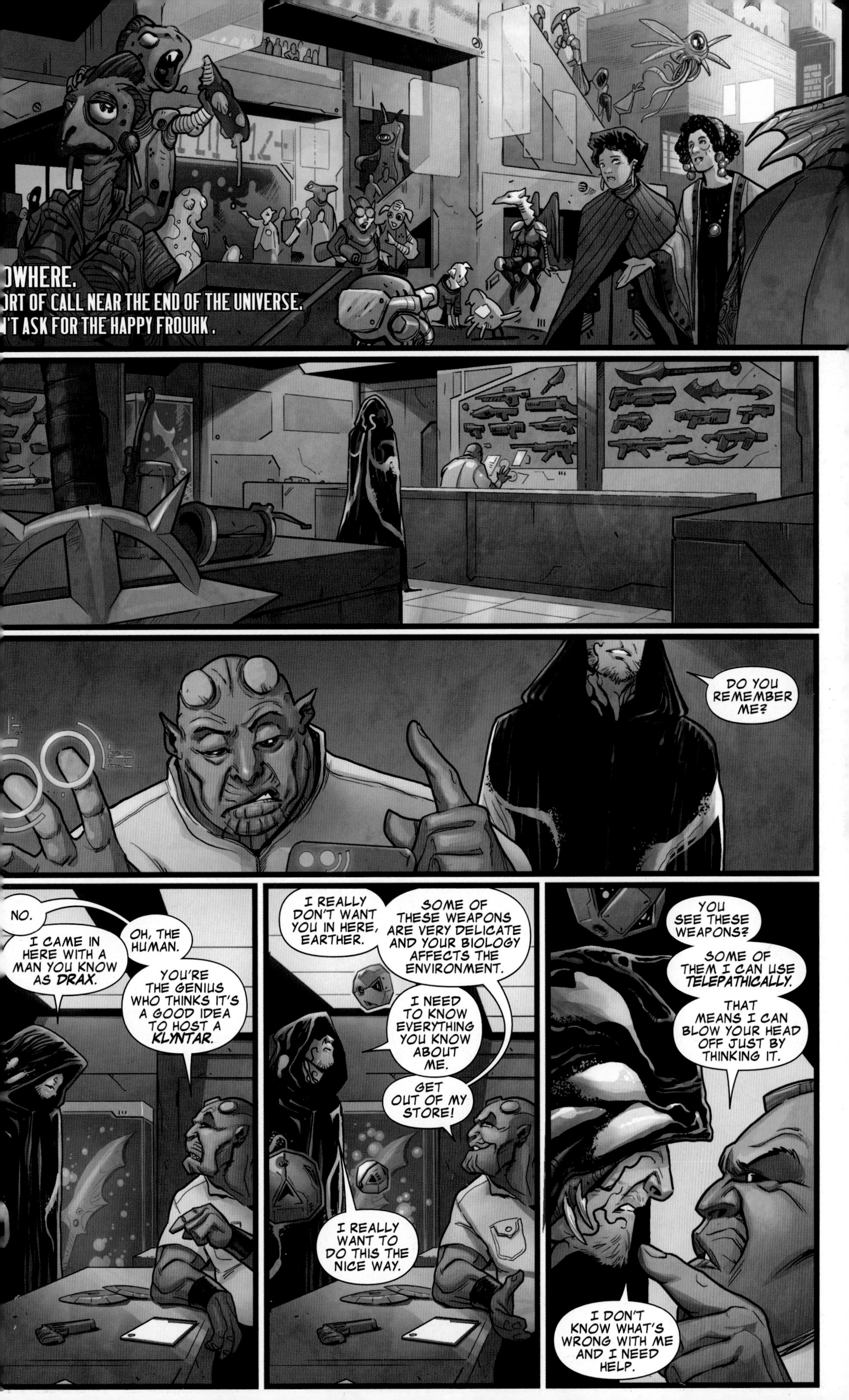

OWHERE.
ORT OF CALL NEAR THE END OF THE UNIVERSE.
'T ASK FOR THE HAPPY FROUHK.
DO YOU REMEMBER ME?
NO.
I CAME IN HERE WITH A MAN YOU KNOW AS DRAX.
OH, THE HUMAN.
YOU'RE THE GENIUS WHO THINKS IT'S A GOOD IDEA TO HOST A KLYNTAR.
I REALLY DON'T WANT YOU IN HERE, EARTHER.
SOME OF THESE WEAPONS ARE VERY DELICATE AND YOUR BIOLOGY AFFECTS THE ENVIRONMENT.
I NEED TO KNOW EVERYTHING YOU KNOW ABOUT ME.
GET OUT OF MY STORE!
I REALLY WANT TO DO THIS THE NICE WAY.
YOU SEE THESE WEAPONS?
SOME OF THEM I CAN USE TELEPATHICALLY.
THAT MEANS I CAN BLOW YOUR HEAD OFF JUST BY THINKING IT.
I DON'T KNOW WHAT'S WRONG WITH ME AND I NEED HELP.

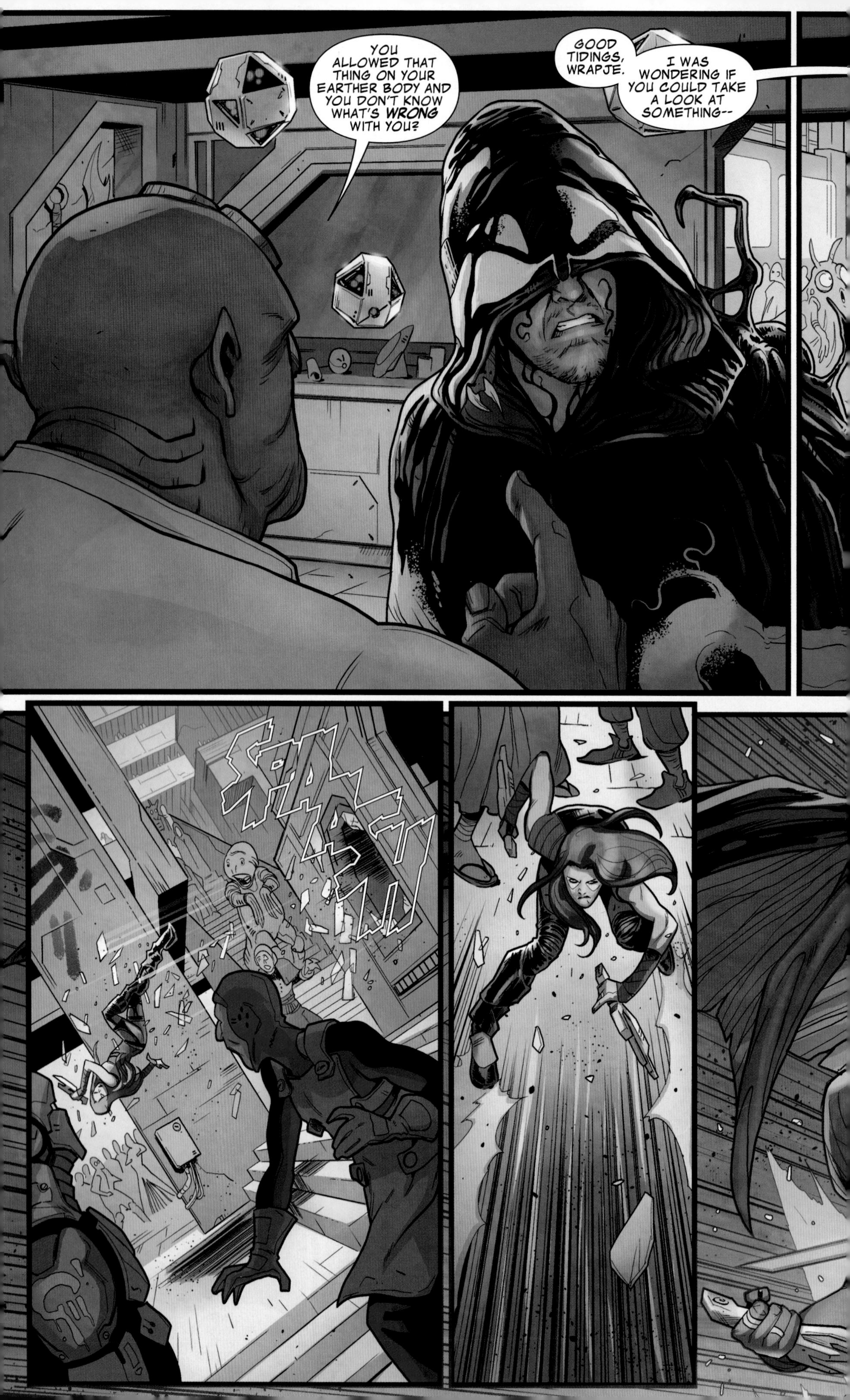
GOOD TIDINGS, WRAPJE.
I WAS WONDERING IF YOU COULD TAKE A LOOK AT SOMETHING--
YOU ALLOWED THAT THING ON YOUR EARTHER BODY AND YOU DON'T KNOW WHAT'S **WRONG** WITH YOU?

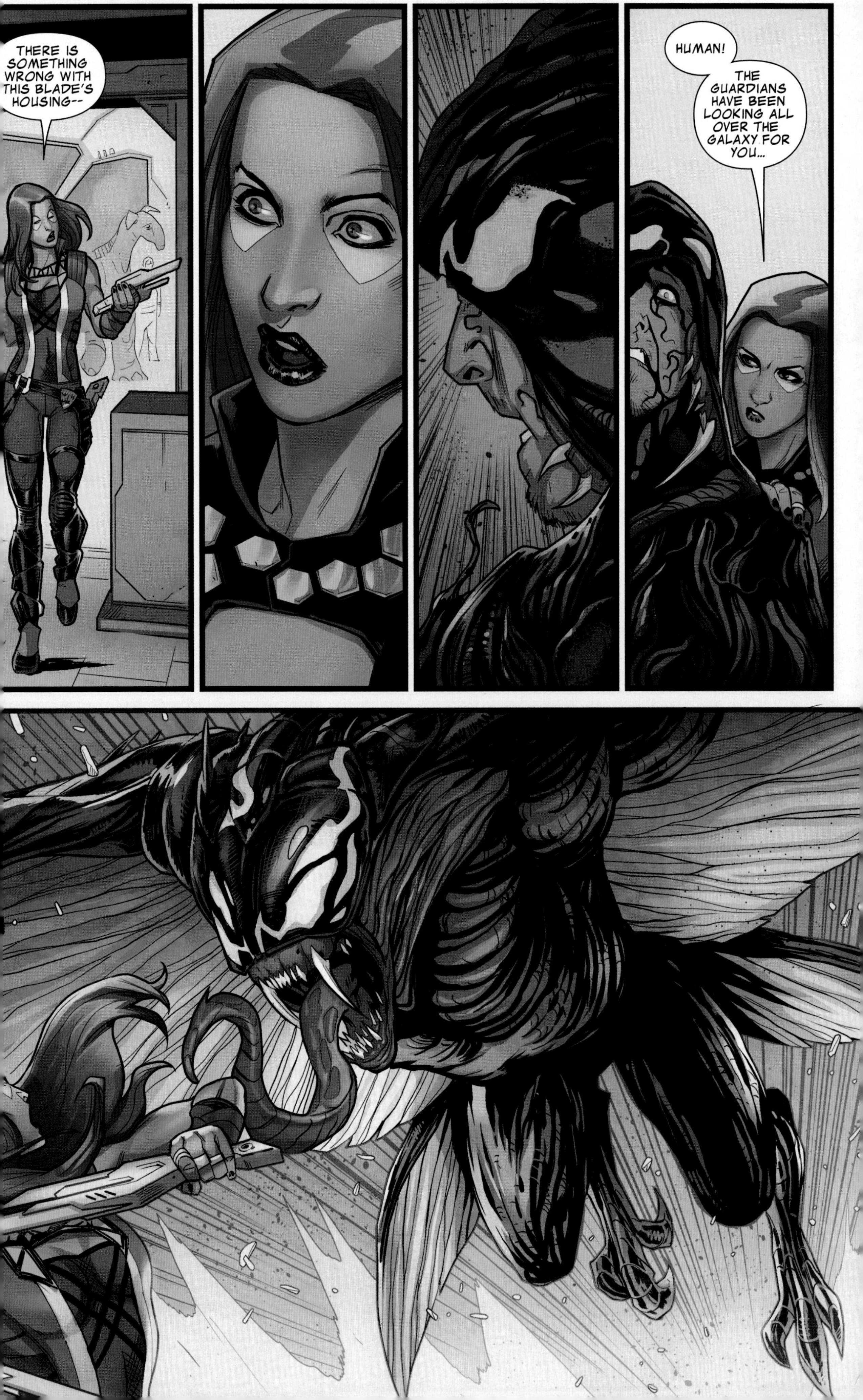
THERE IS SOMETHING WRONG WITH THIS BLADE'S HOUSING--
HUMAN!
THE GUARDIANS HAVE BEEN LOOKING ALL OVER THE GALAXY FOR YOU...

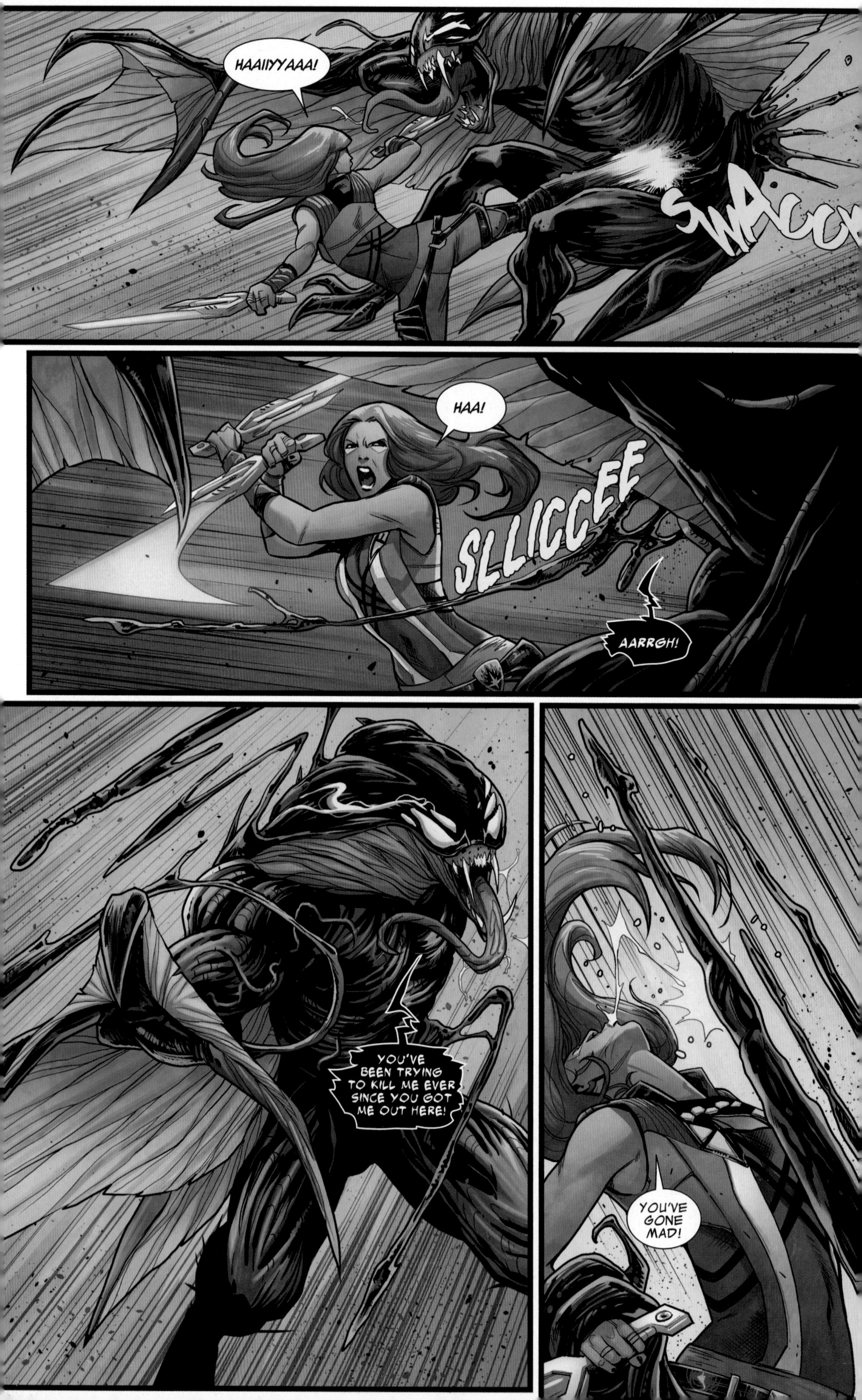
HAAIIYYAAA!
SWACCK
HAA!
SLLICCEE
AARRGH!
YOU'VE BEEN TRYING TO KILL ME EVER SINCE YOU GOT ME OUT HERE!
YOU'VE GONE MAD!

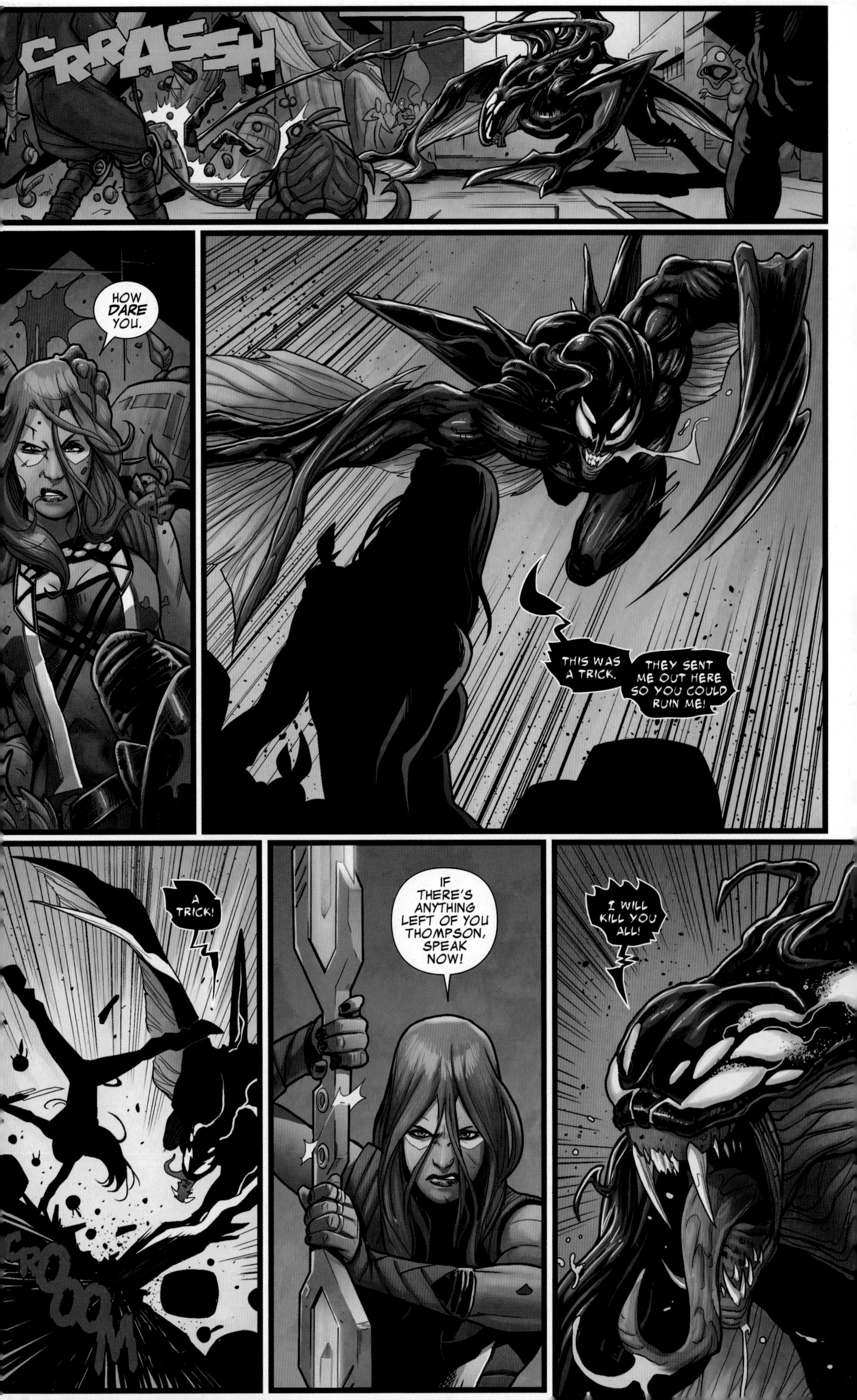
CRRASSH
HOW DARE YOU.
THIS WAS A TRICK.
THEY SENT ME OUT HERE SO YOU COULD RUIN ME!
A TRICK!
CROOOM
IF THERE'S ANYTHING LEFT OF YOU THOMPSON, SPEAK NOW!
I WILL KILL YOU ALL!

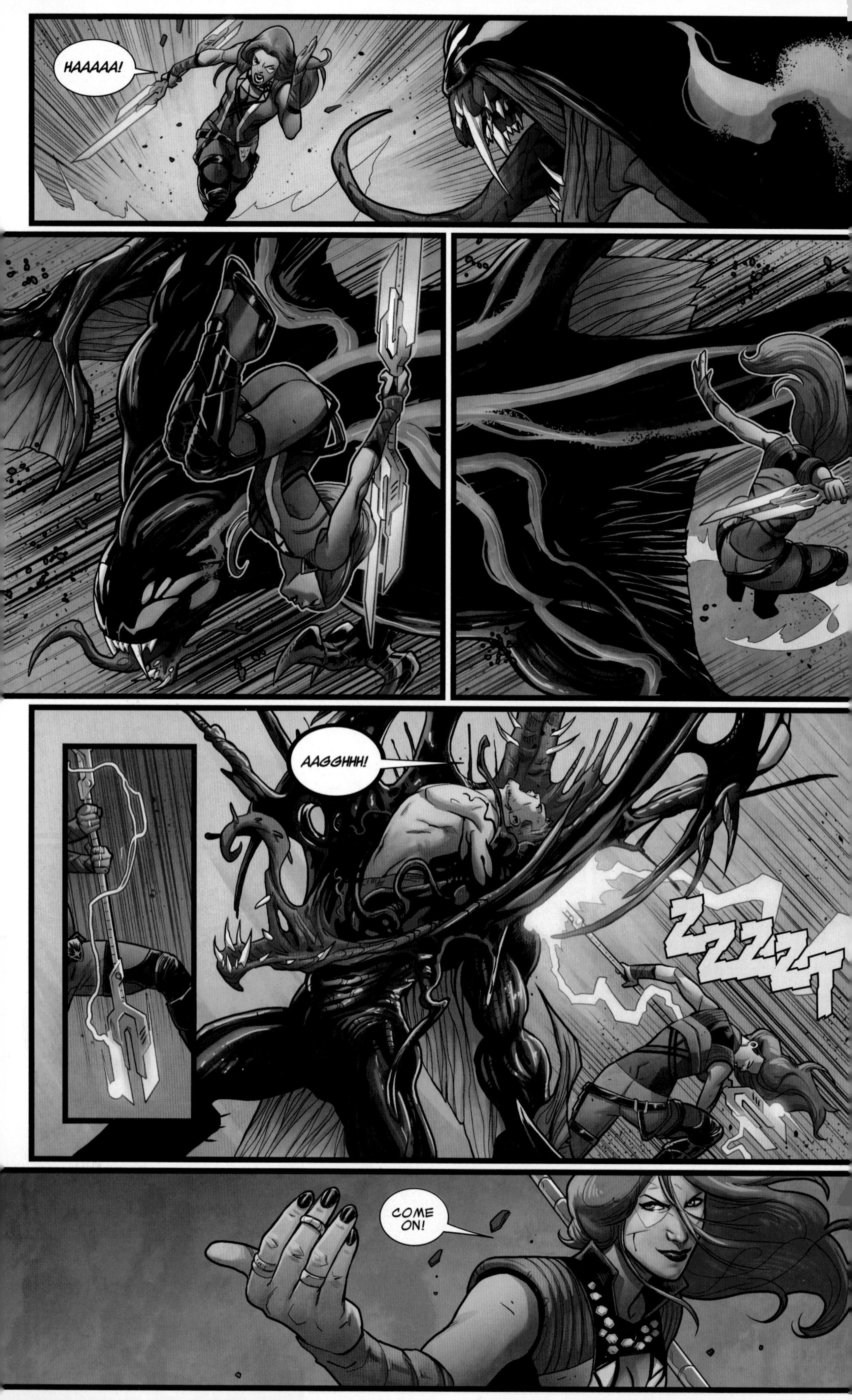
HAAAAA!
AAGGHHH!
ZZZZZT
COME ON!

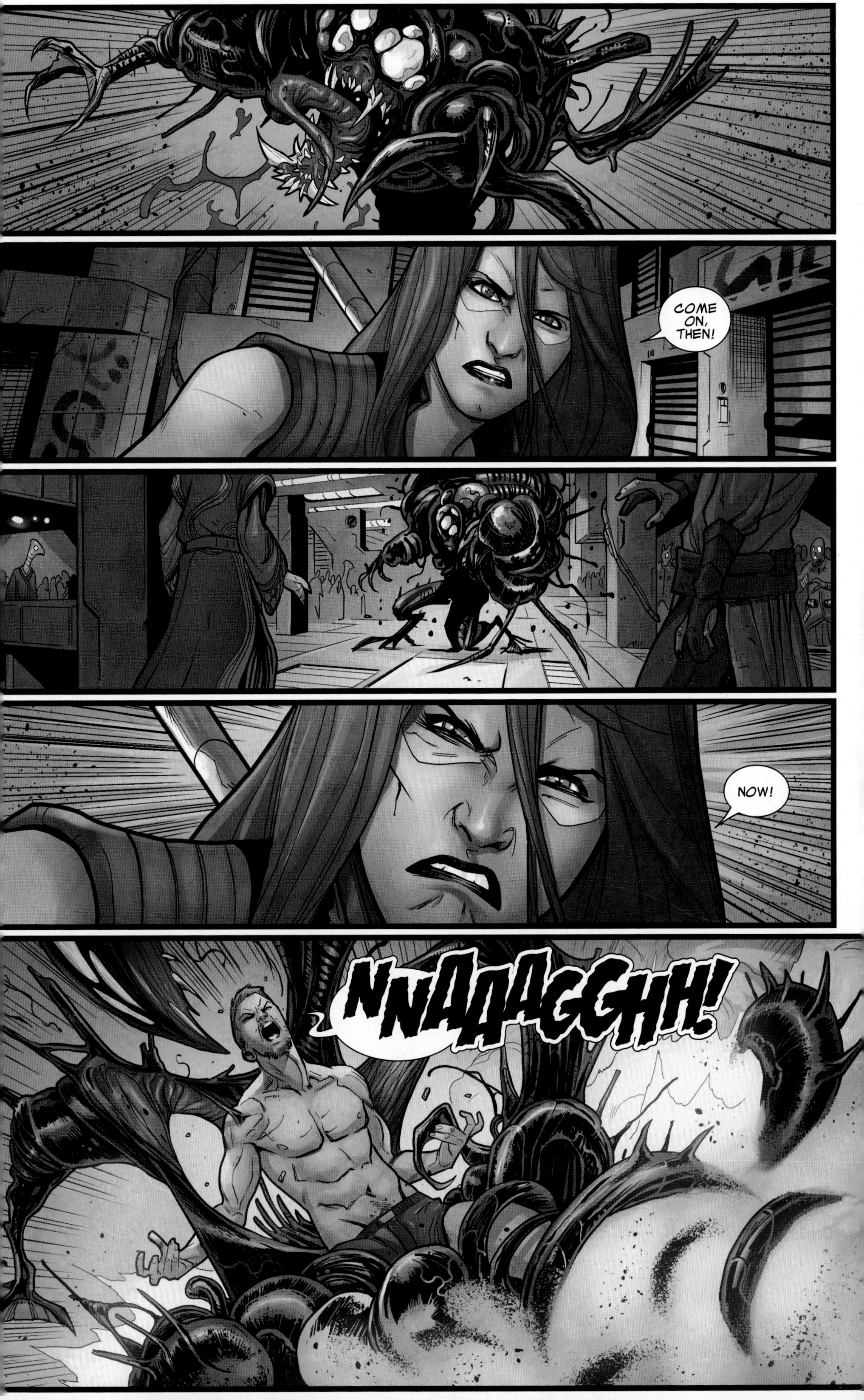
COME ON, THEN!
NOW!
NNAAAGGHH!

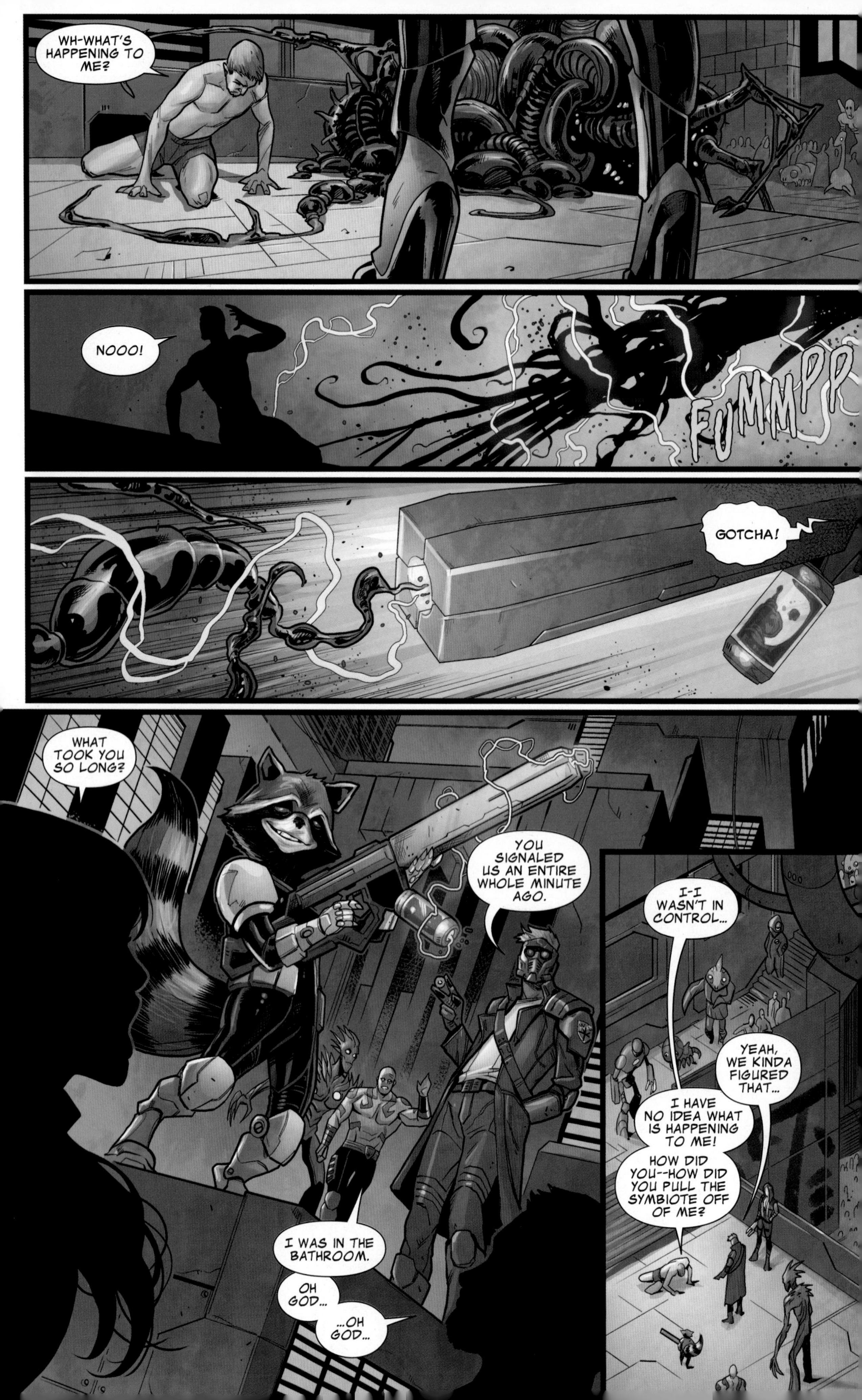
WH-WHAT'S HAPPENING TO ME?
NOOO!
FUMMPP
GOTCHA!
WHAT TOOK YOU SO LONG?
YOU SIGNALED US AN ENTIRE WHOLE MINUTE AGO.
I WAS IN THE BATHROOM.
OH GOD...
...OH GOD...
I-I WASN'T IN CONTROL...
YEAH, WE KINDA FIGURED THAT...
I HAVE NO IDEA WHAT IS HAPPENING TO ME!
HOW DID YOU--HOW DID YOU PULL THE SYMBIOTE OFF OF ME?

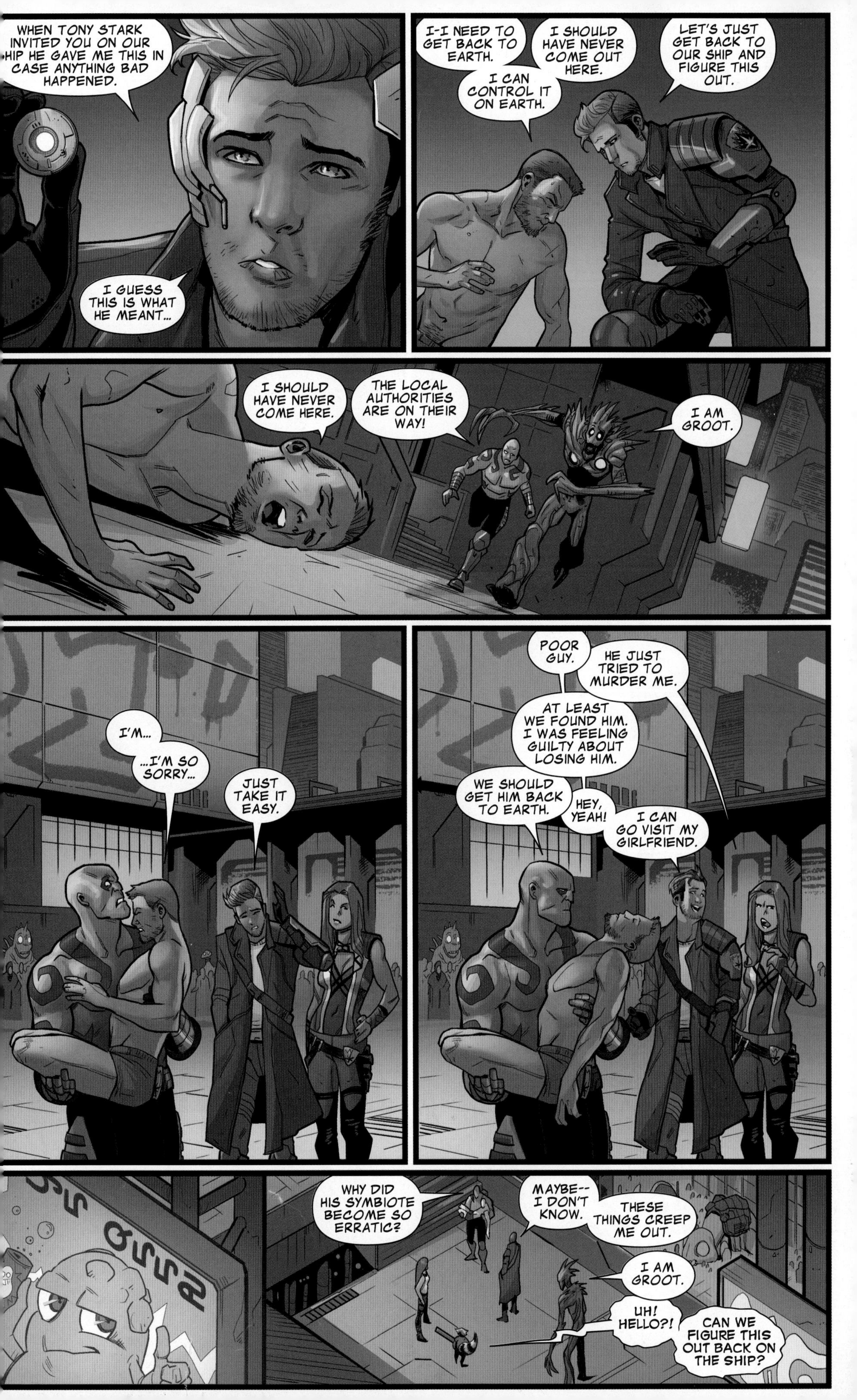
WHEN TONY STARK INVITED YOU ON OUR HIP HE GAVE ME THIS IN CASE ANYTHING BAD HAPPENED.
I GUESS THIS IS WHAT HE MEANT...
I-I NEED TO GET BACK TO EARTH.
I SHOULD HAVE NEVER COME OUT HERE.
I CAN CONTROL IT ON EARTH.
LET'S JUST GET BACK TO OUR SHIP AND FIGURE THIS OUT.
I SHOULD HAVE NEVER COME HERE.
THE LOCAL AUTHORITIES ARE ON THEIR WAY!
I AM GROOT.
I'M...
...I'M SO SORRY...
JUST TAKE IT EASY.
POOR GUY.
HE JUST TRIED TO MURDER ME.
AT LEAST WE FOUND HIM. I WAS FEELING GUILTY ABOUT LOSING HIM.
WE SHOULD GET HIM BACK TO EARTH.
HEY, YEAH!
I CAN GO VISIT MY GIRLFRIEND.
WHY DID HIS SYMBIOTE BECOME SO ERRATIC?
MAYBE-- I DON'T KNOW.
THESE THINGS CREEP ME OUT.
I AM GROOT.
UH! HELLO?!
CAN WE FIGURE THIS OUT BACK ON THE SHIP?

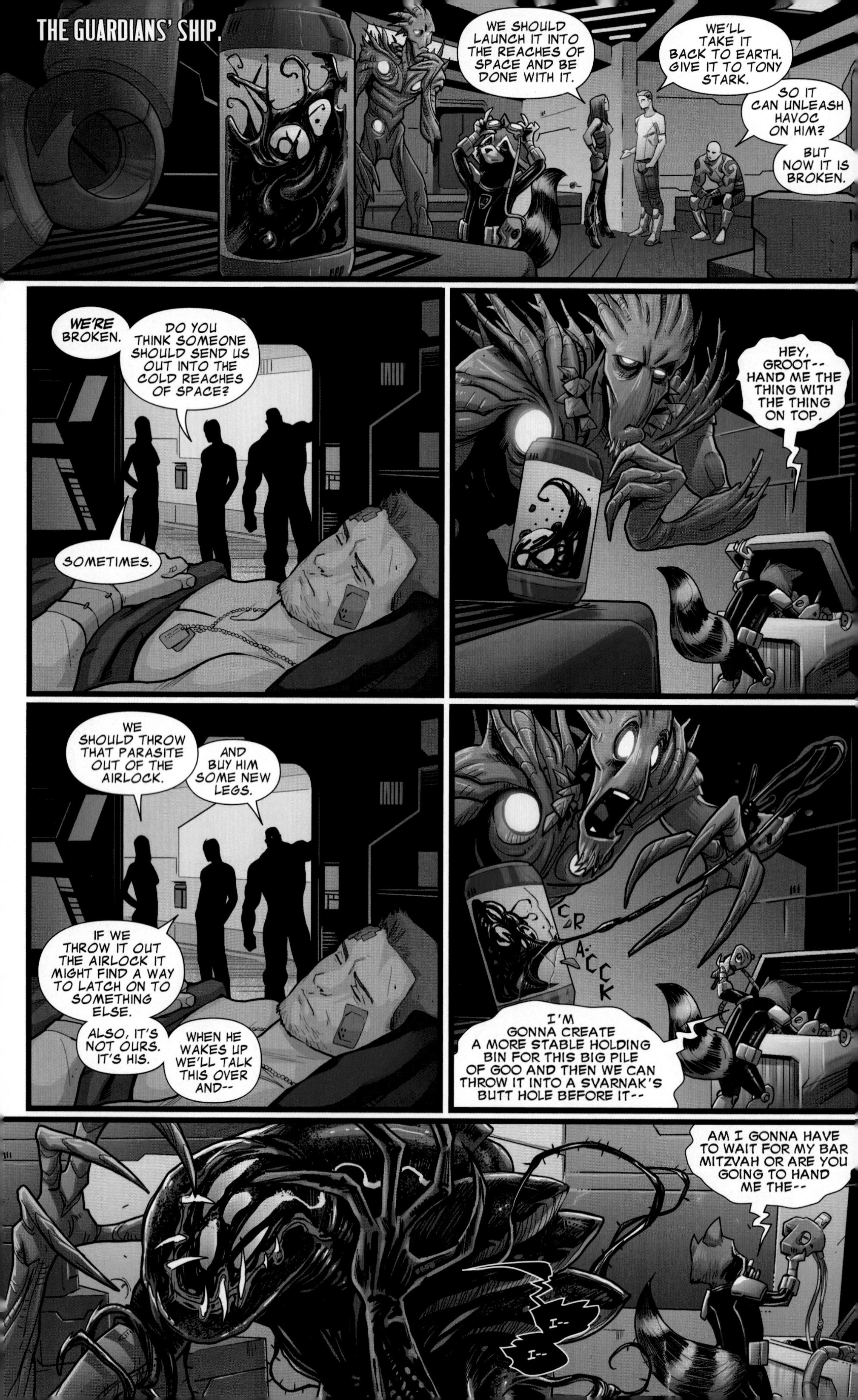
THE GUARDIANS' SHIP.
WE SHOULD LAUNCH IT INTO THE REACHES OF SPACE AND BE DONE WITH IT.
WE'LL TAKE IT BACK TO EARTH. GIVE IT TO TONY STARK.
SO IT CAN UNLEASH HAVOC ON HIM?
BUT NOW IT IS BROKEN.
WE'RE BROKEN.
DO YOU THINK SOMEONE SHOULD SEND US OUT INTO THE COLD REACHES OF SPACE?
SOMETIMES.
HEY, GROOT-- HAND ME THE THING WITH THE THING ON TOP.
WE SHOULD THROW THAT PARASITE OUT OF THE AIRLOCK.
AND BUY HIM SOME NEW LEGS.
IF WE THROW IT OUT THE AIRLOCK IT MIGHT FIND A WAY TO LATCH ON TO SOMETHING ELSE.
ALSO, IT'S NOT OURS. IT'S HIS.
WHEN HE WAKES UP WE'LL TALK THIS OVER AND--
CRACCK
I'M GONNA CREATE A MORE STABLE HOLDING BIN FOR THIS BIG PILE OF GOO AND THEN WE CAN THROW IT INTO A SVARNAK'S BUTT HOLE BEFORE IT--
AM I GONNA HAVE TO WAIT FOR MY BAR MITZVAH OR ARE YOU GOING TO HAND ME THE--
I--
I--

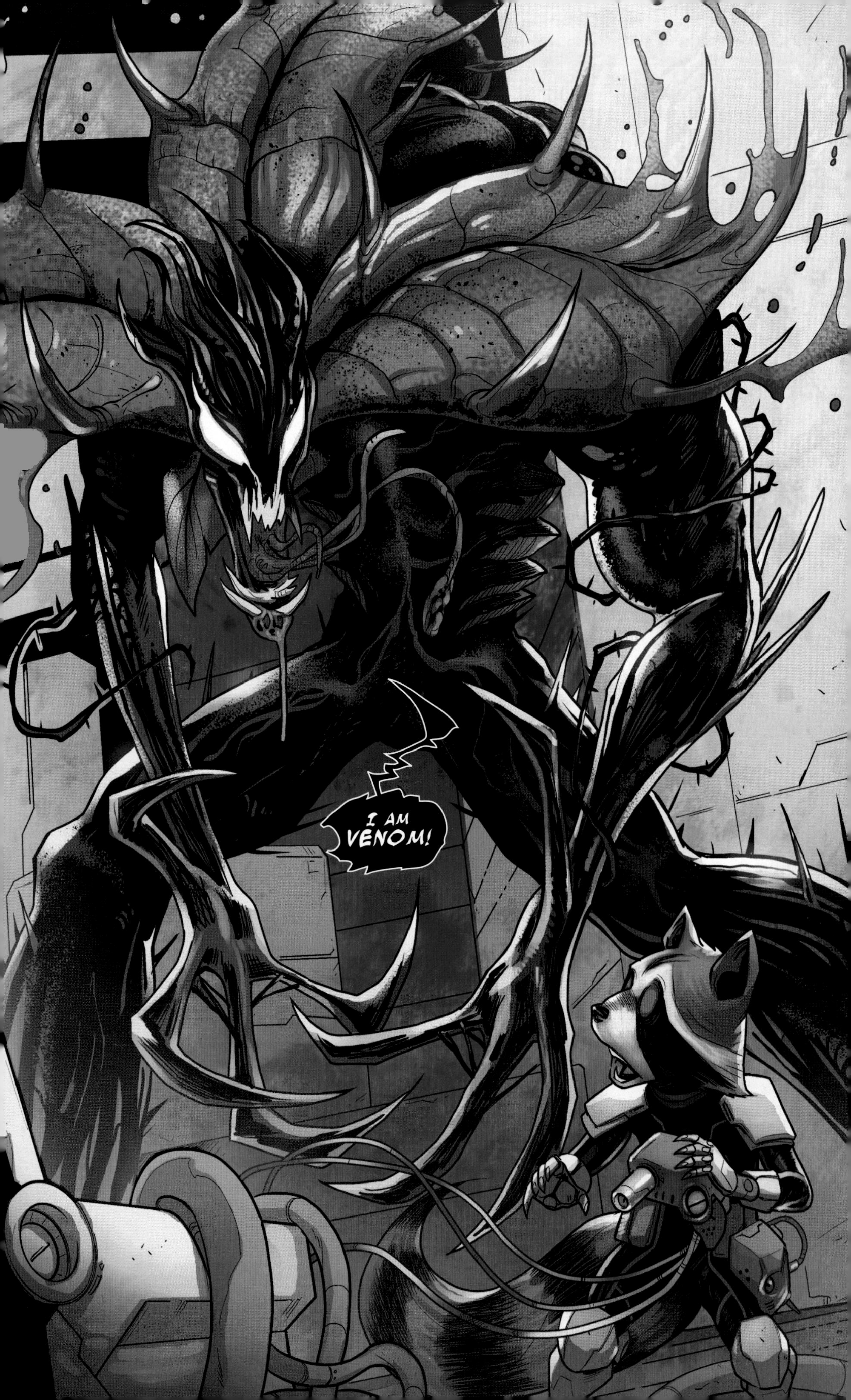
I AM VENOM!

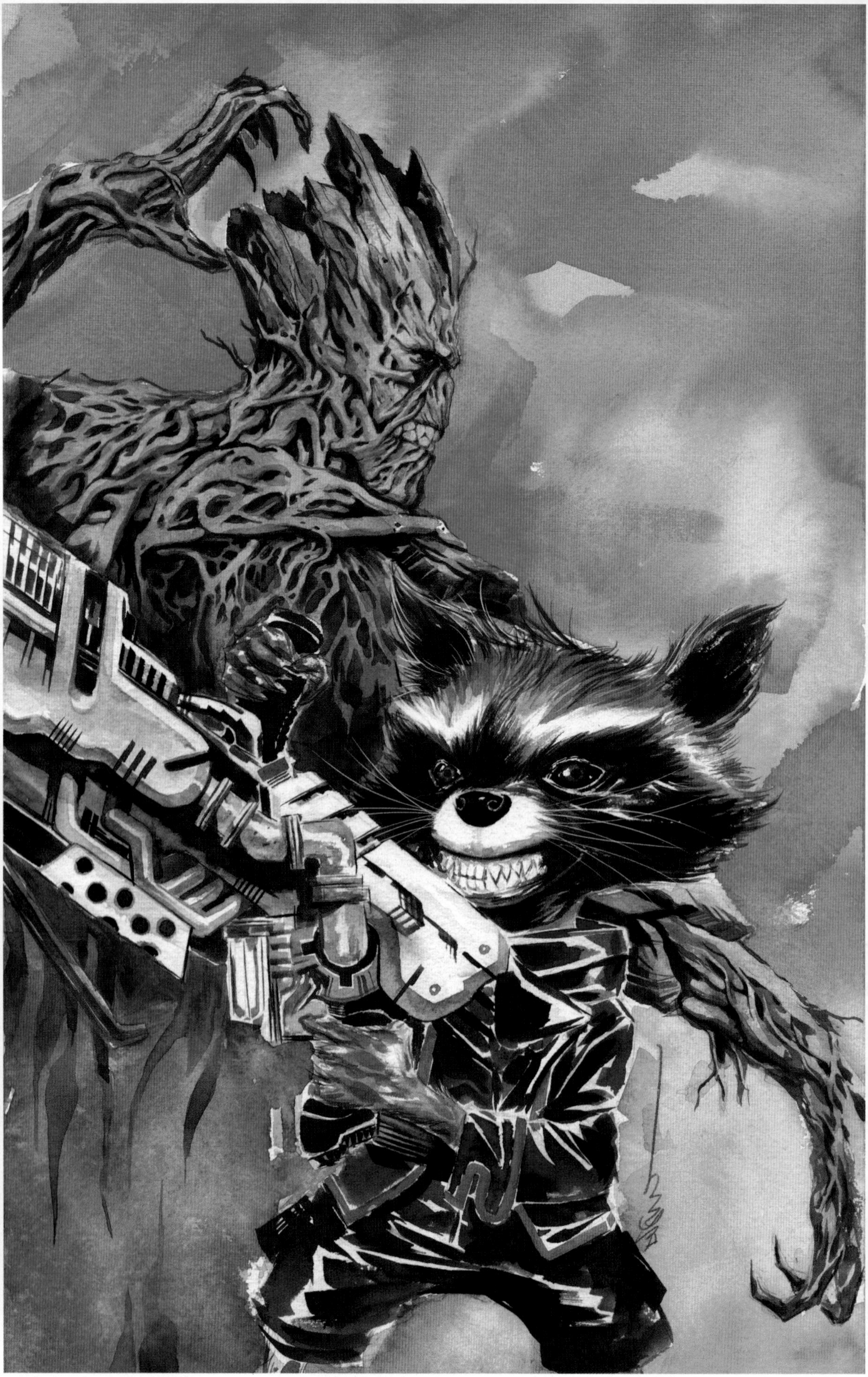

#21 ROCKET RACCOON & GROOT VARIANT BY DUSTIN NGUYEN

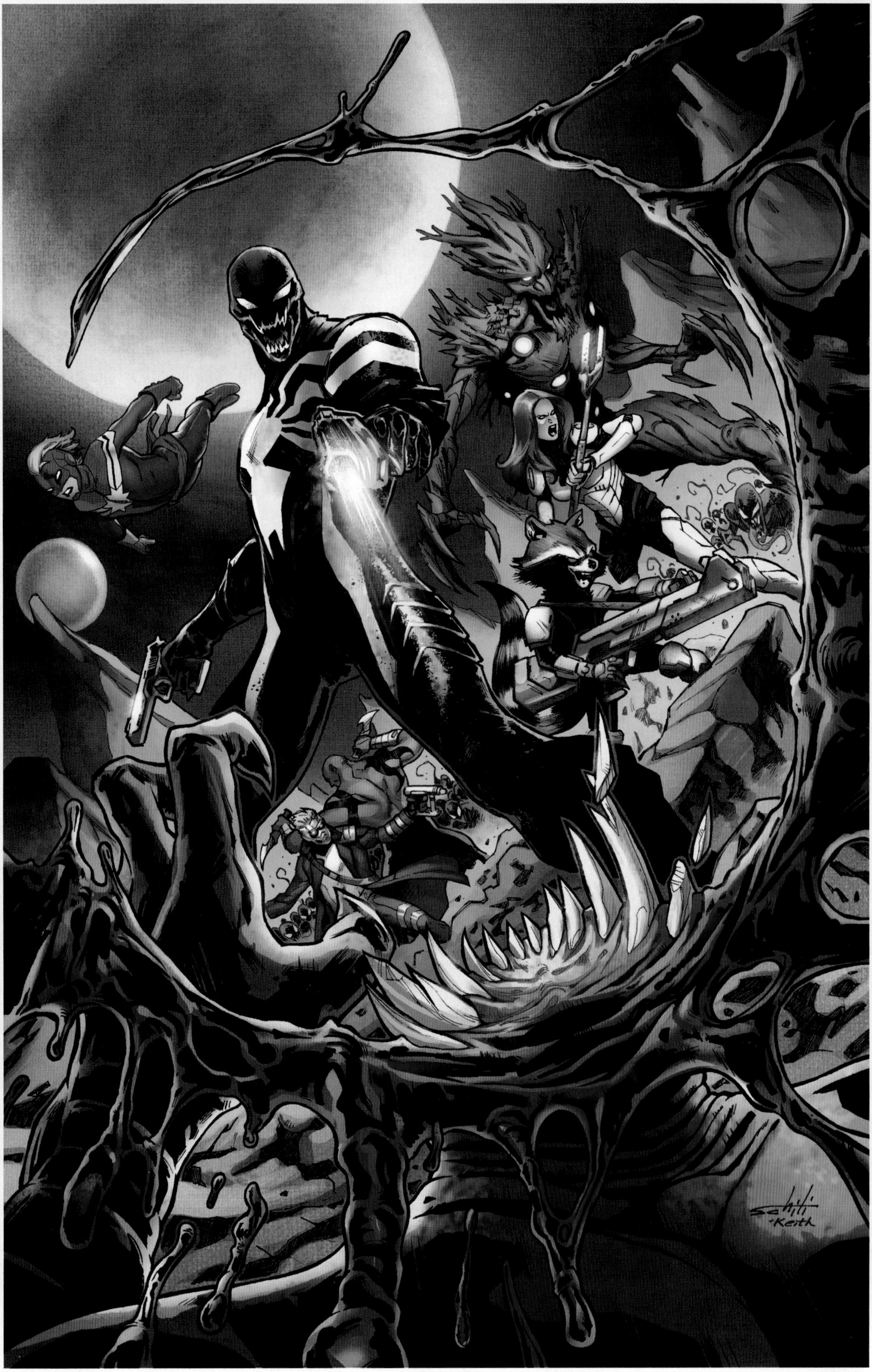
Schiti
+Keith

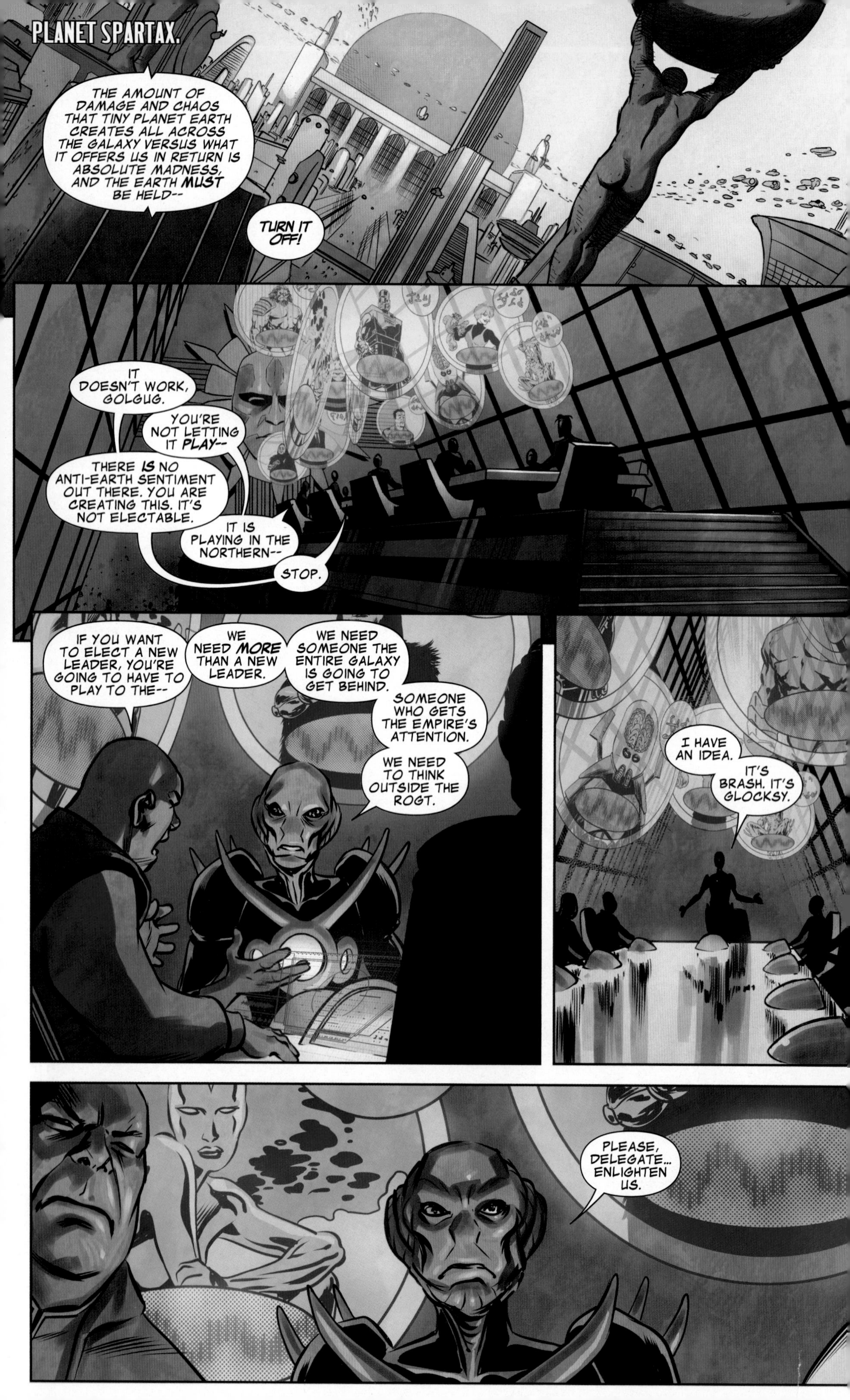
PLANET SPARTAX.
THE AMOUNT OF DAMAGE AND CHAOS THAT TINY PLANET EARTH CREATES ALL ACROSS THE GALAXY VERSUS WHAT IT OFFERS US IN RETURN IS ABSOLUTE MADNESS, AND THE EARTH MUST BE HELD--
TURN IT OFF!
IT DOESN'T WORK, GOLGUG.
YOU'RE NOT LETTING IT PLAY--
THERE IS NO ANTI-EARTH SENTIMENT OUT THERE. YOU ARE CREATING THIS. IT'S NOT ELECTABLE.
IT IS PLAYING IN THE NORTHERN--
STOP.
IF YOU WANT TO ELECT A NEW LEADER, YOU'RE GOING TO HAVE TO PLAY TO THE--
WE NEED MORE THAN A NEW LEADER.
WE NEED SOMEONE THE ENTIRE GALAXY IS GOING TO GET BEHIND.
SOMEONE WHO GETS THE EMPIRE'S ATTENTION.
WE NEED TO THINK OUTSIDE THE ROGT.
I HAVE AN IDEA.
IT'S BRASH. IT'S GLOCKSY.
PLEASE, DELEGATE... ENLIGHTEN US.

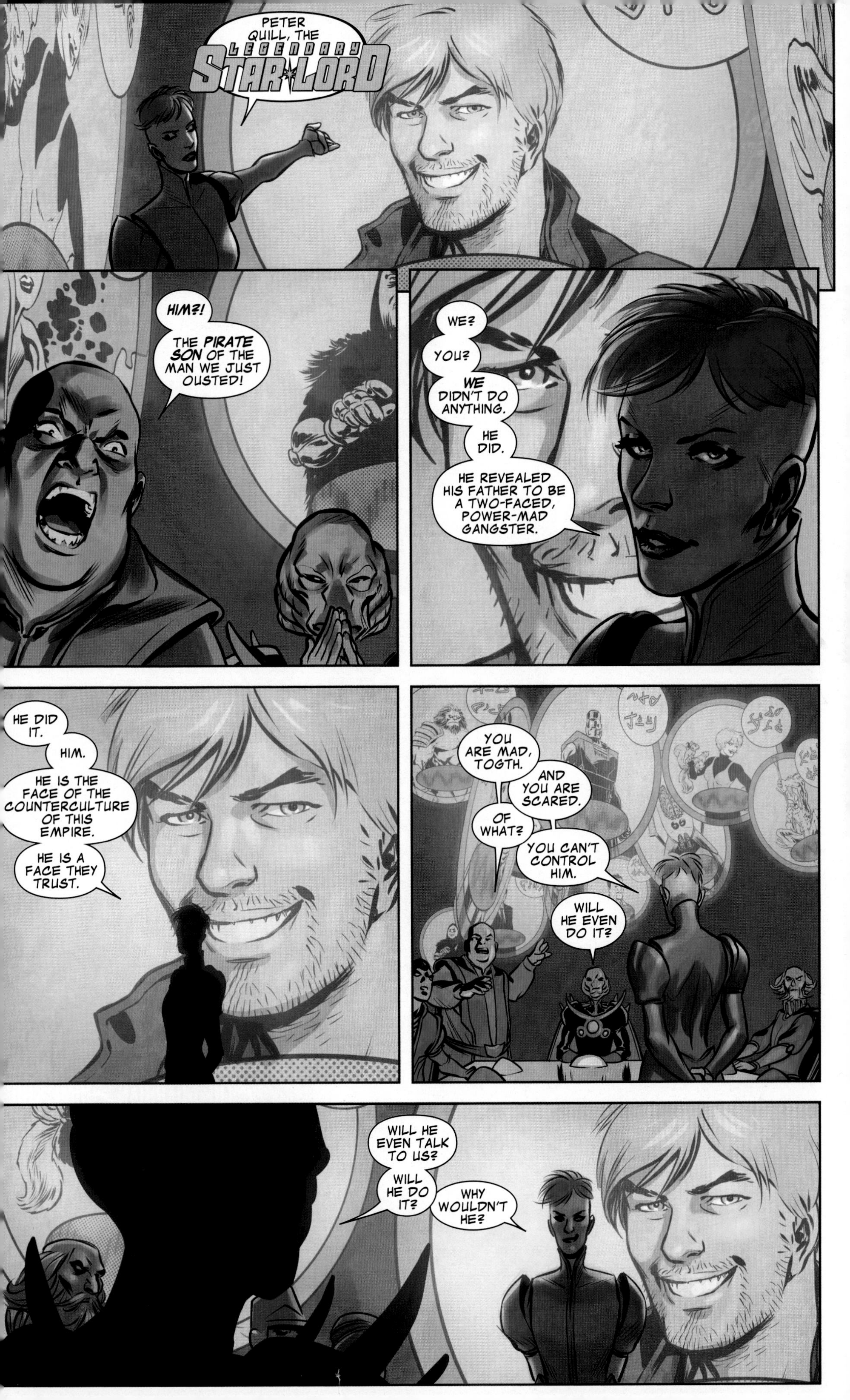
PETER QUILL, THE LEGENDARY STAR-LORD
HIM?!
THE PIRATE SON OF THE MAN WE JUST OUSTED!
WE?
YOU?
WE DIDN'T DO ANYTHING.
HE DID.
HE REVEALED HIS FATHER TO BE A TWO-FACED, POWER-MAD GANGSTER.
HE DID IT.
HIM.
HE IS THE FACE OF THE COUNTERCULTURE OF THIS EMPIRE.
HE IS A FACE THEY TRUST.
YOU ARE MAD, TOGTH.
AND YOU ARE SCARED.
OF WHAT?
YOU CAN'T CONTROL HIM.
WILL HE EVEN DO IT?
WILL HE EVEN TALK TO US?
WILL HE DO IT?
WHY WOULDN'T HE?

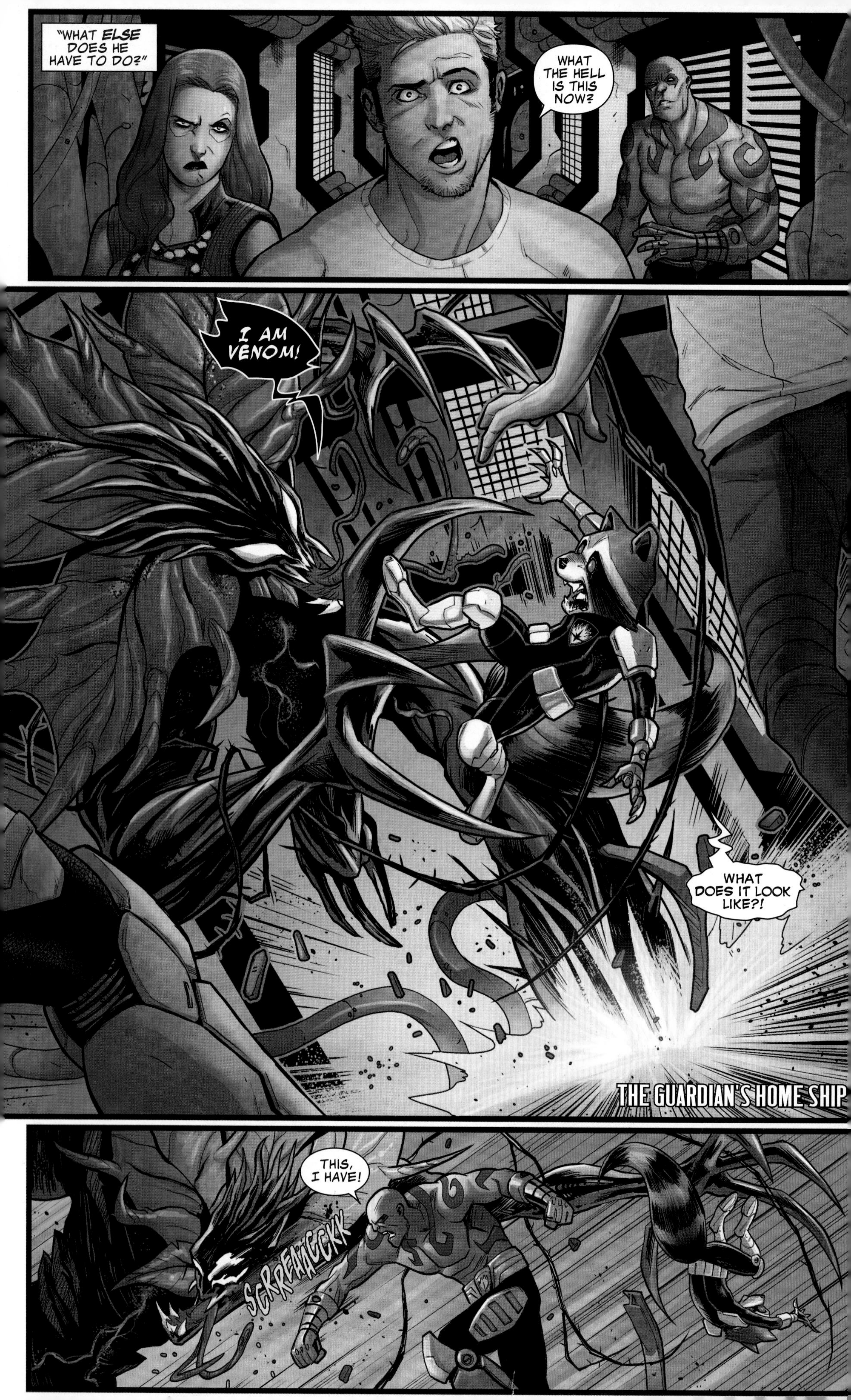
"WHAT ELSE DOES HE HAVE TO DO?"
WHAT THE HELL IS THIS NOW?
I AM VENOM!
WHAT DOES IT LOOK LIKE?!
THE GUARDIAN'S HOME SHIP
THIS, I HAVE!
SCRREAACCKK

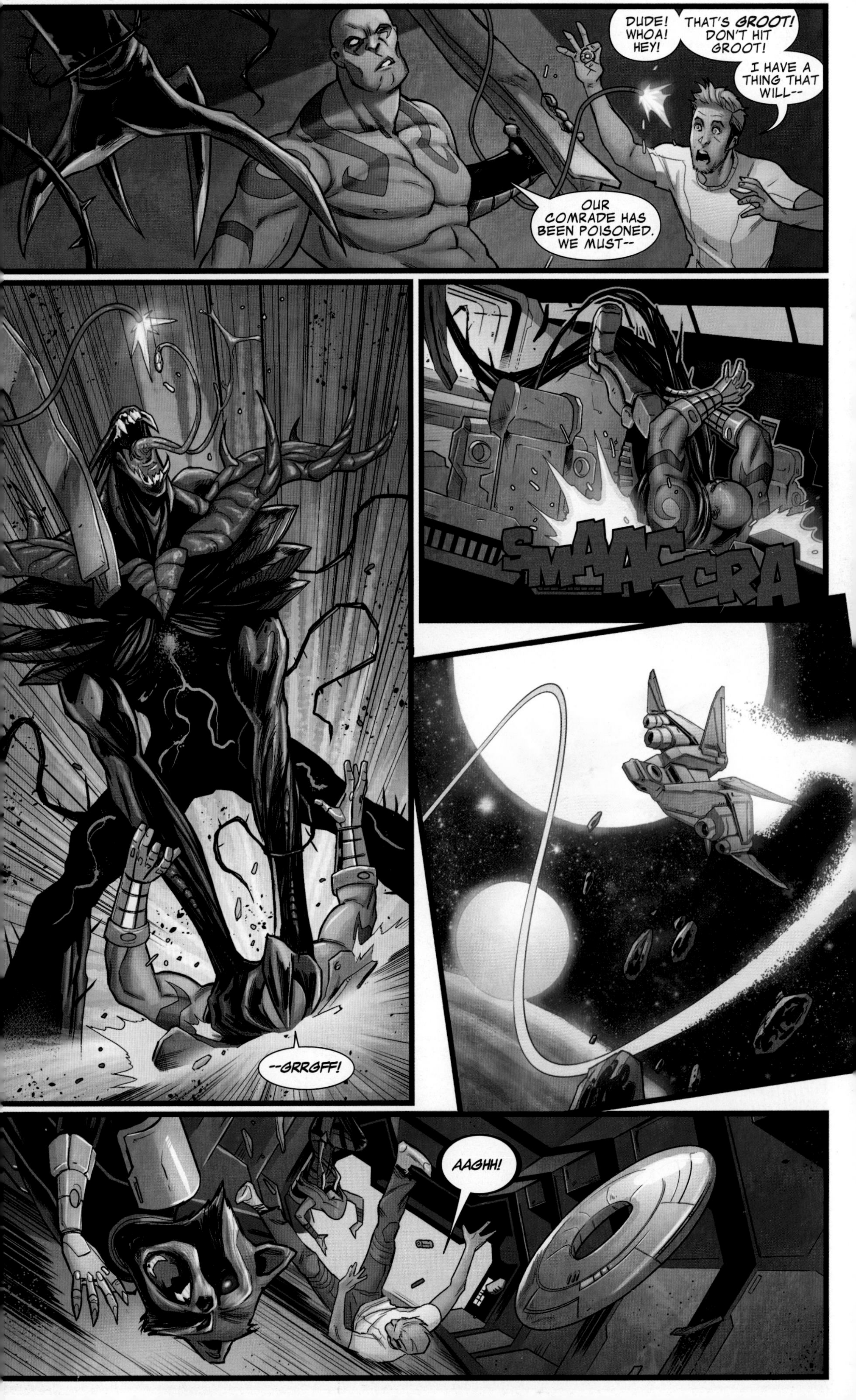
DUDE! WHOA! HEY!
THAT'S GROOT! DON'T HIT GROOT!
I HAVE A THING THAT WILL--
OUR COMRADE HAS BEEN POISONED. WE MUST--
SMAAK
CRA
--GRRGFF!
AAGHH!

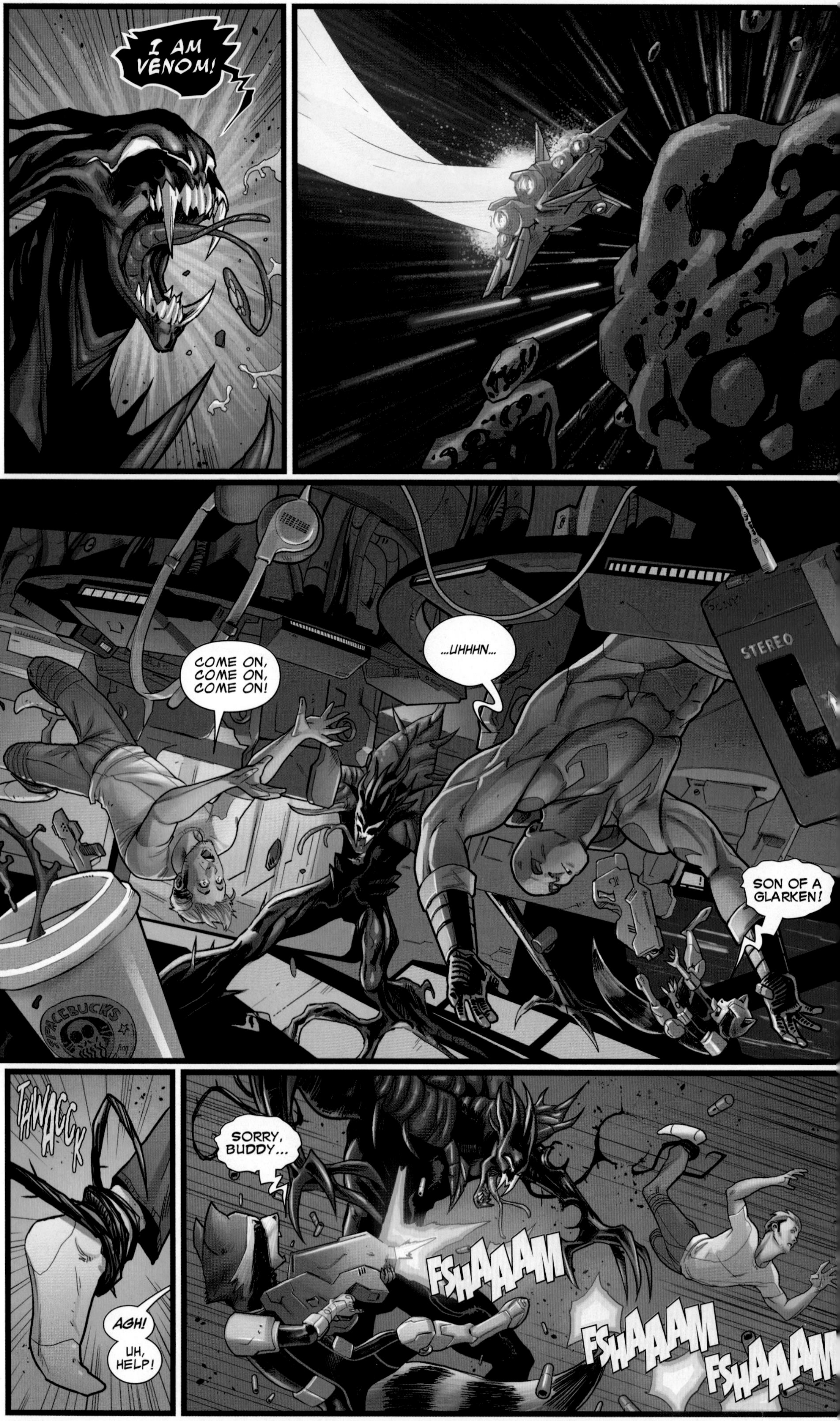
I AM VENOM!
COME ON, COME ON, COME ON!
...UHHHN...
STEREO
SON OF A GLARKEN!
SPACEBUCKS
THWACCK
AGH!
UH, HELP!
SORRY, BUDDY...
FSHAAAM
FSHAAAM
FSHAAAM

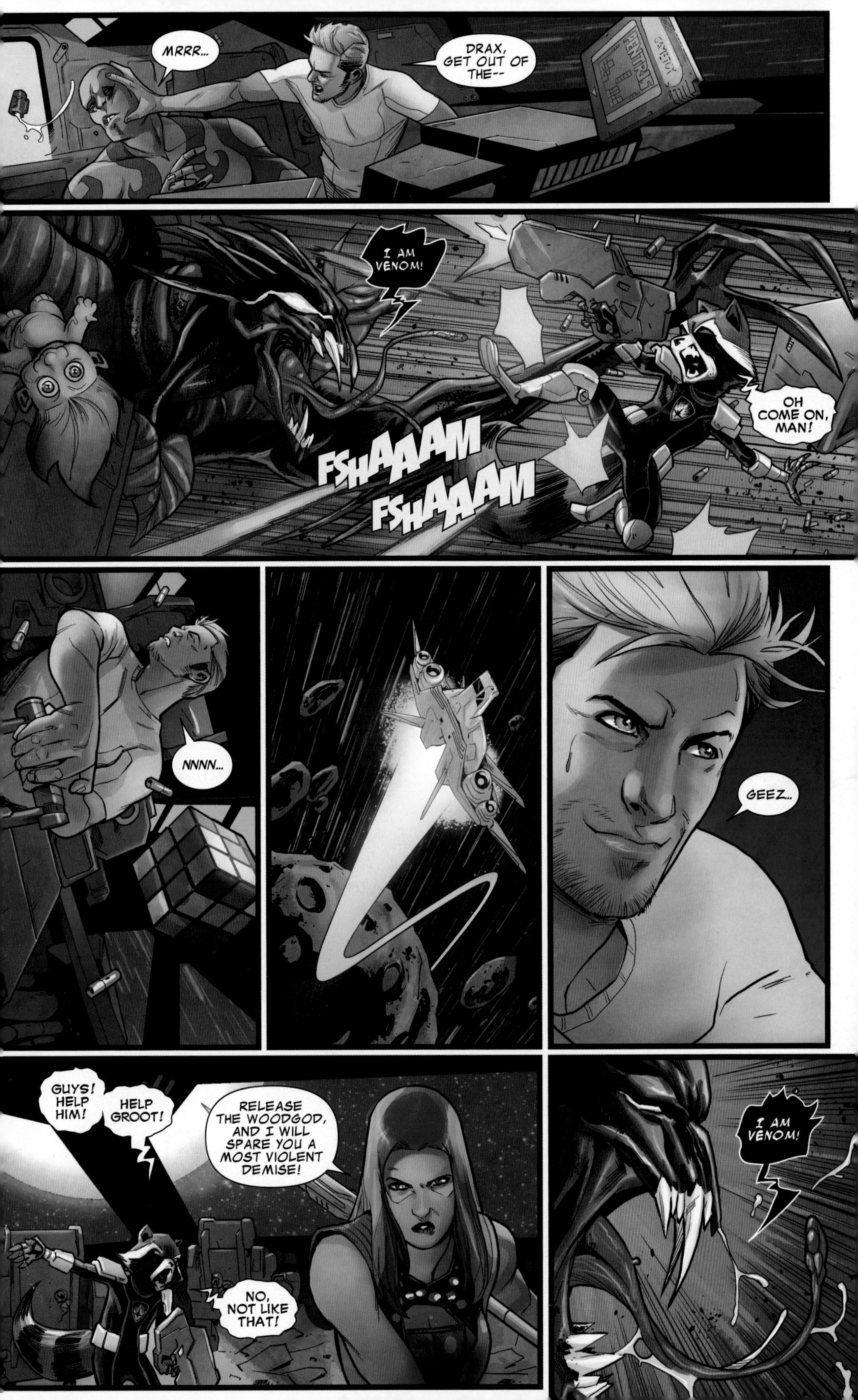
MRRR...
DRAX, GET OUT OF THE--
I AM VENOM!
OH COME ON, MAN!
FSHAAAM
FSHAAAM
NNNN...
GEEZ...
GUYS! HELP HIM!
HELP GROOT!
RELEASE THE WOODGOD, AND I WILL SPARE YOU A MOST VIOLENT DEMISE!
NO, NOT LIKE THAT!
I AM VENOM!

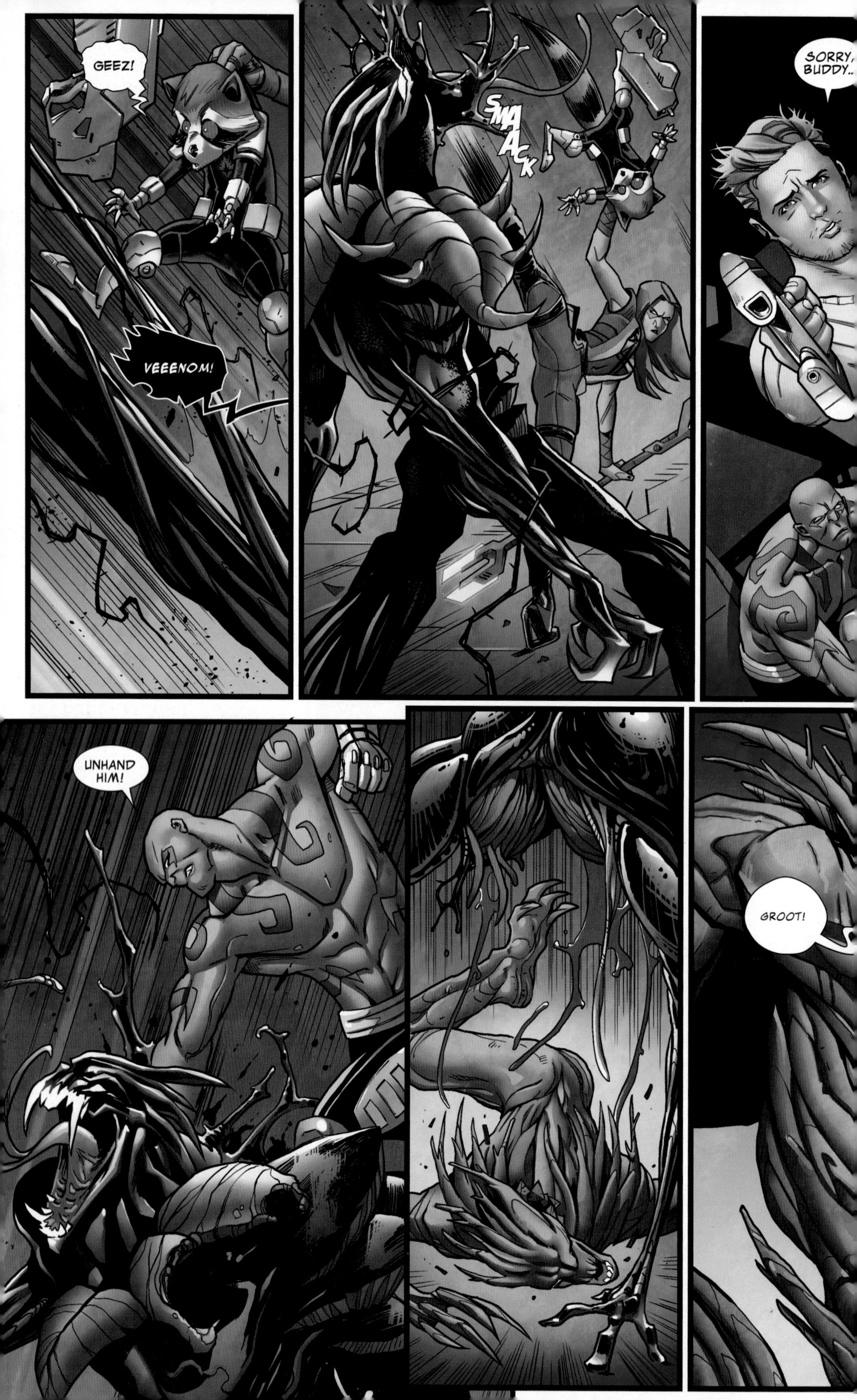
GEEZ!
VEEENOM!
SMAACK
SORRY, BUDDY...
UNHAND HIM!
GROOT!

FSHAAAM

YAAAAGROOOOOT!

FSHAAAM FSHAAAM FSHAAAM FSHAAAM

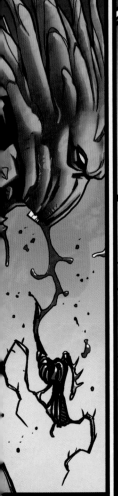

UH, GUYS...

GET AWAY FROM THE SYMBIOTE, ROCKET!

UH, GUYS?!

UH, GUYS?!

FURTRACK YOU!

FSHAAAM

FSHAAAM

FSHAAAM

I AM GROOT!

EASY!

YEAH!

YOU LIKE THAT?!

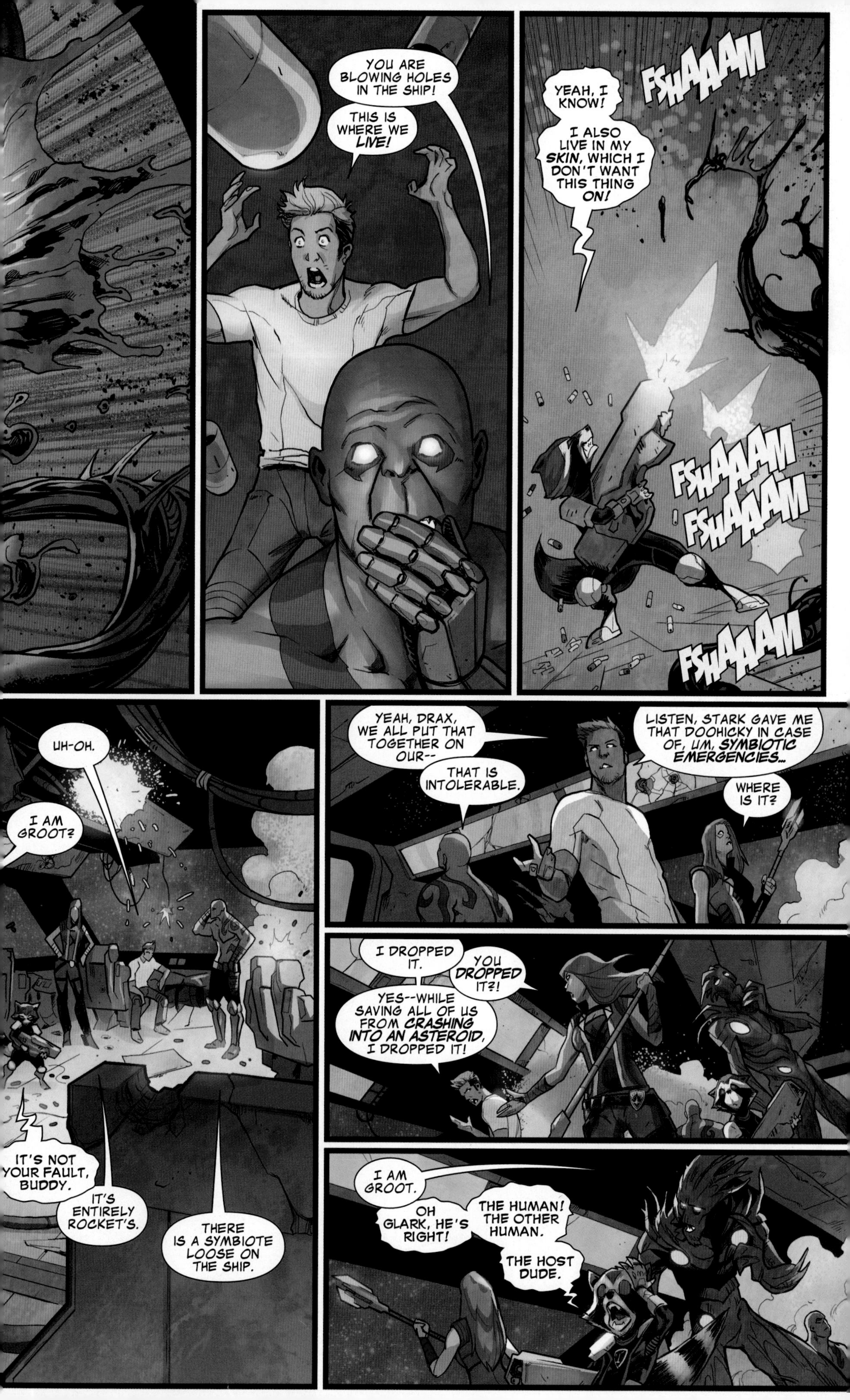
YOU ARE BLOWING HOLES IN THE SHIP!
THIS IS WHERE WE *LIVE!*
FSHAAAM
YEAH, I KNOW!
I ALSO LIVE IN MY *SKIN*, WHICH I DON'T WANT THIS THING *ON!*
FSHAAAM
FSHAAAM
FSHAAAM
UH-OH.
I AM GROOT?
IT'S NOT YOUR FAULT, BUDDY.
IT'S ENTIRELY ROCKET'S.
THERE IS A SYMBIOTE LOOSE ON THE SHIP.
YEAH, DRAX, WE ALL PUT THAT TOGETHER ON OUR--
THAT IS INTOLERABLE.
LISTEN, STARK GAVE ME THAT DOOHICKY IN CASE OF, UM, *SYMBIOTIC EMERGENCIES...*
WHERE IS IT?
I DROPPED IT.
YOU *DROPPED* IT?!
YES--WHILE SAVING ALL OF US FROM *CRASHING INTO AN ASTEROID*, I DROPPED IT!
I AM GROOT.
OH GLARK, HE'S RIGHT!
THE HUMAN! THE OTHER HUMAN.
THE HOST DUDE.

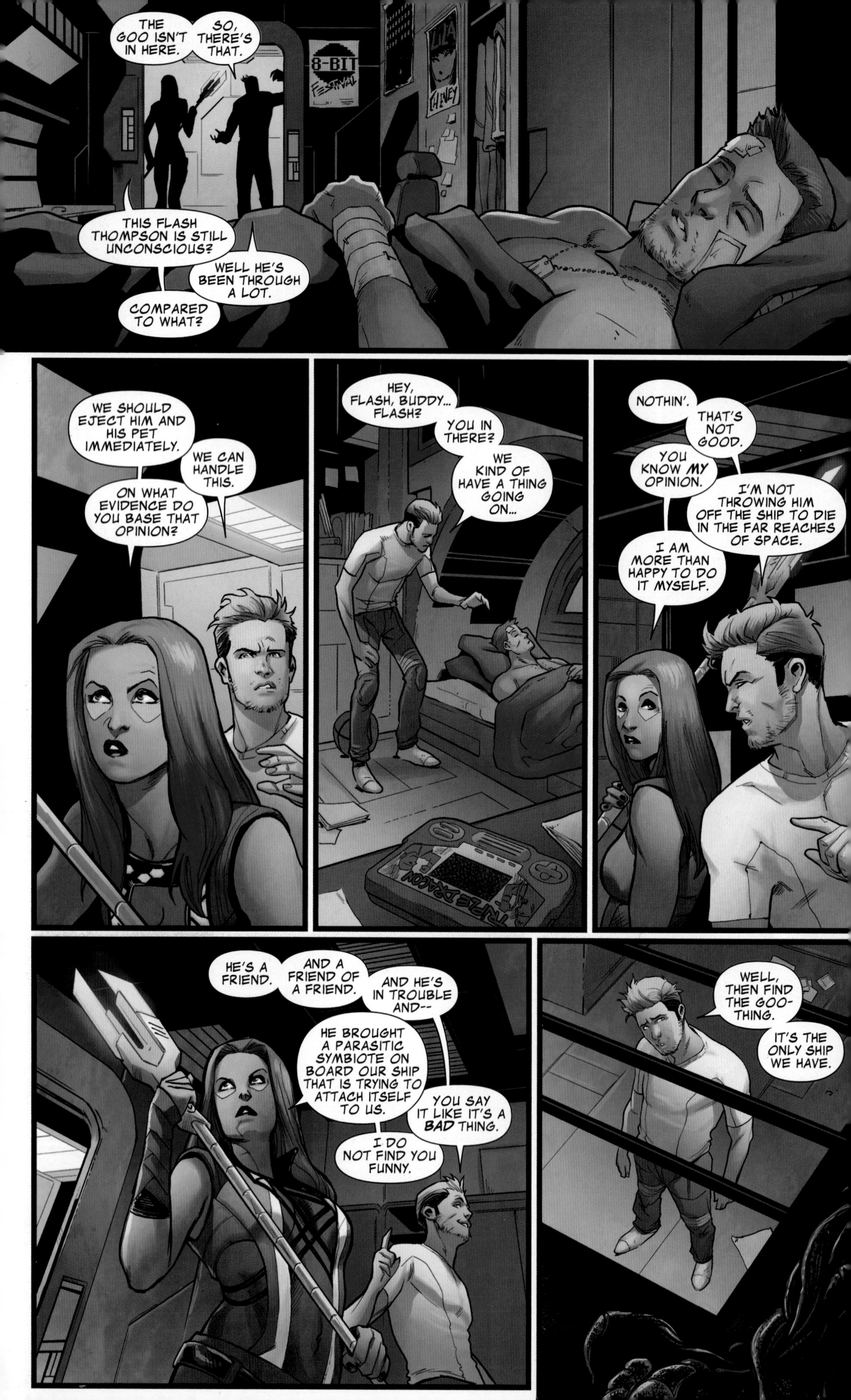
THE GOO ISN'T IN HERE.
SO, THERE'S THAT.
8-BIT FESTIVAL
THIS FLASH THOMPSON IS STILL UNCONSCIOUS?
WELL HE'S BEEN THROUGH A LOT.
COMPARED TO WHAT?
WE SHOULD EJECT HIM AND HIS PET IMMEDIATELY.
WE CAN HANDLE THIS.
ON WHAT EVIDENCE DO YOU BASE THAT OPINION?
HEY, FLASH, BUDDY... FLASH?
YOU IN THERE?
WE KIND OF HAVE A THING GOING ON...
TRIPLE DRAGON
NOTHIN'.
THAT'S NOT GOOD.
YOU KNOW MY OPINION.
I'M NOT THROWING HIM OFF THE SHIP TO DIE IN THE FAR REACHES OF SPACE.
I AM MORE THAN HAPPY TO DO IT MYSELF.
HE'S A FRIEND.
AND A FRIEND OF A FRIEND.
AND HE'S IN TROUBLE AND--
HE BROUGHT A PARASITIC SYMBIOTE ON BOARD OUR SHIP THAT IS TRYING TO ATTACH ITSELF TO US.
YOU SAY IT LIKE IT'S A BAD THING.
I DO NOT FIND YOU FUNNY.
WELL, THEN FIND THE GOO-THING.
IT'S THE ONLY SHIP WE HAVE.

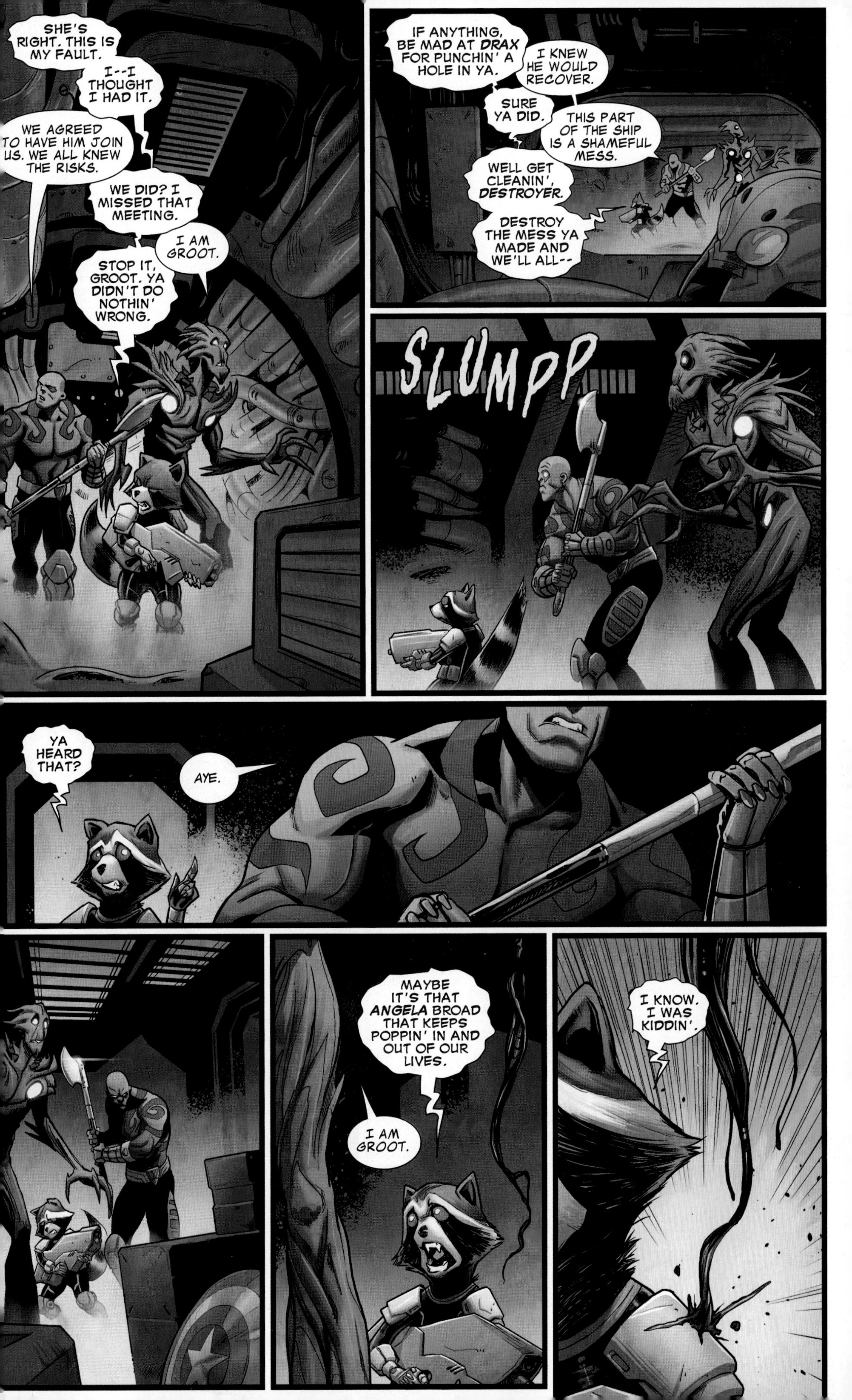
SHE'S RIGHT. THIS IS MY FAULT.
I--I THOUGHT I HAD IT.
WE AGREED TO HAVE HIM JOIN US. WE ALL KNEW THE RISKS.
WE DID? I MISSED THAT MEETING.
I AM GROOT.
STOP IT, GROOT. YA DIDN'T DO NOTHIN' WRONG.
IF ANYTHING, BE MAD AT DRAX FOR PUNCHIN' A HOLE IN YA.
I KNEW HE WOULD RECOVER.
SURE YA DID.
THIS PART OF THE SHIP IS A SHAMEFUL MESS.
WELL GET CLEANIN', DESTROYER.
DESTROY THE MESS YA MADE AND WE'LL ALL--
SLUMPP
YA HEARD THAT?
AYE.
MAYBE IT'S THAT ANGELA BROAD THAT KEEPS POPPIN' IN AND OUT OF OUR LIVES.
I AM GROOT.
I KNOW. I WAS KIDDIN'.

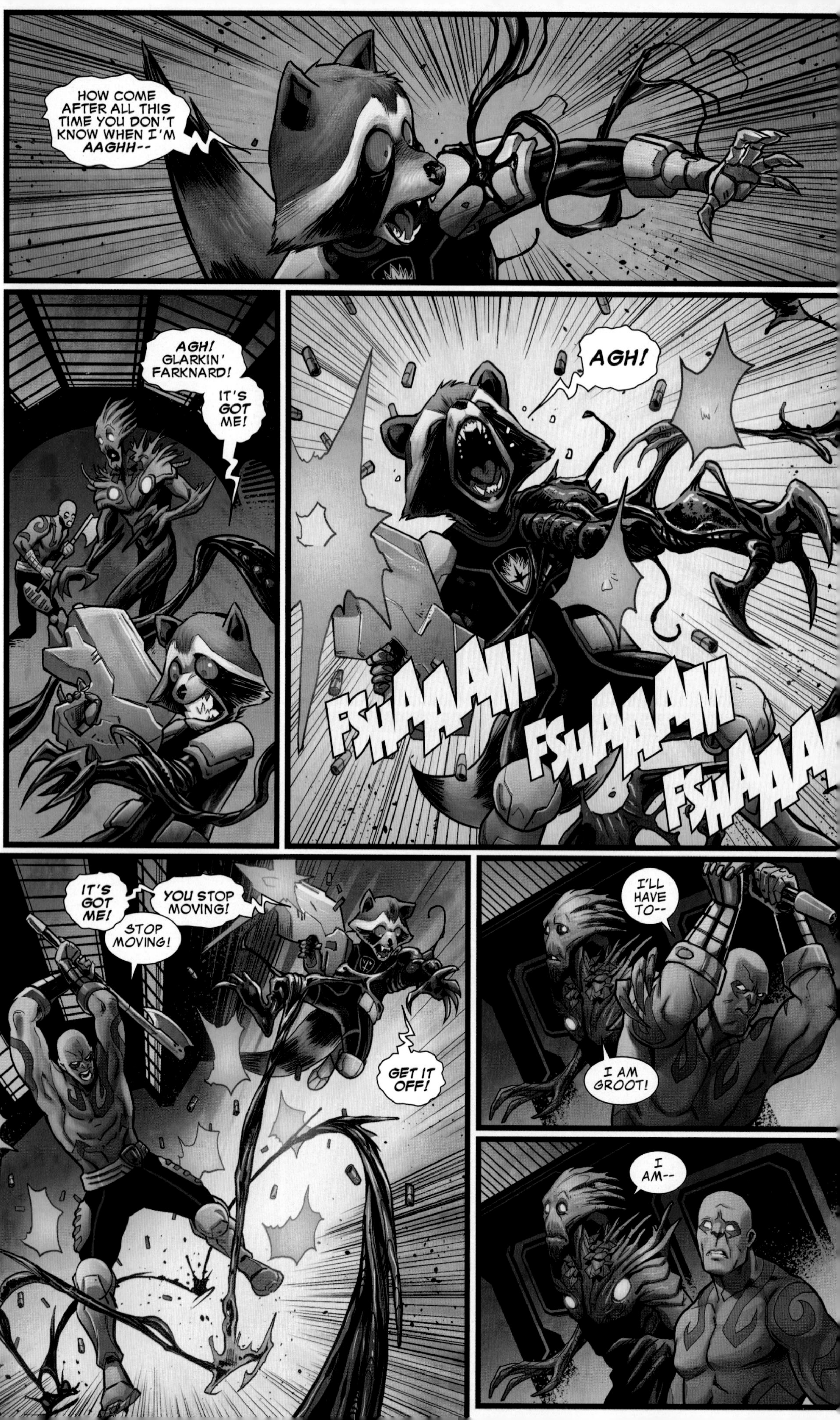
HOW COME AFTER ALL THIS TIME YOU DON'T KNOW WHEN I'M AAGHH--
AGH! GLARKIN' FARKNARD!
IT'S GOT ME!
AGH!
FSHAAAAM
FSHAAAAM
IT'S GOT ME!
YOU STOP MOVING!
STOP MOVING!
GET IT OFF!
I'LL HAVE TO--
I AM GROOT!
I AM--

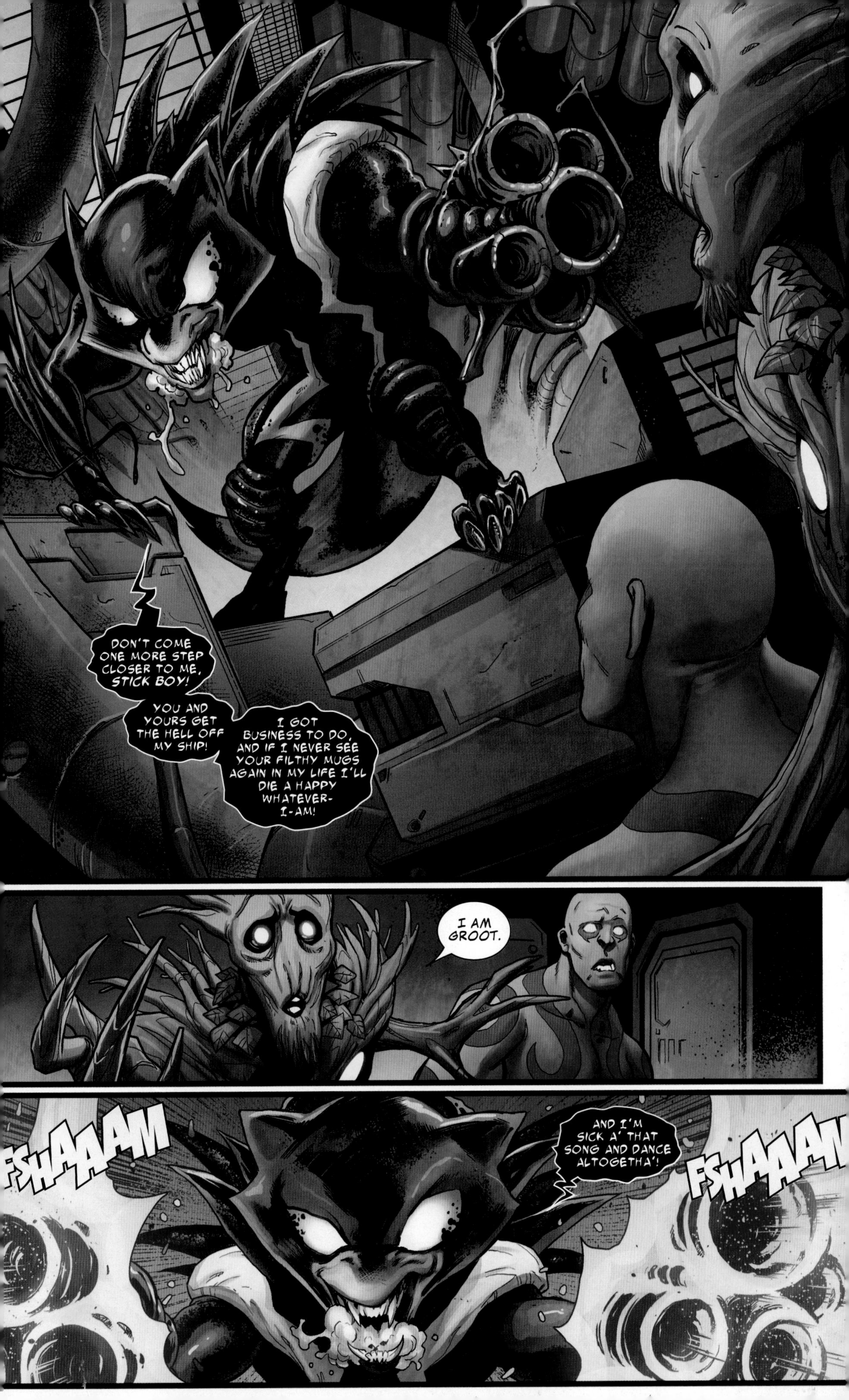
DON'T COME ONE MORE STEP CLOSER TO ME, STICK BOY!
YOU AND YOURS GET THE HELL OFF MY SHIP!
I GOT BUSINESS TO DO, AND IF I NEVER SEE YOUR FILTHY MUGS AGAIN IN MY LIFE I'LL DIE A HAPPY WHATEVER-I-AM!
I AM GROOT.
FSHAAAM
AND I'M SICK A' THAT SONG AND DANCE ALTOGETHA'!
FSHAAAM

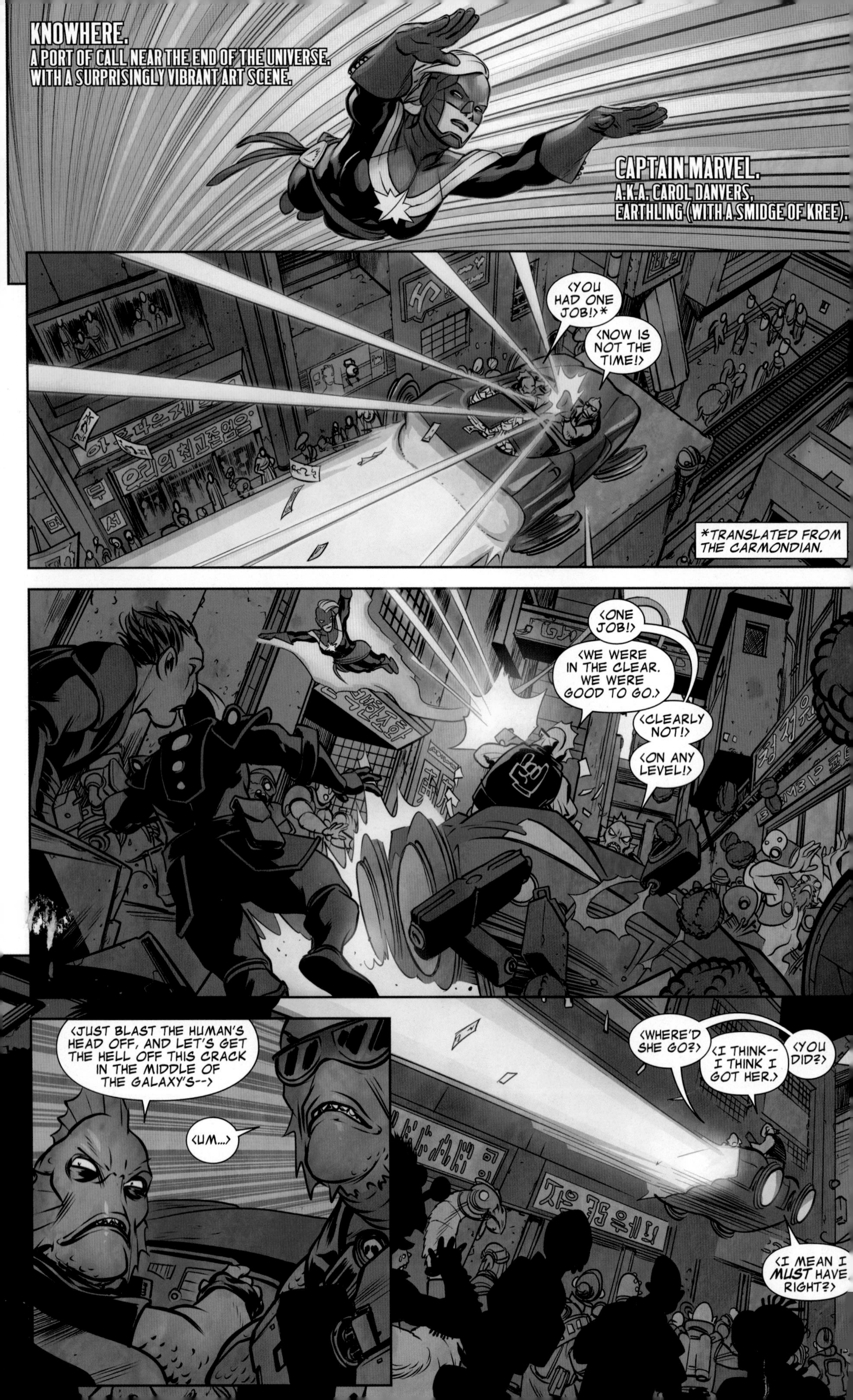
KNOWHERE.
A PORT OF CALL NEAR THE END OF THE UNIVERSE. WITH A SURPRISINGLY VIBRANT ART SCENE.
CAPTAIN MARVEL.
A.K.A. CAROL DANVERS, EARTHLING (WITH A SMIDGE OF KREE).
<YOU HAD ONE JOB!>*
<NOW IS NOT THE TIME!>
*TRANSLATED FROM THE CARMONDIAN.
<ONE JOB!>
<WE WERE IN THE CLEAR. WE WERE GOOD TO GO.>
<CLEARLY NOT!>
<ON ANY LEVEL!>
<JUST BLAST THE HUMAN'S HEAD OFF, AND LET'S GET THE HELL OFF THIS CRACK IN THE MIDDLE OF THE GALAXY'S-->
<UM...>
<WHERE'D SHE GO?>
<I THINK-- I THINK I GOT HER.>
<YOU DID?>
<I MEAN I MUST HAVE, RIGHT?>

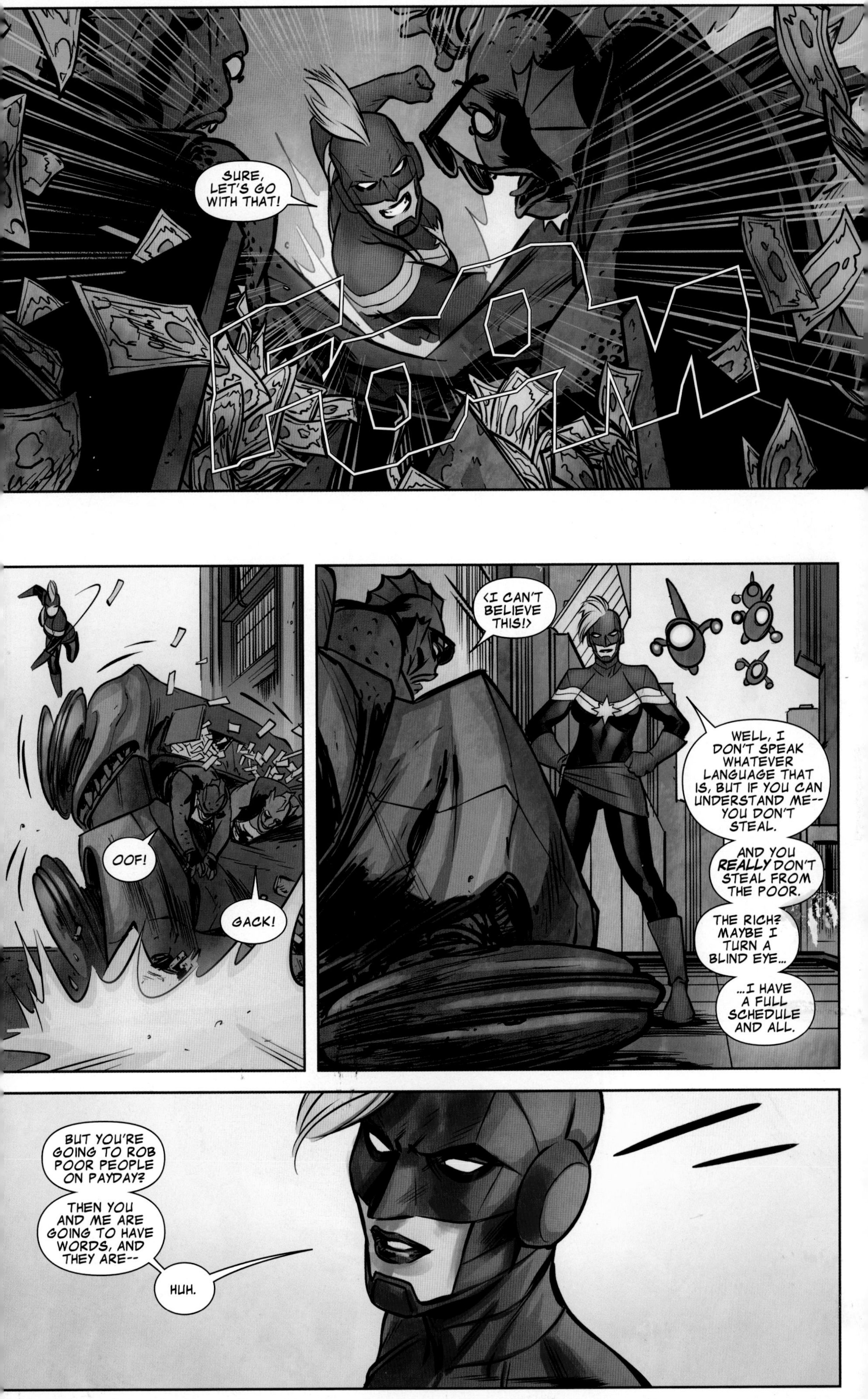
SURE, LET'S GO WITH THAT!
FOOM
OOF!
GACK!
<I CAN'T BELIEVE THIS!>
WELL, I DON'T SPEAK WHATEVER LANGUAGE THAT IS, BUT IF YOU CAN UNDERSTAND ME-- YOU DON'T STEAL.
AND YOU **REALLY** DON'T STEAL FROM THE POOR.
THE RICH? MAYBE I TURN A BLIND EYE...
...I HAVE A FULL SCHEDULE AND ALL.
BUT YOU'RE GOING TO ROB POOR PEOPLE ON PAYDAY?
THEN YOU AND ME ARE GOING TO HAVE WORDS, AND THEY ARE--
HUH.

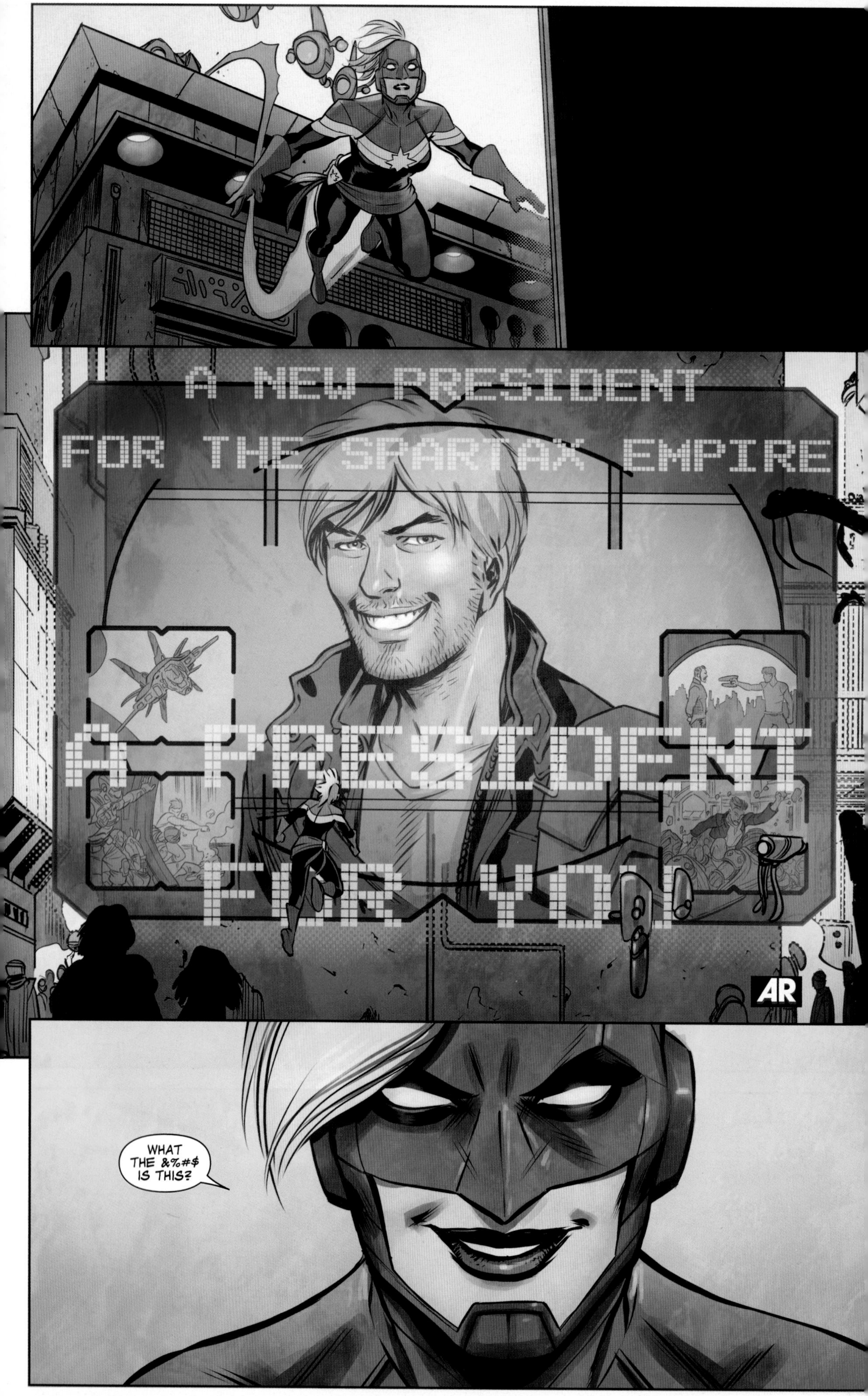
A NEW PRESIDENT
FOR THE SPARTAX EMPIRE
A PRESIDENT
FOR YOU!
AR
WHAT THE &%#$ IS THIS?

WHAT THE GLARK IS THIS?!

WHAT DOES IT *LOOK* LIKE?!

UNBELIEVABLE!

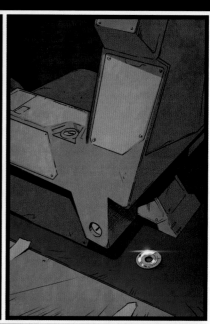

ROCKET, YOU ARE STRONGER THAN THIS!

YOU ARE BETTER THAN THIS!

FIGHT THIS!

I AM EXACTLY THIS, LADY THANOS!

GAARGH!

GOT IT!

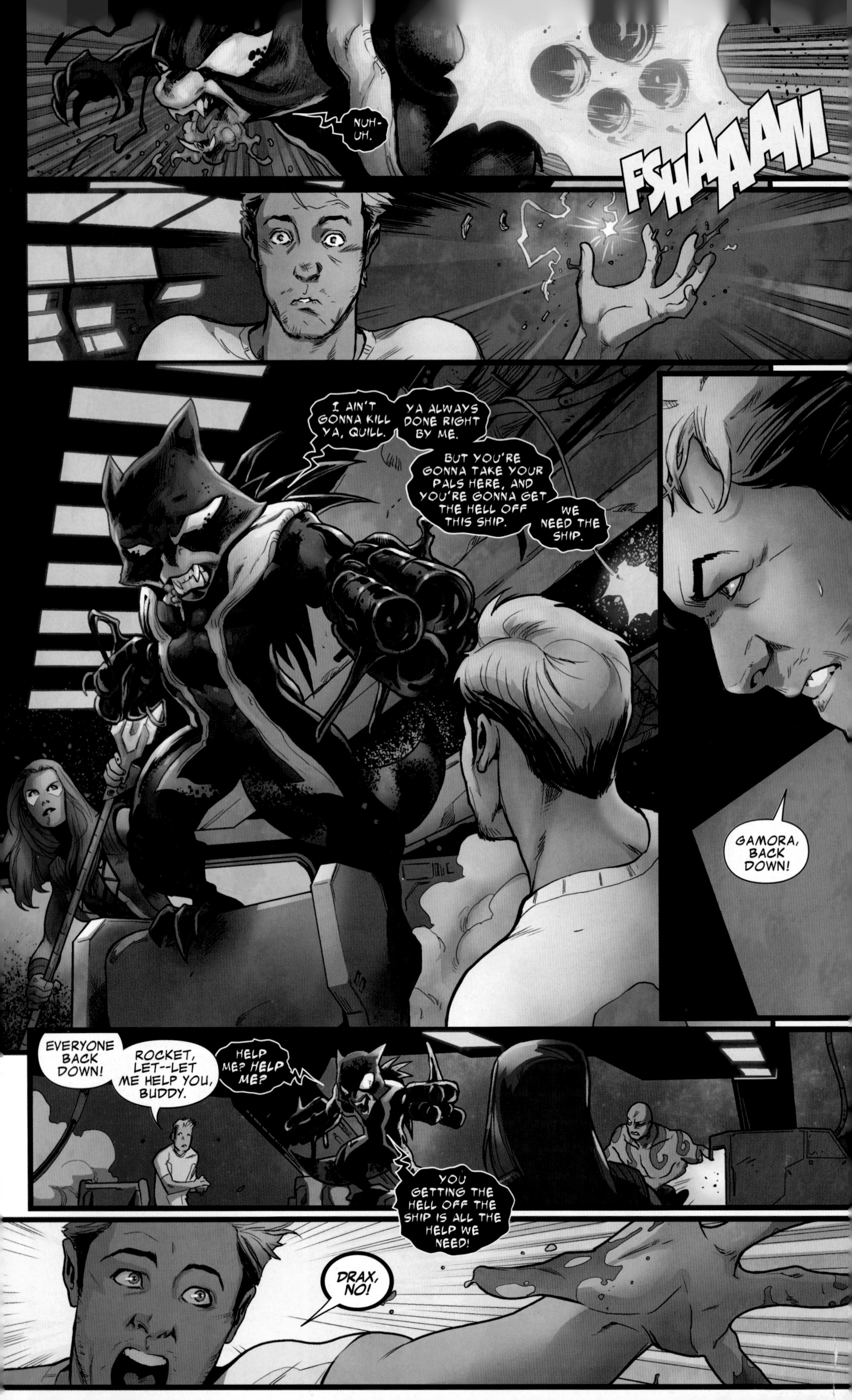
NUH-UH.
FSHAAAAM
I AIN'T GONNA KILL YA, QUILL.
YA ALWAYS DONE RIGHT BY ME.
BUT YOU'RE GONNA TAKE YOUR PALS HERE, AND YOU'RE GONNA GET THE HELL OFF THIS SHIP.
WE NEED THE SHIP.
GAMORA, BACK DOWN!
EVERYONE BACK DOWN!
ROCKET, LET--LET ME HELP YOU, BUDDY.
HELP ME? HELP ME?
YOU GETTING THE HELL OFF THE SHIP IS ALL THE HELP WE NEED!
DRAX, NO!

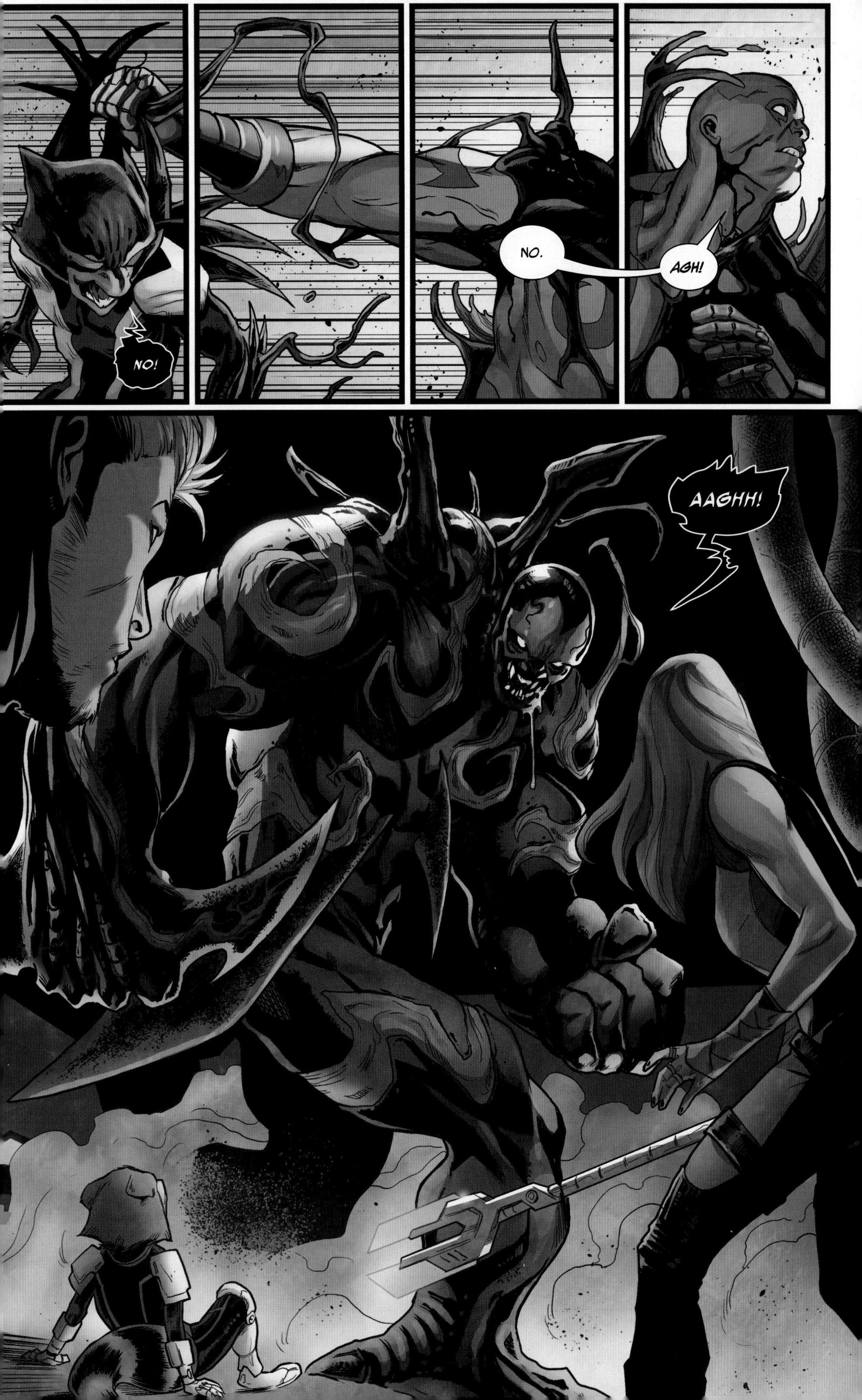
NO!
NO.
AGH!
AAGHH!

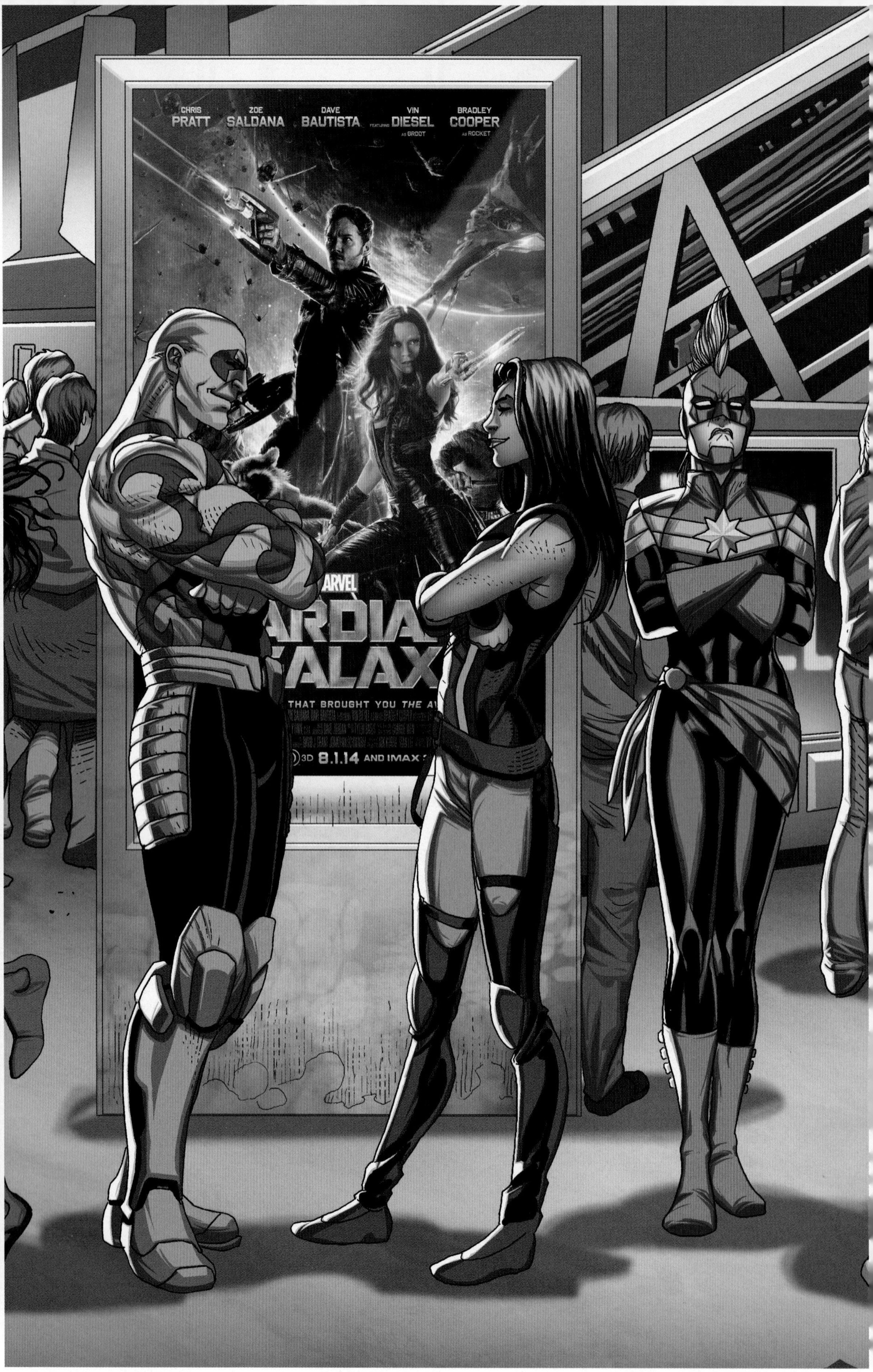
CHRIS
PRATT
ZOE
SALDANA
DAVE
BAUTISTA
VIN
DIESEL
AS GROOT
BRADLEY
COOPER
AS ROCKET
MARVEL
8.1.14 AND IMAX

#23 WELCOME HOME VARIANT BY SALVADOR LARROCA & ISRAEL SILVA

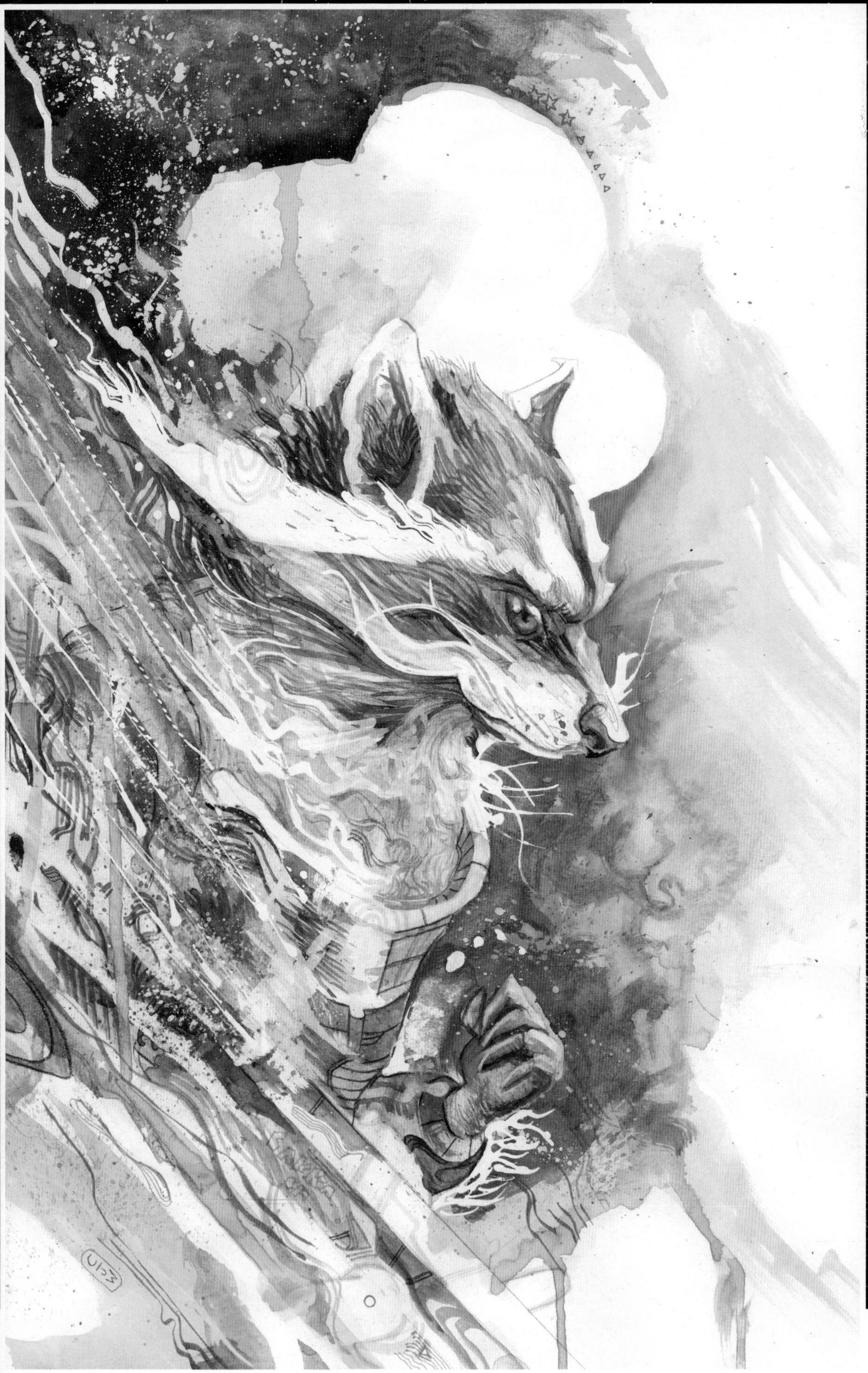

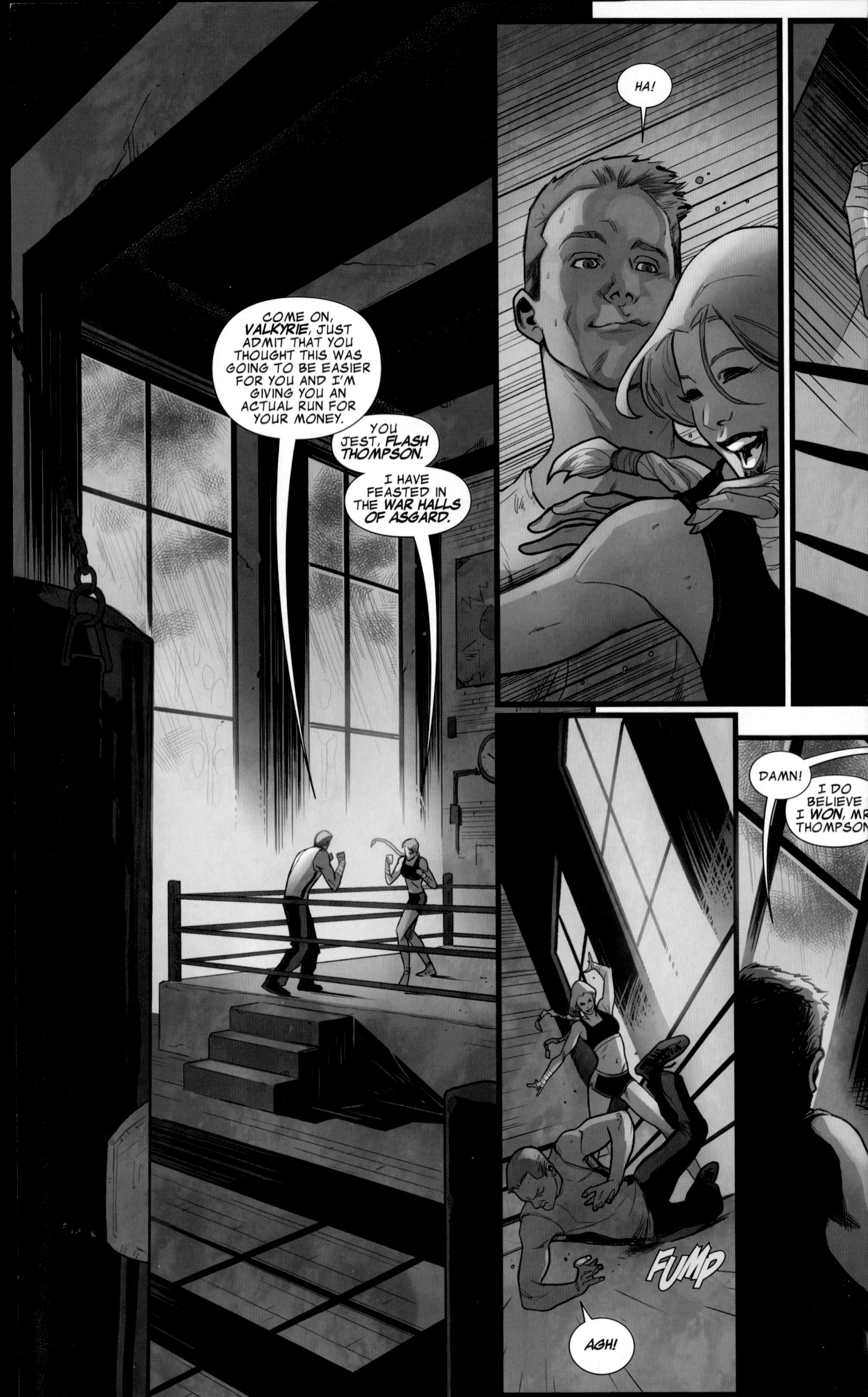

COME ON, VALKYRIE, JUST ADMIT THAT YOU THOUGHT THIS WAS GOING TO BE EASIER FOR YOU AND I'M GIVING YOU AN ACTUAL RUN FOR YOUR MONEY.
YOU JEST, FLASH THOMPSON.
I HAVE FEASTED IN THE WAR HALLS OF ASGARD.
HA!
DAMN!
I DO BELIEVE I WON, MR. THOMPSON
FUMP
AGH!

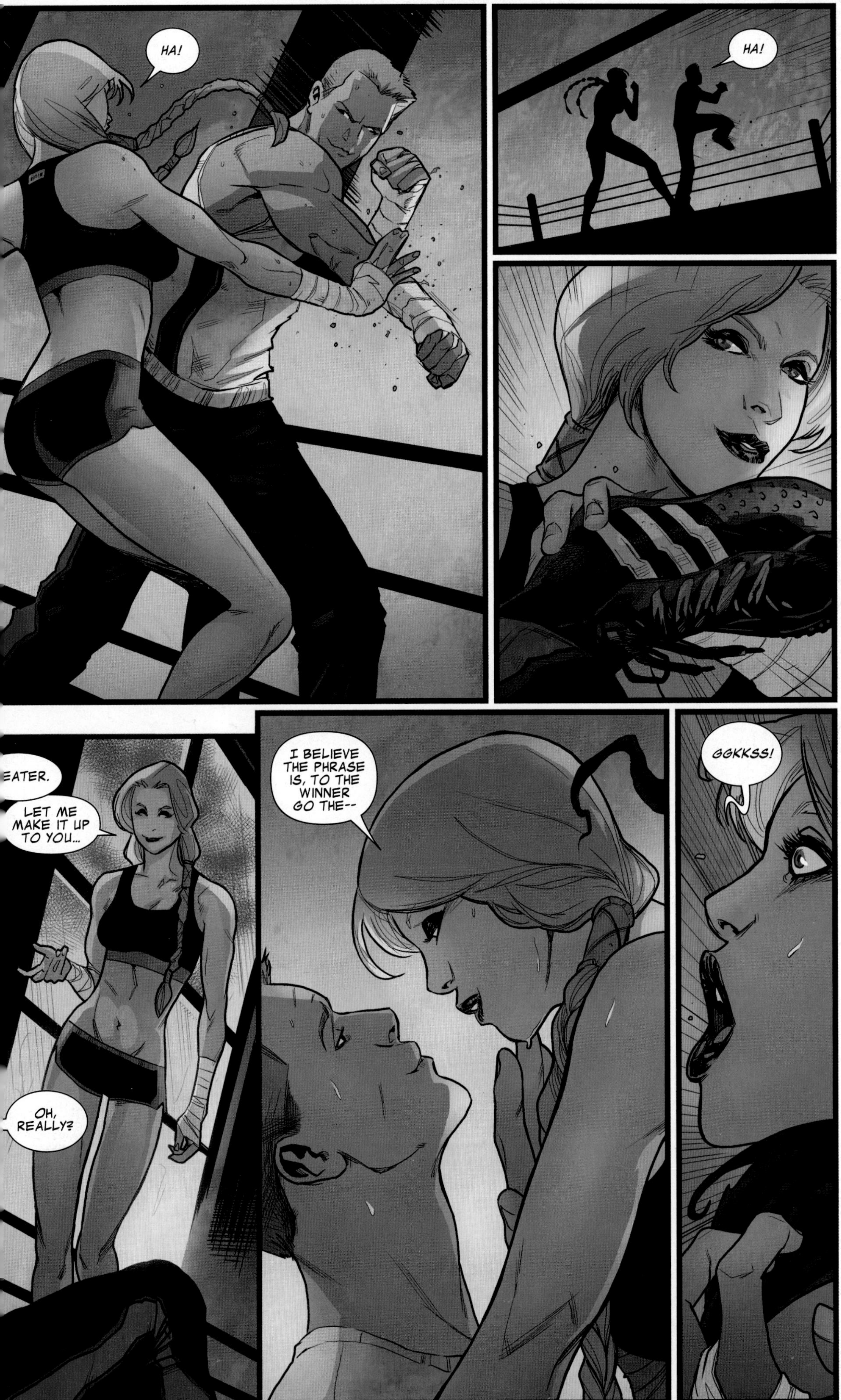
HA!
HA!
EATER.
LET ME MAKE IT UP TO YOU...
OH, REALLY?
I BELIEVE THE PHRASE IS, TO THE WINNER GO THE--
GGKKSS!

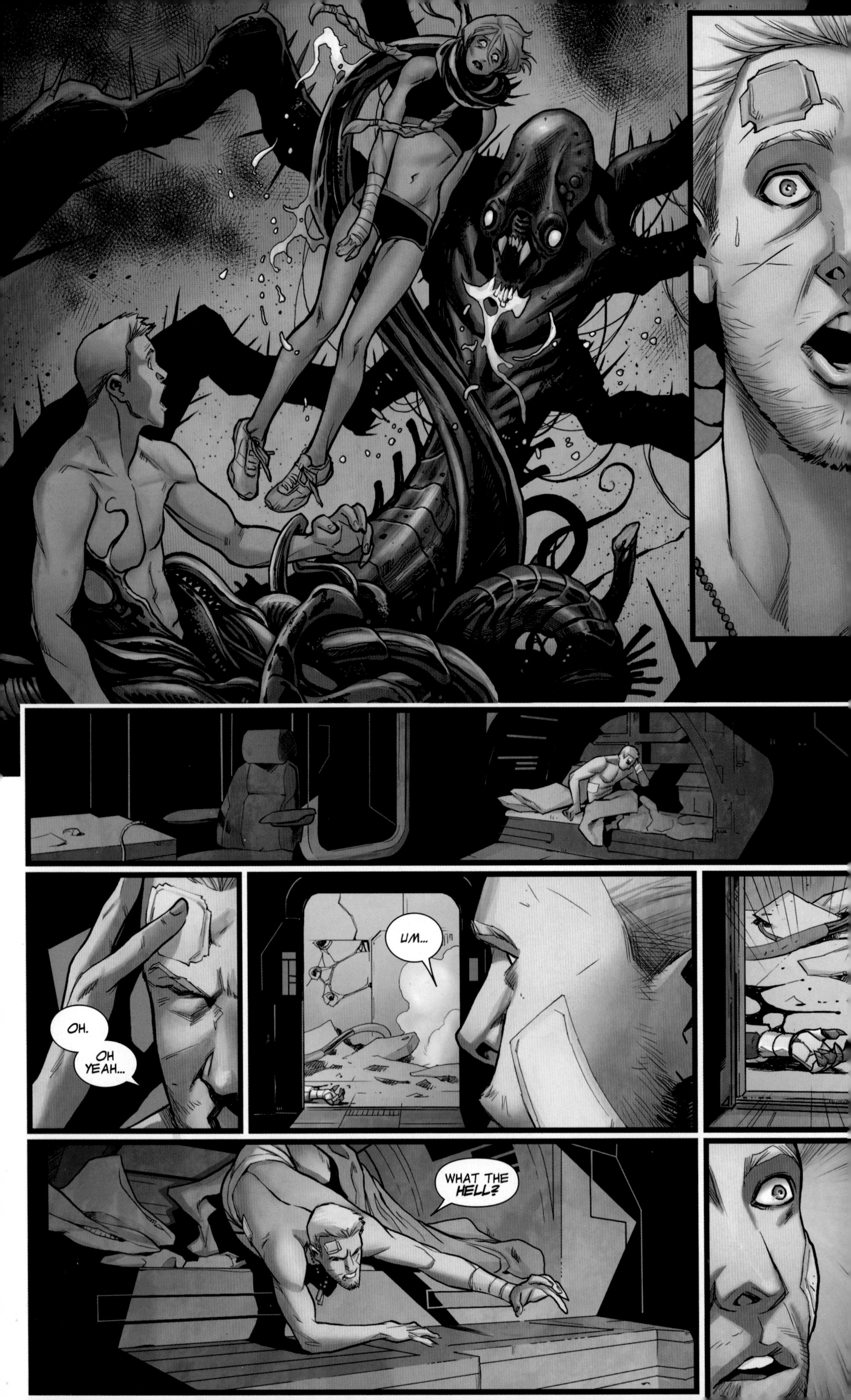
OH.
OH YEAH...
UM...
WHAT THE HELL?

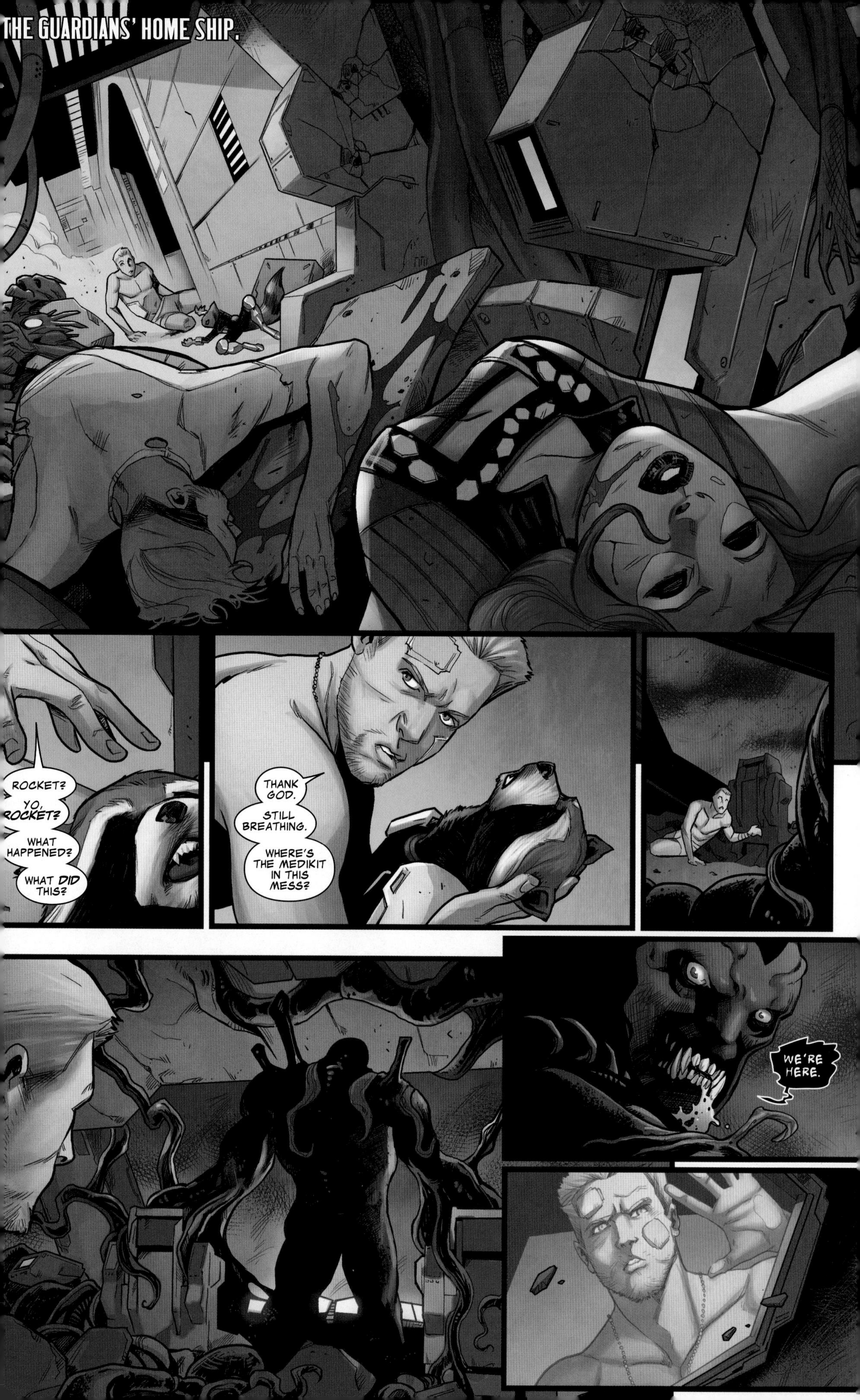
THE GUARDIANS' HOME SHIP.
ROCKET?
YO, ROCKET?
WHAT HAPPENED?
WHAT DID THIS?
THANK GOD.
STILL BREATHING.
WHERE'S THE MEDIKIT IN THIS MESS?
WE'RE HERE.

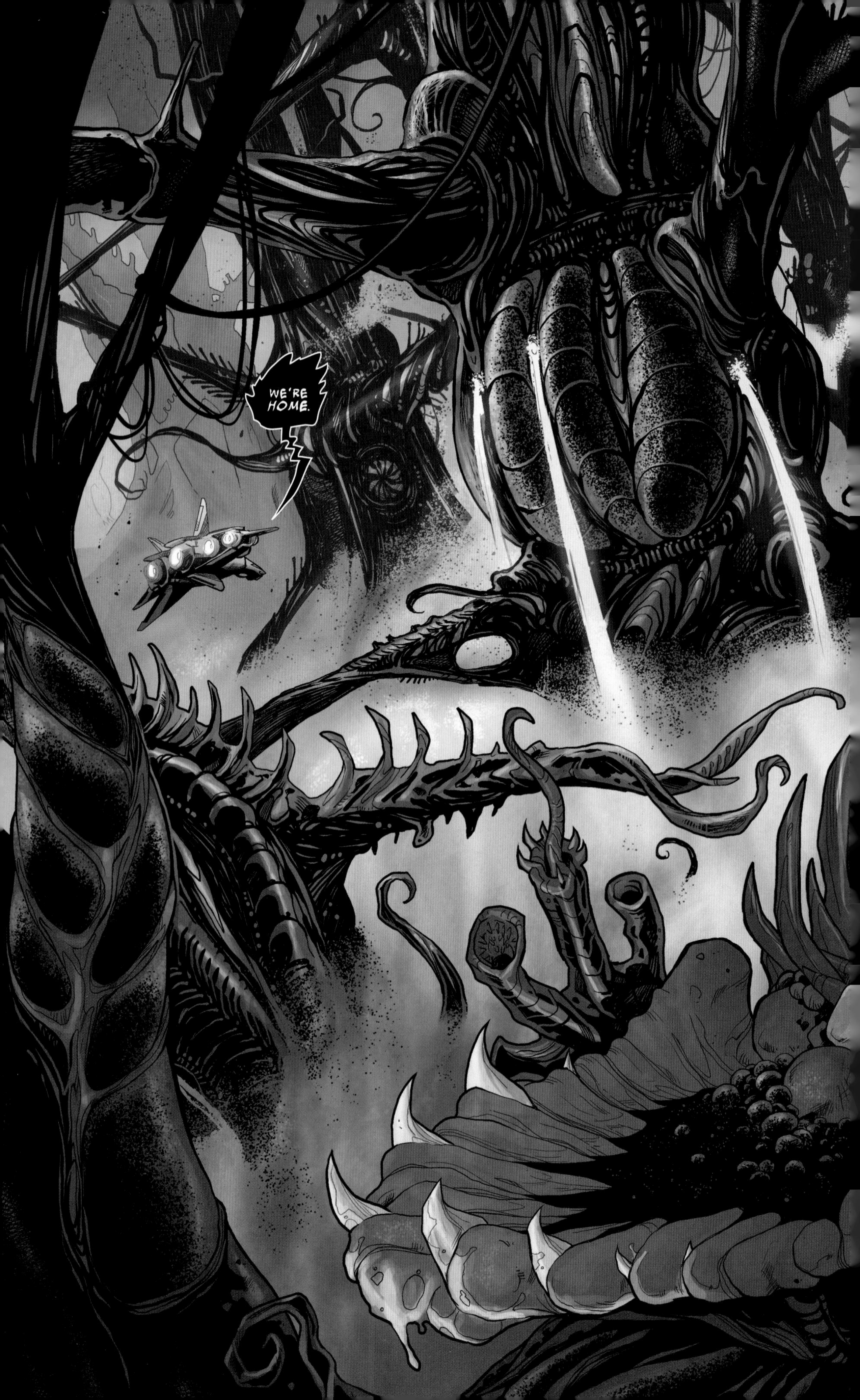
WE'RE HOME.

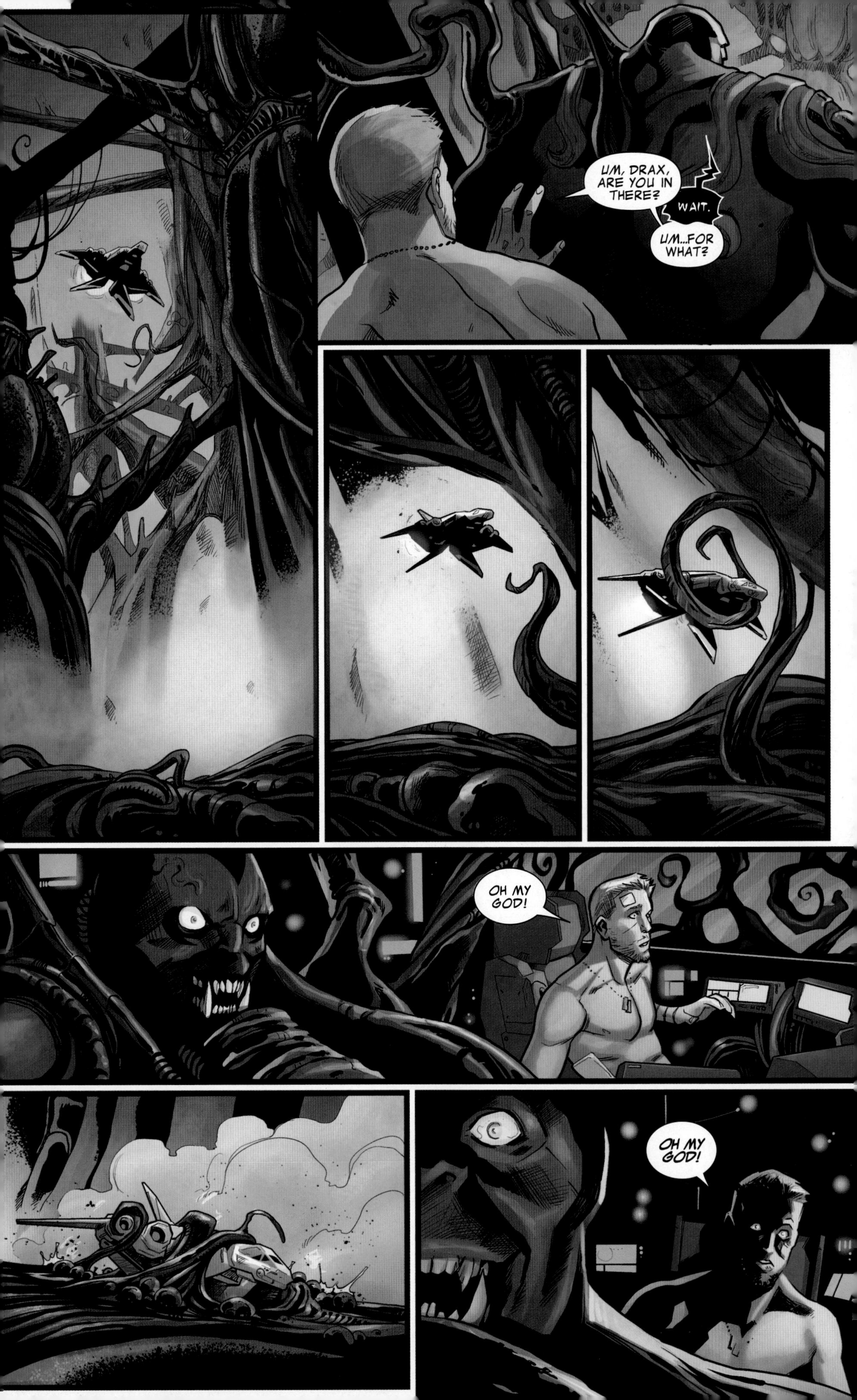
UM, DRAX, ARE YOU IN THERE?
WAIT.
UM...FOR WHAT?
OH MY GOD!
OH MY GOD!

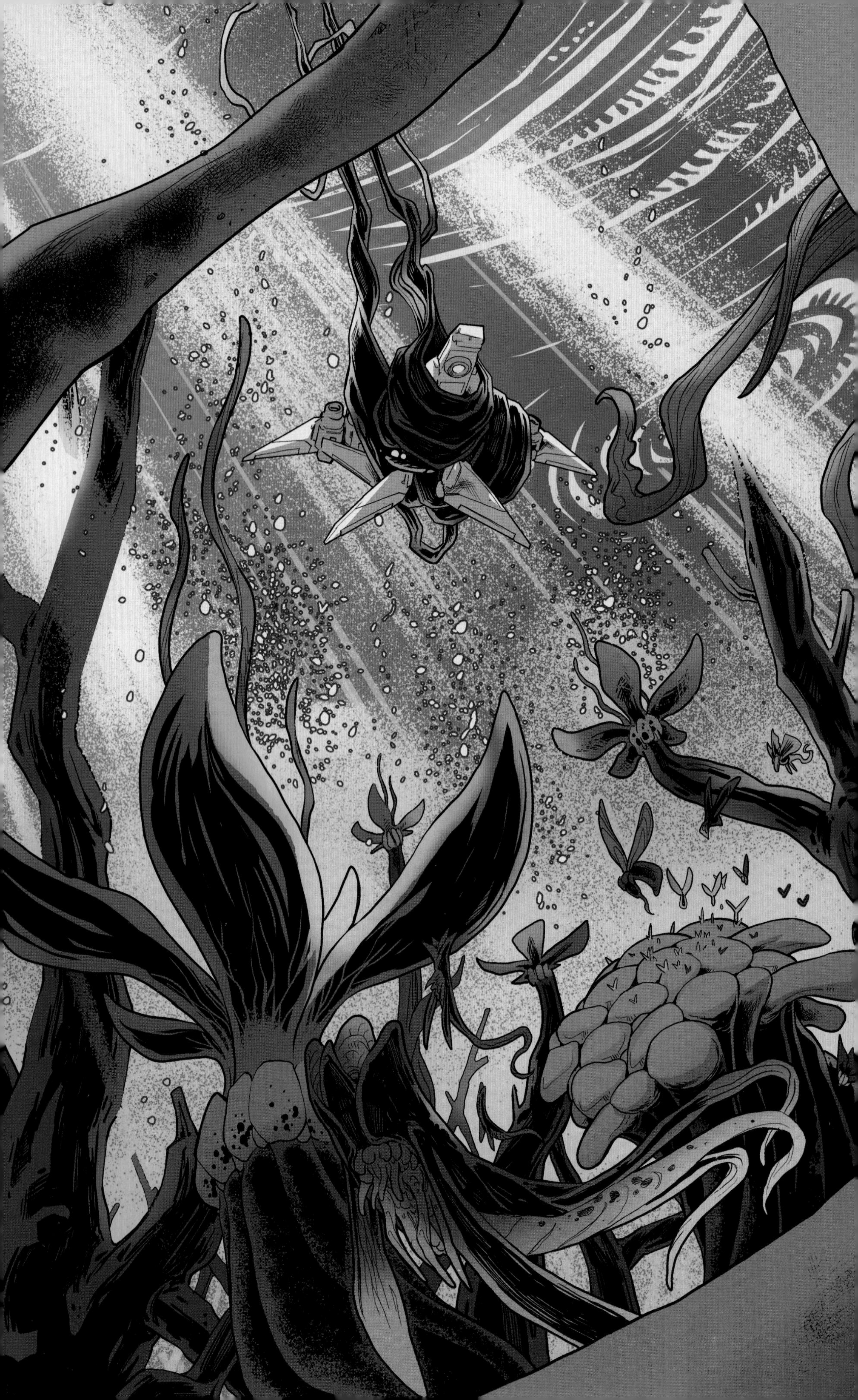

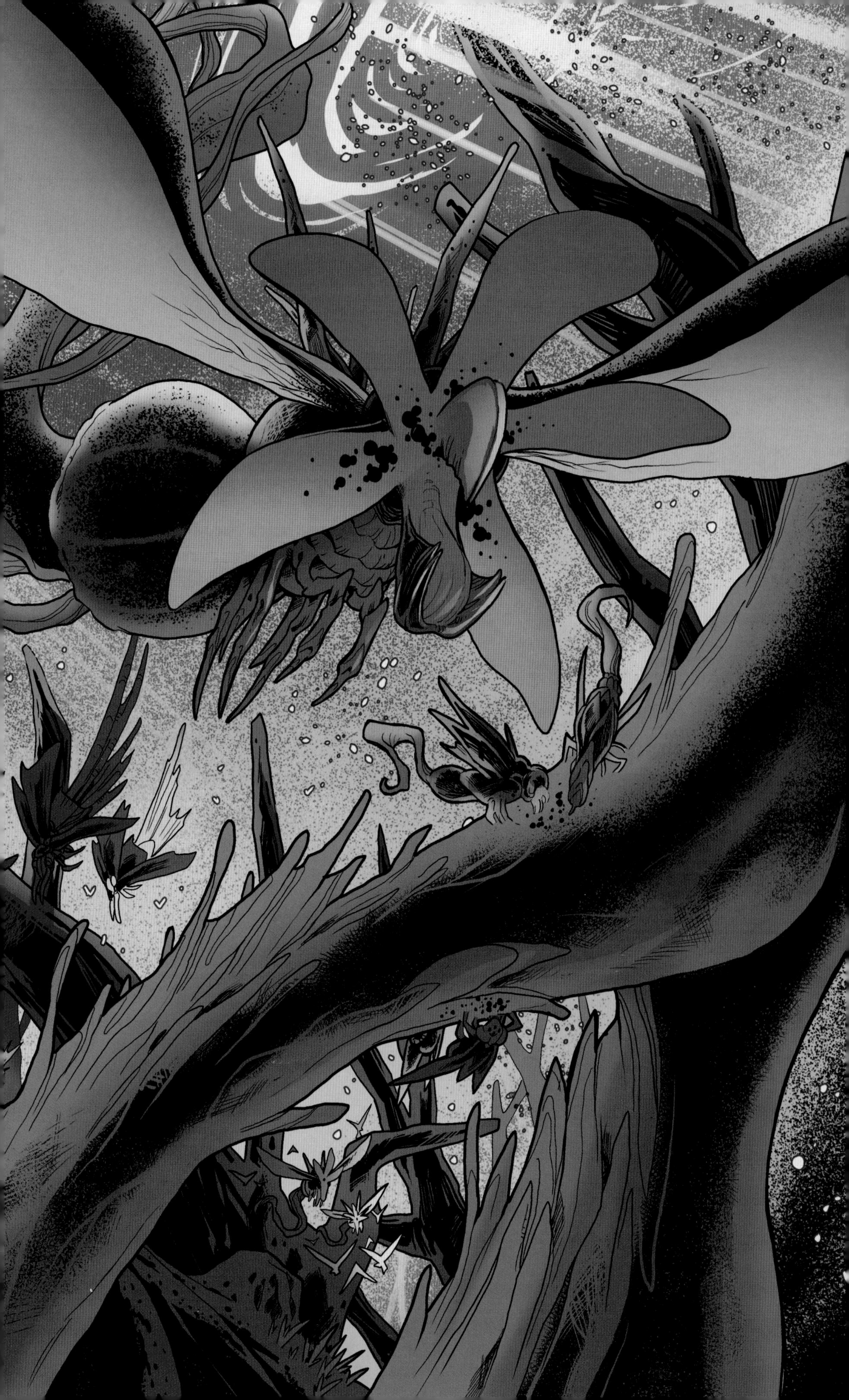

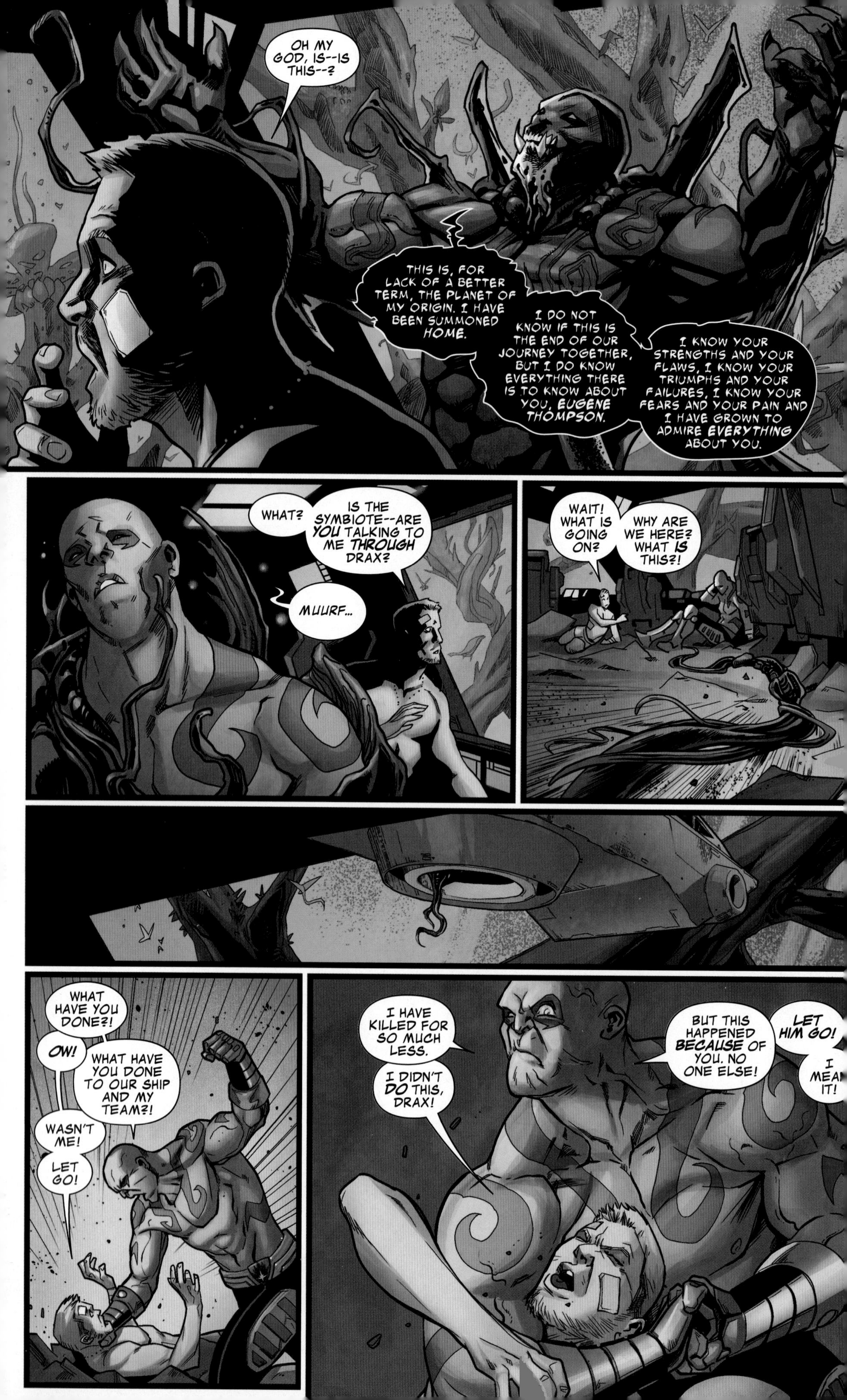

OH MY GOD, IS--IS THIS--?
THIS IS, FOR LACK OF A BETTER TERM, THE PLANET OF MY ORIGIN. I HAVE BEEN SUMMONED HOME.
I DO NOT KNOW IF THIS IS THE END OF OUR JOURNEY TOGETHER, BUT I DO KNOW EVERYTHING THERE IS TO KNOW ABOUT YOU, EUGENE THOMPSON.
I KNOW YOUR STRENGTHS AND YOUR FLAWS, I KNOW YOUR TRIUMPHS AND YOUR FAILURES, I KNOW YOUR FEARS AND YOUR PAIN AND I HAVE GROWN TO ADMIRE EVERYTHING ABOUT YOU.
WHAT?
IS THE SYMBIOTE--ARE YOU TALKING TO ME THROUGH DRAX?
MUURF...
WAIT! WHAT IS GOING ON?
WHY ARE WE HERE? WHAT IS THIS?!
WHAT HAVE YOU DONE?!
OW!
WHAT HAVE YOU DONE TO OUR SHIP AND MY TEAM?!
WASN'T ME!
LET GO!
I HAVE KILLED FOR SO MUCH LESS.
I DIDN'T DO THIS, DRAX!
BUT THIS HAPPENED BECAUSE OF YOU. NO ONE ELSE!
LET HIM GO!
I MEAN IT!

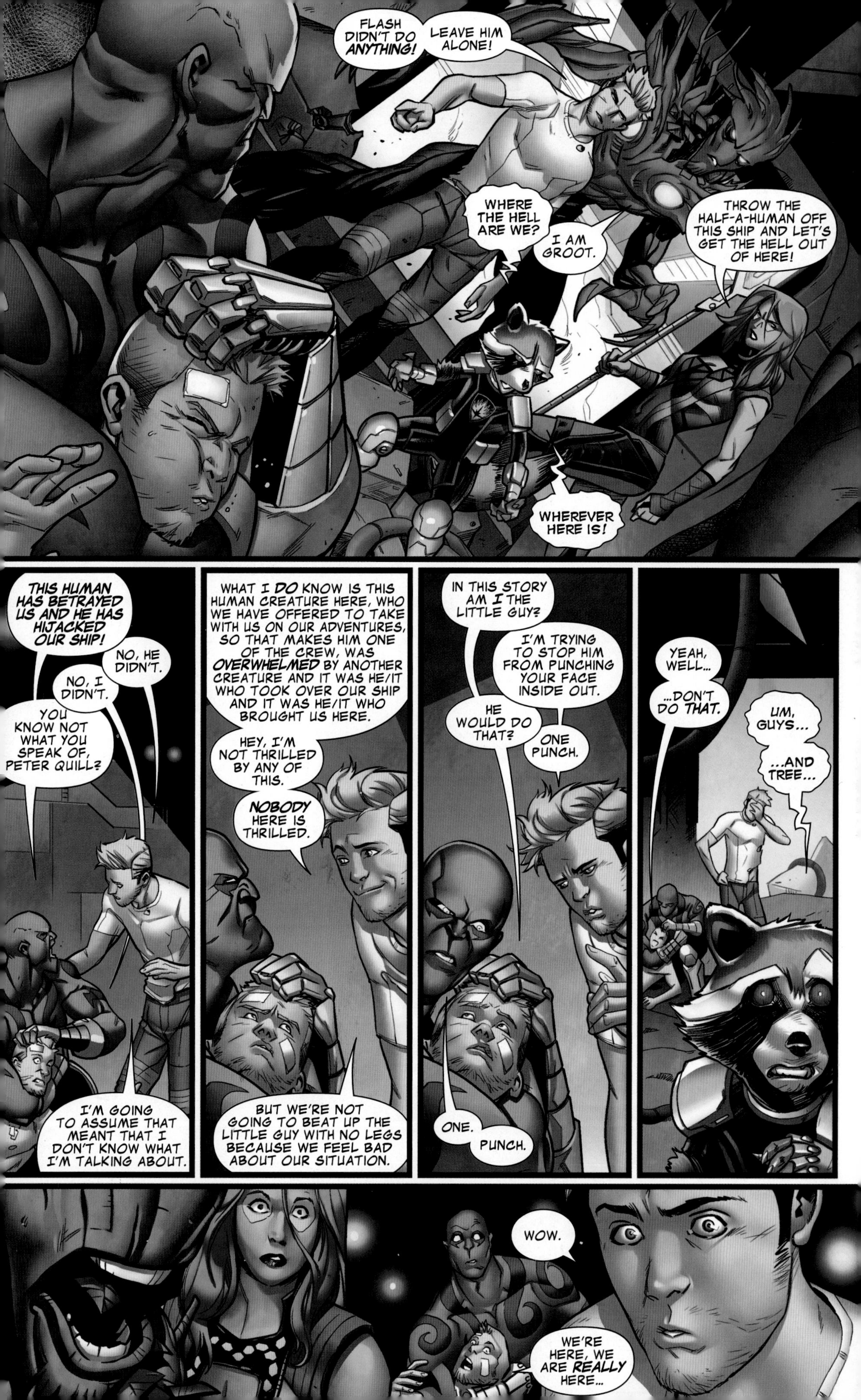

FLASH DIDN'T DO ANYTHING!
LEAVE HIM ALONE!
WHERE THE HELL ARE WE?
I AM GROOT.
THROW THE HALF-A-HUMAN OFF THIS SHIP AND LET'S GET THE HELL OUT OF HERE!
WHEREVER HERE IS!
THIS HUMAN HAS BETRAYED US AND HE HAS HIJACKED OUR SHIP!
NO, HE DIDN'T.
NO, I DIDN'T.
YOU KNOW NOT WHAT YOU SPEAK OF, PETER QUILL?
I'M GOING TO ASSUME THAT MEANT THAT I DON'T KNOW WHAT I'M TALKING ABOUT.
WHAT I DO KNOW IS THIS HUMAN CREATURE HERE, WHO WE HAVE OFFERED TO TAKE WITH US ON OUR ADVENTURES, SO THAT MAKES HIM ONE OF THE CREW, WAS OVERWHELMED BY ANOTHER CREATURE AND IT WAS HE/IT WHO TOOK OVER OUR SHIP AND IT WAS HE/IT WHO BROUGHT US HERE.
HEY, I'M NOT THRILLED BY ANY OF THIS.
NOBODY HERE IS THRILLED.
BUT WE'RE NOT GOING TO BEAT UP THE LITTLE GUY WITH NO LEGS BECAUSE WE FEEL BAD ABOUT OUR SITUATION.
IN THIS STORY AM I THE LITTLE GUY?
I'M TRYING TO STOP HIM FROM PUNCHING YOUR FACE INSIDE OUT.
HE WOULD DO THAT?
ONE PUNCH.
ONE.
PUNCH.
YEAH, WELL...
...DON'T DO THAT.
UM, GUYS...
...AND TREE...
WOW.
WE'RE HERE, WE ARE REALLY HERE...

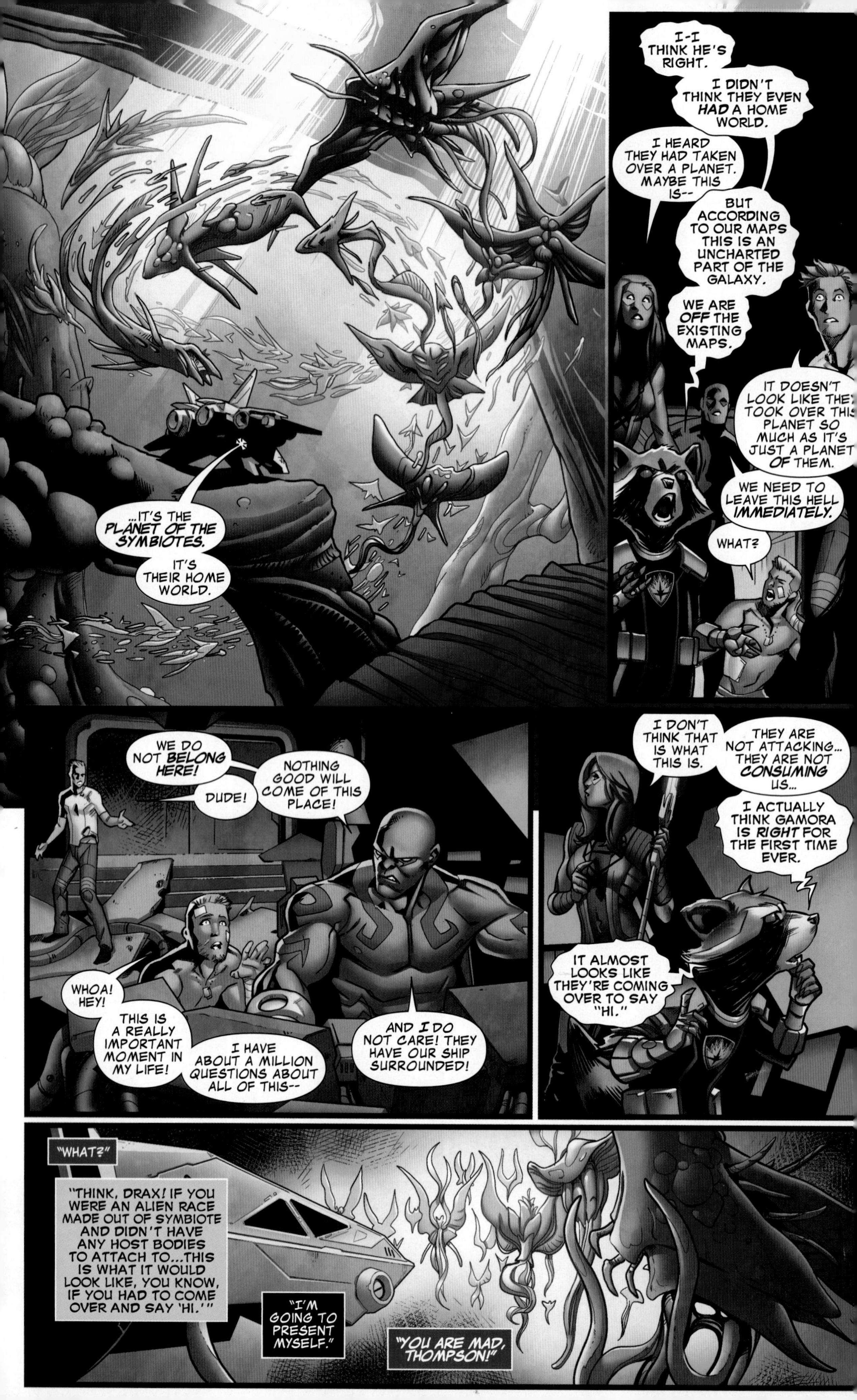
...IT'S THE PLANET OF THE SYMBIOTES.
IT'S THEIR HOME WORLD.
I-I THINK HE'S RIGHT.
I DIDN'T THINK THEY EVEN HAD A HOME WORLD.
I HEARD THEY HAD TAKEN OVER A PLANET. MAYBE THIS IS--
BUT ACCORDING TO OUR MAPS THIS IS AN UNCHARTED PART OF THE GALAXY.
WE ARE OFF THE EXISTING MAPS.
IT DOESN'T LOOK LIKE THEY TOOK OVER THIS PLANET SO MUCH AS IT'S JUST A PLANET OF THEM.
WE NEED TO LEAVE THIS HELL IMMEDIATELY.
WHAT?
WE DO NOT BELONG HERE!
DUDE!
NOTHING GOOD WILL COME OF THIS PLACE!
WHOA! HEY!
THIS IS A REALLY IMPORTANT MOMENT IN MY LIFE!
I HAVE ABOUT A MILLION QUESTIONS ABOUT ALL OF THIS--
AND I DO NOT CARE! THEY HAVE OUR SHIP SURROUNDED!
I DON'T THINK THAT IS WHAT THIS IS.
THEY ARE NOT ATTACKING... THEY ARE NOT CONSUMING US...
I ACTUALLY THINK GAMORA IS RIGHT FOR THE FIRST TIME EVER.
IT ALMOST LOOKS LIKE THEY'RE COMING OVER TO SAY "HI."
"WHAT?"
"THINK, DRAX! IF YOU WERE AN ALIEN RACE MADE OUT OF SYMBIOTE AND DIDN'T HAVE ANY HOST BODIES TO ATTACH TO...THIS IS WHAT IT WOULD LOOK LIKE, YOU KNOW, IF YOU HAD TO COME OVER AND SAY 'HI.'"
"I'M GOING TO PRESENT MYSELF."
"YOU ARE MAD, THOMPSON!"

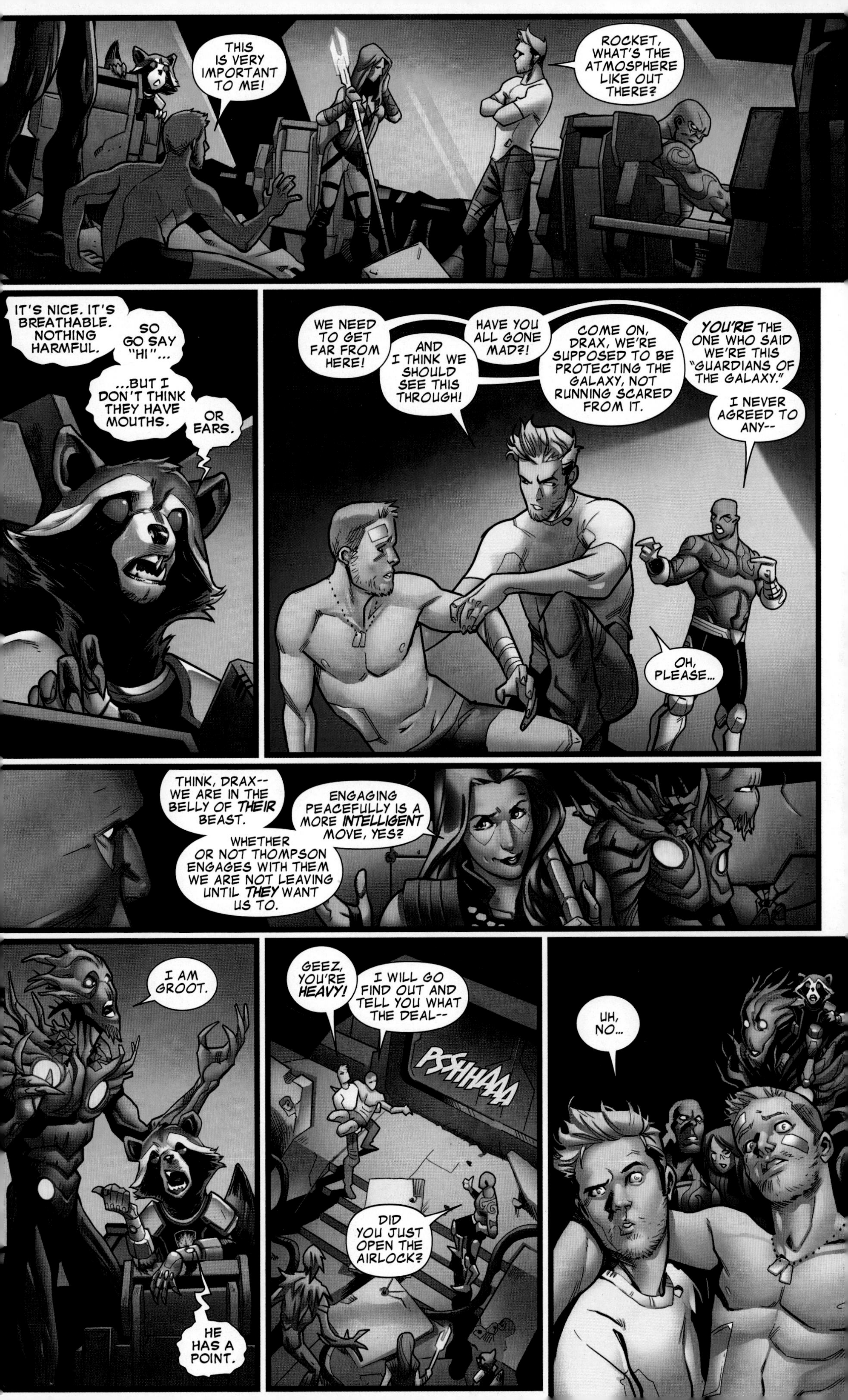
THIS IS VERY IMPORTANT TO ME!
ROCKET, WHAT'S THE ATMOSPHERE LIKE OUT THERE?
IT'S NICE. IT'S BREATHABLE. NOTHING HARMFUL.
SO GO SAY "HI"...
...BUT I DON'T THINK THEY HAVE MOUTHS.
OR EARS.
WE NEED TO GET FAR FROM HERE!
AND I THINK WE SHOULD SEE THIS THROUGH!
HAVE YOU ALL GONE MAD?!
COME ON, DRAX, WE'RE SUPPOSED TO BE PROTECTING THE GALAXY, NOT RUNNING SCARED FROM IT.
YOU'RE THE ONE WHO SAID WE'RE THIS "GUARDIANS OF THE GALAXY."
I NEVER AGREED TO ANY--
OH, PLEASE...
THINK, DRAX-- WE ARE IN THE BELLY OF THEIR BEAST.
WHETHER OR NOT THOMPSON ENGAGES WITH THEM WE ARE NOT LEAVING UNTIL THEY WANT US TO.
ENGAGING PEACEFULLY IS A MORE INTELLIGENT MOVE, YES?
I AM GROOT.
HE HAS A POINT.
GEEZ, YOU'RE HEAVY!
I WILL GO FIND OUT AND TELL YOU WHAT THE DEAL--
PSSHHAAA
DID YOU JUST OPEN THE AIRLOCK?
UH, NO...

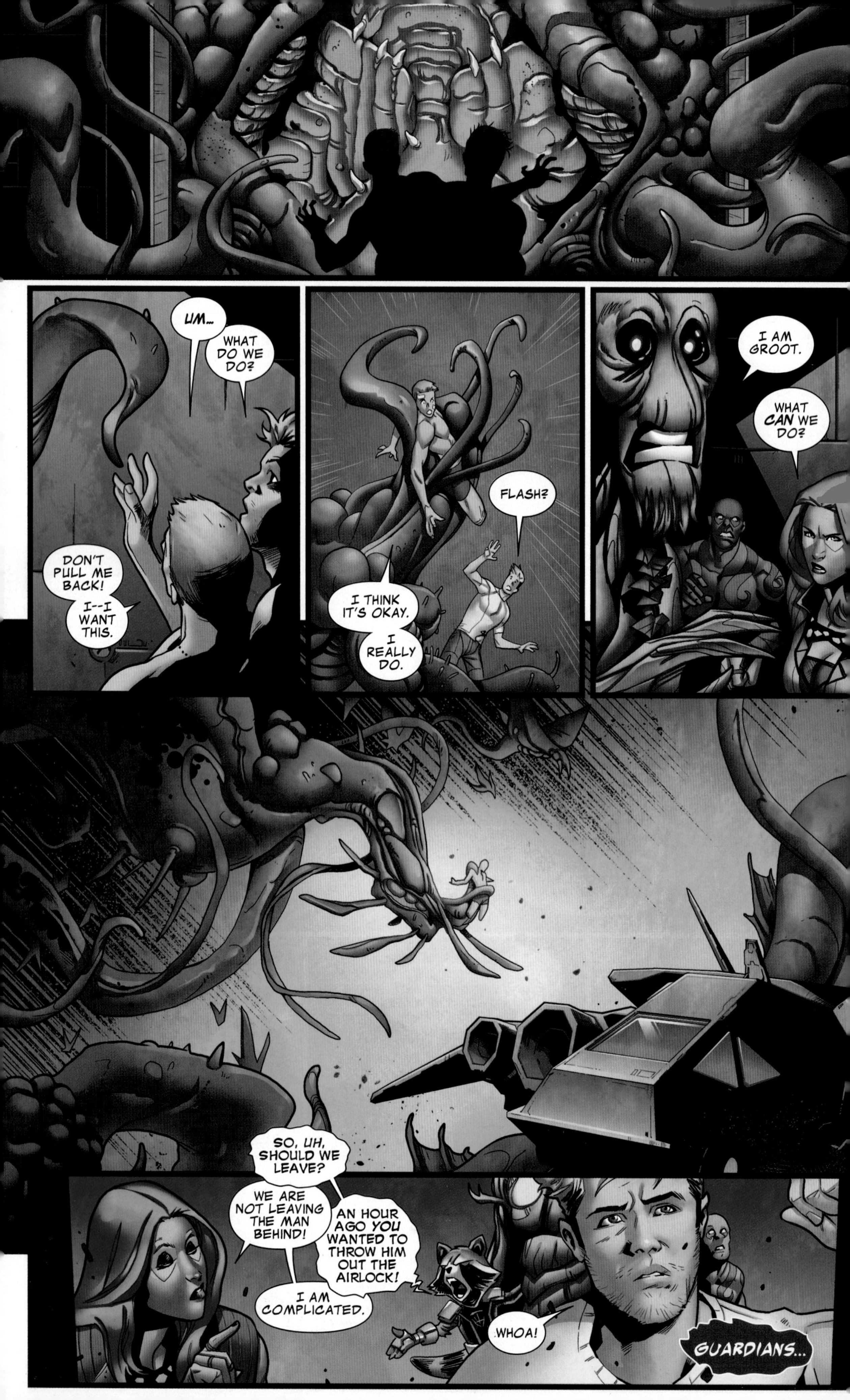
UM...
WHAT DO WE DO?
DON'T PULL ME BACK!
I--I WANT THIS.
FLASH?
I THINK IT'S OKAY.
I REALLY DO.
I AM GROOT.
WHAT CAN WE DO?
SO, UH, SHOULD WE LEAVE?
WE ARE NOT LEAVING THE MAN BEHIND!
AN HOUR AGO YOU WANTED TO THROW HIM OUT THE AIRLOCK!
I AM COMPLICATED.
WHOA!
GUARDIANS...

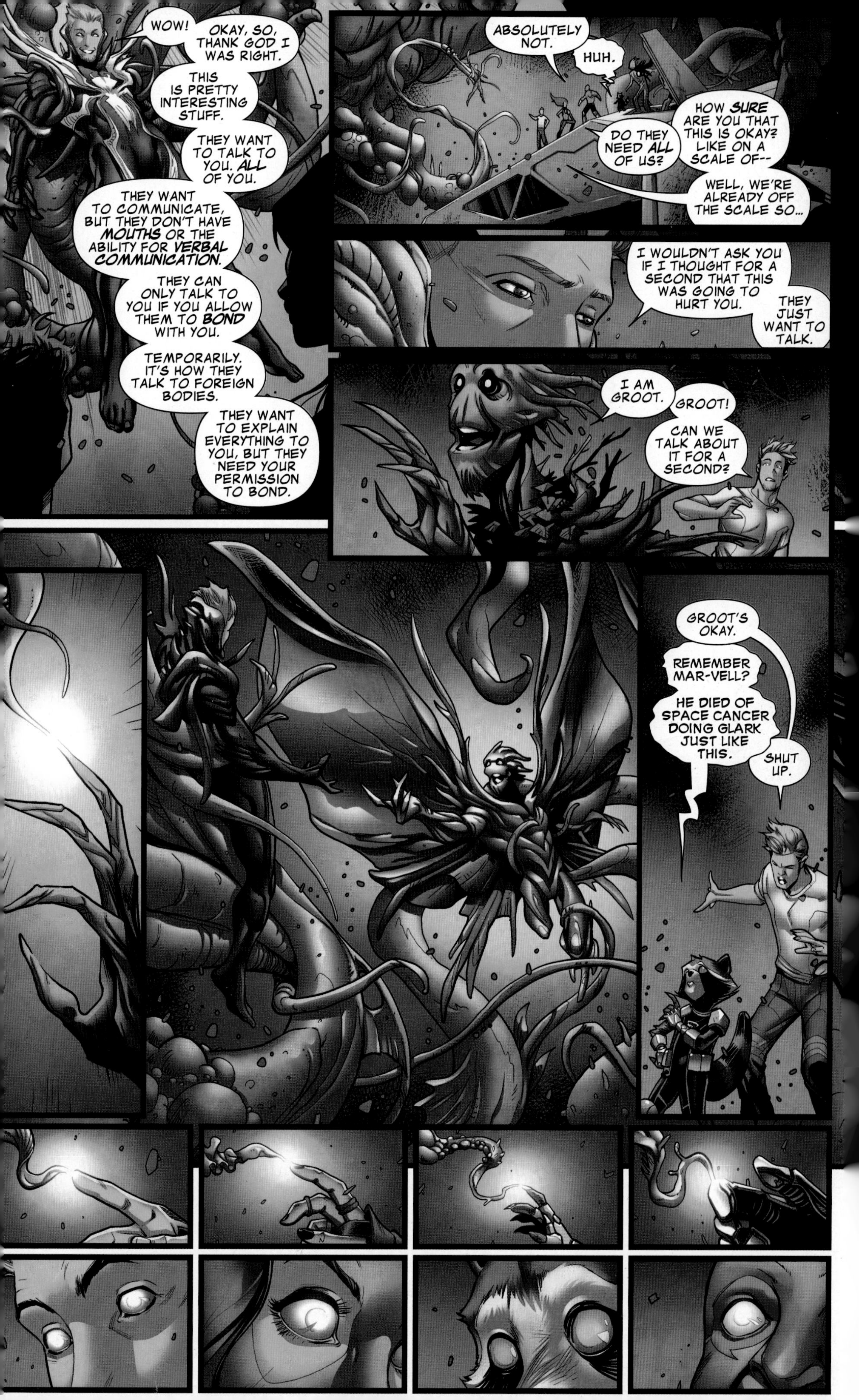

WOW!
OKAY, SO, THANK GOD I WAS RIGHT.
THIS IS PRETTY INTERESTING STUFF.
THEY WANT TO TALK TO YOU. ALL OF YOU.
THEY WANT TO COMMUNICATE, BUT THEY DON'T HAVE MOUTHS OR THE ABILITY FOR VERBAL COMMUNICATION.
THEY CAN ONLY TALK TO YOU IF YOU ALLOW THEM TO BOND WITH YOU.
TEMPORARILY. IT'S HOW THEY TALK TO FOREIGN BODIES.
THEY WANT TO EXPLAIN EVERYTHING TO YOU, BUT THEY NEED YOUR PERMISSION TO BOND.
ABSOLUTELY NOT.
HUH.
DO THEY NEED ALL OF US?
HOW SURE ARE YOU THAT THIS IS OKAY? LIKE ON A SCALE OF--
WELL, WE'RE ALREADY OFF THE SCALE SO...
I WOULDN'T ASK YOU IF I THOUGHT FOR A SECOND THAT THIS WAS GOING TO HURT YOU.
THEY JUST WANT TO TALK.
I AM GROOT.
GROOT!
CAN WE TALK ABOUT IT FOR A SECOND?
GROOT'S OKAY.
REMEMBER MAR-VELL?
HE DIED OF SPACE CANCER DOING GLARK JUST LIKE THIS.
SHUT UP.

THERE ARE MANY STORIES ABOUT
US ACROSS THE GALAXY.

SOME TRUE,
SOME FALSE...

...SOME CONCOCTED BY RENEGADE
MEMBERS OF OUR OWN SPECIES.

AND BECAUSE OF
THIS WE ARE KNOWN
BY MANY NAMES...

...WE PREFER TO BE CALLED
THE KLYNTAR.

ALLOW US TO EXPLAIN
OURSELVES USING FAMILIAR
PERSPECTIVES AND THE
VERNACULAR OF YOUR SPECIES...

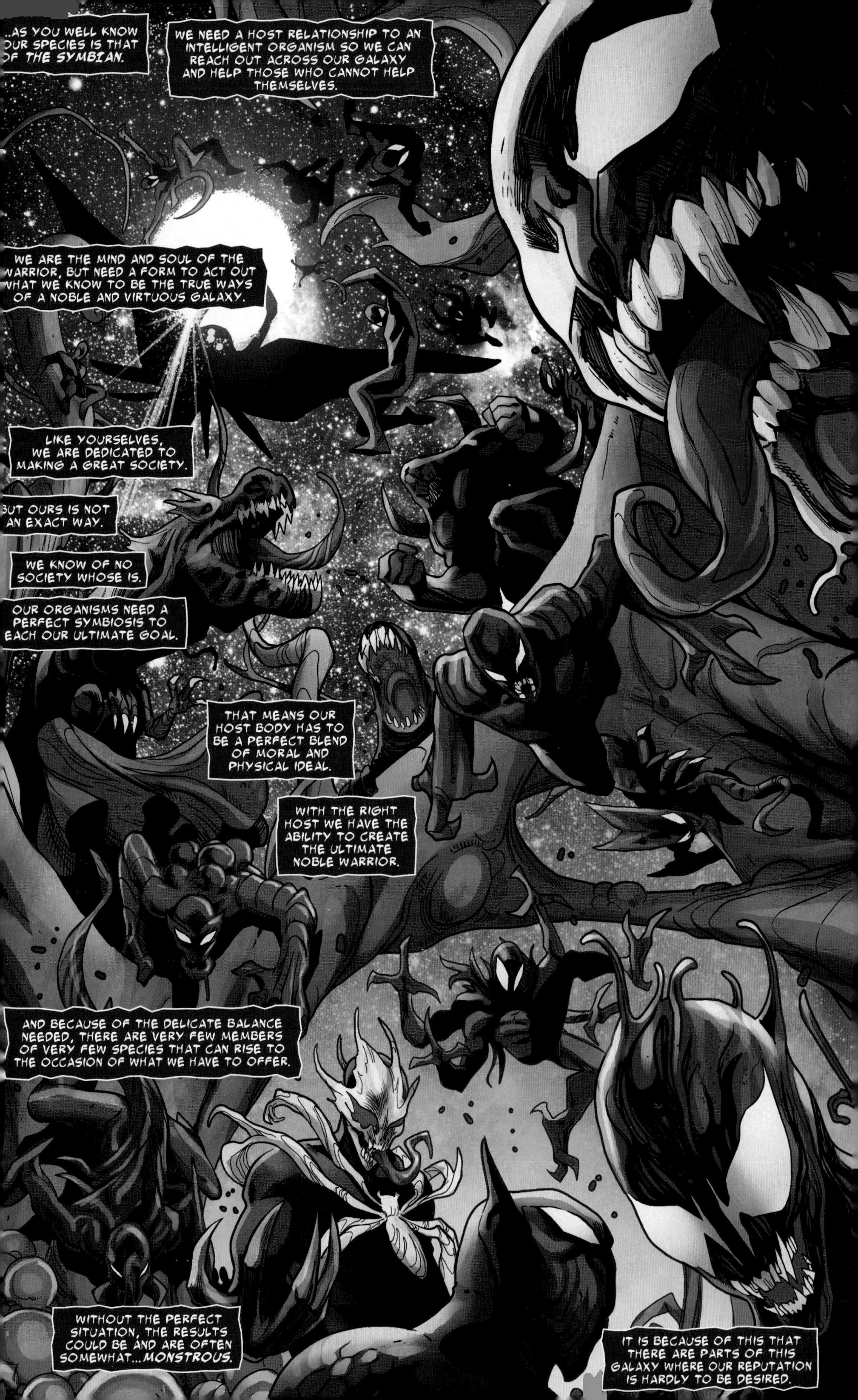
..AS YOU WELL KNOW OUR SPECIES IS THAT OF THE SYMBIAN.
WE NEED A HOST RELATIONSHIP TO AN INTELLIGENT ORGANISM SO WE CAN REACH OUT ACROSS OUR GALAXY AND HELP THOSE WHO CANNOT HELP THEMSELVES.
WE ARE THE MIND AND SOUL OF THE WARRIOR, BUT NEED A FORM TO ACT OUT WHAT WE KNOW TO BE THE TRUE WAYS OF A NOBLE AND VIRTUOUS GALAXY.
LIKE YOURSELVES, WE ARE DEDICATED TO MAKING A GREAT SOCIETY.
BUT OURS IS NOT AN EXACT WAY.
WE KNOW OF NO SOCIETY WHOSE IS.
OUR ORGANISMS NEED A PERFECT SYMBIOSIS TO REACH OUR ULTIMATE GOAL.
THAT MEANS OUR HOST BODY HAS TO BE A PERFECT BLEND OF MORAL AND PHYSICAL IDEAL.
WITH THE RIGHT HOST WE HAVE THE ABILITY TO CREATE THE ULTIMATE NOBLE WARRIOR.
AND BECAUSE OF THE DELICATE BALANCE NEEDED, THERE ARE VERY FEW MEMBERS OF VERY FEW SPECIES THAT CAN RISE TO THE OCCASION OF WHAT WE HAVE TO OFFER.
WITHOUT THE PERFECT SITUATION, THE RESULTS COULD BE AND ARE OFTEN SOMEWHAT...MONSTROUS.
IT IS BECAUSE OF THIS THAT THERE ARE PARTS OF THIS GALAXY WHERE OUR REPUTATION IS HARDLY TO BE DESIRED.

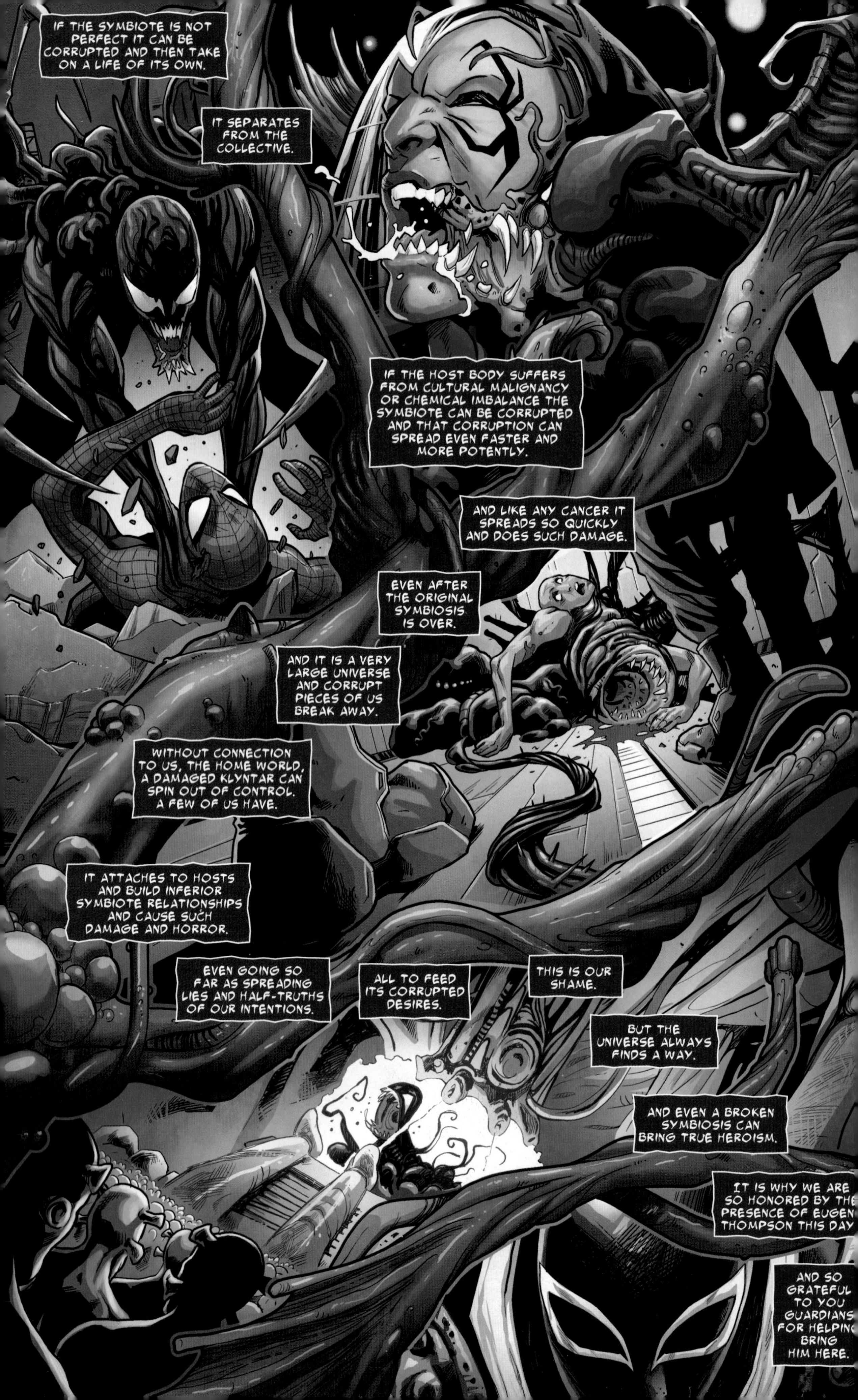
IF THE SYMBIOTE IS NOT PERFECT IT CAN BE CORRUPTED AND THEN TAKE ON A LIFE OF ITS OWN.
IT SEPARATES FROM THE COLLECTIVE.
IF THE HOST BODY SUFFERS FROM CULTURAL MALIGNANCY OR CHEMICAL IMBALANCE THE SYMBIOTE CAN BE CORRUPTED AND THAT CORRUPTION CAN SPREAD EVEN FASTER AND MORE POTENTLY.
AND LIKE ANY CANCER IT SPREADS SO QUICKLY AND DOES SUCH DAMAGE.
EVEN AFTER THE ORIGINAL SYMBIOSIS IS OVER.
AND IT IS A VERY LARGE UNIVERSE AND CORRUPT PIECES OF US BREAK AWAY.
WITHOUT CONNECTION TO US, THE HOME WORLD, A DAMAGED KLYNTAR CAN SPIN OUT OF CONTROL. A FEW OF US HAVE.
IT ATTACHES TO HOSTS AND BUILD INFERIOR SYMBIOTE RELATIONSHIPS AND CAUSE SUCH DAMAGE AND HORROR.
EVEN GOING SO FAR AS SPREADING LIES AND HALF-TRUTHS OF OUR INTENTIONS.
ALL TO FEED ITS CORRUPTED DESIRES.
THIS IS OUR SHAME.
BUT THE UNIVERSE ALWAYS FINDS A WAY.
AND EVEN A BROKEN SYMBIOSIS CAN BRING TRUE HEROISM.
IT IS WHY WE ARE SO HONORED BY THE PRESENCE OF EUGEN THOMPSON THIS DAY
AND SO GRATEFUL TO YOU GUARDIANS FOR HELPING BRING HIM HERE.

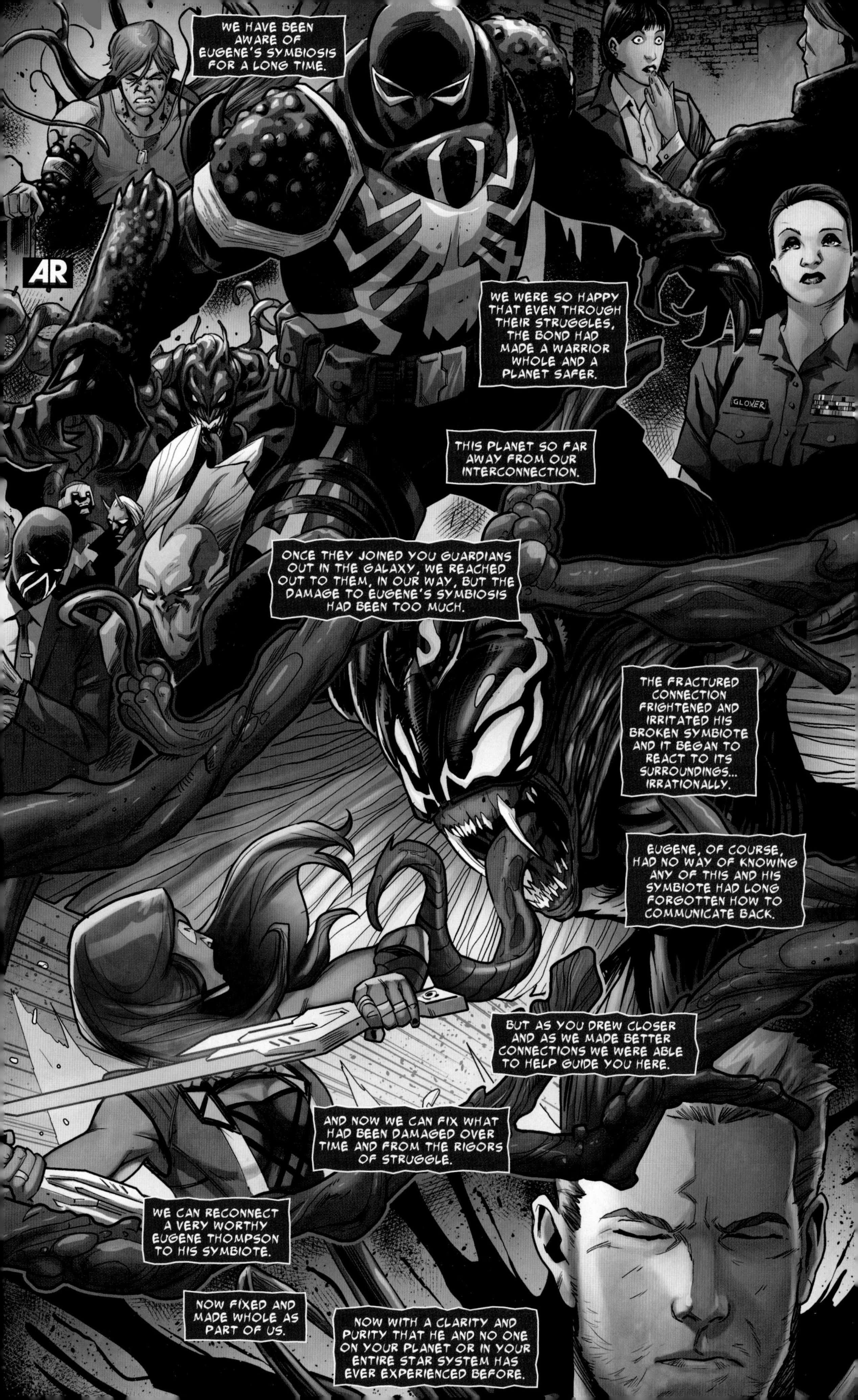
WE HAVE BEEN AWARE OF EUGENE'S SYMBIOSIS FOR A LONG TIME.
AR
WE WERE SO HAPPY THAT EVEN THROUGH THEIR STRUGGLES, THE BOND HAD MADE A WARRIOR WHOLE AND A PLANET SAFER.
GLOVER
THIS PLANET SO FAR AWAY FROM OUR INTERCONNECTION.
ONCE THEY JOINED YOU GUARDIANS OUT IN THE GALAXY, WE REACHED OUT TO THEM, IN OUR WAY, BUT THE DAMAGE TO EUGENE'S SYMBIOSIS HAD BEEN TOO MUCH.
THE FRACTURED CONNECTION FRIGHTENED AND IRRITATED HIS BROKEN SYMBIOTE AND IT BEGAN TO REACT TO ITS SURROUNDINGS... IRRATIONALLY.
EUGENE, OF COURSE, HAD NO WAY OF KNOWING ANY OF THIS AND HIS SYMBIOTE HAD LONG FORGOTTEN HOW TO COMMUNICATE BACK.
BUT AS YOU DREW CLOSER AND AS WE MADE BETTER CONNECTIONS WE WERE ABLE TO HELP GUIDE YOU HERE.
AND NOW WE CAN FIX WHAT HAD BEEN DAMAGED OVER TIME AND FROM THE RIGORS OF STRUGGLE.
WE CAN RECONNECT A VERY WORTHY EUGENE THOMPSON TO HIS SYMBIOTE.
NOW FIXED AND MADE WHOLE AS PART OF US.
NOW WITH A CLARITY AND PURITY THAT HE AND NO ONE ON YOUR PLANET OR IN YOUR ENTIRE STAR SYSTEM HAS EVER EXPERIENCED BEFORE.

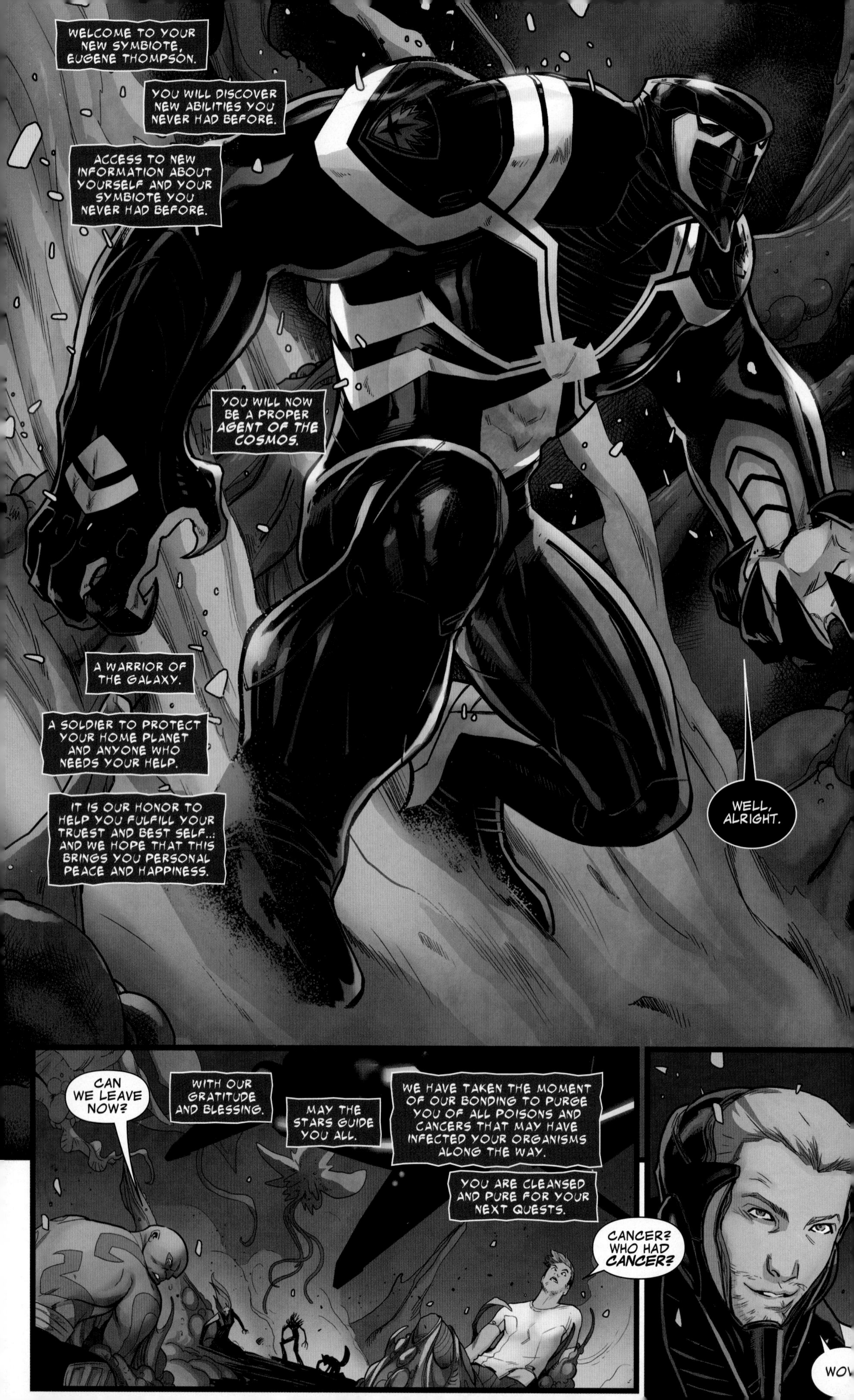
WELCOME TO YOUR NEW SYMBIOTE, EUGENE THOMPSON.
YOU WILL DISCOVER NEW ABILITIES YOU NEVER HAD BEFORE.
ACCESS TO NEW INFORMATION ABOUT YOURSELF AND YOUR SYMBIOTE YOU NEVER HAD BEFORE.
YOU WILL NOW BE A PROPER AGENT OF THE COSMOS.
A WARRIOR OF THE GALAXY.
A SOLDIER TO PROTECT YOUR HOME PLANET AND ANYONE WHO NEEDS YOUR HELP.
IT IS OUR HONOR TO HELP YOU FULFILL YOUR TRUEST AND BEST SELF... AND WE HOPE THAT THIS BRINGS YOU PERSONAL PEACE AND HAPPINESS.
WELL, ALRIGHT.
CAN WE LEAVE NOW?
WITH OUR GRATITUDE AND BLESSING.
MAY THE STARS GUIDE YOU ALL.
WE HAVE TAKEN THE MOMENT OF OUR BONDING TO PURGE YOU OF ALL POISONS AND CANCERS THAT MAY HAVE INFECTED YOUR ORGANISMS ALONG THE WAY.
YOU ARE CLEANSED AND PURE FOR YOUR NEXT QUESTS.
CANCER? WHO HAD CANCER?
WOW

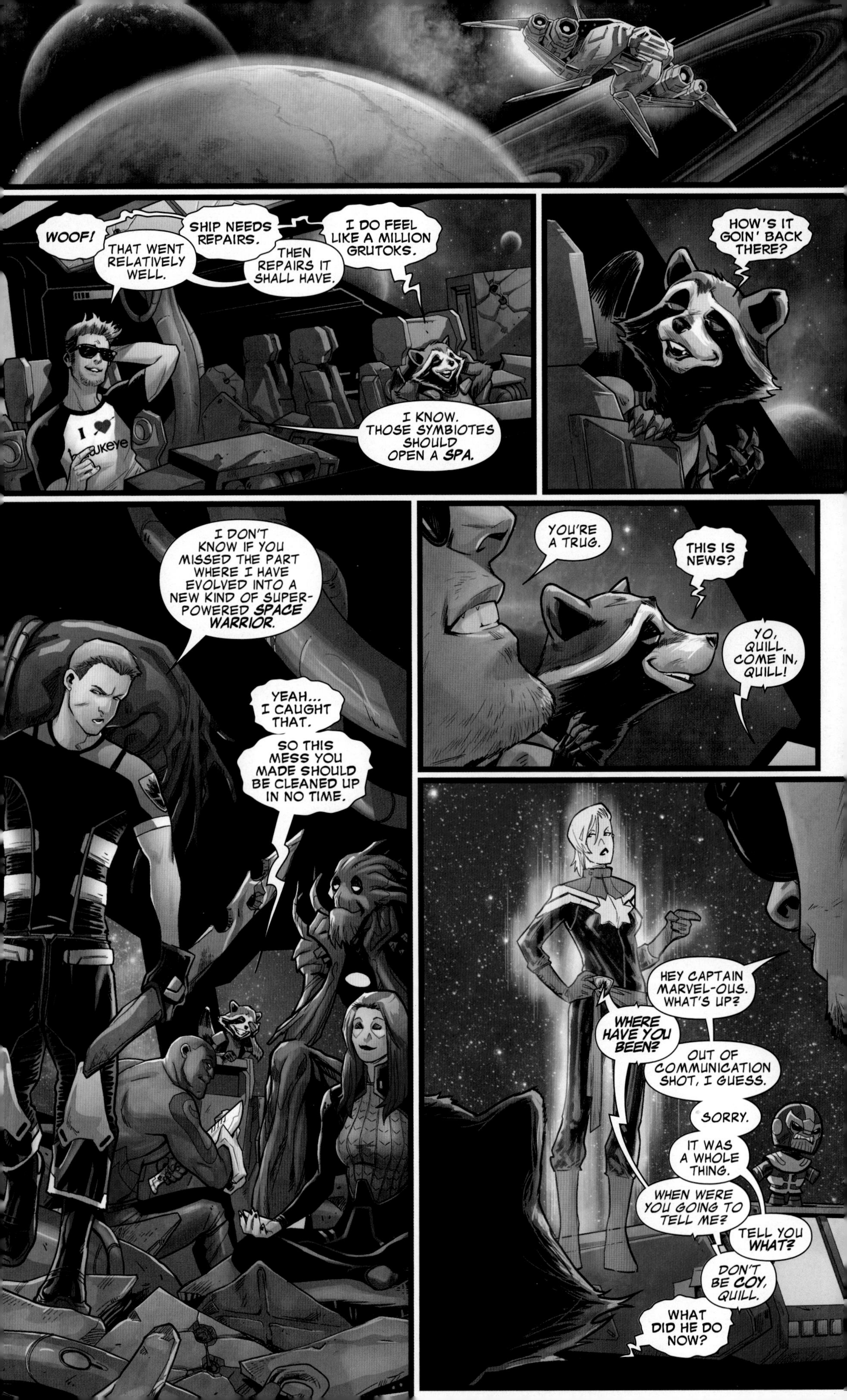
WOOF!
THAT WENT RELATIVELY WELL.
SHIP NEEDS REPAIRS.
THEN REPAIRS IT SHALL HAVE.
I DO FEEL LIKE A MILLION GRUTOKS.
I KNOW. THOSE SYMBIOTES SHOULD OPEN A SPA.
HOW'S IT GOIN' BACK THERE?
I DON'T KNOW IF YOU MISSED THE PART WHERE I HAVE EVOLVED INTO A NEW KIND OF SUPER-POWERED SPACE WARRIOR.
YEAH... I CAUGHT THAT.
SO THIS MESS YOU MADE SHOULD BE CLEANED UP IN NO TIME.
YOU'RE A TRUG.
THIS IS NEWS?
YO, QUILL. COME IN, QUILL!
HEY CAPTAIN MARVEL-OUS. WHAT'S UP?
WHERE HAVE YOU BEEN?
OUT OF COMMUNICATION SHOT, I GUESS.
SORRY.
IT WAS A WHOLE THING.
WHEN WERE YOU GOING TO TELL ME?
TELL YOU WHAT?
DON'T BE COY, QUILL.
WHAT DID HE DO NOW?

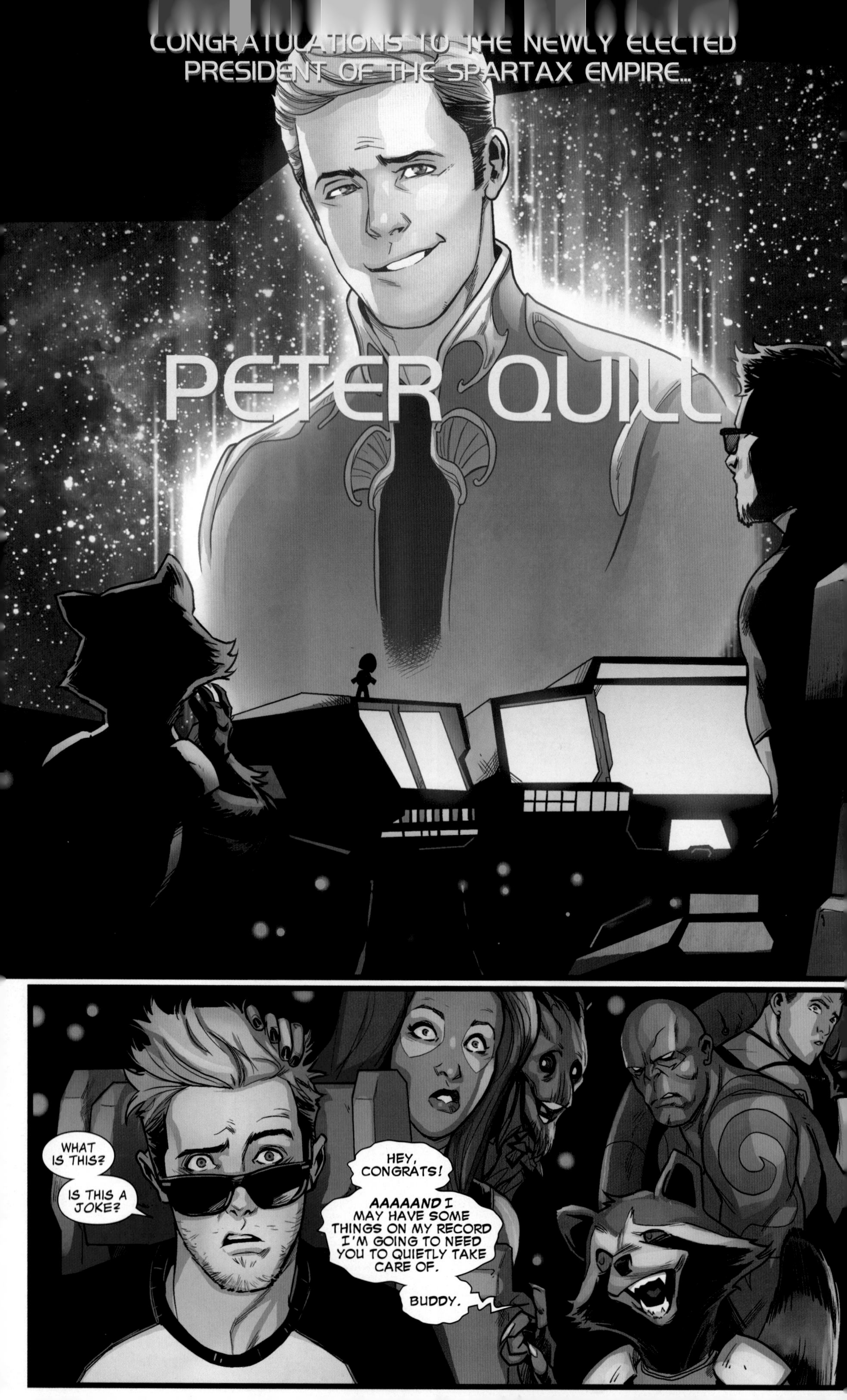
CONGRATULATIONS TO THE NEWLY ELECTED PRESIDENT OF THE SPARTAX EMPIRE...
PETER QUILL
WHAT IS THIS?
IS THIS A JOKE?
HEY, CONGRATS!
AAAAAND I MAY HAVE SOME THINGS ON MY RECORD I'M GOING TO NEED YOU TO QUIETLY TAKE CARE OF.
BUDDY.

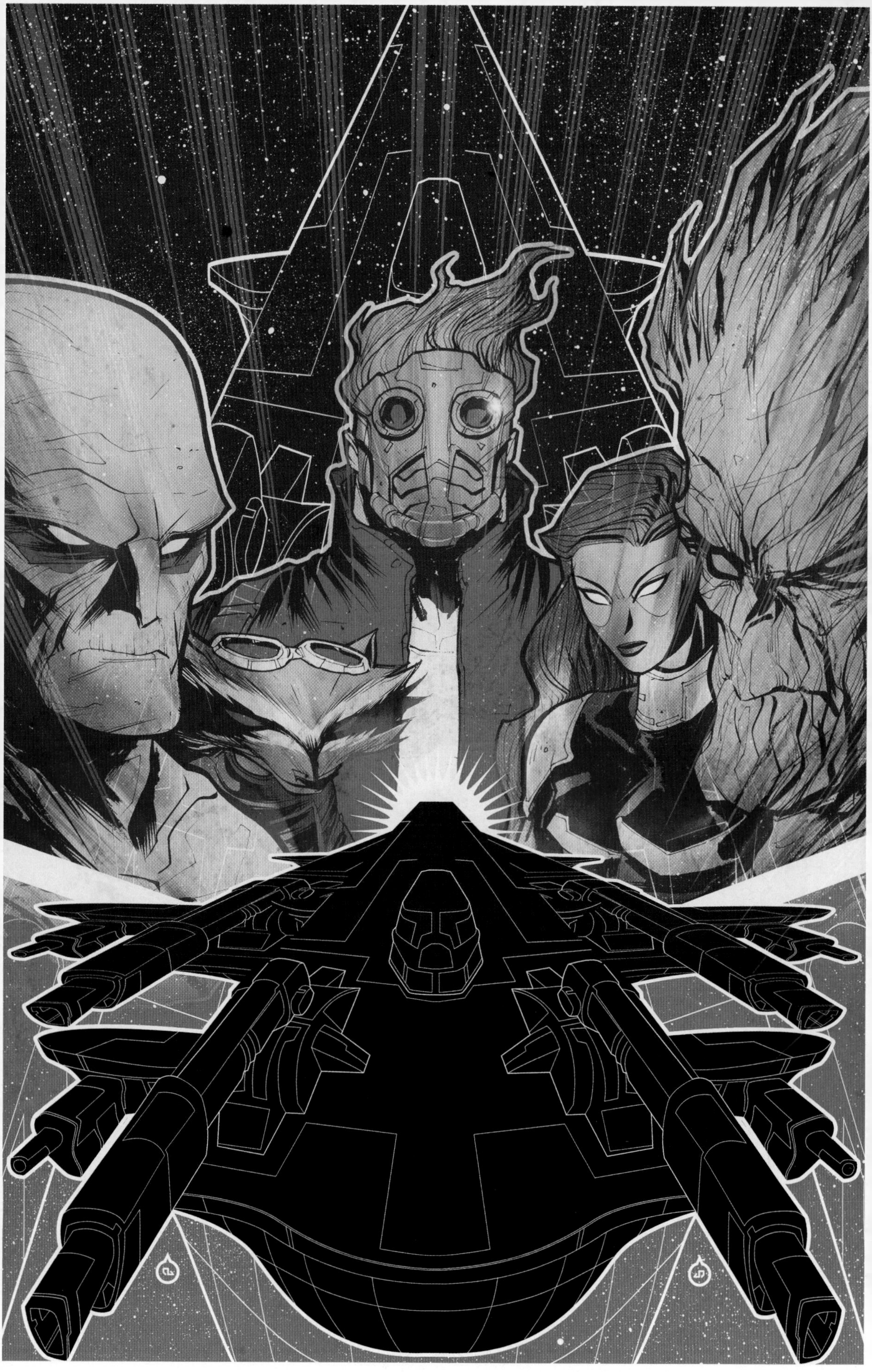

***ANNUAL #1* VARIANT** BY JUAN DOE

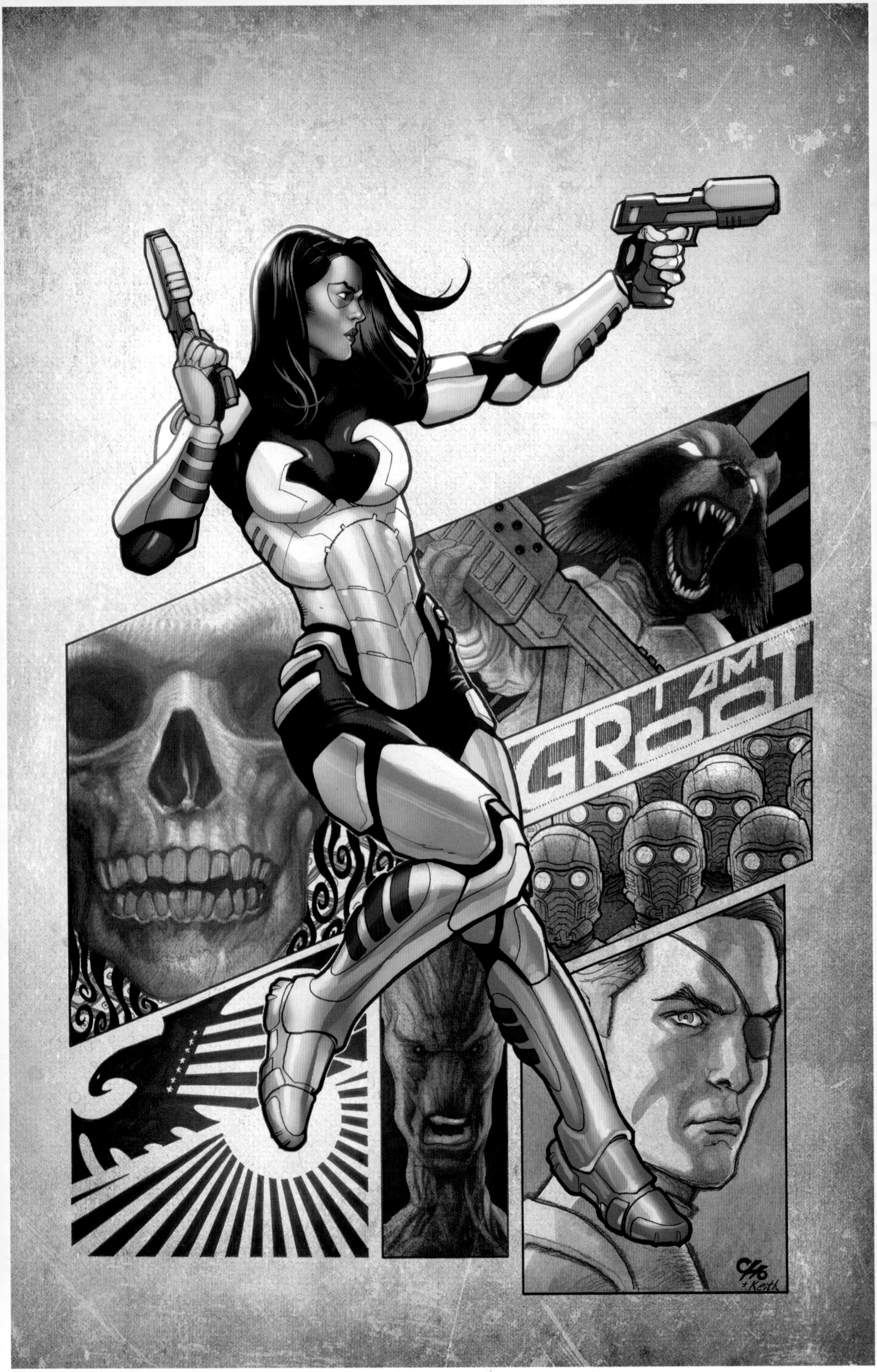
I AM GROOT
CHO + Keith

ANNUAL 1

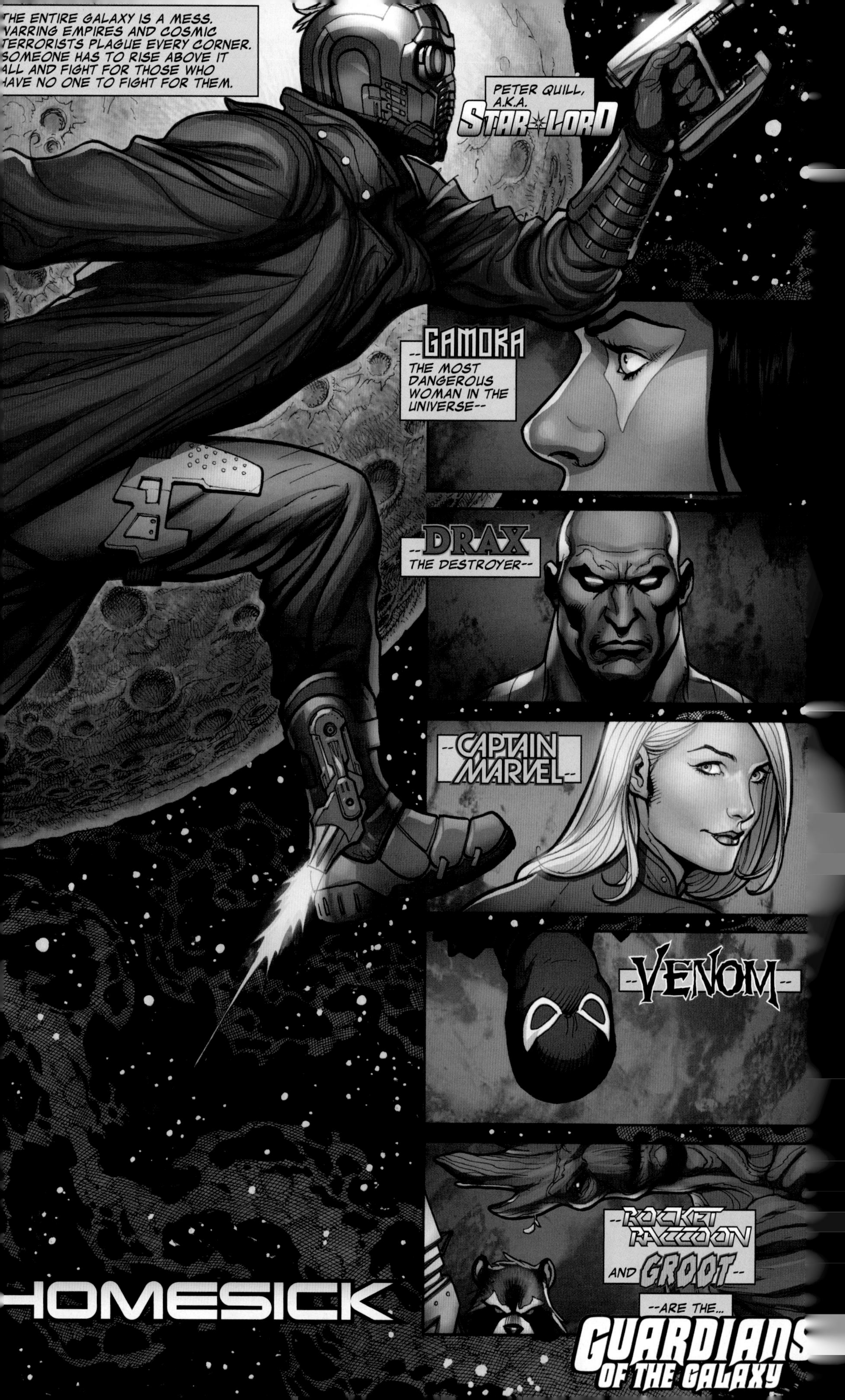

THE ENTIRE GALAXY IS A MESS. WARRING EMPIRES AND COSMIC TERRORISTS PLAGUE EVERY CORNER. SOMEONE HAS TO RISE ABOVE IT ALL AND FIGHT FOR THOSE WHO HAVE NO ONE TO FIGHT FOR THEM.
PETER QUILL, A.K.A. STAR-LORD
--GAMORA THE MOST DANGEROUS WOMAN IN THE UNIVERSE--
--DRAX THE DESTROYER--
--CAPTAIN MARVEL--
--VENOM--
--ROCKET RACCOON AND GROOT--
--ARE THE...
GUARDIANS OF THE GALAXY
HOMESICK

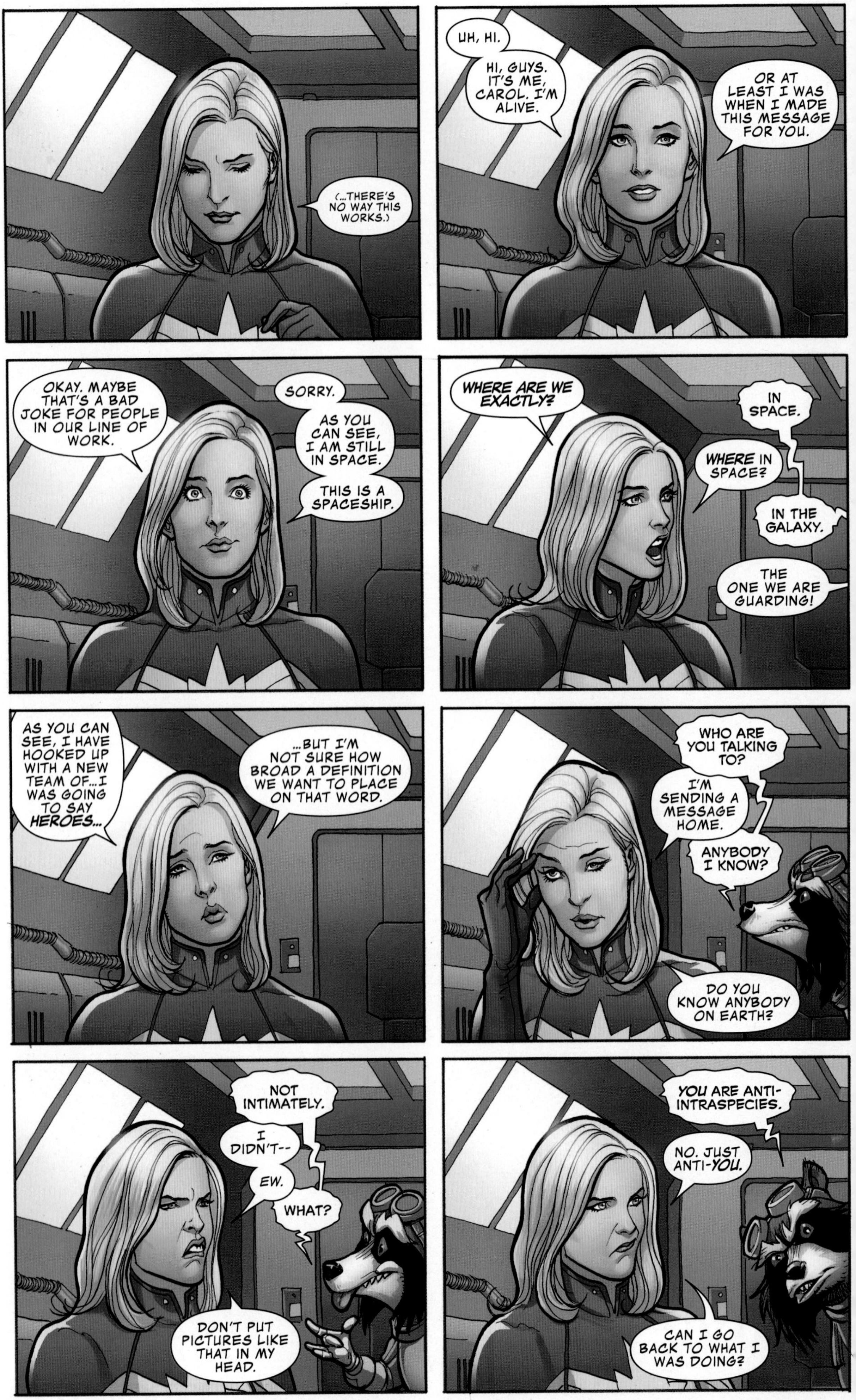
(...THERE'S NO WAY THIS WORKS.)
UH, HI.
HI, GUYS. IT'S ME, CAROL. I'M ALIVE.
OR AT LEAST I WAS WHEN I MADE THIS MESSAGE FOR YOU.
OKAY. MAYBE THAT'S A BAD JOKE FOR PEOPLE IN OUR LINE OF WORK.
SORRY.
AS YOU CAN SEE, I AM STILL IN SPACE.
THIS IS A SPACESHIP.
WHERE ARE WE EXACTLY?
IN SPACE.
WHERE IN SPACE?
IN THE GALAXY.
THE ONE WE ARE GUARDING!
AS YOU CAN SEE, I HAVE HOOKED UP WITH A NEW TEAM OF...I WAS GOING TO SAY HEROES...
...BUT I'M NOT SURE HOW BROAD A DEFINITION WE WANT TO PLACE ON THAT WORD.
WHO ARE YOU TALKING TO?
I'M SENDING A MESSAGE HOME.
ANYBODY I KNOW?
DO YOU KNOW ANYBODY ON EARTH?
NOT INTIMATELY.
I DIDN'T--
EW.
WHAT?
DON'T PUT PICTURES LIKE THAT IN MY HEAD.
YOU ARE ANTI-INTRASPECIES.
NO. JUST ANTI-YOU.
CAN I GO BACK TO WHAT I WAS DOING?

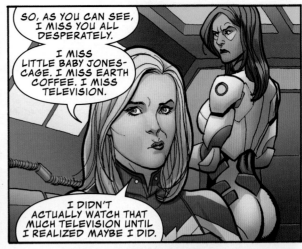
SO, AS YOU CAN SEE, I MISS YOU ALL DESPERATELY.

I MISS LITTLE BABY JONES-CAGE. I MISS EARTH COFFEE. I MISS TELEVISION.

I DIDN'T ACTUALLY WATCH THAT MUCH TELEVISION UNTIL I REALIZED MAYBE I DID.

I'M NOT SURE WHEN I DID, BUT I MUST HAVE BECAUSE I'M REALLY MISSING IT.

OR MAYBE I'M MISSING THE IDEA THAT I COULD WATCH IT.

ANYWAY, I JUST WANTED TO TELL YOU THAT THINGS OUT HERE ARE INTERESTING.

I DON'T KNOW IF YOU KNOW THIS, BUT--

CAN I HELP YOU?

I AM GROOT.

YES.

HE IS GROOT.

ANYWAY, I WAS GOING TO CATCH YOU UP ON ALL MY STUFF, BUT...THAT'S PRETTY MUCH--

HOLY @#$@#$@!

ALL STATIONS!

IS SOMETHING WRONG?

YOU'RE GOING TO WANT TO SEE THIS!

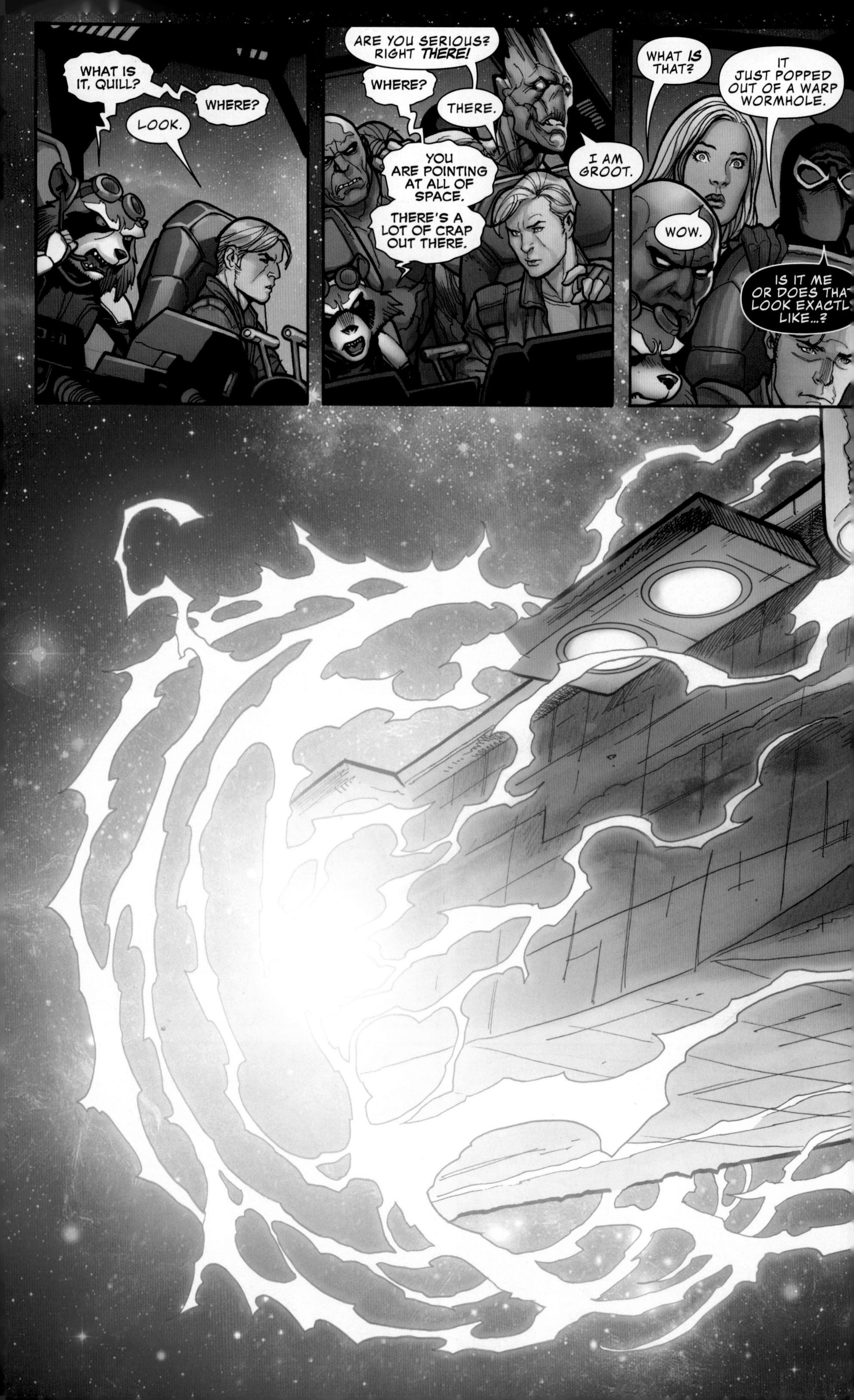
WHAT IS IT, QUILL?
WHERE?
LOOK.
ARE YOU SERIOUS? RIGHT THERE!
WHERE?
THERE.
YOU ARE POINTING AT ALL OF SPACE.
THERE'S A LOT OF CRAP OUT THERE.
I AM GROOT.
WHAT IS THAT?
IT JUST POPPED OUT OF A WARP WORMHOLE.
WOW.
IS IT ME OR DOES THAT LOOK EXACTLY LIKE...?

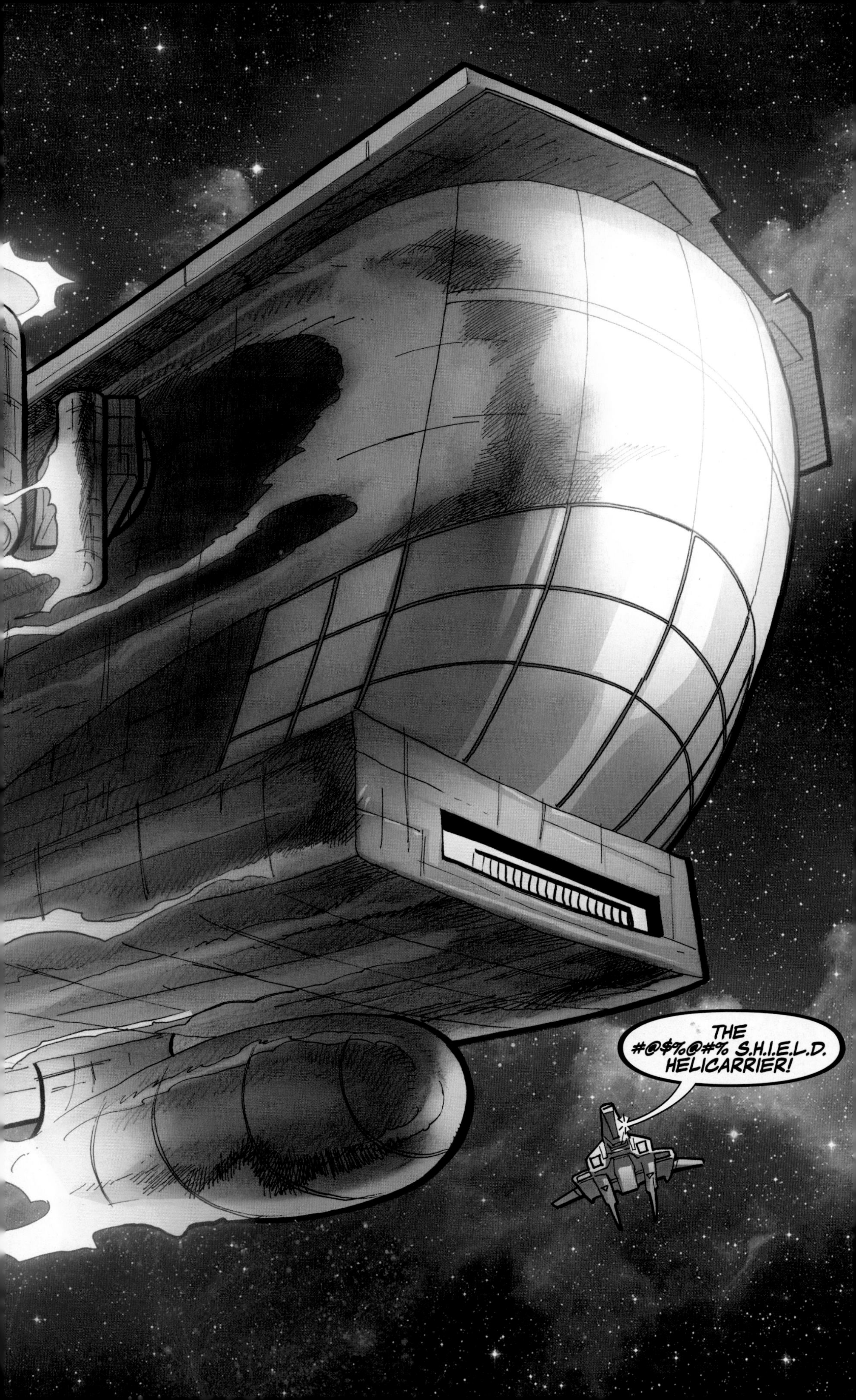
THE #@$%@#% S.H.I.E.L.D. HELICARRIER!

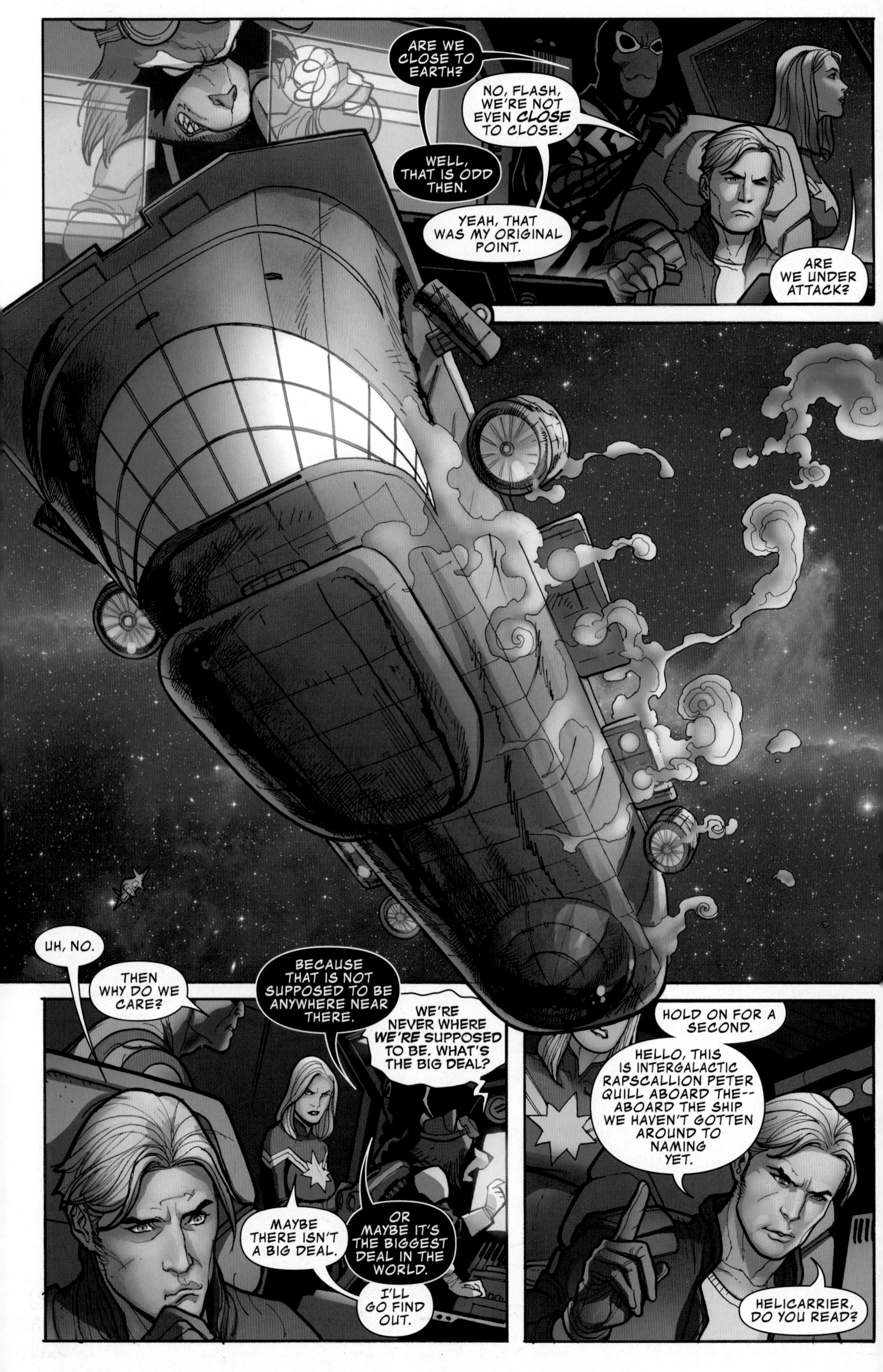
ARE WE CLOSE TO EARTH?
NO, FLASH, WE'RE NOT EVEN CLOSE TO CLOSE.
WELL, THAT IS ODD THEN.
YEAH, THAT WAS MY ORIGINAL POINT.
ARE WE UNDER ATTACK?
UH, NO.
THEN WHY DO WE CARE?
BECAUSE THAT IS NOT SUPPOSED TO BE ANYWHERE NEAR THERE.
WE'RE NEVER WHERE WE'RE SUPPOSED TO BE. WHAT'S THE BIG DEAL?
MAYBE THERE ISN'T A BIG DEAL.
OR MAYBE IT'S THE BIGGEST DEAL IN THE WORLD.
I'LL GO FIND OUT.
HOLD ON FOR A SECOND.
HELLO, THIS IS INTERGALACTIC RAPSCALLION PETER QUILL ABOARD THE SHIP-- ABOARD THE SHIP WE HAVEN'T GOTTEN AROUND TO NAMING YET.
HELICARRIER, DO YOU READ?

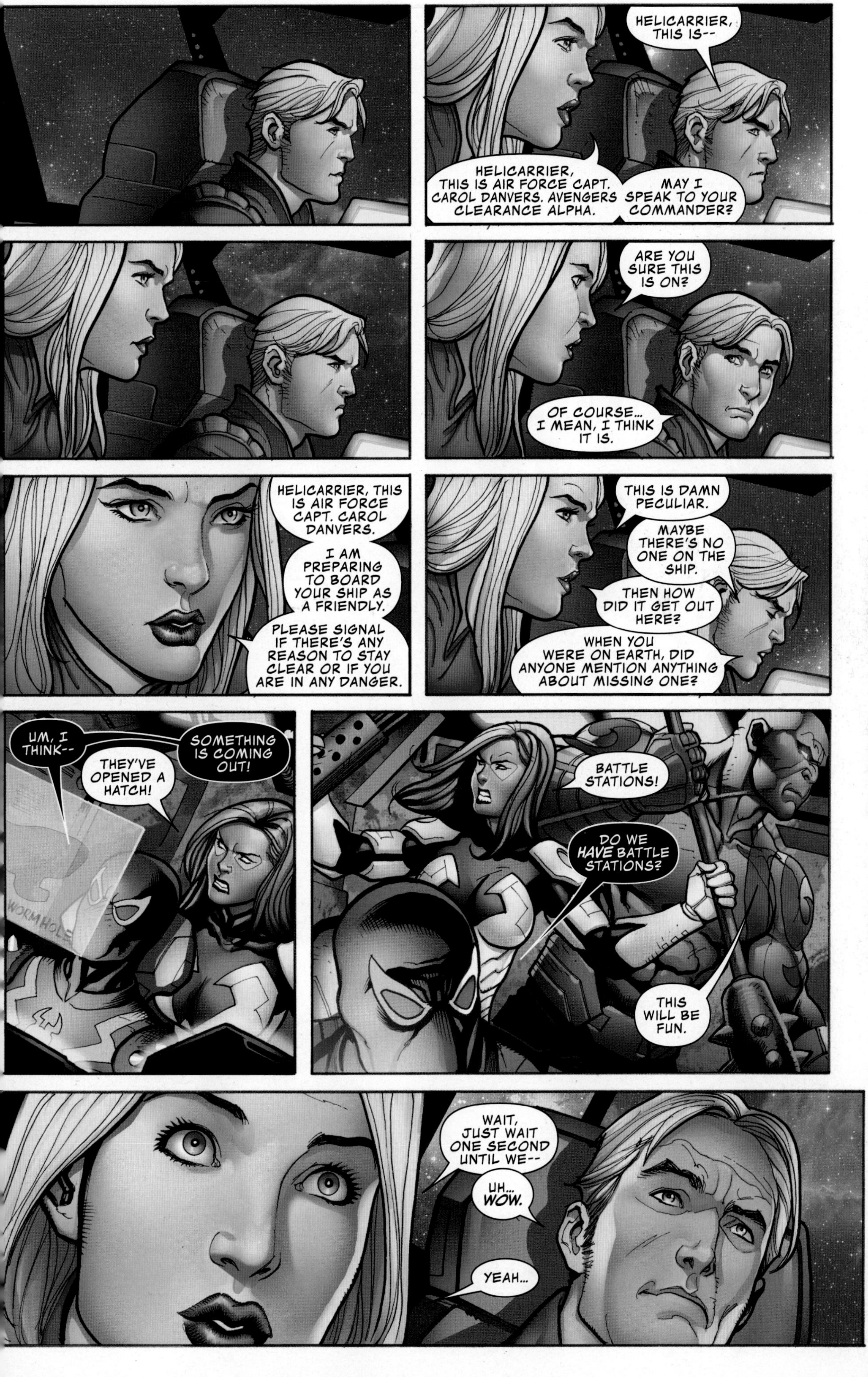
HELICARRIER, THIS IS--
HELICARRIER, THIS IS AIR FORCE CAPT. CAROL DANVERS. AVENGERS CLEARANCE ALPHA.
MAY I SPEAK TO YOUR COMMANDER?
ARE YOU SURE THIS IS ON?
OF COURSE... I MEAN, I THINK IT IS.
HELICARRIER, THIS IS AIR FORCE CAPT. CAROL DANVERS.
I AM PREPARING TO BOARD YOUR SHIP AS A FRIENDLY.
PLEASE SIGNAL IF THERE'S ANY REASON TO STAY CLEAR OR IF YOU ARE IN ANY DANGER.
THIS IS DAMN PECULIAR.
MAYBE THERE'S NO ONE ON THE SHIP.
THEN HOW DID IT GET OUT HERE?
WHEN YOU WERE ON EARTH, DID ANYONE MENTION ANYTHING ABOUT MISSING ONE?
UM, I THINK--
THEY'VE OPENED A HATCH!
SOMETHING IS COMING OUT!
WORMHOLE
BATTLE STATIONS!
DO WE *HAVE* BATTLE STATIONS?
THIS WILL BE FUN.
WAIT, JUST WAIT ONE SECOND UNTIL WE--
UH... *WOW.*
YEAH...

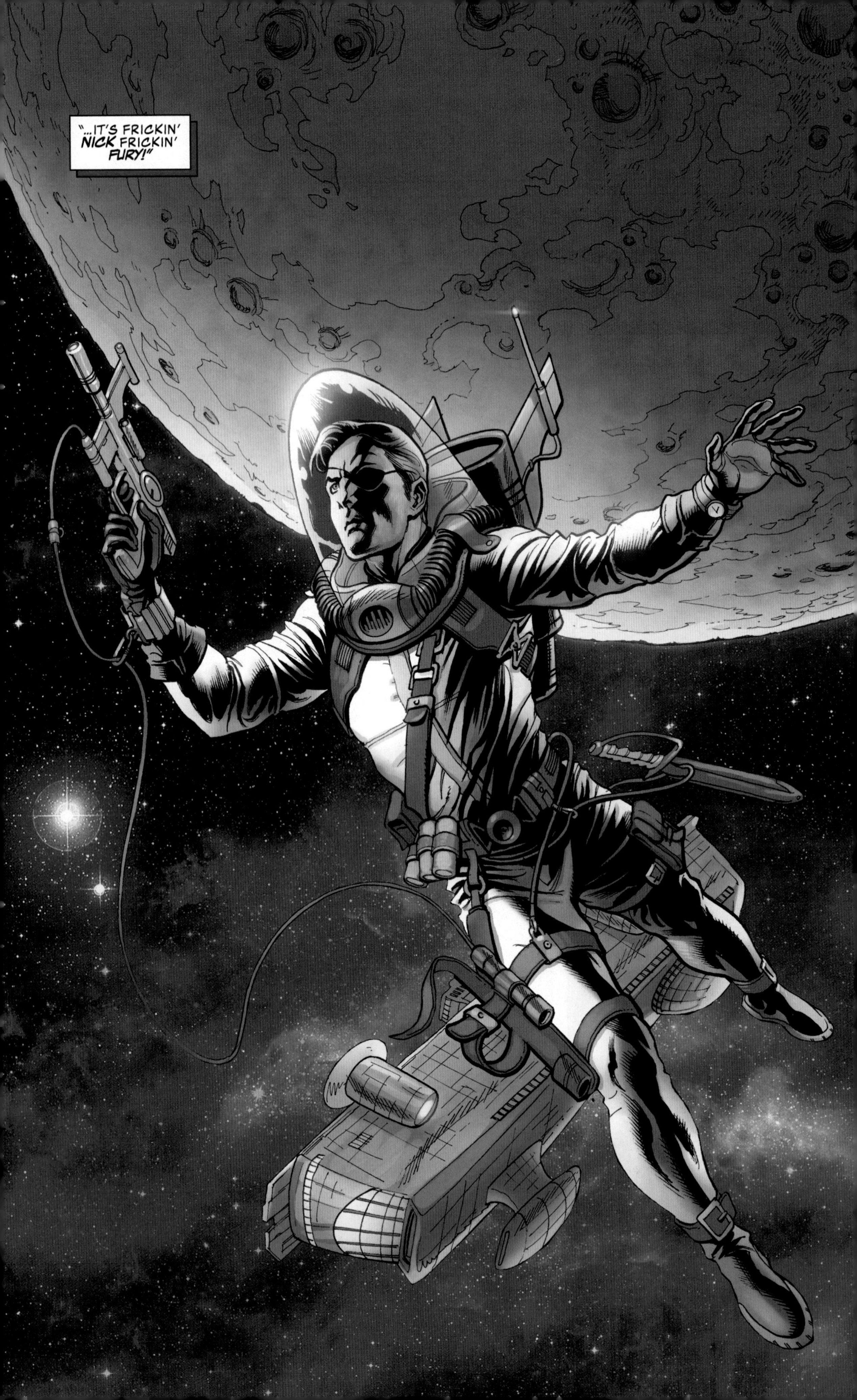
"...IT'S FRICKIN' NICK FRICKIN' FURY!"

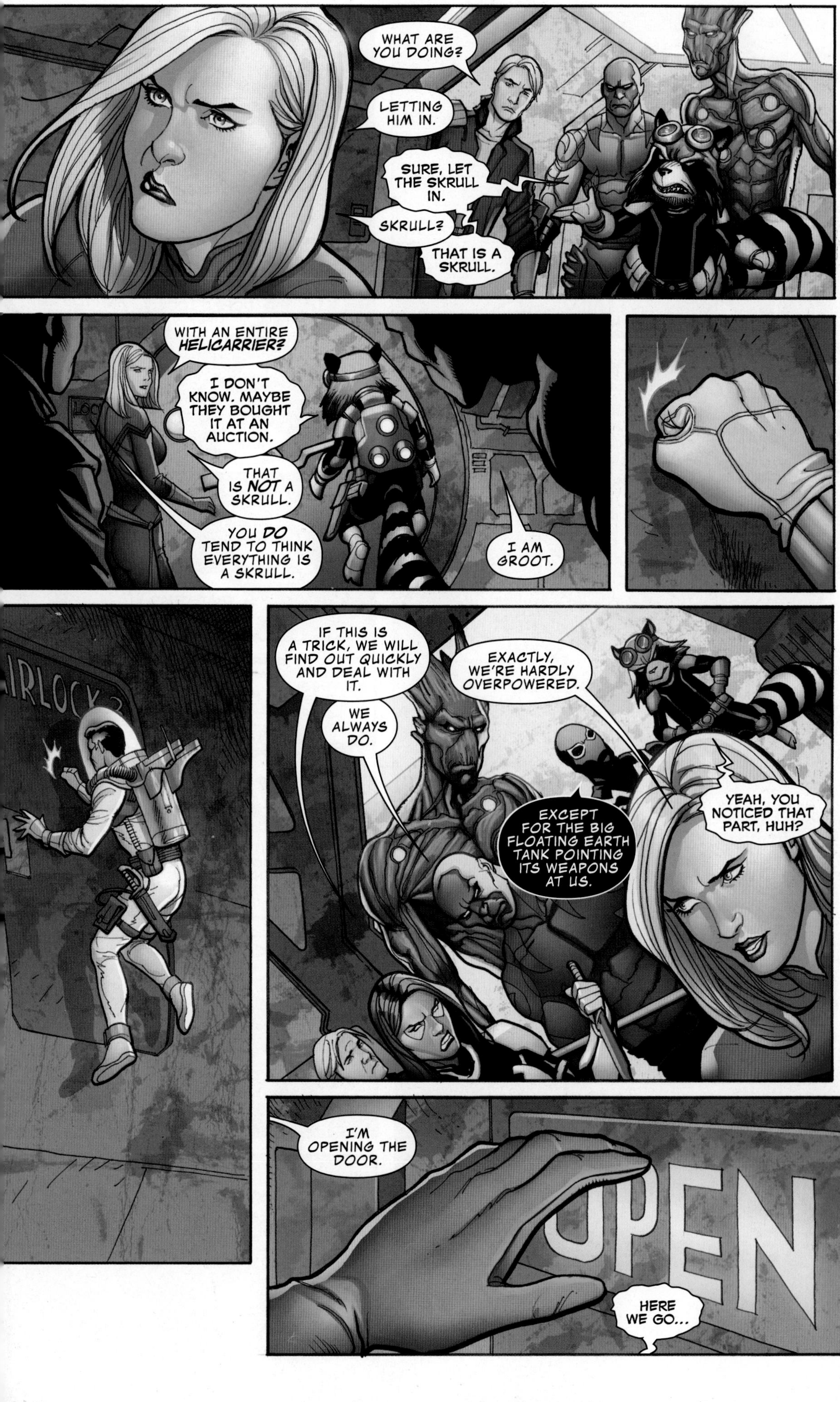
WHAT ARE YOU DOING?
LETTING HIM IN.
SURE, LET THE SKRULL IN.
SKRULL?
THAT IS A SKRULL.
WITH AN ENTIRE HELICARRIER?
I DON'T KNOW. MAYBE THEY BOUGHT IT AT AN AUCTION.
THAT IS NOT A SKRULL.
YOU DO TEND TO THINK EVERYTHING IS A SKRULL.
I AM GROOT.
AIRLOCK 3
IF THIS IS A TRICK, WE WILL FIND OUT QUICKLY AND DEAL WITH IT.
WE ALWAYS DO.
EXACTLY, WE'RE HARDLY OVERPOWERED.
EXCEPT FOR THE BIG FLOATING EARTH TANK POINTING ITS WEAPONS AT US.
YEAH, YOU NOTICED THAT PART, HUH?
I'M OPENING THE DOOR.
OPEN
HERE WE GO...

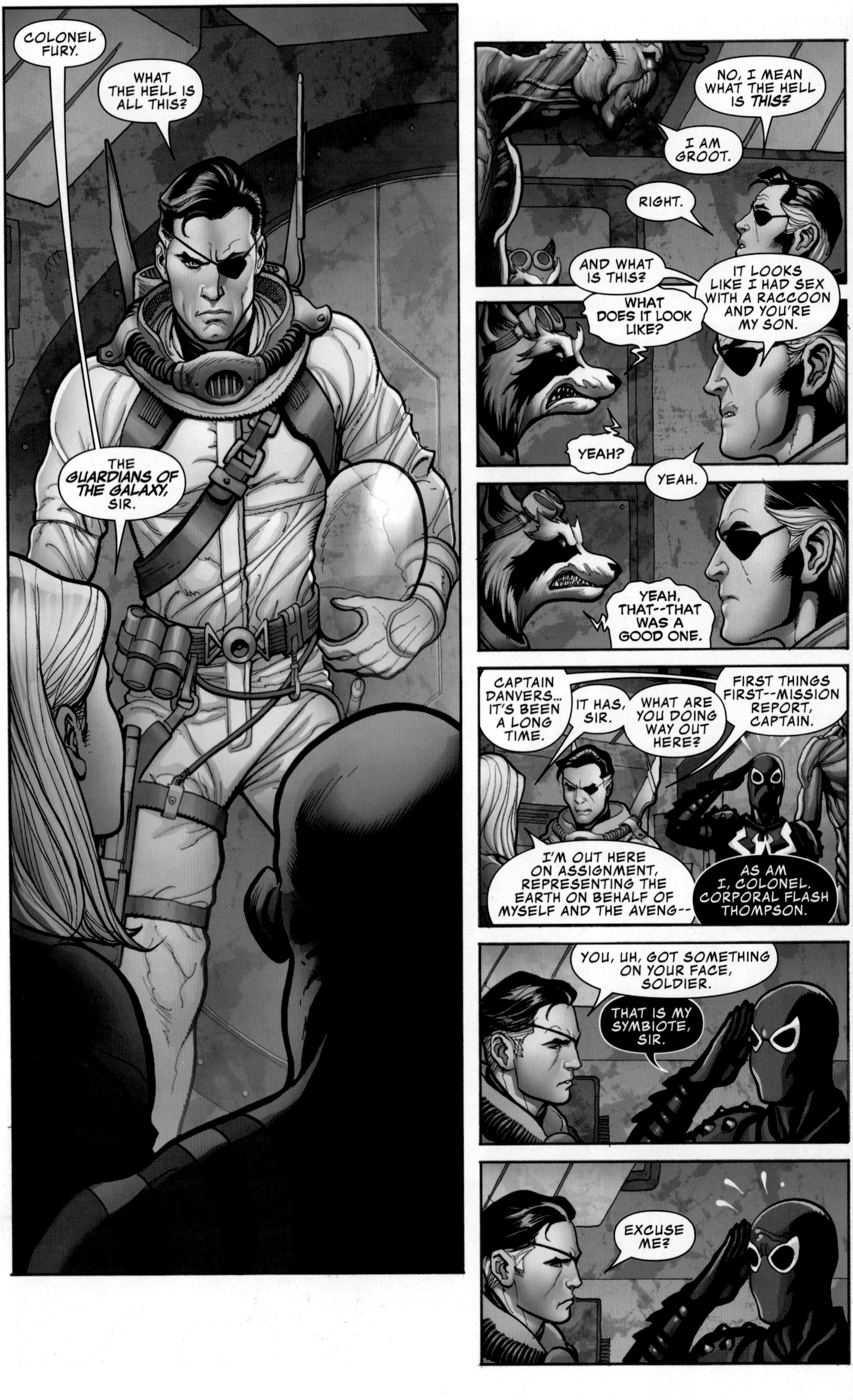

COLONEL FURY.
WHAT THE HELL IS ALL THIS?
THE GUARDIANS OF THE GALAXY, SIR.
NO, I MEAN WHAT THE HELL IS THIS?
I AM GROOT.
RIGHT.
AND WHAT IS THIS?
IT LOOKS LIKE I HAD SEX WITH A RACCOON AND YOU'RE MY SON.
WHAT DOES IT LOOK LIKE?
YEAH?
YEAH.
YEAH, THAT--THAT WAS A GOOD ONE.
CAPTAIN DANVERS... IT'S BEEN A LONG TIME.
IT HAS, SIR.
WHAT ARE YOU DOING WAY OUT HERE?
FIRST THINGS FIRST--MISSION REPORT, CAPTAIN.
I'M OUT HERE ON ASSIGNMENT, REPRESENTING THE EARTH ON BEHALF OF MYSELF AND THE AVENG--
AS AM I, COLONEL. CORPORAL FLASH THOMPSON.
YOU, UH, GOT SOMETHING ON YOUR FACE, SOLDIER.
THAT IS MY SYMBIOTE, SIR.
EXCUSE ME?

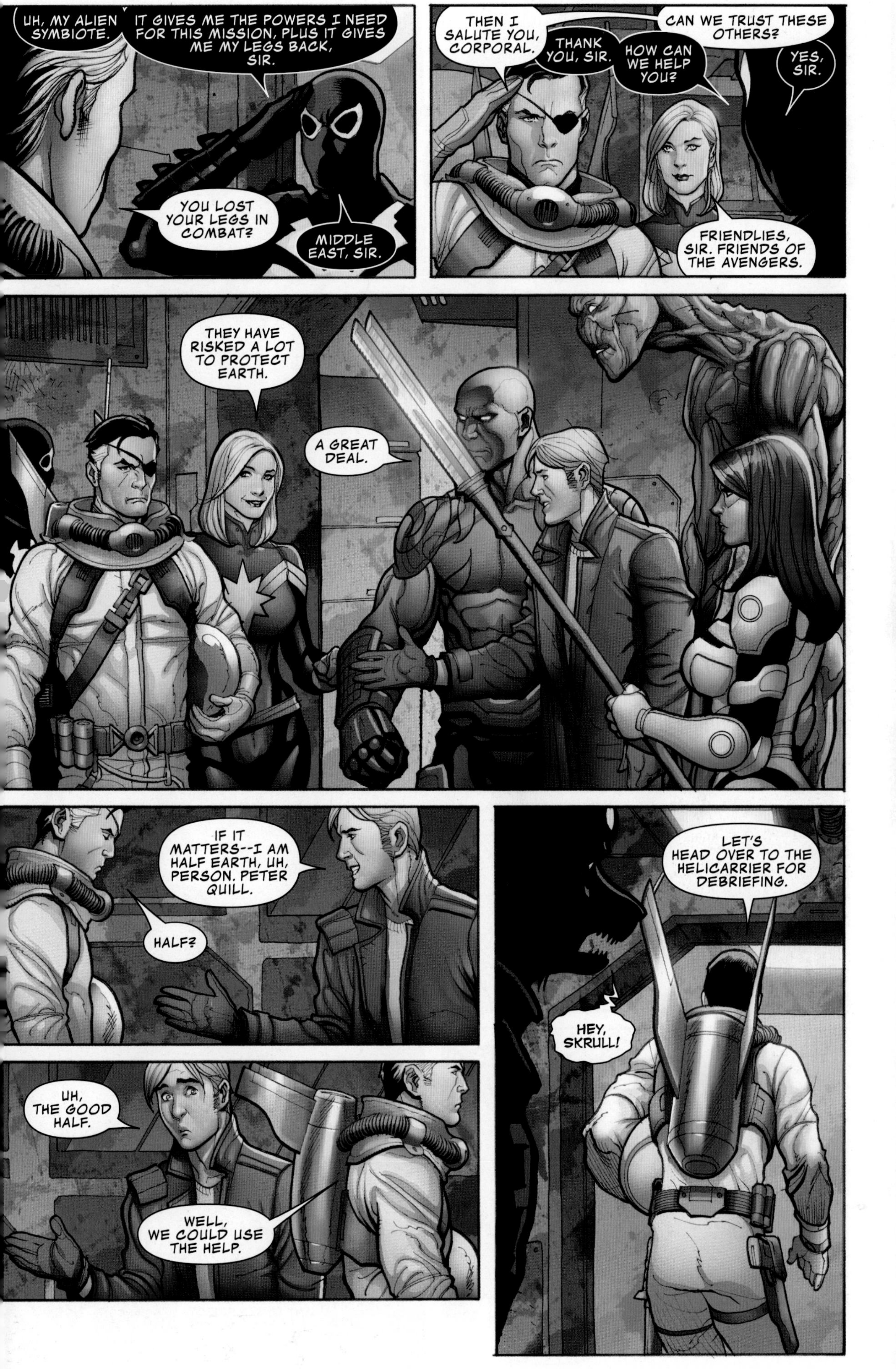

UH, MY ALIEN SYMBIOTE.
IT GIVES ME THE POWERS I NEED FOR THIS MISSION, PLUS IT GIVES ME MY LEGS BACK, SIR.
YOU LOST YOUR LEGS IN COMBAT?
MIDDLE EAST, SIR.
THEN I SALUTE YOU, CORPORAL.
THANK YOU, SIR.
HOW CAN WE HELP YOU?
CAN WE TRUST THESE OTHERS?
YES, SIR.
FRIENDLIES, SIR. FRIENDS OF THE AVENGERS.
THEY HAVE RISKED A LOT TO PROTECT EARTH.
A GREAT DEAL.
IF IT MATTERS--I AM HALF EARTH, UH, PERSON. PETER QUILL.
HALF?
UH, THE GOOD HALF.
WELL, WE COULD USE THE HELP.
LET'S HEAD OVER TO THE HELICARRIER FOR DEBRIEFING.
HEY, SKRULL!

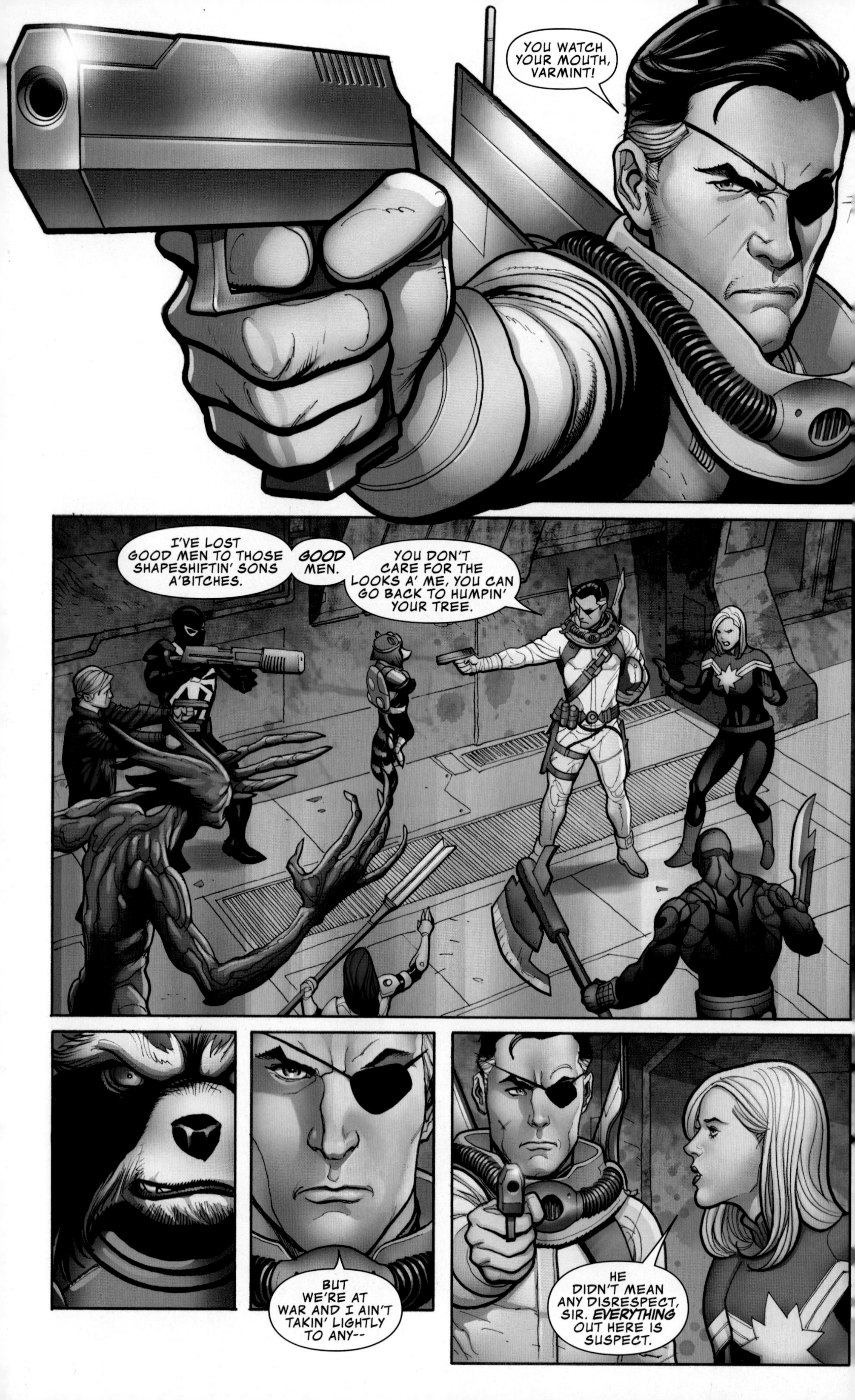
YOU WATCH YOUR MOUTH, VARMINT!
I'VE LOST GOOD MEN TO THOSE SHAPESHIFTIN' SONS A'BITCHES.
GOOD MEN.
YOU DON'T CARE FOR THE LOOKS A' ME, YOU CAN GO BACK TO HUMPIN' YOUR TREE.
BUT WE'RE AT WAR AND I AIN'T TAKIN' LIGHTLY TO ANY--
HE DIDN'T MEAN ANY DISRESPECT, SIR. EVERYTHING OUT HERE IS SUSPECT.

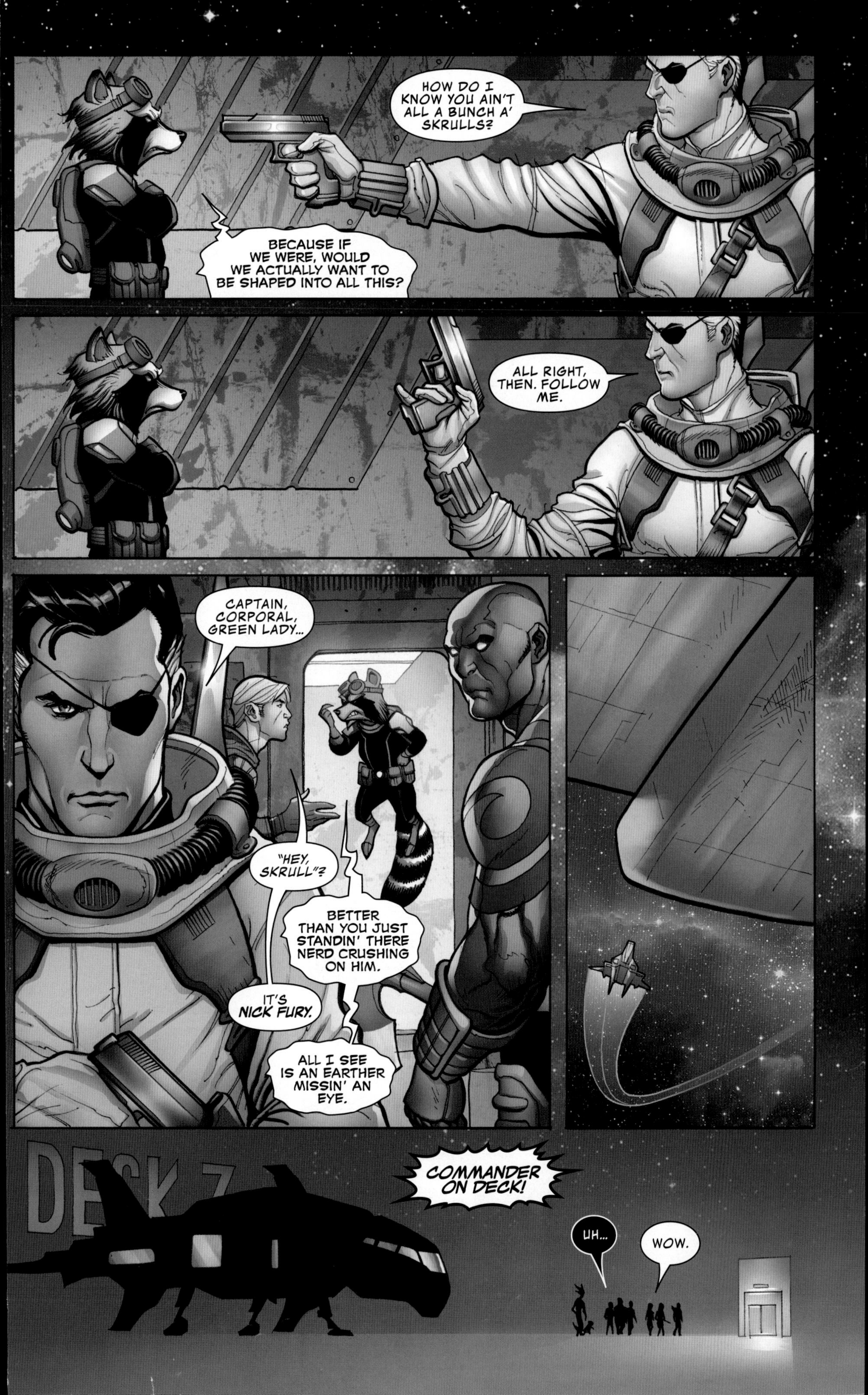
HOW DO I KNOW YOU AIN'T ALL A BUNCH A' SKRULLS?
BECAUSE IF WE WERE, WOULD WE ACTUALLY WANT TO BE SHAPED INTO ALL THIS?
ALL RIGHT, THEN. FOLLOW ME.
CAPTAIN, CORPORAL, GREEN LADY...
"HEY, SKRULL"?
BETTER THAN YOU JUST STANDIN' THERE NERD CRUSHING ON HIM.
IT'S NICK FURY.
ALL I SEE IS AN EARTHER MISSIN' AN EYE.
COMMANDER ON DECK!
UH...
WOW.

NICK, WHAT IS THIS?

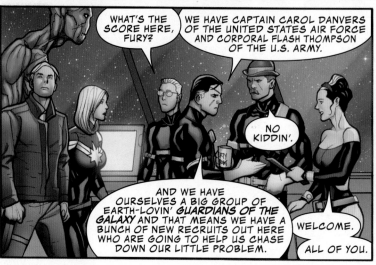

WHAT'S THE SCORE HERE, FURY?

WE HAVE CAPTAIN CAROL DANVERS OF THE UNITED STATES AIR FORCE AND CORPORAL FLASH THOMPSON OF THE U.S. ARMY.

NO KIDDIN'.

AND WE HAVE OURSELVES A BIG GROUP OF EARTH-LOVIN' *GUARDIANS OF THE GALAXY* AND THAT MEANS WE HAVE A BUNCH OF NEW RECRUITS OUT HERE WHO ARE GOING TO HELP US CHASE DOWN OUR LITTLE PROBLEM.

WELCOME. ALL OF YOU.

GUARDIANS OF THE GALAXY.

WHY DIDN'T WE THINK TO CALL OURSELVES THAT?

COLONEL FURY, WHAT AR YOU ALL *DOIN* OUT HERE?

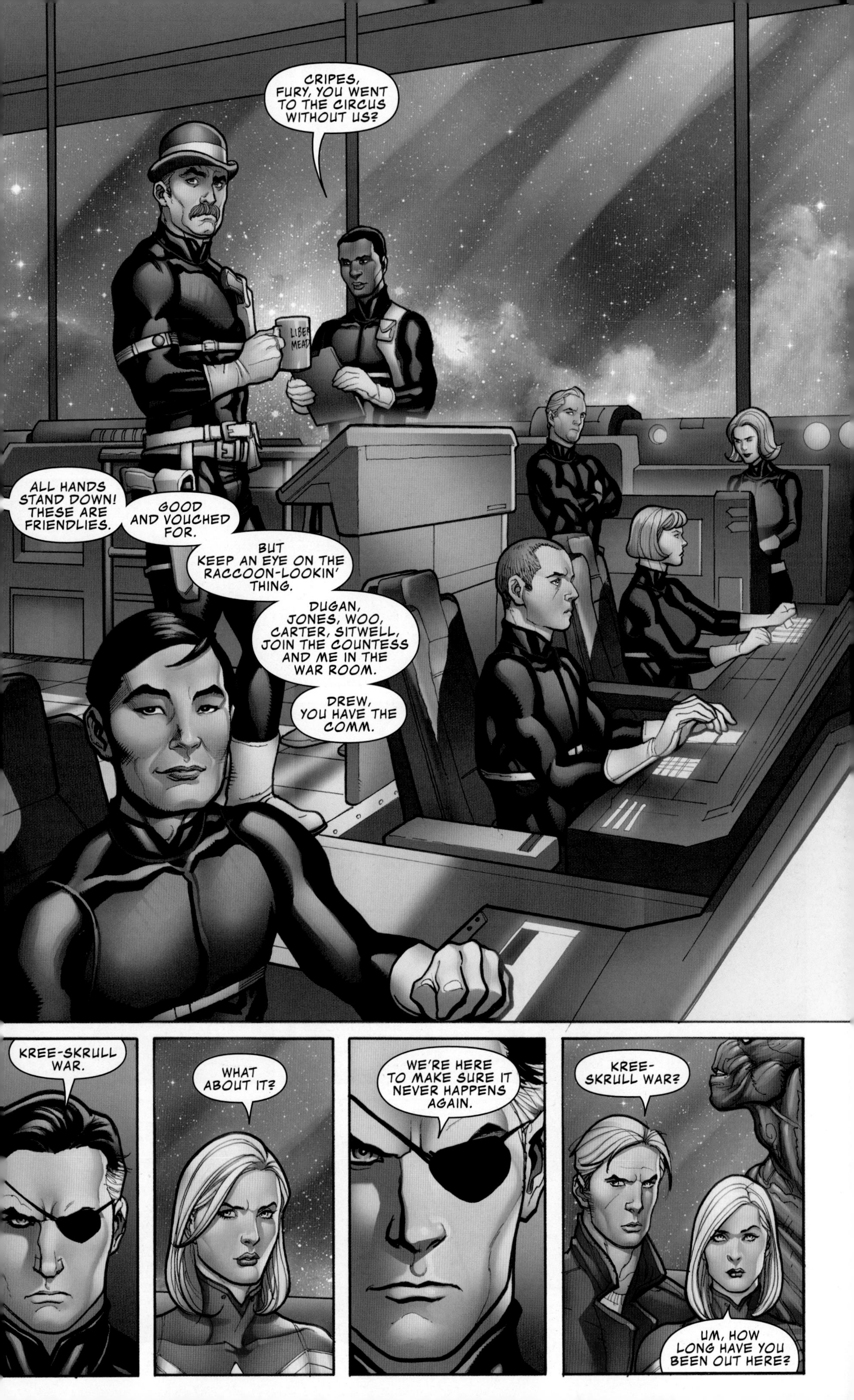

CRIPES, FURY, YOU WENT TO THE CIRCUS WITHOUT US?
ALL HANDS STAND DOWN! THESE ARE FRIENDLIES.
GOOD AND VOUCHED FOR.
BUT KEEP AN EYE ON THE RACCOON-LOOKIN' THING.
DUGAN, JONES, WOO, CARTER, SITWELL, JOIN THE COUNTESS AND ME IN THE WAR ROOM.
DREW, YOU HAVE THE COMM.
KREE-SKRULL WAR.
WHAT ABOUT IT?
WE'RE HERE TO MAKE SURE IT NEVER HAPPENS AGAIN.
KREE-SKRULL WAR?
UM, HOW LONG HAVE YOU BEEN OUT HERE?

THE KREE AND THE SKRULLS BOTH PLANTED THEIR FLAG ON EARTH.

JUST DECIDED IT WAS THEIRS.

WHEN WAS THIS?

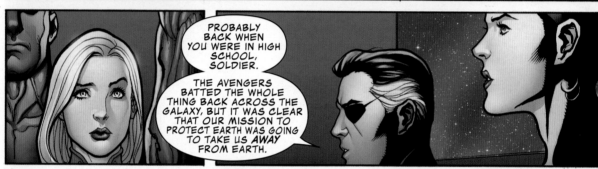

PROBABLY BACK WHEN YOU WERE IN HIGH SCHOOL, SOLDIER.

THE AVENGERS BATTED THE WHOLE THING BACK ACROSS THE GALAXY, BUT IT WAS CLEAR THAT OUR MISSION TO PROTECT EARTH WAS GOING TO TAKE US *AWAY* FROM EARTH.

THE THREAT TO OUR FREEDOM AIN'T JUST COMIN' FROM MOTHER RUSSIA AND HYDRA...

...IT'S COMIN' FROM ALL ANGLES AND ALL SPACES.

THERE ARE PLAYERS OUT HERE WE DON'T EVEN KNOW ABOUT YET.

SO WE SET OUT TO TAKE THE FIGHT HEAD ON.

WE GAVE UP A LOT TO BE HERE.

ALL OF US.

THESE ARE THE FINEST, MOST DEDICATED SOLDIERS I HAVE EVER HAD THE DAMN HONOR OF SERVIN' WITH.

NO ONE ON EARTH KNOWS ABOUT THIS, DO THEY?

I DON'T KNOW WHAT THEY KNOW.

BUT PROBABLY NOT.

HAVE YOU HAD ANY RUN-INS WITH SKRULLS?

BECAUSE WE'RE HUNTIN' THEM DOWN, EACH AND EVERY ONE.

AND THEY AIN'T THAT EASY TO SPOT.

BATTLE STATIONS!

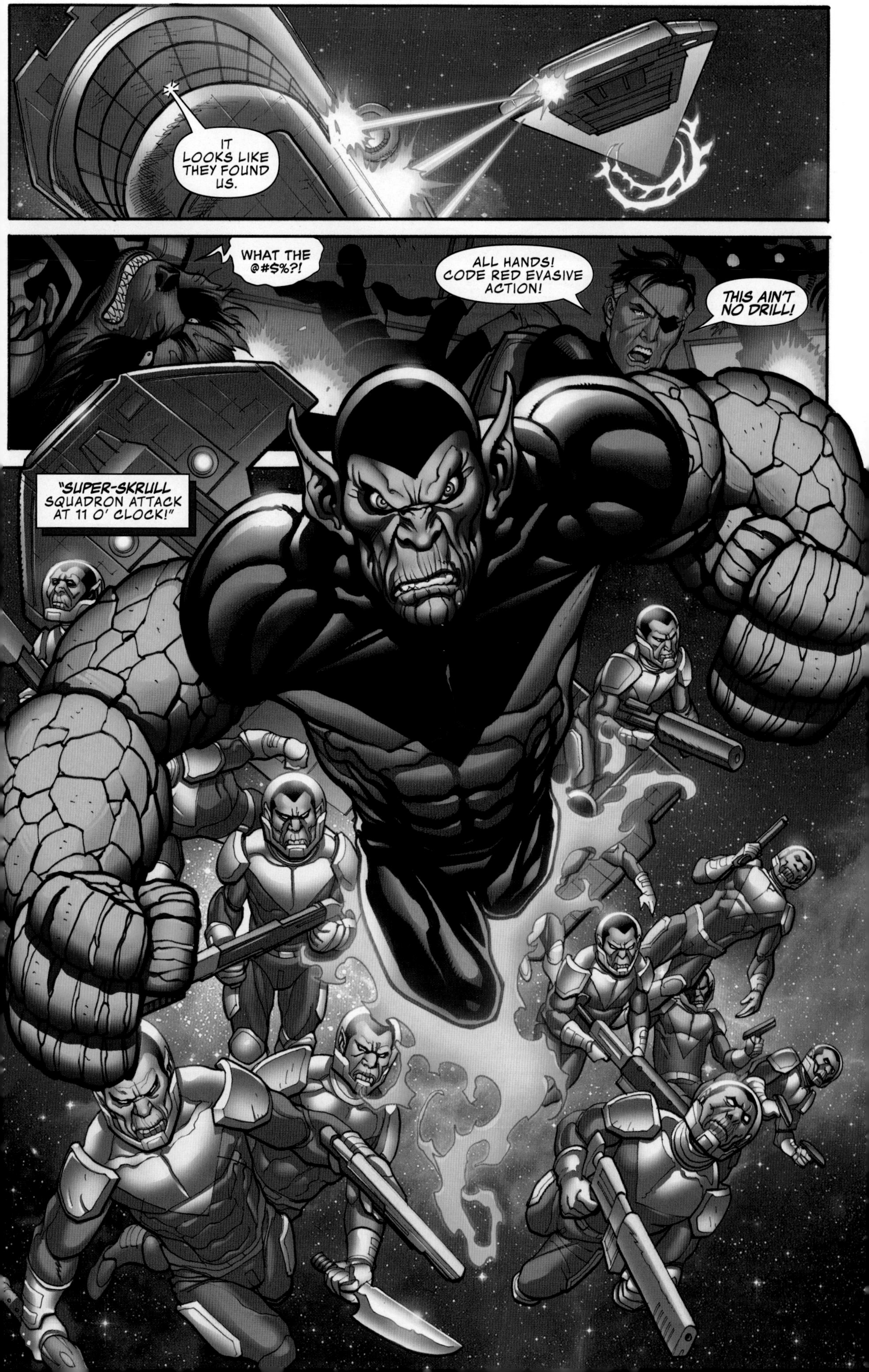
IT LOOKS LIKE THEY FOUND US.
WHAT THE @#$%?!
ALL HANDS! CODE RED EVASIVE ACTION!
THIS AIN'T NO DRILL!
"SUPER-SKRULL SQUADRON ATTACK AT 11 O' CLOCK!"

SKRULLS? FOR REAL?!

MY FAVORITE SPORT.

WE SHOULD HAVE NEVER LEFT OUR SHIP! THIS IS WHY YOU NEVER LEAVE THE SHIP!

THE SHIP IS CLOAKED! STOP YOUR WHINING.

YEAH, BUT I'M NOT!

GUYS, THIS ALL FEELS REALLY OFF TO ME!

HEY! STOP THEM! THEY MIGHT BE SKRULLS SENT HERE TO DISTRACT US!

STOP RIGHT THERE, SKRULLS!

WE'RE NOT SKRULLS, YA DUMB FRATAKI!

IF WE WERE SKRULLS, WOULD WE BE SHAPESHIFTING INTO THIS?!

YOU USED THAT LINE ALREADY.

MAYBE THAT'S EXACTLY WHAT YOU'D SHAPESHIFT INTO. SOMETHING WE WOULDN'T--

GET OUT OF THE WAY. WE CAN HELP YOU.

GET BACK!

IF I WAS HERE TO HARM YOU, YOU'D BE HARMED!

BOOM

AGH!

GUARDIANS!

WE'RE OKAY!

LET'S GO!

I AM GROOT!

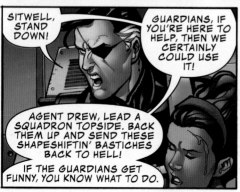

SITWELL, STAND DOWN!

GUARDIANS, IF YOU'RE HERE TO HELP, THEN WE CERTAINLY COULD USE IT!

AGENT DREW, LEAD A SQUADRON TOPSIDE. BACK THEM UP AND SEND THESE SHAPESHIFTIN' BASTICHES BACK TO HELL!

IF THE GUARDIANS GET FUNNY, YOU KNOW WHAT TO DO.

I'M ON IT, COLONEL!

AGENT DREW?!

FOLLOW ME! WE'LL STOP THEM ON THE AIRFIELD.

JESSICA?

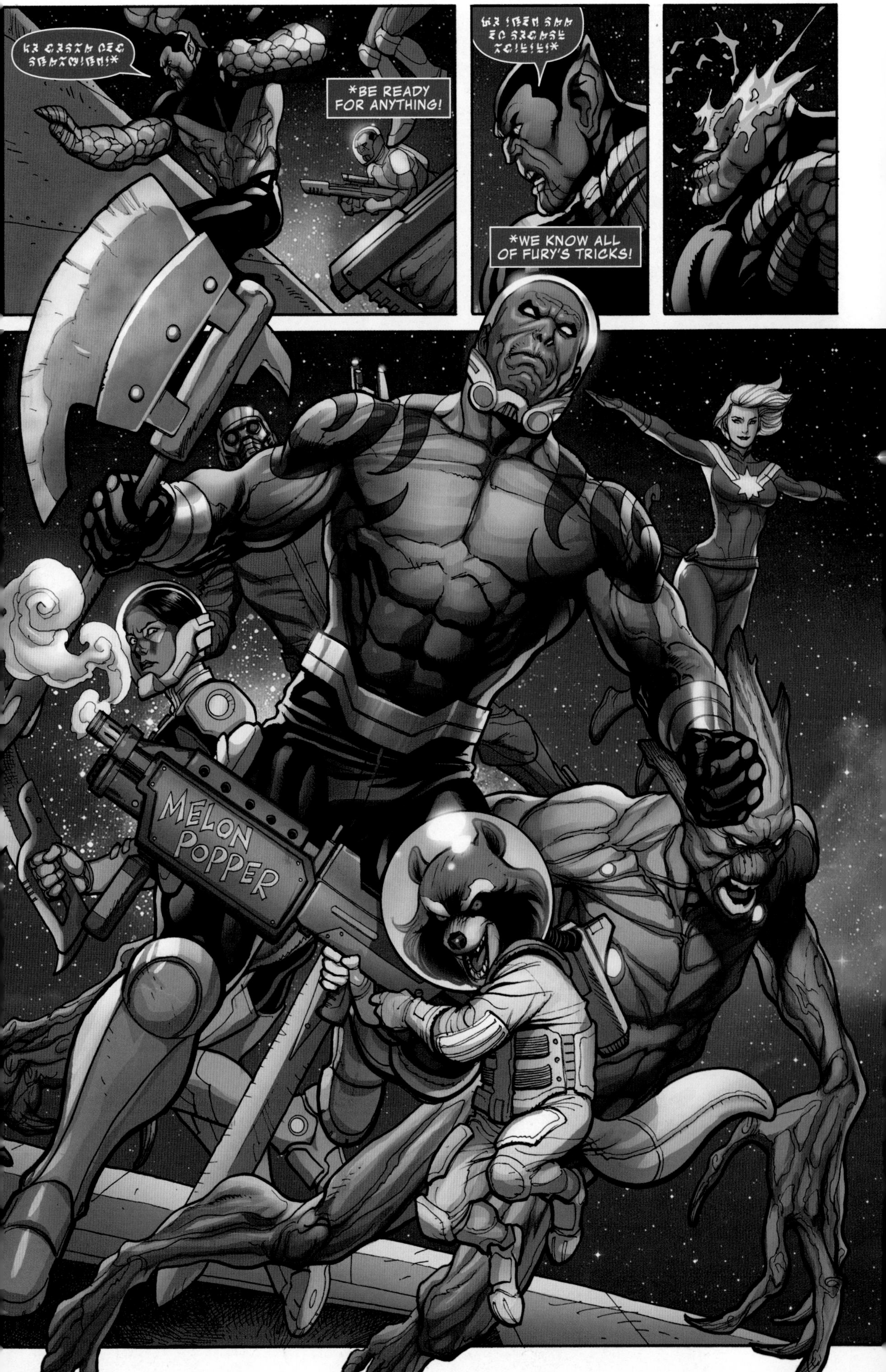

*BE READY FOR ANYTHING!
*WE KNOW ALL OF FURY'S TRICKS!
MELON POPPER

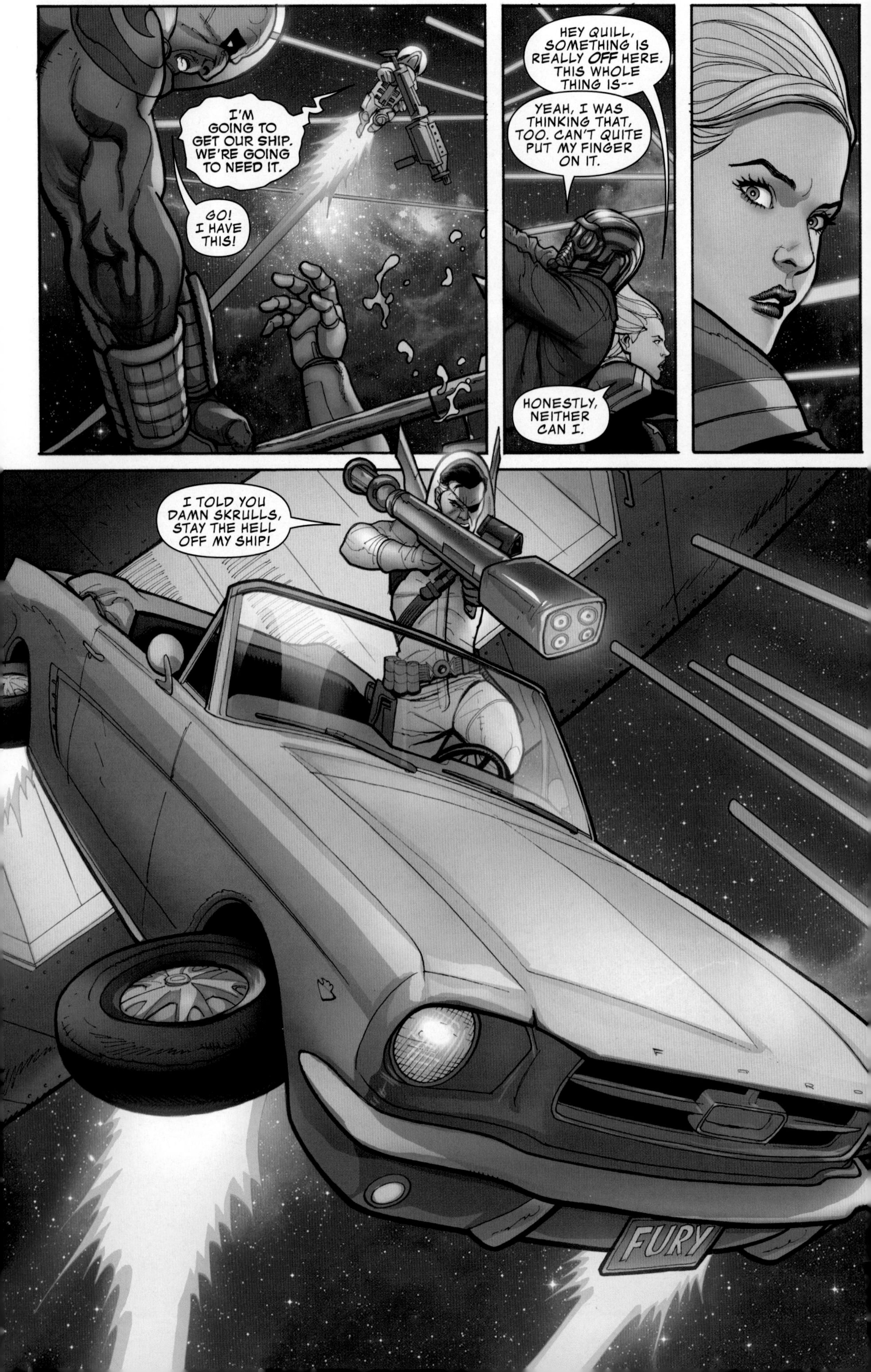
I'M GOING TO GET OUR SHIP. WE'RE GOING TO NEED IT.
GO! I HAVE THIS!
HEY QUILL, SOMETHING IS REALLY OFF HERE. THIS WHOLE THING IS--
YEAH, I WAS THINKING THAT, TOO. CAN'T QUITE PUT MY FINGER ON IT.
HONESTLY, NEITHER CAN I.
I TOLD YOU DAMN SKRULLS, STAY THE HELL OFF MY SHIP!
FORD
FURY

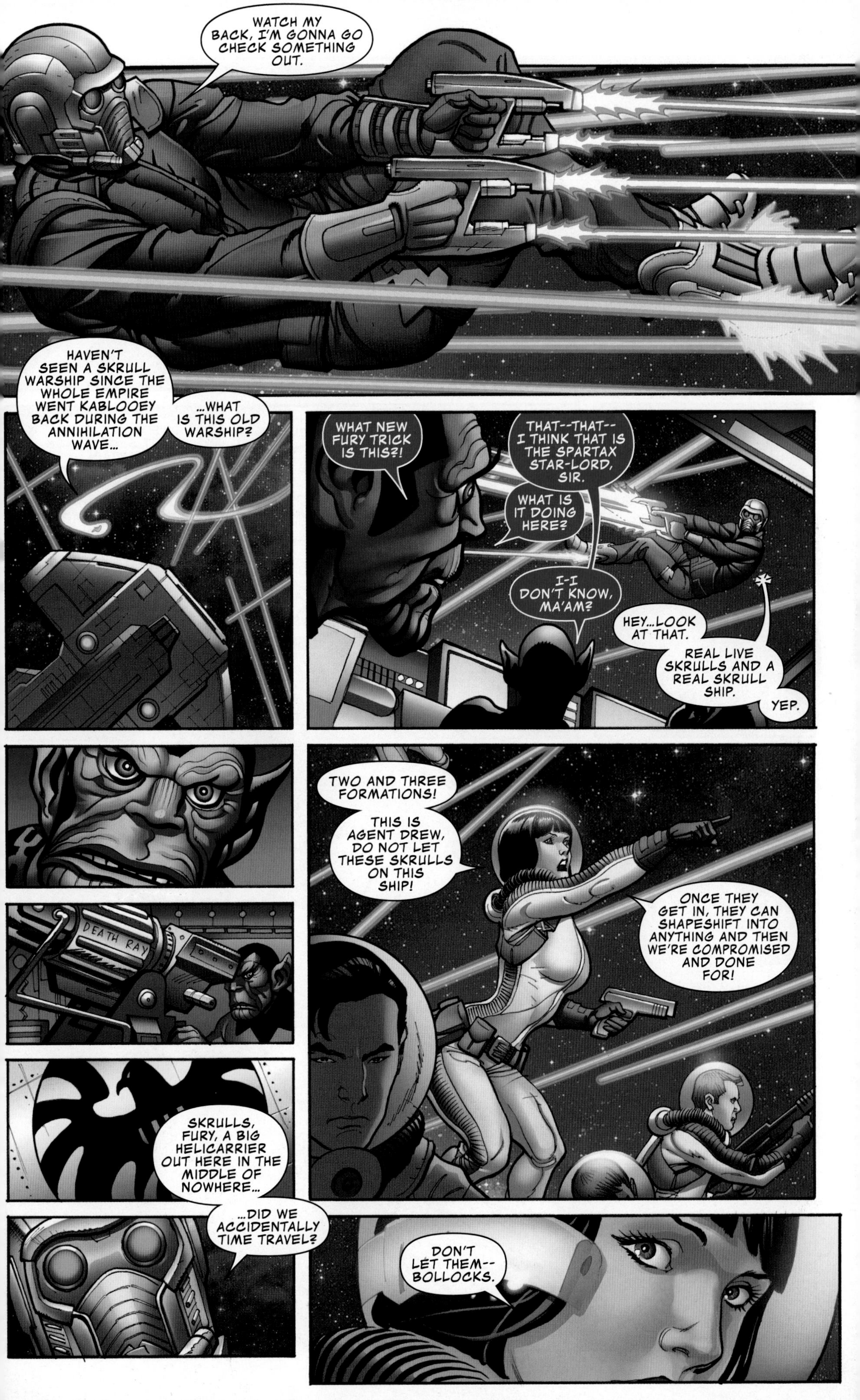
WATCH MY BACK, I'M GONNA GO CHECK SOMETHING OUT.
HAVEN'T SEEN A SKRULL WARSHIP SINCE THE WHOLE EMPIRE WENT KABLOOEY BACK DURING THE ANNIHILATION WAVE...
...WHAT IS THIS OLD WARSHIP?
WHAT NEW FURY TRICK IS THIS?!
THAT--THAT--I THINK THAT IS THE SPARTAX STAR-LORD, SIR.
WHAT IS IT DOING HERE?
I-I DON'T KNOW, MA'AM?
HEY...LOOK AT THAT.
REAL LIVE SKRULLS AND A REAL SKRULL SHIP.
YEP.
DEATH RAY
TWO AND THREE FORMATIONS!
THIS IS AGENT DREW, DO NOT LET THESE SKRULLS ON THIS SHIP!
ONCE THEY GET IN, THEY CAN SHAPESHIFT INTO ANYTHING AND THEN WE'RE COMPROMISED AND DONE FOR!
SKRULLS, FURY, A BIG HELICARRIER OUT HERE IN THE MIDDLE OF NOWHERE...
...DID WE ACCIDENTALLY TIME TRAVEL?
DON'T LET THEM--BOLLOCKS.

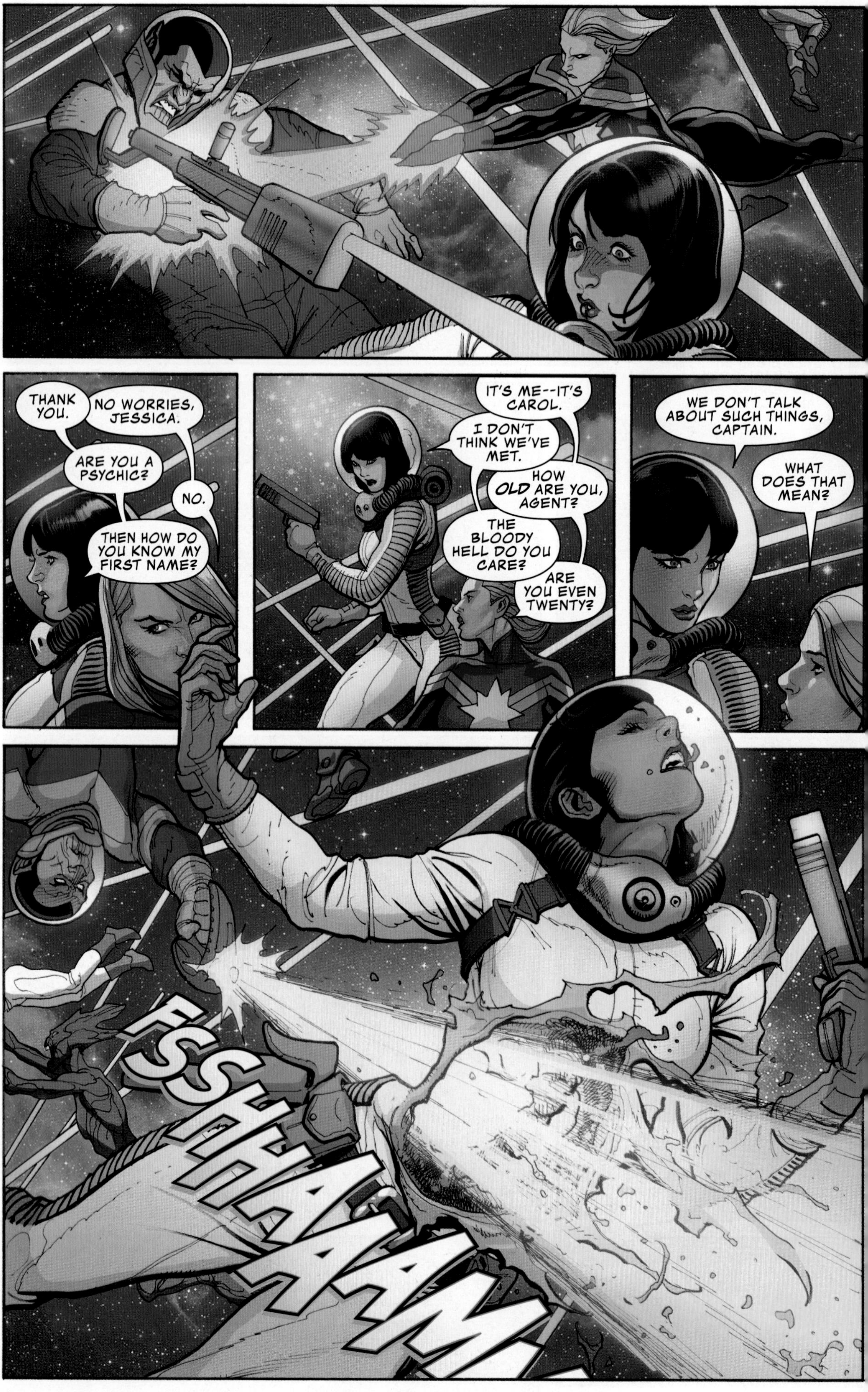
THANK YOU.
NO WORRIES, JESSICA.
ARE YOU A PSYCHIC?
NO.
THEN HOW DO YOU KNOW MY FIRST NAME?
IT'S ME--IT'S CAROL.
I DON'T THINK WE'VE MET.
HOW OLD ARE YOU, AGENT?
THE BLOODY HELL DO YOU CARE?
ARE YOU EVEN TWENTY?
WE DON'T TALK ABOUT SUCH THINGS, CAPTAIN.
WHAT DOES THAT MEAN?
FSSHAAM!

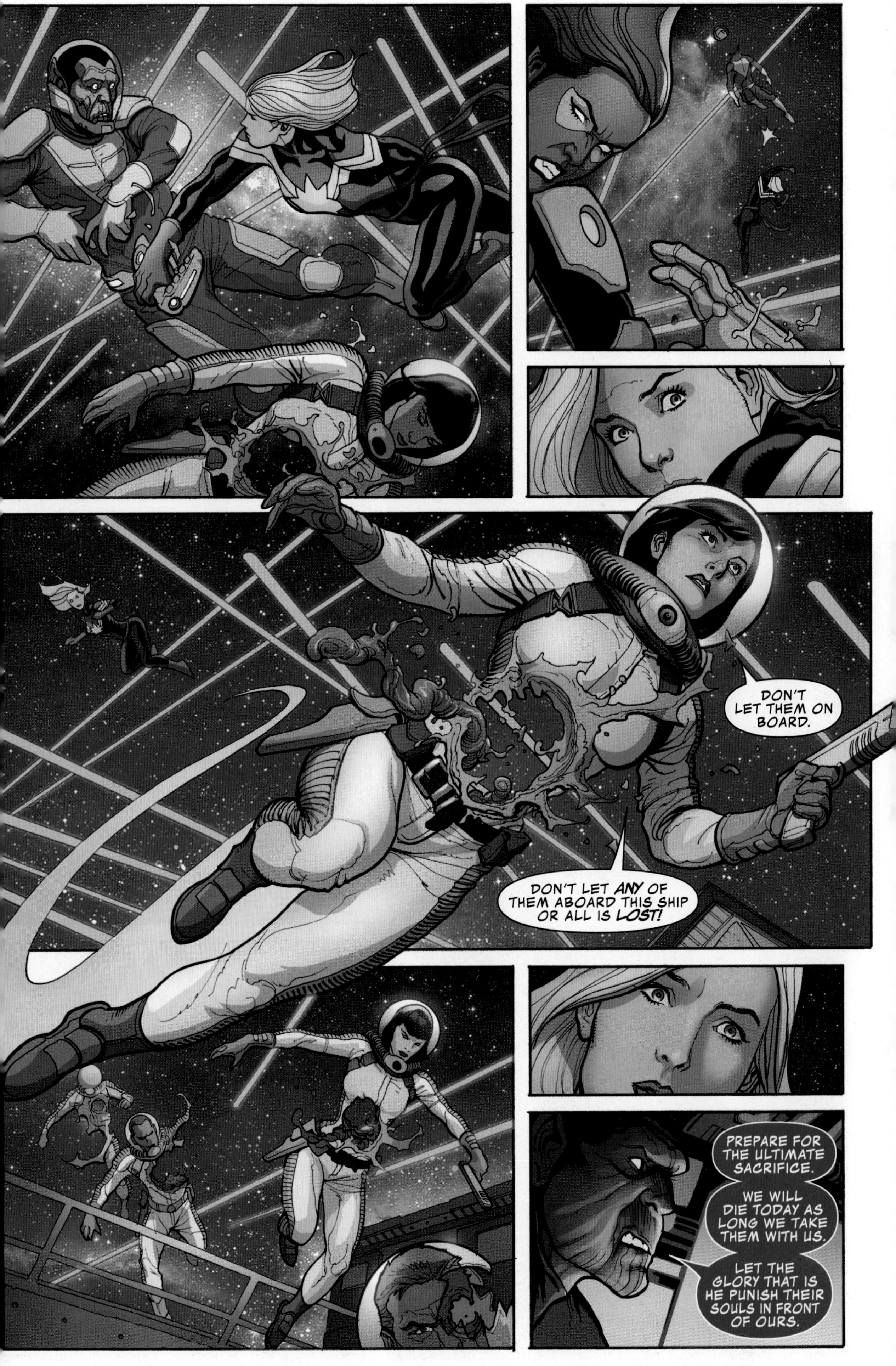
DON'T LET THEM ON BOARD.
DON'T LET *ANY* OF THEM ABOARD THIS SHIP OR ALL IS *LOST!*
PREPARE FOR THE ULTIMATE SACRIFICE.
WE WILL DIE TODAY AS LONG WE TAKE THEM WITH US.
LET THE GLORY THAT IS HE PUNISH THEIR SOULS IN FRONT OF OURS.

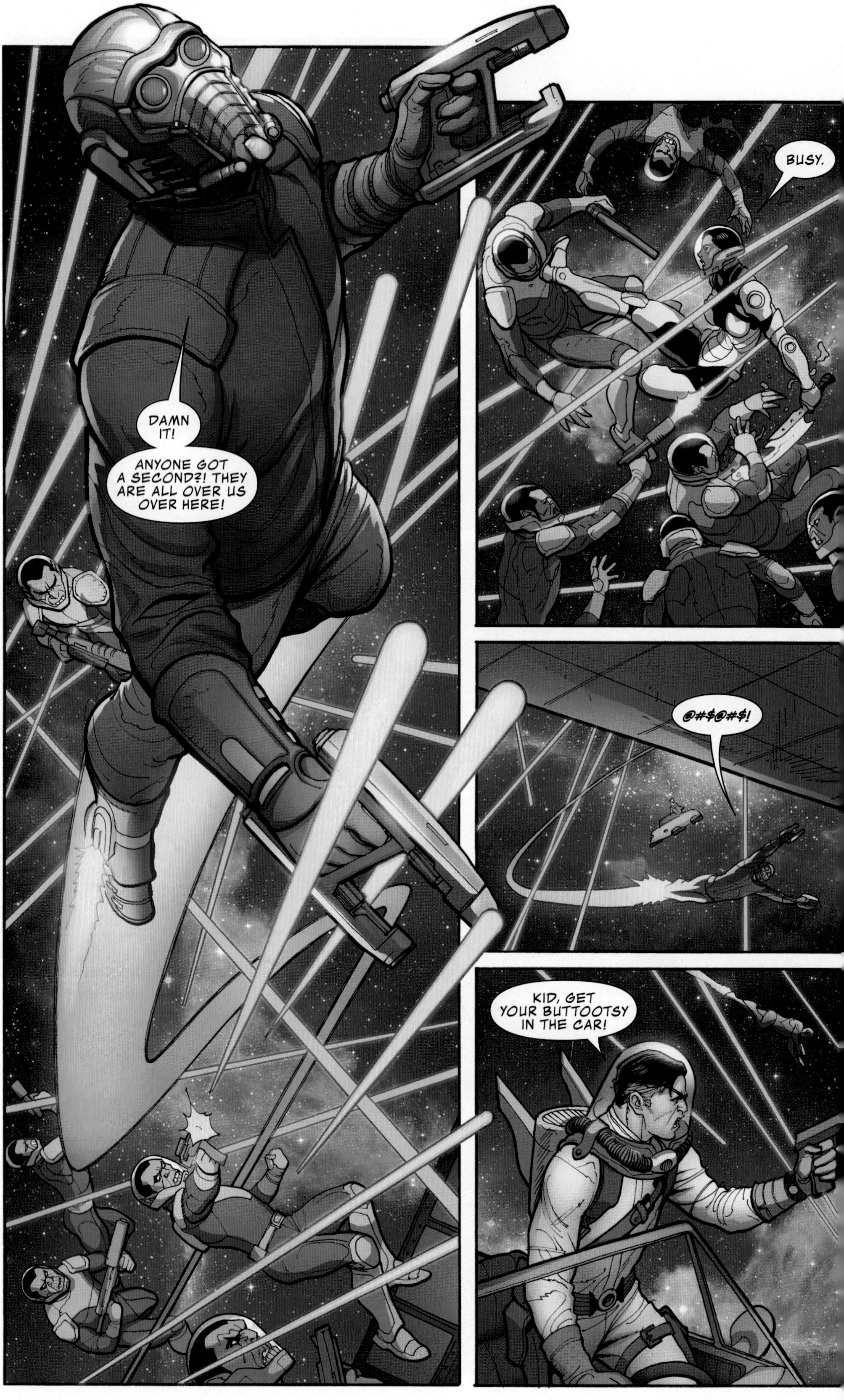
DAMN IT!
ANYONE GOT A SECOND?! THEY ARE ALL OVER US OVER HERE!
BUSY.
@#$@#$!
KID, GET YOUR BUTTOOTSY IN THE CAR!

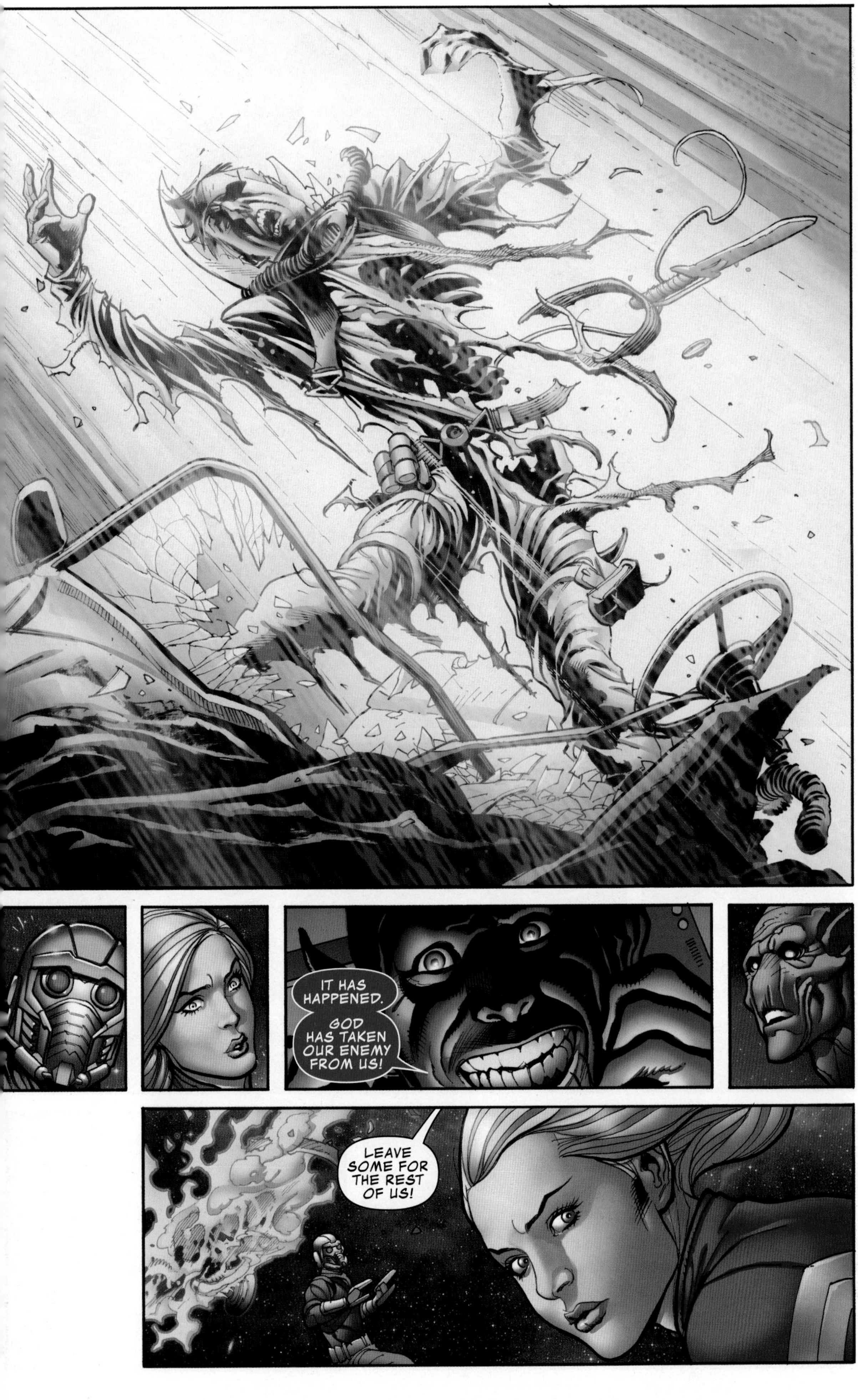
IT HAS HAPPENED.
GOD HAS TAKEN OUR ENEMY FROM US!
LEAVE SOME FOR THE REST OF US!

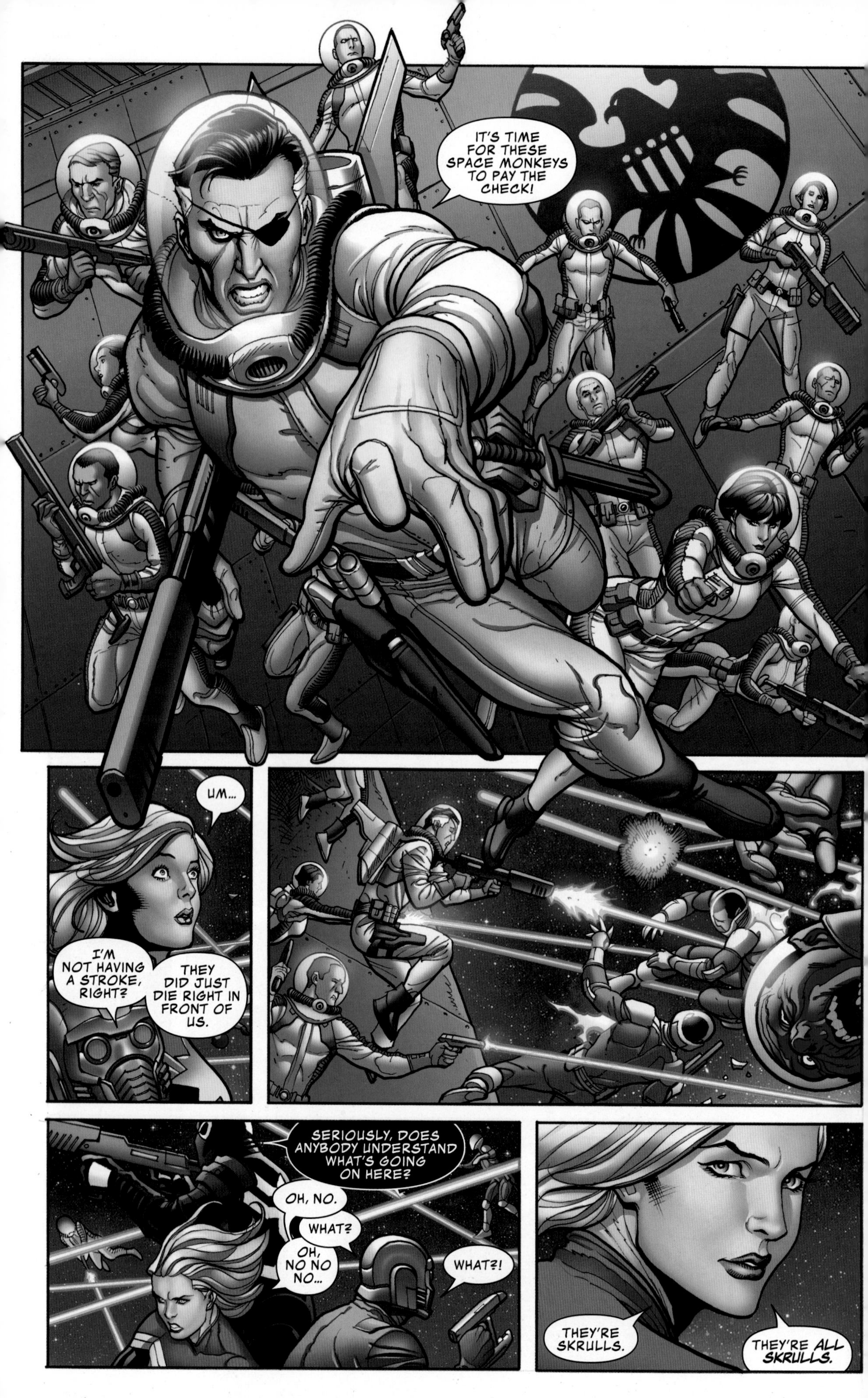
IT'S TIME FOR THESE SPACE MONKEYS TO PAY THE CHECK!
UM...
I'M NOT HAVING A STROKE, RIGHT?
THEY DID JUST DIE RIGHT IN FRONT OF US.
SERIOUSLY, DOES ANYBODY UNDERSTAND WHAT'S GOING ON HERE?
OH, NO.
WHAT?
OH, NO NO NO...
WHAT?!
THEY'RE SKRULLS.
THEY'RE *ALL* *SKRULLS.*

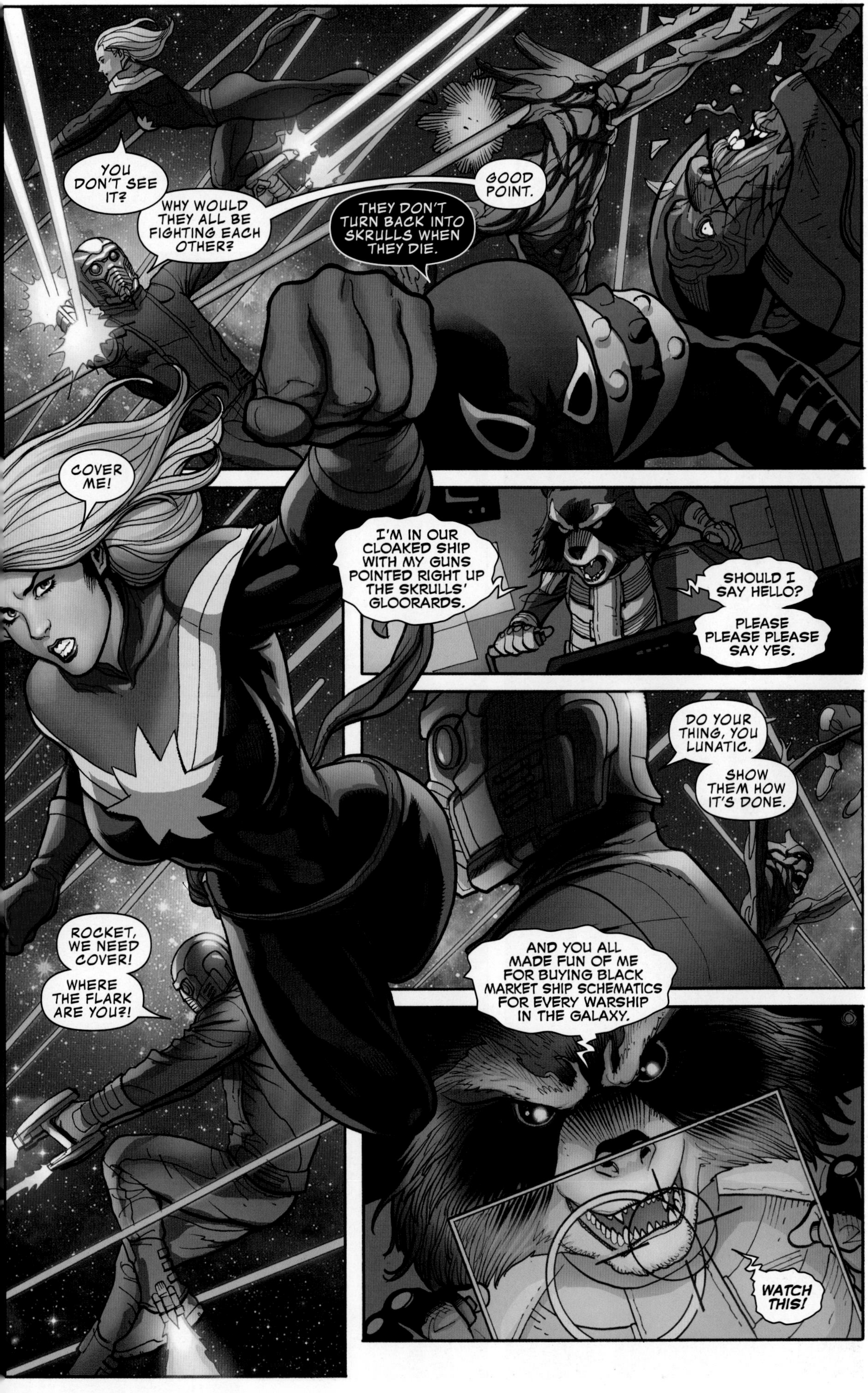

YOU DON'T SEE IT?
WHY WOULD THEY ALL BE FIGHTING EACH OTHER?
GOOD POINT.
THEY DON'T TURN BACK INTO SKRULLS WHEN THEY DIE.
COVER ME!
I'M IN OUR CLOAKED SHIP WITH MY GUNS POINTED RIGHT UP THE SKRULLS' GLOORARDS.
SHOULD I SAY HELLO?
PLEASE PLEASE PLEASE SAY YES.
DO YOUR THING, YOU LUNATIC.
SHOW THEM HOW IT'S DONE.
ROCKET, WE NEED COVER!
WHERE THE FLARK ARE YOU?!
AND YOU ALL MADE FUN OF ME FOR BUYING BLACK MARKET SHIP SCHEMATICS FOR EVERY WARSHIP IN THE GALAXY.
WATCH THIS!

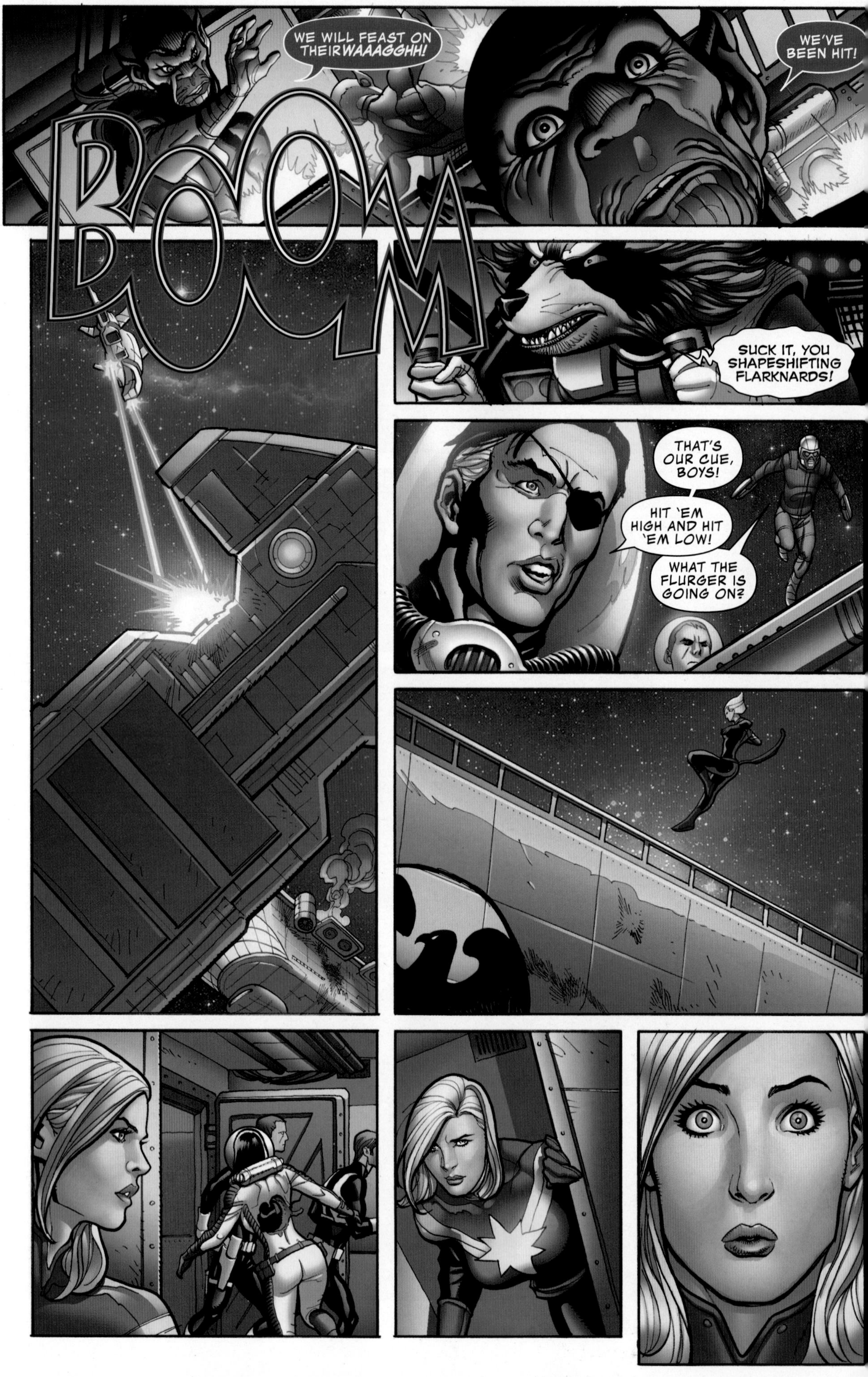
WE WILL FEAST ON THEIRWAAAGGHH!
BOOM
WE'VE BEEN HIT!
SUCK IT, YOU SHAPESHIFTING FLARKNARDS!
THAT'S OUR CUE, BOYS!
HIT 'EM HIGH AND HIT 'EM LOW!
WHAT THE FLURGER IS GOING ON?

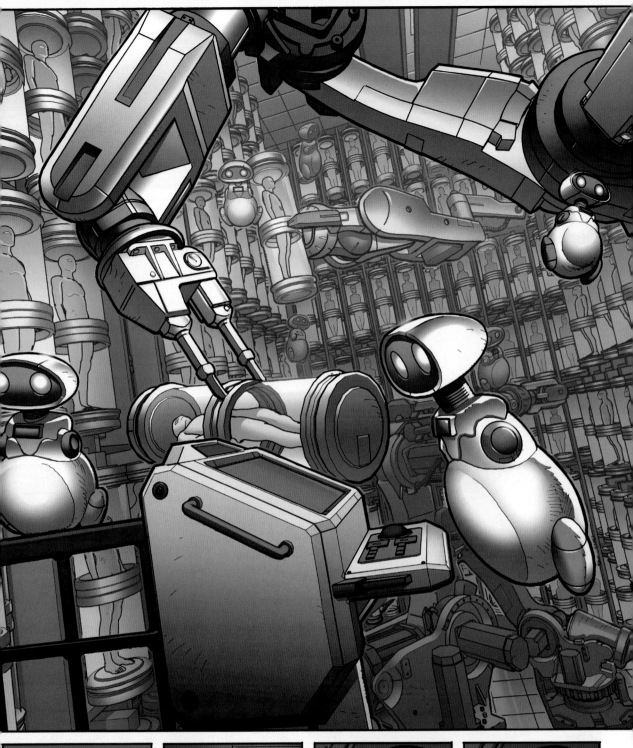

TIMOTHY ALOYSIUS
CADWALLANDER DUGAN

ALIAS: DUM DUM

RANK: S.H.I.E.L.D.
DEPUTY DIRECTOR

TIMOTHY ALOYSIUS
CADWALLANDER DUGAN

DECEASED

RANK: S.H.I.E.L.D.
DEPUTY DIRECTOR

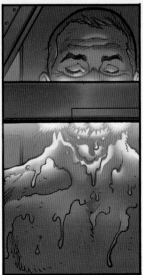

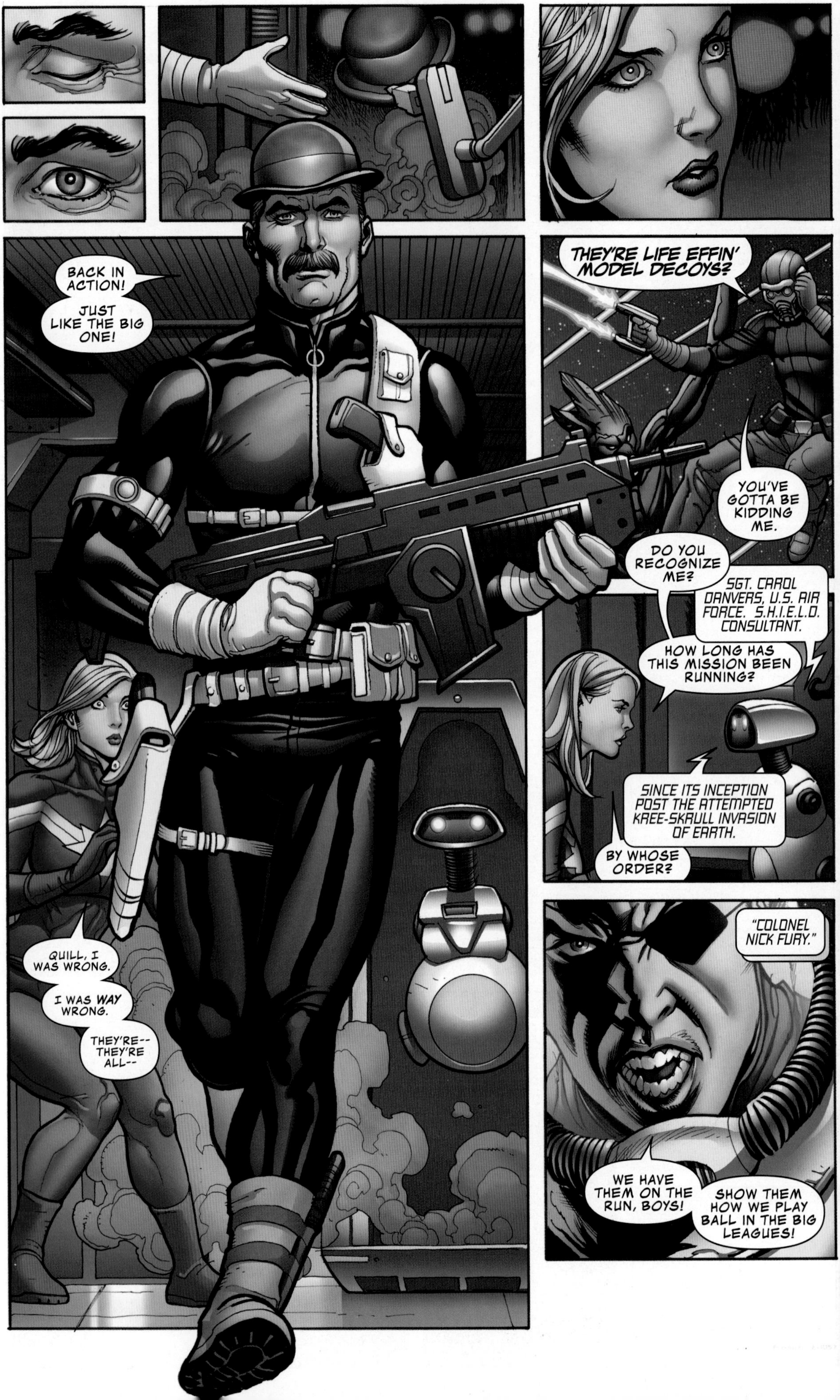
BACK IN ACTION!
JUST LIKE THE BIG ONE!
QUILL, I WAS WRONG.
I WAS WAY WRONG.
THEY'RE--THEY'RE ALL--
THEY'RE LIFE EFFIN' MODEL DECOYS?
YOU'VE GOTTA BE KIDDING ME.
DO YOU RECOGNIZE ME?
SGT. CAROL DANVERS, U.S. AIR FORCE. S.H.I.E.L.D. CONSULTANT.
HOW LONG HAS THIS MISSION BEEN RUNNING?
SINCE ITS INCEPTION POST THE ATTEMPTED KREE-SKRULL INVASION OF EARTH.
BY WHOSE ORDER?
"COLONEL NICK FURY."
WE HAVE THEM ON THE RUN, BOYS!
SHOW THEM HOW WE PLAY BALL IN THE BIG LEAGUES!

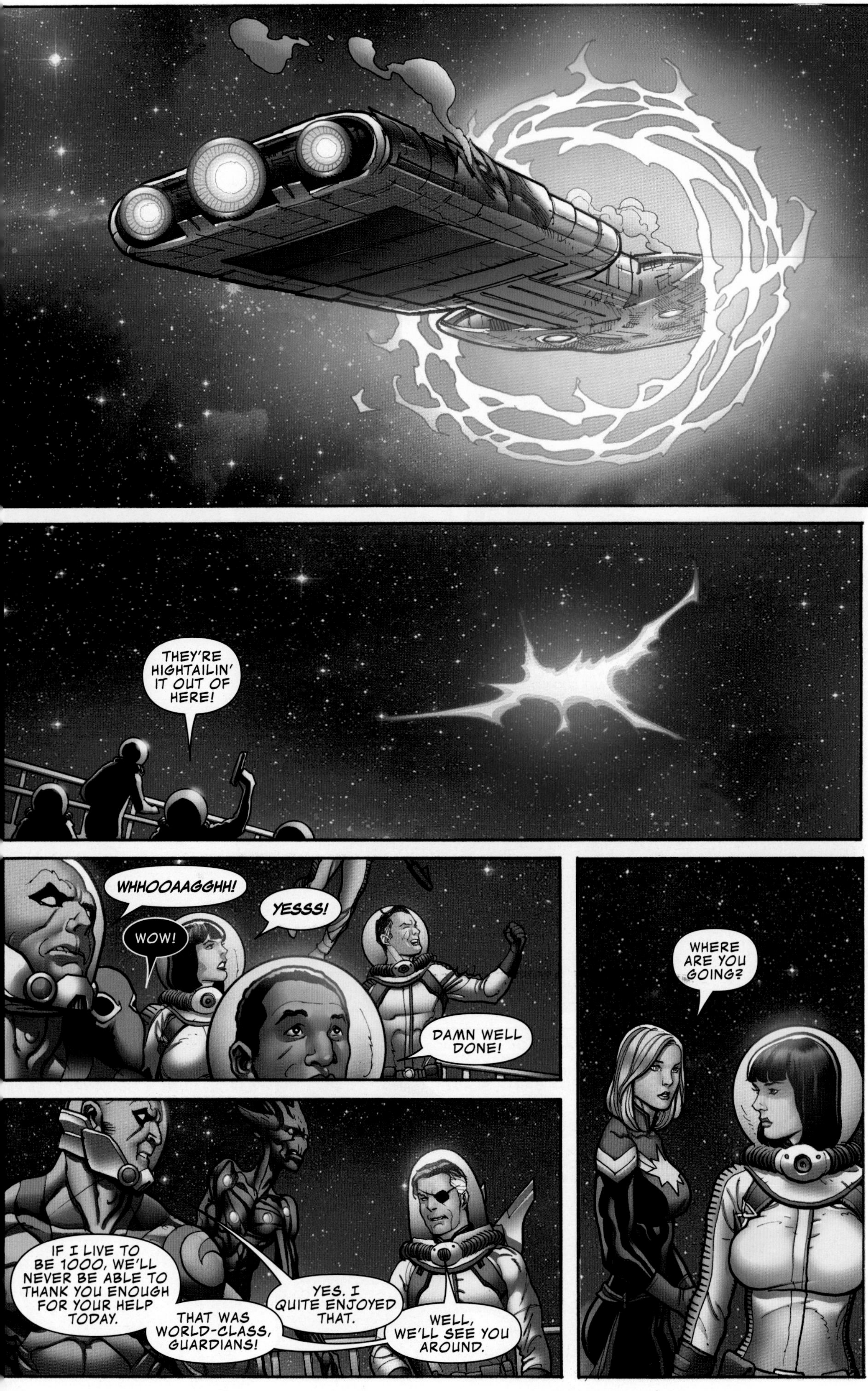
THEY'RE HIGHTAILIN' IT OUT OF HERE!
WHHOOAAGGHH!
WOW!
YESSS!
DAMN WELL DONE!
IF I LIVE TO BE 1000, WE'LL NEVER BE ABLE TO THANK YOU ENOUGH FOR YOUR HELP TODAY.
THAT WAS WORLD-CLASS, GUARDIANS!
YES. I QUITE ENJOYED THAT.
WELL, WE'LL SEE YOU AROUND.
WHERE ARE YOU GOING?

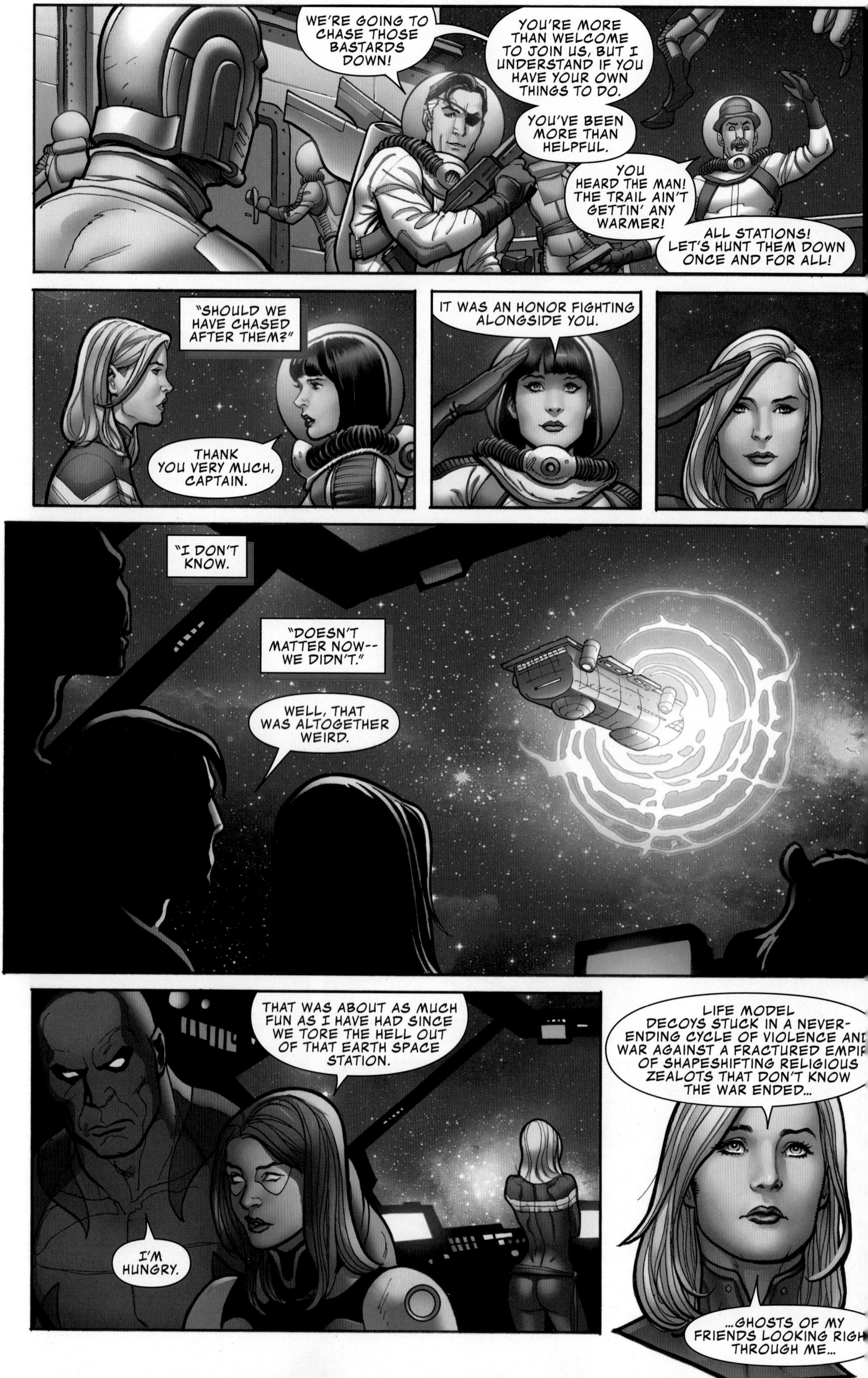
WE'RE GOING TO CHASE THOSE BASTARDS DOWN!
YOU'RE MORE THAN WELCOME TO JOIN US, BUT I UNDERSTAND IF YOU HAVE YOUR OWN THINGS TO DO.
YOU'VE BEEN MORE THAN HELPFUL.
YOU HEARD THE MAN! THE TRAIL AIN'T GETTIN' ANY WARMER!
ALL STATIONS! LET'S HUNT THEM DOWN ONCE AND FOR ALL!
"SHOULD WE HAVE CHASED AFTER THEM?"
THANK YOU VERY MUCH, CAPTAIN.
IT WAS AN HONOR FIGHTING ALONGSIDE YOU.
"I DON'T KNOW.
"DOESN'T MATTER NOW-- WE DIDN'T."
WELL, THAT WAS ALTOGETHER WEIRD.
THAT WAS ABOUT AS MUCH FUN AS I HAVE HAD SINCE WE TORE THE HELL OUT OF THAT EARTH SPACE STATION.
I'M HUNGRY.
LIFE MODEL DECOYS STUCK IN A NEVER-ENDING CYCLE OF VIOLENCE AND WAR AGAINST A FRACTURED EMPIR OF SHAPESHIFTING RELIGIOUS ZEALOTS THAT DON'T KNOW THE WAR ENDED...
...GHOSTS OF MY FRIENDS LOOKING RIGH THROUGH ME...

TODAY I WISH YOU GUYS WERE OUT HERE, BECAUSE TODAY WAS REALLY HARD.

I'M TRYING NOT TO SAY THESE WORDS OUT LOUD, BUT-- THOSE THINGS... IS THAT ALL WE ARE?

ALL THE PUNCHES TO THE FACE. ALL THE RUNNING AROUND...

...AND ALL OF IT JUST TO KEEP THE BAD GUYS ONE INCH AWAY.

JUST TO KEEP THE WORLD TURNING FOR TEN MORE MINUTES TILL THE NEXT THING.

I CAN'T BELIEVE IT, BUT I ACTUALLY MISS SITTING AROUND THE DINING ROOM TABLE IN AVENGERS MANSION WATCHING WOLVERINE EAT THOSE DISGUSTING THINGS.

I MISS YOU AND LUKE CAGE GIVING EACH OTHER THAT LOOK. THAT AMAZING LOOK OF TOTAL LOVE.

A LOOK I HAVE YET TO INSPIRE OUT OF ANOTHER PERSON.

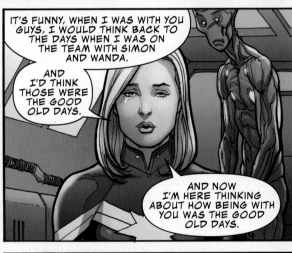

IT'S FUNNY, WHEN I WAS WITH YOU GUYS, I WOULD THINK BACK TO THE DAYS WHEN I WAS ON THE TEAM WITH SIMON AND WANDA.

AND I'D THINK THOSE WERE THE GOOD OLD DAYS.

AND NOW I'M HERE THINKING ABOUT HOW BEING WITH YOU WAS THE GOOD OLD DAYS.

I WONDER WHERE I'LL BE NEXT YEAR THINKING THAT THIS IS THE GOOD OLD DAYS.

I MISS YOU. I LIKE THESE GUYS BUT THEY ARE CLEARLY NOT HUGGERS.

I DON'T THINK THEY KNOW WHAT A HUG IS.

BUT SOMETIMES YOU JUST NE-- AGH.

I AM GROOT.

YEAH.

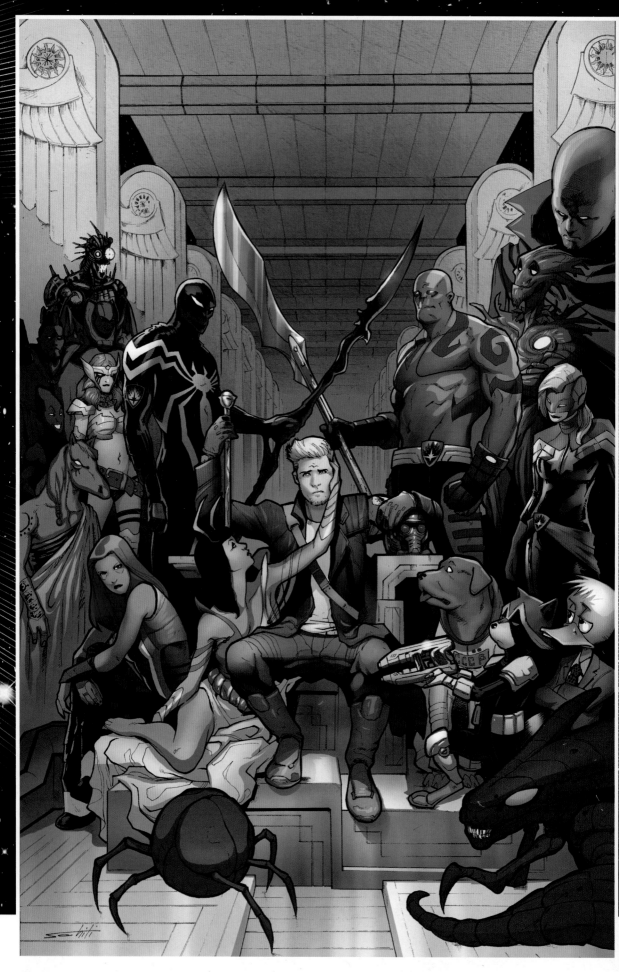

GUARDIANS OF THE GALAXY & X-MEN

THE BLACK VORTEX

CHAPTER 2

Previously in *The Black Vortex*...

Billions of years ago, an ancient race named the Viscardi were gifted an object
of immense cosmic power by a Celestial. This artifact, known as the Black
Vortex, transforms the user, imbuing them with cosmic energy. However, the
power of this object caused the Viscardi to turn on each other, annihilating
their own race from within.

In the present day, Peter Quill has been hounded by a mysterious villain named
Mister Knife. Upon being captured by Knife, Peter discovered him to actually be
his father, J-Son, the deposed Emperor of Spartax. With the help of Kitty Pryde,
Peter escaped Knife's clutches. Seeking revenge, Peter and Kitty returned to
Knife's fortress. However, while spying on Mister Knife's conversations, they
discovered that he had recovered the Black Vortex and watched as he used
it to enhance his henchmen, christening them, in their new forms, as the
Slaughter Lords. Not willing to leave such power in the hands of his father,
Peter stole the Black Vortex. In need of help, Peter and Kitty summoned the
Guardians of the Galaxy and members of the X-Men. But while they argued
over what to do with the object, the Slaughter Lords arrived and began to lay
waste to the heroes. Seeking to save her friends, Gamora took matters into her
own hands and submitted to the power of the Black Vortex.

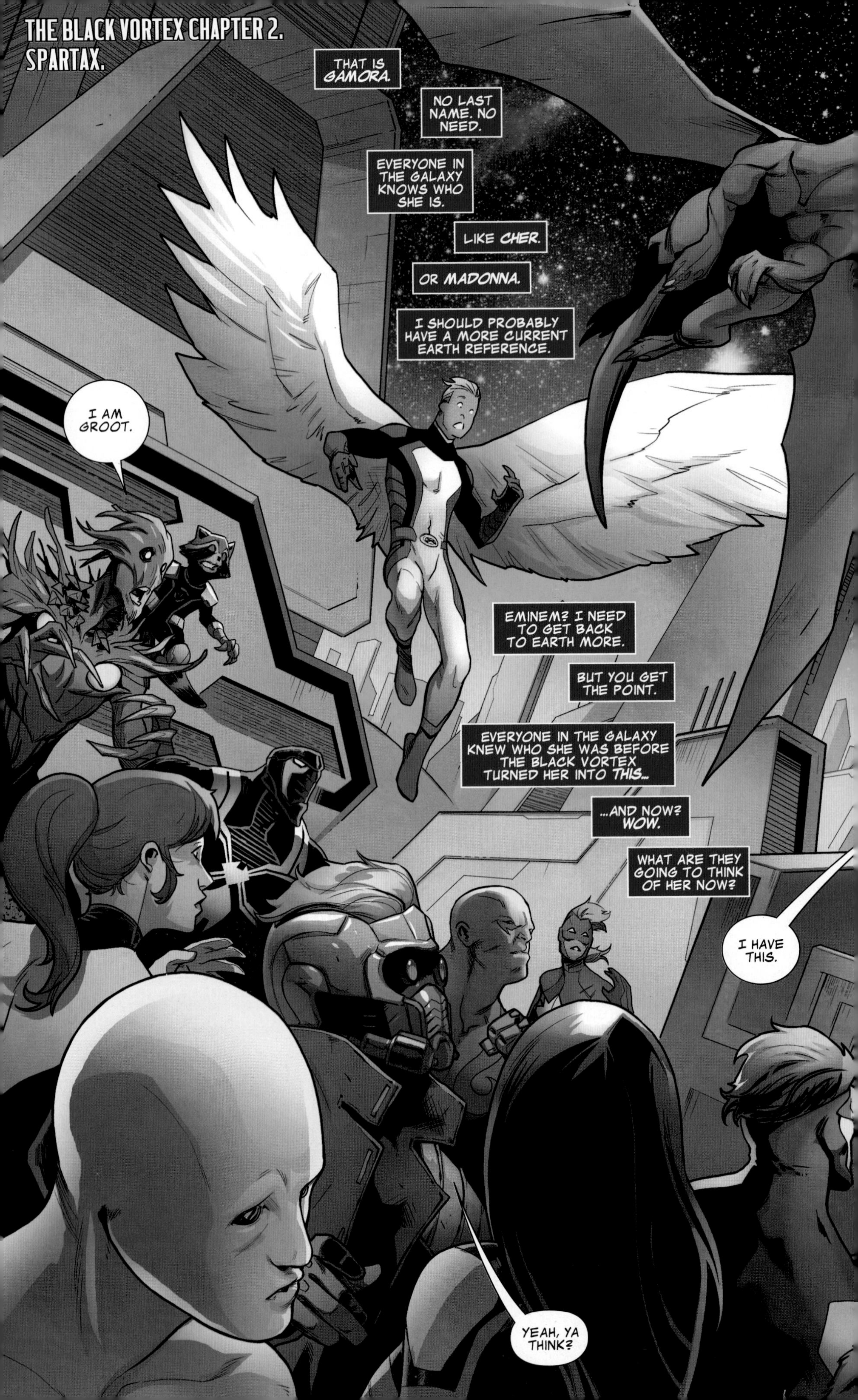
THE BLACK VORTEX CHAPTER 2.
SPARTAX.
THAT IS GAMORA.
NO LAST NAME. NO NEED.
EVERYONE IN THE GALAXY KNOWS WHO SHE IS.
LIKE CHER.
OR MADONNA.
I SHOULD PROBABLY HAVE A MORE CURRENT EARTH REFERENCE.
I AM GROOT.
EMINEM? I NEED TO GET BACK TO EARTH MORE.
BUT YOU GET THE POINT.
EVERYONE IN THE GALAXY KNEW WHO SHE WAS BEFORE THE BLACK VORTEX TURNED HER INTO THIS...
...AND NOW? WOW.
WHAT ARE THEY GOING TO THINK OF HER NOW?
I HAVE THIS.
YEAH, YA THINK?

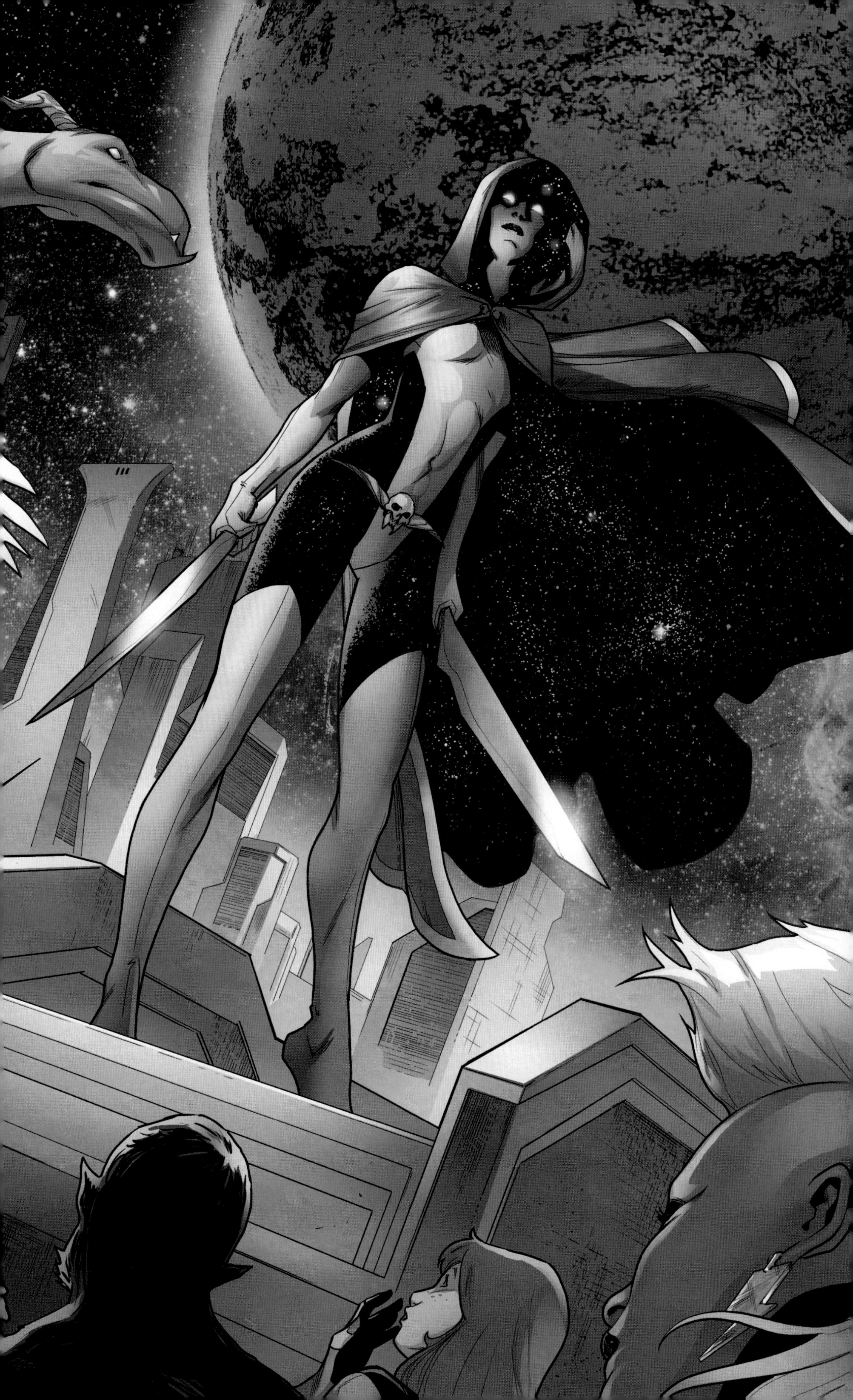

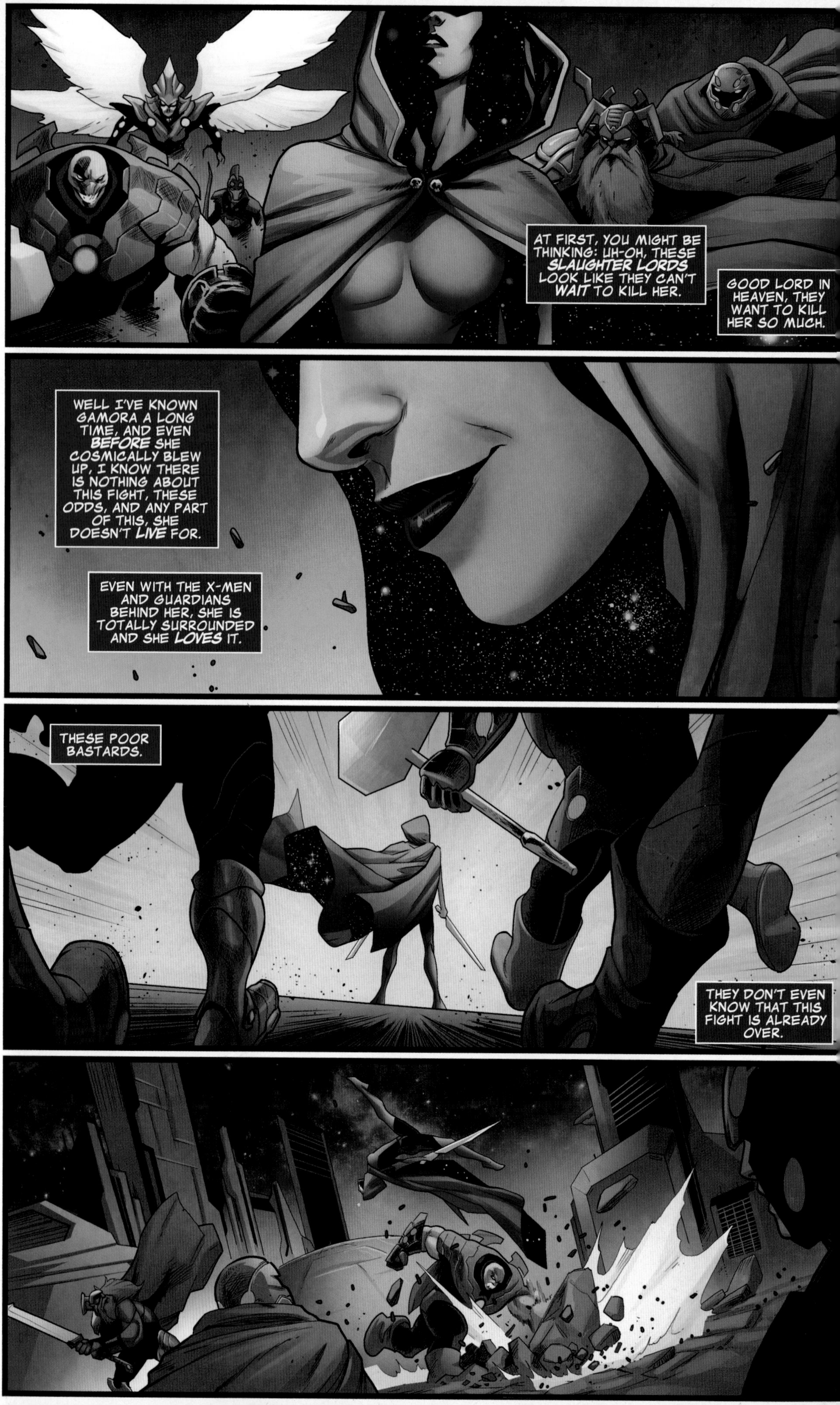
AT FIRST, YOU MIGHT BE THINKING: UH-OH, THESE SLAUGHTER LORDS LOOK LIKE THEY CAN'T WAIT TO KILL HER.
GOOD LORD IN HEAVEN, THEY WANT TO KILL HER SO MUCH.
WELL I'VE KNOWN GAMORA A LONG TIME, AND EVEN BEFORE SHE COSMICALLY BLEW UP, I KNOW THERE IS NOTHING ABOUT THIS FIGHT, THESE ODDS, AND ANY PART OF THIS, SHE DOESN'T LIVE FOR.
EVEN WITH THE X-MEN AND GUARDIANS BEHIND HER, SHE IS TOTALLY SURROUNDED AND SHE LOVES IT.
THESE POOR BASTARDS.
THEY DON'T EVEN KNOW THAT THIS FIGHT IS ALREADY OVER.

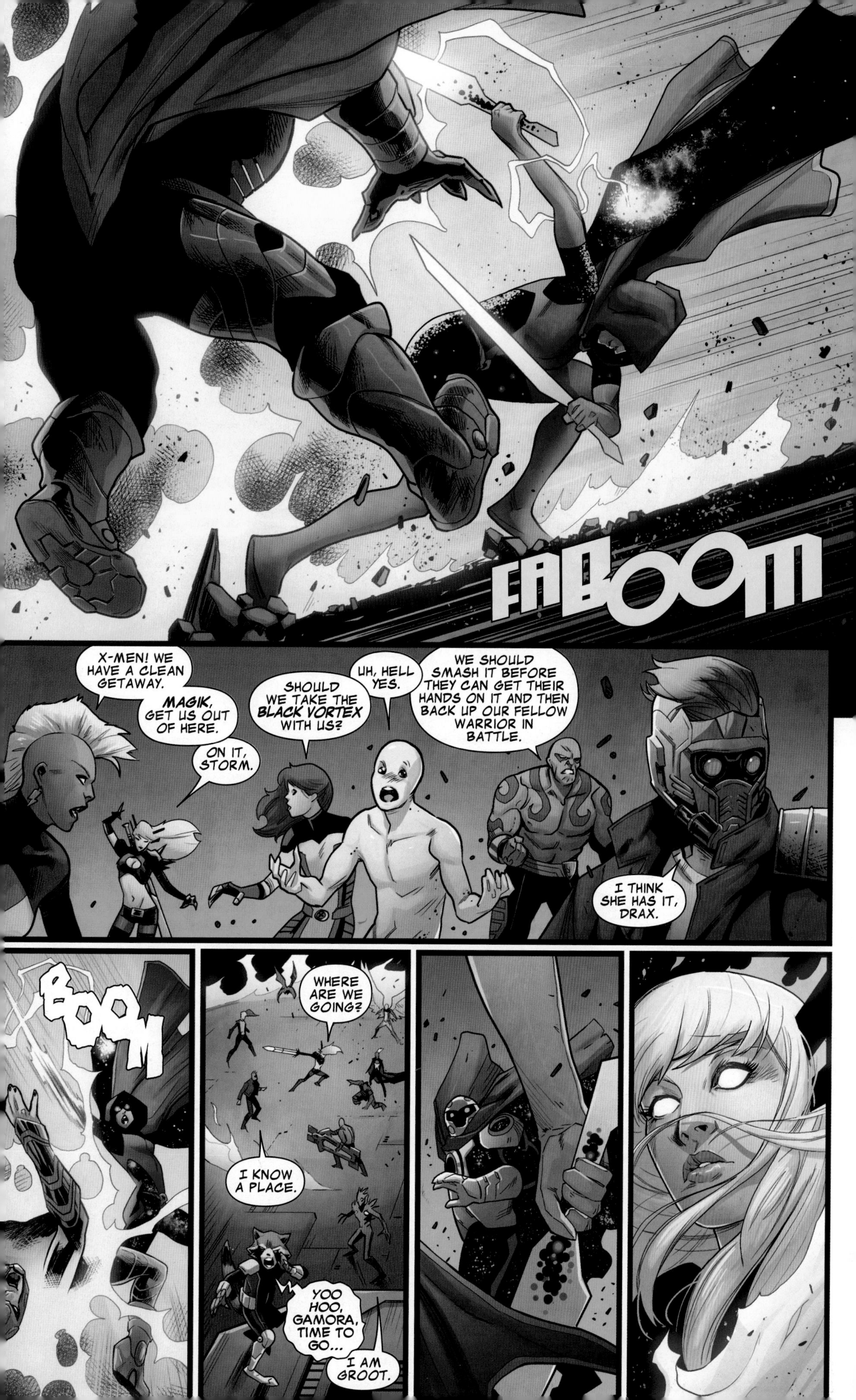
FABOOM
X-MEN! WE HAVE A CLEAN GETAWAY.
MAGIK, GET US OUT OF HERE.
ON IT, STORM.
SHOULD WE TAKE THE BLACK VORTEX WITH US?
UH, HELL YES.
WE SHOULD SMASH IT BEFORE THEY CAN GET THEIR HANDS ON IT AND THEN BACK UP OUR FELLOW WARRIOR IN BATTLE.
I THINK SHE HAS IT, DRAX.
BOOM
WHERE ARE WE GOING?
I KNOW A PLACE.
YOO HOO, GAMORA, TIME TO GO...
I AM GROOT.

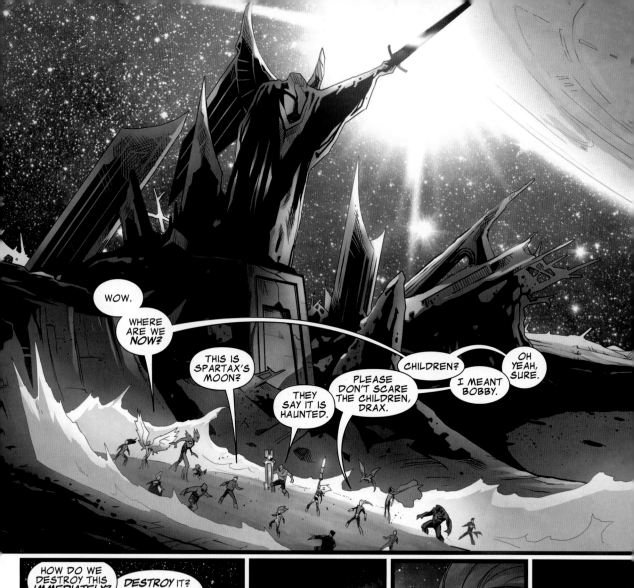

WOW.

WHERE ARE WE *NOW?*

THIS IS SPARTAX'S MOON?

THEY SAY IT IS HAUNTED.

PLEASE DON'T SCARE THE CHILDREN, DRAX.

CHILDREN?

I MEANT BOBBY.

OH YEAH, SURE.

HOW DO WE DESTROY THIS *IMMEDIATELY?*

DESTROY IT? THIS IS TOO FASCINATING TO DESTROY.

I COULD STUDY IT FOR THE REST OF MY LIFE.

HOW "HANK McCOY" OF YOU.

THANK YOU.

WE LINE UP AND WE ALL POWER THE HELL UP.

WHAT?

WHAT?

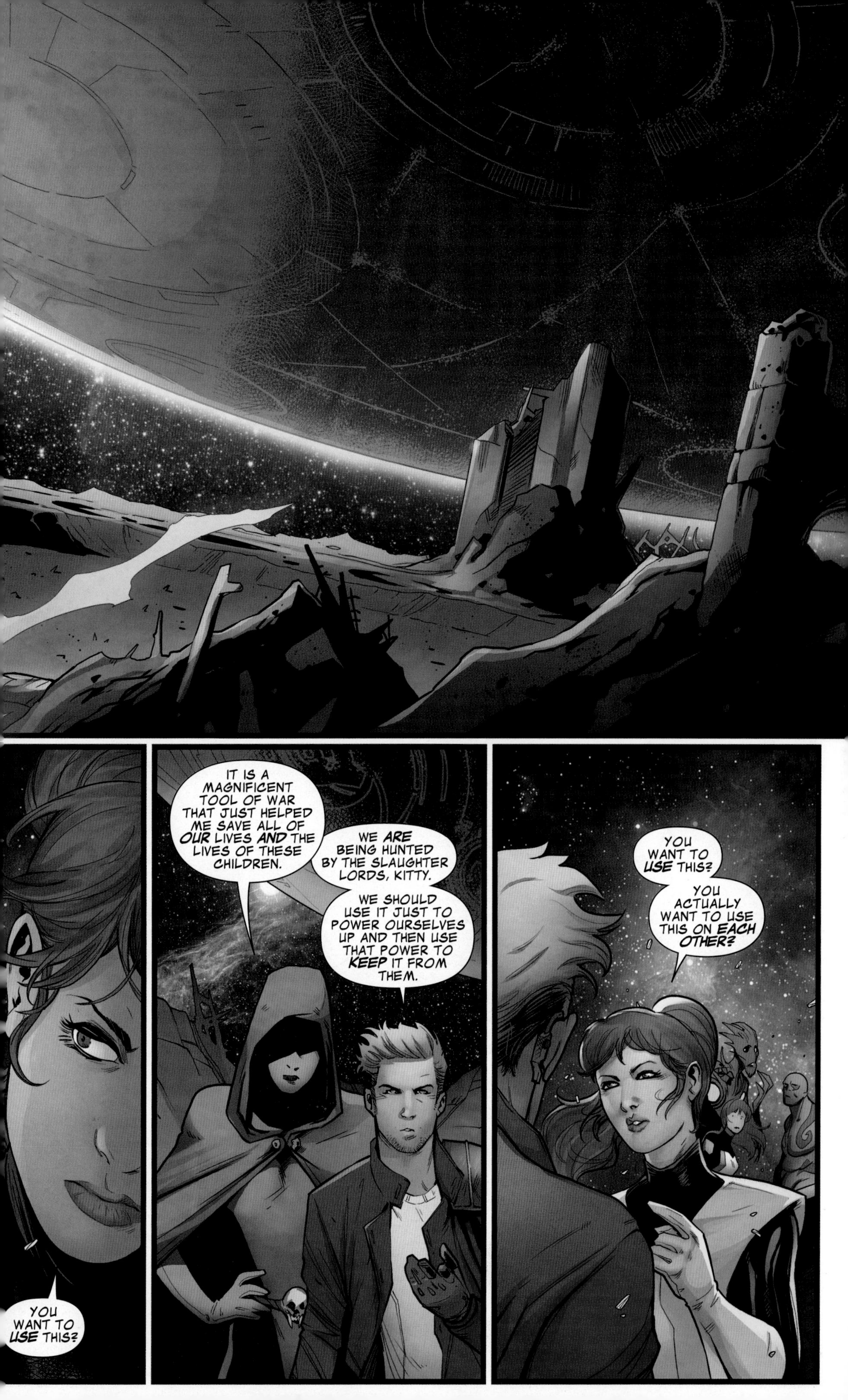
IT IS A MAGNIFICENT TOOL OF WAR THAT JUST HELPED ME SAVE ALL OF OUR LIVES AND THE LIVES OF THESE CHILDREN.
WE ARE BEING HUNTED BY THE SLAUGHTER LORDS, KITTY.
WE SHOULD USE IT JUST TO POWER OURSELVES UP AND THEN USE THAT POWER TO KEEP IT FROM THEM.
YOU WANT TO USE THIS?
YOU WANT TO USE THIS?
YOU ACTUALLY WANT TO USE THIS ON EACH OTHER?

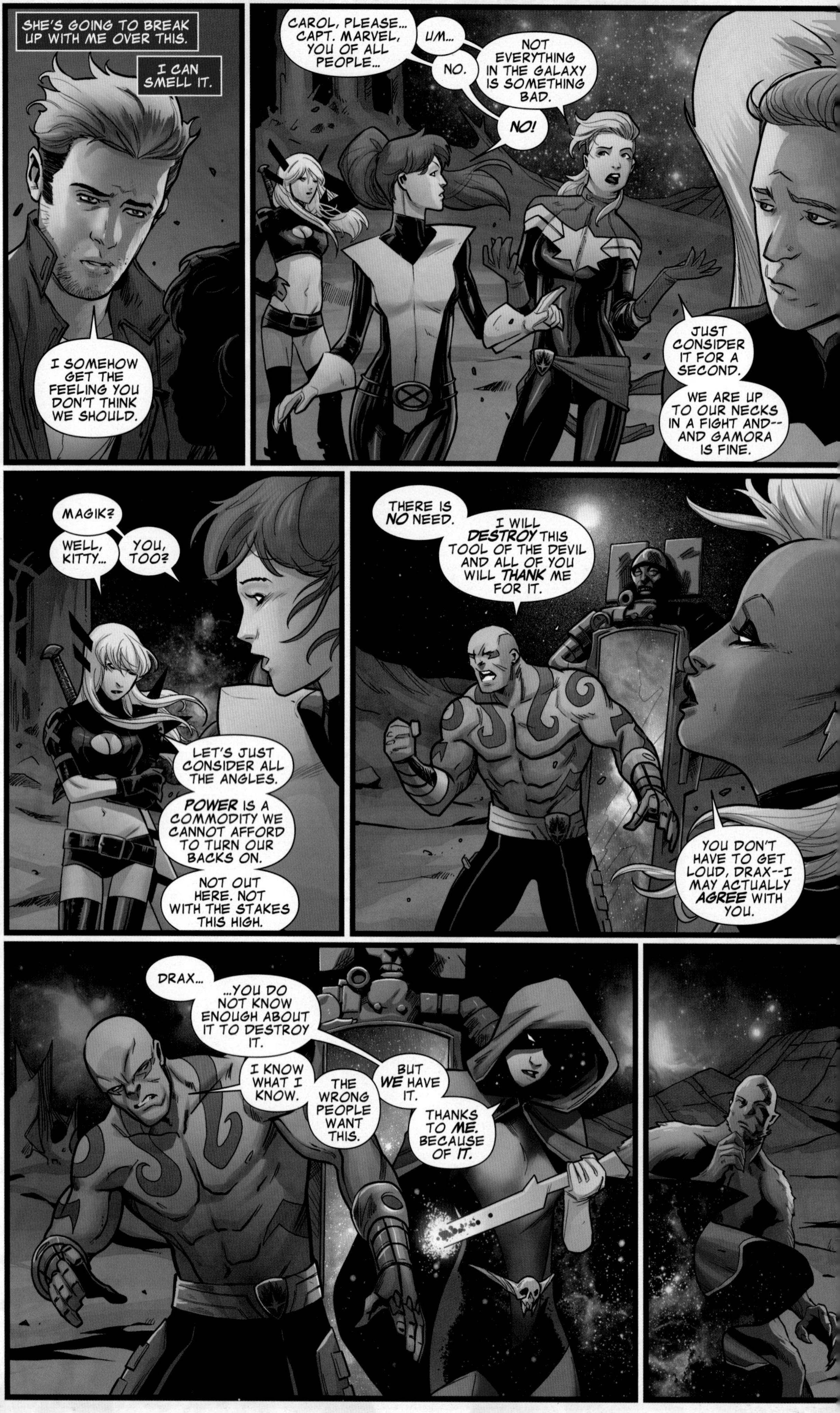
SHE'S GOING TO BREAK UP WITH ME OVER THIS.
I CAN SMELL IT.
I SOMEHOW GET THE FEELING YOU DON'T THINK WE SHOULD.
CAROL, PLEASE... CAPT. MARVEL, YOU OF ALL PEOPLE...
UM...
NO.
NOT EVERYTHING IN THE GALAXY IS SOMETHING BAD.
NO!
JUST CONSIDER IT FOR A SECOND.
WE ARE UP TO OUR NECKS IN A FIGHT AND-- AND GAMORA IS FINE.
MAGIK?
WELL, KITTY...
YOU, TOO?
LET'S JUST CONSIDER ALL THE ANGLES.
POWER IS A COMMODITY WE CANNOT AFFORD TO TURN OUR BACKS ON.
NOT OUT HERE. NOT WITH THE STAKES THIS HIGH.
THERE IS NO NEED.
I WILL DESTROY THIS TOOL OF THE DEVIL AND ALL OF YOU WILL THANK ME FOR IT.
YOU DON'T HAVE TO GET LOUD, DRAX--I MAY ACTUALLY AGREE WITH YOU.
DRAX...
...YOU DO NOT KNOW ENOUGH ABOUT IT TO DESTROY IT.
I KNOW WHAT I KNOW.
THE WRONG PEOPLE WANT THIS.
BUT WE HAVE IT.
THANKS TO ME. BECAUSE OF IT.

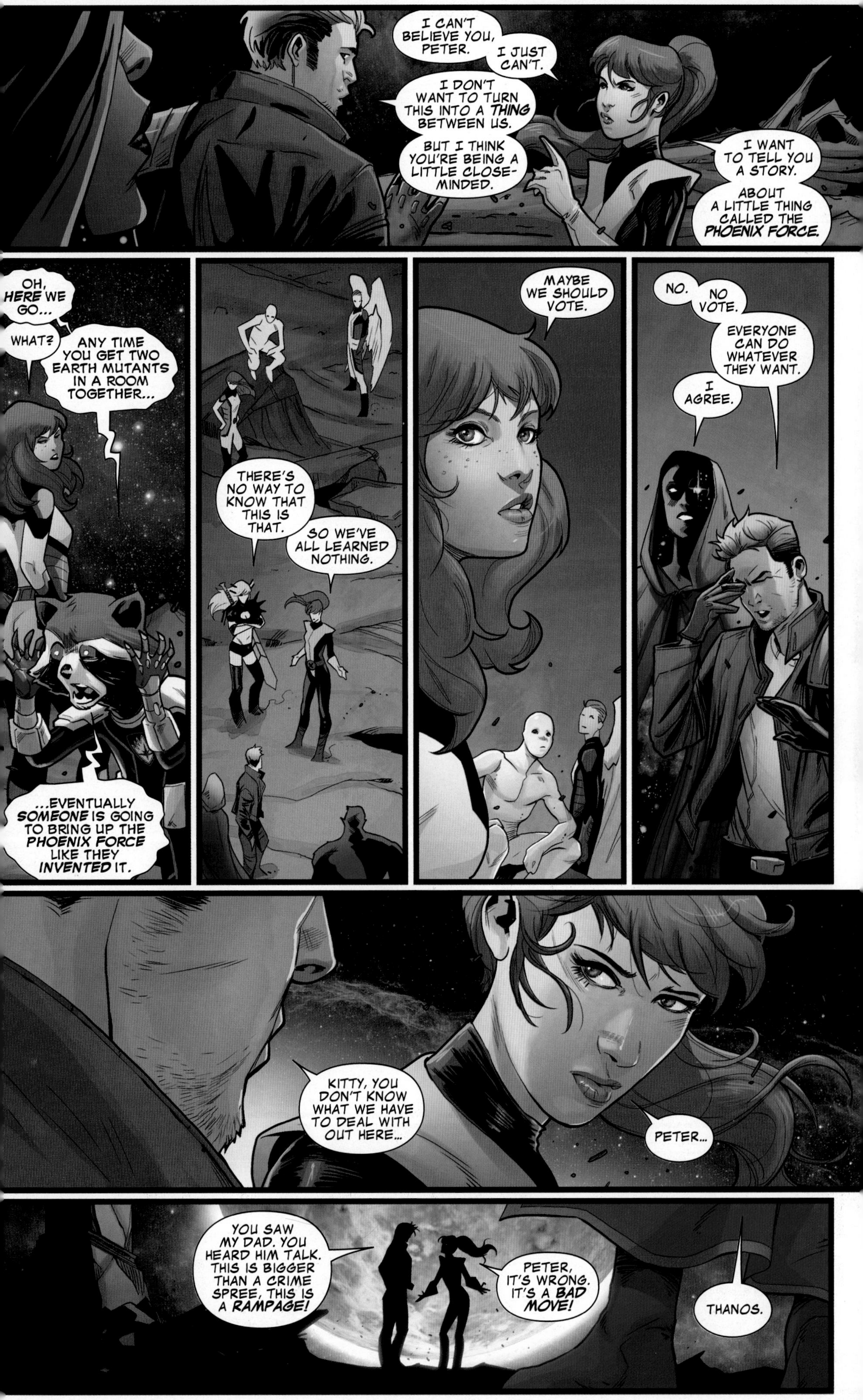

I CAN'T BELIEVE YOU, PETER.
I JUST CAN'T.
I DON'T WANT TO TURN THIS INTO A *THING* BETWEEN US.
BUT I THINK YOU'RE BEING A LITTLE CLOSE-MINDED.
I WANT TO TELL YOU A STORY.
ABOUT A LITTLE THING CALLED THE *PHOENIX FORCE.*
OH, *HERE* WE GO...
WHAT?
ANY TIME YOU GET TWO EARTH MUTANTS IN A ROOM TOGETHER...
...EVENTUALLY *SOMEONE* IS GOING TO BRING UP THE *PHOENIX FORCE* LIKE THEY *INVENTED* IT.
THERE'S NO WAY TO KNOW THAT THIS IS THAT.
SO WE'VE ALL LEARNED NOTHING.
MAYBE WE SHOULD VOTE.
NO.
NO VOTE.
EVERYONE CAN DO WHATEVER THEY WANT.
I AGREE.
KITTY, YOU DON'T KNOW WHAT WE HAVE TO DEAL WITH OUT HERE...
PETER...
YOU SAW MY DAD. YOU HEARD HIM TALK. THIS IS BIGGER THAN A CRIME SPREE, THIS IS A *RAMPAGE!*
PETER, IT'S WRONG. IT'S A *BAD MOVE!*
THANOS.

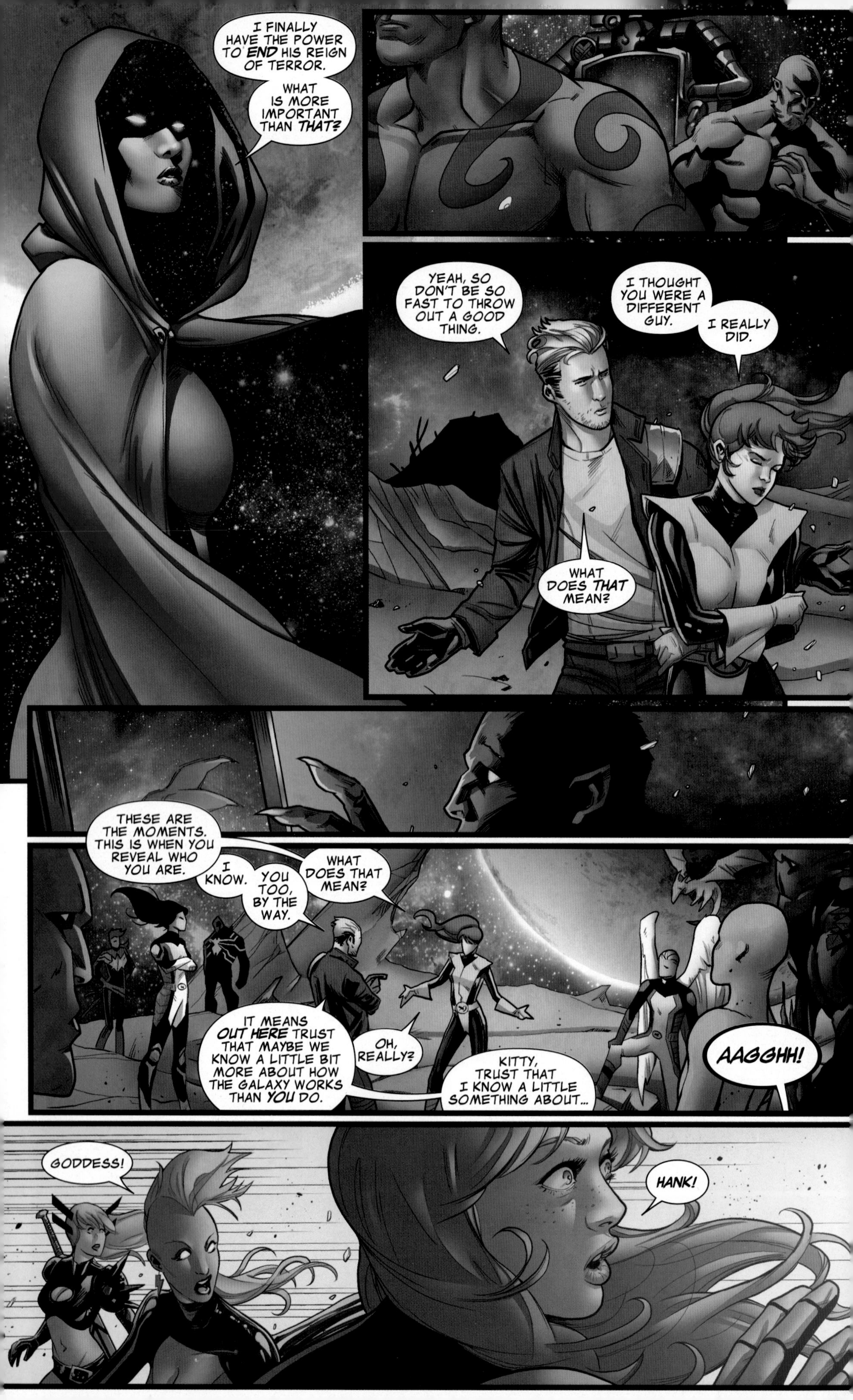

I FINALLY HAVE THE POWER TO END HIS REIGN OF TERROR.
WHAT IS MORE IMPORTANT THAN THAT?
YEAH, SO DON'T BE SO FAST TO THROW OUT A GOOD THING.
I THOUGHT YOU WERE A DIFFERENT GUY.
I REALLY DID.
WHAT DOES THAT MEAN?
THESE ARE THE MOMENTS. THIS IS WHEN YOU REVEAL WHO YOU ARE.
I KNOW.
YOU TOO, BY THE WAY.
WHAT DOES THAT MEAN?
IT MEANS OUT HERE TRUST THAT MAYBE WE KNOW A LITTLE BIT MORE ABOUT HOW THE GALAXY WORKS THAN YOU DO.
OH, REALLY?
KITTY, TRUST THAT I KNOW A LITTLE SOMETHING ABOUT...
AAGGHH!
GODDESS!
HANK!

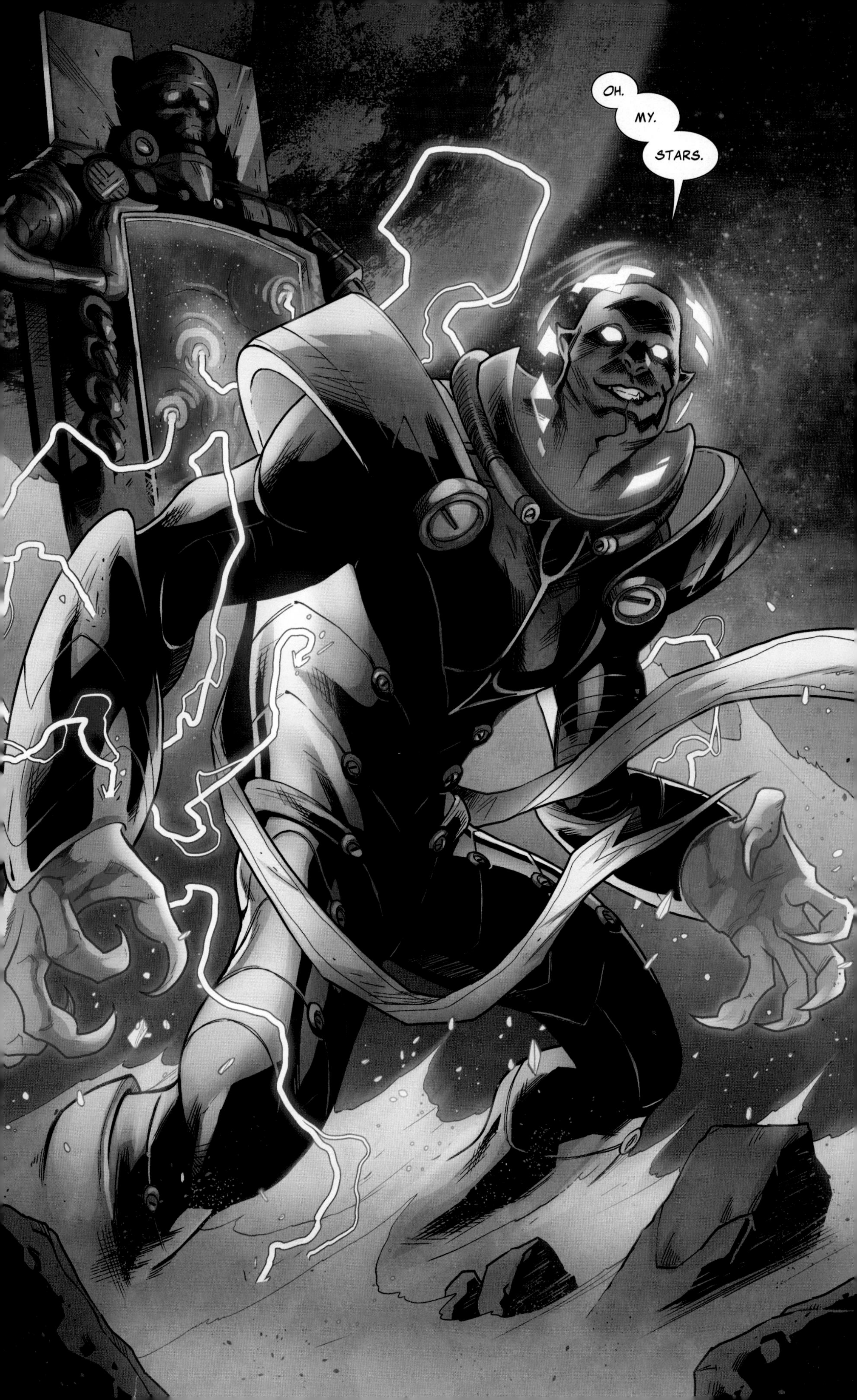
OH.
MY.
STARS.

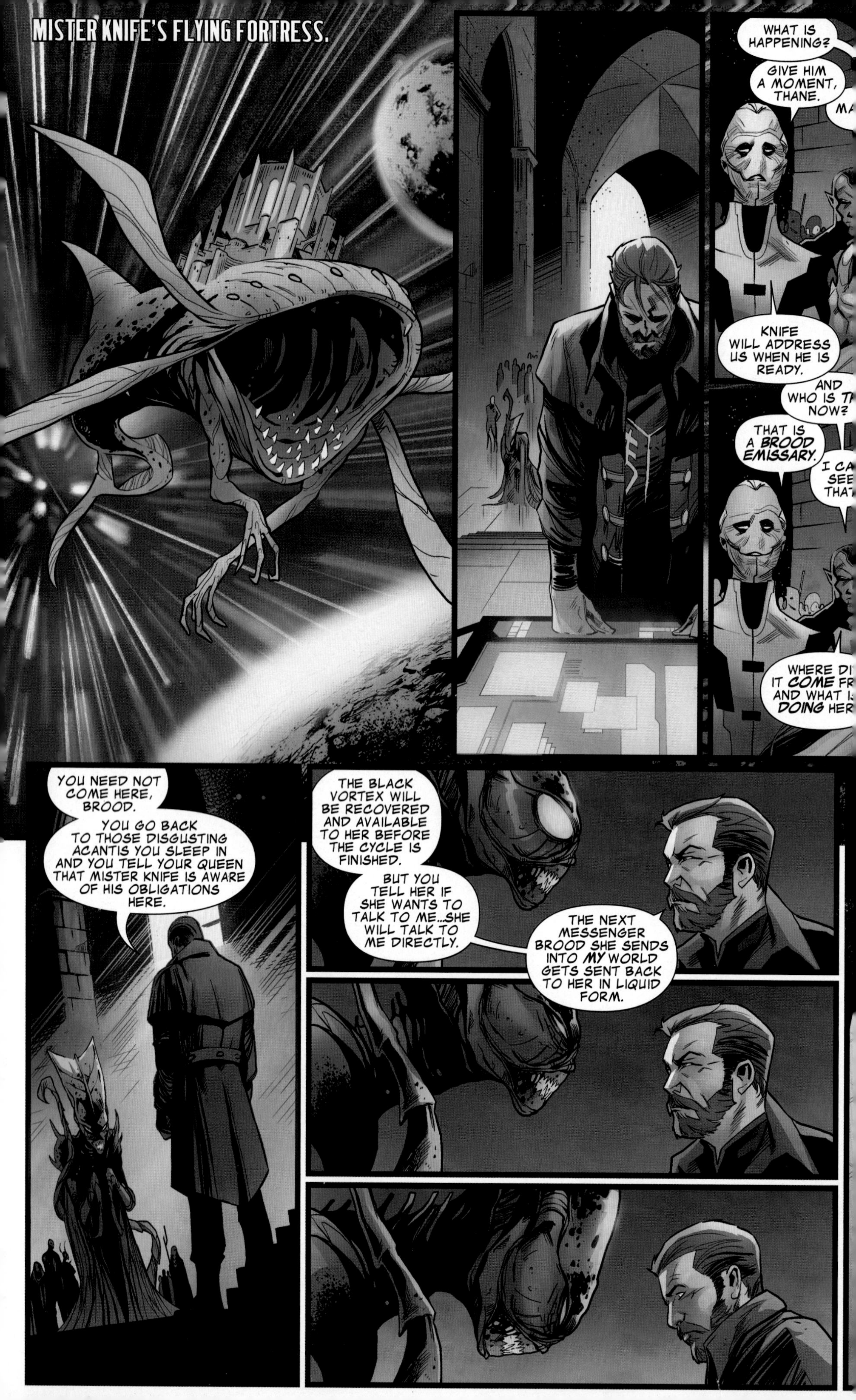
MISTER KNIFE'S FLYING FORTRESS.
WHAT IS HAPPENING?
GIVE HIM A MOMENT, THANE.
KNIFE WILL ADDRESS US WHEN HE IS READY.
AND WHO IS TH NOW?
THAT IS A BROOD EMISSARY.
I CA SEE THAT
WHERE DI IT COME FR AND WHAT I DOING HER
YOU NEED NOT COME HERE, BROOD.
YOU GO BACK TO THOSE DISGUSTING ACANTIS YOU SLEEP IN AND YOU TELL YOUR QUEEN THAT MISTER KNIFE IS AWARE OF HIS OBLIGATIONS HERE.
THE BLACK VORTEX WILL BE RECOVERED AND AVAILABLE TO HER BEFORE THE CYCLE IS FINISHED.
BUT YOU TELL HER IF SHE WANTS TO TALK TO ME...SHE WILL TALK TO ME DIRECTLY.
THE NEXT MESSENGER BROOD SHE SENDS INTO MY WORLD GETS SENT BACK TO HER IN LIQUID FORM.

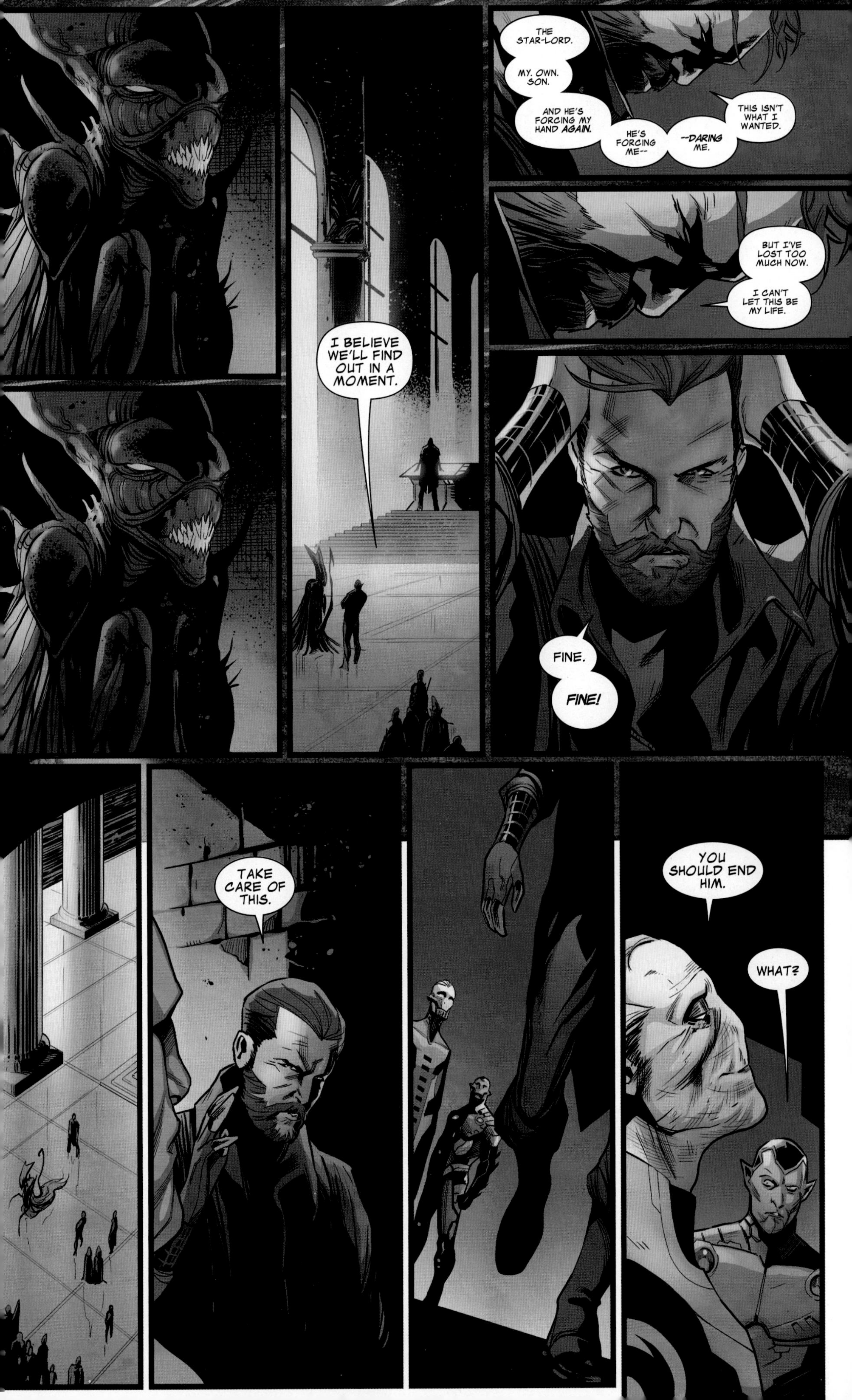
I BELIEVE WE'LL FIND OUT IN A MOMENT.
THE STAR-LORD.
MY. OWN. SON.
AND HE'S FORCING MY HAND AGAIN.
HE'S FORCING ME--
--DARING ME.
THIS ISN'T WHAT I WANTED.
BUT I'VE LOST TOO MUCH NOW.
I CAN'T LET THIS BE MY LIFE.
FINE.
FINE!
TAKE CARE OF THIS.
YOU SHOULD END HIM.
WHAT?

YOU HEARD ME.

WE ARE BUILDING SOMETHING HERE.

SOMETHING TO FEAR. SOMETHING OF MATTER.

OF IMPORT.

WE ARE CHANGING THE BALANCE OF POWER IN THE GALAXY AND THAT IS SOMETHING THIS GALAXY *DESPERATELY* NEEDS.

AND HE, THAT *MAN*, WITH EVERY STEP FORWARD IS REVEALING THAT HE IS NOT THE MAN TO TAKE US THERE.

SO WE *KILL* HIM?

THAT'S NOT NICE.

YOUR FATHER IS A MAD TITAN. NO ONE WOULD ARGUE THAT.

BUT IF HE HAD THE VISION AND CLARITY YOU HAVE...HE WOULD OWN THIS GALAXY.

HE WOULD ABSOLUTELY *OWN* IT.

THANE... YOU HAVE ALL OF YOUR FATHER'S *STRENGTH OF SPIRIT* AND NONE OF HIS *DEFECTS*.

YOU...CAN *LEAD*.

GO BACK TO WHEREVER YOU *DISAPPEAR* TO.

YOU WILL NOT SPEAK THESE WORDS TO ME AGAIN.

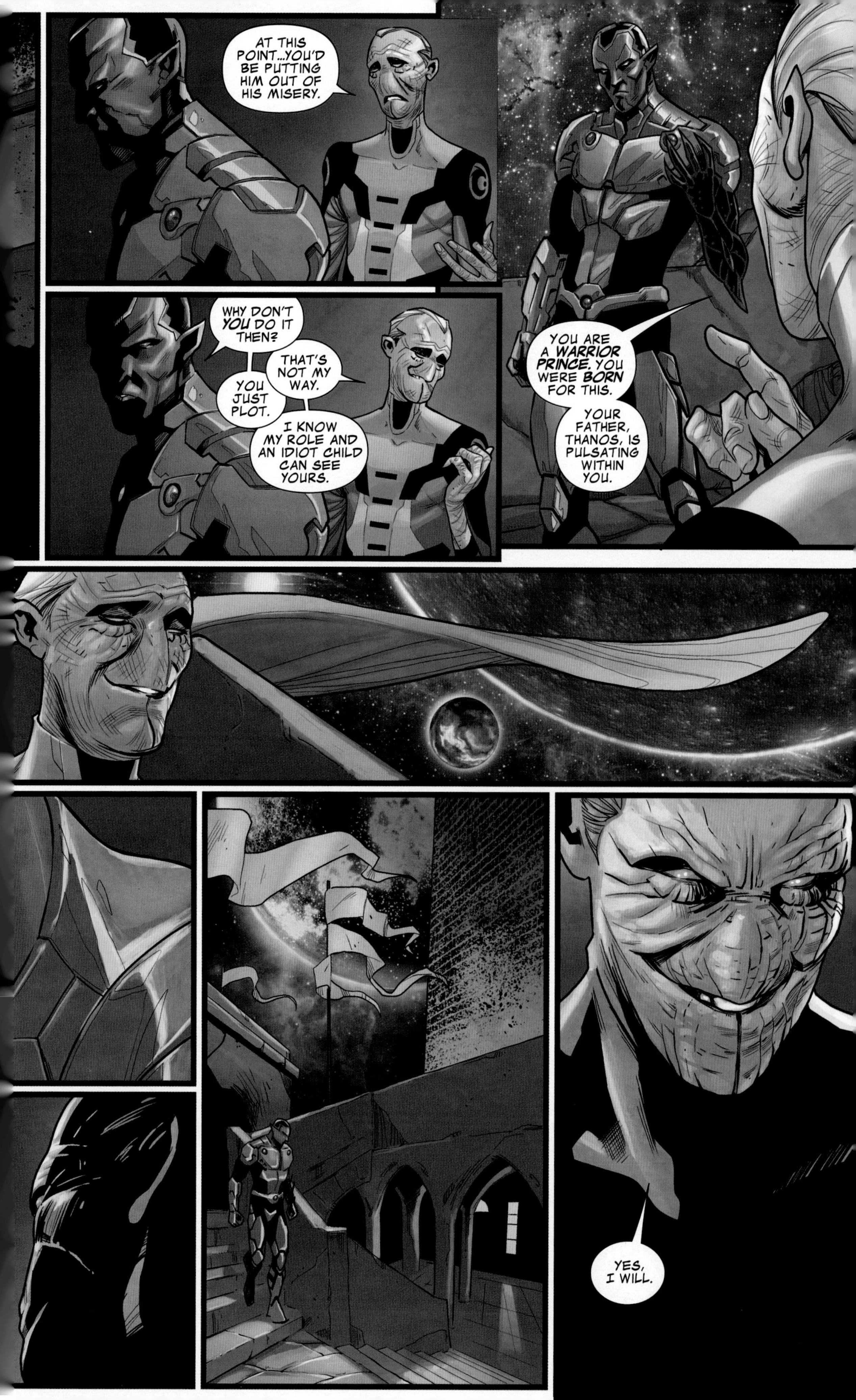
AT THIS POINT...YOU'D BE PUTTING HIM OUT OF HIS MISERY.
WHY DON'T YOU DO IT THEN?
YOU JUST PLOT.
THAT'S NOT MY WAY.
I KNOW MY ROLE AND AN IDIOT CHILD CAN SEE YOURS.
YOU ARE A WARRIOR PRINCE. YOU WERE BORN FOR THIS.
YOUR FATHER, THANOS, IS PULSATING WITHIN YOU.
YES, I WILL.

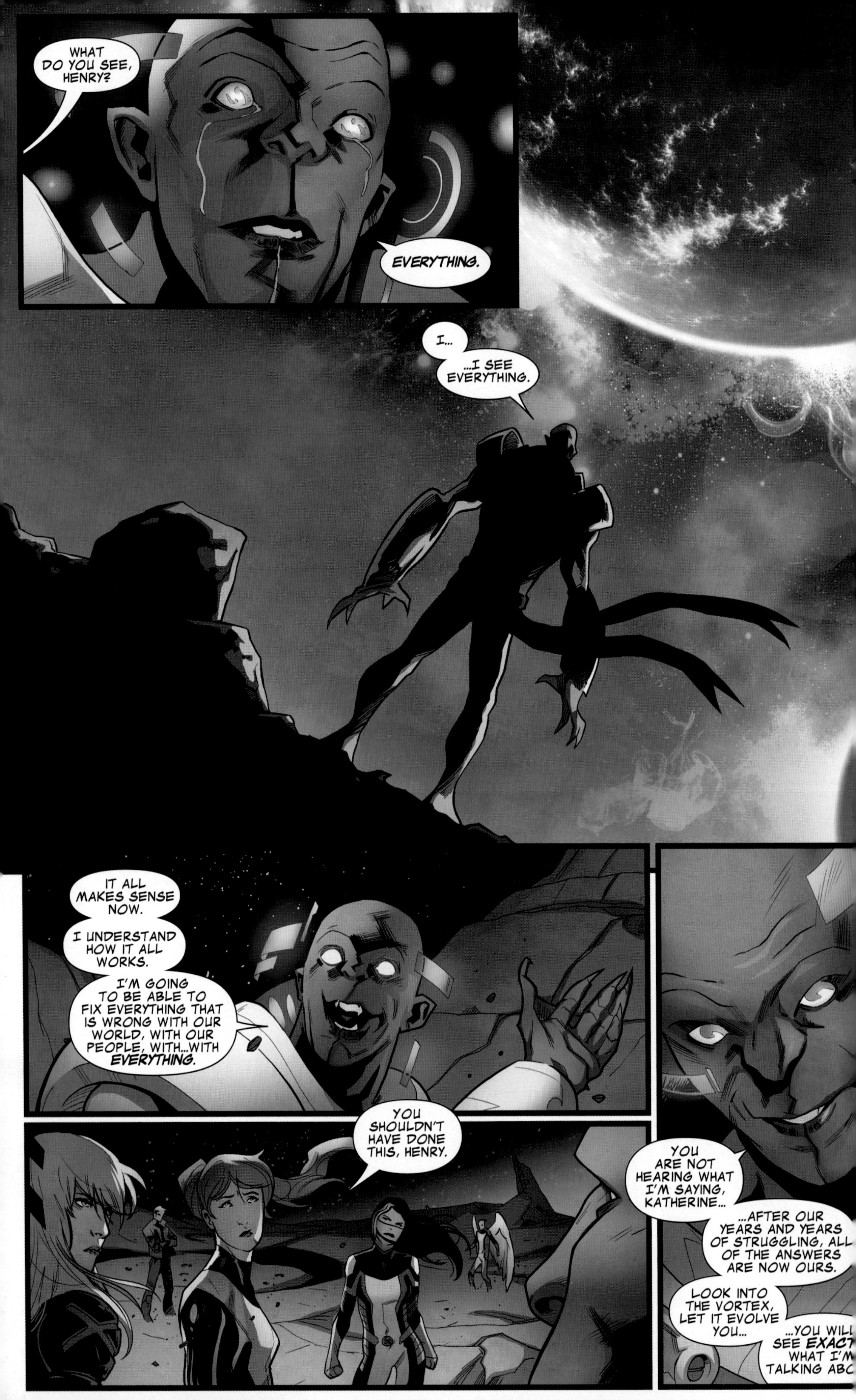
WHAT DO YOU SEE, HENRY?
EVERYTHING.
I...
...I SEE EVERYTHING.
IT ALL MAKES SENSE NOW.
I UNDERSTAND HOW IT ALL WORKS.
I'M GOING TO BE ABLE TO FIX EVERYTHING THAT IS WRONG WITH OUR WORLD, WITH OUR PEOPLE, WITH...WITH EVERYTHING.
YOU SHOULDN'T HAVE DONE THIS, HENRY.
YOU ARE NOT HEARING WHAT I'M SAYING, KATHERINE...
...AFTER OUR YEARS AND YEARS OF STRUGGLING, ALL OF THE ANSWERS ARE NOW OURS.
LOOK INTO THE VORTEX, LET IT EVOLVE YOU...
...YOU WILL SEE EXACT WHAT I'M TALKING ABO

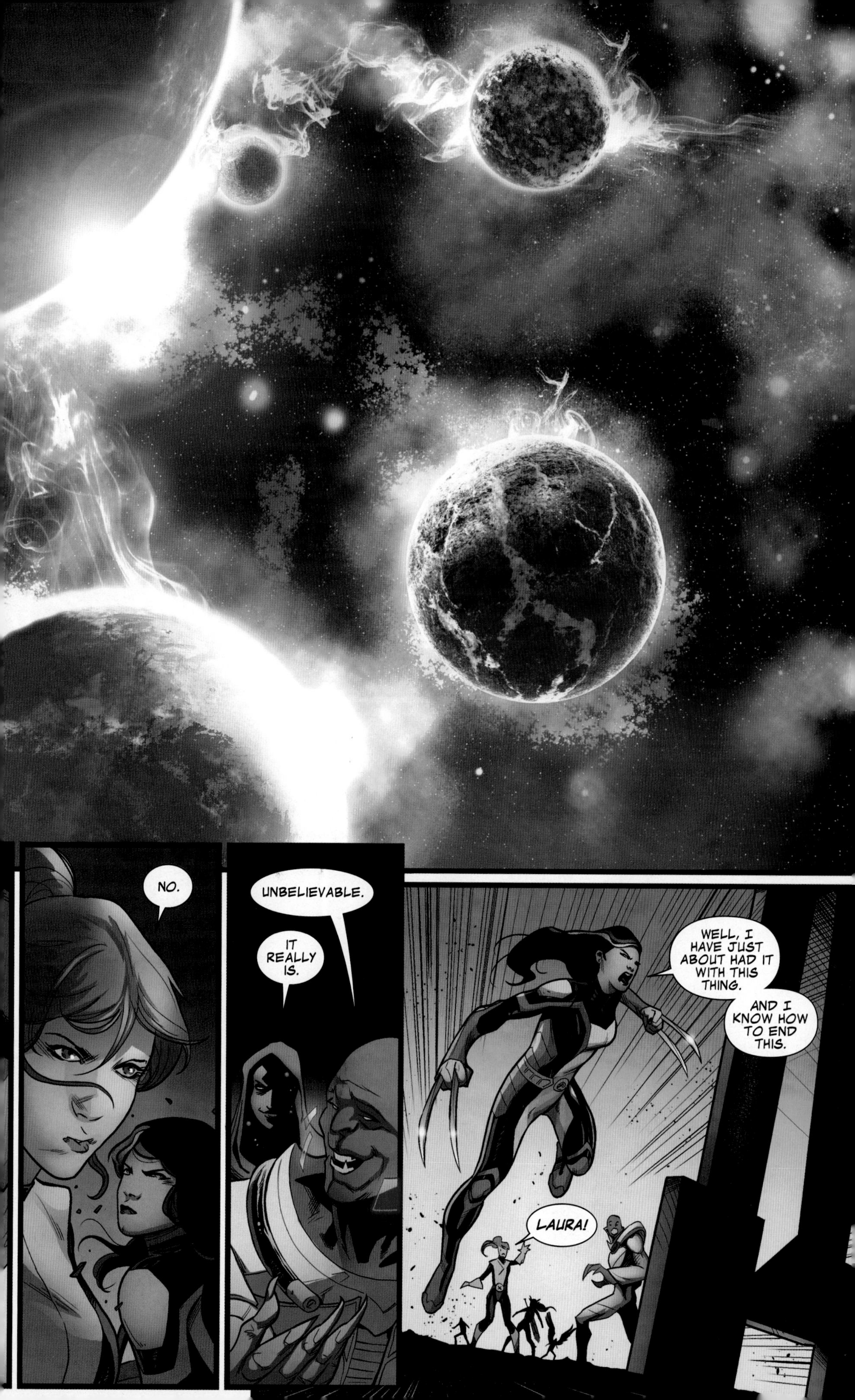
NO.
UNBELIEVABLE.
IT REALLY IS.
WELL, I HAVE JUST ABOUT HAD IT WITH THIS THING.
AND I KNOW HOW TO END THIS.
LAURA!

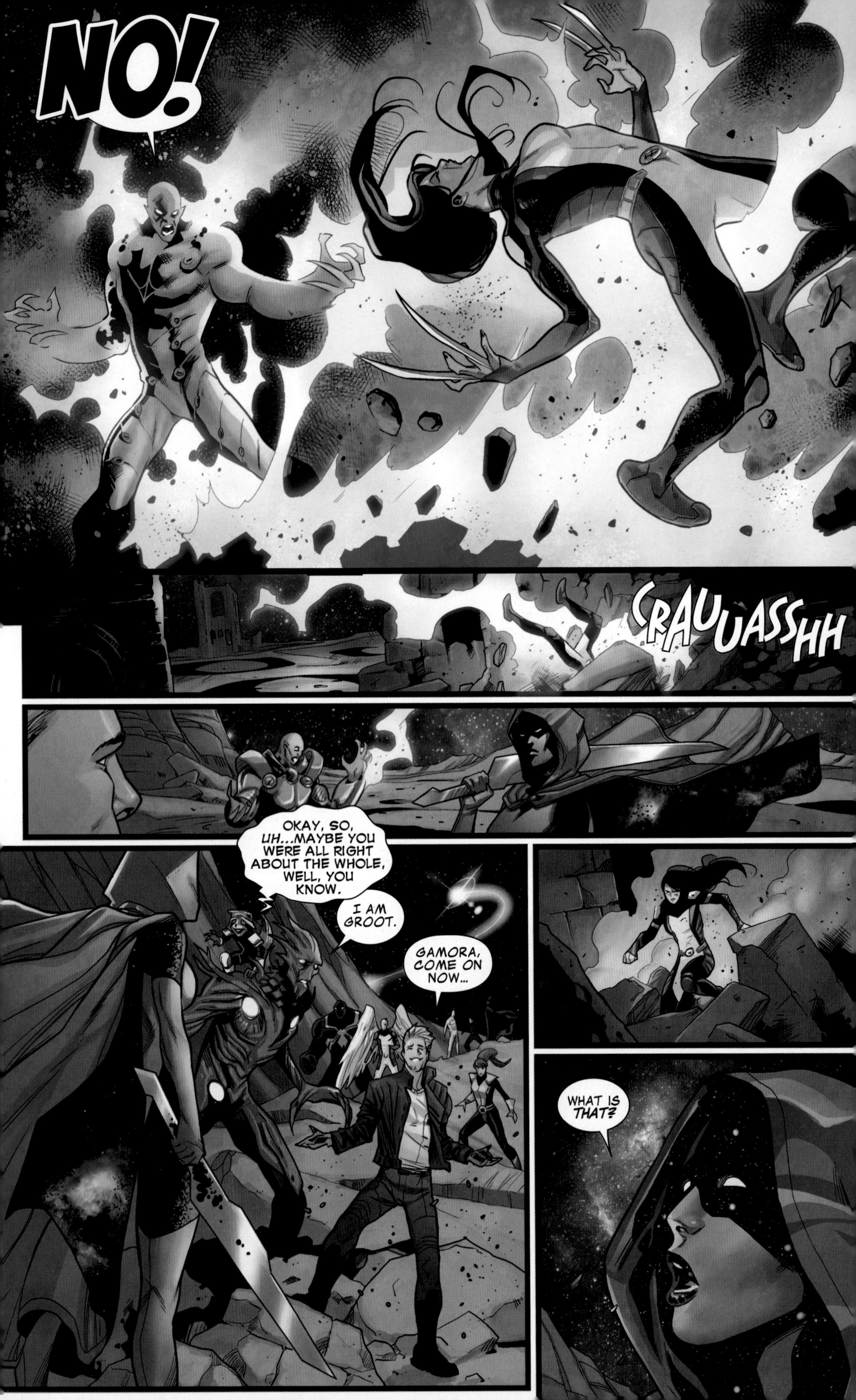
NO!
CRAUUASSHH
OKAY, SO, UH...MAYBE YOU WERE ALL RIGHT ABOUT THE WHOLE, WELL, YOU KNOW.
I AM GROOT.
GAMORA, COME ON NOW...
WHAT IS THAT?

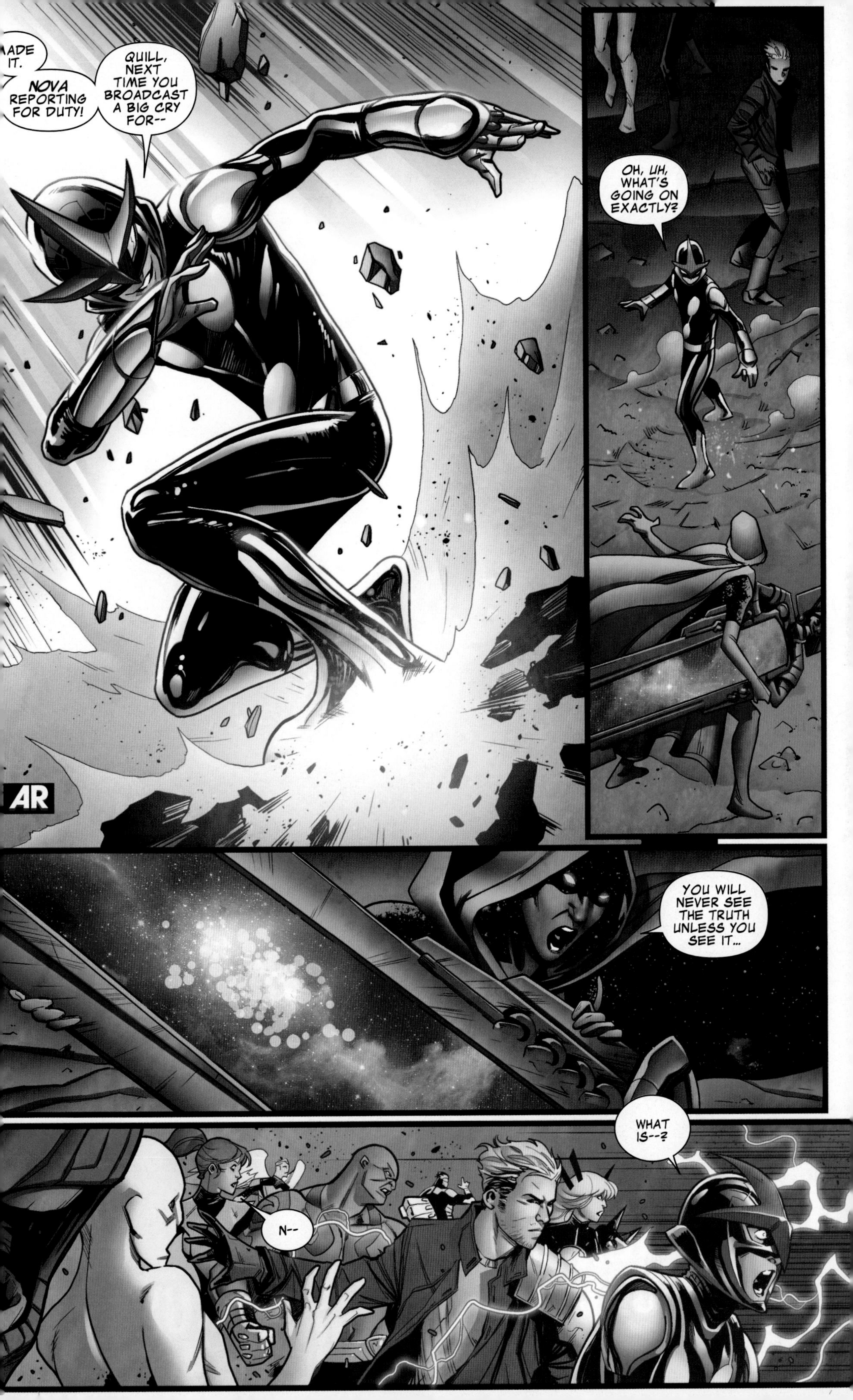
MADE IT. NOVA REPORTING FOR DUTY!
QUILL, NEXT TIME YOU BROADCAST A BIG CRY FOR--
OH, UH, WHAT'S GOING ON EXACTLY?
YOU WILL NEVER SEE THE TRUTH UNLESS YOU SEE IT...
WHAT IS--?
N--

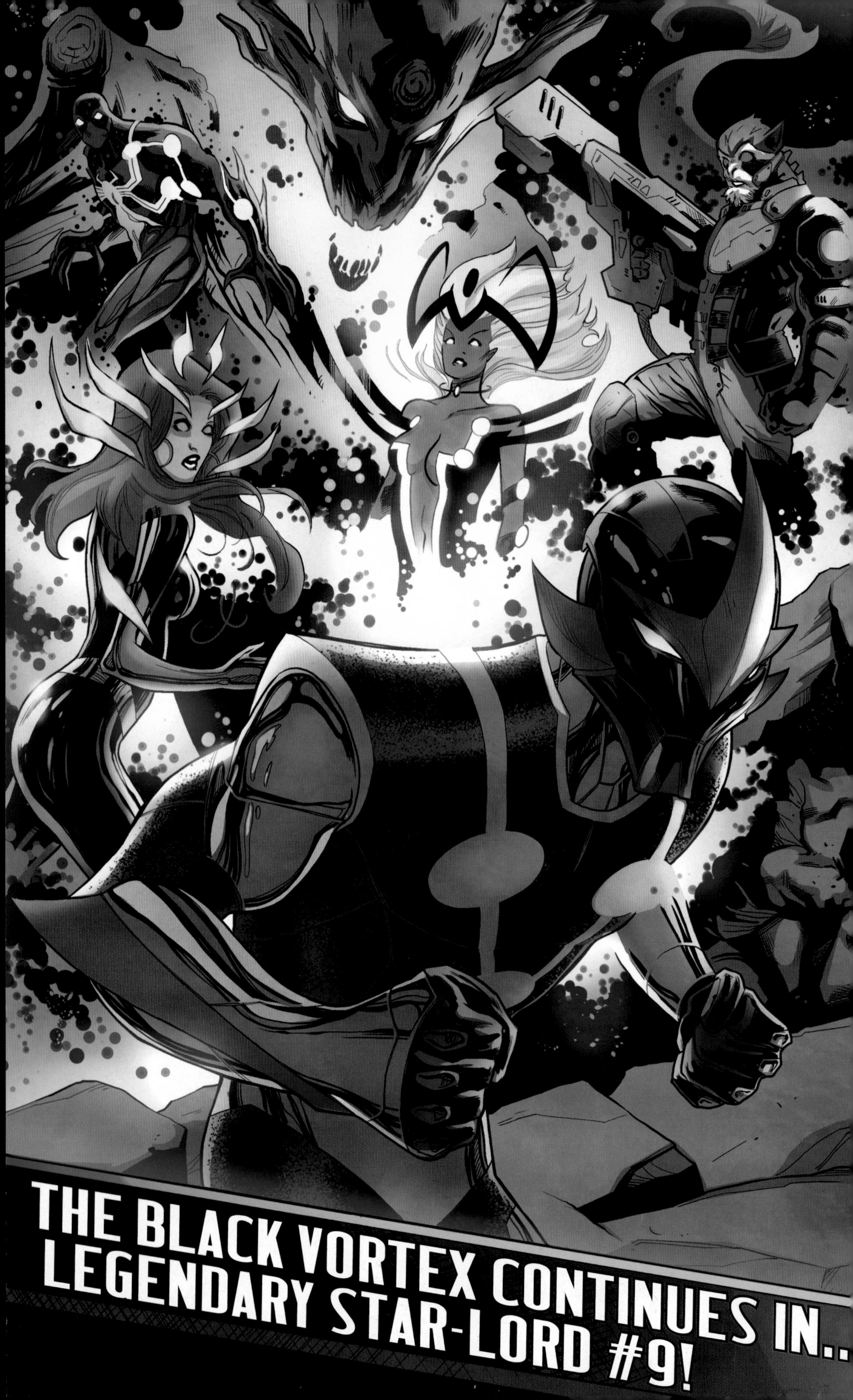
THE BLACK VORTEX CONTINUES IN...
LEGENDARY STAR-LORD #9!

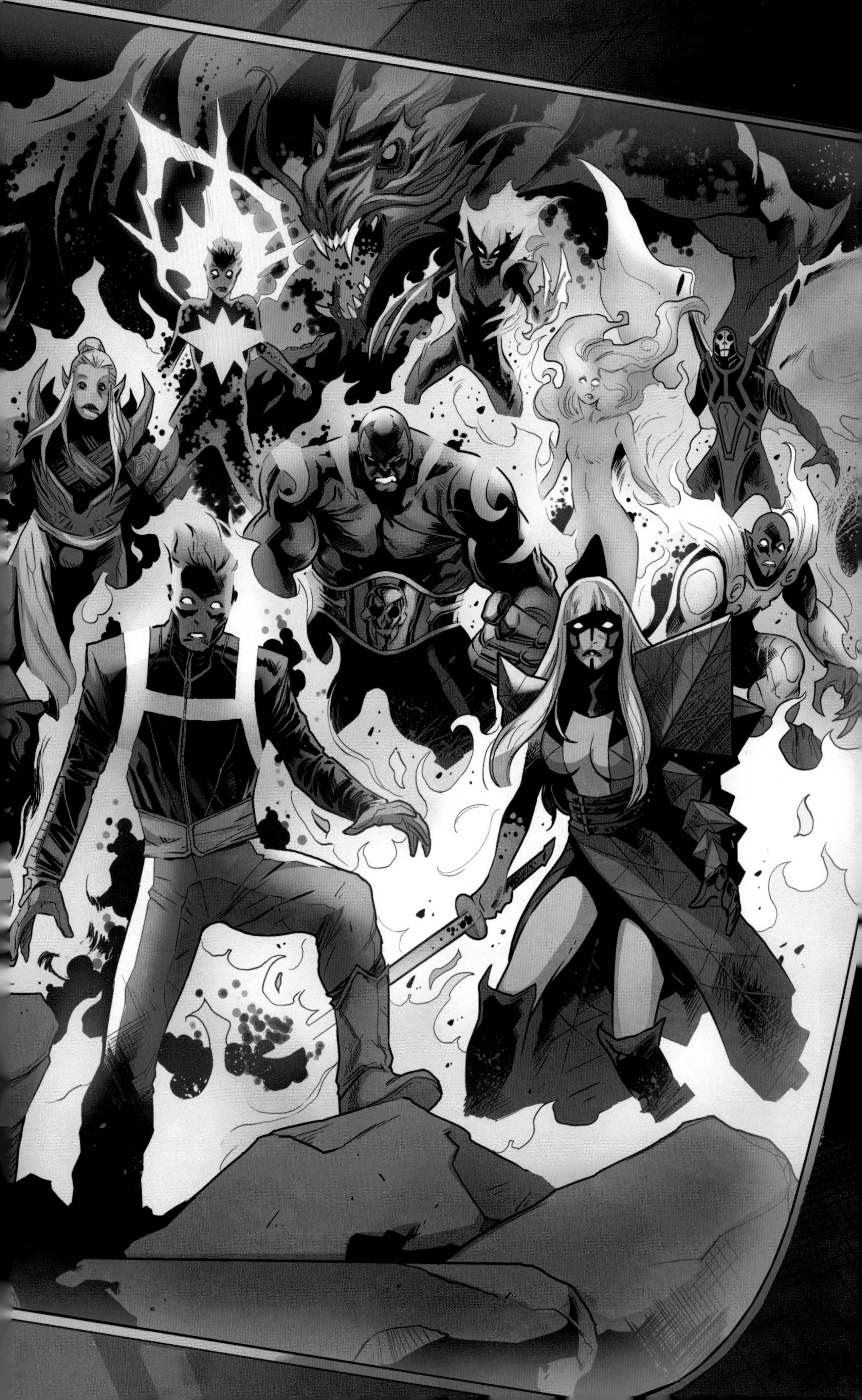

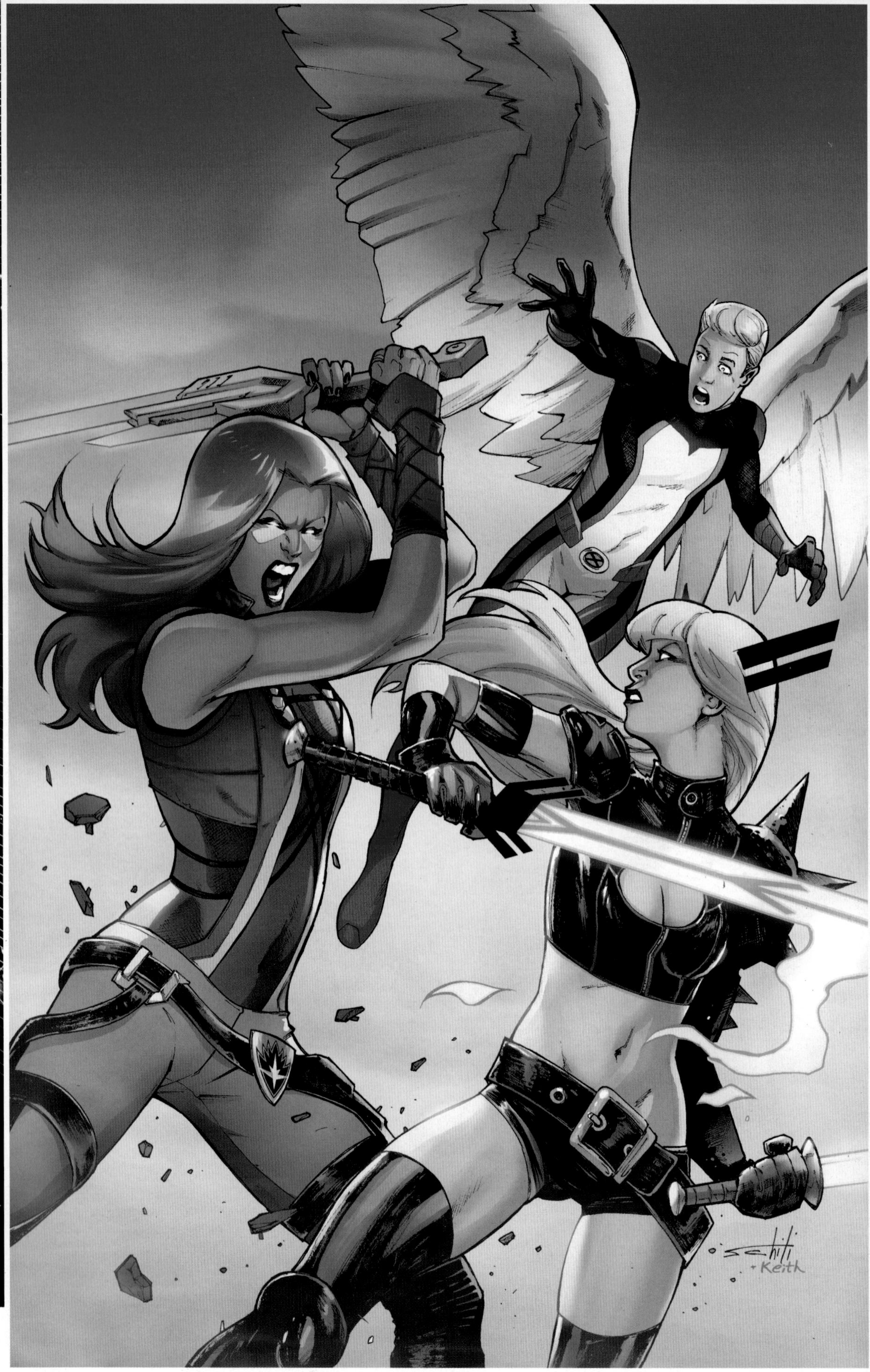
Schiti
+Keith

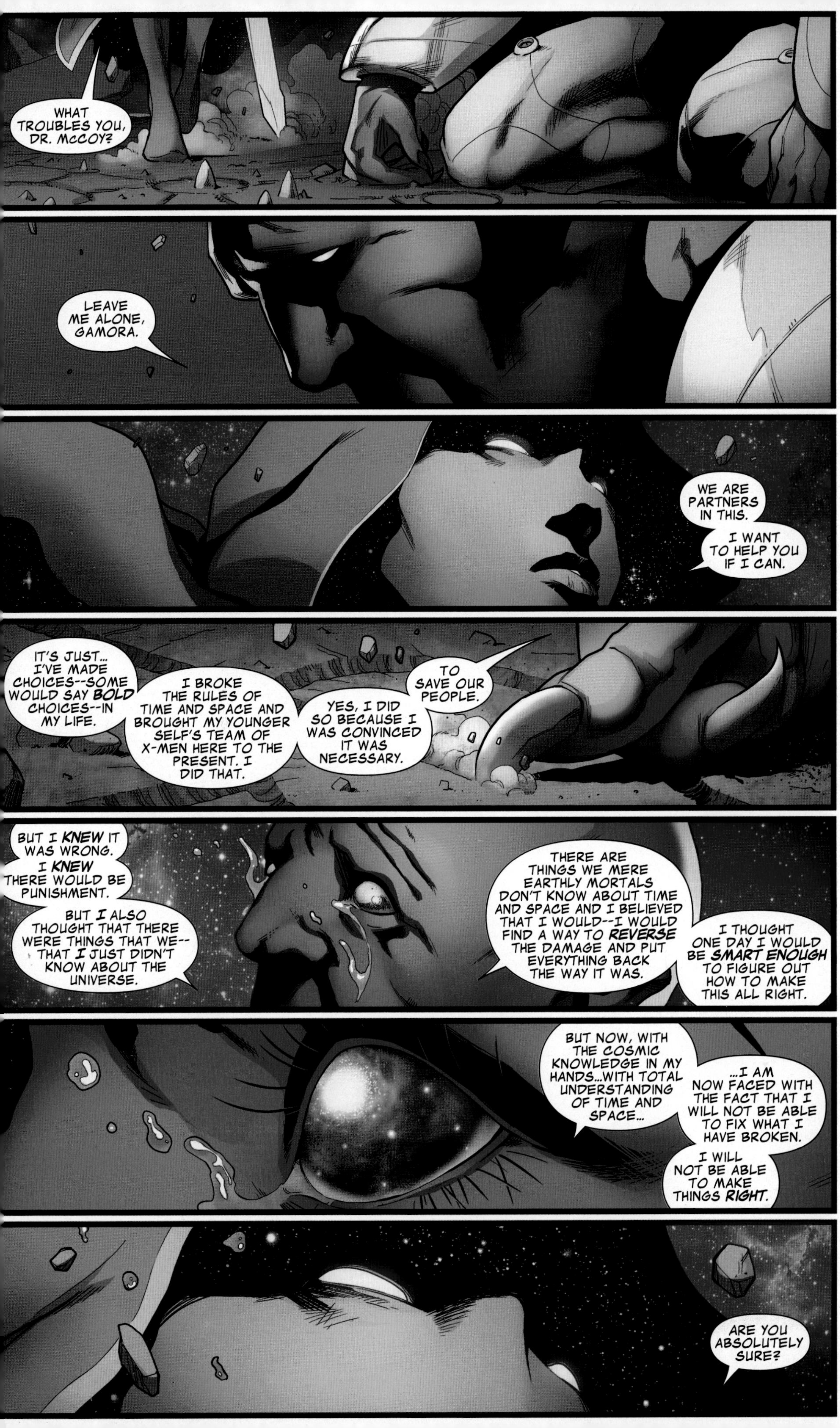
WHAT TROUBLES YOU, DR. McCOY?
LEAVE ME ALONE, GAMORA.
WE ARE PARTNERS IN THIS.
I WANT TO HELP YOU IF I CAN.
IT'S JUST... I'VE MADE CHOICES--SOME WOULD SAY BOLD CHOICES--IN MY LIFE.
I BROKE THE RULES OF TIME AND SPACE AND BROUGHT MY YOUNGER SELF'S TEAM OF X-MEN HERE TO THE PRESENT. I DID THAT.
YES, I DID SO BECAUSE I WAS CONVINCED IT WAS NECESSARY.
TO SAVE OUR PEOPLE.
BUT I KNEW IT WAS WRONG.
I KNEW THERE WOULD BE PUNISHMENT.
BUT I ALSO THOUGHT THAT THERE WERE THINGS THAT WE-- THAT I JUST DIDN'T KNOW ABOUT THE UNIVERSE.
THERE ARE THINGS WE MERE EARTHLY MORTALS DON'T KNOW ABOUT TIME AND SPACE AND I BELIEVED THAT I WOULD--I WOULD FIND A WAY TO REVERSE THE DAMAGE AND PUT EVERYTHING BACK THE WAY IT WAS.
I THOUGHT ONE DAY I WOULD BE SMART ENOUGH TO FIGURE OUT HOW TO MAKE THIS ALL RIGHT.
BUT NOW, WITH THE COSMIC KNOWLEDGE IN MY HANDS...WITH TOTAL UNDERSTANDING OF TIME AND SPACE...
...I AM NOW FACED WITH THE FACT THAT I WILL NOT BE ABLE TO FIX WHAT I HAVE BROKEN.
I WILL NOT BE ABLE TO MAKE THINGS RIGHT.
ARE YOU ABSOLUTELY SURE?

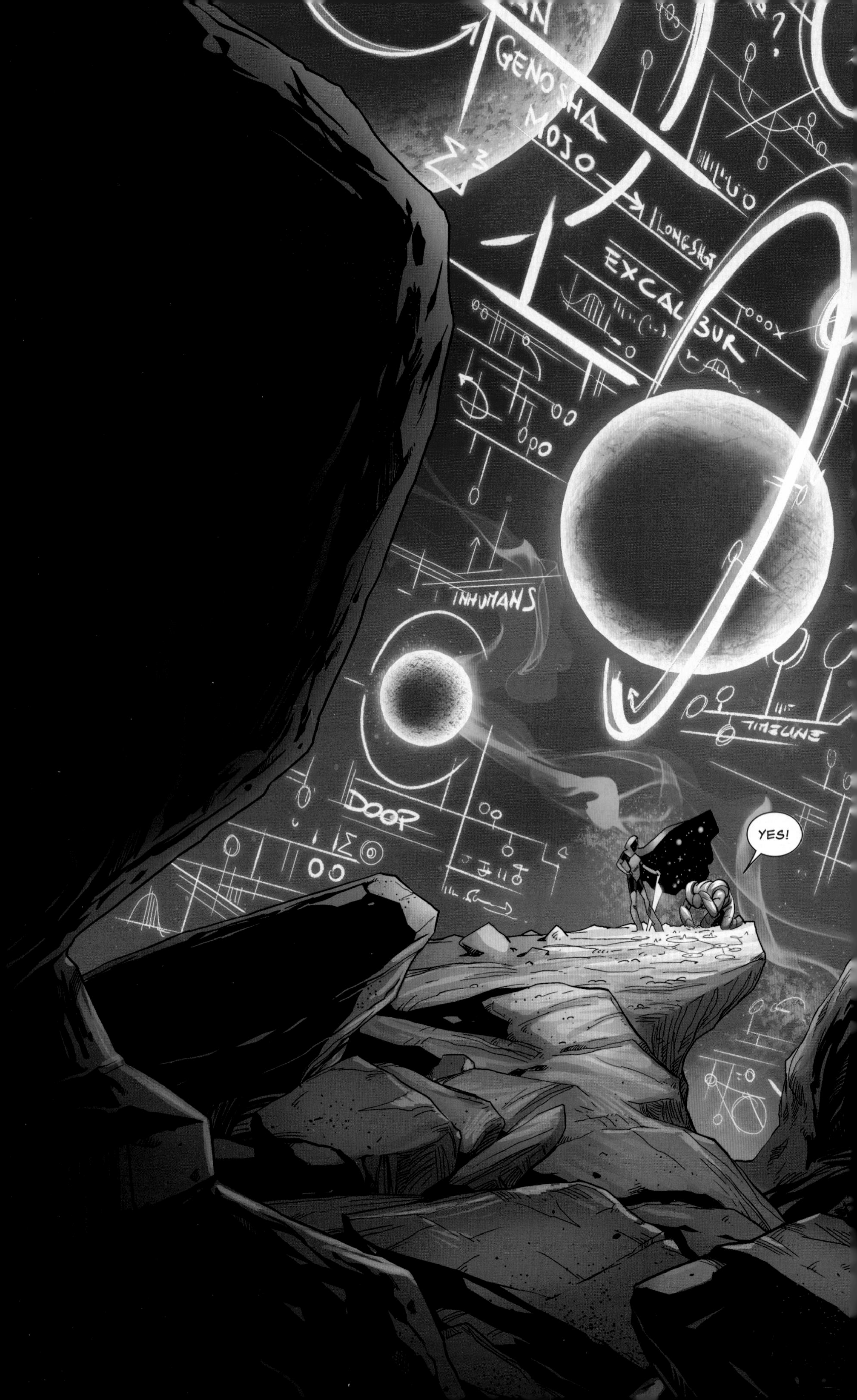
GENOSHA
MOJO
LONGSHOT
EXCALIBUR
INHUMANS
TIMELINE
DOOP
YES!

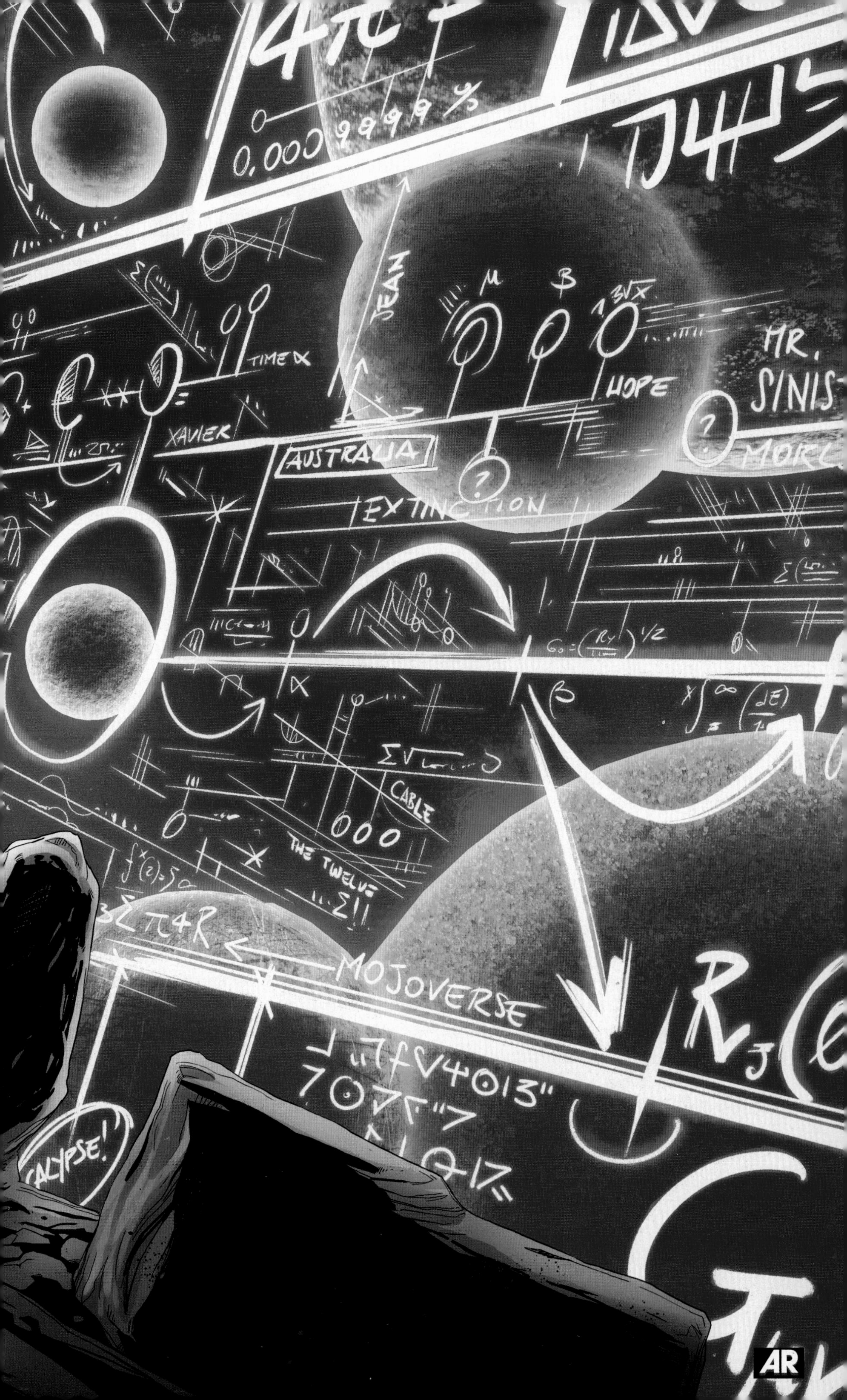

JEAN
HOPE
MR. SINIS-
TIME
XAVIER
AUSTRALIA
EXTINCTION
CABLE
THE TWELVE
MOJOVERSE
CALYPSE!

GUARDIANS OF THE GALAXY & X-MEN

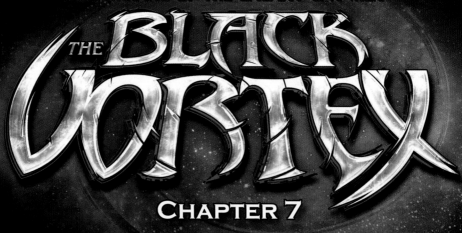

THE BLACK VORTEX

CHAPTER 7

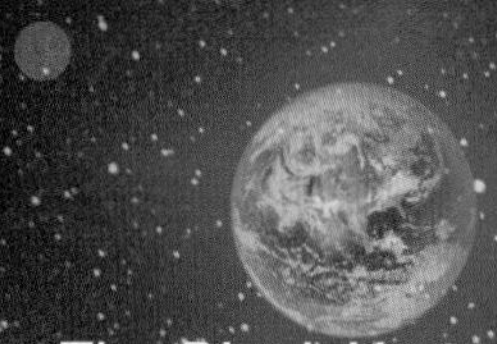

Previously in *The Black Vortex*...

Billions of years ago, an ancient race named the Viscardi were gifted an object of immense cosmic power by a Celestial. This artifact, known as the Black Vortex, transformed the user, imbuing them with cosmic energy. However, the power of this object caused the Viscardi to turn on each other, annihilating their own race from within.

When Mister Knife, a.k.a. J'Son, Peter Quill's father, obtained the Black Vortex, Peter and Kitty Pryde stole the artifact and recruited the Guardians of the Galaxy and the X-Men for help. Gamora, the elder Beast, and Angel chose to submit to the Vortex and the three cosmically enhanced heroes took the artifact and left, intending to reshape the universe in their image. But when Ronan the Accuser stole the Vortex from them, they retaliated by assaulting the Kree homeworld, Hala. Fearing total annihilation, Ronan used the Vortex to enhance himself against the Supreme Intelligence's wishes. As Ronan used his new powers to hold off the three enhanced heroes, the elder Beast was horrified to discover that he could not fix the damage he had done to space-time and fled with the other two in tow.

Meanwhile, the Guardians and X-Men escaped Knife's henchmen and were joined by the young Cyclops and his father, Corsair. Receiving multiple distress signals, they split into three groups. Cyclops, Iceman, and Groot stayed behind to delay the Slaughter Lords, but were quickly overpowered and are now prisoners of Mister Knife!

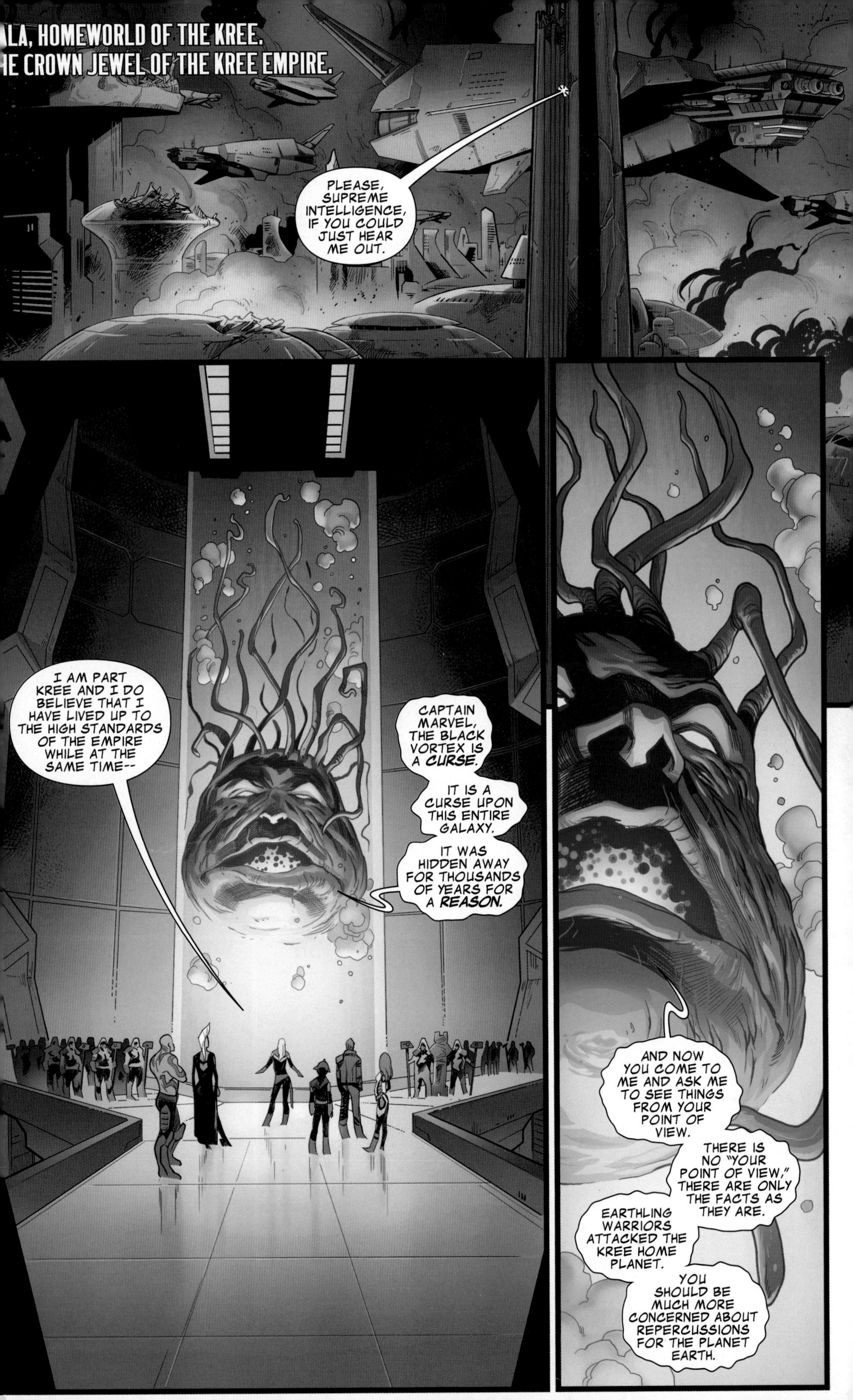
LA, HOMEWORLD OF THE KREE.
IE CROWN JEWEL OF THE KREE EMPIRE.
PLEASE, SUPREME INTELLIGENCE, IF YOU COULD JUST HEAR ME OUT.
I AM PART KREE AND I DO BELIEVE THAT I HAVE LIVED UP TO THE HIGH STANDARDS OF THE EMPIRE WHILE AT THE SAME TIME--
CAPTAIN MARVEL, THE BLACK VORTEX IS A CURSE.
IT IS A CURSE UPON THIS ENTIRE GALAXY.
IT WAS HIDDEN AWAY FOR THOUSANDS OF YEARS FOR A REASON.
AND NOW YOU COME TO ME AND ASK ME TO SEE THINGS FROM YOUR POINT OF VIEW.
THERE IS NO "YOUR POINT OF VIEW," THERE ARE ONLY THE FACTS AS THEY ARE.
EARTHLING WARRIORS ATTACKED THE KREE HOME PLANET.
YOU SHOULD BE MUCH MORE CONCERNED ABOUT REPERCUSSIONS FOR THE PLANET EARTH.

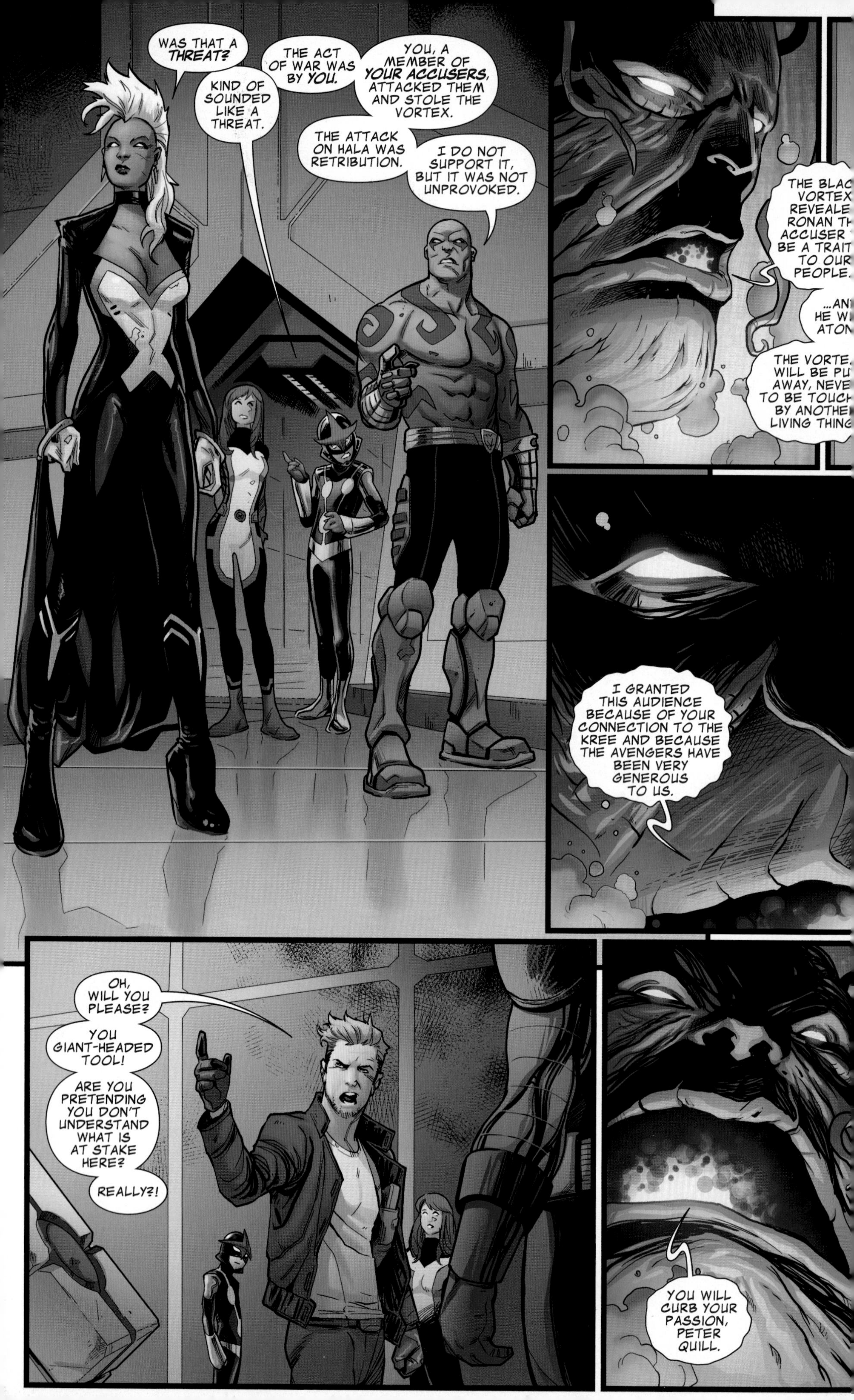
WAS THAT A THREAT?
KIND OF SOUNDED LIKE A THREAT.
THE ACT OF WAR WAS BY YOU.
YOU, A MEMBER OF YOUR ACCUSERS, ATTACKED THEM AND STOLE THE VORTEX.
THE ATTACK ON HALA WAS RETRIBUTION.
I DO NOT SUPPORT IT, BUT IT WAS NOT UNPROVOKED.
THE BLAC VORTEX REVEALE RONAN TH ACCUSER BE A TRAIT TO OUR PEOPLE.
...AN HE WI ATON
THE VORTE WILL BE PU AWAY, NEVE TO BE TOUCH BY ANOTHE LIVING THING
I GRANTED THIS AUDIENCE BECAUSE OF YOUR CONNECTION TO THE KREE AND BECAUSE THE AVENGERS HAVE BEEN VERY GENEROUS TO US.
OH, WILL YOU PLEASE?
YOU GIANT-HEADED TOOL!
ARE YOU PRETENDING YOU DON'T UNDERSTAND WHAT IS AT STAKE HERE?
REALLY?!
YOU WILL CURB YOUR PASSION, PETER QUILL.

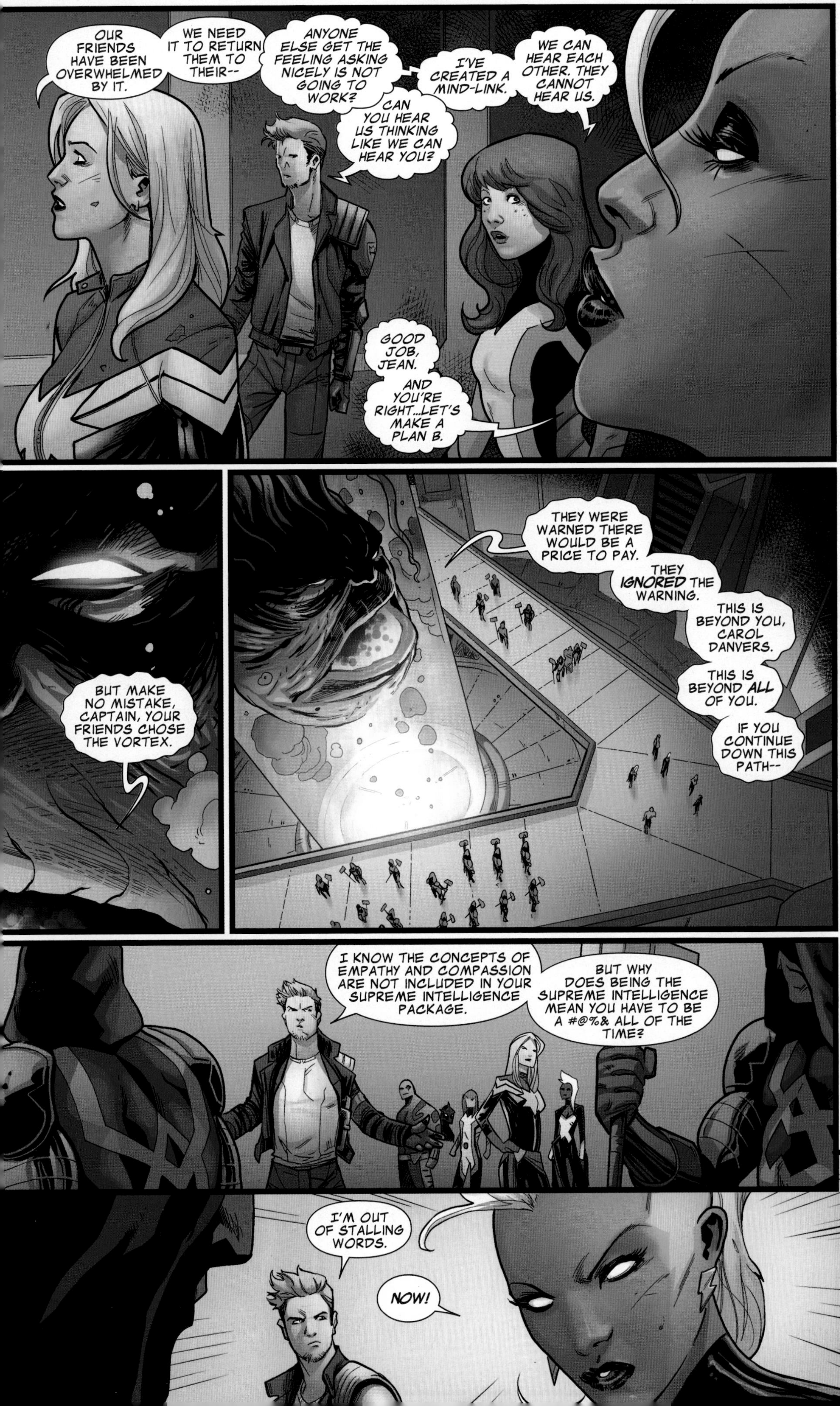
OUR FRIENDS HAVE BEEN OVERWHELMED BY IT.
WE NEED IT TO RETURN THEM TO THEIR--
ANYONE ELSE GET THE FEELING ASKING NICELY IS NOT GOING TO WORK?
I'VE CREATED A MIND-LINK.
WE CAN HEAR EACH OTHER. THEY CANNOT HEAR US.
CAN YOU HEAR US THINKING LIKE WE CAN HEAR YOU?
GOOD JOB, JEAN.
AND YOU'RE RIGHT...LET'S MAKE A PLAN B.
BUT MAKE NO MISTAKE, CAPTAIN, YOUR FRIENDS CHOSE THE VORTEX.
THEY WERE WARNED THERE WOULD BE A PRICE TO PAY.
THEY IGNORED THE WARNING.
THIS IS BEYOND YOU, CAROL DANVERS.
THIS IS BEYOND ALL OF YOU.
IF YOU CONTINUE DOWN THIS PATH--
I KNOW THE CONCEPTS OF EMPATHY AND COMPASSION ARE NOT INCLUDED IN YOUR SUPREME INTELLIGENCE PACKAGE.
BUT WHY DOES BEING THE SUPREME INTELLIGENCE MEAN YOU HAVE TO BE A #@%& ALL OF THE TIME?
I'M OUT OF STALLING WORDS.
NOW!

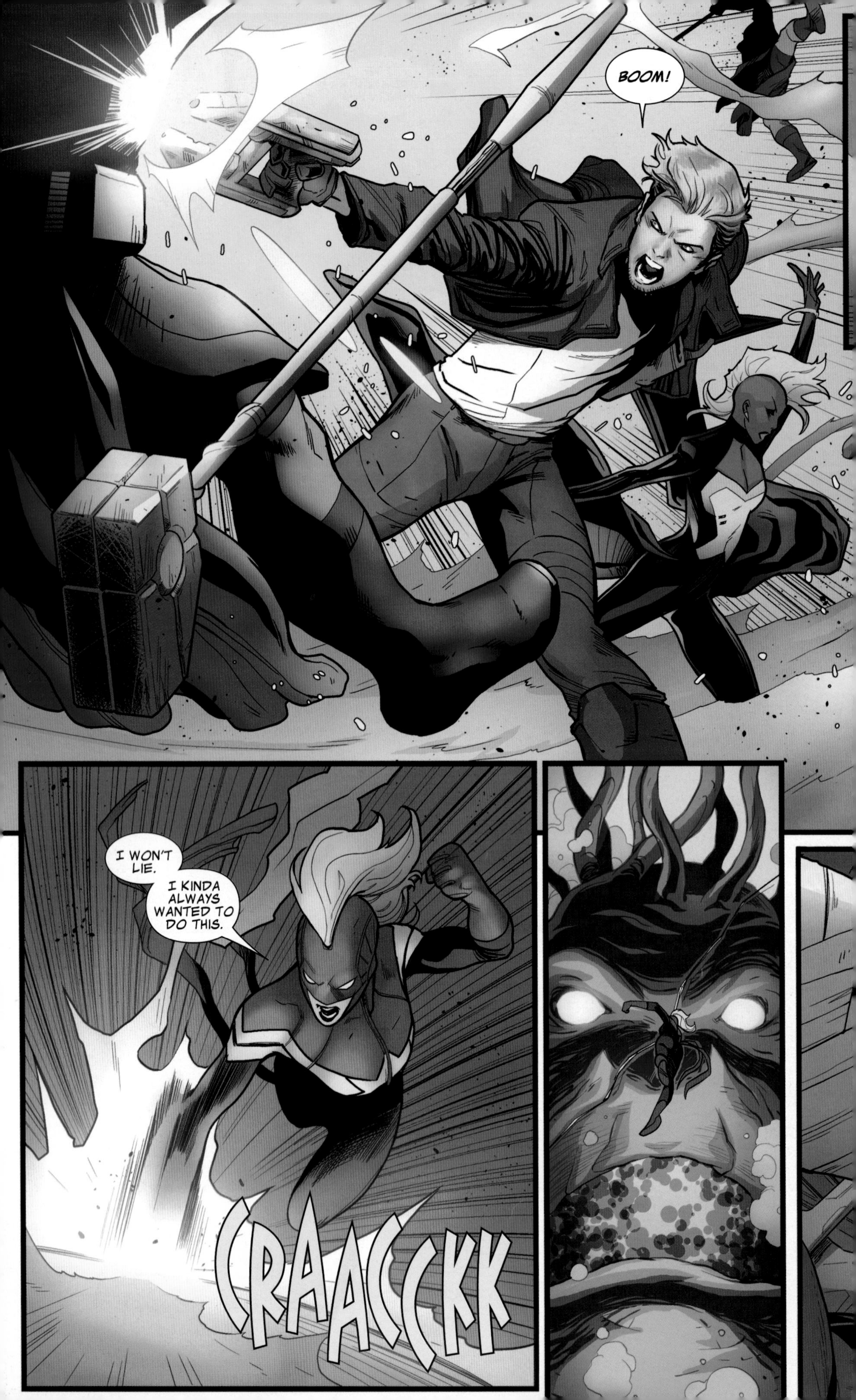
BOOM!
I WON'T LIE.
I KINDA ALWAYS WANTED TO DO THIS.
CRAACCKK

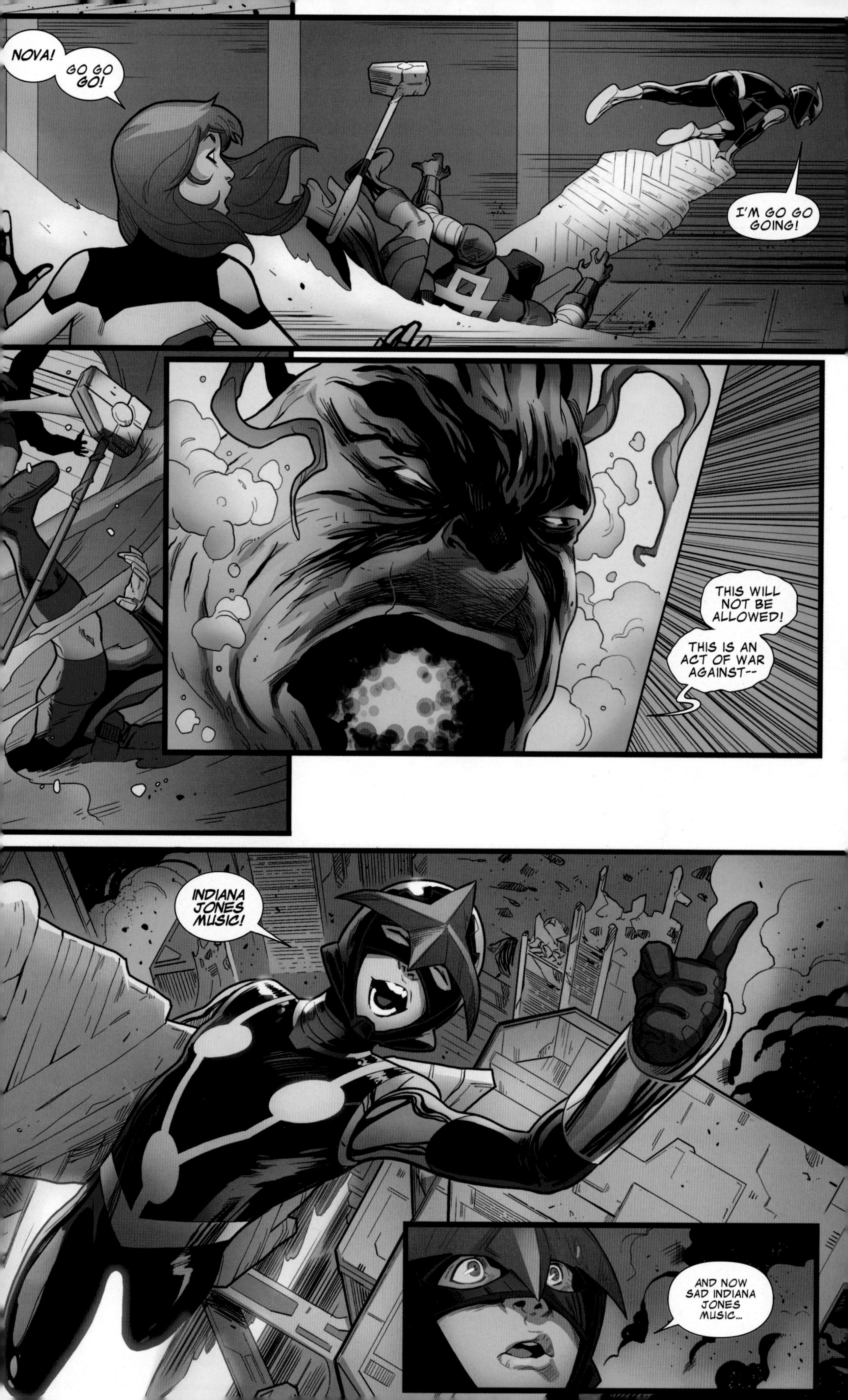
NOVA!
GO GO GO!
I'M GO GO GOING!
THIS WILL NOT BE ALLOWED!
THIS IS AN ACT OF WAR AGAINST--
INDIANA JONES MUSIC!
AND NOW SAD INDIANA JONES MUSIC...

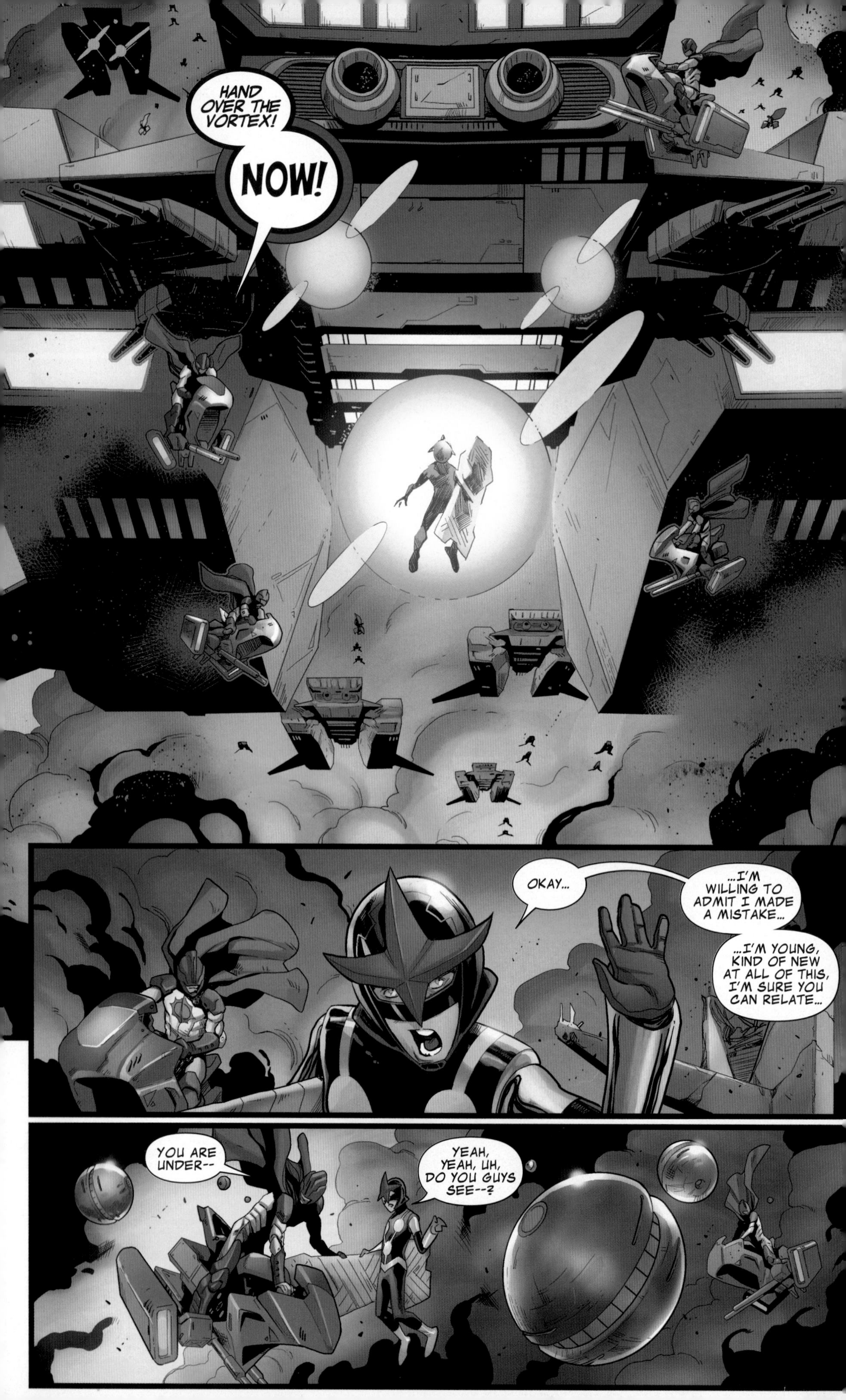
HAND OVER THE VORTEX!
NOW!
OKAY...
...I'M WILLING TO ADMIT I MADE A MISTAKE...
...I'M YOUNG, KIND OF NEW AT ALL OF THIS, I'M SURE YOU CAN RELATE...
YOU ARE UNDER--
YEAH, YEAH, UH, DO YOU GUYS SEE--?

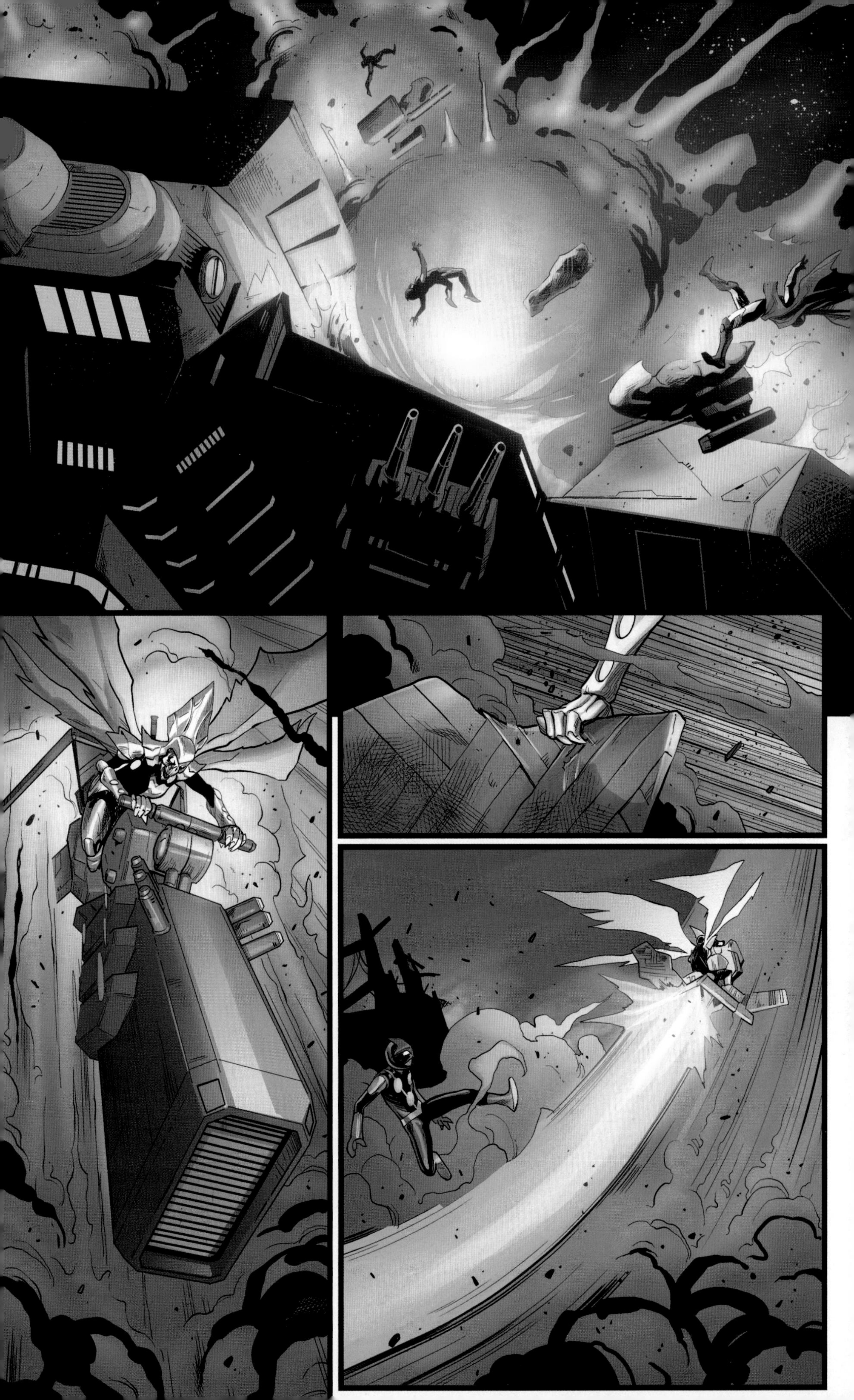

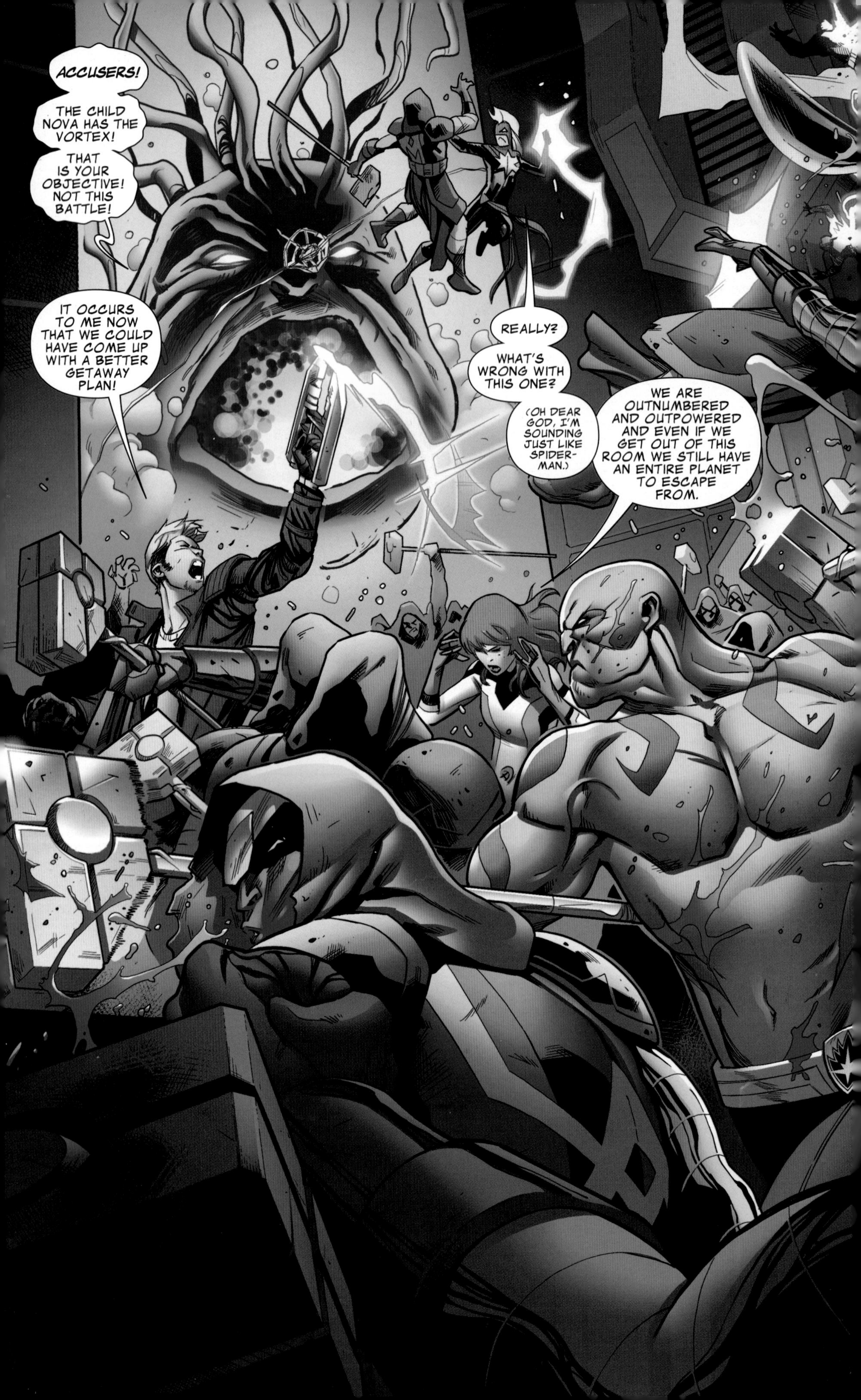
ACCUSERS!
THE CHILD NOVA HAS THE VORTEX!
THAT IS YOUR OBJECTIVE! NOT THIS BATTLE!
IT OCCURS TO ME NOW THAT WE COULD HAVE COME UP WITH A BETTER GETAWAY PLAN!
REALLY?
WHAT'S WRONG WITH THIS ONE?
(OH DEAR GOD, I'M SOUNDING JUST LIKE SPIDER-MAN.)
WE ARE OUTNUMBERED AND OUTPOWERED AND EVEN IF WE GET OUT OF THIS ROOM WE STILL HAVE AN ENTIRE PLANET TO ESCAPE FROM.

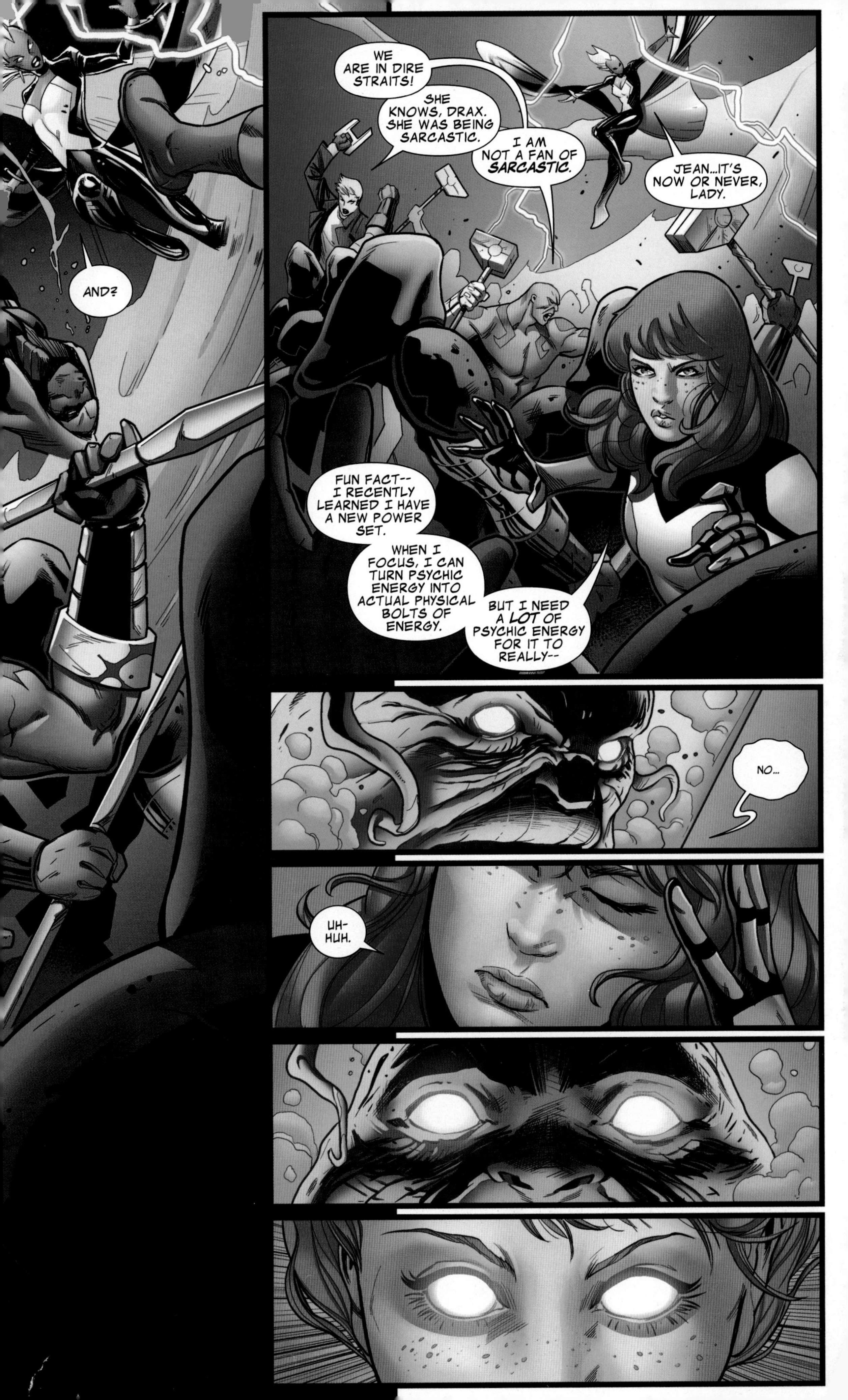

AND?
WE ARE IN DIRE STRAITS!
SHE KNOWS, DRAX. SHE WAS BEING SARCASTIC.
I AM NOT A FAN OF SARCASTIC.
JEAN...IT'S NOW OR NEVER, LADY.
FUN FACT-- I RECENTLY LEARNED I HAVE A NEW POWER SET.
WHEN I FOCUS, I CAN TURN PSYCHIC ENERGY INTO ACTUAL PHYSICAL BOLTS OF ENERGY.
BUT I NEED A LOT OF PSYCHIC ENERGY FOR IT TO REALLY--
NO...
UH-HUH.

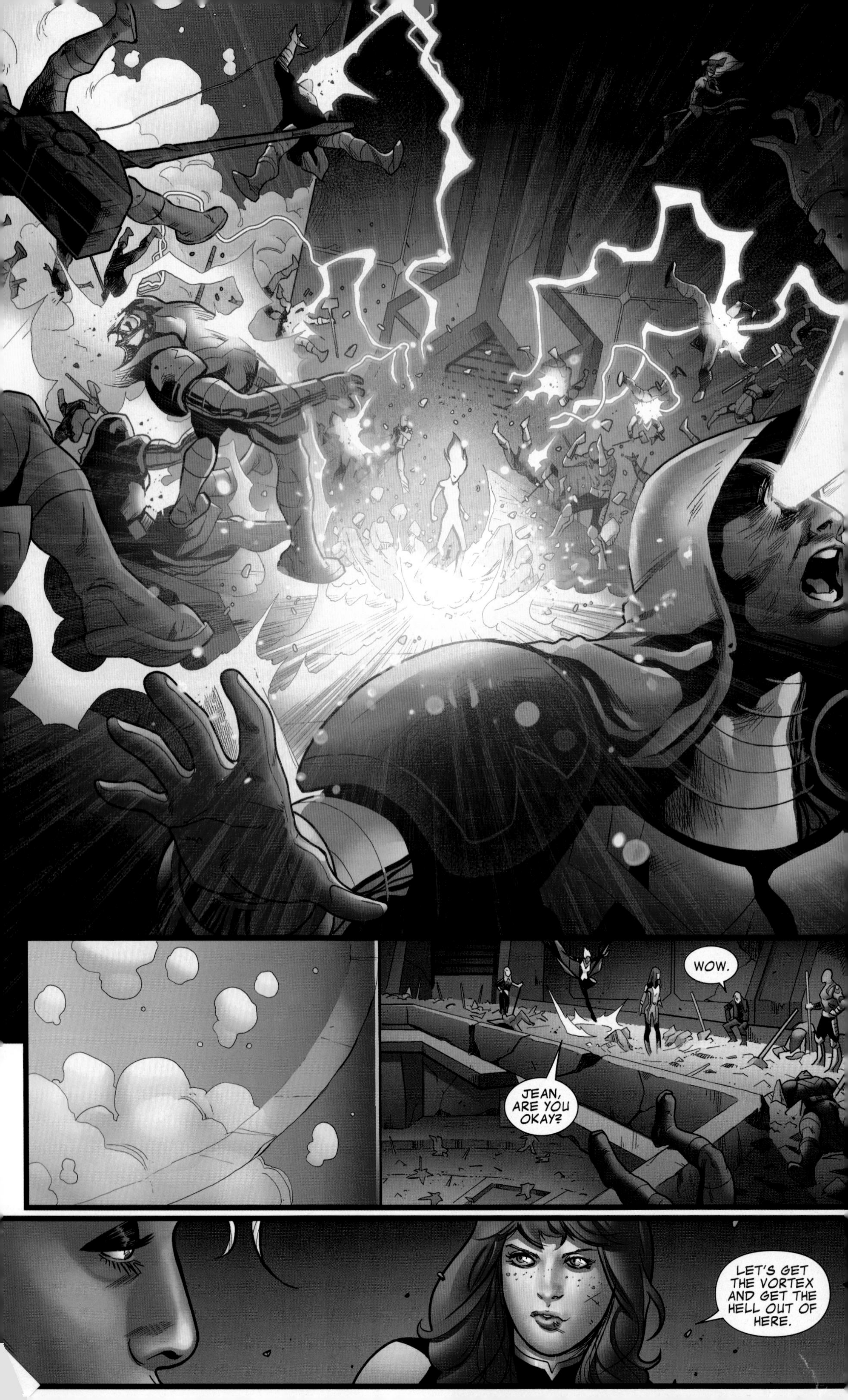
WOW.
JEAN, ARE YOU OKAY?
LET'S GET THE VORTEX AND GET THE HELL OUT OF HERE.

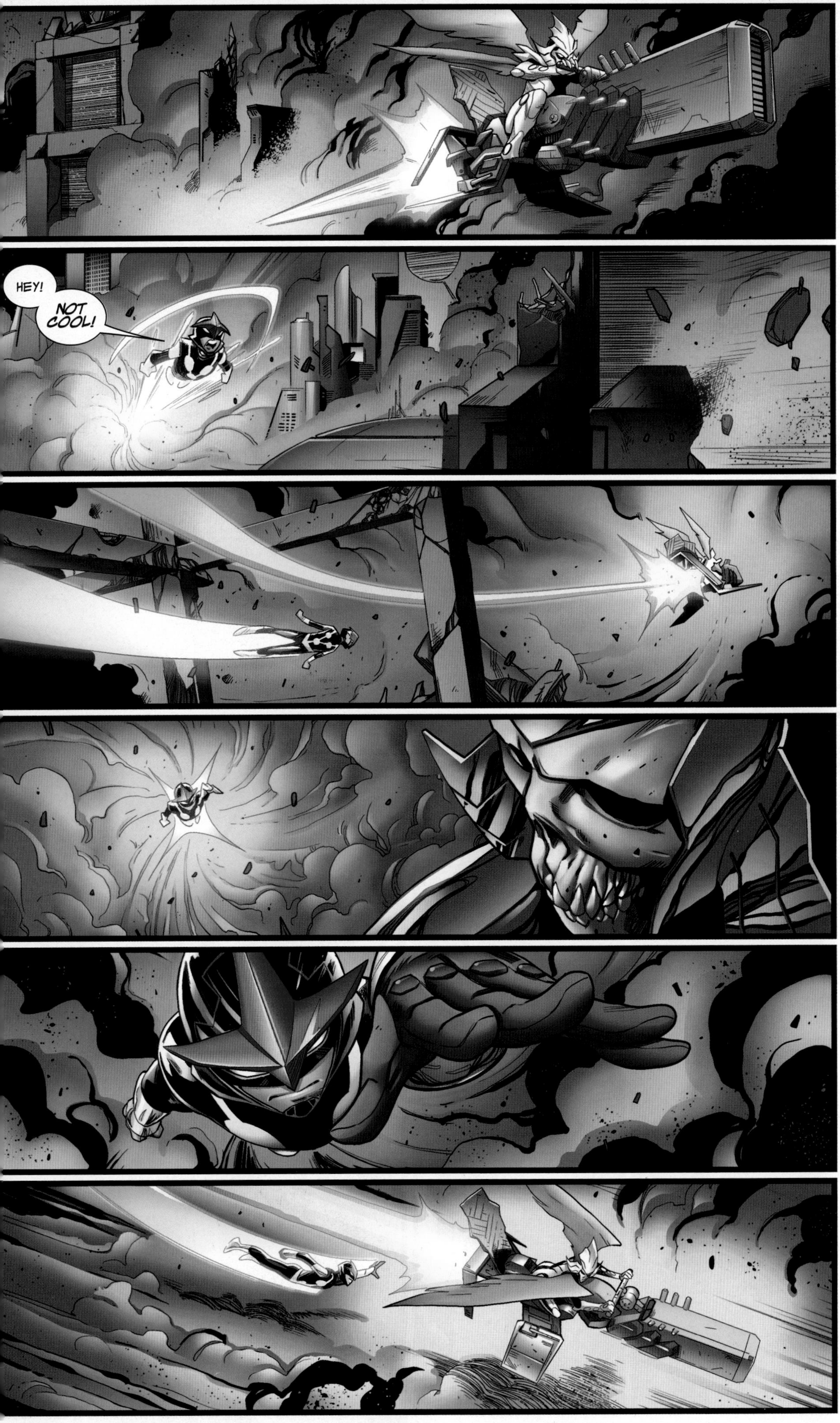
HEY!
NOT COOL!

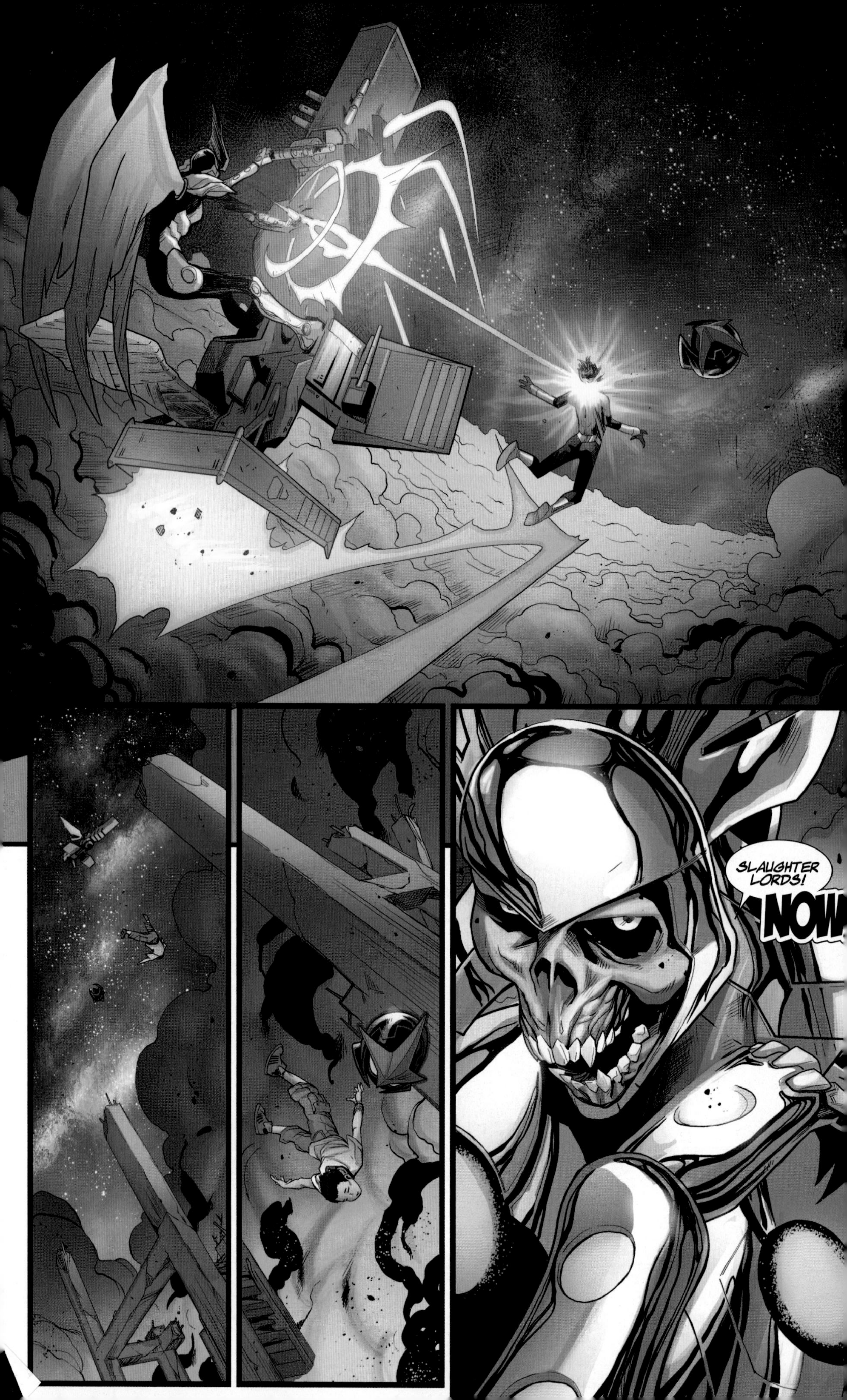
SLAUGHTER LORDS!
NOW

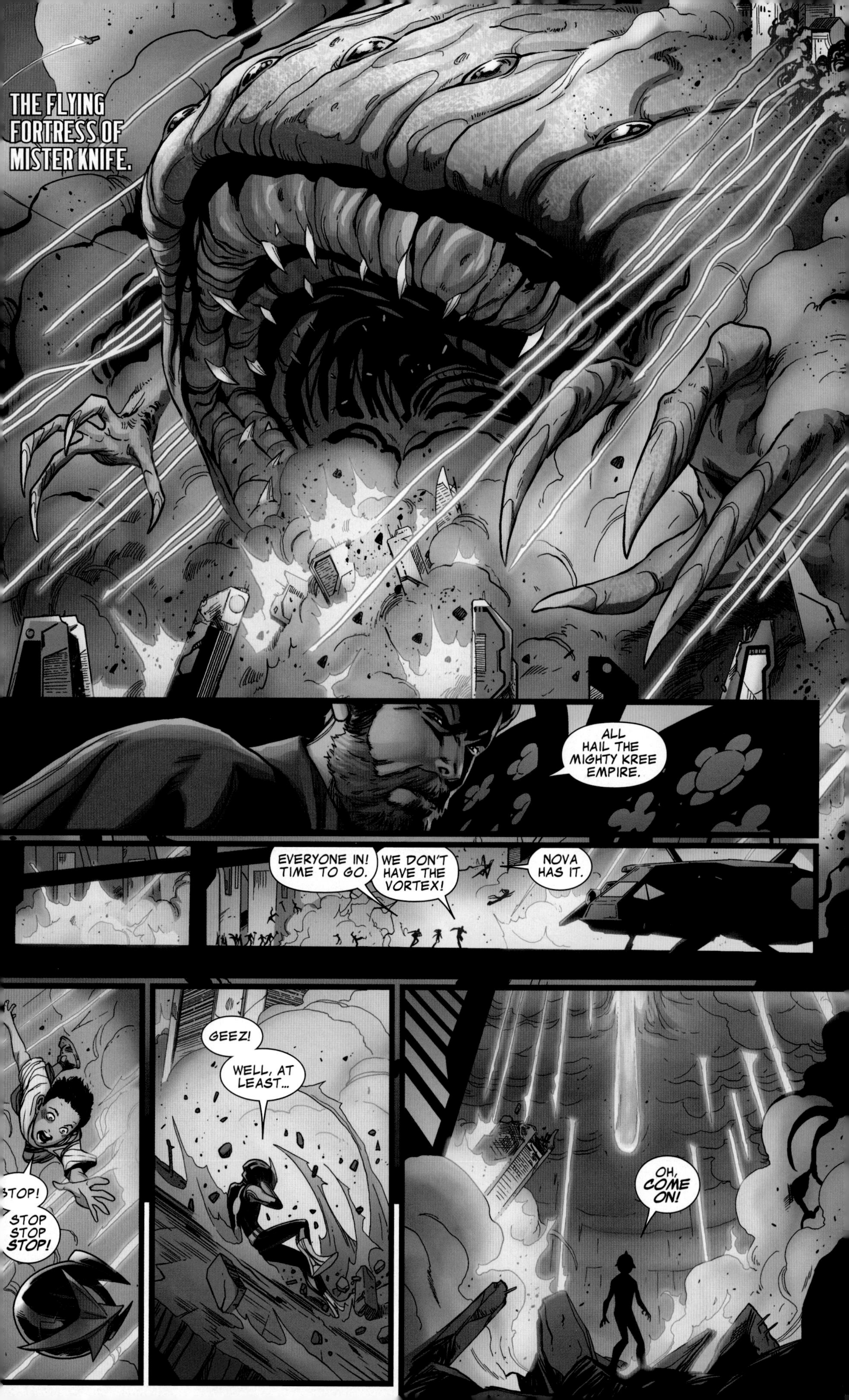
THE FLYING FORTRESS OF MISTER KNIFE.
ALL HAIL THE MIGHTY KREE EMPIRE.
EVERYONE IN! TIME TO GO.
WE DON'T HAVE THE VORTEX!
NOVA HAS IT.
STOP!
STOP STOP STOP!
GEEZ!
WELL, AT LEAST...
OH, COME ON!

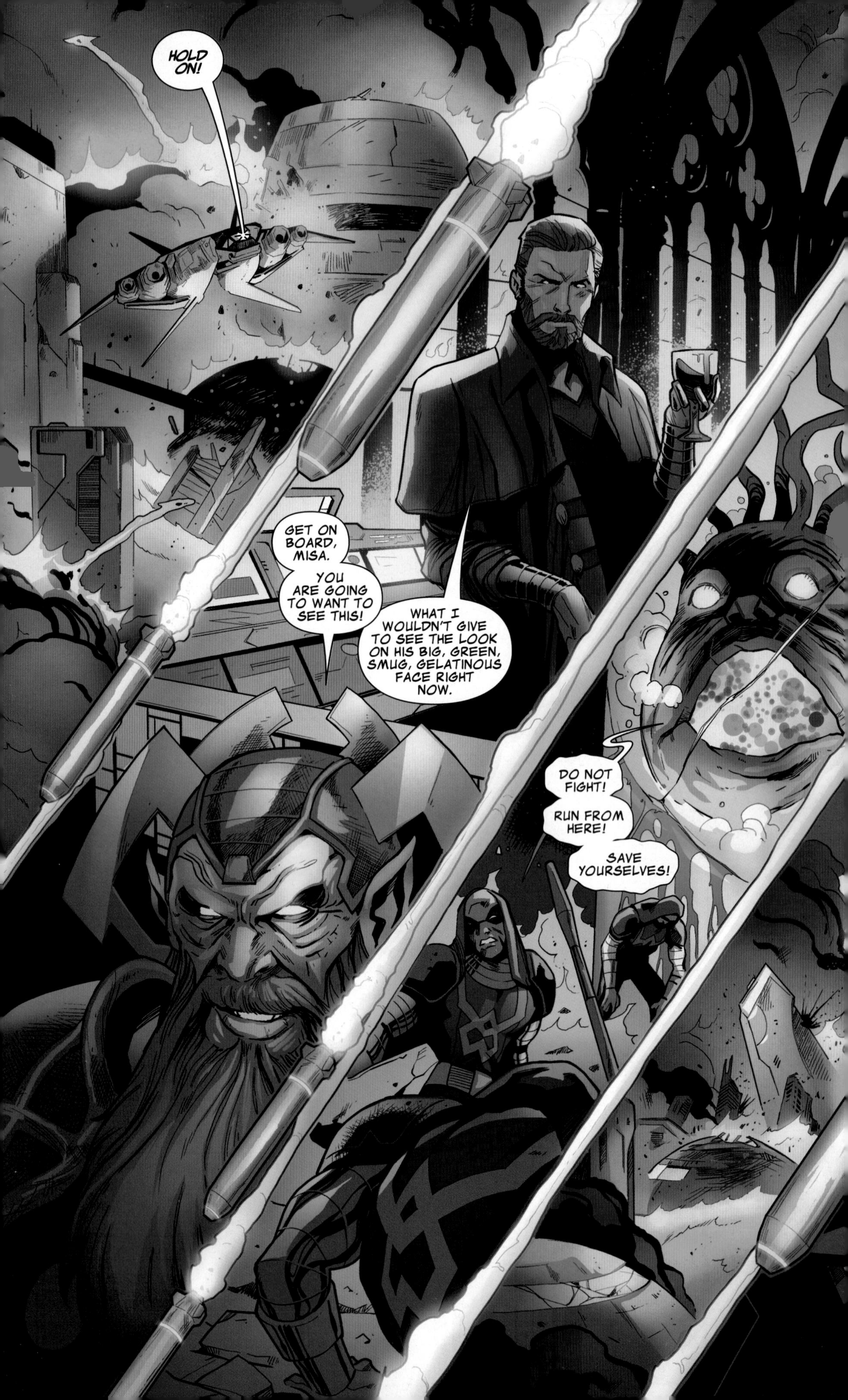
HOLD ON!
GET ON BOARD, MISA.
YOU ARE GOING TO WANT TO SEE THIS!
WHAT I WOULDN'T GIVE TO SEE THE LOOK ON HIS BIG, GREEN, SMUG, GELATINOUS FACE RIGHT NOW.
DO NOT FIGHT!
RUN FROM HERE!
SAVE YOURSELVES!

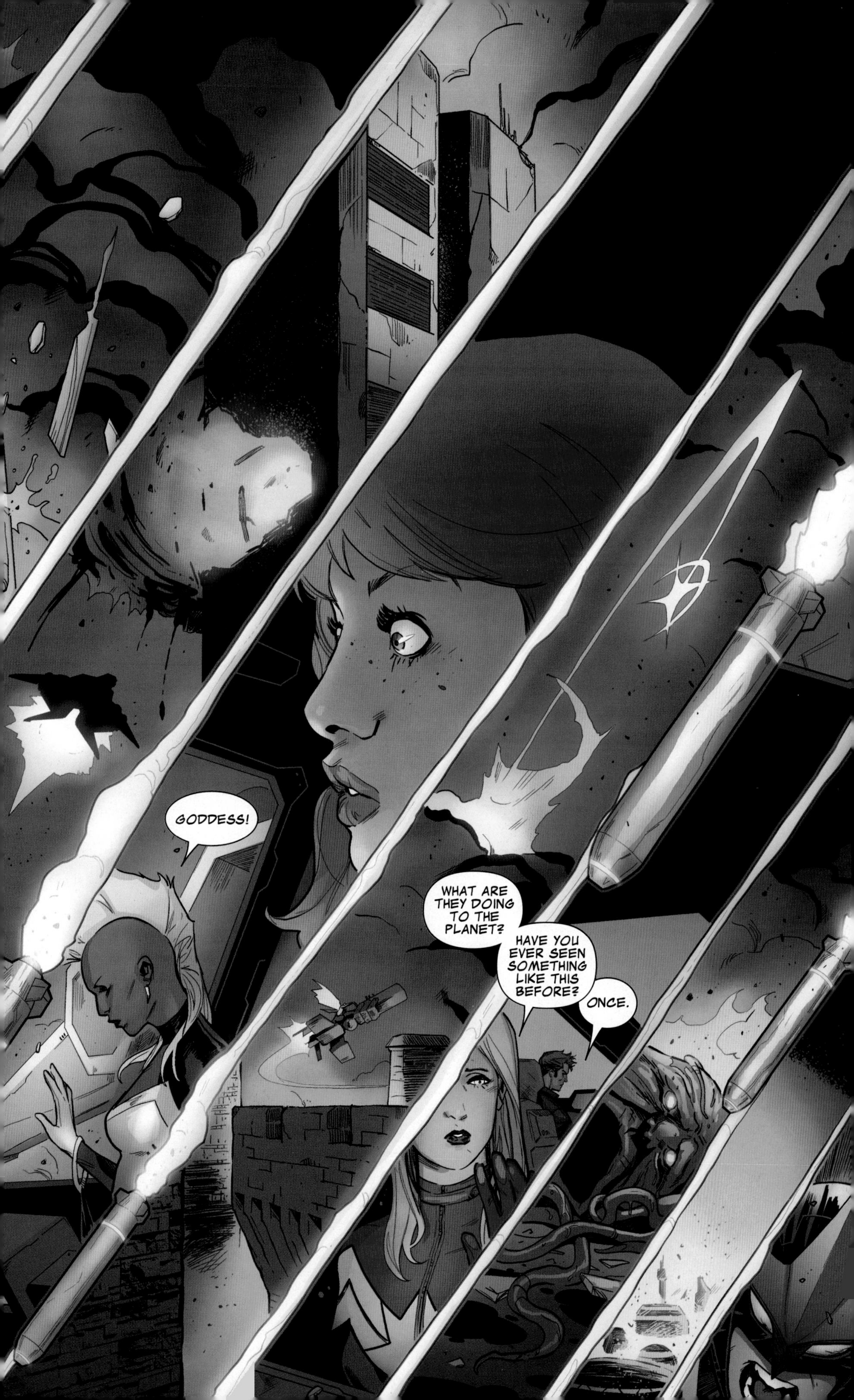
GODDESS!
WHAT ARE THEY DOING TO THE PLANET?
HAVE YOU EVER SEEN SOMETHING LIKE THIS BEFORE?
ONCE.

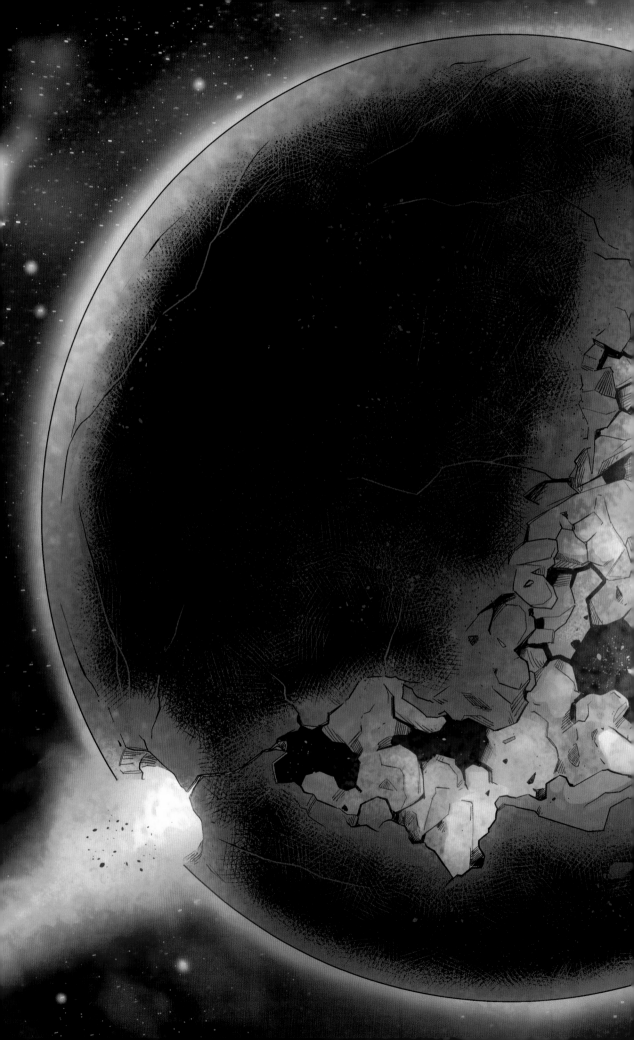

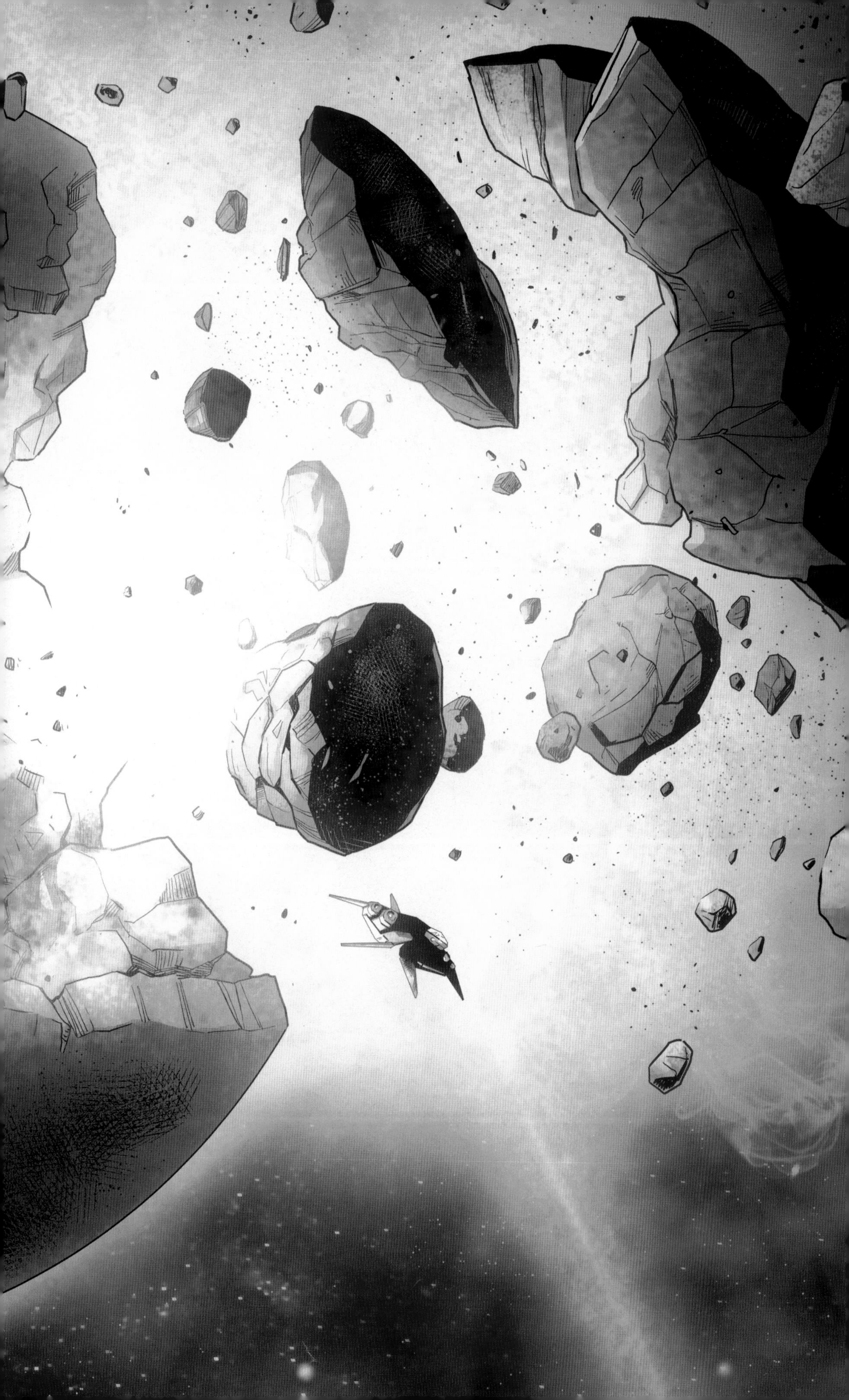

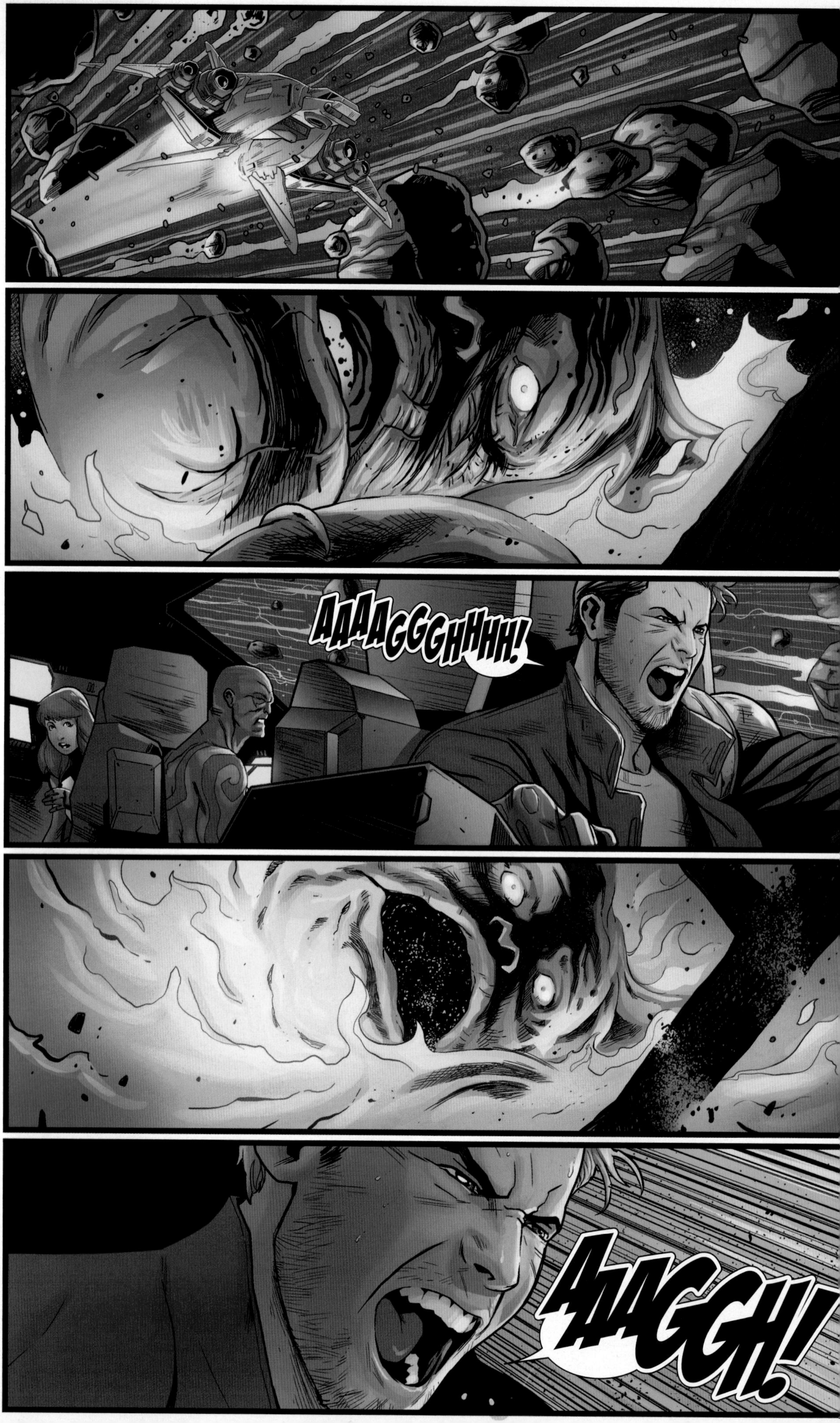
AAAAGGGHHHH!
AAAGGH!

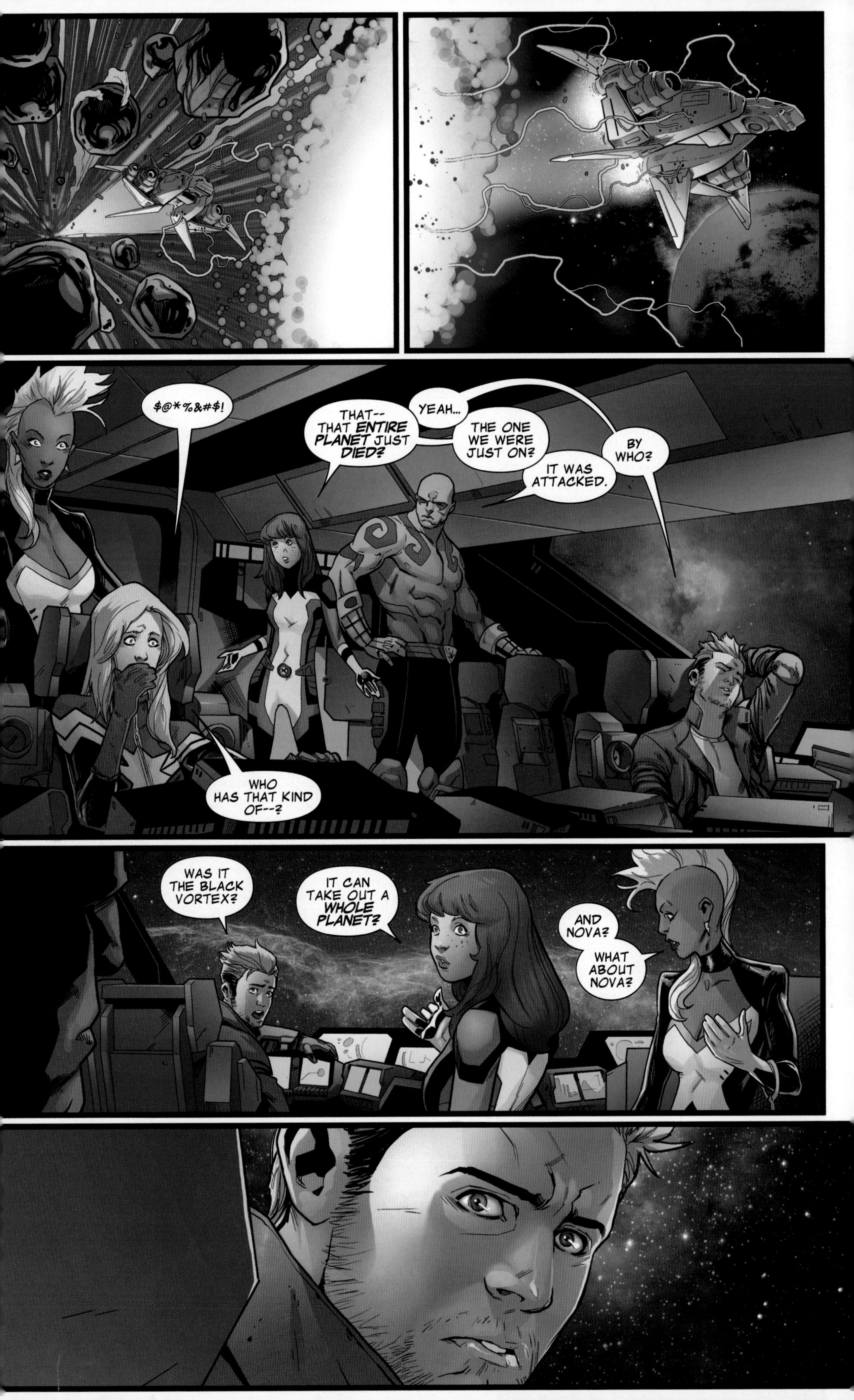
$@*%&#$!
THAT-- THAT ENTIRE PLANET JUST DIED?
YEAH...
THE ONE WE WERE JUST ON?
BY WHO?
IT WAS ATTACKED.
WHO HAS THAT KIND OF--?
WAS IT THE BLACK VORTEX?
IT CAN TAKE OUT A WHOLE PLANET?
AND NOVA?
WHAT ABOUT NOVA?

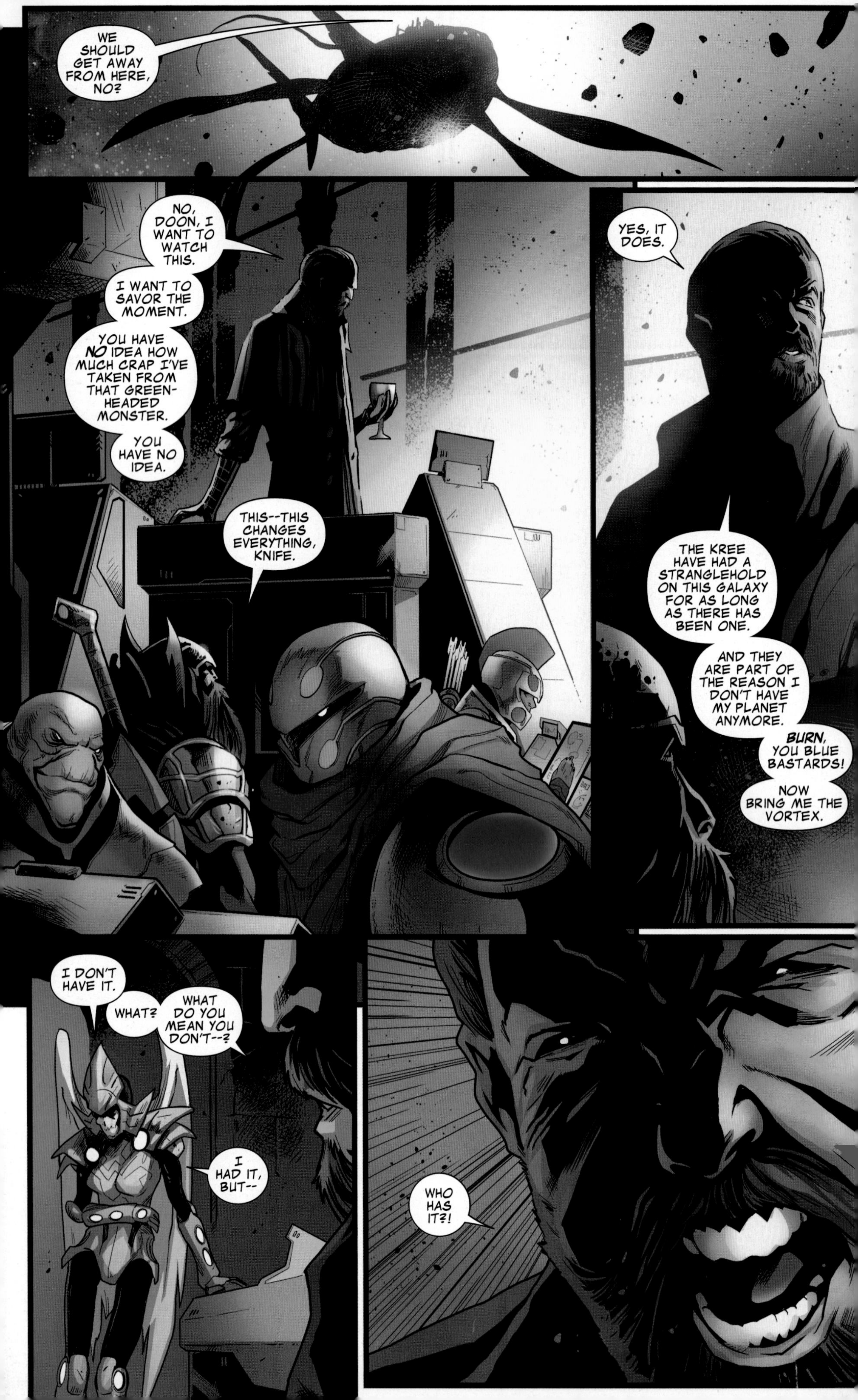
WE SHOULD GET AWAY FROM HERE, NO?
NO, DOON, I WANT TO WATCH THIS.
I WANT TO SAVOR THE MOMENT.
YOU HAVE NO IDEA HOW MUCH CRAP I'VE TAKEN FROM THAT GREEN-HEADED MONSTER.
YOU HAVE NO IDEA.
THIS--THIS CHANGES EVERYTHING, KNIFE.
YES, IT DOES.
THE KREE HAVE HAD A STRANGLEHOLD ON THIS GALAXY FOR AS LONG AS THERE HAS BEEN ONE.
AND THEY ARE PART OF THE REASON I DON'T HAVE MY PLANET ANYMORE.
BURN, YOU BLUE BASTARDS!
NOW BRING ME THE VORTEX.
I DON'T HAVE IT.
WHAT?
WHAT DO YOU MEAN YOU DON'T--?
I HAD IT, BUT--
WHO HAS IT?!

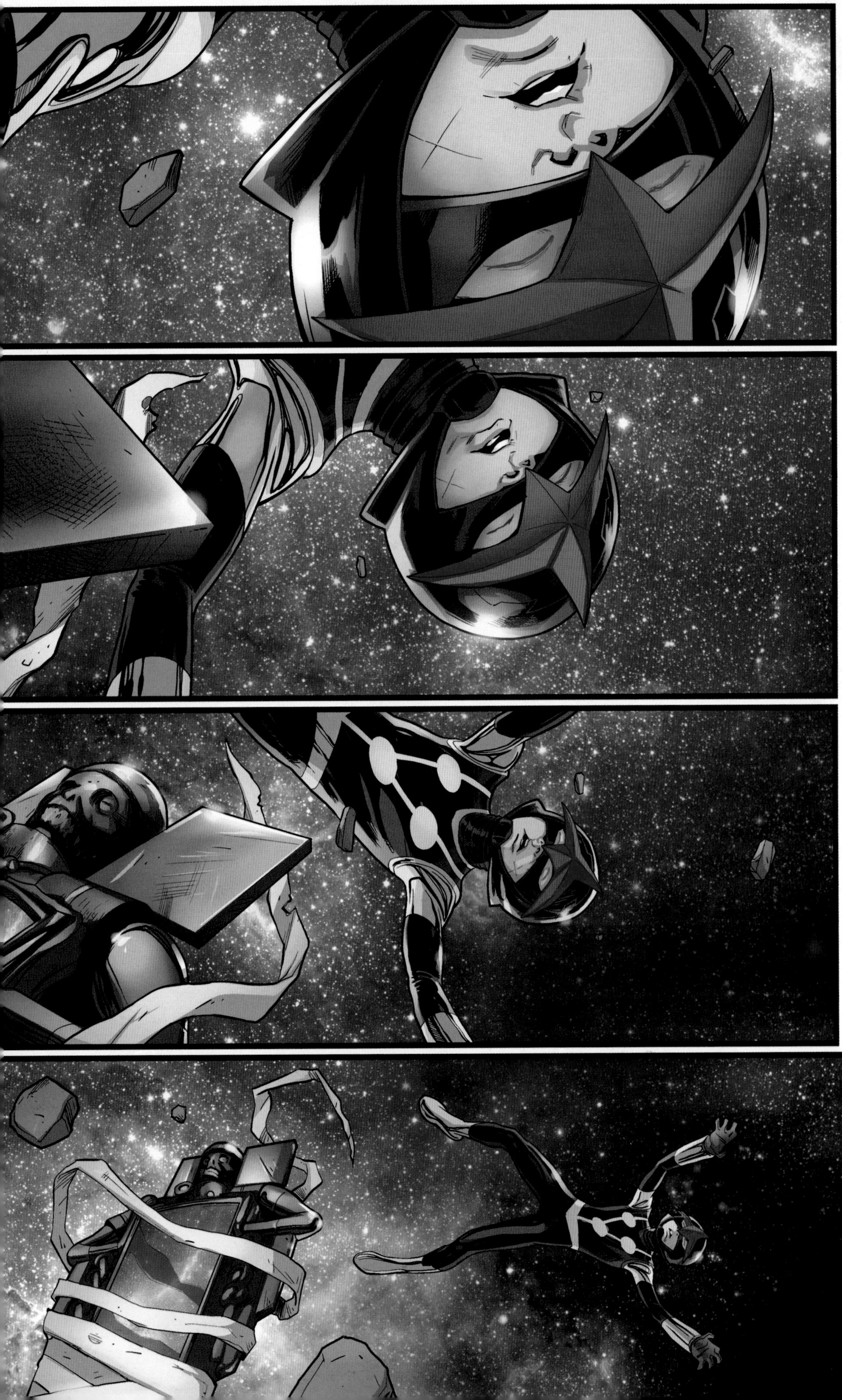

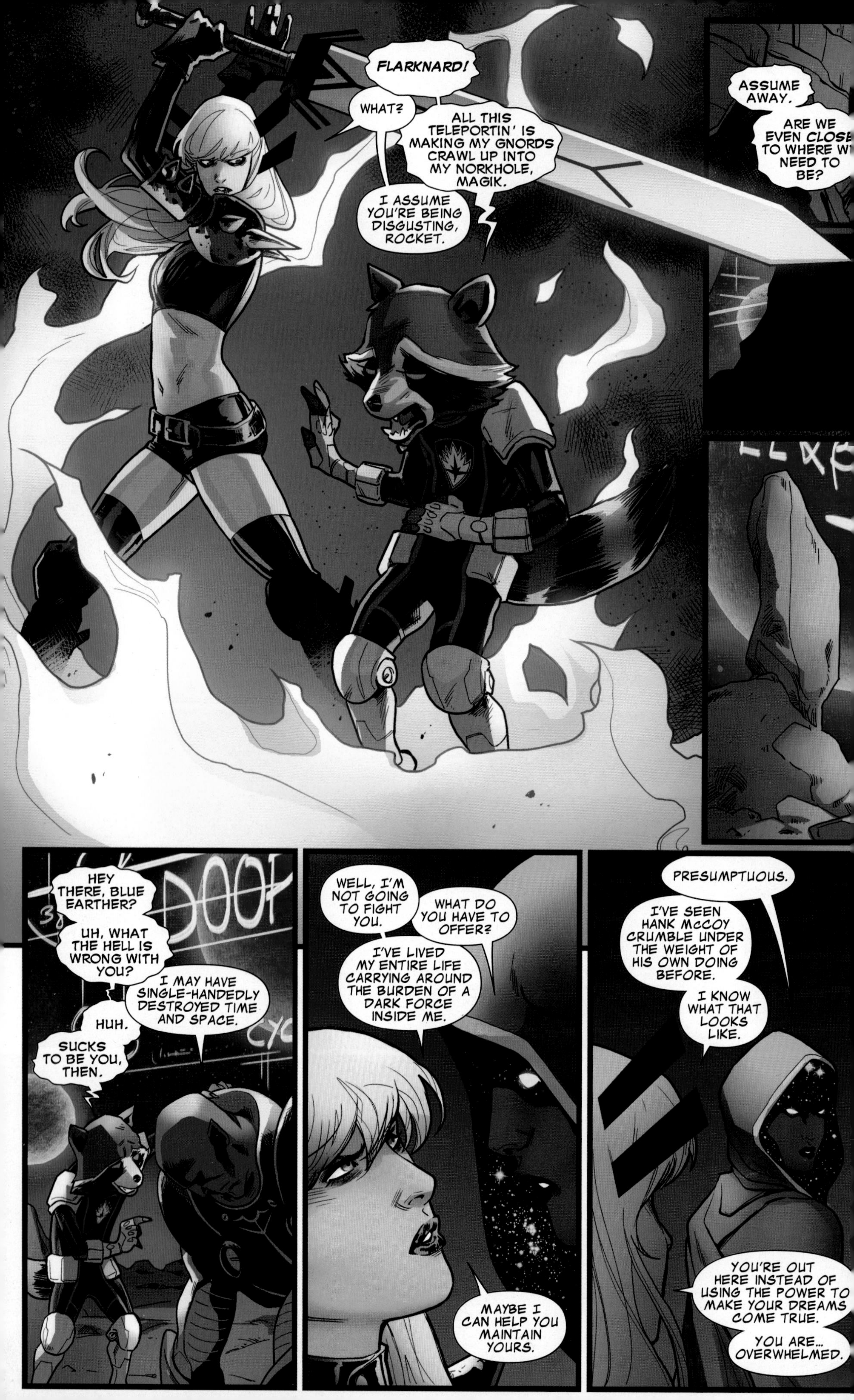
FLARKNARD!
WHAT?
ALL THIS TELEPORTIN' IS MAKING MY GNORDS CRAWL UP INTO MY NORKHOLE, MAGIK.
I ASSUME YOU'RE BEING DISGUSTING, ROCKET.
ASSUME AWAY.
ARE WE EVEN CLOSE TO WHERE WE NEED TO BE?
HEY THERE, BLUE EARTHER?
UH, WHAT THE HELL IS WRONG WITH YOU?
I MAY HAVE SINGLE-HANDEDLY DESTROYED TIME AND SPACE.
HUH.
SUCKS TO BE YOU, THEN.
WELL, I'M NOT GOING TO FIGHT YOU.
WHAT DO YOU HAVE TO OFFER?
I'VE LIVED MY ENTIRE LIFE CARRYING AROUND THE BURDEN OF A DARK FORCE INSIDE ME.
MAYBE I CAN HELP YOU MAINTAIN YOURS.
PRESUMPTUOUS.
I'VE SEEN HANK McCOY CRUMBLE UNDER THE WEIGHT OF HIS OWN DOING BEFORE.
I KNOW WHAT THAT LOOKS LIKE.
YOU'RE OUT HERE INSTEAD OF USING THE POWER TO MAKE YOUR DREAMS COME TRUE.
YOU ARE... OVERWHELMED.

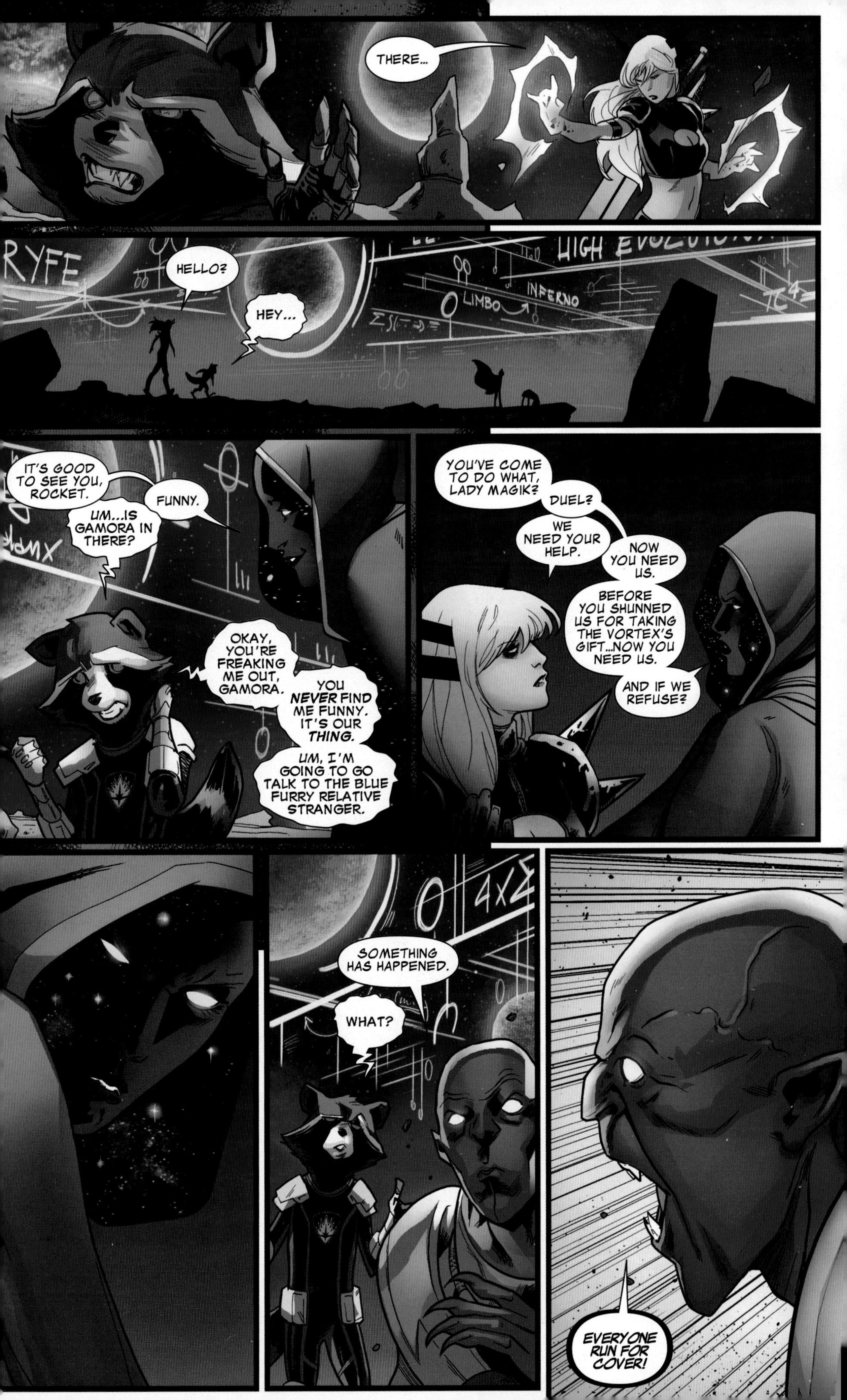
THERE...
RYFE
HIGH EVOLUTION
LIMBO
INFERNO
HELLO?
HEY...
IT'S GOOD TO SEE YOU, ROCKET.
FUNNY.
UM...IS GAMORA IN THERE?
OKAY, YOU'RE FREAKING ME OUT, GAMORA.
YOU *NEVER* FIND ME FUNNY. IT'S OUR *THING.*
UM, I'M GOING TO GO TALK TO THE BLUE FURRY RELATIVE STRANGER.
YOU'VE COME TO DO WHAT, LADY MAGIK?
DUEL?
WE NEED YOUR HELP.
NOW YOU NEED US.
BEFORE YOU SHUNNED US FOR TAKING THE VORTEX'S GIFT...NOW YOU NEED US.
AND IF WE REFUSE?
4xΣ
SOMETHING HAS HAPPENED.
WHAT?
EVERYONE RUN FOR COVER!

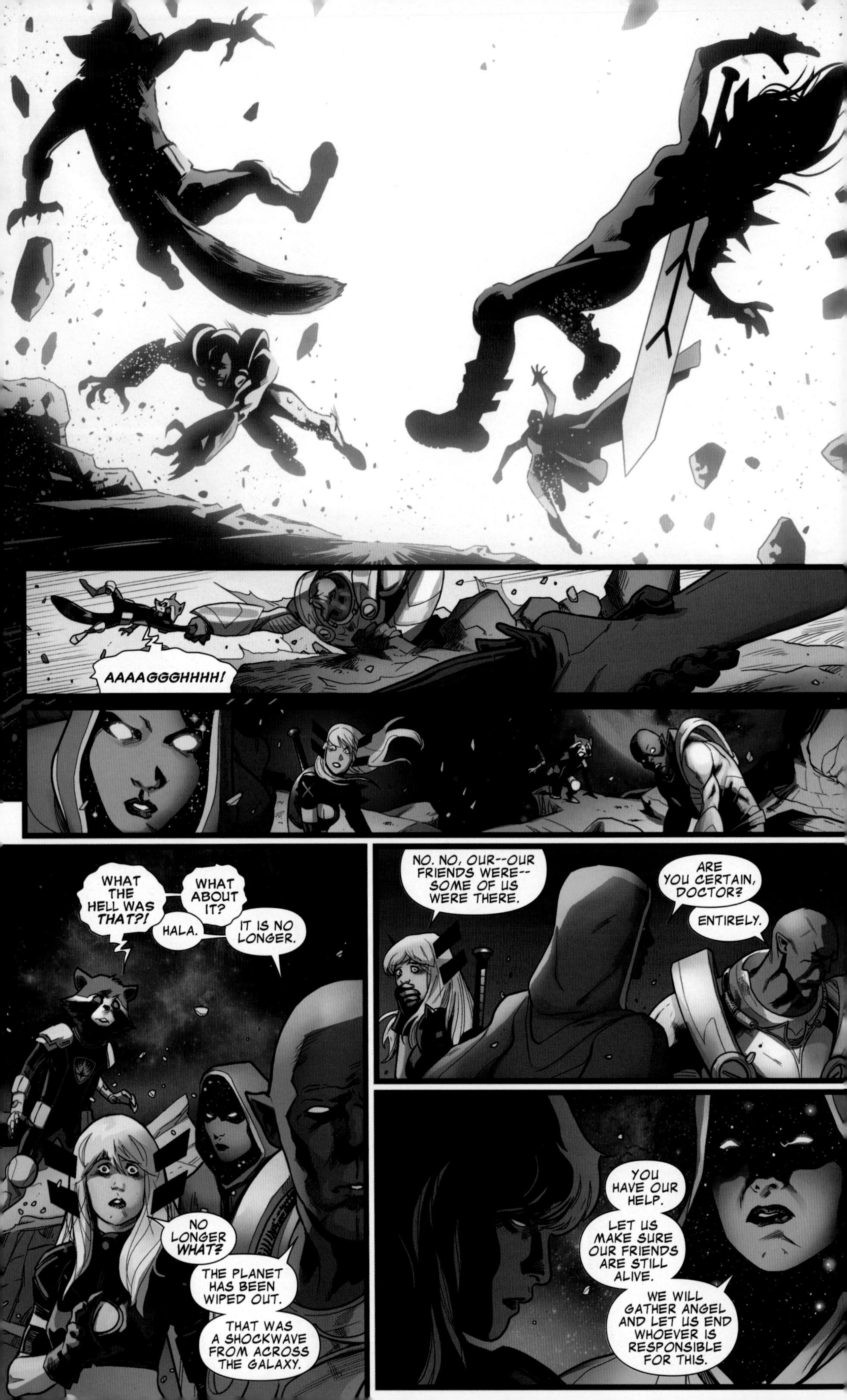
AAAAGGGHHHH!
WHAT THE HELL WAS THAT?!
WHAT ABOUT IT?
HALA.
IT IS NO LONGER.
NO LONGER WHAT?
THE PLANET HAS BEEN WIPED OUT.
THAT WAS A SHOCKWAVE FROM ACROSS THE GALAXY.
NO. NO, OUR--OUR FRIENDS WERE-- SOME OF US WERE THERE.
ARE YOU CERTAIN, DOCTOR?
ENTIRELY.
YOU HAVE OUR HELP.
LET US MAKE SURE OUR FRIENDS ARE STILL ALIVE.
WE WILL GATHER ANGEL AND LET US END WHOEVER IS RESPONSIBLE FOR THIS.

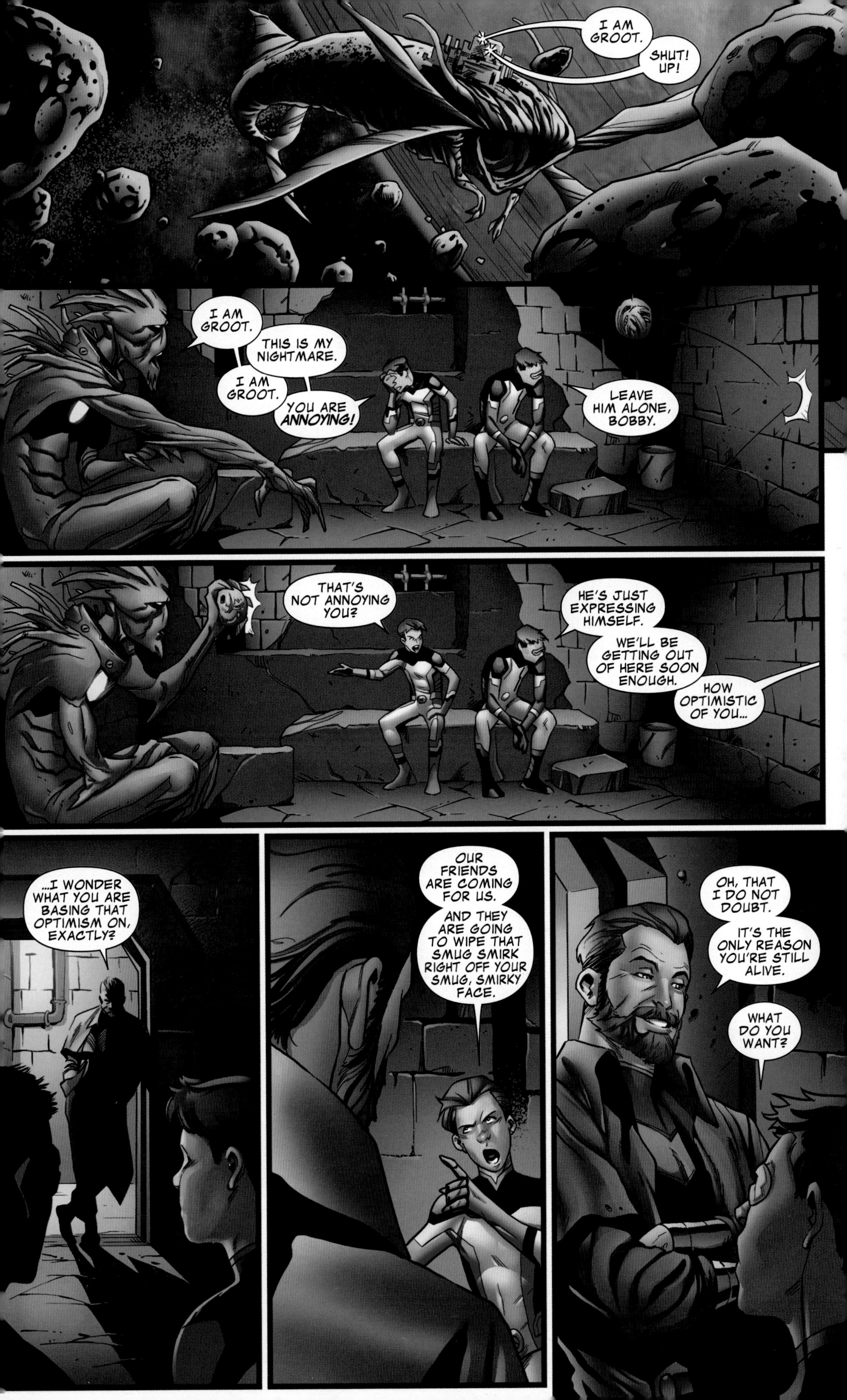

I AM GROOT.
SHUT! UP!
I AM GROOT.
THIS IS MY NIGHTMARE.
I AM GROOT.
YOU ARE ANNOYING!
LEAVE HIM ALONE, BOBBY.
THAT'S NOT ANNOYING YOU?
HE'S JUST EXPRESSING HIMSELF.
WE'LL BE GETTING OUT OF HERE SOON ENOUGH.
HOW OPTIMISTIC OF YOU...
...I WONDER WHAT YOU ARE BASING THAT OPTIMISM ON, EXACTLY?
OUR FRIENDS ARE COMING FOR US.
AND THEY ARE GOING TO WIPE THAT SMUG SMIRK RIGHT OFF YOUR SMUG, SMIRKY FACE.
OH, THAT I DO NOT DOUBT.
IT'S THE ONLY REASON YOU'RE STILL ALIVE.
WHAT DO YOU WANT?

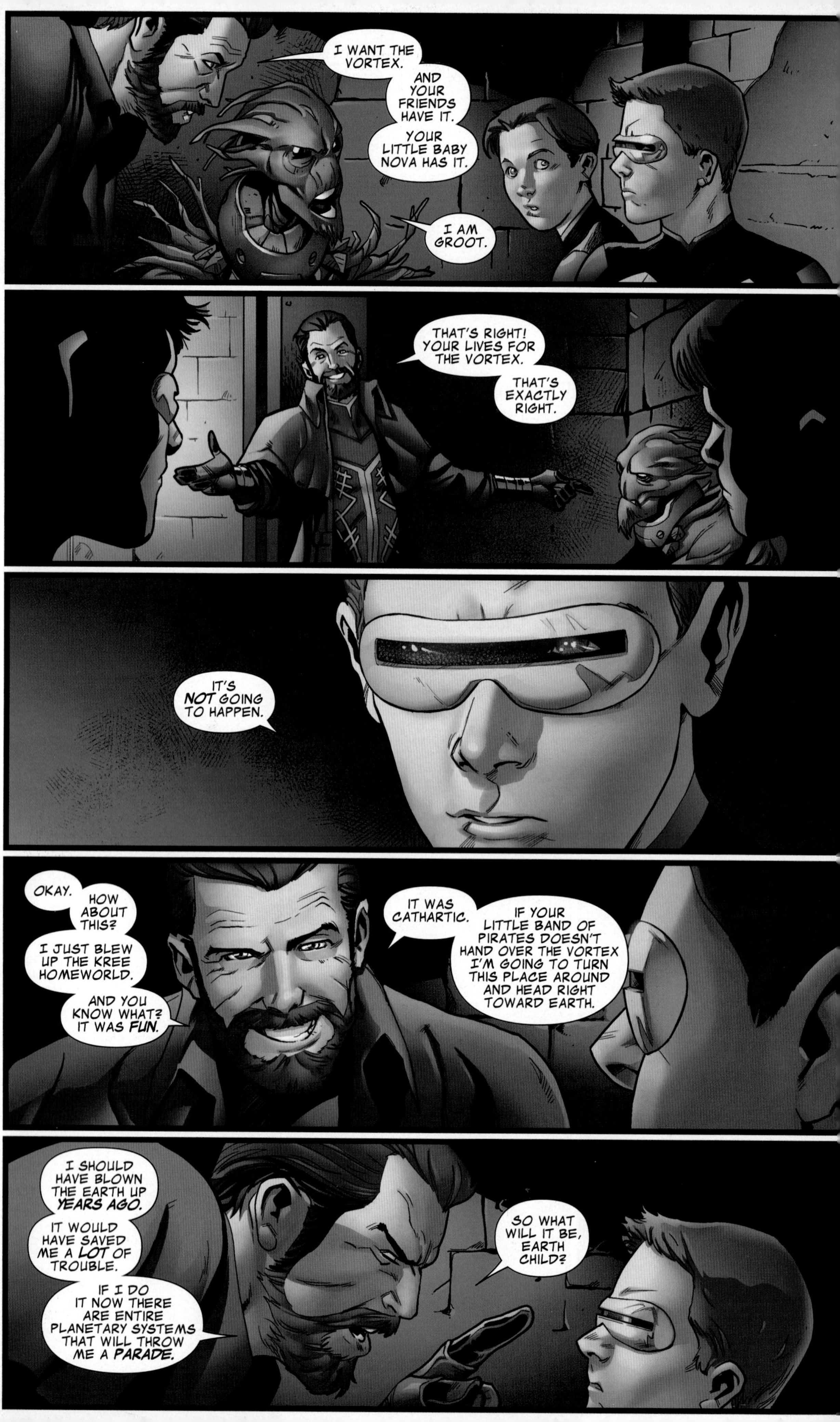
I WANT THE VORTEX.
AND YOUR FRIENDS HAVE IT.
YOUR LITTLE BABY NOVA HAS IT.
I AM GROOT.
THAT'S RIGHT! YOUR LIVES FOR THE VORTEX.
THAT'S EXACTLY RIGHT.
IT'S NOT GOING TO HAPPEN.
OKAY.
HOW ABOUT THIS?
I JUST BLEW UP THE KREE HOMEWORLD.
AND YOU KNOW WHAT? IT WAS FUN.
IT WAS CATHARTIC.
IF YOUR LITTLE BAND OF PIRATES DOESN'T HAND OVER THE VORTEX I'M GOING TO TURN THIS PLACE AROUND AND HEAD RIGHT TOWARD EARTH.
I SHOULD HAVE BLOWN THE EARTH UP YEARS AGO.
IT WOULD HAVE SAVED ME A LOT OF TROUBLE.
IF I DO IT NOW THERE ARE ENTIRE PLANETARY SYSTEMS THAT WILL THROW ME A PARADE.
SO WHAT WILL IT BE, EARTH CHILD?

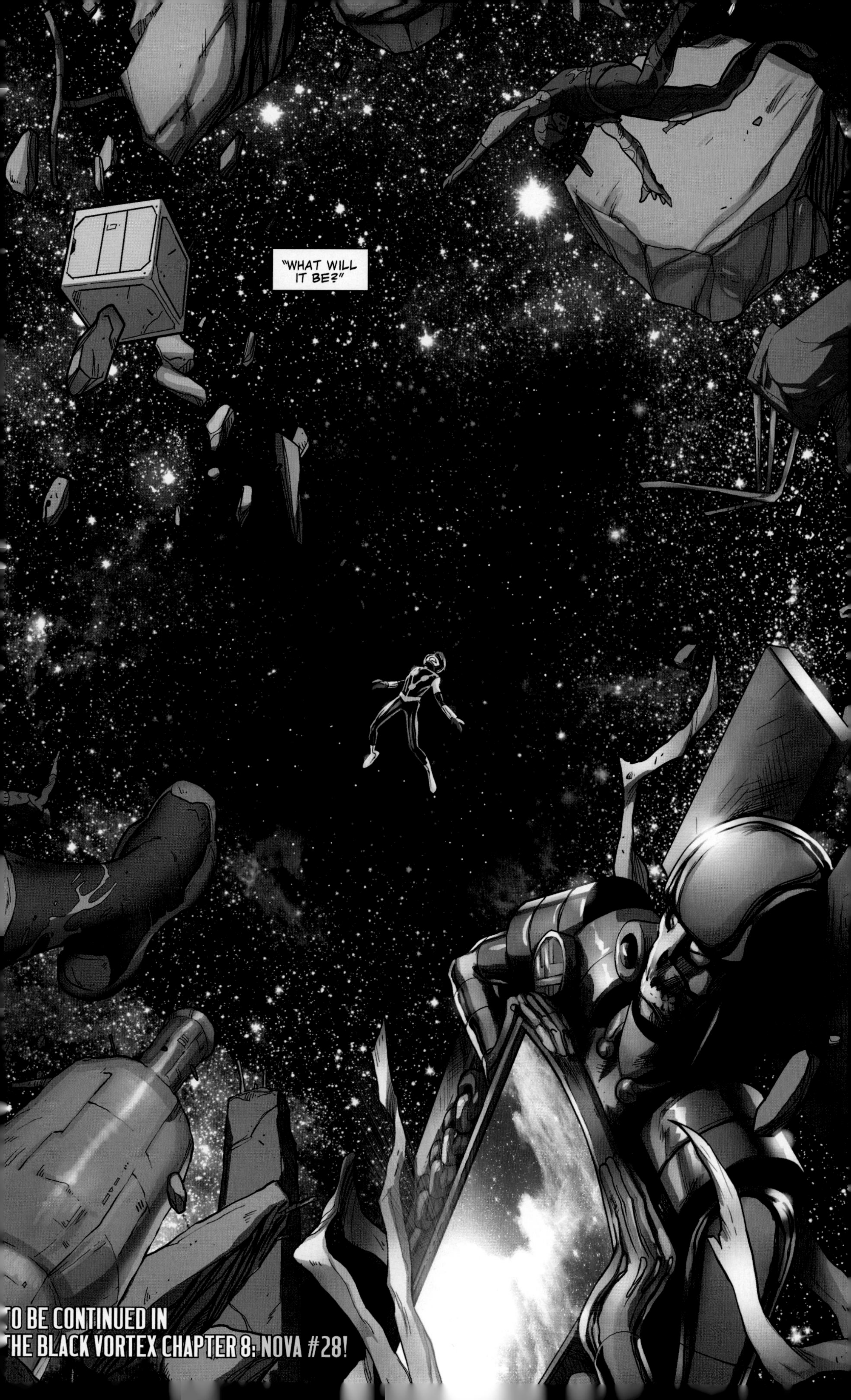
"WHAT WILL IT BE?"
TO BE CONTINUED IN
THE BLACK VORTEX CHAPTER 8: NOVA #28!

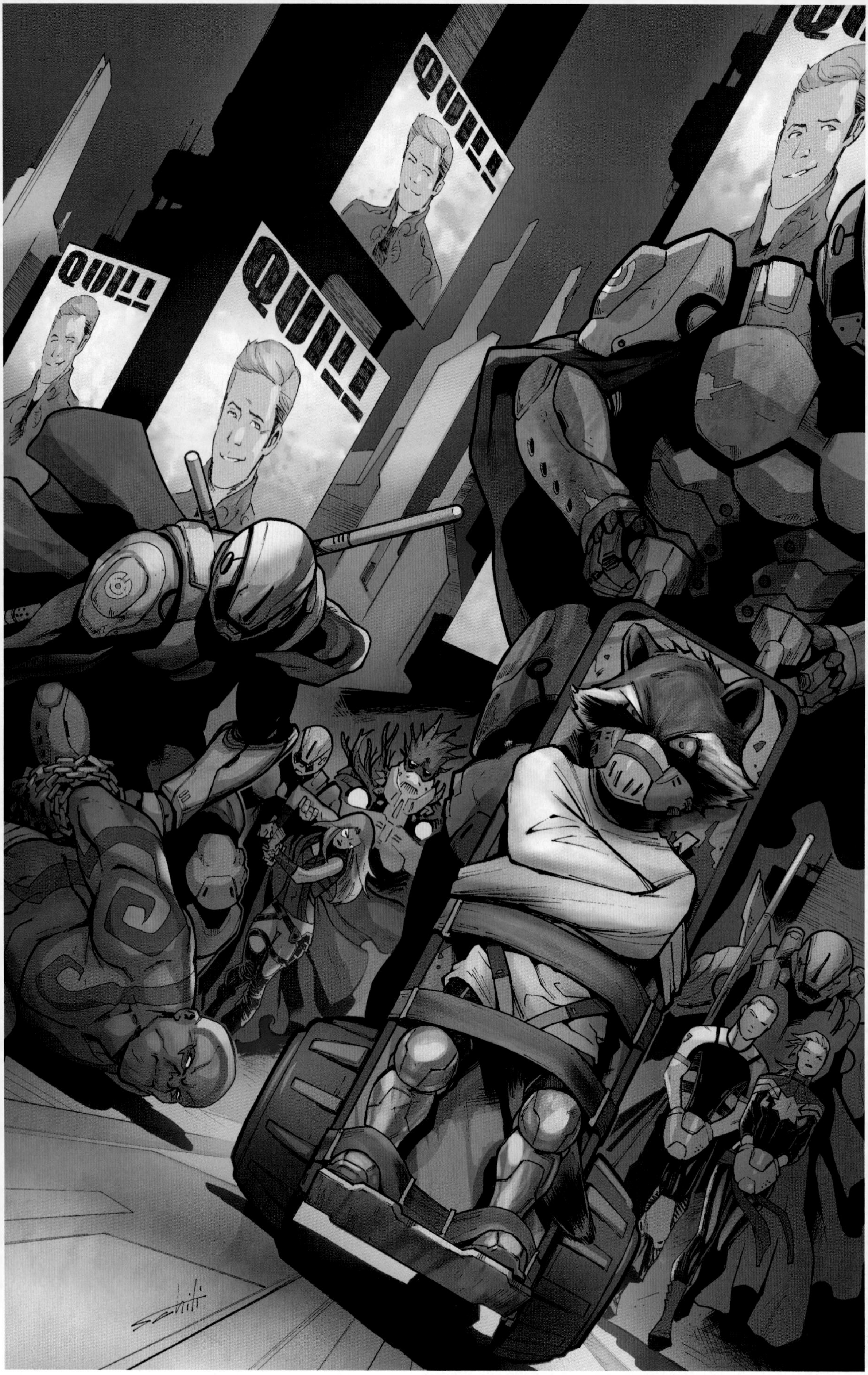
QUILL!
QUILL!
QUILL!

PREVIOUSLY...

RECENTLY, PETER QUILL'S FATHER, J'SON, ACQUIRED AN ANCIENT AND POWERFUL ARTIFACT, THE BLACK VORTEX. USING THE VORTEX TO IMBUE THANOS' SON THANE WITH COSMIC POWER, J'SON HAD THANE SEAL THE PLANET SPARTAX IN AMBER. J'SON INTENDED TO GIFT THE PLANET TO THE BROOD SO THAT THEY MIGHT USE THE CITIZENS TO INCUBATE THEIR EGGS. FACED WITH THE PROSPECT OF A PLANET-WIDE EXTINCTION, AND NOT TO MENTION AN OVERWHELMING ARMY OF BROOD SOLDIERS, KITTY PRYDE CHOSE TO SUBMIT TO THE BLACK VORTEX. SHE THEN USED HER ENHANCED POWERS TO PHASE THE PLANET OUT OF ITS AMBER PRISON, SAVING THE PEOPLE OF SPARTAX.

WITH THE BATTLE OVER CONTROL OF THE COSMICALLY POWERED BLACK VORTEX NOW FINISHED, THINGS SEEM TO HAVE SETTLED DOWN A LITTLE BIT FOR THE GUARDIANS. ALTHOUGH THERE IS ONE SLIGHT CHANGE, WHAT WITH PETER GETTING ENGAGED TO THE NOW COSMICALLY ENHANCED KITTY PRYDE. BUT IN ALL THE MESS CAUSED BY THE BLACK VORTEX, PETER HAS CONVENIENTLY FORGOTTEN THE OTHER RECENT EVENTS ON HIS HOME PLANET OF SPARTAX...

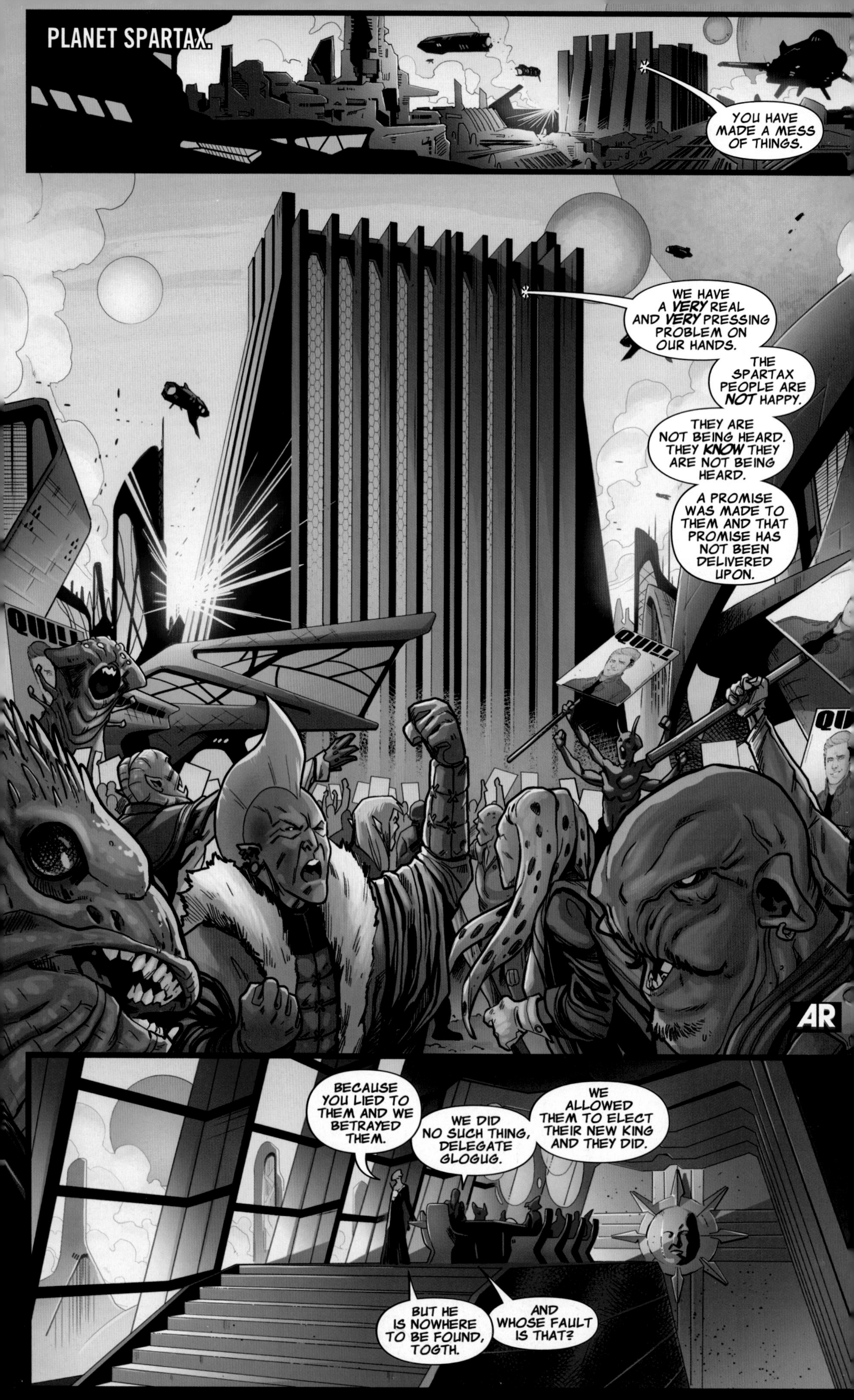
PLANET SPARTAX.
YOU HAVE MADE A MESS OF THINGS.
WE HAVE A VERY REAL AND VERY PRESSING PROBLEM ON OUR HANDS.
THE SPARTAX PEOPLE ARE NOT HAPPY.
THEY ARE NOT BEING HEARD. THEY KNOW THEY ARE NOT BEING HEARD.
A PROMISE WAS MADE TO THEM AND THAT PROMISE HAS NOT BEEN DELIVERED UPON.
BECAUSE YOU LIED TO THEM AND WE BETRAYED THEM.
WE DID NO SUCH THING, DELEGATE GLOGUG.
WE ALLOWED THEM TO ELECT THEIR NEW KING AND THEY DID.
BUT HE IS NOWHERE TO BE FOUND, TOGTH.
AND WHOSE FAULT IS THAT?

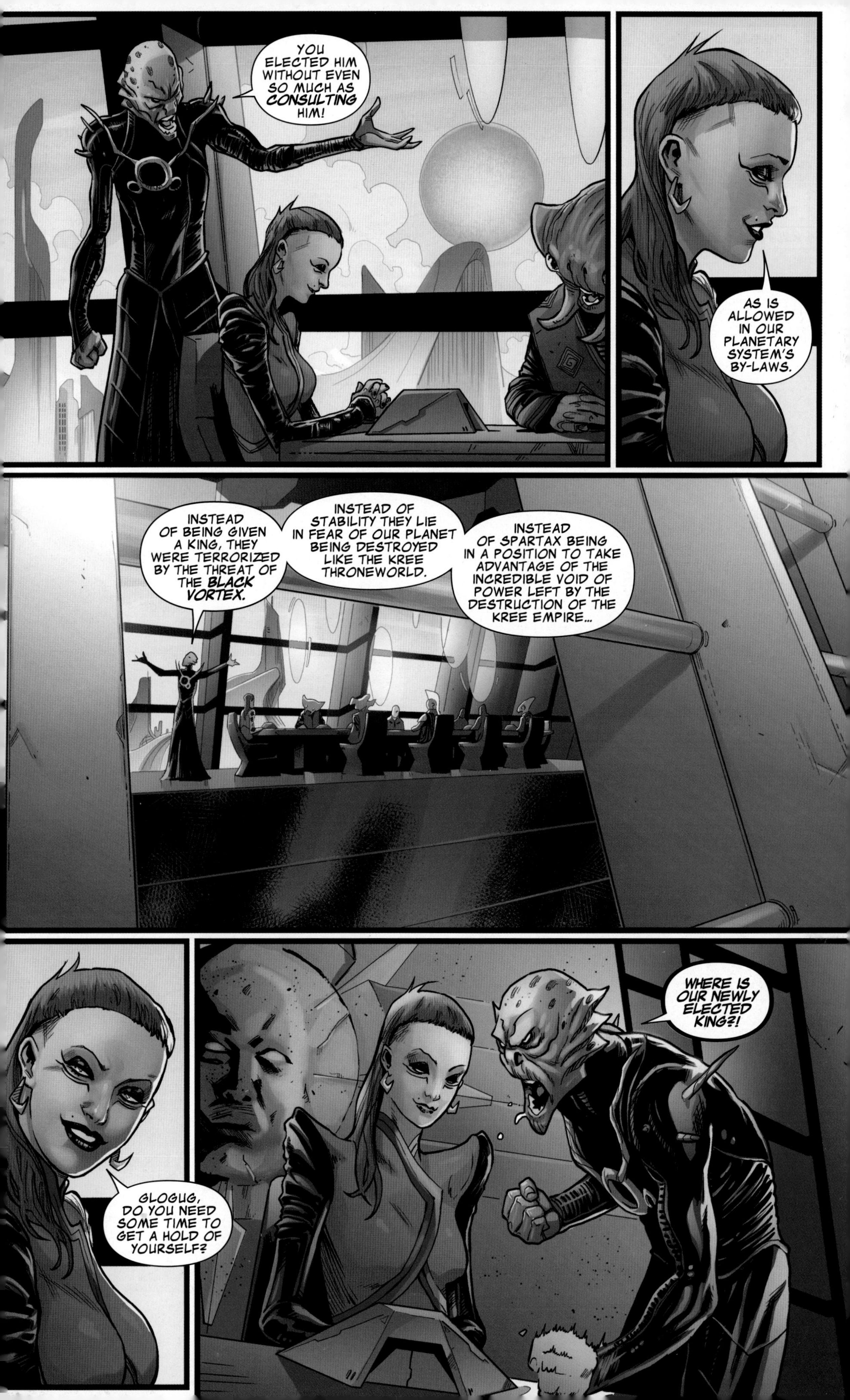
YOU ELECTED HIM WITHOUT EVEN SO MUCH AS CONSULTING HIM!
AS IS ALLOWED IN OUR PLANETARY SYSTEM'S BY-LAWS.
INSTEAD OF BEING GIVEN A KING, THEY WERE TERRORIZED BY THE THREAT OF THE BLACK VORTEX.
INSTEAD OF STABILITY THEY LIE IN FEAR OF OUR PLANET BEING DESTROYED LIKE THE KREE THRONEWORLD.
INSTEAD OF SPARTAX BEING IN A POSITION TO TAKE ADVANTAGE OF THE INCREDIBLE VOID OF POWER LEFT BY THE DESTRUCTION OF THE KREE EMPIRE...
GLOGUG, DO YOU NEED SOME TIME TO GET A HOLD OF YOURSELF?
WHERE IS OUR NEWLY ELECTED KING?!

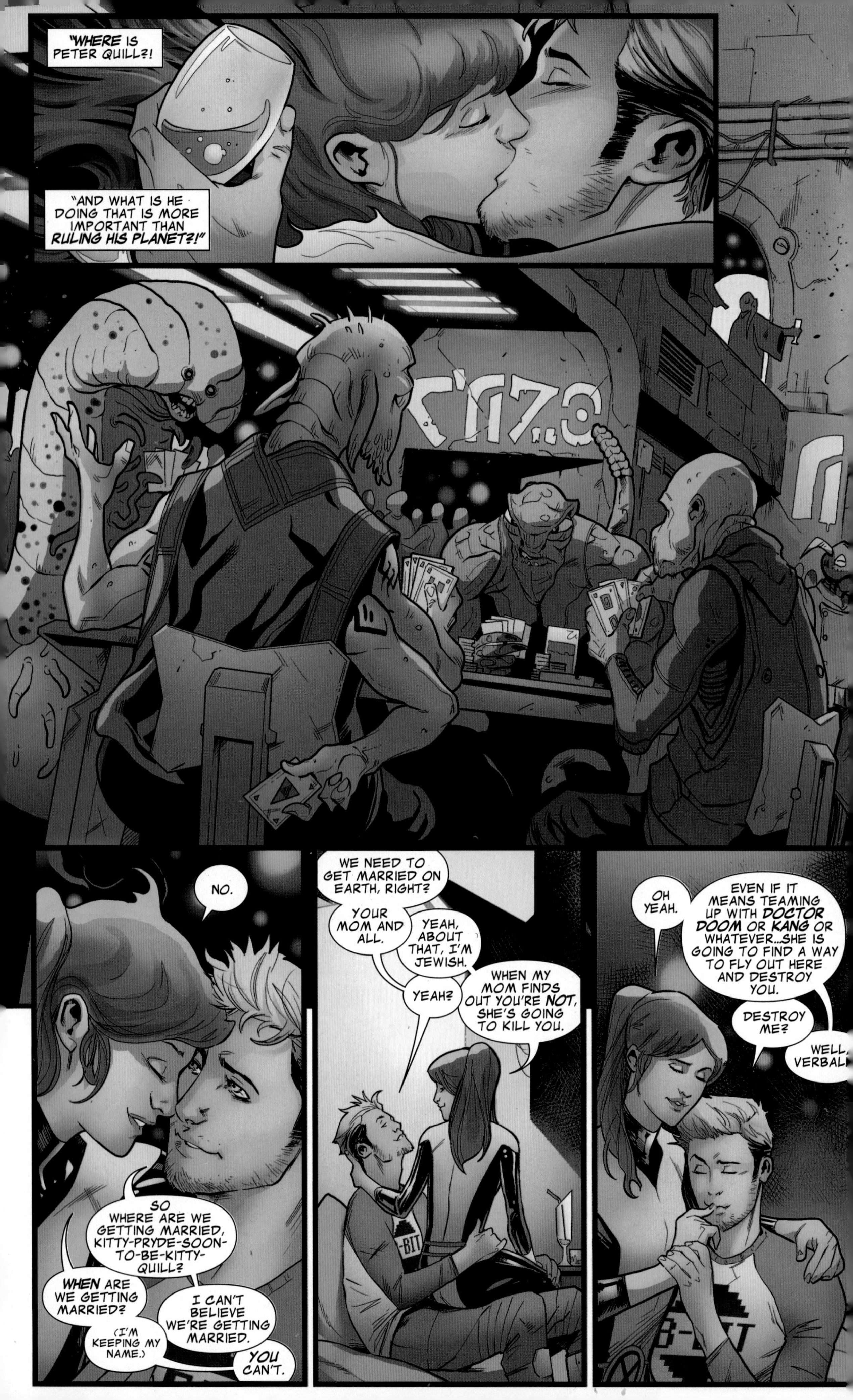
"WHERE IS PETER QUILL?!
"AND WHAT IS HE DOING THAT IS MORE IMPORTANT THAN RULING HIS PLANET?!"
NO.
SO WHERE ARE WE GETTING MARRIED, KITTY-PRYDE-SOON-TO-BE-KITTY-QUILL?
WHEN ARE WE GETTING MARRIED?
(I'M KEEPING MY NAME.)
I CAN'T BELIEVE WE'RE GETTING MARRIED.
YOU CAN'T.
WE NEED TO GET MARRIED ON EARTH, RIGHT?
YOUR MOM AND ALL.
YEAH, ABOUT THAT, I'M JEWISH.
YEAH?
WHEN MY MOM FINDS OUT YOU'RE NOT, SHE'S GOING TO KILL YOU.
OH YEAH.
EVEN IF IT MEANS TEAMING UP WITH DOCTOR DOOM OR KANG OR WHATEVER...SHE IS GOING TO FIND A WAY TO FLY OUT HERE AND DESTROY YOU.
DESTROY ME?
WELL, VERBAL

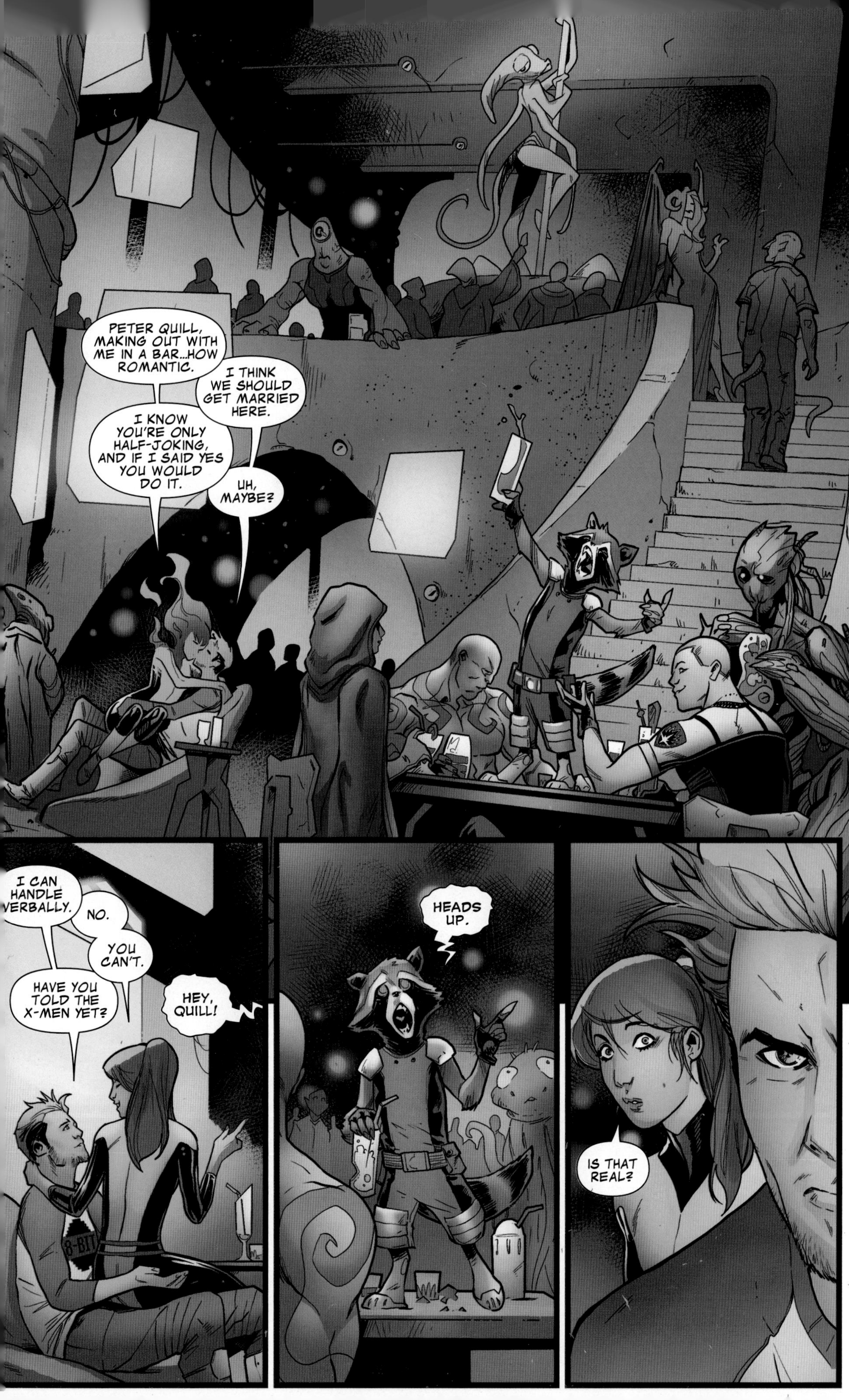
PETER QUILL, MAKING OUT WITH ME IN A BAR...HOW ROMANTIC.
I THINK WE SHOULD GET MARRIED HERE.
I KNOW YOU'RE ONLY HALF-JOKING, AND IF I SAID YES YOU WOULD DO IT.
UH, MAYBE?
I CAN HANDLE VERBALLY.
NO.
YOU CAN'T.
HAVE YOU TOLD THE X-MEN YET?
HEY, QUILL!
8-BIT
HEADS UP.
IS THAT REAL?

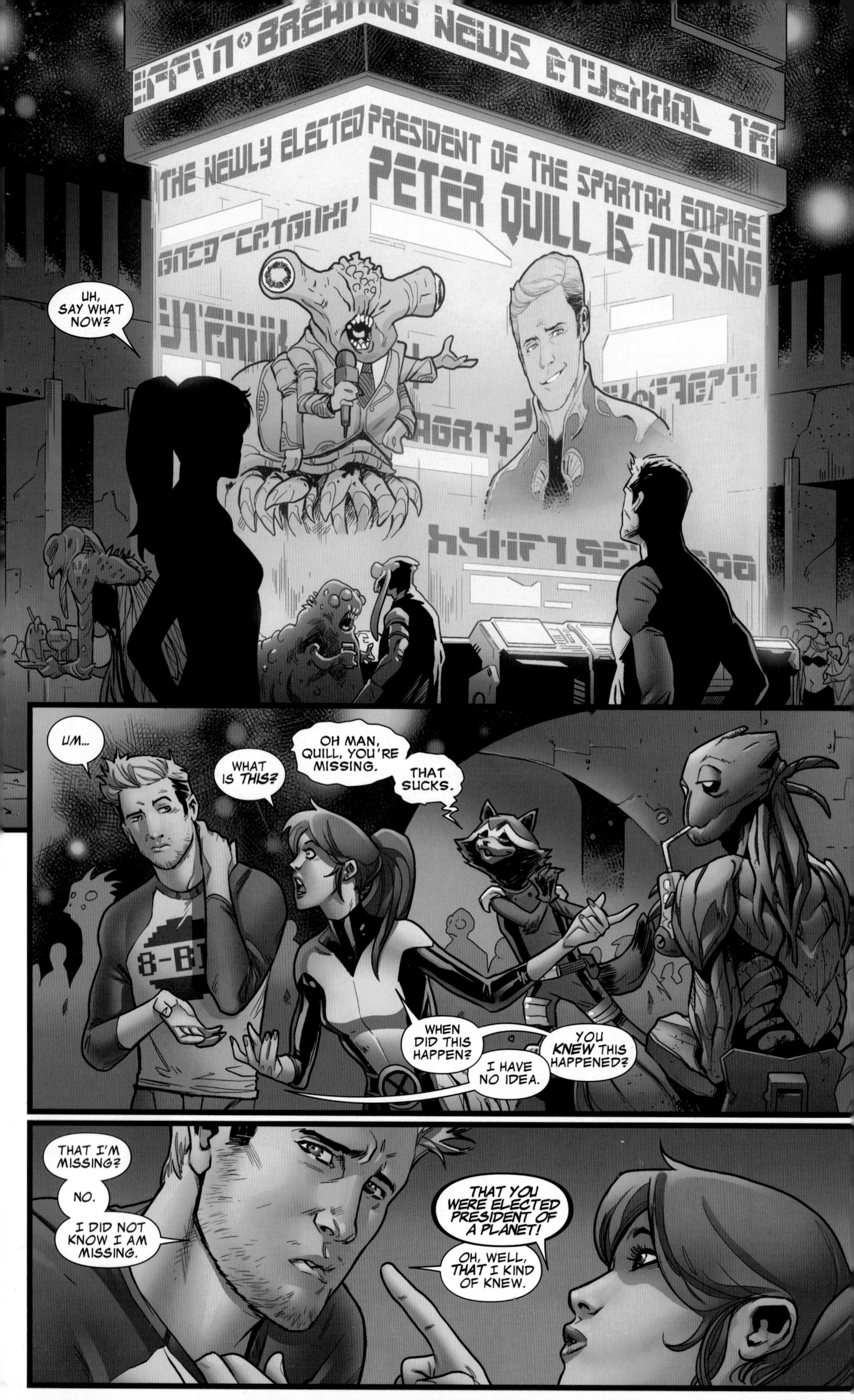
BREAKING NEWS
THE NEWLY ELECTED PRESIDENT OF THE SPARTAX EMPIRE
PETER QUILL IS MISSING
UH, SAY WHAT NOW?
UM...
WHAT IS THIS?
OH MAN, QUILL, YOU'RE MISSING.
THAT SUCKS.
8-BI
WHEN DID THIS HAPPEN?
YOU KNEW THIS HAPPENED?
I HAVE NO IDEA.
THAT I'M MISSING?
NO.
I DID NOT KNOW I AM MISSING.
THAT YOU WERE ELECTED PRESIDENT OF A PLANET!
OH, WELL, THAT I KIND OF KNEW.

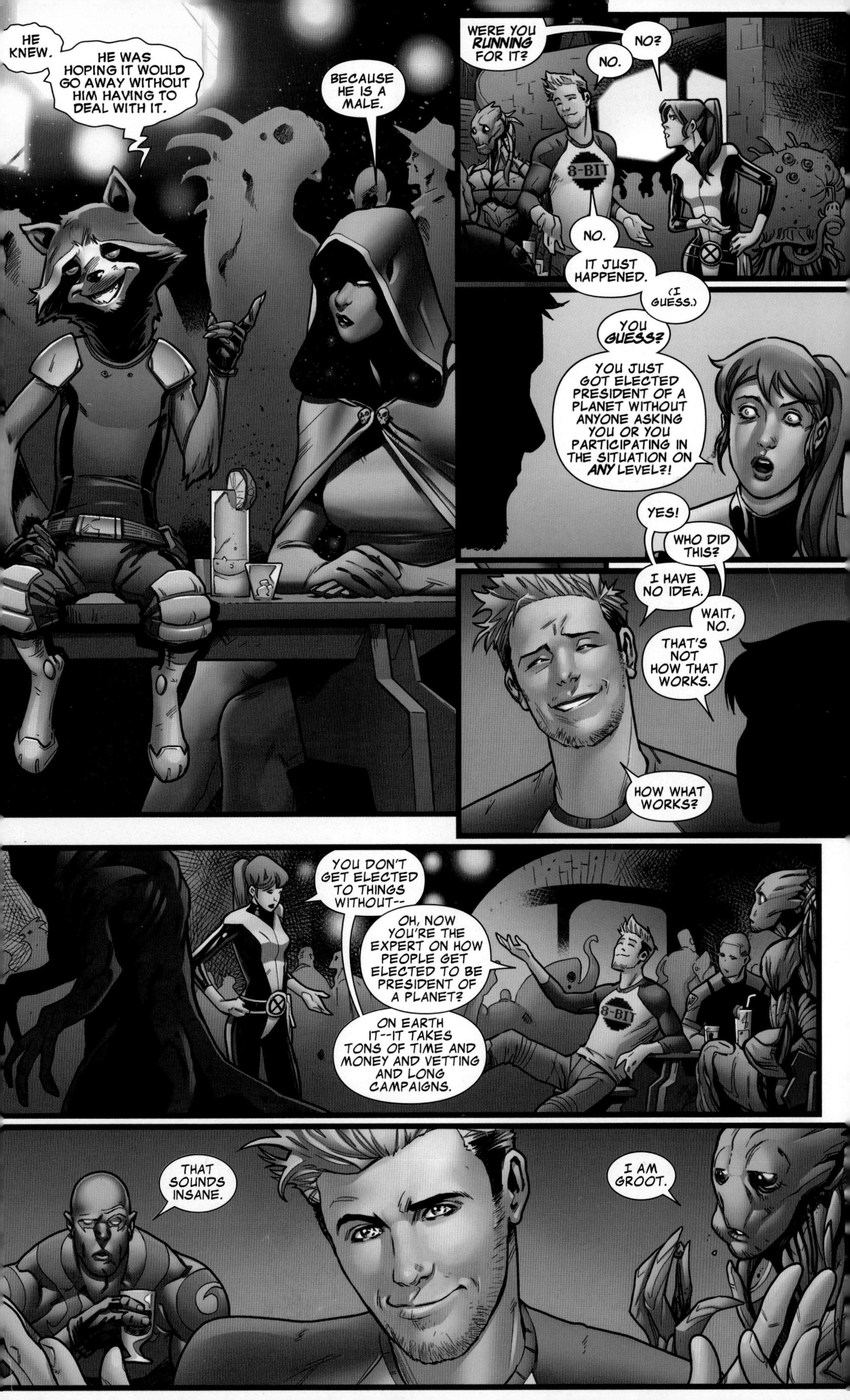
HE KNEW.
HE WAS HOPING IT WOULD GO AWAY WITHOUT HIM HAVING TO DEAL WITH IT.
BECAUSE HE IS A MALE.
WERE YOU RUNNING FOR IT?
NO?
NO.
NO.
IT JUST HAPPENED.
(I GUESS.)
YOU GUESS?
YOU JUST GOT ELECTED PRESIDENT OF A PLANET WITHOUT ANYONE ASKING YOU OR YOU PARTICIPATING IN THE SITUATION ON ANY LEVEL?!
YES!
WHO DID THIS?
I HAVE NO IDEA.
WAIT, NO.
THAT'S NOT HOW THAT WORKS.
HOW WHAT WORKS?
YOU DON'T GET ELECTED TO THINGS WITHOUT--
OH, NOW YOU'RE THE EXPERT ON HOW PEOPLE GET ELECTED TO BE PRESIDENT OF A PLANET?
ON EARTH IT--IT TAKES TONS OF TIME AND MONEY AND VETTING AND LONG CAMPAIGNS.
THAT SOUNDS INSANE.
I AM GROOT.

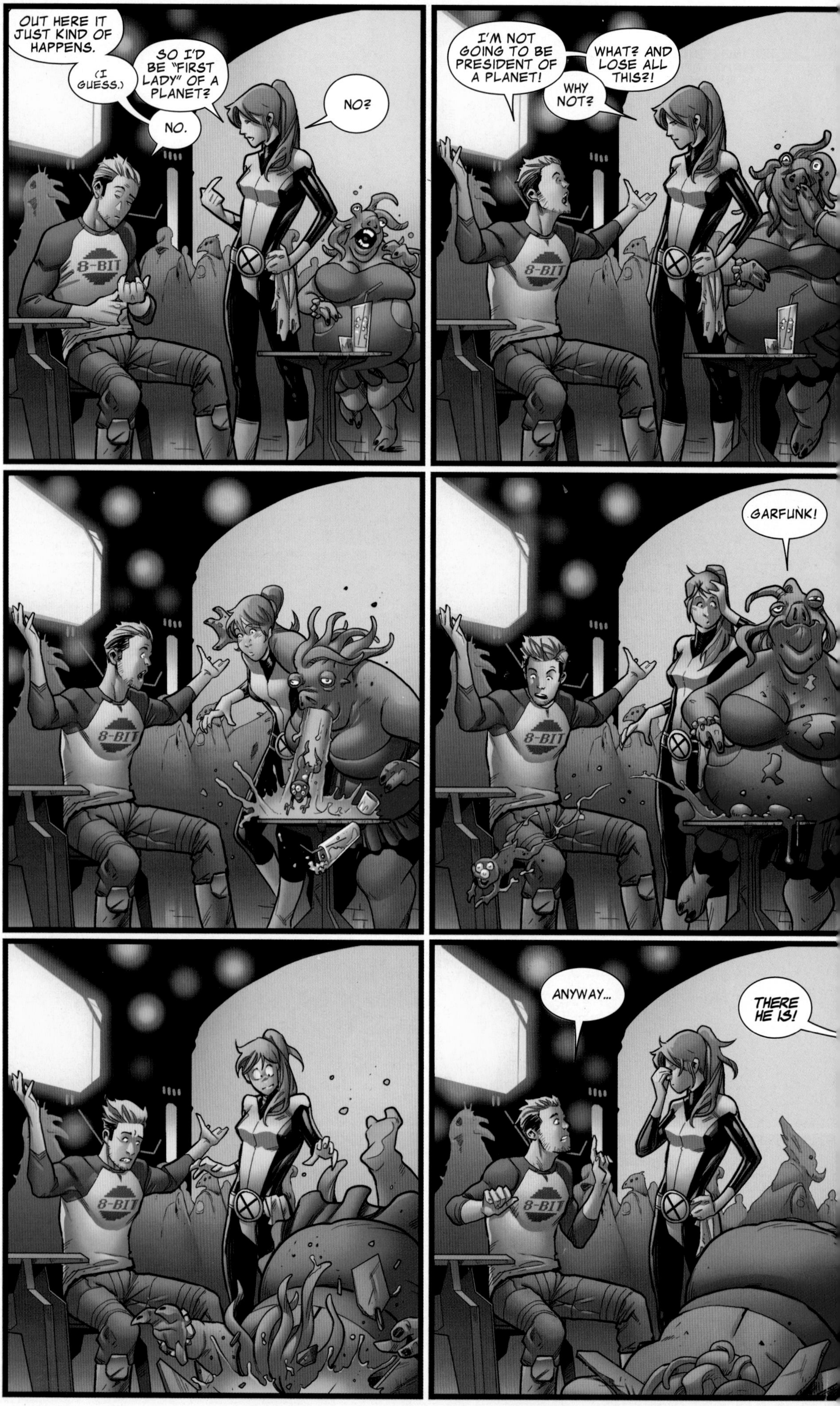
OUT HERE IT JUST KIND OF HAPPENS.
(I GUESS.)
SO I'D BE "FIRST LADY" OF A PLANET?
NO.
NO?
I'M NOT GOING TO BE PRESIDENT OF A PLANET!
WHY NOT?
WHAT? AND LOSE ALL THIS?!
GARFUNK!
ANYWAY...
THERE HE IS!
8-BIT

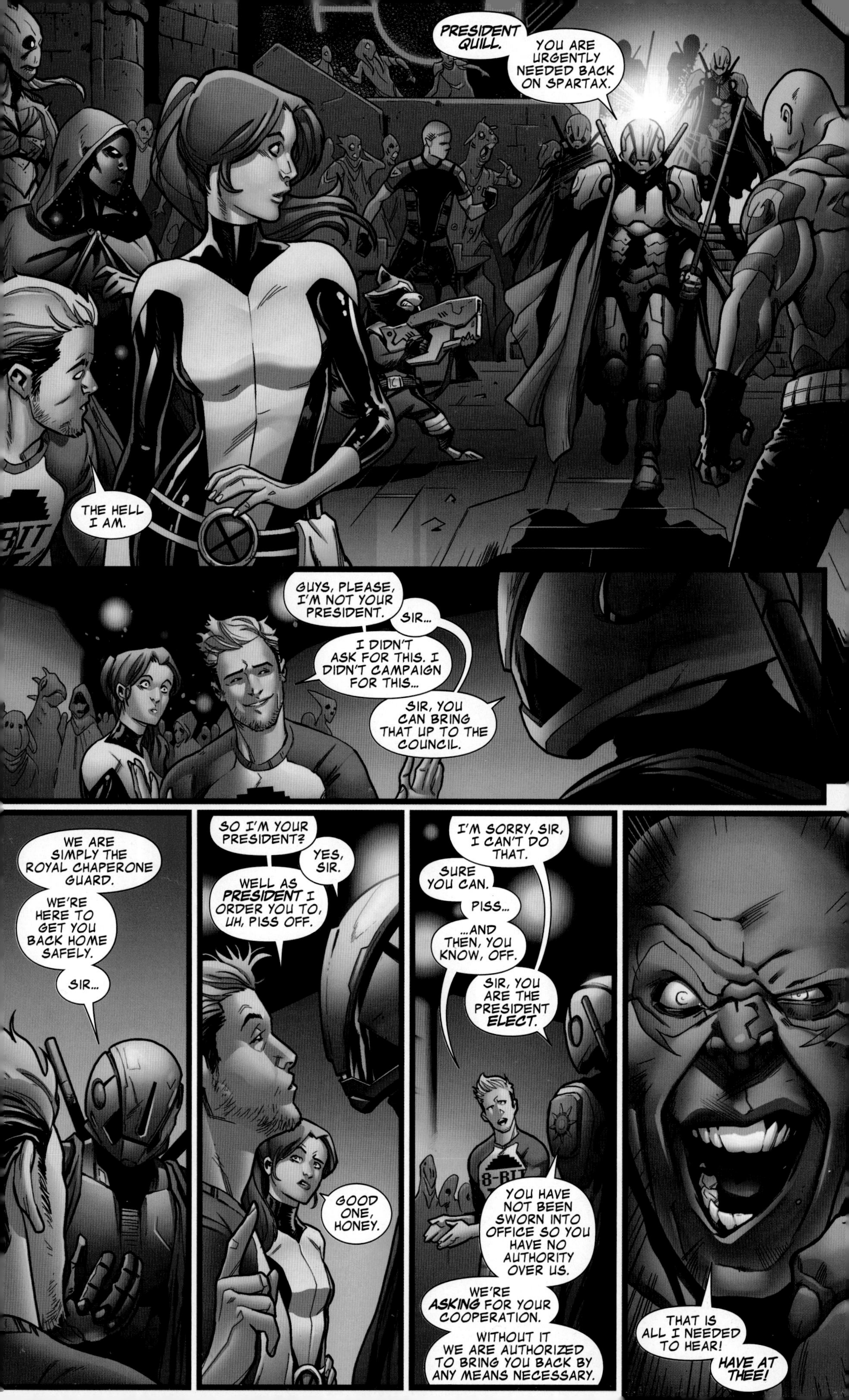
PRESIDENT QUILL.
YOU ARE URGENTLY NEEDED BACK ON SPARTAX.
THE HELL I AM.
GUYS, PLEASE, I'M NOT YOUR PRESIDENT.
SIR...
I DIDN'T ASK FOR THIS. I DIDN'T CAMPAIGN FOR THIS...
SIR, YOU CAN BRING THAT UP TO THE COUNCIL.
WE ARE SIMPLY THE ROYAL CHAPERONE GUARD.
WE'RE HERE TO GET YOU BACK HOME SAFELY.
SIR...
SO I'M YOUR PRESIDENT?
YES, SIR.
WELL AS PRESIDENT I ORDER YOU TO, UH, PISS OFF.
GOOD ONE, HONEY.
I'M SORRY, SIR, I CAN'T DO THAT.
SURE YOU CAN.
PISS...
...AND THEN, YOU KNOW, OFF.
SIR, YOU ARE THE PRESIDENT ELECT.
YOU HAVE NOT BEEN SWORN INTO OFFICE SO YOU HAVE NO AUTHORITY OVER US.
WE'RE ASKING FOR YOUR COOPERATION.
WITHOUT IT WE ARE AUTHORIZED TO BRING YOU BACK BY ANY MEANS NECESSARY.
THAT IS ALL I NEEDED TO HEAR!
HAVE AT THEE!

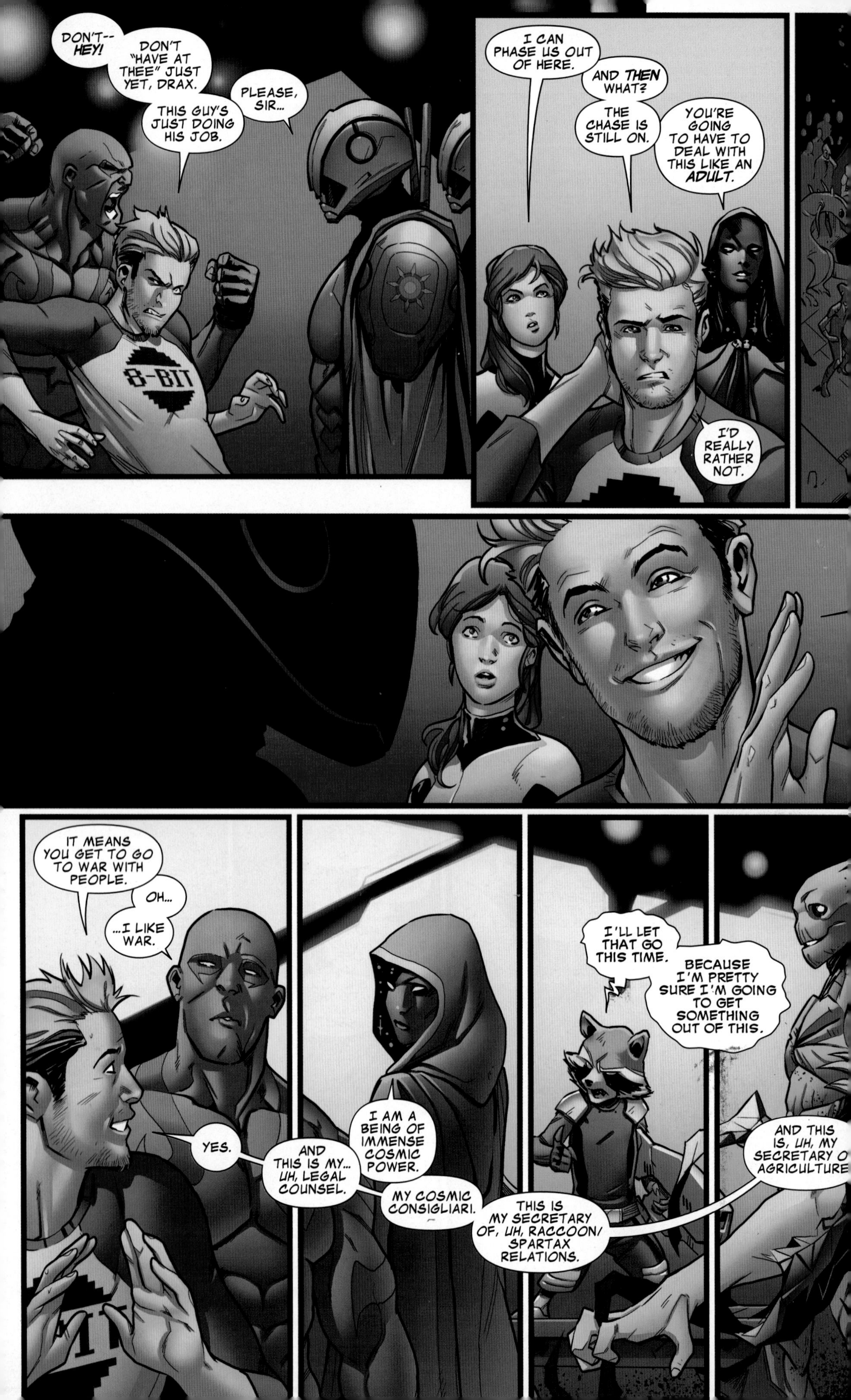

DON'T-- HEY!
DON'T "HAVE AT THEE" JUST YET, DRAX.
THIS GUY'S JUST DOING HIS JOB.
PLEASE, SIR...
8-BIT
I CAN PHASE US OUT OF HERE.
AND THEN WHAT?
THE CHASE IS STILL ON.
YOU'RE GOING TO HAVE TO DEAL WITH THIS LIKE AN ADULT.
I'D REALLY RATHER NOT.
IT MEANS YOU GET TO GO TO WAR WITH PEOPLE.
OH...
...I LIKE WAR.
YES.
AND THIS IS MY... UH, LEGAL COUNSEL.
I AM A BEING OF IMMENSE COSMIC POWER.
MY COSMIC CONSIGLIARI.
THIS IS MY SECRETARY OF, UH, RACCOON/ SPARTAX RELATIONS.
I'LL LET THAT GO THIS TIME.
BECAUSE I'M PRETTY SURE I'M GOING TO GET SOMETHING OUT OF THIS.
AND THIS IS, UH, MY SECRETARY O AGRICULTURE

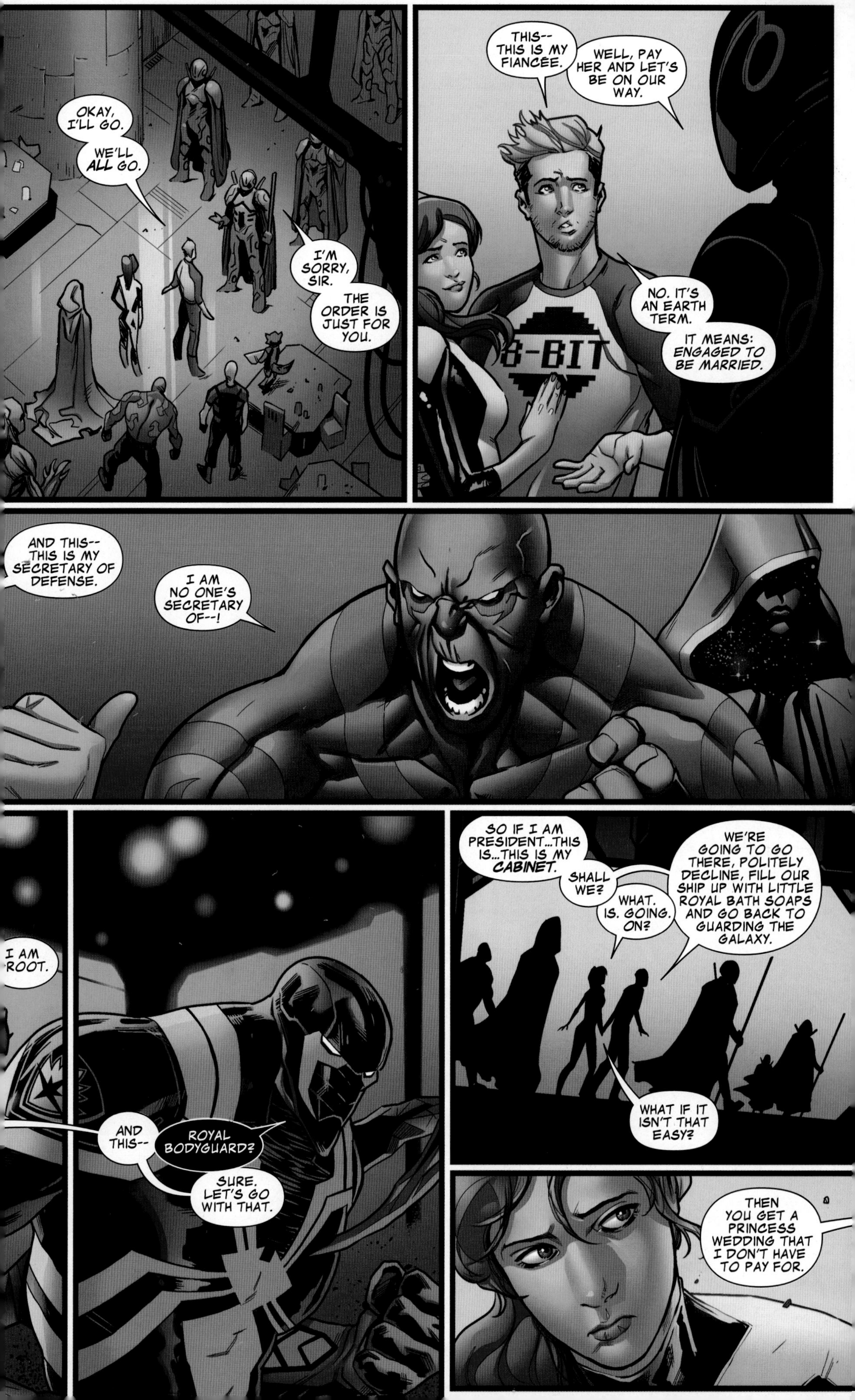
OKAY, I'LL GO.
WE'LL ALL GO.
I'M SORRY, SIR.
THE ORDER IS JUST FOR YOU.
THIS-- THIS IS MY FIANCÉE.
WELL, PAY HER AND LET'S BE ON OUR WAY.
NO. IT'S AN EARTH TERM.
IT MEANS: ENGAGED TO BE MARRIED.
8-BIT
AND THIS-- THIS IS MY SECRETARY OF DEFENSE.
I AM NO ONE'S SECRETARY OF--!
I AM ROOT.
AND THIS--
ROYAL BODYGUARD?
SURE. LET'S GO WITH THAT.
SO IF I AM PRESIDENT...THIS IS...THIS IS MY CABINET.
SHALL WE?
WHAT. IS. GOING. ON?
WE'RE GOING TO GO THERE, POLITELY DECLINE, FILL OUR SHIP UP WITH LITTLE ROYAL BATH SOAPS AND GO BACK TO GUARDING THE GALAXY.
WHAT IF IT ISN'T THAT EASY?
THEN YOU GET A PRINCESS WEDDING THAT I DON'T HAVE TO PAY FOR.

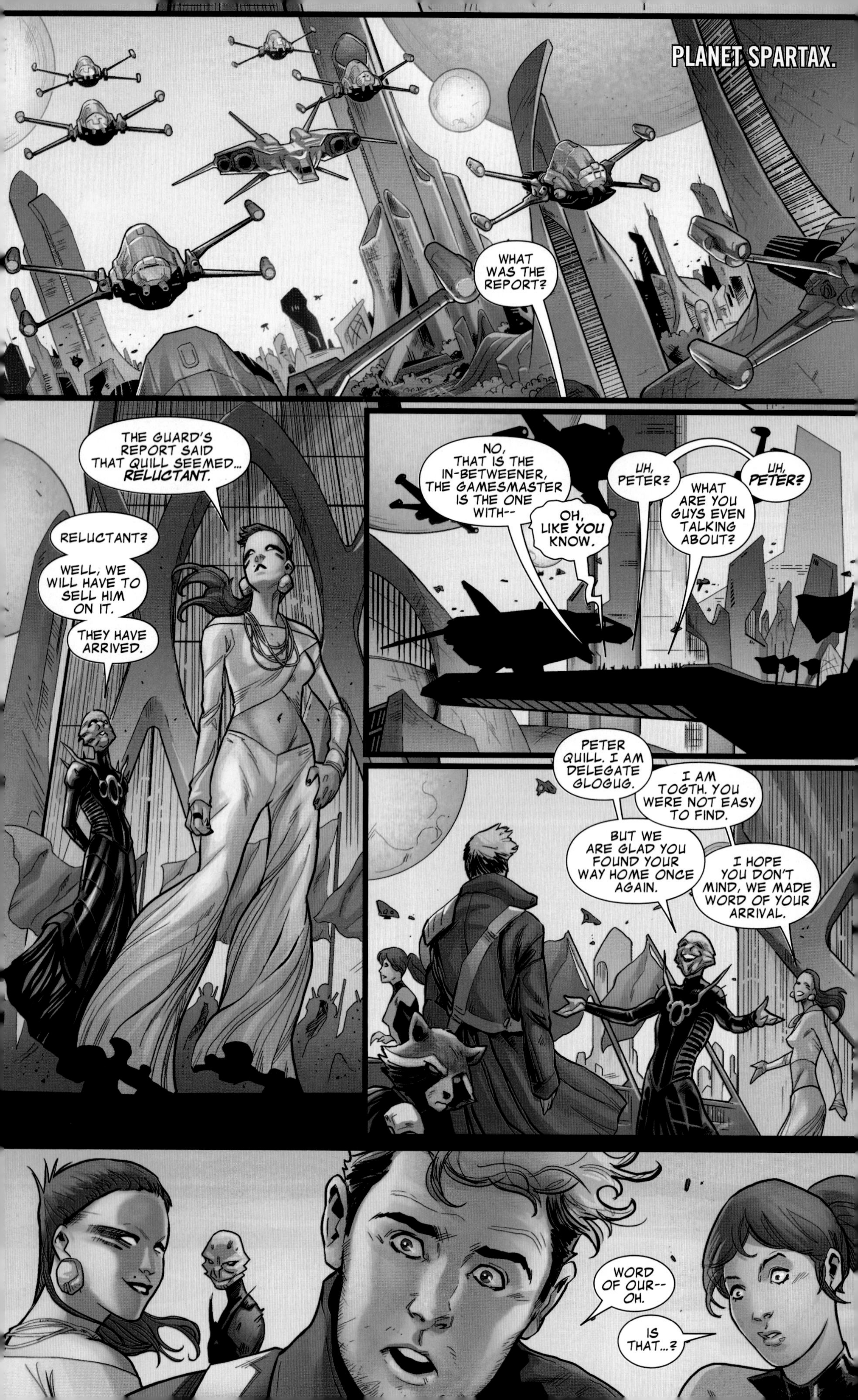
PLANET SPARTAX.
WHAT WAS THE REPORT?
THE GUARD'S REPORT SAID THAT QUILL SEEMED... RELUCTANT.
RELUCTANT?
WELL, WE WILL HAVE TO SELL HIM ON IT.
THEY HAVE ARRIVED.
NO, THAT IS THE IN-BETWEENER, THE GAMESMASTER IS THE ONE WITH--
OH, LIKE YOU KNOW.
UH, PETER?
UH, PETER?
WHAT ARE YOU GUYS EVEN TALKING ABOUT?
PETER QUILL. I AM DELEGATE GLOGUG.
I AM TOGTH. YOU WERE NOT EASY TO FIND.
BUT WE ARE GLAD YOU FOUND YOUR WAY HOME ONCE AGAIN.
I HOPE YOU DON'T MIND, WE MADE WORD OF YOUR ARRIVAL.
WORD OF OUR-- OH.
IS THAT...?

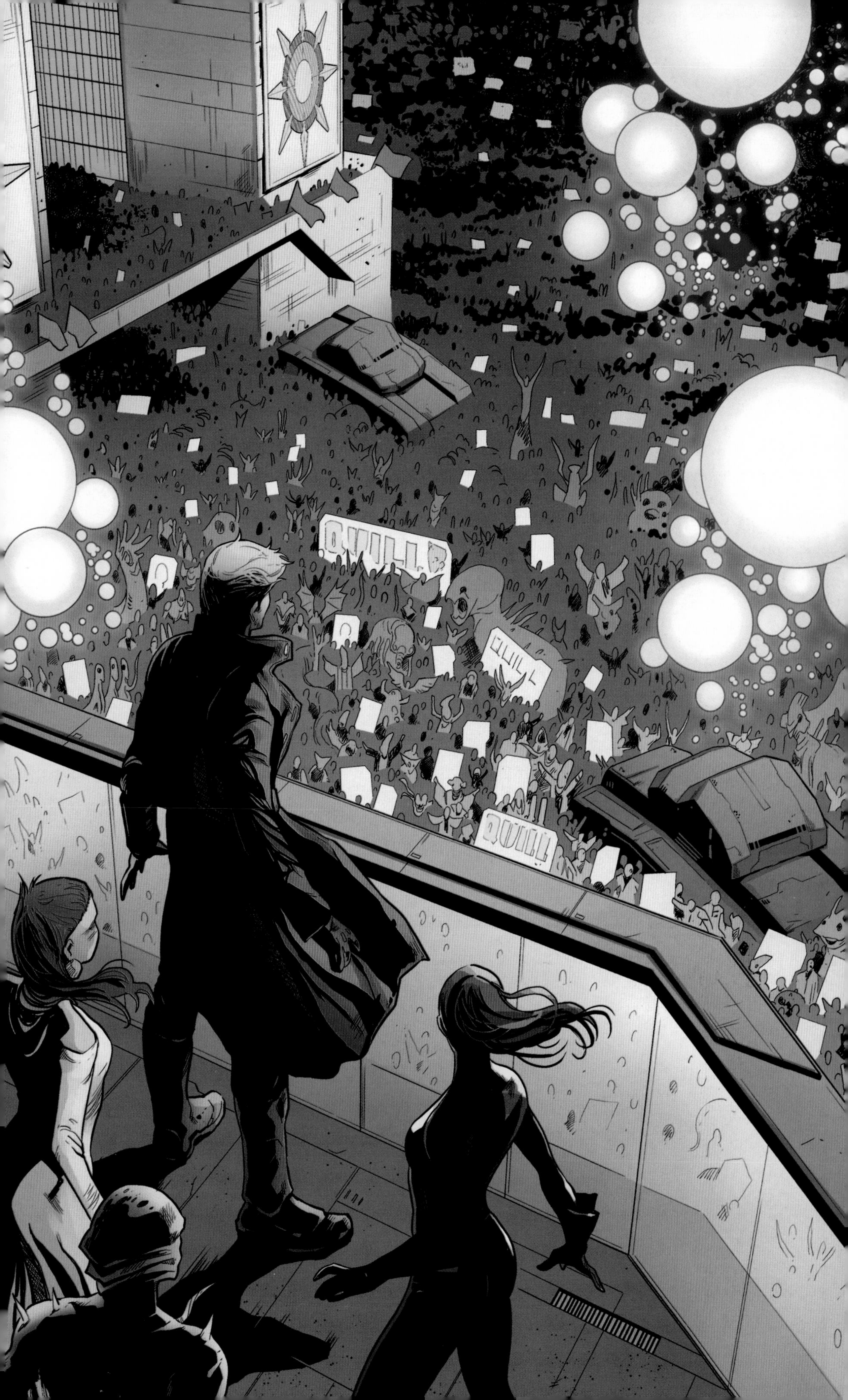
QUILL
QUILL
QUILL

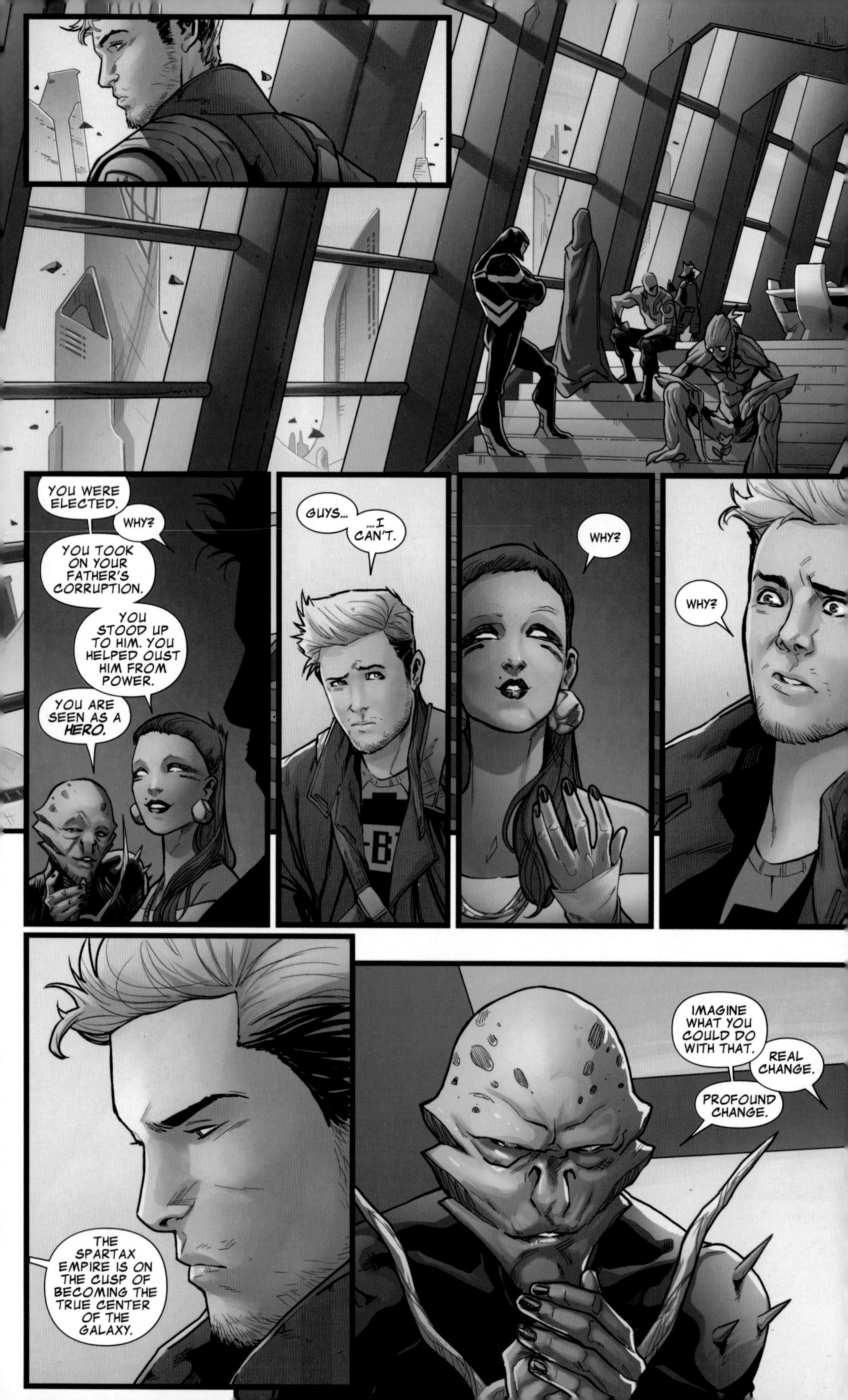
YOU WERE ELECTED.
WHY?
YOU TOOK ON YOUR FATHER'S CORRUPTION.
YOU STOOD UP TO HIM. YOU HELPED OUST HIM FROM POWER.
YOU ARE SEEN AS A HERO.
GUYS...
...I CAN'T.
WHY?
WHY?
IMAGINE WHAT YOU COULD DO WITH THAT.
REAL CHANGE.
PROFOUND CHANGE.
THE SPARTAX EMPIRE IS ON THE CUSP OF BECOMING THE TRUE CENTER OF THE GALAXY.

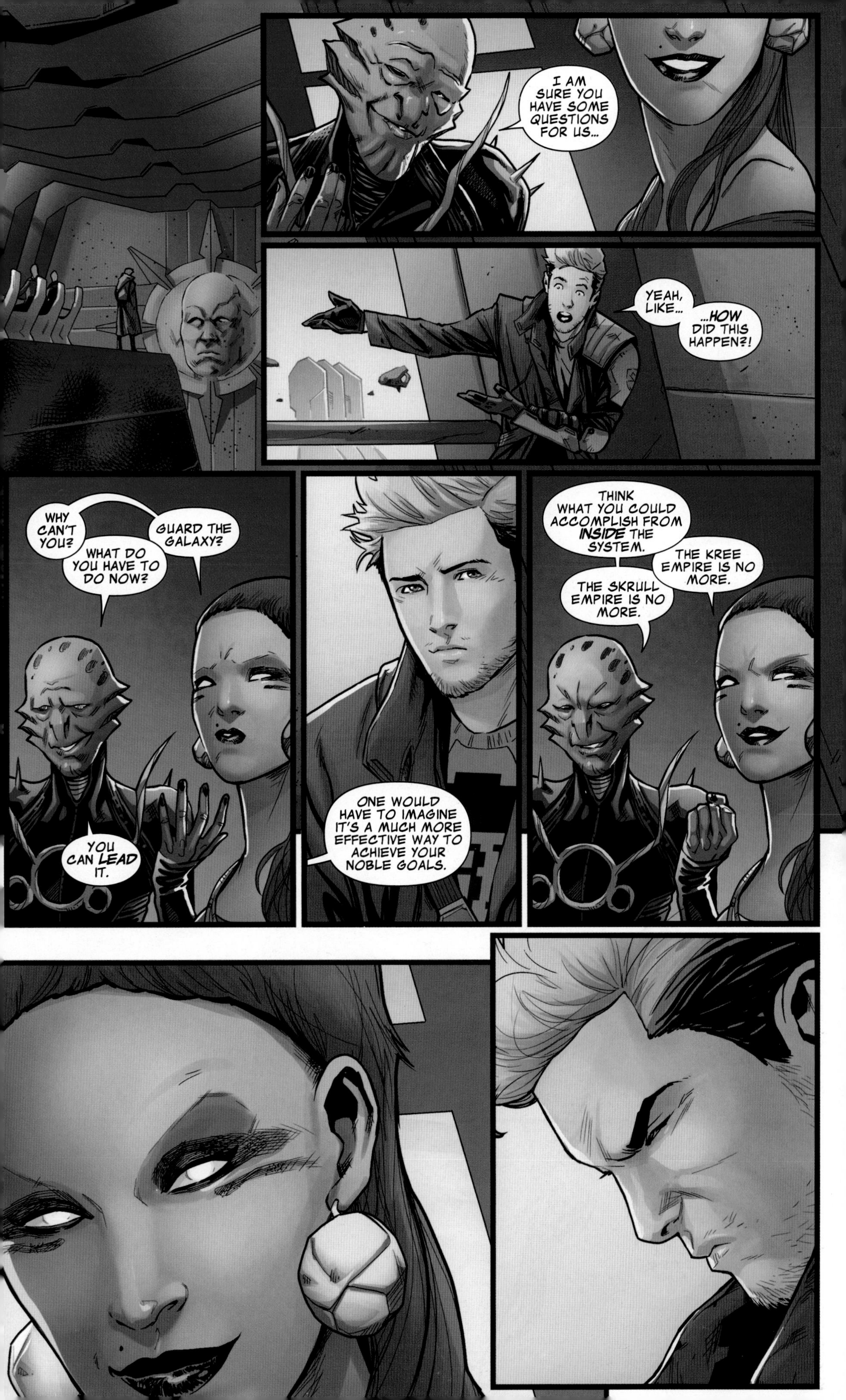

I AM SURE YOU HAVE SOME QUESTIONS FOR US...
YEAH, LIKE...
...HOW DID THIS HAPPEN?!
WHY CAN'T YOU?
GUARD THE GALAXY?
WHAT DO YOU HAVE TO DO NOW?
YOU CAN LEAD IT.
ONE WOULD HAVE TO IMAGINE IT'S A MUCH MORE EFFECTIVE WAY TO ACHIEVE YOUR NOBLE GOALS.
THINK WHAT YOU COULD ACCOMPLISH FROM INSIDE THE SYSTEM.
THE KREE EMPIRE IS NO MORE.
THE SKRULL EMPIRE IS NO MORE.

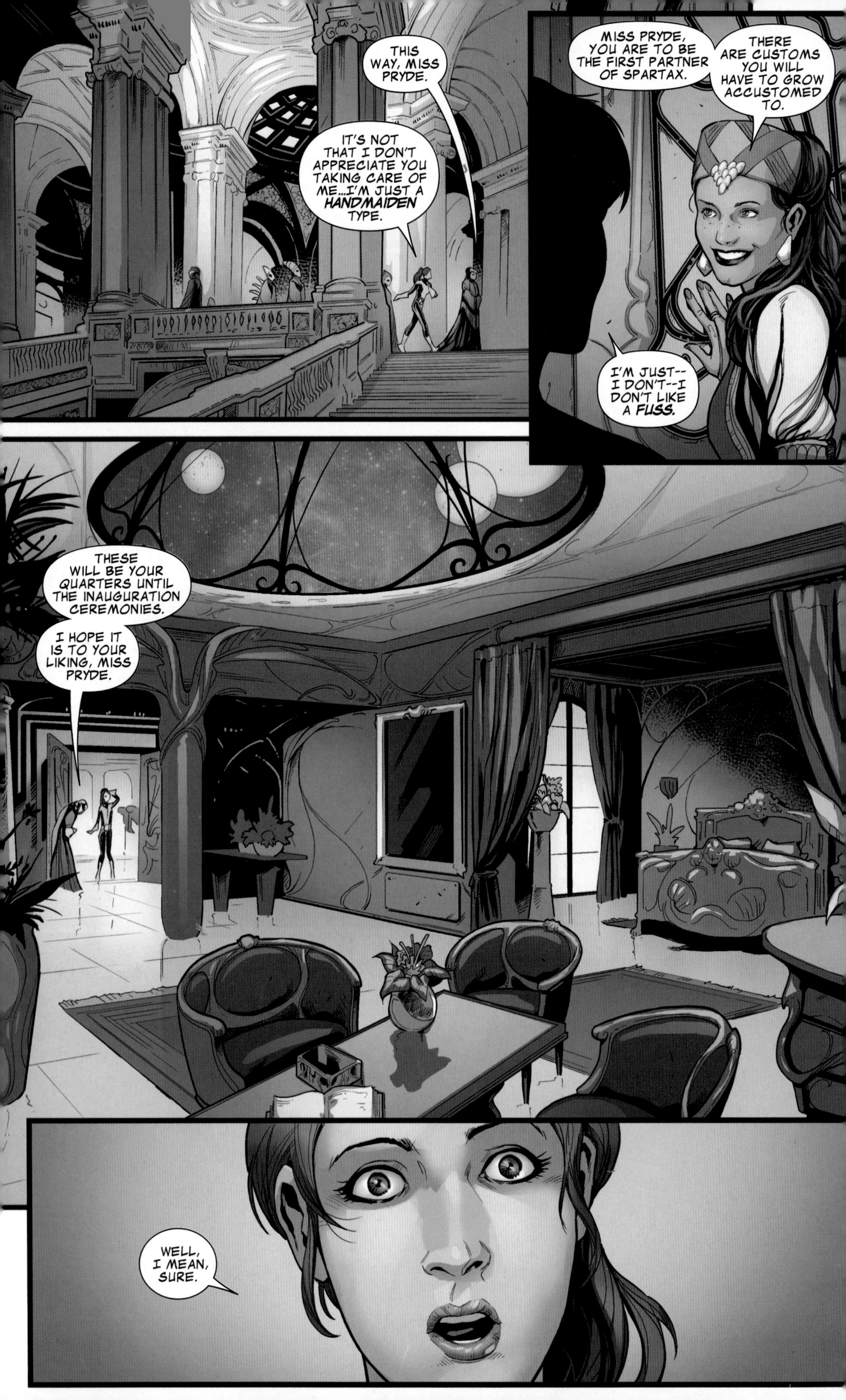
THIS WAY, MISS PRYDE.
IT'S NOT THAT I DON'T APPRECIATE YOU TAKING CARE OF ME...I'M JUST A HANDMAIDEN TYPE.
MISS PRYDE, YOU ARE TO BE THE FIRST PARTNER OF SPARTAX.
THERE ARE CUSTOMS YOU WILL HAVE TO GROW ACCUSTOMED TO.
I'M JUST-- I DON'T--I DON'T LIKE A FUSS.
THESE WILL BE YOUR QUARTERS UNTIL THE INAUGURATION CEREMONIES.
I HOPE IT IS TO YOUR LIKING, MISS PRYDE.
WELL, I MEAN, SURE.

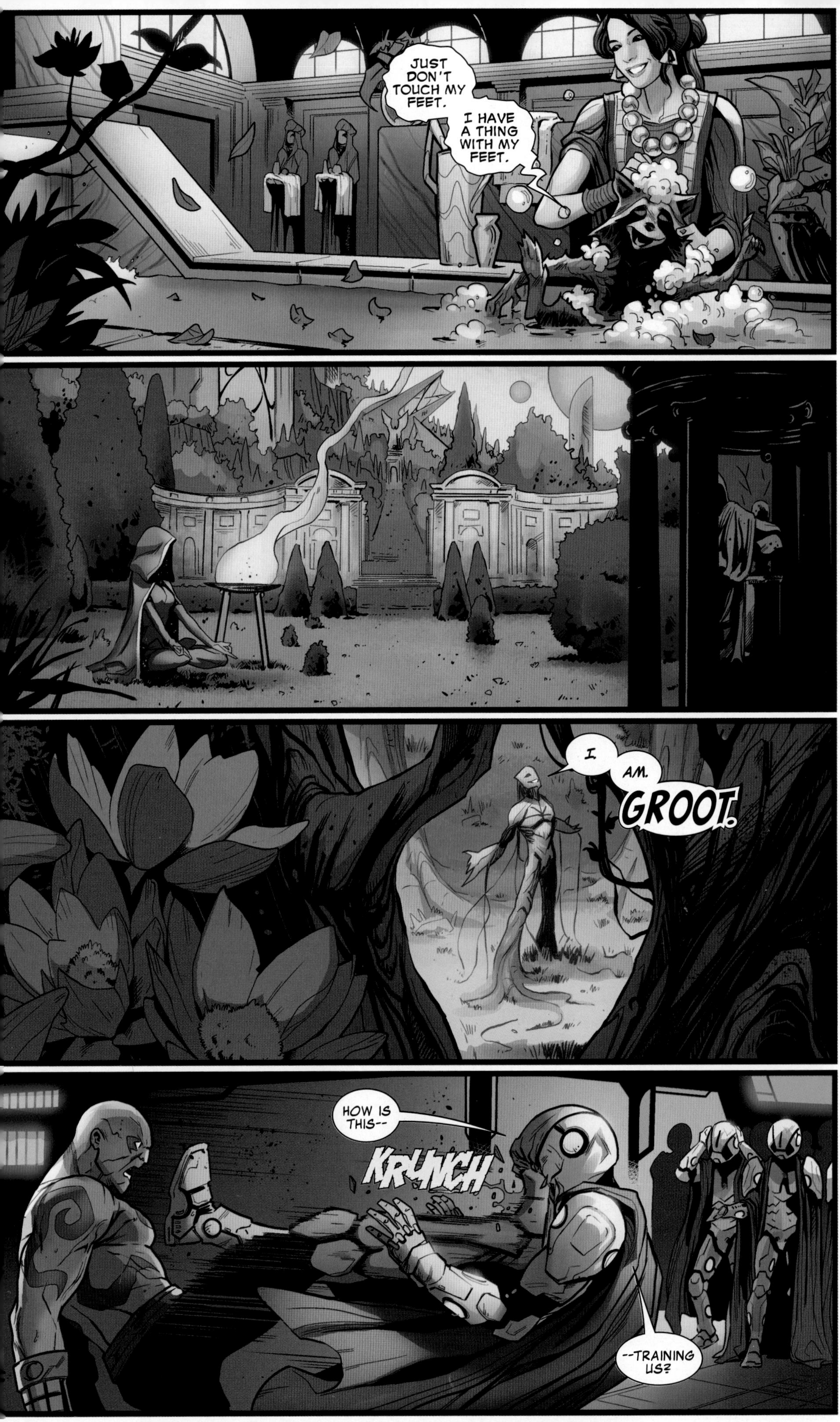
JUST DON'T TOUCH MY FEET.
I HAVE A THING WITH MY FEET.
I
AM.
GROOT.
HOW IS THIS--
KRUNCH
--TRAINING US?

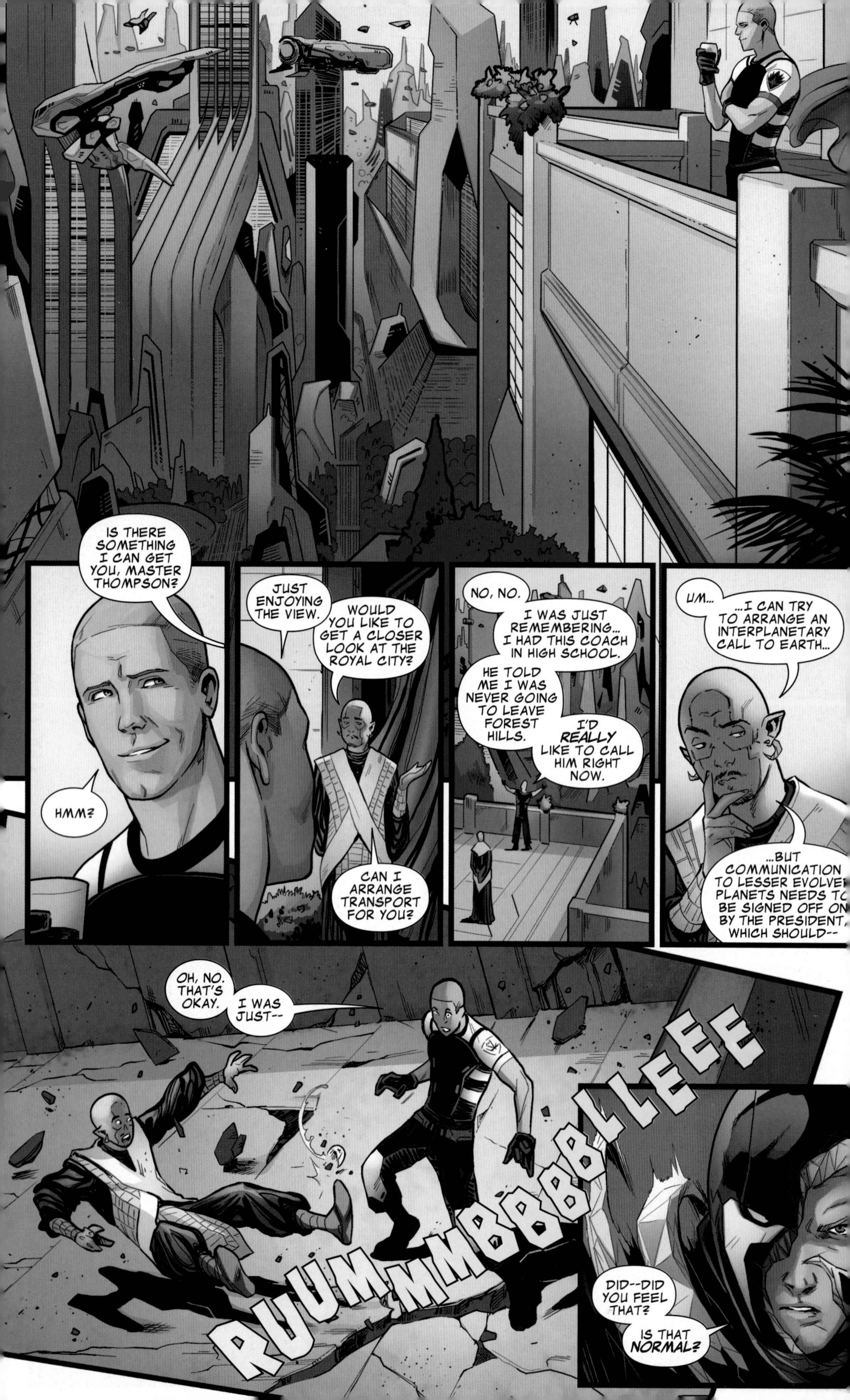
IS THERE SOMETHING I CAN GET YOU, MASTER THOMPSON?
HMM?
JUST ENJOYING THE VIEW.
WOULD YOU LIKE TO GET A CLOSER LOOK AT THE ROYAL CITY?
CAN I ARRANGE TRANSPORT FOR YOU?
NO, NO.
I WAS JUST REMEMBERING... I HAD THIS COACH IN HIGH SCHOOL.
HE TOLD ME I WAS NEVER GOING TO LEAVE FOREST HILLS.
I'D REALLY LIKE TO CALL HIM RIGHT NOW.
UM...
...I CAN TRY TO ARRANGE AN INTERPLANETARY CALL TO EARTH...
...BUT COMMUNICATION TO LESSER EVOLVE PLANETS NEEDS TO BE SIGNED OFF ON BY THE PRESIDENT, WHICH SHOULD--
OH, NO. THAT'S OKAY.
I WAS JUST--
RUUMMMBBBBLLEEE
DID--DID YOU FEEL THAT?
IS THAT NORMAL?

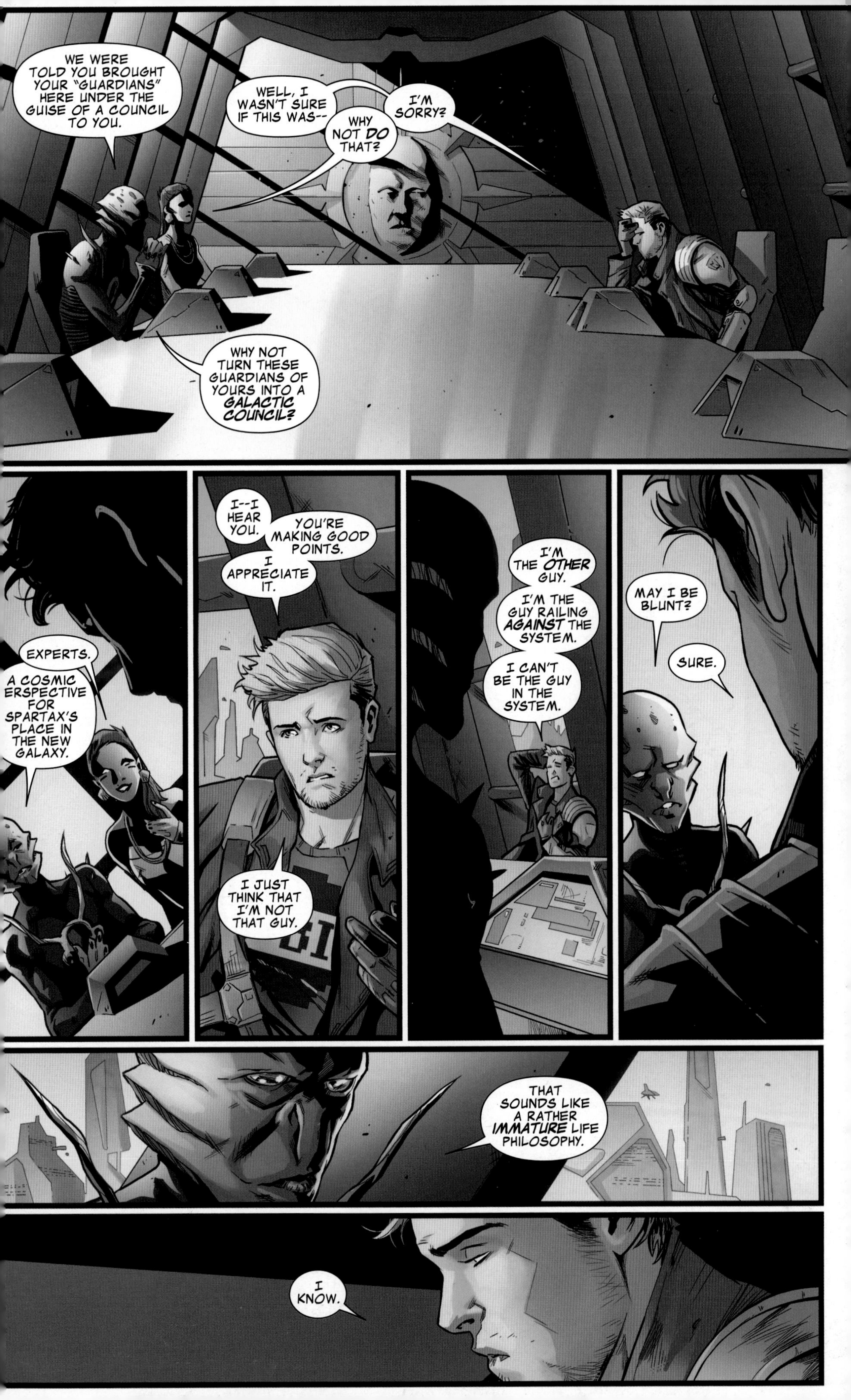
WE WERE TOLD YOU BROUGHT YOUR "GUARDIANS" HERE UNDER THE GUISE OF A COUNCIL TO YOU.
WELL, I WASN'T SURE IF THIS WAS--
WHY NOT DO THAT?
I'M SORRY?
WHY NOT TURN THESE GUARDIANS OF YOURS INTO A GALACTIC COUNCIL?
EXPERTS.
A COSMIC ERSPECTIVE FOR SPARTAX'S PLACE IN THE NEW GALAXY.
I--I HEAR YOU.
YOU'RE MAKING GOOD POINTS.
I APPRECIATE IT.
I JUST THINK THAT I'M NOT THAT GUY.
I'M THE OTHER GUY.
I'M THE GUY RAILING AGAINST THE SYSTEM.
I CAN'T BE THE GUY IN THE SYSTEM.
MAY I BE BLUNT?
SURE.
THAT SOUNDS LIKE A RATHER IMMATURE LIFE PHILOSOPHY.
I KNOW.

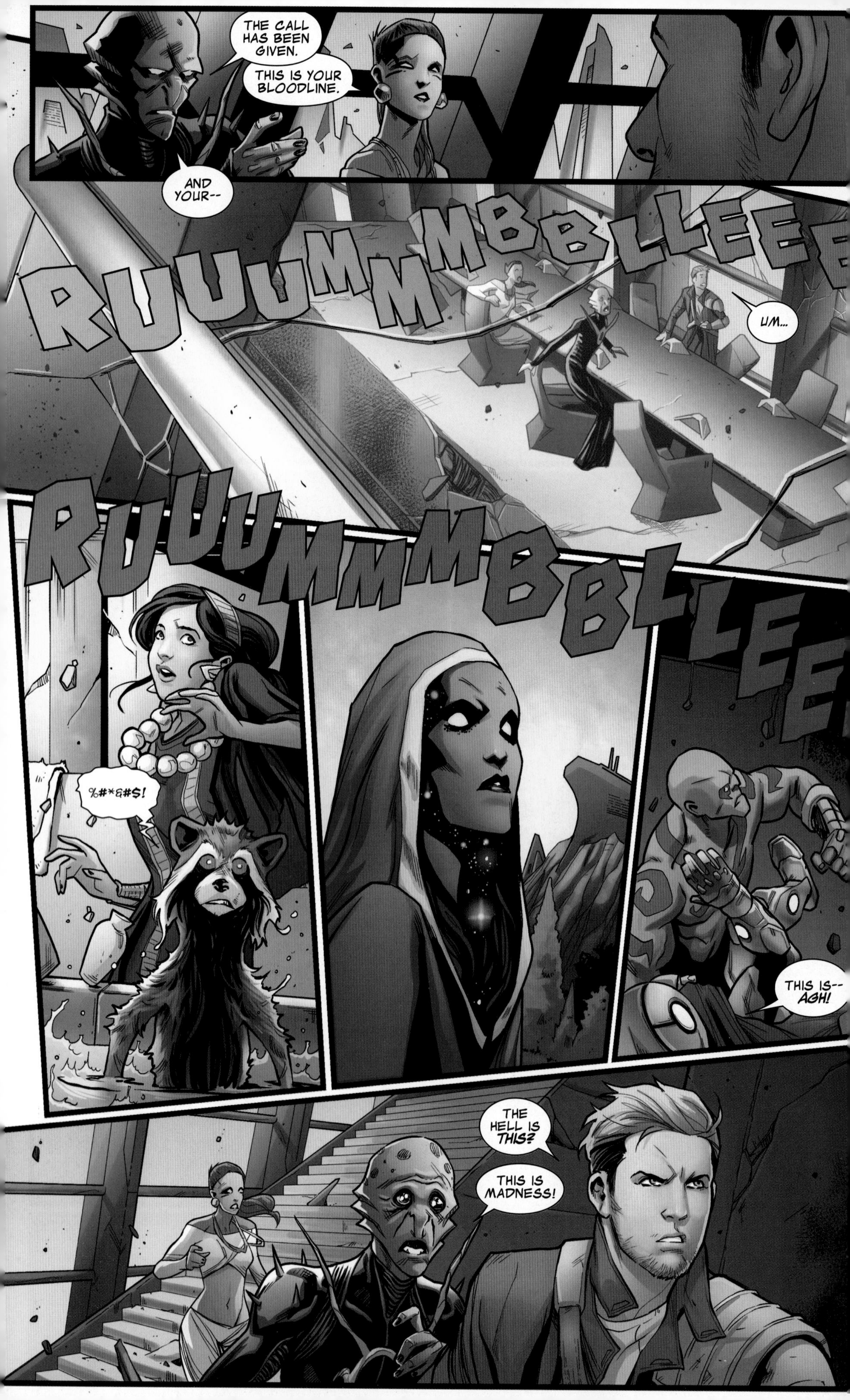
THE CALL HAS BEEN GIVEN.
THIS IS YOUR BLOODLINE.
AND YOUR--
RUUUMMMBBLLEEE
UM...
RUUUMMMMBBLLEEE
%#*ß#$!
THIS IS-- AGH!
THE HELL IS THIS?
THIS IS MADNESS!

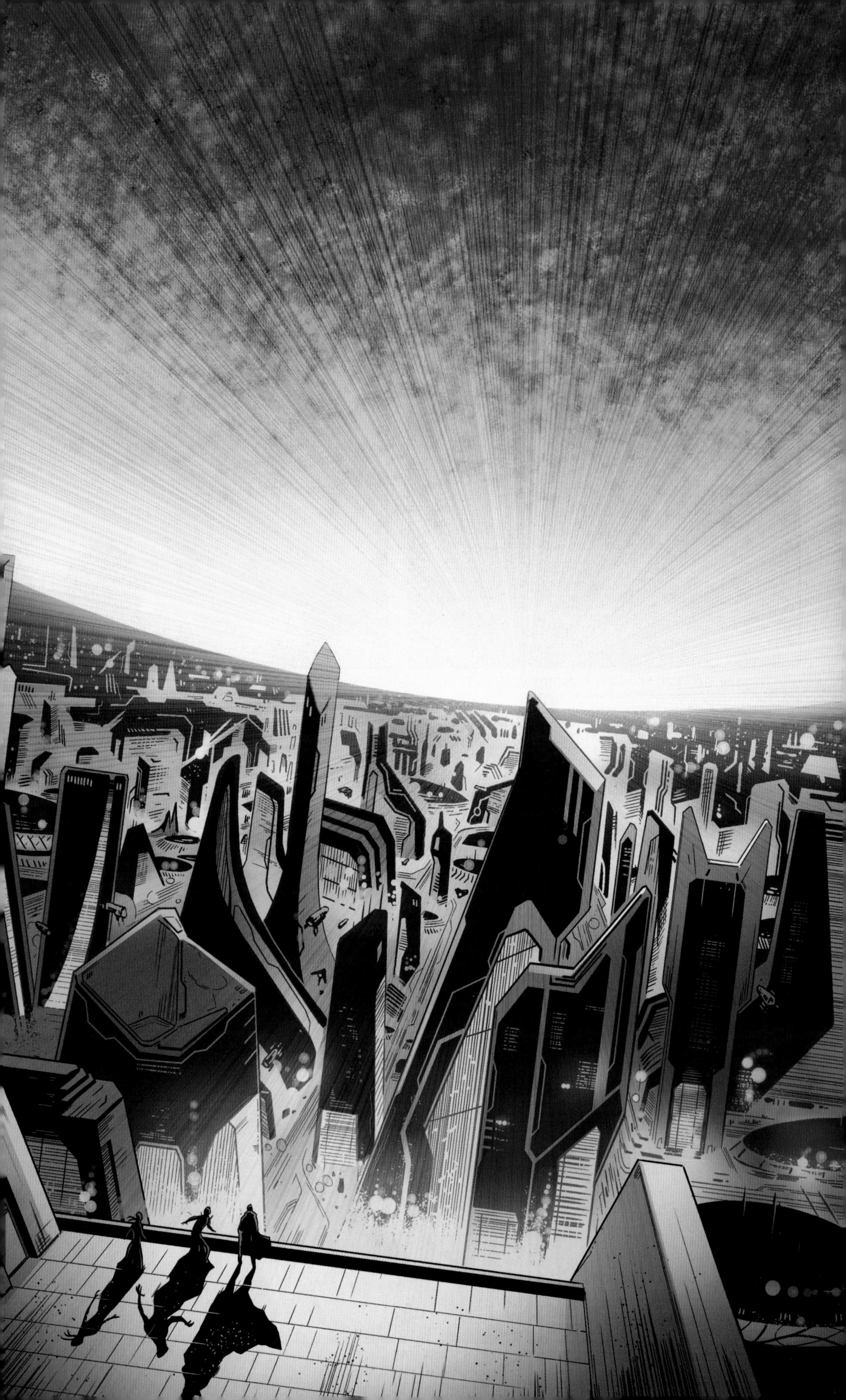

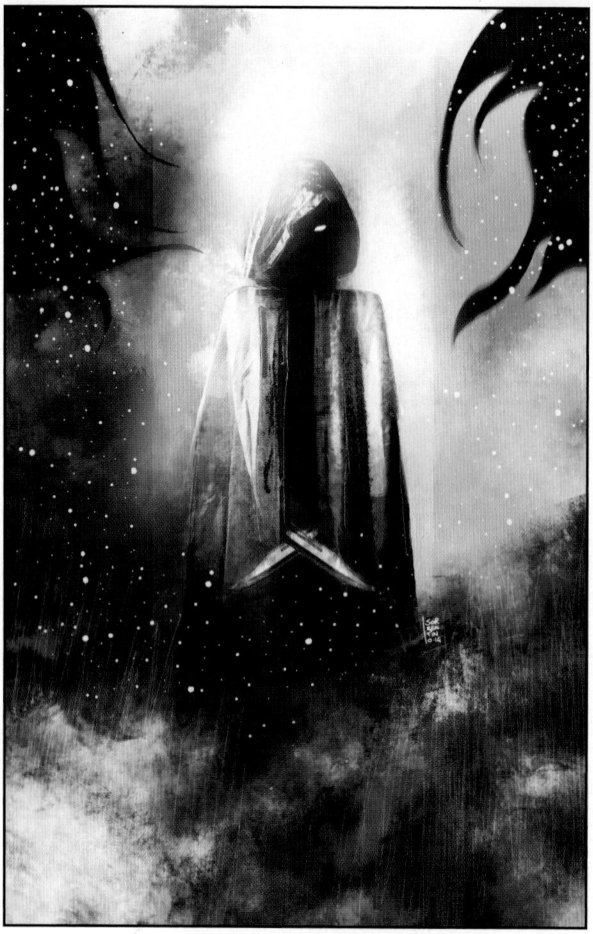

#24 COSMICALLY ENHANCED VARIANT
BY ANDREA SORRENTINO

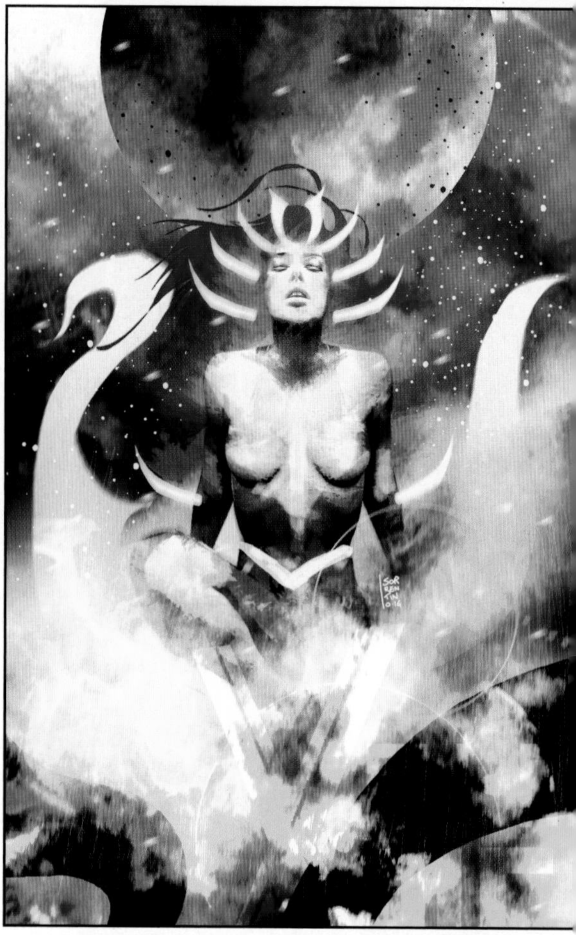

#25 COSMICALLY ENHANCED VARIANT
BY ANDREA SORRENTINO

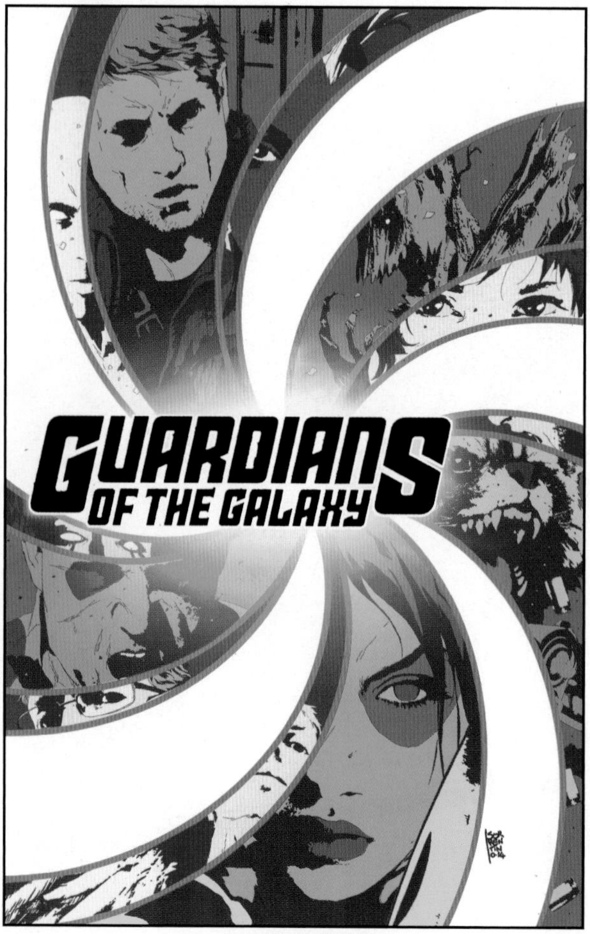
GUARDIANS
OF THE GALAXY

#25 VARIANT
BY ANDREA SORRENTINO

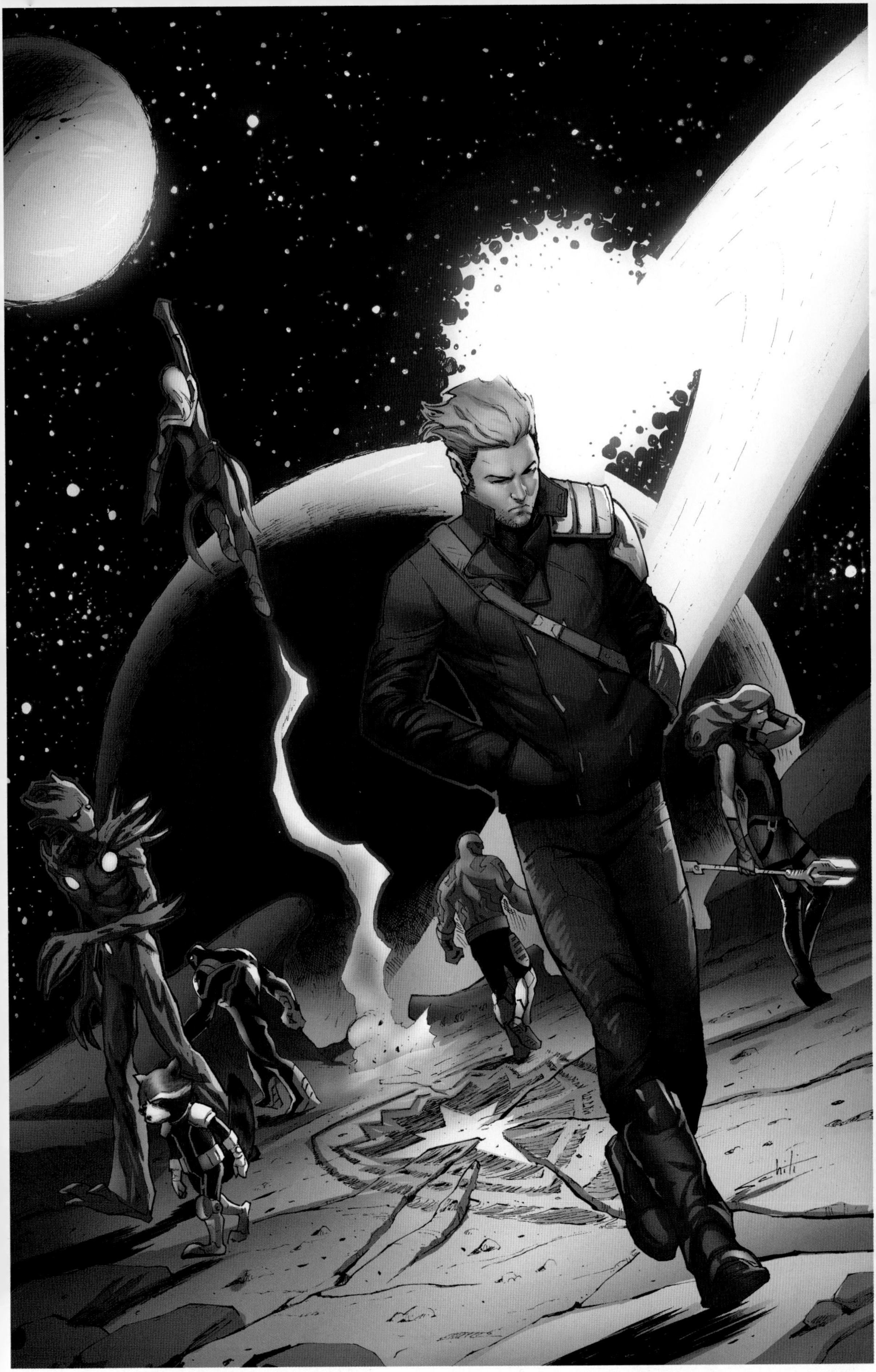

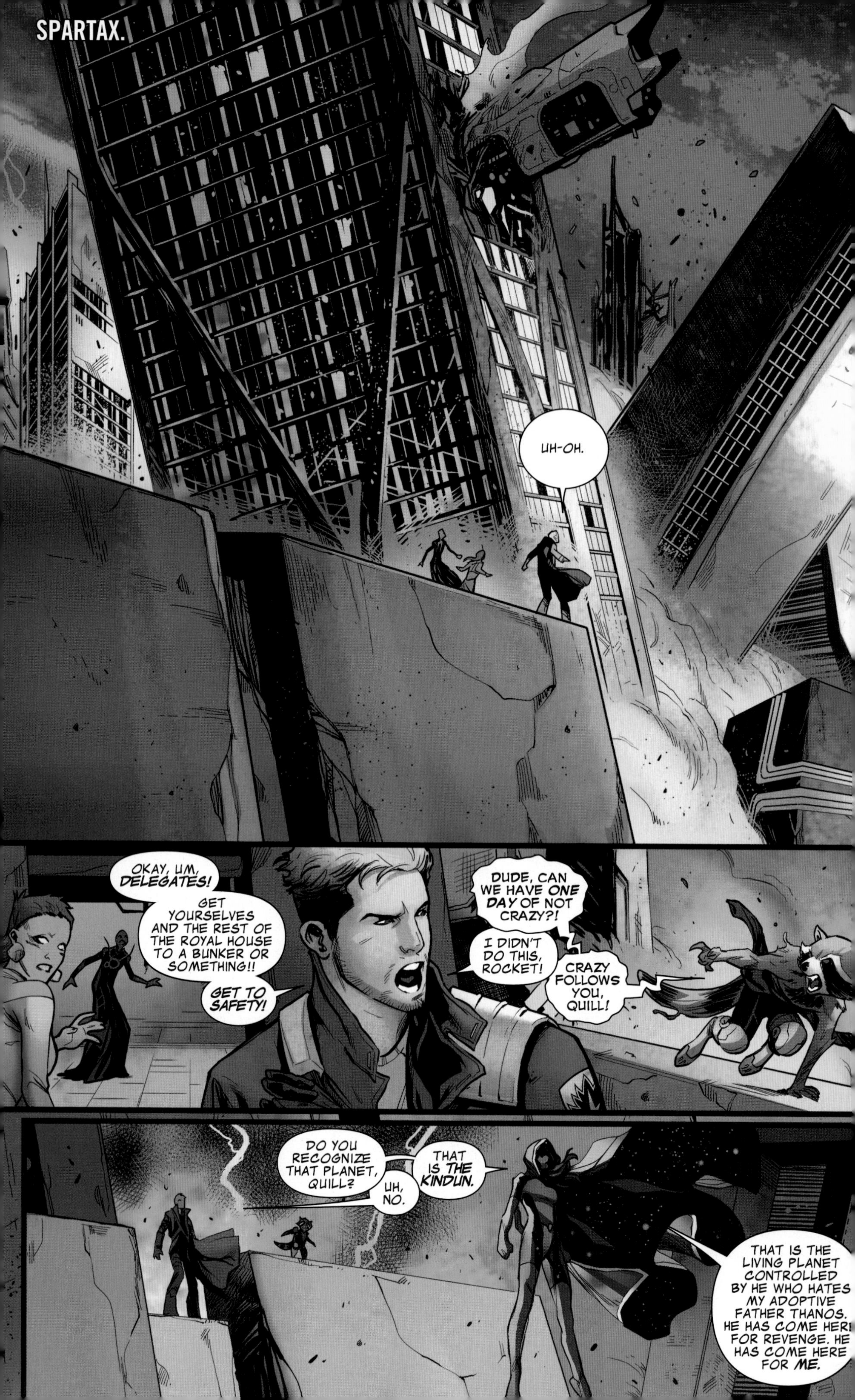
SPARTAX.
UH-OH.
OKAY, UM, DELEGATES!
GET YOURSELVES AND THE REST OF THE ROYAL HOUSE TO A BUNKER OR SOMETHING!!
GET TO SAFETY!
DUDE, CAN WE HAVE ONE DAY OF NOT CRAZY?!
I DIDN'T DO THIS, ROCKET!
CRAZY FOLLOWS YOU, QUILL!
DO YOU RECOGNIZE THAT PLANET, QUILL?
UH, NO.
THAT IS THE KINDUN.
THAT IS THE LIVING PLANET CONTROLLED BY HE WHO HATES MY ADOPTIVE FATHER THANOS. HE HAS COME HERE FOR REVENGE. HE HAS COME HERE FOR ME.

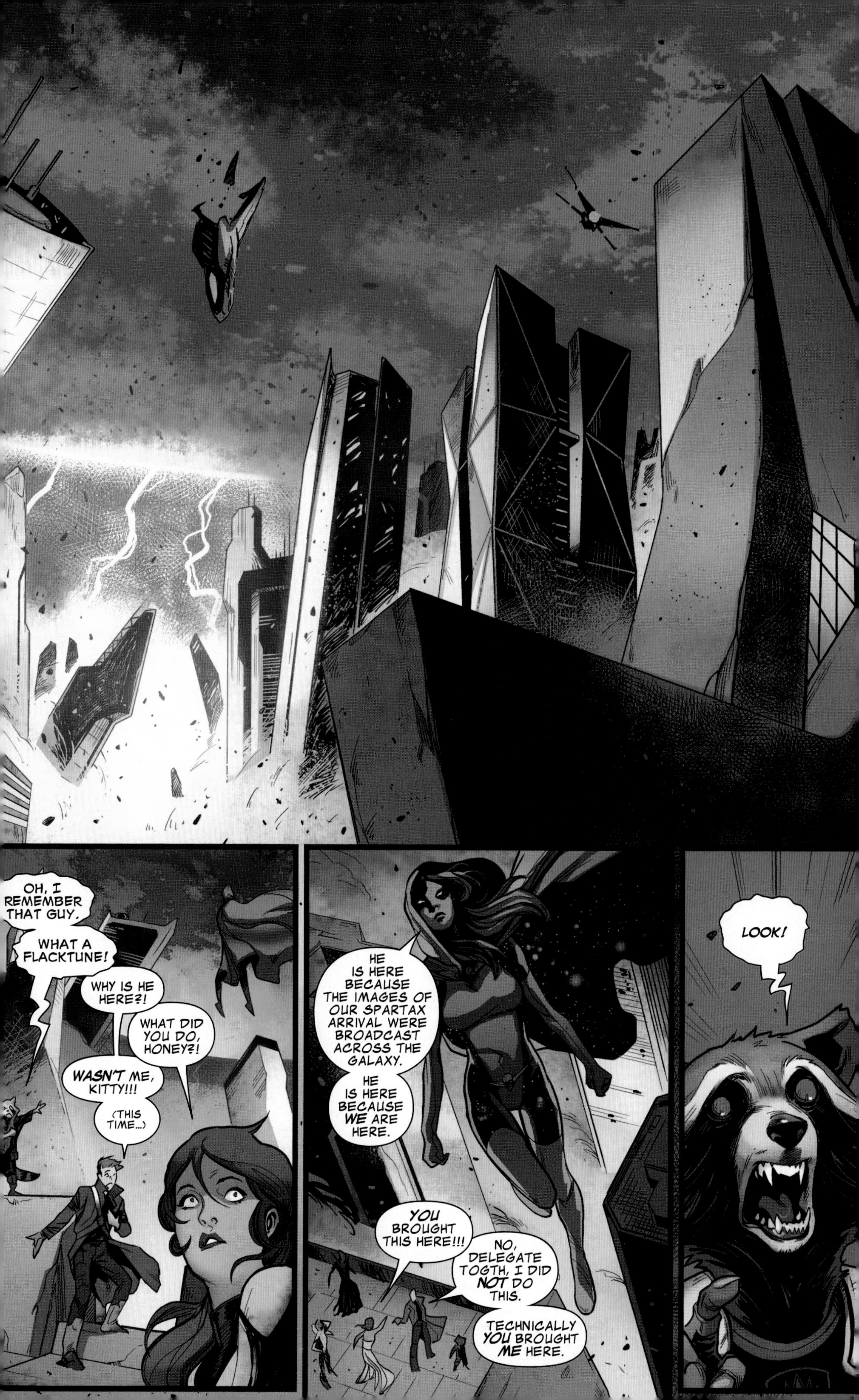
OH, I REMEMBER THAT GUY.
WHAT A FLACKTUNE!
WHY IS HE HERE?!
WHAT DID YOU DO, HONEY?!
WASN'T ME, KITTY!!!
(THIS TIME...)
HE IS HERE BECAUSE THE IMAGES OF OUR SPARTAX ARRIVAL WERE BROADCAST ACROSS THE GALAXY.
HE IS HERE BECAUSE WE ARE HERE.
YOU BROUGHT THIS HERE!!!
NO, DELEGATE TOGTH, I DID NOT DO THIS.
TECHNICALLY YOU BROUGHT ME HERE.
LOOK!

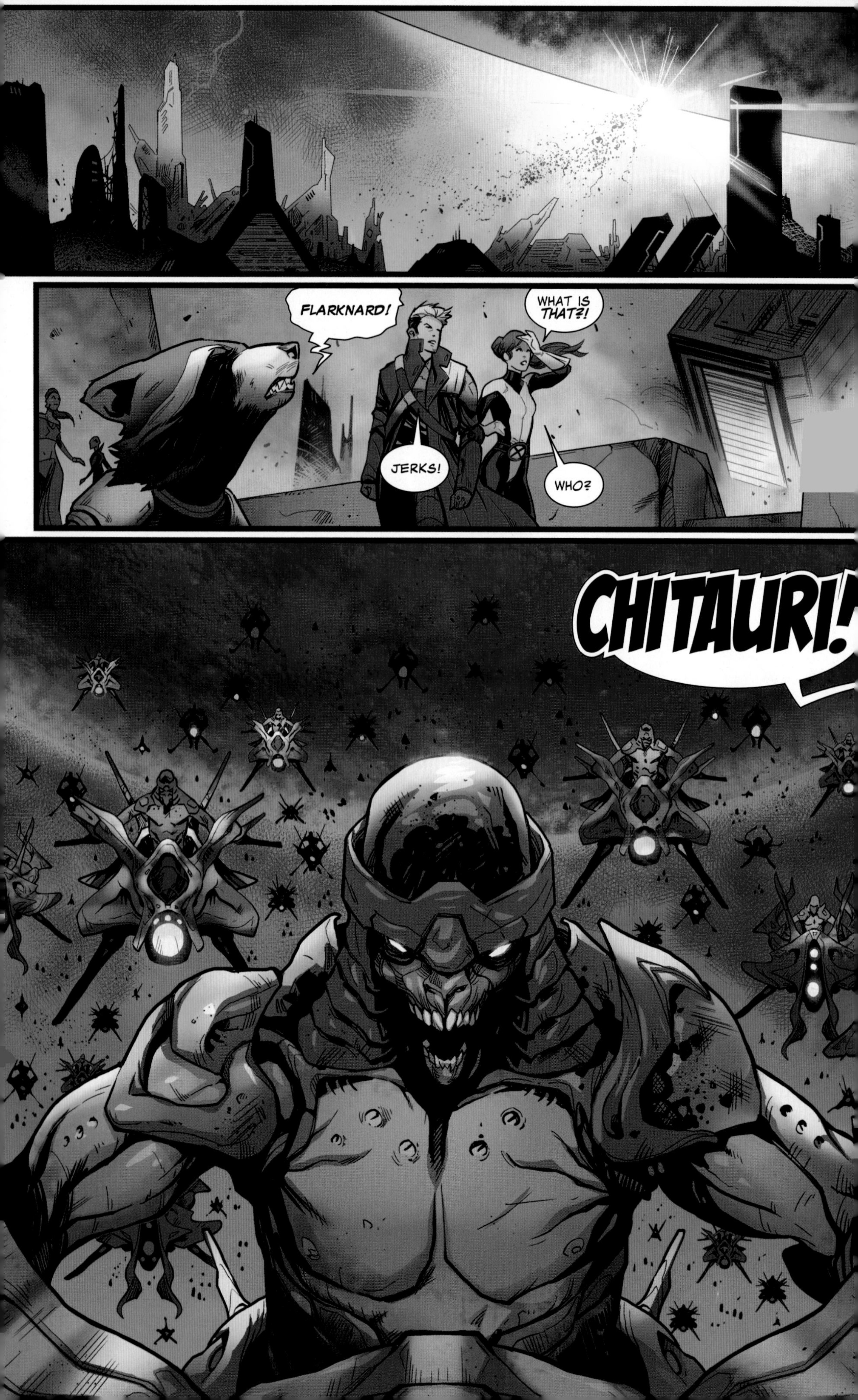
FLARKNARD!
WHAT IS THAT?!
JERKS!
WHO?
CHITAURI!

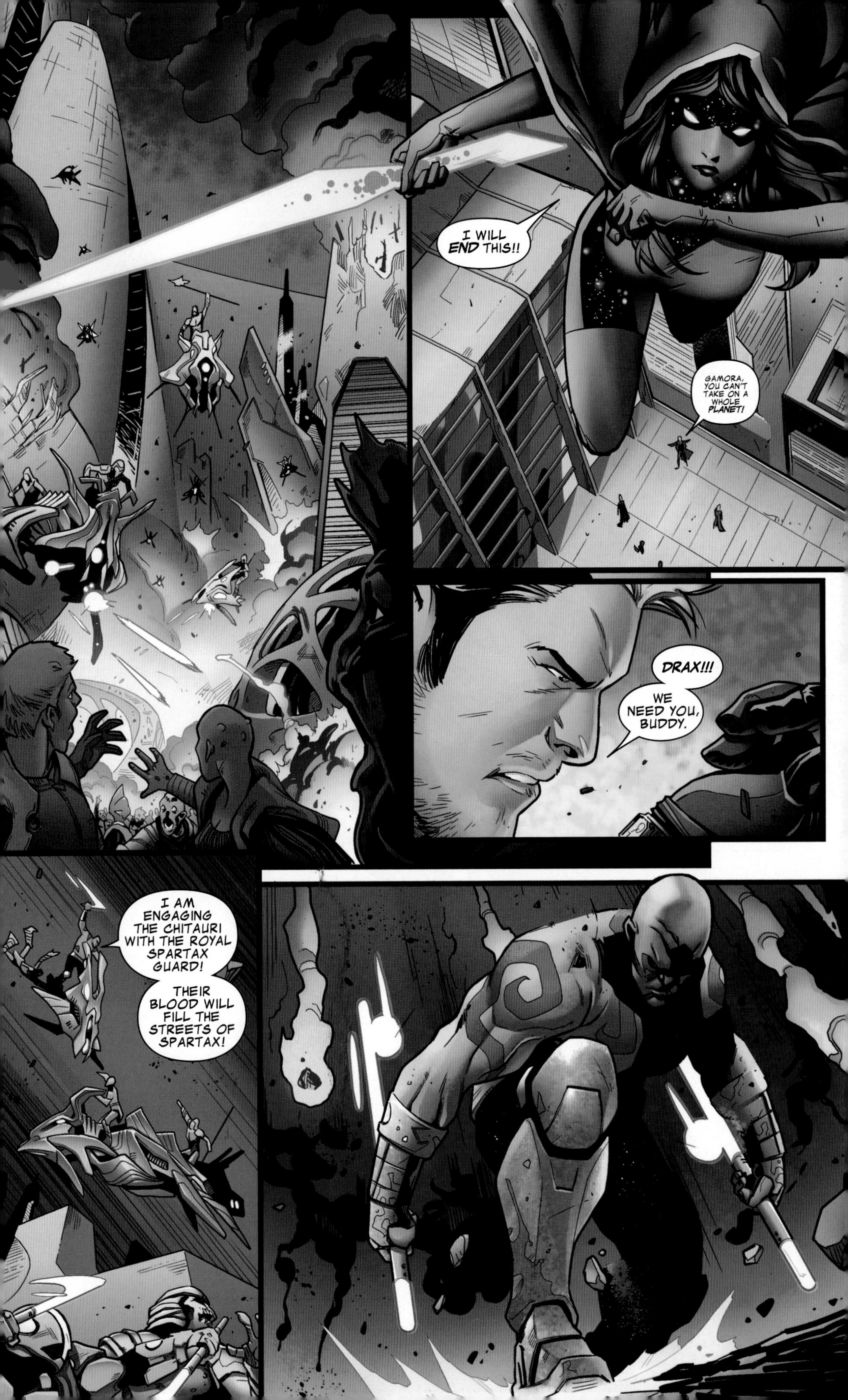

I WILL END THIS!!
GAMORA, YOU CAN'T TAKE ON A WHOLE PLANET!
DRAX!!!
WE NEED YOU, BUDDY.
I AM ENGAGING THE CHITAURI WITH THE ROYAL SPARTAX GUARD!
THEIR BLOOD WILL FILL THE STREETS OF SPARTAX!

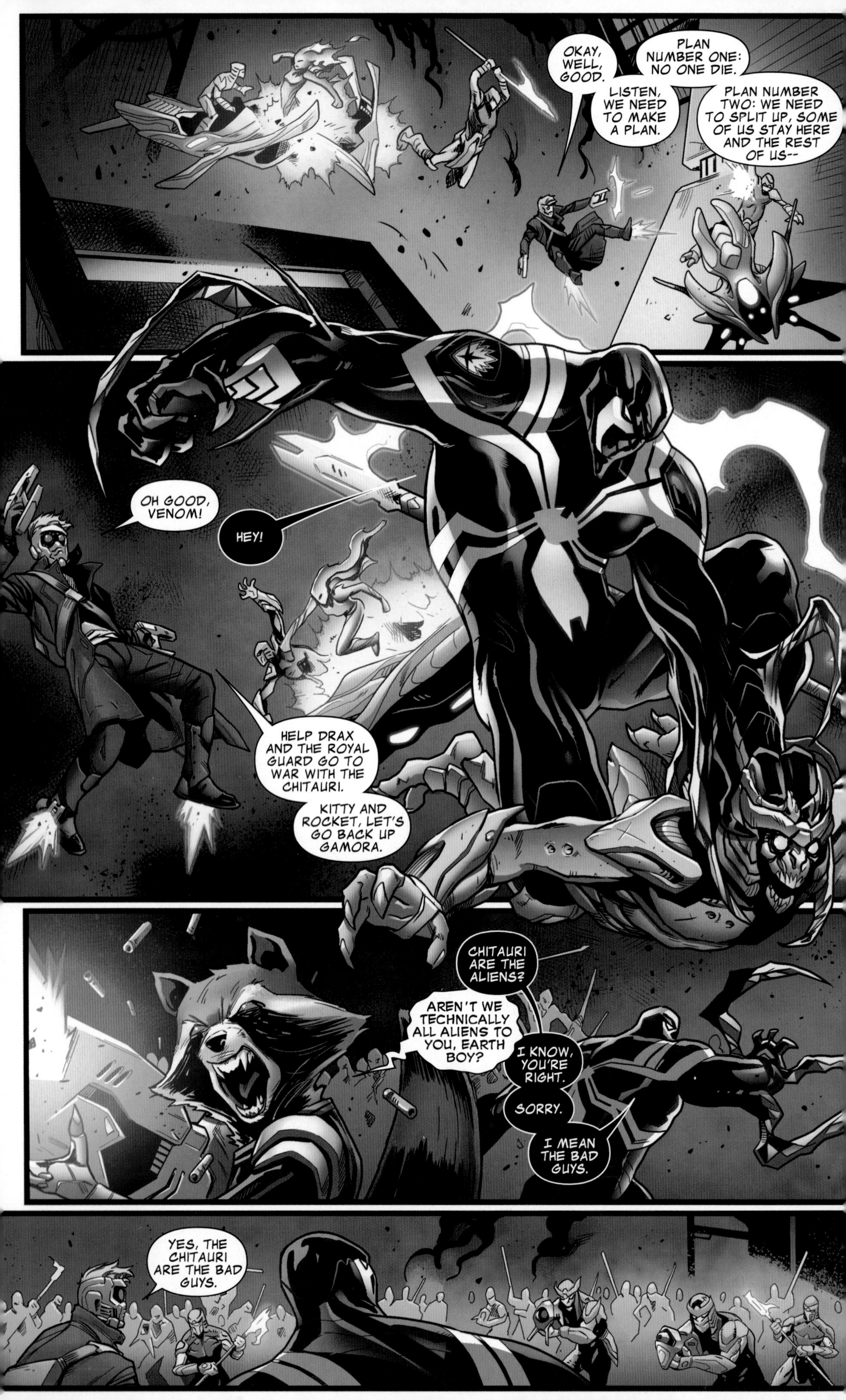

OKAY, WELL, GOOD.
PLAN NUMBER ONE: NO ONE DIE.
LISTEN, WE NEED TO MAKE A PLAN.
PLAN NUMBER TWO: WE NEED TO SPLIT UP, SOME OF US STAY HERE AND THE REST OF US--
OH GOOD, VENOM!
HEY!
HELP DRAX AND THE ROYAL GUARD GO TO WAR WITH THE CHITAURI.
KITTY AND ROCKET, LET'S GO BACK UP GAMORA.
CHITAURI ARE THE ALIENS?
AREN'T WE TECHNICALLY ALL ALIENS TO YOU, EARTH BOY?
I KNOW, YOU'RE RIGHT.
SORRY.
I MEAN THE BAD GUYS.
YES, THE CHITAURI ARE THE BAD GUYS.

KINDUN,
THE LIVING PLANET.

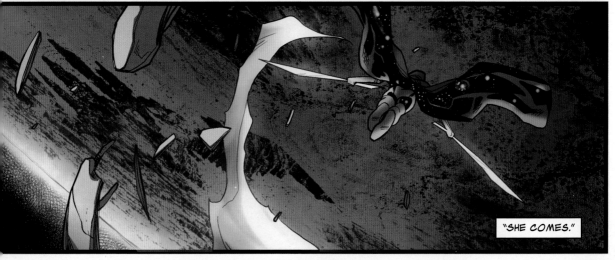

"SHE COMES."

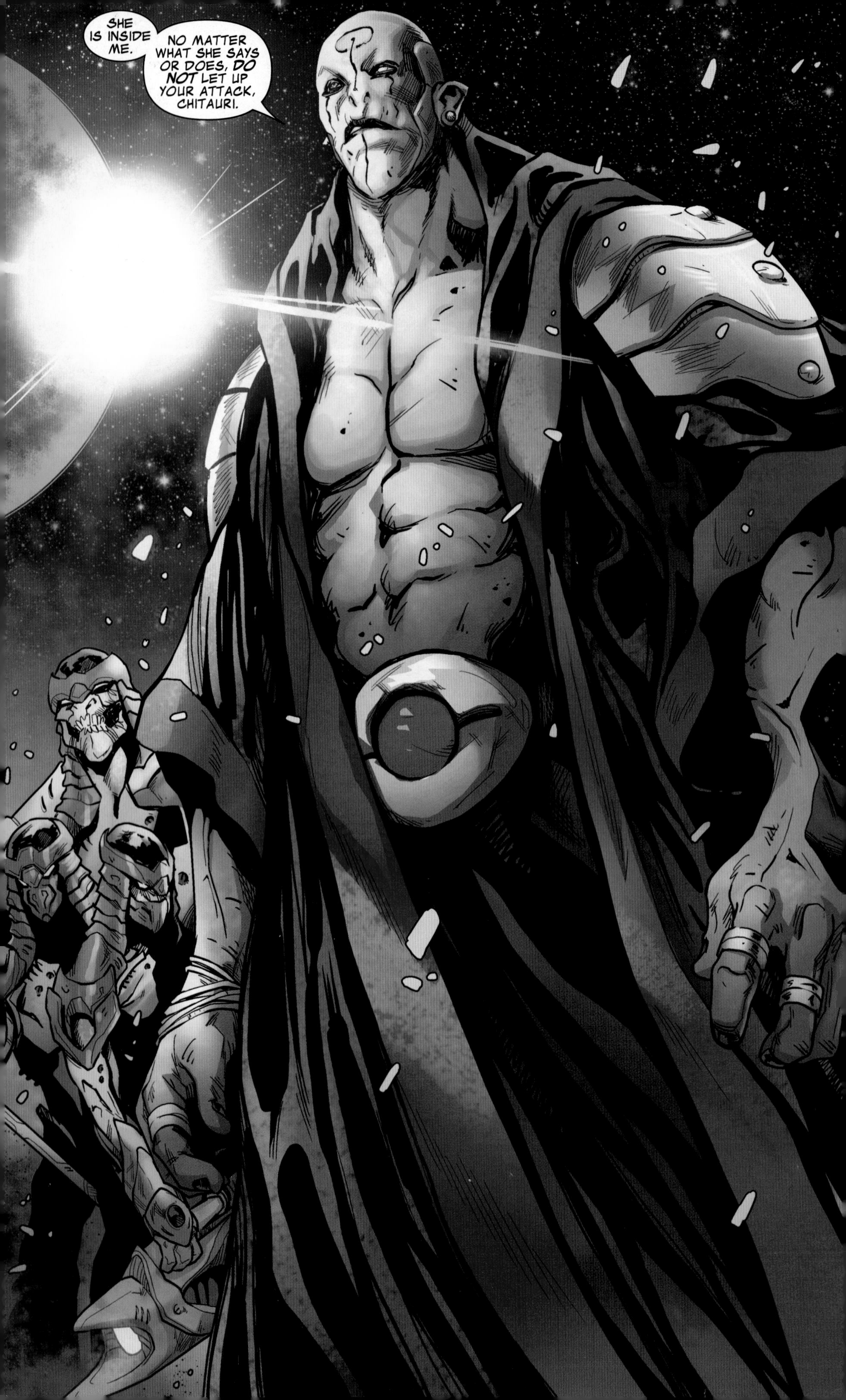
SHE IS INSIDE ME.
NO MATTER WHAT SHE SAYS OR DOES, DO NOT LET UP YOUR ATTACK, CHITAURI.

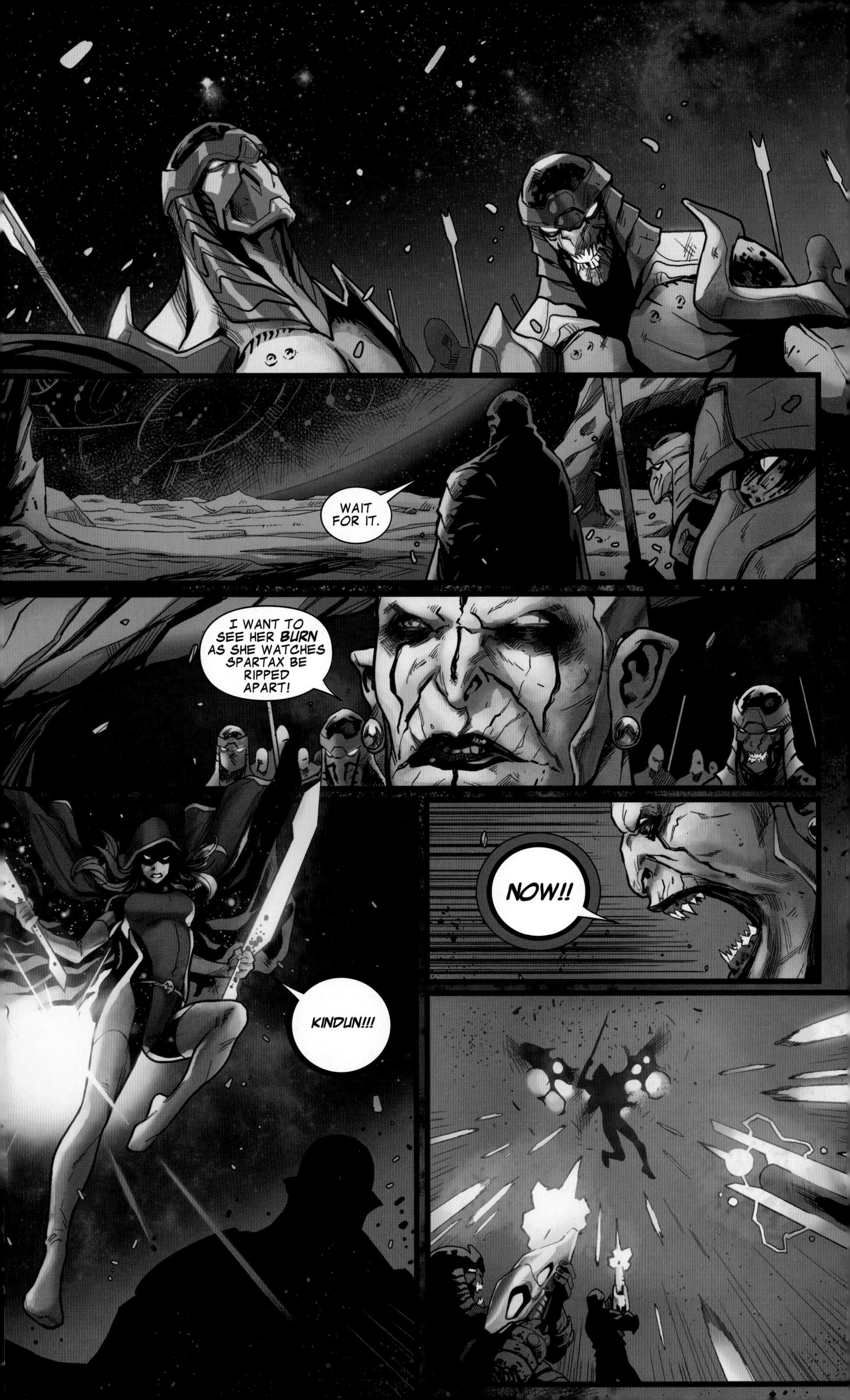
WAIT FOR IT.
I WANT TO SEE HER BURN AS SHE WATCHES SPARTAX BE RIPPED APART!
NOW!!
KINDUN!!!

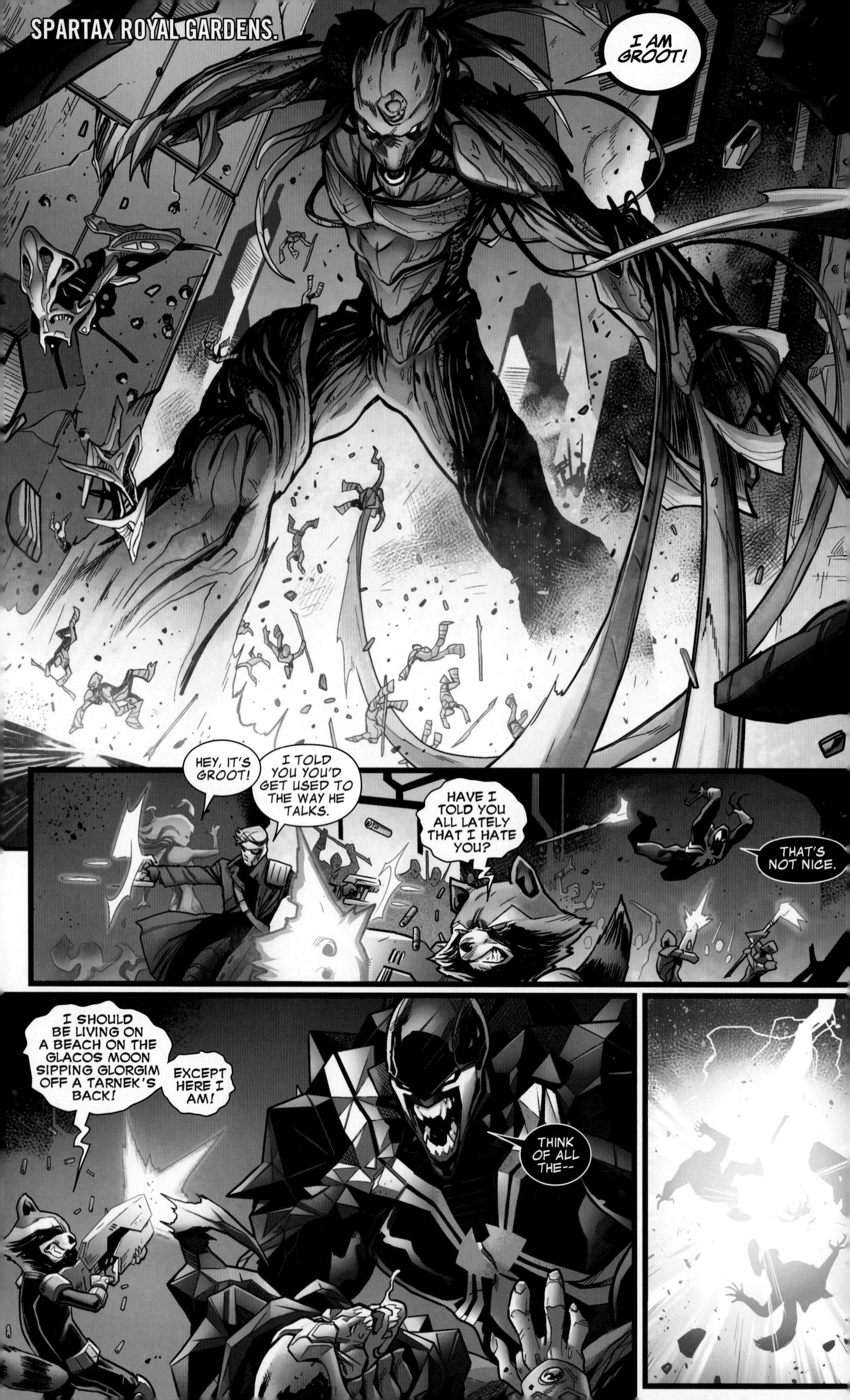
SPARTAX ROYAL GARDENS.
I AM GROOT!
HEY, IT'S GROOT!
I TOLD YOU YOU'D GET USED TO THE WAY HE TALKS.
HAVE I TOLD YOU ALL LATELY THAT I HATE YOU?
THAT'S NOT NICE.
I SHOULD BE LIVING ON A BEACH ON THE GLACOS MOON SIPPING GLORGIM OFF A TARNEK'S BACK!
EXCEPT HERE I AM!
THINK OF ALL THE--

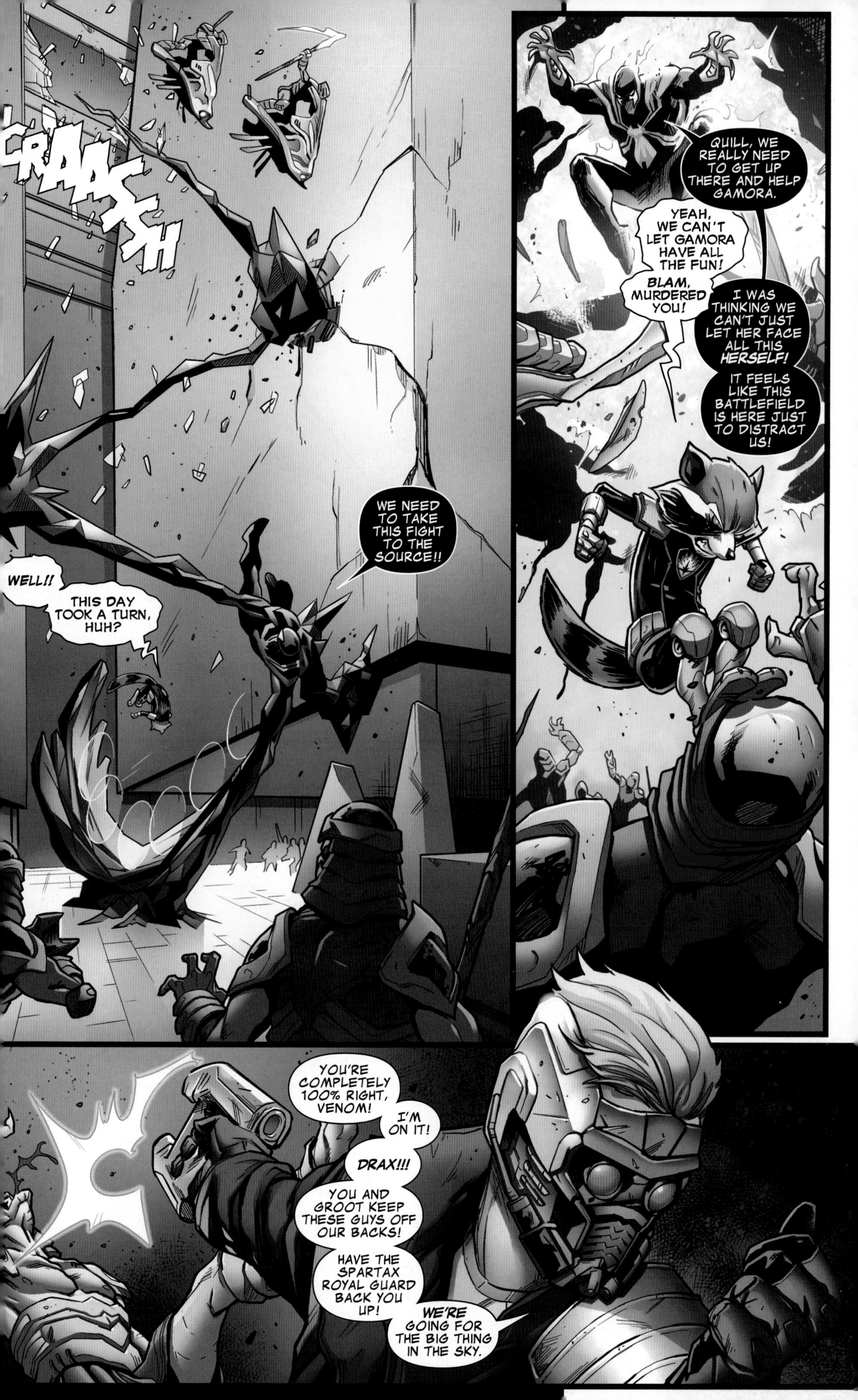
CRAAASHH
WE NEED TO TAKE THIS FIGHT TO THE SOURCE!!
WELL!! THIS DAY TOOK A TURN, HUH?
QUILL, WE REALLY NEED TO GET UP THERE AND HELP GAMORA.
YEAH, WE CAN'T LET GAMORA HAVE ALL THE FUN!
BLAM, MURDERED YOU!
I WAS THINKING WE CAN'T JUST LET HER FACE ALL THIS HERSELF!
IT FEELS LIKE THIS BATTLEFIELD IS HERE JUST TO DISTRACT US!
YOU'RE COMPLETELY 100% RIGHT, VENOM!
I'M ON IT!
DRAX!!!
YOU AND GROOT KEEP THESE GUYS OFF OUR BACKS!
HAVE THE SPARTAX ROYAL GUARD BACK YOU UP!
WE'RE GOING FOR THE BIG THING IN THE SKY.

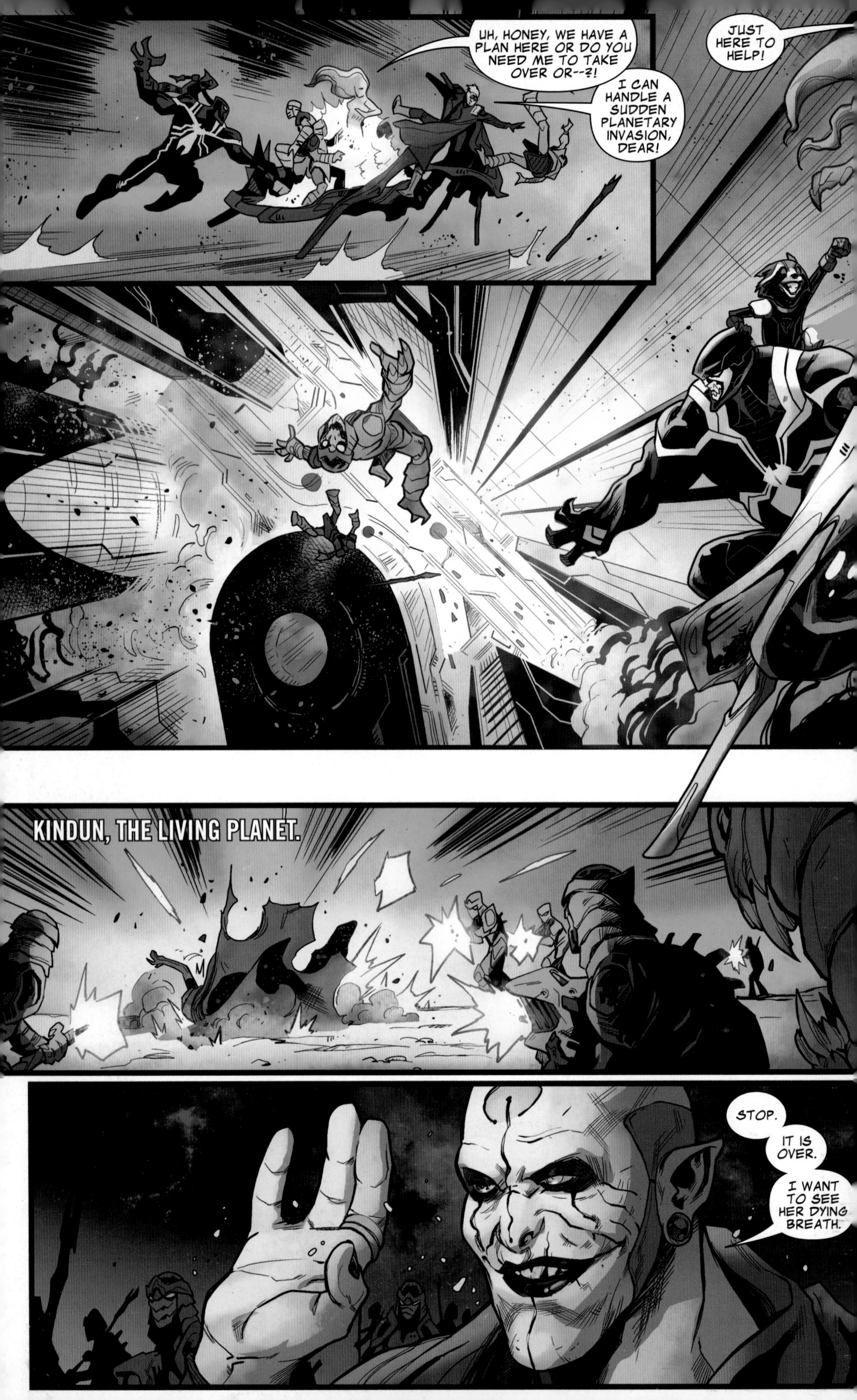
UH, HONEY, WE HAVE A PLAN HERE OR DO YOU NEED ME TO TAKE OVER OR--?!
I CAN HANDLE A SUDDEN PLANETARY INVASION, DEAR!
JUST HERE TO HELP!
KINDUN, THE LIVING PLANET.
STOP.
IT IS OVER.
I WANT TO SEE HER DYING BREATH.

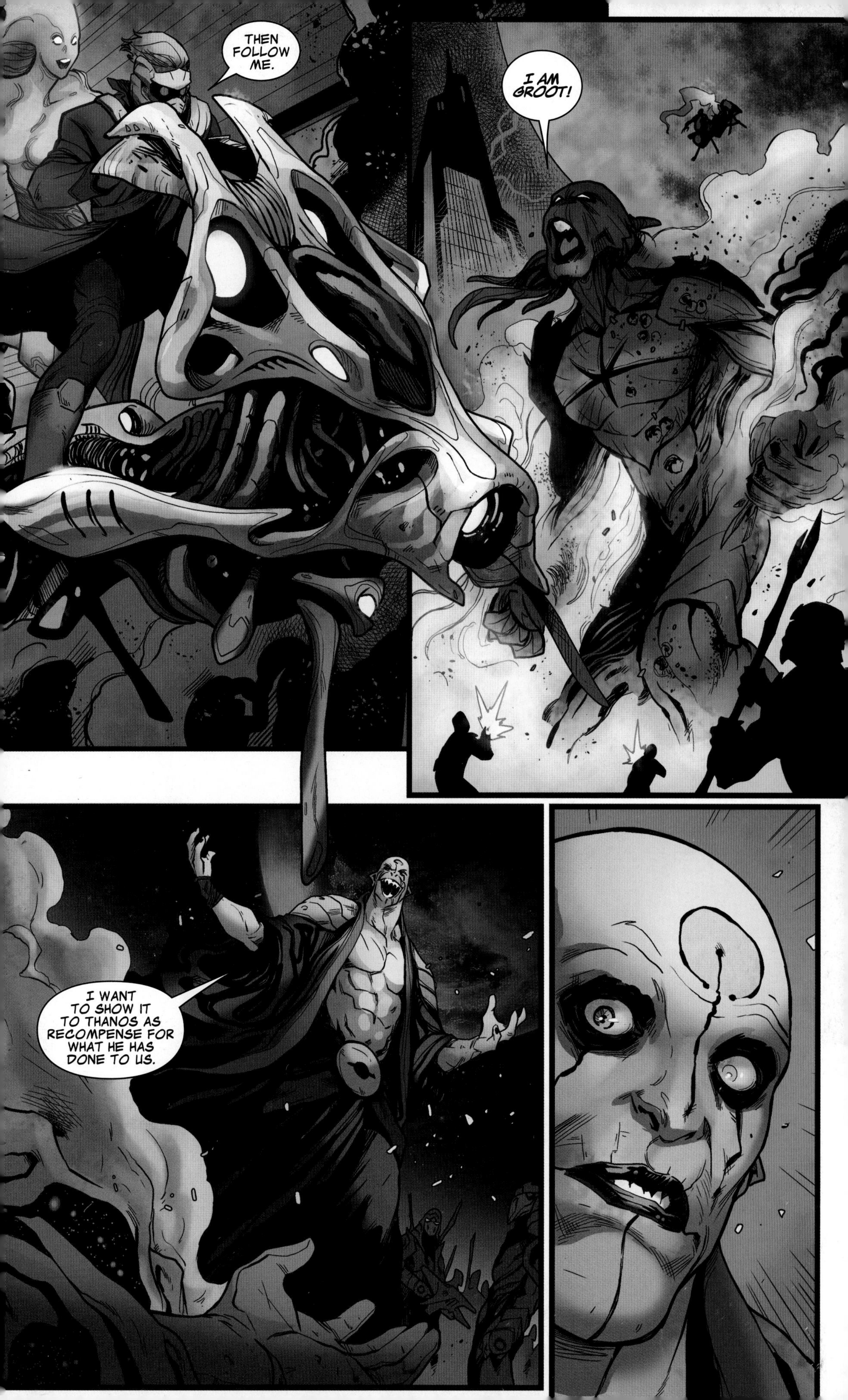
THEN FOLLOW ME.
I AM GROOT!
I WANT TO SHOW IT TO THANOS AS RECOMPENSE FOR WHAT HE HAS DONE TO US.

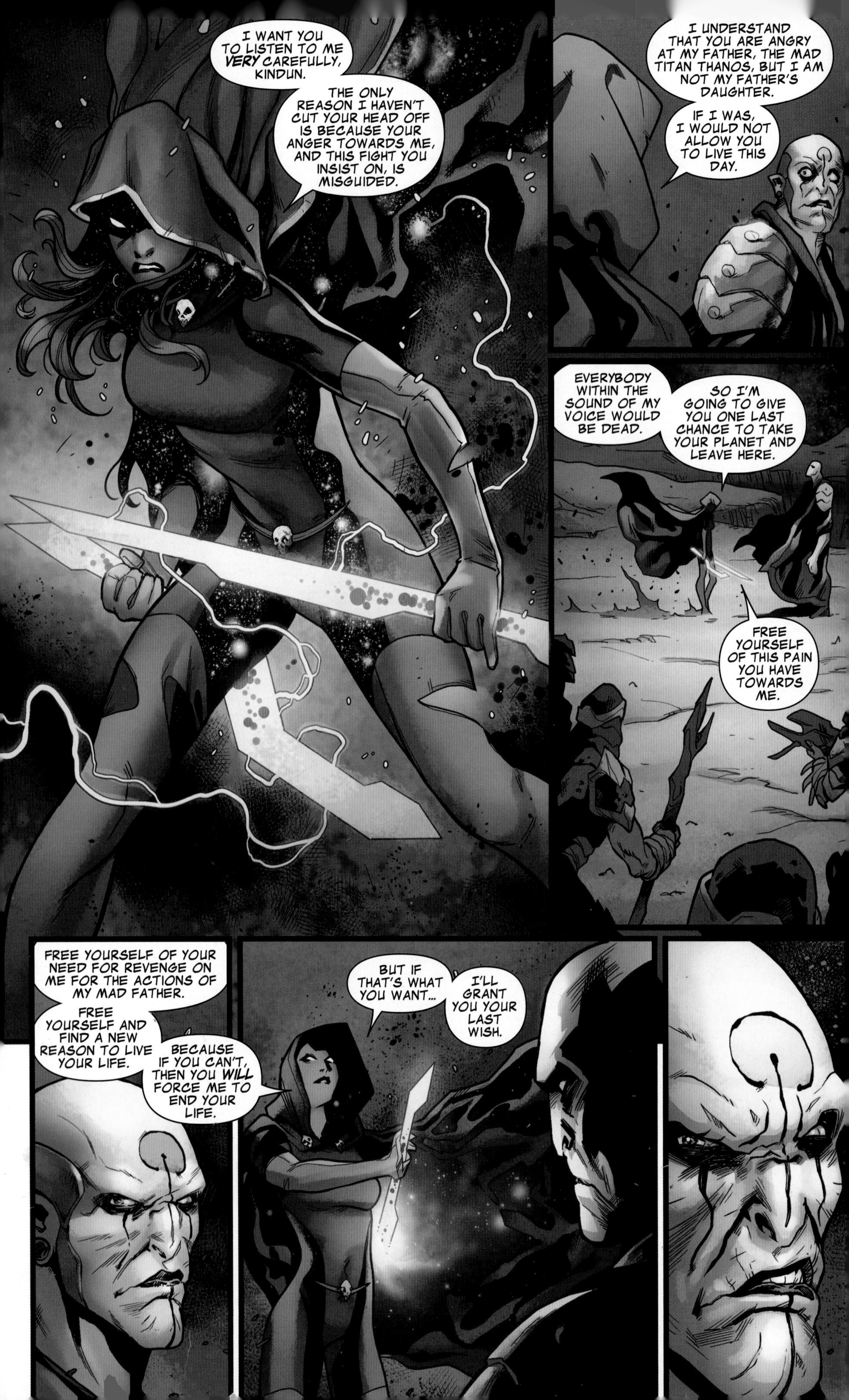
I WANT YOU TO LISTEN TO ME VERY CAREFULLY, KINDUN.
THE ONLY REASON I HAVEN'T CUT YOUR HEAD OFF IS BECAUSE YOUR ANGER TOWARDS ME, AND THIS FIGHT YOU INSIST ON, IS MISGUIDED.
I UNDERSTAND THAT YOU ARE ANGRY AT MY FATHER, THE MAD TITAN THANOS, BUT I AM NOT MY FATHER'S DAUGHTER.
IF I WAS, I WOULD NOT ALLOW YOU TO LIVE THIS DAY.
EVERYBODY WITHIN THE SOUND OF MY VOICE WOULD BE DEAD.
SO I'M GOING TO GIVE YOU ONE LAST CHANCE TO TAKE YOUR PLANET AND LEAVE HERE.
FREE YOURSELF OF THIS PAIN YOU HAVE TOWARDS ME.
FREE YOURSELF OF YOUR NEED FOR REVENGE ON ME FOR THE ACTIONS OF MY MAD FATHER.
FREE YOURSELF AND FIND A NEW REASON TO LIVE YOUR LIFE.
BECAUSE IF YOU CAN'T, THEN YOU WILL FORCE ME TO END YOUR LIFE.
BUT IF THAT'S WHAT YOU WANT...
I'LL GRANT YOU YOUR LAST WISH.

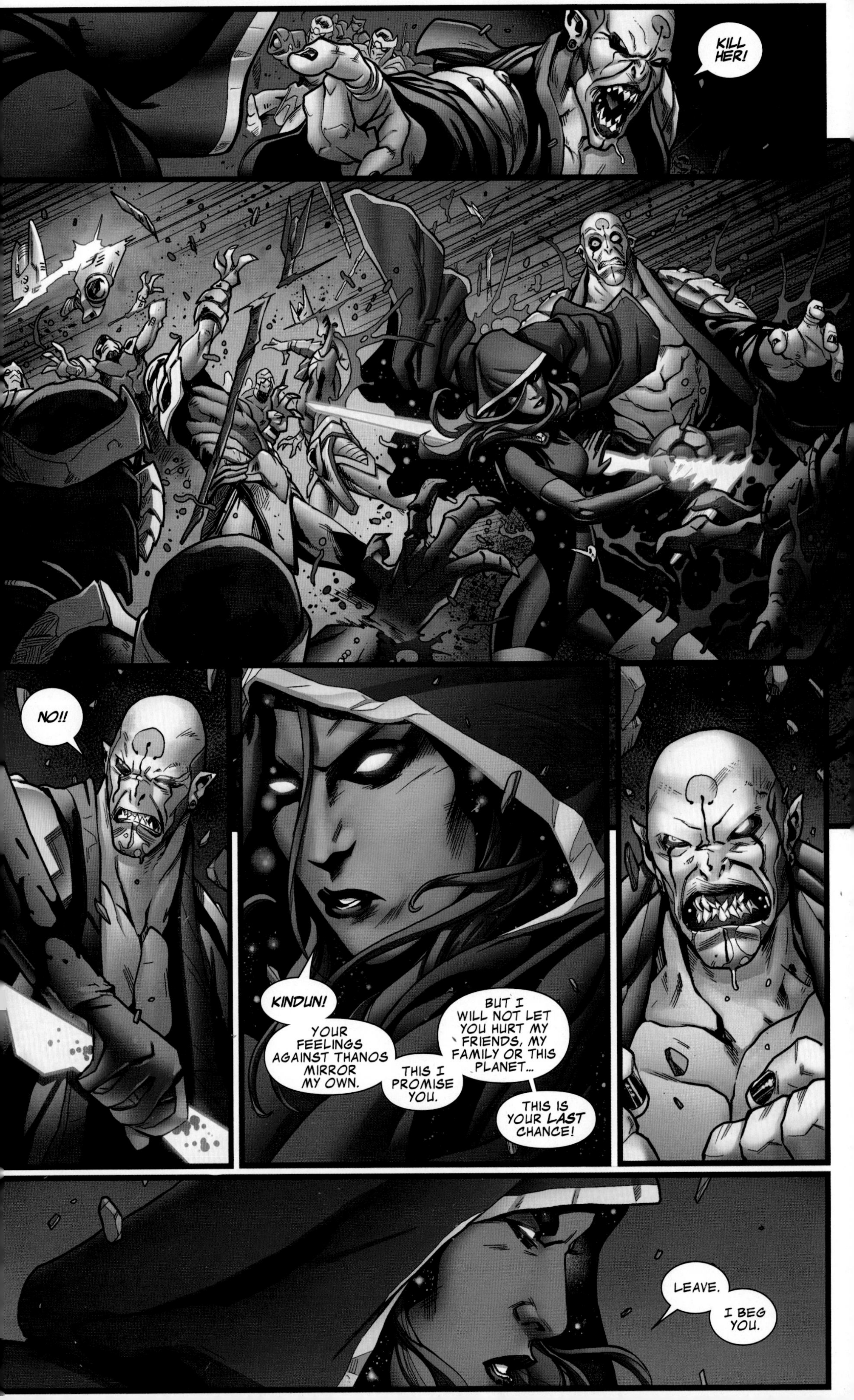

KILL HER!
NO!!
KINDUN!
YOUR FEELINGS AGAINST THANOS MIRROR MY OWN.
THIS I PROMISE YOU.
BUT I WILL NOT LET YOU HURT MY FRIENDS, MY FAMILY OR THIS PLANET...
THIS IS YOUR LAST CHANCE!
LEAVE.
I BEG YOU.

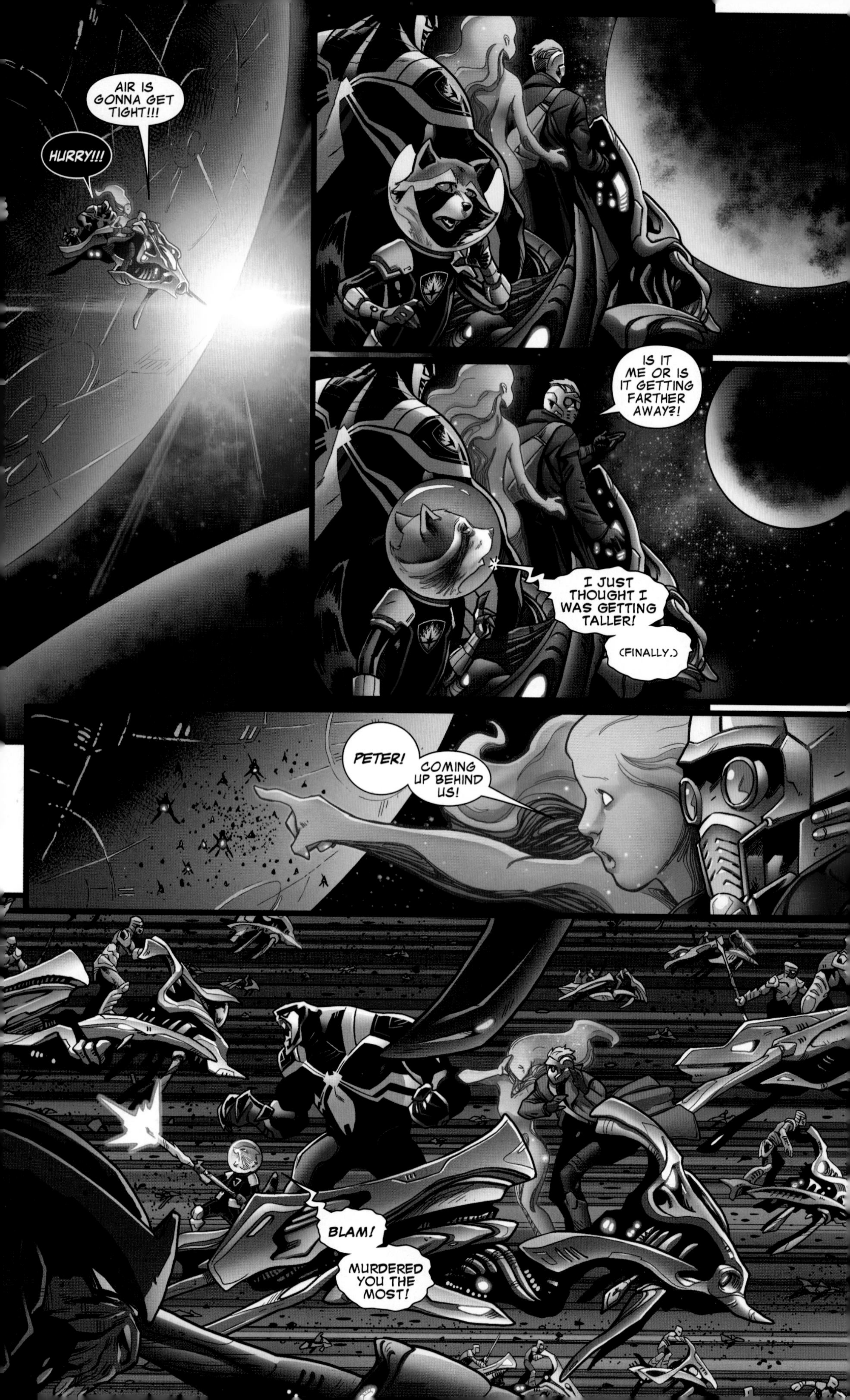

AIR IS GONNA GET TIGHT!!!
HURRY!!!
IS IT ME OR IS IT GETTING FARTHER AWAY?!
I JUST THOUGHT I WAS GETTING TALLER!
(FINALLY.)
PETER!
COMING UP BEHIND US!
BLAM!
MURDERED YOU THE MOST!

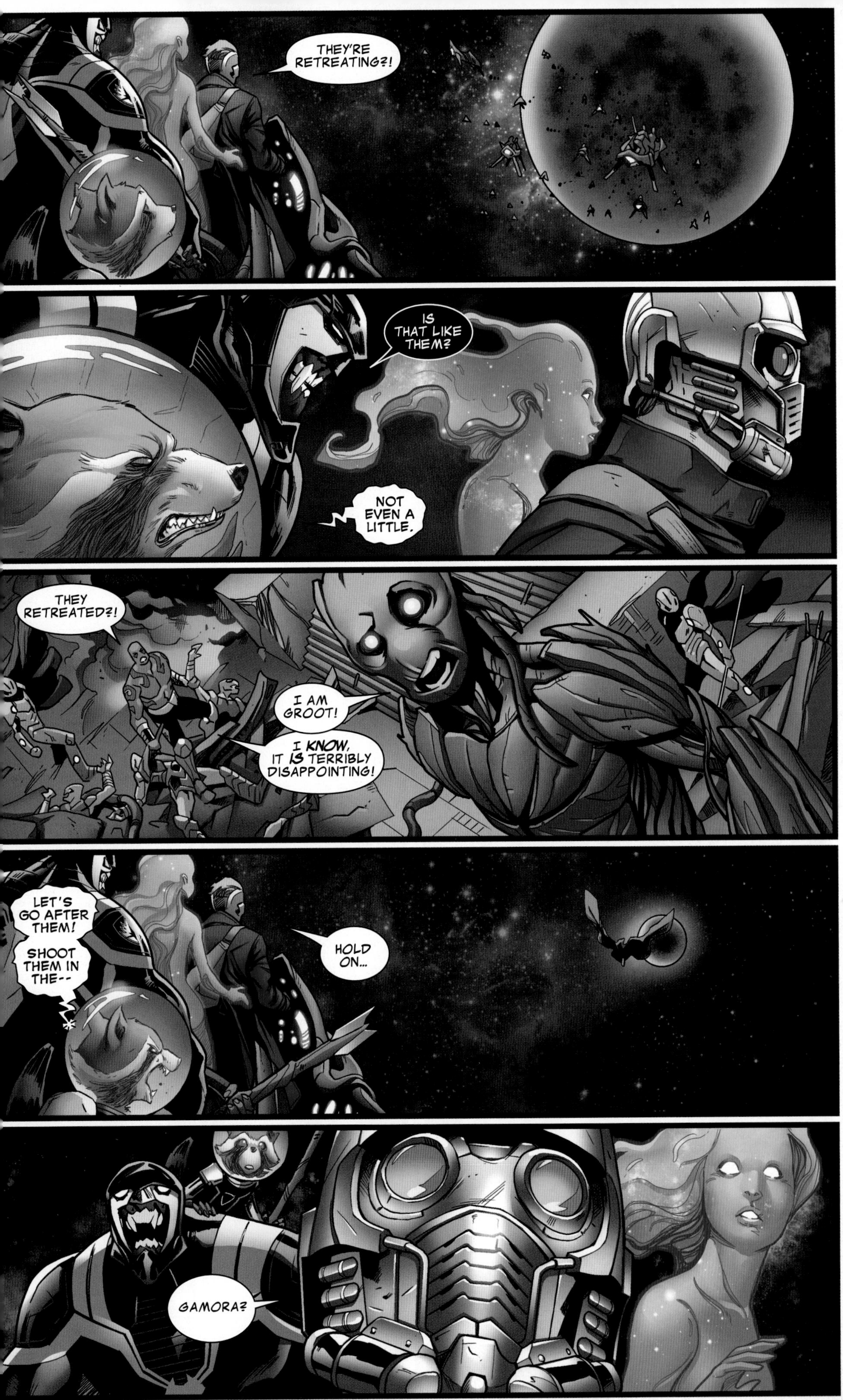
THEY'RE RETREATING?!
IS THAT LIKE THEM?
NOT EVEN A LITTLE.
THEY RETREATED?!
I AM GROOT!
I KNOW, IT IS TERRIBLY DISAPPOINTING!
LET'S GO AFTER THEM!
SHOOT THEM IN THE--
HOLD ON...
GAMORA?

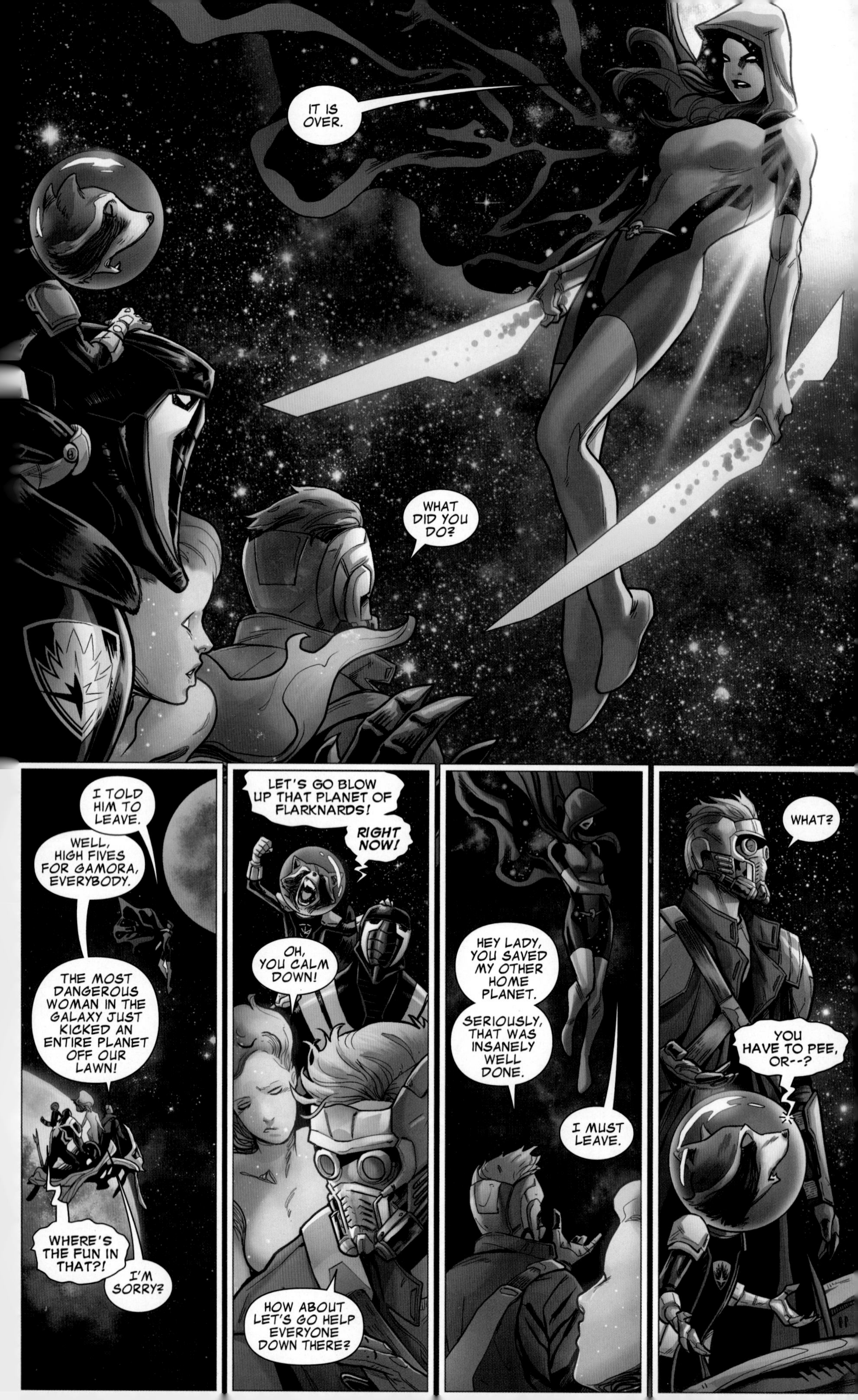
IT IS OVER.
WHAT DID YOU DO?
I TOLD HIM TO LEAVE.
WELL, HIGH FIVES FOR GAMORA, EVERYBODY.
THE MOST DANGEROUS WOMAN IN THE GALAXY JUST KICKED AN ENTIRE PLANET OFF OUR LAWN!
WHERE'S THE FUN IN THAT?!
I'M SORRY?
LET'S GO BLOW UP THAT PLANET OF FLARKNARDS!
RIGHT NOW!
OH, YOU CALM DOWN!
HOW ABOUT LET'S GO HELP EVERYONE DOWN THERE?
HEY LADY, YOU SAVED MY OTHER HOME PLANET.
SERIOUSLY, THAT WAS INSANELY WELL DONE.
I MUST LEAVE.
WHAT?
YOU HAVE TO PEE, OR--?

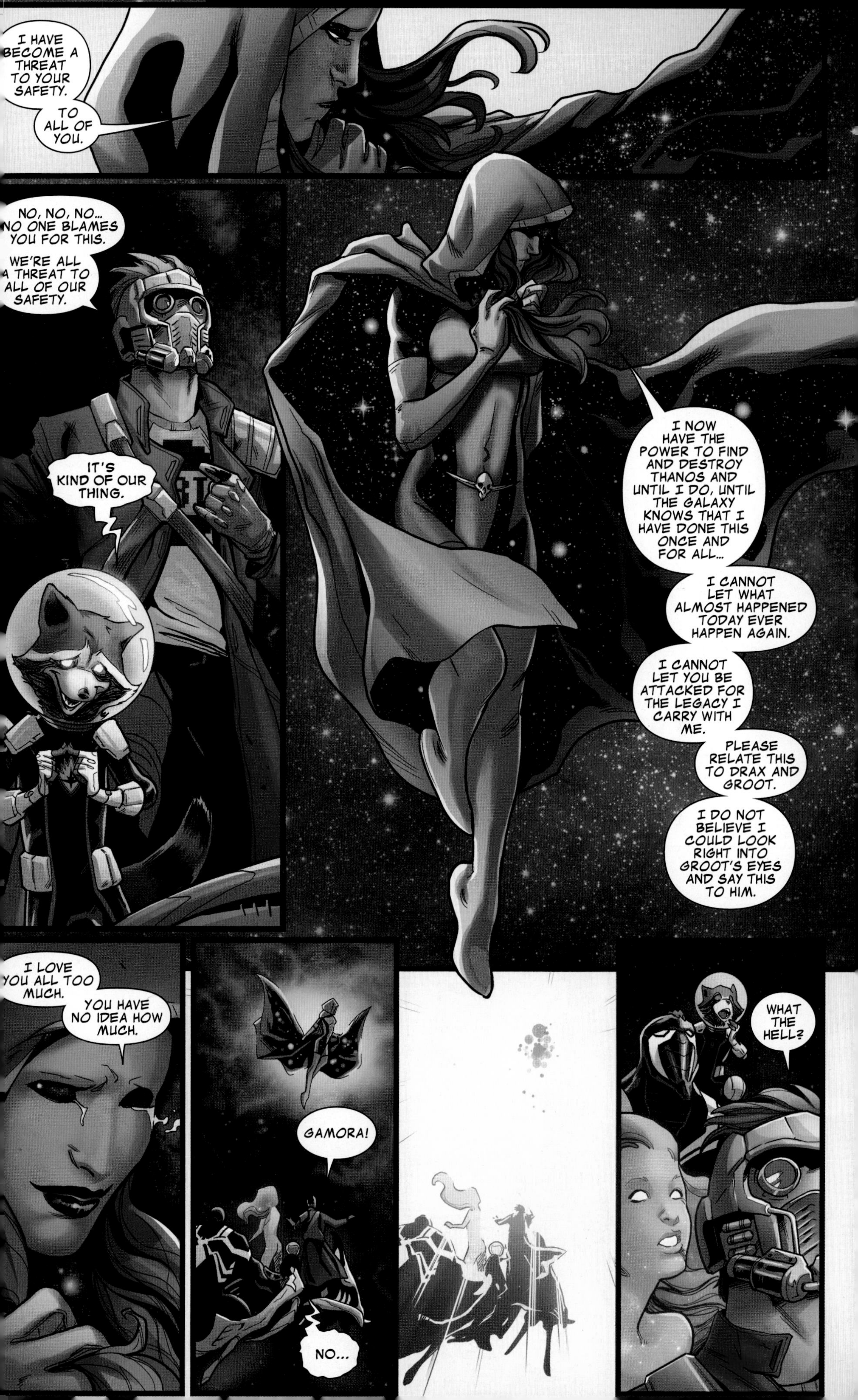
I HAVE BECOME A THREAT TO YOUR SAFETY.
TO ALL OF YOU.
NO, NO, NO... NO ONE BLAMES YOU FOR THIS.
WE'RE ALL A THREAT TO ALL OF OUR SAFETY.
IT'S KIND OF OUR THING.
I NOW HAVE THE POWER TO FIND AND DESTROY THANOS AND UNTIL I DO, UNTIL THE GALAXY KNOWS THAT I HAVE DONE THIS ONCE AND FOR ALL...
I CANNOT LET WHAT ALMOST HAPPENED TODAY EVER HAPPEN AGAIN.
I CANNOT LET YOU BE ATTACKED FOR THE LEGACY I CARRY WITH ME.
PLEASE RELATE THIS TO DRAX AND GROOT.
I DO NOT BELIEVE I COULD LOOK RIGHT INTO GROOT'S EYES AND SAY THIS TO HIM.
I LOVE YOU ALL TOO MUCH.
YOU HAVE NO IDEA HOW MUCH.
GAMORA!
NO...
WHAT THE HELL?

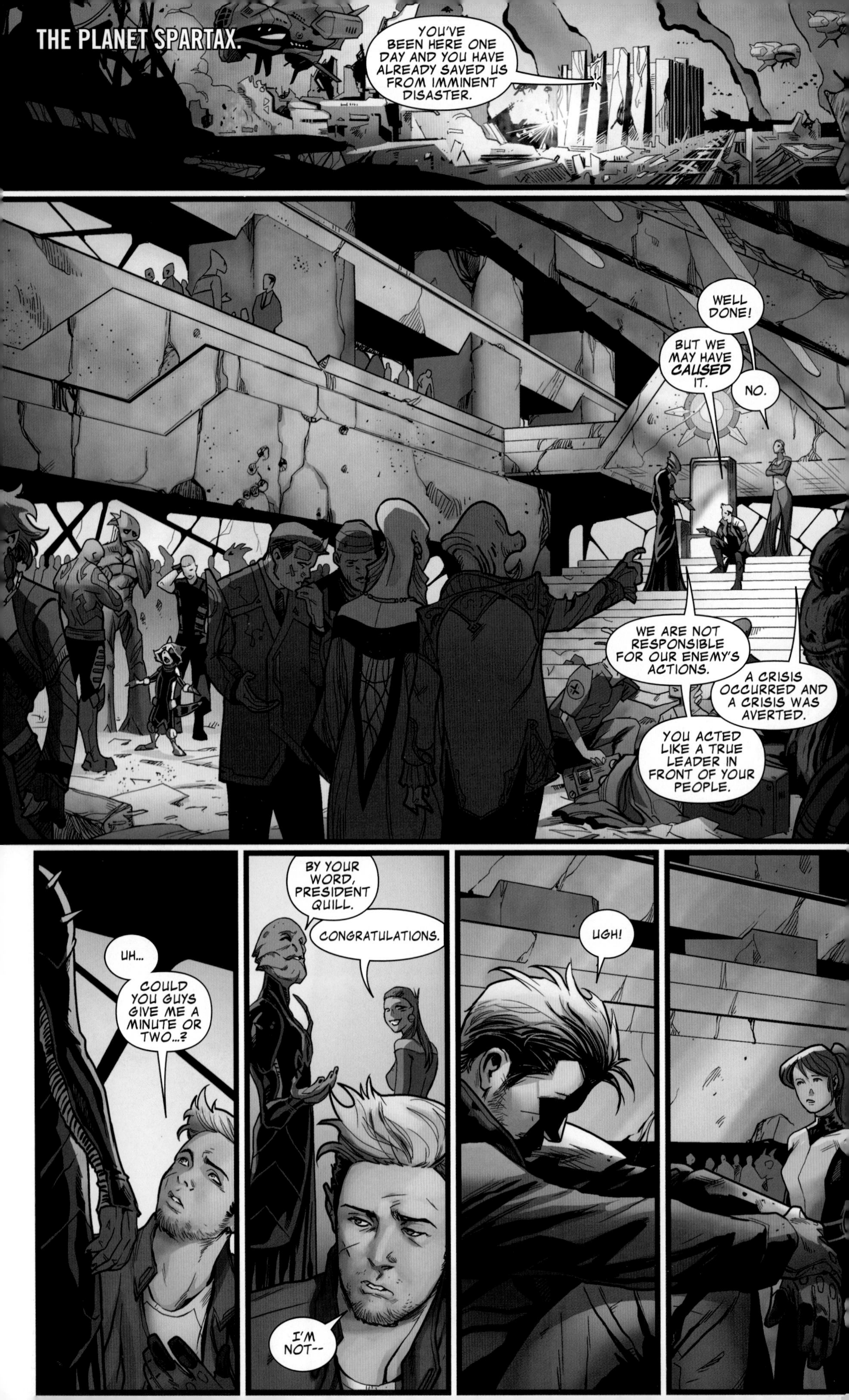
THE PLANET SPARTAX.
YOU'VE BEEN HERE ONE DAY AND YOU HAVE ALREADY SAVED US FROM IMMINENT DISASTER.
WELL DONE!
BUT WE MAY HAVE CAUSED IT.
NO.
WE ARE NOT RESPONSIBLE FOR OUR ENEMY'S ACTIONS.
A CRISIS OCCURRED AND A CRISIS WAS AVERTED.
YOU ACTED LIKE A TRUE LEADER IN FRONT OF YOUR PEOPLE.
UH...
COULD YOU GUYS GIVE ME A MINUTE OR TWO...?
BY YOUR WORD, PRESIDENT QUILL.
CONGRATULATIONS.
I'M NOT--
UGH!

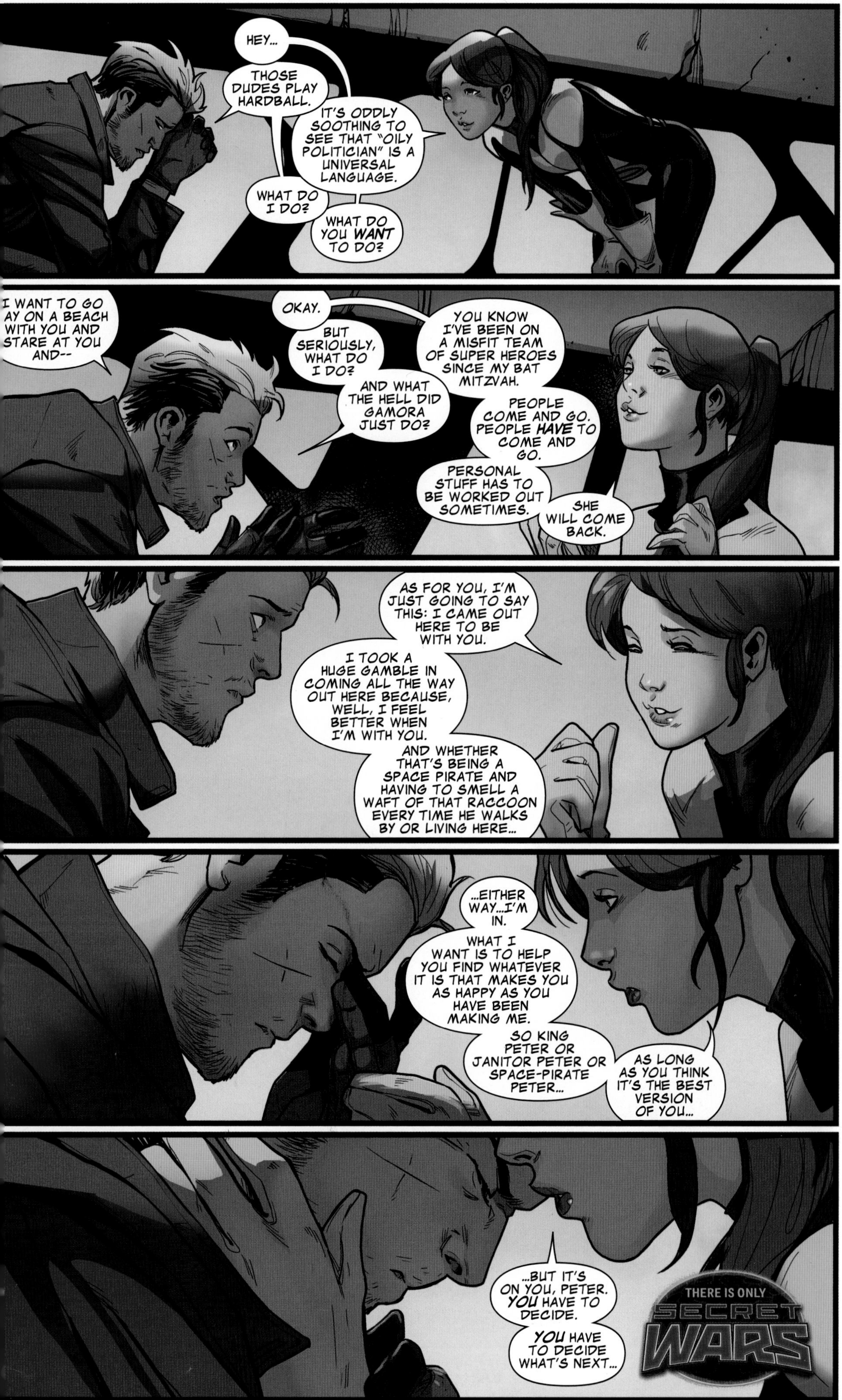
HEY...
THOSE DUDES PLAY HARDBALL.
IT'S ODDLY SOOTHING TO SEE THAT "OILY POLITICIAN" IS A UNIVERSAL LANGUAGE.
WHAT DO I DO?
WHAT DO YOU WANT TO DO?
I WANT TO GO AY ON A BEACH WITH YOU AND STARE AT YOU AND--
OKAY.
BUT SERIOUSLY, WHAT DO I DO?
AND WHAT THE HELL DID GAMORA JUST DO?
YOU KNOW I'VE BEEN ON A MISFIT TEAM OF SUPER HEROES SINCE MY BAT MITZVAH.
PEOPLE COME AND GO. PEOPLE HAVE TO COME AND GO.
PERSONAL STUFF HAS TO BE WORKED OUT SOMETIMES.
SHE WILL COME BACK.
AS FOR YOU, I'M JUST GOING TO SAY THIS: I CAME OUT HERE TO BE WITH YOU.
I TOOK A HUGE GAMBLE IN COMING ALL THE WAY OUT HERE BECAUSE, WELL, I FEEL BETTER WHEN I'M WITH YOU.
AND WHETHER THAT'S BEING A SPACE PIRATE AND HAVING TO SMELL A WAFT OF THAT RACCOON EVERY TIME HE WALKS BY OR LIVING HERE...
...EITHER WAY...I'M IN.
WHAT I WANT IS TO HELP YOU FIND WHATEVER IT IS THAT MAKES YOU AS HAPPY AS YOU HAVE BEEN MAKING ME.
SO KING PETER OR JANITOR PETER OR SPACE-PIRATE PETER...
AS LONG AS YOU THINK IT'S THE BEST VERSION OF YOU...
...BUT IT'S ON YOU, PETER. YOU HAVE TO DECIDE.
YOU HAVE TO DECIDE WHAT'S NEXT...
THERE IS ONLY SECRET WARS

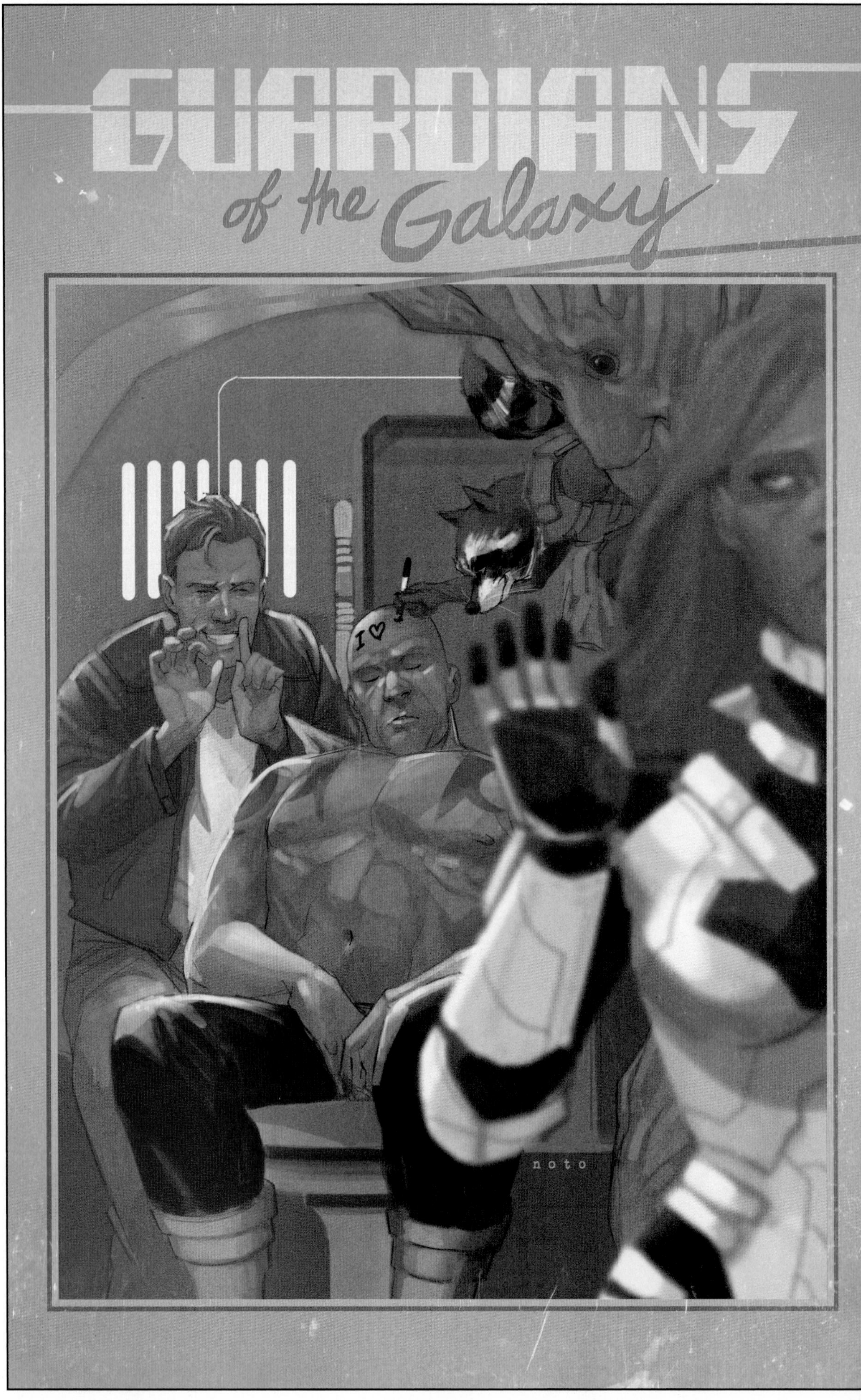
GUARDIANS
of the Galaxy
I ♡
noto

#24 VARIANT BY PHIL NOTO

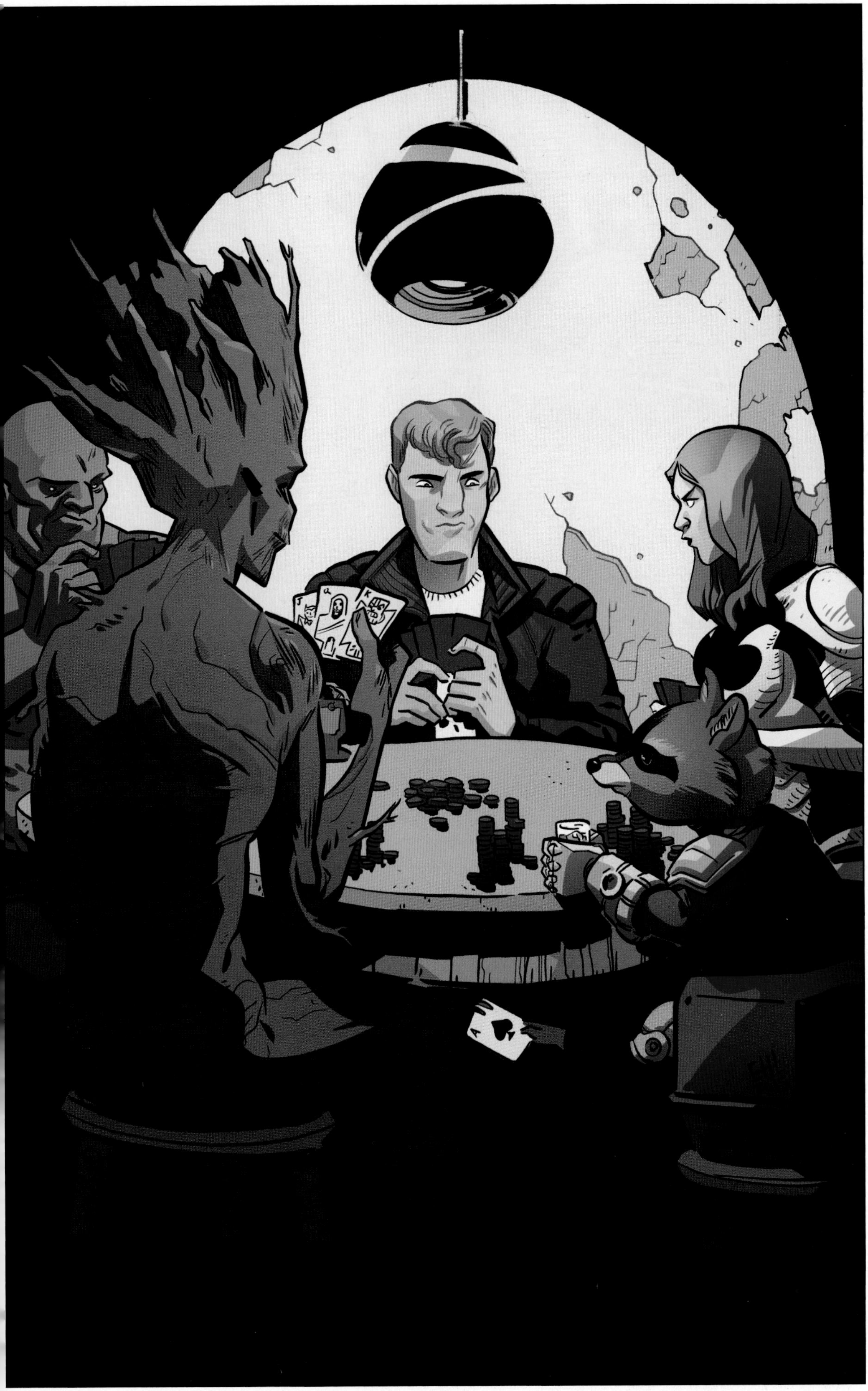

#25 WOMEN OF MARVEL VARIANT BY ERICA HENDERSON

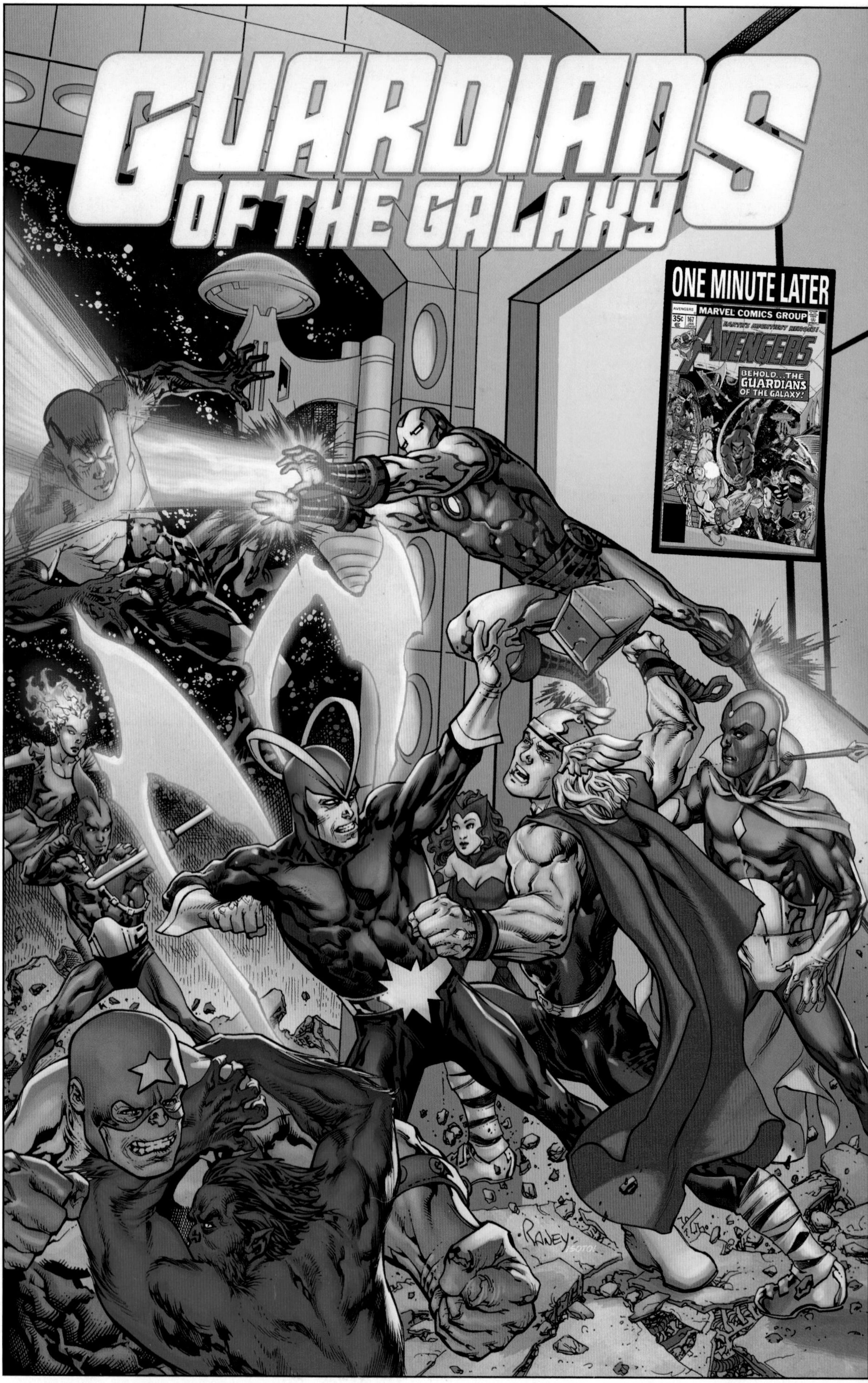
GUARDIANS OF THE GALAXY
ONE MINUTE LATER
AVENGERS
MARVEL COMICS GROUP
35¢
167
AVENGERS
BEHOLD...THE GUARDIANS OF THE GALAXY!
RANEY

#26 ONE MINUTE LATER VARIANT BY TOM RANEY & CHRIS SOTOMAYOR

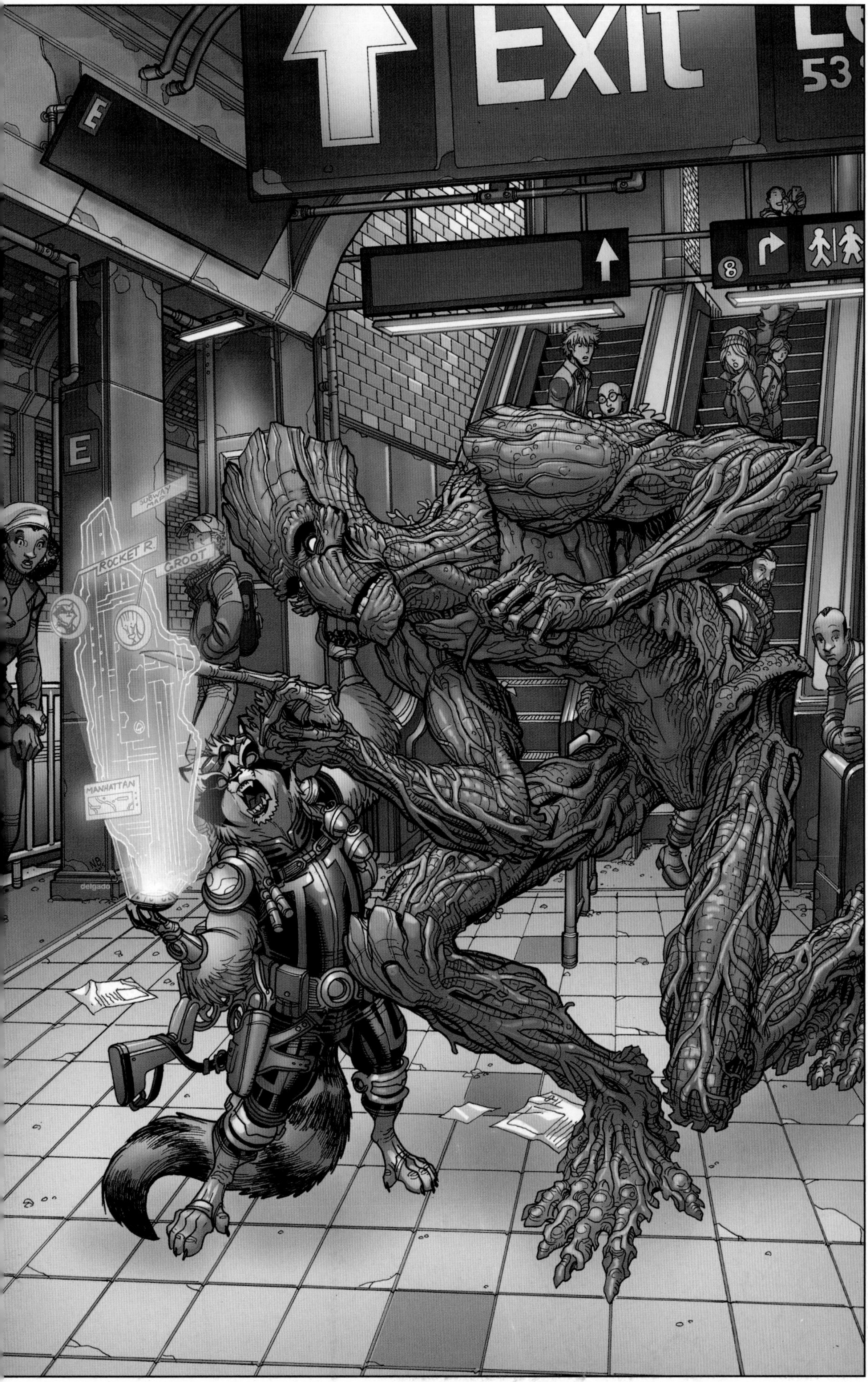

Exit
SUBWAY MAP
ROCKET R.
GROOT
MANHATTAN

#27 NYC VARIANT BY NICK BRADSHAW & EDGAR DELGADO

**MARVEL AUGMENTED REALITY (AR)
ENHANCES AND CHANGES THE WAY
YOU EXPERIENCE COMICS!**

TO ACCESS THE FREE MARVEL AR CONTENT IN THIS BOOK*:

1. Locate the **AR** logo within the comic.
2. Go to Marvel.com/AR in your web browser.
3. Search by series title to find the corresponding AR.
4. Enjoy Marvel AR!

*All AR content that appears in this book has been archived and will be available only at Marvel.com/AR – no longer in the Marvel AR App. Content subject to change and availability.

GUARDIANS OF THE GALAXY
AR INDEX